£7.50
GW00675575

# THE BRITISH GENERAL ELECTION OF 1970

*Other books in this series*

THE BRITISH GENERAL ELECTION OF 1945
*R. B. McCallum and Alison Readman*

THE BRITISH GENERAL ELECTION OF 1950
*H. G. Nicholas*

THE BRITISH GENERAL ELECTION OF 1951
*D. E. Butler*

THE BRITISH GENERAL ELECTION OF 1955
*D. E. Butler*

THE BRITISH GENERAL ELECTION OF 1959
*D. E. Butler and Richard Rose*

THE BRITISH GENERAL ELECTION OF 1964
*D. E. Butler and Anthony King*

THE BRITISH GENERAL ELECTION OF 1966
*D. E. Butler and Anthony King*

* *

POLITICAL CHANGE IN BRITAIN
*David Butler and Donald Stokes*

# THE BRITISH GENERAL ELECTION OF 1970

*By*

DAVID BUTLER

*Fellow of Nuffield College, Oxford*

*and*

MICHAEL PINTO-DUSCHINSKY

*Research Fellow of Pembroke College, Oxford*

MACMILLAN

ST MARTIN'S PRESS

© David Butler and Michael Pinto-Duschinsky 1971

All rights reserved. No part of this publication may be reproduced or transmitted, in any form or by any means, without permission.

*First published 1971 by*
THE MACMILLAN PRESS LTD
*London and Basingstoke*
*Associated companies in New York Toronto*
*Dublin Melbourne Johannesburg and Madras*

Library of Congress catalog card no. 70–145587

SBN 333 12142 2 (hard cover)

*Printed in Great Britain by*
RICHARD CLAY (THE CHAUCER PRESS) LTD
*Bungay, Suffolk*

# CONTENTS

## CARTOONS



## PHOTOGRAPHS



## DIAGRAMS



## MAP

# ACKNOWLEDGMENTS

THE authors and publishers wish to thank the following for permission to reproduce the photographs: Associated Press, Camera Press, Central Press, Percy Clarke, the Conservative Party, *Daily Telegraph*, Douglas Hurd, *Guardian*, Keystone, the Labour Party, *London Express*, Press Association, Terry Pitt, *Reading Evening Post*, Roy Squire, Topix, Universal Pictorial.

# INTRODUCTION

At 10.30 p.m. on Thursday June 18, 1970, Mr. Wilson was in the Adelphi Hotel at Liverpool, chatting with journalists in cheerful anticipation; the reports from Transport House had confirmed the broad message of the opinion polls — victory was in the bag. Mr. Heath at Bexley showed no anxiety but he was virtually alone in his defiance of the general expectation; at least one of his aides had gone home to sleep because he could not bear the prospect of the night. Top civil servants prepared for a quiet weekend undisturbed by the flurry of a changeover of government.

Half an hour later, the returning officer at Guildford appeared on the nation's television screens to declare the first result; it showed a greatly increased majority for David Howell, the Conservative candidate. Within minutes the swing at Guildford was repeated in Cheltenham, and then in the Salford and Wolverhampton seats. It was plain to Mr. Wilson and to everyone else who was watching that he was heading for a totally unexpected defeat.

Yet had the election taken place on June 18, 1969, just a year earlier and on the very day of the government's capitulation over the Industrial Relations Bill, there would have been equal amazement — but for the opposite reason. Mr. Wilson's administration had sunk so low in the opinion polls that anyone who said that a year later it would come within 29 seats of retaining its majority would have been regarded as out of touch with reality.

Therefore our central tasks in this book are to see why Labour went into the depths of public disfavour; to show how it recovered; and then to examine the way in which the Conservatives won after all.

It is twenty-five years since the first Nuffield election study was written. In 1945 there was no precedent for such a venture. Its inspiration came from the fact that a college, newly founded to study the contemporary world, accepted the suggestion of R. B. McCallum, who was by profession a historian of the recent past, that it had a duty to chronicle an event of such importance and to kill at birth any myths of the sort that had grown up about the election of 1918. The 1945 study was concerned mainly to record the events of the campaign itself and to provide a document setting out, for the convenience of future historians, publicly available information about the election.

These aims have ranked high in the minds of authors of subsequent Nuffield studies, and readers of earlier volumes will see a large element of continuity in *The British General Election of 1970*. There have, however, been important innovations. On the one hand, elections nowadays are much more fully recorded and analysed in the press and there is less need to provide the detailed documentation that can be found elsewhere. On the other hand, previous Nuffield books as well as other psephological studies have shown how misleading it can be to confine attention to the campaign period or to those elements of electioneering which are already on public record.[1]

[1] We should perhaps add a parenthetical word on a current debate. We are aware that students of elections are often classed with the surveyors of public opinion. It is understandable that the psephologists and the pollsters should be lumped together in praise, or, more often, in obloquy, but it is not fair to either trade, even though they use many of the same tools. The justification for the systematic study of party campaigning and political persuasion and for the exhaustive analysis of election results does not rest on the success or failure of opinion poll predictions — nor does the pollster's achievement rest upon the quality of academic work in psephology. Elections demand study because they serve as the focus for so much of democratic activity. How politicians prepare for campaigns and conduct them, and what consequences their activities have, raise problems that are central to any understanding of our government and society. If erroneous conclusions are sometimes reached by psephologists, it in no way vitiates the *raison d'être* for their activity.

Yet there are two challenges to the study of elections which must be faced. The first is that the observer affects his subject-matter. It can be argued that, by looking at and writing about electioneering so publicly, the psephologist alters the nature of the thing he is describing. 'Elections are primarily decided over the long haul.' 'Candidates seldom change votes.' By reaching and documenting such conclusions, it is argued, the psephologist leads politicians and party officials to act differently: moreover, by inducing the mass media to fill their space with psephological technicalities rather than with news of the campaign and the issues, he leads discussion of the election into the wrong channels. Even if this were true, it would not follow that the study of elections should be abandoned. But in fact it greatly overrates the importance and the impact of psephology. Having had close contact with people in the parties and with the academic discipline, we can confidently assert that the latter has as yet had but limited effect. Polls are, it is true, a different matter: they attract much more attention and have a far greater potential for influencing conduct. As the 1970 election showed, their influence, too, may be overrated, but it cannot be so lightly ignored. In Chapter VIII we discuss it and whether it calls for any remedy.

The second challenge to psephology is a wider one. Do elections really matter? Britain, some would say, is now so much in the grip externally of international economic circumstances, and internally of five-year 'rolling programmes' devised and administered by civil servants, that it matters little which of two surprisingly similar parties is in fact in power. Our answer is not to claim that a vast amount turns on the outcome of a general election. The difference that a new government can make to the direction taken by the country may indeed be much more limited than most people imagine. But it is far from negligible. Even if the range of choice in short-term policy is limited, those in power can

If previous studies have had one developing theme, it is that election campaigns offer very insufficient explanations of election results. We have become more and more aware of the extent to which party choice is made over the long run, and usually over the very long run.[1] To give a simple example: when voters were asked after the 1970 election when they had finally made up their minds how they would vote, only 11% said it was during the campaign; 67% dated their partisanship back more than five years, a majority of them saying, 'All my life.' 1970 provided one of the rare examples of an election that may have been finally decided by what happened during the campaign; but it would be misleading to focus too much attention on the events of the last few weeks. Even if there was a late movement to the Conservatives, it is still necessary to explain the gradual build-up of circumstance which put voters in a mood to make last-minute switches so easily.

Elections are complex events which can never yield to a simple or single theory of how they are won and lost. As the successive British election studies have shown, it is necessary to examine them in several time scales and at several levels. Among the subjects that have an obvious relevance are the politicians' views of the electorate and how these influence their tactics; the use of parliament as a forum for long-term campaigning; the mobilisation of the central party organisations; the activities in the constituencies; the reactions of ordinary voters; and the behaviour of the mass media.

Our broad strategy has been to accept the variety of facets to the situation and to deal with them separately. Firstly we have outlined the events of 1966–69, the period of Labour decline, in so far as they bore on the election, separating the impact of national events and the policy-making difficulties of the parties from the organisational challenges; secondly we have recorded the Labour

---

do much to condition the climate of thought within which social change takes place. While that is so, the struggles to become the new government are worthy of study as real struggles for power. And even if they were not real struggles but only thought to be so by the participants they would be worthy of detailed examination as significant manifestations of contemporary human behaviour.

[1] See e.g. David Butler and Donald Stokes, *Political Change in Britain* (Macmillan, 1969) chaps. 3 and 19. In other countries, such as the United States, there is evidence of a similar tendency for voters to decide their party affiliations over a long term. Nevertheless, the campaign period in the United States is, comparatively speaking, of greater importance than in Britain. Cf. A. Campbell *et al. The American Voter* (New York, 1960).

recovery during the run-up and offered a description of the campaign and the opinion polls and the way they were presented by the mass media; thirdly we have discussed organisation at the local level, before and during the campaign; and fourthly we have examined the outcome. We have reserved to appendices some material too technical to fit into the broad sweep of the main story: the statistical examination of the results and their link to census data, the content analysis of speeches and manifestos, and the role of Scottish nationalism.

In the early chapters we have focused closely on the two party leaders not because we subscribe to the currently fashionable theories of the presidentialisation of British politics but because our interviews with their colleagues and other evidence convince us that Mr. Wilson and Mr. Heath each exercised, in the particular circumstances of 1966 to 1970, a quite exceptional pre-eminence in shaping the situation. We have also concentrated very heavily on economic questions in our description of how party fortunes and policies evolved because at the time politicians plainly saw them as of overriding importance in determining how, in the end, voters would react; our later chapters suggest that they were probably right.[1]

We should add a word about the sources on which we have depended in the pages that follow. The press has, of course, been essential. There are few countries where so much of the story we seek to tell would be reported so fully and accurately in the newspapers. But the reports do at times conflict and there are aspects of party activities which are never covered in detail.[2] To check and supplement the news and analysis made available to the public day by day, we have had recourse to extensive interviewing. Between January 1968 and October 1970 we carried out 305 inter-

[1] We should make plain that we have aimed to write about the election and the events leading up to it as they appeared in June 1970. Although we have not ignored new evidence as it has become available we have tried to avoid being distracted by the changing perspectives that come inevitably with the passage of time as the forecasts and promises offered during the campaign about the state of the economy and other matters have been vindicated or falsified.

[2] In our work we have been made very strongly aware of the difficulties faced by lobby correspondents who have only a few hours to finalise their story if they are to be topical. With the passage of time politicians become much more forthcoming. We would not ourselves claim to match the experienced lobby correspondent who told us that given two weeks he could unlock any cabinet secret (unfortunately his editor lost interest after two days). The contemporary historian lacks the immediacy of access granted to the journalist; he has to rely on politicians' hindsight — which has its dangers as well as its advantages.

views (excluding those at regional and local levels). 137 of them were with national politicians, including a majority of the cabinet and most senior shadow ministers. 135 were with officials at party headquarters, and 33 were with civil servants or other observers. With their aid, supported by analysis of published and unpublished documents, we have tried to sort out what seemed to us the key events and factors in the 1970 campaign and in the four years that preceded it. In the narrative chapters that follow there are few assertions that could not be traced directly to our interview notes, even though the interviews were conducted on understandings which debar us from citing our authority. Nor, of course, is something said in a confidential interview necessarily a reliable piece of historical evidence. Almost everyone to whom we spoke was an interested party and, like all of us, was subject to the selectivity and the fallibility of memory. (Once, four out of five participants interviewed named a different person as chairman of an important meeting three months earlier.) We have tried to double- and triple-check wherever possible and we have often omitted interesting and plausible material because we could not fully satisfy ourselves of its truth. We have tried to be especially careful not to impute intentions to individuals unless we felt we had really solid warrant for doing so and we have tried to preserve forms of words close to those they might have used themselves. The writing of contemporary history has its inevitable frustrations. We feel, however, that the gaps that have to be left may be no more serious than those forced on the more distant chronicler and that the insights are more than sufficient to justify the enterprise academically.

An election is of course not confined to the *haute politique* of Whitehall, Westminster and Smith Square. Unlike previous studies which have included sketches of particular constituency campaigns, we have attempted to give politics at the local level a more general and possibly a more systematic treatment. In addition to over a hundred interviews with local agents and regional organisers before the election, we carried out, with the help of a dozen colleagues, 237 interviews in 130 constituencies during the campaign, mostly with agents and candidates. After the election 109 candidates replied to private letters and about 40 agents, mainly in marginal seats, sent technical details in answer to a questionnaire.

Anyone who seeks in this book a final answer to what happened on June 18, 1970, will be disappointed. We have gathered together as much factual material as we could; we have set out the background to the event; we have asked what seem to us to be the relevant questions and we have explored the hypotheses which have been put forward to meet them, adding some of our own. We hope we have made a substantial contribution to the argument and provided evidence which proponents of any point of view can cite. But on such central questions as the cause of the Labour recovery from March to early June or of the Conservative recovery in the final days, as well as the extent of those movements and how far they were inevitable, we remain very ready to be corrected as the analysis of survey data continues or as participants in the affair offer new insights into their conduct.

We do not mention all this data-gathering either as evidence of our industry or proof of our infallibility: much more could have been collected and, even so, it would still have been subject to the limitations of our interpretation. We merely feel that the reader, particularly when some years have passed, is entitled to know the basis for what follows.

We are describing an election in which, as always, government and opposition emphasised their differences and sought to convince the public that their vote represented a choice between two widely different paths. We ourselves did not see the contest so starkly. The leaders of both parties, either from principle or with their eyes on the electorate, had in practice, if not explicitly, steered towards the middle. The real clashes of principle in 1966–70 and in the campaign seemed extraordinarily few; the divide between the rival manifestos and election addresses was also small, as a study of their content shows; the voters showed that they were not deeply aroused; their volatility, as measured by the polls before and during the campaign, showed a new lack of fixity or depth of reaction. They were choosing, as Mr. Wilson admitted, 'the lesser evil'. Indeed if we were to append a sub-title to this book it would be 'The unpopularity contest'. We are describing why on June 18, 1970, those who bothered to vote decided that by a narrow margin Mr. Heath and the Conservatives were probably the lesser evil.

In this, the eighth in the series of general election studies sponsored by Nuffield College, the authors' debt to the College both officially and personally is very great. Inevitably a work such as this has to be a collaborative venture and it is not possible to name all those who have contributed to our labours.

We should, however, like to thank, in addition to those whose names appear in the table of contents, those who collected material for us in the constituencies. An exceptional burden fell on Elizabeth Balson (who covered the South West), Alan Butt Philip (Wales), William Johnson (East Anglia), Iain McLean (Scotland), John Ramsden (Yorkshire and Wessex) and David Wilson (the Midlands), but we are also most grateful to Hugh Berrington, Martin Ceadel, Chris Cook, Ivor Crewe, Alan Sked and Robert Taylor. Michael Ashley did much work on the background of candidates and John O'Sullivan on newspaper archives. We are indebted to Hannan Rose for information on problems of race relations, to Roger Scott for information on Northern Ireland and to Lewis Chester for information on candidates. Clive Payne lightened all our statistical burdens to an enormous degree: Angela Weight arranged the illustrations. Austin Mitchell played a major part in the inception of this book. Merton College was generous with secretarial help and in the last phase of writing one of us returned to Pembroke College where, in 1945, R. B. McCallum composed so much of the first volume in this series. The patience and resourcefulness of Mrs. Gay Swabey, our research assistant, and of Mrs. Ann Taylor and Mrs. Audrey Skeats were beyond praise. Hugh Berrington, Samuel Brittan, Martin Ceadel, Anthony King, Dick Leonard, Shelley Markham, Janet Morgan, Peter Pulzer, John Ramsden, Stan Taylor, and Philip Williams were invaluable critics of our manuscript.

Our thanks are also due to many people in the wider world of politics and the mass media. We owe a debt to many journalists and broadcasters not only for their published work but for much private guidance as well. We should also thank the pollsters who have been unfailingly courteous in providing additional details on their findings. The General Register Office and the Home Office, too, were very helpful.

But it is the politicians and party officials whom we should thank most of all. Very few leading figures in the party hierarchies have escaped our importunities over the past three years. The party headquarters on both sides of Smith Square have gone to unprecedented lengths in giving us time and information about matters that used to be veiled in secrecy. We are very deeply grateful for all those hours spent in answering our questions and in reading our manuscript. At the constituency level too we have asked and received far more than ever before from agents and candidates; one of the most agreeable features of our task was the welcome that we always seemed to be given, even in the busiest moments of the campaign, when we drifted unannounced into their offices.

Psephology can be a demanding pursuit. We are much indebted for the kindness and forbearance of our academic colleagues and, even more, of Marilyn Butler and her sons.

DAVID BUTLER
MICHAEL PINTO-DUSCHINSKY

*Nuffield College,*
*Oxford*
*November 9, 1970*

[*Punch*, May 20, 1970

CHAPTER I

# THE WOUNDS OF GOVERNMENT 1966–1969

IN 1960 an imaginary constitution for the Conservative party was prepared for the *New Statesman*. '. . . When the Party is in Opposition,' started one of the clauses, '. . . the Party shall not normally be in Opposition.' The article, which for diplomatic reasons was not published, was written by Harold Wilson. At this early stage he had already formulated his main long-term aim — possibly his only one — to build Labour into the natural governing party and to transfer its heritage of protest and internal dissent to the Conservatives. Britain was to follow the example of Sweden where the Social Democratic party had continued in power without a break since 1936. From 1964 onwards, this motive governed the actions of Mr. Wilson, and thus of the whole administration of which he was the moving force.[1]

How was this to be achieved? Opinion surveys (which Mr. Wilson invariably examined in considerable detail) regularly showed that a majority of the electorate thought Labour's heart was in the right place and that it was more likely than the Conservatives to improve pensions, education, health and housing. But it suffered from the reputation of being unable to manage the economy or to handle foreign affairs. Admittedly, Ramsay MacDonald could not be blamed for the world slump which engulfed the Labour government in 1931; nor did Clement Attlee bear the main responsibility for post-war austerity, the convertibility fiasco of 1947, the devaluation of 1949 or the sterling crisis which

[1] By no means all the cabinet shared Mr. Wilson's aims, but they tended to be too busily engaged in their departmental activities to give thought to the general direction which the government might take. As a cabinet minister wrote privately after the election

> 'The real weakness lay [in the fact that] the Government did not operate politically at the centre. It accepted the pattern of departmental structure and advice and never really provided the central strategic thinking that was necessary on a whole host of issues . . . Labour Ministers, with a few exceptions, locked themselves up in Departments.'

Mr. Wilson is reported to have remarked soon after the 1964 election that there were only two people besides himself who thought in terms of governmental activity as a whole: his private secretary, Derek Mitchell and Sir Burke Trend (Secretary of the Cabinet).

followed the outbreak of the Korean War. Yet the fact remained that every previous Labour government — and there had been only three — had encountered grave difficulties and the public still needed to be convinced that the art of government was not confined to the Conservatives. Mr. Wilson was now determined to show that his Labour cabinet was superior in competence as well as in worthy ideals. He thought that the British people cared comparatively little about specific policies or issues. They wanted an administration in which they could have general confidence and a Prime Minister able to react to events in a statesmanlike manner. ('You Know Labour Government Works' was the party slogan in 1966.) If this meant reinterpreting socialism and abandoning some of its basic tenets, he was quite willing to do so.[1]

Accordingly, the maintenance of intimate relationships with Washington was a cornerstone of the incoming Labour government's policy, with Mr. Wilson committed to an active British role East of Suez. It was only after considerable pressure from the Treasury that the cabinet agreed in February 1965 to limit defence spending to £2,000 million a year. The Rhodesian 'Unilateral Declaration of Independence' in November 1965 gave Mr. Wilson an ideal opportunity to show himself in the role of a moderate, firm, national leader. He duly dismissed the use of force against the Smith regime, rejected offers of help from the United Nations and confined himself to the imposition of partial economic sanctions. Within days of the 1966 election, there were informal talks with the Rhodesians at official level. These led to direct negotiations between Mr. Wilson and Mr. Smith, on HMS *Tiger* in December 1966 and on HMS *Fearless* in October 1968. On both occasions, Mr. Wilson offered terms which granted much that the Rhodesians were asking. It was mainly pressure from extremists within Mr. Smith's cabinet, who insisted on the outward form as well as the substance of victory, that prevented a settlement.

In home affairs 'competence' and 'responsibility' were likewise

[1] Paul Foot argues in *The Politics of Harold Wilson* (Penguin, 1968) that he did not 'abandon' socialism in the 1960s as he had never been a doctrinaire socialist in the first place, despite his connections with the Labour left. There is considerable evidence for this view. Indeed, Mr. Wilson certainly spoke of the wealth tax and the mildly left-wing measures which some wished to include in the 1970 manifesto as 'wild Hampstead stuff . . . already refuted in the 1940s'. His priorities as Prime Minister are perhaps illustrated in the Transport House handouts of his speeches and statements during the 1970 campaign. The word 'responsibility' (and its variations such as 'Tory irresponsibility') occurred 21 times and the word 'socialism' only once.

to be the aim. Mr. Wilson felt it was therefore necessary at all costs — and the cost became ever higher — to prevent the devaluation of the pound. He also resisted pressure, particularly from Transport House and from left-wing M.P.s, to extend public ownership to new industries such as North Sea gas. An industrial economist by training, he felt that neither nationalisation nor devaluation provided answers to Britain's economic problems. These would be solved by restructuring and modernising British industry. The government was to use its influence to improve the quality of management and to streamline industries in which there were too many competing firms. It was to achieve a technological revolution. The Prime Minister's faith in 'restructuring' was convenient in two ways. It suggested, firstly, that the painful policies of devaluation and deflation could both be avoided. It was also a handy substitute for the traditional, abstract and politically disadvantageous socialist values of equality and common ownership. For he consciously rejected the principles of Professor Tawney whose writings on *Equality* had been so influential during his youth. Instead, he considered that the Labour party would be much better served by placing successful managers such as Arnold Weinstock and Sir Donald Stokes at the head of the great combines GEC/AEI (formed in November 1967) and British Leyland Motor Corporation (formed in January 1968).[1]

While he prepared to occupy the centre ground of politics and to forsake some of the principles the party had held most sacred, Mr. Wilson did not allow himself to forget the fate of Ramsay MacDonald and the troubled career of Hugh Gaitskell. He believed

[1] One of Mr. Wilson's many 'technological socialism' speeches is quoted at length on pp. 123–4. Despite the wide gulf that separated it from traditional socialism, it is important to recognise the radical social ethic encompassed by his vision of technological revolution. The modernisation of Britain would bring, he hoped, not only wealth (and therefore social welfare) but it would advance into positions of responsibility men who had risen by their merits, such as many of those whom the government now favoured in top positions in industry. In this process, the bastions of class privilege such as the public schools and the merchant banks, would lose much of their power.

The new establishment, upon which Mr. Wilson concentrated his honours lists and government awards, consisted largely of self-made industrialists and managers. Other fields such as sport or entertainment in which success was dictated by personal merits rather than elite upbringing were also well represented. His personal friends and those who received invitations to receptions at Downing Street tended to be marked by their professionalism on the one hand and their unconcern for social graces on the other. The fact that he evidently was not seduced by the established class system did much to preserve his emotional rapport with the Labour left, even though many of his policies accorded more closely with the Labour right.

that no leader of the Labour party could afford totally to alienate the left-wing minority in parliament. Besides, he owed a great personal debt to left-wingers. They had been his companions in the early fifties, when he resigned along with Aneurin Bevan from the Attlee government; they supported him in the early sixties in his assault on Hugh Gaitskell; and they voted for him when he stood against George Brown for the party leadership in 1963. Mr. Wilson could hardly expect any loyalty from the Gaitskellites; if the left turned against him as well, he would have no base of support in the Parliamentary Labour Party. Fortunately, he was to find the left was not persistent in its demands. It lacked leaders and members often seemed more concerned to clear their consciences than to put embarrassing pressure on the government.[1] There is only one known occasion when left-wingers threatened to abstain in sufficient numbers to defeat the government. This occurred when the introduction of a compulsory wages freeze was being considered in the autumn of 1965; the plan was then quietly dropped. It is significant, however, that Mr. Wilson was particularly anxious to secure his political base on the left during the months after devaluation when he was most vulnerable. This is the most plausible explanation of his curious behaviour, described later, in the winter of 1967 when the cabinet was discussing the possibility of selling arms to South Africa.

To lead Labour to the right while keeping the left in tow nevertheless required political artistry of a high order. No one was better equipped for the task than the Prime Minister. His memory and his virtuosity in quoting figures were unparalleled; as he often

[1] The most coherent voice of the left was the '*Tribune* Group' (sometimes known in its early days as the 'Monday Group'). It was organised in 1964 and, throughout the Labour government, it met regularly on Monday afternoons. Among its leading figures were Ian Mikardo, Eric Heffer, Stan Orme, James Dickens and, of course, Michael Foot. The number on the circulation list for the meetings was 30 to 35 and was, by pruning, confined to regular attenders. The group registered with the Whips in 1966 and invited the Chief Whip to attend (he came only once). Although the aim of the group was to reach an agreed point of view on important issues and although at times there was a show of hands they did not try to impose any line on their members. On the whole, they felt that they achieved very little because, in the last resort, they could not use their ultimate weapons — voting in a way that would bring the government to defeat. A further handicap to their effectiveness was that they were themselves divided on some issues, such as Europe. However, they considered that they might have contributed something to modifying government policy over the abandonment of so much of the 1968 Prices and Incomes Bill and to frustrating the penal legislation proposed for trade unions in 1969, as well as to the ultimate adoption of some policies they had long advocated — for example, devaluation, scrapping the F-111 contract and withdrawing from East of Suez.

liked to mention, he was a Fellow of the Royal Statistical Society. He was as adept in the Byzantine arts of managing Whitehall committees and of playing off his colleagues against each other as in the gentler techniques of appealing to ordinary people on television. His avuncular, humorous public style masked a complete dedication to his work, for he disdained the social prizes which go with political success and which have an allure that some Labour leaders have found difficult to resist. Even by many Tories he was accepted as the most brilliant politician in the land, and he knew it.

In April 1966 he was at the height of his powers. No Prime Minister in the twentieth century had managed to direct his party to a second election victory with an increased majority. Mr. Wilson had succeeded in doing this despite a succession of economic crises and a parliamentary majority of only three. He had performed the feat of pleasing moderate opinion in his handling of the Rhodesian crisis without provoking the left or the black Commonwealth. He had defused the colour issue which threatened in 1964 to become a serious threat to the Labour party in several parts of the country. He had averted more than one strike by his well-publicised last-minute interventions. Yet it was precisely his agility in short-term manoeuvre that was to cause many of the troubles that were to hound him during the next three years. It made him overconfident and acted as a substitute for strategic decisions. His state of mind was expressed in his dictum, which he often repeated, 'a week in politics is a long time', and in his boast that, like President Johnson, he flew the political plane by the seat of his pants. There is evidence that he actually believed that his diplomatic efforts might lead to peace in Vietnam.[1] His optimism led him to postpone unpleasant choices about the economy. His confidence in his powers of persuasion allowed him in May 1967 to apply for British membership of the Common Market despite the overwhelming evidence that General de Gaulle had no intention of lifting his veto. When he was finally compelled to agree to the devaluation of sterling in November 1967, he calmly assured the British people that the pound in their pockets[2] had not been devalued, and when nine

[1] See G. McDermott, 'The Wilson-Kosygin Peace Bid', *New Statesman*, December 18, 1970.

[2] Mr. Wilson has frequently complained that the 'pound in your pocket' quotation was misleadingly removed from its context and that, in accordance with a Treasury brief, it was intended to explain how devaluation would work. The full paragraph reads: '*Tonight we must face the new situation. First, what this means. From now on the pound abroad is worth 14 per cent or so less in terms of*

days later de Gaulle ended the Common Market talks, he insisted, with notable insouciance, that the British application remained on the table and would be pursued anew at a future date. Throughout his premiership, his belief that Labour success at the polls depended on his personal appeal allowed him to ignore the pressing need to strengthen the party organisation and led to the sorry state of affairs at Transport House which is described in the next chapter.

Mr. Wilson was to attribute his defeat in the 1970 election to the fact that the scar tissue of the wounds the British people had received during 1966 to 1969 had not sufficiently healed. He was probably right. Had he tackled the unpleasant problems facing the country immediately after obtaining a working majority in April 1966; had he, for example, agreed to devaluation in July 1966, he would in all likelihood have won the 1970 general election and become at the age of 54 the first Prime Minister since Lord Liverpool in the 1820s to win three elections in a row. As it was, he very nearly succeeded: had the swing to the Conservatives been 1·5% less, he would have come near to his goal of making Labour the normal governing party.[1]

The Labour government, which was returned to office on April 1, 1966, with a handsome majority of 97, ran into serious trouble within four months. On Wednesday, July 20, the Prime Minister, faced by exceptionally severe speculation against sterling, presented a £500 million package of 'swingeing cuts' to parliament. The July measures, more harshly deflationary than any since 1949,

---

*other currencies. It does not mean, of course, that the pound here in Britain, in your pocket or purse or in your bank, has been devalued. What it does mean is that we shall now be able to sell more goods abroad on a competitive basis'.* Later in his broadcast he foreshadowed future cuts in public expenditure, especially on defence, but gave an assurance (incorrectly) that 'the priority programmes of housing, school building, and hospital building will be safeguarded in all these measures'. The broadcast contained no direct reference to possible tax increases. While he was preparing his statement, he is known to have been advised by Mr. Crossman, and possibly by other senior colleagues, to start with 'two minutes of the white sheet', to inject a firmer tone throughout and to eliminate the 'pound in your pocket' phrase which was bound to be quoted on its own. Mr. Wilson refused.

[1] Specially useful among the many sketches of Mr. Wilson are Ian Trethowan, 'Five Years of Mr. Wilson', *The Times*, January 29, 30, 31, 1968, Peter Jenkins, *The Battle of Downing Street*, Chapter 6 (Charles Knight, 1970), Ronald Butt, 'Profile', *Sunday Times*, May 24, 1970. Patrick Gordon Walker describes the working of the cabinet under Mr. Wilson in *The Cabinet* (Cape, 1970).

included restrictions on hire purchase, a surcharge on alcohol, beer and petrol, increased postal charges, tightened building controls, cuts in public investment and overseas expenditure and a statutory wages freeze to last for six months. The root cause of the crisis was the failure to prevent wage rises during the period before the 1966 general election. When Mr. Wilson had announced on February 28 that the old parliament would be dissolved, there were already signs that inflation would soon be uncontrollable if the government remained inactive. Mr. Callaghan, the Chancellor of the Exchequer, knowing full well that the state of the economy was bound to be a major election issue, wished to make as reassuring a statement as possible. His Treasury advisers indicated that the post-election Budget would need to be deflationary. But it was agreed that he could declare in his major pre-election pronouncement on March 1 that he did not 'foresee the need for severe increases in taxation', on the ground that the official forecasts, if interpreted most optimistically, brought the statement within the bounds of possibility. But it clearly contained an element of recklessness, constituting in Treasury opinion a 'high risk policy'.

After the election, the Treasury recommended an orthodox deflationary Budget. However, the triumvirate which controlled economic policy, the Prime Minister, James Callaghan and George Brown, felt this was unacceptable in view of their statements during the campaign and the Treasury was given the task of preparing at a few days' notice a set of measures that tackled inflation without appearing too obviously restrictive. The midnight oil burned until one of the many ideas of Nicholas Kaldor found general acceptance. Professor Kaldor was one of the most influential of the economic advisers brought in by the new government in 1964. He proposed that a tax should be paid by employers for each of their employees. The brunt of the tax was to fall on the service industries — 25*s.* per person per week. Employment in manufacturing, which was considered more conducive to growth and higher exports, was to be encouraged by the remission of the tax and the payment of a premium of 7*s.* 6*d.* a week for each employee. This Selective Employment Tax was acceptable to the Treasury as it would yield over £300 million in a full year and was therefore a deflationary measure. It was also acceptable to the Department of Economic Affairs which calculated that it would foster the restructuring of the economy and would, unlike conventional taxes, encourage increased productivity. Indeed, the new tax had considerable theoretical and practical advantages, which were later to be emphasised in an independent study by Professor Reddaway.[1] In the short run, however, it had three major disadvantages. Firstly, the rush and the necessary secrecy with which the SET was prepared left a host of minor anomalies. Secondly, it left inflation unchecked over the difficult summer months as it did not come into force until September. Thirdly, and most important, SET appeared too painless.[2] It seemed, as was intended, a soft substitute for conventional deflation. The conviction soon spread among the international banking community that the Labour government was still reluctant to take the measures necessary to defend the pound despite its newly found freedom from electoral pressures. In June, when the central bankers met at Basle, it was widely expected that sterling would be devalued by the autumn.

Matters were not improved by a seamen's strike which lasted from May 16 until July 2. Although the strike affected no foreign shipping and less than half of British shipping, the economy was in too precarious a state to withstand even a moderate blow at this time. The £38 million deficit in the balance of payments in May was followed by a £49 million deficit in June. The publication at the end of June of bad trade figures for the first quarter of 1966 led to speculation against the pound. This became severe on Monday, July 11, following an article in the *Observer* advocating devaluation. The cabinet meeting on Tuesday produced no more than an announcement from the Chancellor that bank credit would be restricted. In the evening, Mr. Wilson was due to give a speech at a dinner for the visiting Australian Prime Minister. He took the opportunity to compensate by harsh words for the lack of governmental action. In typical style he attributed the bout of speculation to the British press:

> 'the defeatist cries, the moaning minnies, the wet editorials — yes, the Sundays as well — of those who will seek any opportunity to sell Britain short at home or abroad.'

[1] *A First Report on the Effects of the Selective Employment Tax*, March 4, 1970.
[2] According to a senior Treasury official:

> 'After the 1966 election, we thought that substantial increases in taxes were necessary. In view of their previous statements, the Government felt it could not do this. The way out was SET. It had a bad psychological effect. It was a new tax, and it did not hurt soon enough. A bad atmosphere of lack of impact was produced.'

The foreign bankers were not impressed. When the markets opened next morning, sterling suffered heavy losses and the Treasury received urgent warnings from the Bank of England that it was 'bleeding to death'.

Meanwhile, unknown to the public and to most of the cabinet as well, matters were coming to a head within the Treasury and the Department of Economic Affairs. The DEA was committed to a National Plan envisaging a growth of 25% between 1964 and 1970. Ever since the formation of the DEA in October 1964, its economic advisers had been united in their view that this target would be unattainable if the economy continued to shoulder the burden of defending sterling at its existing parity. Mr. Brown, Secretary of State for Economic Affairs, and the architect of the National Plan, had been slow to accept this analysis, but faced by the prospect of deflationary measures that would completely destroy it, he finally became committed to devaluation. At the Treasury, Mr. Callaghan also began to have doubts, though of a very different kind. Basically he was wholly committed to the $2.80 parity. He did not want to be remembered as the Chancellor who devalued the pound. Yet, the 'creative tension' between the DEA and the Treasury, skilfully encouraged for nearly two years by the Prime Minister, had prevented the introduction of the deflationary measures which were advocated by the Treasury and which Mr. Callaghan considered to be the only viable alternative. Even in the present crisis, he feared that it would be impossible to impose sufficiently severe cuts. If negotiations with the Prime Minister, the DEA and the spending ministries produced a half-baked set of measures, he would lose out in personal terms in all directions: within the Labour party, he would be seen as an axing Chancellor — the force of evil — as against George Brown who would be the advocate of economic expansion — the force for good. At the same time, compromise measures would not solve the problem of sterling and there would be future crises which would force him to devalue after all. If, therefore, he could not enforce the full package which the Treasury had in mind, he would support George Brown's case for an immediate devaluation.

On Thursday, July 14 Bank Rate was raised from 6% to 7%. There was a cabinet meeting in the morning but no further measures were announced. It was during the same morning, it seems, that Mr. Callaghan played his hand. He let it be known to the Prime Minister that he was 'wobbling' in his determination to avoid devaluation. The implication was that he would join Mr. Brown unless the Prime Minister supported the Treasury proposals to the full.[1] Faced by the possibility of the combined opposition of his two most senior ministers (who had been his opponents during the leadership struggle in 1963), Mr. Wilson had to make the choice between devaluation and deflation which he had been avoiding for nearly two years.[2] He chose the latter. He assured the Chancellor of his complete support for the measures the Treasury would be proposing. Indeed, he would shield Mr. Callaghan from the odium of the cuts by announcing them to parliament himself. Confident of Mr. Wilson's backing, Mr. Callaghan hauled down his devaluationist kite. In the afternoon Mr. Wilson accordingly told the House of Commons that deflationary measures would be announced in about two weeks' time. Unfortunately, this statement did not calm the exchange market and speculation against the pound intensified on Friday, July 15.

Mr. Wilson was due to visit Moscow on Saturday. He was reluctant to postpone his meeting with Mr. Kosygin as the need for a settlement of the Vietnam war had become even more pressing when U.S. jets had bombed oil installations near Hanoi and Haiphong on June 29. He also wanted to show the left-wingers who had refused to support his moderate policy in the vote after the Commons debate on July 7 that he sympathised with their concern. On Friday night, he issued a statement that the promised economic cuts would be brought forward and announced to parliament the following Wednesday, July 20, a day after his return from Russia. To assure the smooth passage of the package through the cabinet, its preparation was entrusted to the most senior civil servants available: Sir Burke Trend (Secretary of the Cabinet), Sir William Armstrong (Permanent Secretary of the Treasury) and Sir Eric Roll (Permanent Secretary of the Department of Economic Affairs). On Monday the proposals were despatched by envoy to Mr.

[1] Recollections of the exact turn of events are vague, but it has been alleged that Mr. Callaghan and Mr. Brown planned a demarche with the Prime Minister when they would jointly demand devaluation. According to this version, news of their intentions travelled, probably as Mr. Callaghan intended, to the Prime Minister; the Prime Minister then saw Mr. Brown and Mr. Callaghan separately and gave in to Mr. Callaghan's demands for deflation as this was now the only way he could split the temporary Brown/Callaghan axis.

[2] As its advocates recognised, devaluation would itself have involved at least a degree of deflation, but, they argued, with happier consequences than deflation on its own.

Wilson. Meanwhile, Mr. Brown tried to rally support for devaluation, though he must have known that the combined opposition of the Prime Minister and the Chancellor made his chances of success slim. Over the weekend key members of the cabinet were widely dispersed. Mr. Brown was in Durham addressing the Miners' Gala where he was letting it be known that he would resign from the government. Mr. Benn was there too. Mr. Jenkins was at a country house party. Others were at their homes or with friends. It was thus impossible to organise a cabal and, while there were a number of consultations by telephone, the later talk of a plot was clearly exaggerated, though it certainly worried the Prime Minister.[1] When on Tuesday afternoon, July 19, within hours of Mr. Wilson's return to London, the cabinet gathered to discuss the statement he was to make the following day, only a minority had a clear impression of the issues involved in the choice between deflation and devaluation; some may even have had no notion that devaluation, 'the great unmentionable', was one of the alternatives before them. The meeting lasted four and a half hours. Several members were absent at a state dinner for King Hussein. The cabinet met again on Wednesday morning. Mr. Callaghan presented the package of deflationary measures, making it clear with the Prime Minister's support that they were put forward as a whole on a non-negotiable basis. Individual items could not be discussed, and perhaps rejected, separately.

Mr. Brown presented the case against the Treasury proposals in characteristically emotional fashion, arguing for the preservation of the expansion envisaged in the National Plan even if this involved devaluation. He was supported by Roy Jenkins and Anthony Crosland, both Gaitskellites who had been convinced by the economic arguments for devaluation. Two personal allies of the Prime Minister, Mr. Crossman and Mrs. Castle, whose departments suffered from the proposed cuts in public expenditure, expressed concern that matters had reached such a point without the cabinet being consulted. They complained that the option of devaluation had been effectively excluded as it was by then too late to obtain the necessary information on which to base a rational decision or to carry out the administrative preparations that devaluation would involve. There was further support from

[1] Cf. Andrew Roth, 'Plots against Wilson', *New Outlook*, November 1966.

Anthony Wedgwood Benn, who had joined the cabinet barely two weeks earlier as Minister of Technology.[1]

Against the devaluationists stood the Chancellor and the Prime Minister. They were backed by the passive majority of the cabinet who did not pretend to understand the economic technicalities involved and were therefore unwilling to oppose the Treasury recommendations. The President of the Board of Trade, Douglas Jay, who had been involved in the 1949 devaluation and whose voice might have been influential against the Treasury, advocated the imposition of import quotas as an alternative to deflation and devaluation. Doubts about altering the parity were also expressed by more than one of the non-departmental ministers on the ground that its effectiveness would be nullified by retaliatory devaluation by other countries and that it would anyway involve the betrayal of foreign holders of sterling. The Prime Minister warned the cabinet against the implication that devaluation would be an easy option, arguing that deflation would be equally necessary whether the parity was changed or not.[2] George Brown again made clear his threat to resign if the cabinet refused to accept his case and at one point in the confused discussion ceremoniously moved his chair away from the table to indicate that he was no longer a member. However, his resignation did not become public until Wednesday afternoon. By that time the cabinet had inevitably accepted the deflationary package and it had been announced to parliament. In the course of Wednesday evening Mr. Brown's

[1] Mr. Cousins resigned on July 4 in protest against the introduction of the Prices and Incomes Bill which gave some statutory powers to the government to delay wage rises. He had made known his objections to the proposals at a much earlier stage and his departure from the cabinet had been predicted for some months.

[2] Even after 1967, Mr. Wilson continued to defend the decision against devaluation in July 1966 on economic grounds. He argued that devaluation in 1966 would have been regarded as premature by the international bankers, and would have led immediately to retaliatory devaluation and after a few months to renewed speculation and a second devaluation (probably after the Six Day War in 1967).

A more widely held view, however, is that Mr. Wilson had from the outset excluded the possibility of devaluation, irrespective of the economic arguments, for political reasons. This is certainly a popular Treasury view. See also Peter Jay, 'Devaluation — Who was to Blame?' *The Times*, November 23, 1967. Mr. Jay, who was previously private secretary to Sir William Armstrong, Permanent Secretary of the Treasury, maintains that in October 1964 'a firm, irrevocable' decision was taken on 'political grounds' that devaluation had to be avoided . . . 'The Prime Minister decided from the outset on his personal authority that devaluation was out: and the machine was given the job of carrying out the policy right or wrong.'

supporters collected a round robin urging him to remain in the government despite the rejection of his expansionist policy. When this reached him late in the night, he relented and went to Number 10 to make his peace with the Prime Minister, stopping afterwards to announce his change of mind to the journalists waiting outside.[1]

With this *opéra bouffe* episode, the drama came to an end. On July 29 Mr. Brown introduced a White Paper incorporating proposals for a compulsory wages freeze. These were added to the Prices and Incomes Bill which had been introduced at the beginning of July and whose passage had been interrupted by the economic difficulties. When the bill came before parliament on August 4, 25 Labour M.P.s, mostly left-wingers, ostentatiously abstained. But this was a minor irritation. Public spirits were high following Britain's magnificent victory on July 30 in the final of the World Cup. Britain's triumph at football, a sport with which the Prime Minister was closely associated, showed that the Dunkirk spirit (to which he was fond of appealing) was not dead. Besides, the frayed tempers at Westminster would be eased by the relaxations of the summer. Before departing for the Scilly Isles, the Prime Minister announced a cabinet reshuffle. Mr. Brown was moved to the Foreign Office, and Mr. Stewart took Mr. Brown's place at the DEA. Mr. Crossman became Lord President of the Council and Leader of the House. Mr. Callaghan, who had appeared to request a move to the Foreign Office in an interview with Mr. William Davis of the *Guardian*, remained at the Treasury. 'Now I've got four heirs apparent instead of one', Mr. Wilson was rumoured to remark.

Mr. Wilson had some grounds for satisfaction. The main danger to his position, a Brown/Callaghan axis, had been eliminated. For the time being the pound was safe. The events of July had not seriously harmed his dominance over the cabinet. Admittedly he

[1] Mr. Brown's uninformative version of the July crisis is given in the *Sunday Times*, October 18, 1970. He discusses relationships between the DEA and the Treasury in 'Why the DEA lost to the Treasury Knights', the *Sunday Times*, March 31, 1968. Mr. Callaghan's views are reflected by William Davis, 'What Really Happened', *Guardian*, July 23, 1966. Magnus Turnstile gives a useful summary of the reporting of the crisis in 'The Fleet Street Version', *New Statesman* July 29, 1966. Cabinet dispositions are reviewed in 'What happened in the Cabinet', *Statist*, July 22, 1966. The role of the Bank and the Treasury Knights is described (and possibly overemphasised) in 'How the bubble burst' by the *Sunday Times* 'Insight' team, July 24, 1966. The case for devaluation from both a right-wing and a left-wing point of view is given by Nigel Lawson and Richard Pryke in the *Spectator*, July 29, 1966.

had agreed to set up a Strategic Economic Policy Committee aimed at preventing the cabinet's being surprised by an economic crisis once again. But this SEP Committee would be under his own chairmanship and its meetings would be irregular. The compulsory wages and prices freeze had been accepted by the TUC and the CBI and was opposed by only a limited group in parliament.

There were other factors, however, which gave cause for alarm. Mr. Wilson's victory in the cabinet debate on devaluation was not unconditional. He had aimed all along to prevent the subject from being discussed or even mentioned in the fear that it would lead to speculation and make it more difficult to avoid a change in the parity. The cabinet debates of July 19 and July 20 would now set the passive majority thinking and improve the chances of the devaluationists if the deflationary package did not work. More generally, it would become harder to control cabinet proceedings as tightly as in the past. His relationships with the TUC, the CBI and the Labour party were likely to worsen as the economic cuts led — as they inevitably would — to higher unemployment during the winter. As it was, the General Council of the TUC had 'acquiesced' in the freeze only after a disputed vote and against the advice of the General Secretary, George Woodcock. The support of the CBI was equally grudging. Although the opinion polls indicated that Labour was still comfortably in the lead (only one poll during 1966, Gallup in August, gave the Conservatives a bare lead of ½%) there had been a hint of the shaky state of opinion in the loss of Carmarthen to the Welsh Nationalists in the first by-election of the new parliament on July 14. The deepest effect of the July crisis was to put the new government on to the defensive and prevent it from taking control of events at a time when the removal of electoral pressures ought to have given it the greatest scope.

Realising that his new ministry was unlikely to be marked by its economic triumphs, Mr. Wilson looked for other opportunities to dish the Tories. In the role of peacemaker, he paid a brief visit to Washington on July 29 to give Mr. Johnson a report on his discussions with Mr. Kosygin about the fighting in Vietnam. At a lunch in his honour the United States President showered praise on Mr. Wilson: 'a nation that has given . . . the courage of a Churchill . . . is blessed now as it was then, with gallant and hardy leadership. In you, sir, she has a man of mettle.' In private, the President was less enthusiastic, preferring Britain to send a token force to Vietnam rather than make futile, embarrassing attempts to secure a peace settlement.[1]

The hopes of obtaining an agreement with the Rhodesians appeared better. Arthur Bottomley was replaced at the Commonwealth Relations Office by Herbert Bowden, whom Mr. Wilson considered less antipathetic to Ian Smith. Talks between officials continued at a higher level over the summer and in August the RAF Squadron was removed from Zambia. In September and again in November Mr. Bowden visited Salisbury and prepared the ground for the summit meeting which took place on HMS *Tiger* in December. Here again, Mr. Wilson was cheated of the dramatic triumph which seemed within his grasp during the negotiations.[2]

Mr. Wilson's most far-reaching enterprise was his attempt to secure admission to the Common Market. Three explanations have sometimes been given for his conversion from his former anti-Europeanism:[3] (i) Growing disillusion with the Commonwealth forced Mr. Wilson to re-examine his priorities; in particular the reappraisal of Britain's defence policies focused attention on Europe. (ii) Mr. Brown agreed to accept the Foreign Office in August 1966 only on condition that the Common Market became a high priority. (iii) It was a consequence of the search for new policies after the sterling crisis of July 1966.

It is argued that throughout the sixties economic and cultural links between Britain and the Commonwealth were becoming tenuous. The decline in British influence, which must have been brought sharply home to Mr. Wilson in the autumn of 1965 when India and Pakistan preferred the services of Mr. Kosygin as mediator in the Kashmir dispute, gradually undermined the rationale of a military presence East of Suez. The decisions in 1965 to limit military spending and to scrap the TSR-2 were followed in February 1966 by the further decisions to withdraw from Aden by 1968 and to drop plans for new aircraft carriers. It was the end of

[1] President Johnson requested a British military contribution to the Vietnam War as early as 1964. See Patrick Gordon Walker, *The Cabinet* (Cape, 1970) (p. 125) and Louis Heren, *No Hail, No Farewell* (Weidenfeld and Nicolson, 1970), p. 183.

[2] See 'Rhodesia: Documents relating to proposal for a settlement, 1966', HMSO December 1966 (Cmnd. 3171). For the Rhodesian view, see 'Statement on Anglo-Rhodesia relations, December 1966 to May 1969', Prime Minister's Office, Salisbury (C.S.R. 36–1969).

[3] See e.g. Nora Beloff, 'What Happened in Britain after the General said No', in Pierre Uri, *From Commonwealth to Common Market* (Penguin, 1968) and Brian Lapping, *The Labour Government, 1964–70* (Penguin, 1970).

the fighting between Malaysia and Indonesia in August 1966 which removed the last major obstacle to the ultimate withdrawal of British troops from S.E. Asia. This was duly heralded in the Defence White Paper of July 1967. It is therefore easy to see the Common Market application as an attempt to substitute a European for a Commonwealth role. A closer look at the evidence suggests, however, that there was little connection between the cabinet's slow acceptance of withdrawal from Asia and its agreement to negotiate with the Six, apart from the fact that they were both consequences of Britain's economic predicament. When the decision to apply for membership of the EEC was taken in principle in October 1966, the government was still committed to maintaining its role East of Suez. The policy was unsuccessfully defended at the Labour Party Conference in October 1966 which passed a hostile motion, and it was vigorously expounded in the Defence White Paper published on February 16, 1967. This led to acrimonious discussion within the Parliamentary Labour Party and to large Labour abstentions when it was debated in the House of Commons. Had the decision to withdraw from East of Suez already been reached as part of the Common Market policy, there would have been every motive for giving some indication of it in Spring 1967. The government's determination to withstand such strong internal pressures suggests that it had not yet made up its mind. Furthermore, it is difficult to detect any link in the attitudes of individual cabinet members or ministries to withdrawal from Asia and to entry into Europe. Some of the most active proponents of a British presence East of Suez were among the keenest Marketeers — notably Mr. Wilson and Mr. Stewart. Others favoured withdrawal from Asia but opposed entry into Europe.

It is also wrong to emphasise the significance of Mr. Brown's move to the Foreign Office. He had just been badly defeated in cabinet and his public standing had not been improved by the affair of his non-resignation on July 20. In any case, the previous Foreign Secretary, Michael Stewart, had also been persuaded to become a supporter of the Common Market.

One underlying motive for the Prime Minister's new-found Europeanism was outlined in his speech at the Lord Mayor's Guildhall banquet on November 14, 1966:

> 'I would like to see . . . a drive to create a new technological community to pool within Europe the enormous technological inventive-

ness of Britain and other European countries. . . . In this field of technological cooperation no one has more to contribute than Britain.'

He was also persuaded by the tactical advantages of applying for EEC membership. He was conscious of the need to 'do something else' following the economic defeat of July 1966. As one of his closest personal advisers later explained, his reasoning was like Mr. Macmillan's in 1961. At that time Mr. Macmillan had seen the Common Market application as a dramatic distraction from burgeoning domestic difficulties, a means of renewing the wilting public image of his party. He too wished 'to break out of a situation of economic crisis and find something new to do'. The Common Market became peculiarly attractive to the Prime Minister as it was the most fundamental shift open to him at the time and also — paradoxically — because it enjoyed Conservative support. Mr. Heath had been so closely involved in the earlier Common Market talks that he could hardly afford to go back on his publicly stated principles for the sake of opposing a Labour move into Europe. His most recognisable political garment would thus (to use words current in No. 10 at the time) be stolen by Labour. A further benefit of the move into Europe, if it succeeded, was that it would give an additional outlet for the British premier to play a world role, for Mr. Wilson realised that the General could not continue indefinitely and he hoped to step into the vacuum himself.

By summer 1966, Mr. Wilson's conversion was already well advanced. He had been thinking along European lines since the previous economic crisis in the autumn of 1965. Shortly before the 1966 election he commissioned an informal high level group of civil servants to examine long-term economic and foreign policy; the Common Market was one of the subjects on its agenda. The trend of his thinking was indicated by the appointment in his post-election government of George Thomson as Chancellor of the Duchy of Lancaster with specific responsibility for relations with Europe. But it was the economic crisis which brought the subject to the centre of politics although, in European eyes, Britain's new attachment to the principles of European union remained only 'skin-deep'.[1]

[1] See U. W. Kitzinger, *The Second Try: Labour and the EEC* (Pergamon, 1968), pp. 3–17. Public opinion on entry into Europe proved very fickle as this Gallup series shows:

| | July 1966 | April 1967 | December 1967 | February 1970 |
|---|---|---|---|---|
| For entry | 71% | 43% | 43% | 22% |
| Against entry | 12% | 30% | 40% | 57% |
| 'Don't know' | 17% | 27% | 17% | 21% |

This analysis may appear to underestimate the policy grounds for Mr. Wilson's change of mind, and it may be objected that some at least of the cabinet held deeper commitment to a united Europe. This is probably correct. Yet it was the Prime Minister himself who determined the pace of the cabinet discussions and the exploratory visits which finally resulted in the announcement on May 2, 1967 that Britain would be making a formal application to the Six. And, unless the tactical nature of the moves is appreciated, it becomes impossible to explain why so little attention was paid to the question of whether the initiative was likely to succeed or not. There were obvious short-term advantages to Mr. Wilson in proceeding with the talks even if they seemed doomed to failure: attention would be distracted from the home front and Europe would be defused as a political issue. In any case, his natural optimism enabled him to go ahead without thinking too hard about failure.

Mr. Wilson's method of carrying his cabinet was a replica of Mr. Macmillan's before the previous EEC application. Each minister and each department was invited to put forward detailed questions and to make thorough enquiries about specific consequences of British entry. These were discussed at a weekend meet-

Eastward Ho!

[*Daily Express*, April 28, 1967

ing of the cabinet and its advisers at Chequers in October 1966. 'If someone wanted to know the effect on Manchester United of joining the Common Market,' the Prime Minister later commented 'we would have a paper for him'. The result, as he intended all along, was that the moves leading to the application had a momentum of their own and at no time was it possible to deploy large questions of principle in opposition. By a narrow vote it was decided at the autumn Chequers weekend to proceed with a high level reconnaisance of the European capitals in the New Year by the Foreign Secretary. The anti-Marketeers won the assurance that entry would be considered only if 'essential British and Commonwealth interests' could be safeguarded. In order to keep a check on Mr. Brown's European proclivities, Mr. Wilson would — so he assured the anti-Marketeers — accompany him on his tour. In fact Mr. Wilson's presence in Europe made the exploratory talks more important and when the cabinet met again for a further conference at Chequers at the end of April matters had already passed the point of no return.[1]

Even Mr. Wilson could not have had high hopes of success. As before, the main barrier was General de Gaulle. When, together with Mr. Brown, he visited him in January, the General gave them a polite reception. On his return to London Mr. Wilson gave the cabinet an enthusiastic description of the meeting, but he had to admit to himself that the General would only let matters go as far as a formal application before applying a further veto. This impression was shared by officials in the British Embassy in Paris. Influential members of the Foreign Office in London, however, were so deeply committed to the European Community that they preferred the application to proceed even if its chances of success were minimal as they wished both major parties to be publicly committed to British entry at some future date. At the Treasury there were serious doubts. Senior officials gave continuous warnings that entry into the EEC would impose a heavy burden of some £500 million per annum on sterling and make devaluation unavoidable. They feared that negotiations themselves would lead to further speculation. The insistence of Mr. Wilson on announcing the British application was an important factor in making some of them advocates of devaluation during the summer of 1967. But their arguments did not persuade Mr. Wilson who took comfort in

[1] The *Guardian* of May 1, 1967, suggested that the dispositions within the cabinet on the Common Market were:

| *Yes* | *Yes, if* | *Maybe* | *No, unless* | *No* |
|---|---|---|---|---|
| Brown | Wilson | Callaghan | Gardiner | Greenwood |
| Crosland | Wedgwood Benn | | Crossman | Ross |
| Jenkins | Gordon Walker | | Marsh | Castle |
| Longford | Stewart | | Bowden | Peart |
| Hughes | | | | Healey |
| Gunter | | | | Jay |

the fact that Britain would not be entering Europe before 1972 at the earliest. Anyway, devaluation would not be the same catastrophically damaging symbol if it came as the price of membership of the Community.

From May 8 to May 10, 1967 the application was debated in parliament. Thirty-five Labour M.P.s voted against the government and about fifty others abstained. Twenty-six Conservatives and a Liberal also voted against. On May 11, seven Parliamentary Private Secretaries were dismissed for supporting the Labour rebels. On May 16 General de Gaulle gave a press conference during the course of which he suggested that Britain was not yet ready to join the Six. The following day, the Prime Minister retorted that he would not take no for an answer. Diplomatic manoeuvres continued over the summer until the General pronounced a firm veto at a further press conference on November 27.

On the home front the wages freeze (July 1966–January 1967) and the 'period of severe restraint' (February to July 1967) provided a temporary relief. In the fourth quarter of 1966 there was a heartening surplus of £141 million in the balance of payments. Despite the fact that this was followed by only a meagre surplus in the first quarter of 1967, the Chancellor prepared his Budget amid a mood of optimism. This was partly because the Treasury forecasts suggested that prospects were much better than they actually turned out to be. It was in May 1967 that the difficulties started to re-emerge.

The deflationary measures of July 1966 thus secured the position of sterling, for a few months at least, but at a political price. The march of unemployed car-workers which interrupted the Labour Party Conference in October 1966 had presaged increasing bitterness as the numbers out of work grew during the winter and spring. In parliament the Labour backbenchers were becoming restive and there were revolts on several major items of government policy including prices and incomes, the Common Market, and defence. Although these had no chance of success they badly damaged morale. At a meeting of the Parliamentary Labour Party on March 2 following the vote on the Defence White Paper (upon which there had been 42 Labour abstentions) Mr. Wilson gave a warning (see *The Times*, March 3, 1967) that 'every dog is allowed one bite, but a different view is taken of a dog that goes on biting all the time. . . .

He may not get his licence renewed when it falls due'. He was unwise to express his annoyance in this way[1] as it was not the Prime Minister but the constituency parties who gave the nomination — the 'licence'— to a candidate, and they were more than likely to sympathise in existing circumstances with the dissident M.P.s. Mr. Wilson's schoolmasterly speech was made largely at the urging of right-wing Labour loyalists, including Emanuel Shinwell. However, reaction was so strong that Mr. Shinwell was edged out of the PLP chairmanship. The more conciliatory Douglas Houghton, who had recently been dropped from the cabinet, was elected in his place.

Over the winter of 1966–67 Mr. Wilson could console himself with the fact that the opinion polls showed that Labour was maintaining its lead. But in the spring they turned for the worse. The first clear sign of the shift in public mood came on March 9, 1967 when a by-election almost converted rock-solid Rhondda West into a second Welsh nationalist gain.[2] On the same day the Conservatives captured Glasgow Pollok. In further by-elections at Honiton on March 16 and Brierley Hill on April 27, the Conservatives handsomely increased their majorities. Greater shocks were in store in the local elections. The Conservatives gained control of 18 county councils and on April 13, they almost swept the board in the Greater London Council elections, winning 82 seats to Labour's 18; it was the first time since 1934 that Labour had lost control of London. In the borough elections on May 12, there was a net Conservative gain of 535 seats. Labour won only 846 seats, fewer than in any year since the war. For the next two years the local elections were to become a recurring nightmare. In April the opinion polls also moved to the Conservatives, although the picture here was less gloomy for Labour than in the local elections.[3]

[1] According to a senior minister 'This speech did him more damage than he ever realised'. Emrys Hughes' biography '*Sydney Silverman: Rebel in Parliament*' (Shilton, 1969) contains Mr. Silverman's well-publicised letter attacking the Prime Minister's speech.

[2] See p. 383.

[3] A simple index of Labour's fortunes is offered by the number of Labour councillors elected for the 3,000 or so seats at stake in the borough elections in England and Wales in May each year (seats in Outer London are subtracted 1950–63).

| | | | | | | |
|---|---|---|---|---|---|---|
| (Worst in 1950s) | 1950 | 993 | 1963 | 1,525 | 1967 | 846 |
| (2nd worst in 1950s) | 1951 | 883 | 1964 | 1,484 | 1968 | 450 |
| (Best in 1950s) | 1952 | 1,507 | 1965 | 1,027 | 1969 | 540 |
| (2nd best in 1950s) | 1958 | 1,483 | 1966 | 1,259 | 1970 | 1,207 |

Throughout the summer of 1967 speculation against the pound remained within manageable proportions. On the surface, therefore, the economic situation — difficult though it was — seemed better than during the previous July. In reality, it was much graver. In 1966, it could at least be argued that there was trouble because no concerted attempt at deflation had been made. But now it had been tried for a whole year and some relaxations would have to be made before long. In July the highest summer unemployment for 27 years was recorded, and it was thought that it would grow to unacceptable proportions by the winter if the restrictions were not relaxed. In July, the 'period of severe restraint' of prices and incomes was due to be replaced by a 'period of moderation'. There could be few illusions as to what this would mean. Indeed, hourly wage rates were to rise by an astonishing 9·2% between July 1967 and March 1968.

Extra burdens were provided by the closure of the Suez Canal after the Arab–Israeli War in June and the unofficial dock strikes from September onwards. However, as Samuel Brittan has pointed out,[1] the position of sterling began to worsen three weeks before the Middle East fighting, which cannot be blamed, any more than the dock strike, for the deeper weaknesses in the economic situation.

The government's dilemma was that economic expansion held as many dangers as economic restriction. The balance of payments was rapidly worsening and there was bound to be renewed speculation before long if the government shrank from applying a further dose of deflation.

During the summer, however, there were relaxations of hire purchase credit controls (on June 7 and August 29) *and* both an increase in pensions (announced on July 21 to apply from October 30) *and* an increase in family allowances (enacted on July 3 to apply from October 1967 or April 1968). Admittedly, a milestone was reached with the acceptance in July of a Defence White Paper proposing the eventual withdrawal of British troops from Malaysia and Singapore; but the resultant savings would come too slowly to help in the immediate future.

The failure of the July 1966 measures became evident during July and August to the government's permanent economic adviser and to senior Treasury officials. This appeared to show that the economy was in a position of fundamental disequilibrium which

[1] S. Brittan, *Steering the Economy* (Penguin, 1971), p. 348.

could be righted only by devaluation. Meanwhile, how did the Prime Minister intend to guard sterling? As before, he relied on his general belief in physical intervention as a substitute for more conventional measures. On August 28 Michael Stewart was removed from the Department of Economic Affairs and the Prime Minister took personal charge with one of his closest political followers, Peter Shore, as his assistant with the rank of Secretary of State. But if the new arrangement indicated that the Prime Minister thought he could rescue sterling by promoting more efficient industrial management, the attempt was bound to fail. Structural changes would take several years and the balance of payments was deteriorating so rapidly that time was running out.

The final manoeuvres leading to devaluation of the pound from \$2·80 to \$2·40 on November 18, 1967, are described by Samuel Brittan in *Steering the Economy*. For present purposes, it is enough to make five general observations. (i) Devaluation was not just the consequence of a run on the pound. It became necessary as the country could no longer pay its way without running the economy at an artificially low level and with high unemployment: had the November crisis been caused by speculation it would have been in the government's interest to accept the American offer of a loan. But it was realised that this would not cure the underlying structural problem. (ii) Agreement to devaluation was not given by Mr. Callaghan until the autumn. Mr. Wilson was finally converted only in November. (iii) By the time the subject was discussed in the cabinet, the point of decision had already passed. (iv) Nevertheless, the discussions about devaluation in July 1966 made it more understandable and acceptable to the cabinet in November 1967. (v) There was support from all the main groupings of the PLP: from the young intellectuals on economic grounds, and from the trade unionists and the left-wingers on the grounds that it would eliminate the need for a harsh and unpopular deflation.

So great had been the Prime Minister's personal commitment to avoid devaluation, so clear a symbol had it become of his competence as a national leader, that the startling announcement of Saturday, November 18, 1967, would inevitably be seen as a major defeat. Nor would Mr. Wilson have the support of his senior colleagues. Mr. Brown could justifiably say, 'I told you so.' Mr. Callaghan would continue to bear a grudge for the refusal to sanction deflation before July 1966. And the passive majority of the

## *Economic and political indicators*

| | 1 | 2 | 3 | 4 | 5 | 6 | 7 | 8 | 9 | 10 | 11 | 12 |
|---|---|---|---|---|---|---|---|---|---|---|---|---|
| | Balance of payments on current account (seasonally adjusted) £m. | FT ordinary share index 1962 = 100 | Real gross domestic product (seasonally adjusted) 1963 = 100 | Public expenditure | | Total retail consumer expenditure at constant prices 1966 = 100 | Retail price index 1963 = 100 | Index of weekly earnings 1963 = 100 | % of labour force unemployed (seasonally adjusted) | Gallup findings | | |
| | | | | £'000 | as % of GNP | | | | | Voting intention Con. % lead over Labour | Satisfied with Mr. Wilson as PM % | Satisfied with Mr. Heath as Ldr. of op. % |
| 1966 I | − 49 | 114 | 110 | 15·3 | 46·4 | 103 | 112 | 120 | 1·18 | − 8 | 63 | 44 |
| II | − 63 | 116 | 110 | | | 100 | 113 | 124 | 1·20 | −15 | 63 | 39 |
| III | − 24 | 104 | 109 | | | 98 | 114 | 123 | 1·37 | − 3 | 54 | 34 |
| IV | +179 | 97 | 110 | | | 99 | 114 | 122 | 1·77 | − 1 | 47 | 38 |
| 1967 I | + 32 | 103 | 111 | 17·5 | 50·3 | 99 | 115 | 122 | 1·97 | − 4½ | 54 | 26 |
| II | − 97 | 111 | 112 | | | 102 | 116 | 126 | 2·18 | 5½ | 44 | 35 |
| III | − 2 | 117 | 112 | | | 103 | 115 | 128 | 2·38 | 2½ | 44 | 30 |
| IV | −245 | 130 | 113 | | | 103 | 116 | 130 | 2·31 | 11½ | 38 | 40 |
| 1968 I | −111 | 135 | 115 | 19·1 | 51·8 | 104 | 118 | 134 | 2·35 | 15½ | 35 | 31 |
| II | −118 | 159 | 114 | | | 103 | 121 | 136 | 2·34 | 25½ | 29 | 29 |
| III | − 29 | 177 | 116 | | | 103 | 121 | 137 | 2·36 | 15 | 31 | 27 |
| IV | − 63 | 178 | 118 | | | 104 | 123 | 140 | 2·30 | 17½ | 32 | 31 |
| 1969 I | + 13 | 183 | 116 | 19·7 | 51·0 | 104 | 125 | 143 | 2·31 | 21 | 34 | 32 |
| II | + 76 | 166 | 118 | | | 103 | 127 | 147 | 2·25 | 19½ | 31 | 29 |
| III | +153 | 148 | 119 | | | 103 | 127 | 148 | 2·37 | 15 | 35 | 33 |
| IV | +174 | 149 | 119 | | | 105 | 129 | 152 | 2·36 | 5½ | 41 | 33 |
| 1970 I | +153 | 155 | 119 | | | 106 | 132 | 156 | 2·43 | 6½ | 42 | 39 |
| II | + 53 | 137 | 120 | | | 108 | 135 | 164 | 2·57 | − 1½ | 47 | 31 |

Sources: 1. *Economic Trends* (CSO). 2. *Financial Times*. 3. *National Institute Economic Review* (*NIER*) (Compromise index of GDP). 4 and 5. *National Income and Expenditure 1970* (CSO), Table 48 for column 4 which comprises the expenditures (including debt interest, national insurance benefits and other transfers of central government and local authorities and capital outlays of public corporations). Column 5 is derived by dividing Column 4 by line 12 of Table 1 in *National Income and Expenditure*. 6. *Economic Trends*, October 1970, Table E last column adjusted on basis 1966 = 100. 7, 8, 9. *NIER*. 10, 11, 12. *Election '70* (Gallup Pre-Election Handbook).

cabinet, who trusted Mr. Wilson because of his uncanny capacity for success, would henceforth be more likely to question his judgement. Sensing the weakness of his position, Mr. Wilson was to attempt in the next weeks to show that the consequences of devaluation were not, after all, as damaging as he had previously suggested. During the discussions in July 1966, one of his most telling arguments against Mr. Brown had been that devaluation was no substitute for deflation. If the pound was to succeed at its new parity, it would be necessary (so he had then maintained) to move productive capacity from the home consumption to the exporting sectors of the economy — there would, in other words, have to be a restriction on the domestic standard of living. But now, in November 1967, he did not have the courage to squash the suggestion that devaluation was a convenient, soft option.[1] Unemployment was already 581,600 (2·5%) and the Gallup Poll showed the Conservatives 10½% in the lead.

In these threatening conditions, he hesitated to face the unpopularity that further curbs on demand would bring. Obligingly, the Treasury had some technical reasons for delaying the imposition of the required cuts. By Christmas there were still no new limits on consumption despite a sensational holiday spending spree. It was not until January 16, 1968, that cuts in public expenditure were announced and it was only in the Budget on March 19 — four months after devaluation — that a heavy deflationary package was introduced. The delay in taking action after November 18 when its psychological impact would have been greatest was one of the gravest failures of the Labour government and was substantially responsible for the catalogue of woe during the next two years, to which the remainder of this chapter is devoted.

Before proceeding with this gloomy story, it should be pointed out that the Labour ministry from 1966 to 1969 was not one of unrelieved failure. It is right to draw attention to some of the important pieces of legislation which were passed during these years and the significant improvements which were made in the machinery of government. The merging of the service departments

[1] Also, Mr. Callaghan was unwilling to bring forward cuts in his last days as Chancellor feeling that it was fairer that the unpleasant task should be left to his successor. In bringing in devaluation, for which he thought he would be unjustly blamed, he had 'done enough'. Mr. Jenkins, as Home Secretary, had not been privy to detailed information about the state of the economy and apparently required time to accustom himself to his Treasury responsibilities.

Consumer Expenditure 1966–70.[1]

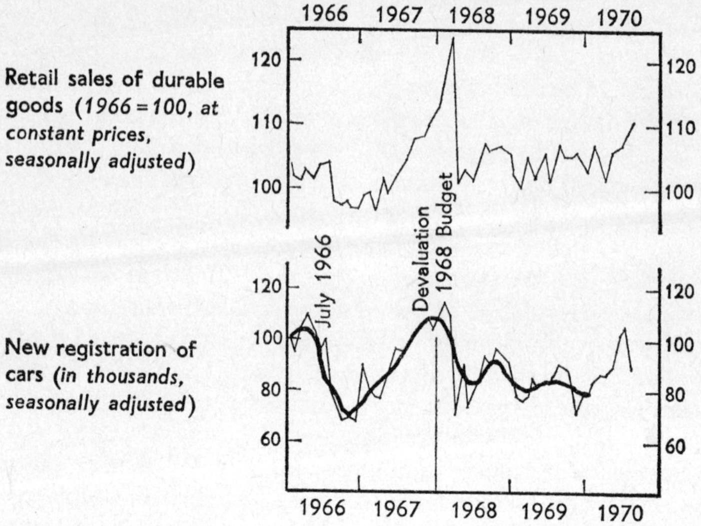


into a unified Ministry of Defence, the coordination of the social services and the overseas affairs departments, the creation of the Civil Service Department and the new methods of assessing and presenting public expenditure were all major developments. So, to a lesser extent, were the reforms in parliamentary procedure and the new parliamentary committees. Had Mr. Wilson been asked to outline the achievements of his government, he would undoubtedly have emphasised its success in developing more effective industrial management — in securing the formation of a British computer firm ICL capable of competing with IBM, in encouraging mergers in the motor and electrical engineering industries and in obtaining a huge American order for aero-engines for Rolls-Royce;

[1] Apart from its temporary fall after the July 1966 measures and its rise immediately after devaluation, consumption remained relatively constant despite the successive government restrictions. There was thus a steady accumulation of consumer durables as shown by these figures derived from the Department of Employment and Productivity's Family Expenditure Surveys:

*Percentage of households using selected consumer durables*

| | Telephone | Washing machine | Refrigerator | Car | Central heating | Television |
|---|---|---|---|---|---|---|
| 1964 | 22 | 53 | 34 | 37 | 7 | 80 |
| 1969 | 32 | 63 | 60 | 51 | 25 | 91 |
| change | +10 | +10 | +26 | +14 | +18 | +11 |

its regional policy; and its increased provision for the social services. But most of these achievements passed unnoticed by the general public and did not affect its attitude to the government. The same applies to such a monumental piece of legislation as Barbara Castle's Transport Bill, which occupied so much parliamentary time in 1968. It was equally inconvenient to the government, which claimed the bill as a major advance, and to the opposition, which complained that it constituted a tyrannical extension of state power, that the public neither knew nor cared about it. The long and sometimes bitter debates in committee and on the floor of the House belonged to a private world confined to the Palace of Westminster, the specific interest groups affected and the Young Conservatives, who were running a campaign against the bill. To the electorate, the name of Barbara Castle meant not the Transport Bill but the breathalyser test to detect drunken driving which she had introduced in October 1967. The fundamental changes which were gradually taking place in secondary and further education also had a minor part in public consciousness. The same can be said of most of the other specific 'issues' and bills which were considered during these years. Even the spate of legislation concerning individual behaviour — the bill legalising homosexual acts between consenting adults, the Abortion Law Reform Bill, the relaxation of restrictions on Sunday entertainments, the Divorce Bill, the abolition of censorship by the Lord Chamberlain, were of comparatively little importance in the ebb and flow of party politics. Only after a number of drugs cases involving pop stars such as Mick Jagger and Marianne Faithfull and a series of student demonstrations imitating the violence in Paris in May 1968 and in Chicago in August, were there serious complaints about the so-called 'permissive society'. It is significant that these complaints took a generalised form and it was only briefly in 1969, when the question of capital punishment was due to come again before parliament, that they appeared likely to be concentrated against a specific measure.[1]

[1] The permissiveness, long hair, mini-skirts, student rebellions and football hooliganism that marked this period are regarded by some as important social developments and it is suggested that they are signs of increasing isolationism following the break-up of the British Empire and the gradual dilution of Commonwealth ties. Others prefer to find an explanation that covers similar phenomena in almost all other advanced Western countries.

In narrowly political terms, these changes in social attitudes had little direct effect. They did not weaken the Labour government in the same way as the 'anti-establishment' feelings and the satire of the early 1960s had undermined

It would be wrong for an election study, therefore, to dwell upon the record of the Labour government from 1966–69 in terms of its specific triumphs and failures. It is necessary to consider the events which bore most closely on the general mood or those which best reveal the overall political strategy of the Labour leaders. In such a survey the desire of the Prime Minister to create an impression of his party's 'responsibility' and his failure to do so must be the predominant themes.[1]

The first major crisis after devaluation concerned a comparatively small matter and was only briefly noticed by the public. But it had such a deep impact on Labour politics and throws such significant light on relationships within the cabinet that it must be considered in detail. In 1964, the government had banned the sale of arms to South Africa, in accordance with a resolution of the United Nations, although it continued to fulfil existing contracts

---

Mr. Macmillan. If anything they tended, particularly among the young, to produce lack of interest in party politics as a whole. Indeed, there was a notable absence of political protests. The function of the Aldermaston marches previously organised by the Campaign for Nuclear Disarmament was largely taken over by pop festivals or university sit-ins, and only to a lesser extent by rallies against the war in Vietnam.

There were a number of occasions when protests threatened to become a political problem. In April 1967 a long series of troubles started at the London School of Economics with the first of several sit-ins; the culmination came in January 1969 with a three-week closure of the school. On October 27, 1968, a large rally was organised against the Vietnam War and there were fears that it would be uncontrollable, like the Chicago violence during the Democratic Party Convention two months previously. In September 1969 the inability of police to eject hippies who were occupying Number 144 Piccadilly highlighted the shortcomings of the laws in relation to trespass.

There was a chance that there would be a reaction from the middle-aged and the middle class, beneficial to the Conservatives, if these were not handled firmly by the government. Mr. Callaghan's calm, solid and well-judged actions as Home Secretary prevented any of these incidents getting out of hand.

The unruly behaviour at some meetings during 1966–70 did have a minor political side-effect. It led Conservative and Labour party organisers, who were planning for the election, to expect violence and heavy heckling during election meetings. It was a surprise and a relief that this did not materialise.

[1] This distinction emerges clearly from the assessment of a Labour supporter, Brian Lapping:

> 'Although the chain of events had become enormous and heavy, a skilful minister could still swing it . . . Roy Jenkins did this in race relations . . . Barbara Castle brought about changes of comparable magnitude in two ministries. . . . As Minister of Education (Anthony Crosland) cudgelled autonomous local authorities into creating comprehensive secondary schools. . . . Richard Crossman's performance as a creator of major and lasting change was perhaps the most impressive. . . . This list of ministerial achievements, even when filled out with many more to the credit of the Labour Government, does not add up to a successful overall government strategy. Too many of the really big strategic decisions . . . failed.' *The Labour Government, 1964–70*, pp. 13–14.

and even continued to sell military aircraft. In the summer of 1967, the South Africans, emboldened by the closure of the Suez Canal which increased the importance of the Simonstown base, and by Britain's economic difficulties, made an approach to the government with a view to persuading it to lift the ban. The request was under consideration by the Defence and Overseas Committee of the cabinet at the time of devaluation. This influenced the discussion in opposite ways. On the one hand it strengthened the economic case for selling arms. The government would soon have to consider how it could least damagingly cut public expenditure. The profit derived from these sales might make it possible to avoid, say, prescription charges. On the other hand, the weak political position of the government made it all the harder to offend the conscience of the PLP.

On December 8, the Defence and Overseas Committee decided to defer its decision. This was a victory for the powerful group of senior ministers led by George Brown and Denis Healey who favoured the relaxation of the ban.[1] For if the possibility of selling arms were not immediately excluded, as the left-wing minority desired, there would be increasing pressures to come to a deal with the South Africans as a convenient substitute for some of the painful domestic cuts that were due to be debated in cabinet after Christmas.

The following Monday, December 11, Mr. Callaghan addressed a private meeting of a group of M.P.s aged under 40. Their gatherings, unlike those of other groups of Labour M.P.s, had a reputation for being leak-free. In the course of questioning, Mr. Callaghan, who was now the Home Secretary and had not been at the Defence and Overseas Committee, was asked about the arms ban and indicated that it might be reversed. This shocked some of the backbenchers, and two of them prepared an Early Day Motion. The Prime Minister was not slow to sense the danger to his own position, knowing that much of the left-wing anger would be directed against him if it was thought that he had associated himself with the move. But he could hardly come out at this stage in favour of a categorical ban as it was still under discussion in the cabinet which seemed more than likely to decide in favour of making the sales. He therefore encouraged the backbench moves

[1] Their support in cabinet reputedly included Mr. Callaghan, Mr. Gordon Walker, Mr. Crosland and Mr. Gunter.

against the imminent proposal. Mr. Silkin, the Chief Whip, obligingly urged Labour M.P.s to support the Early Day Motion in Mr. Kevin McNamara's name which called on the government to uphold the arms ban.[1] Mr. Wilson would thus be able to use the backbench revolt as a lever in cabinet against the ministers who were opposing him.

When questions were asked in parliament on Wednesday, December 13, Mr. Roy Mason stonewalled. But Mr. Wilson, addressing a meeting of Labour M.P.s from Northern constituencies in the evening, had fewer inhibitions. He said:

> 'that the Government had no intention of changing their policy on the supply of arms to South Africa. (It) would continue to support the United Nations' resolution calling for an embargo.'[2]

The following morning, Thursday, December 14, the cabinet discussion had to be unexpectedly postponed until Friday as fog prevented Mr. Brown's return from a NATO meeting in Brussels. In the afternoon, Mr. Wilson told the House of Commons that he had hoped to make a statement,

> 'but my right hon. Friend the Foreign Secretary, who is very much concerned with these matters, was prevented by weather conditions from getting back. I think it right that these matters should be the subject of consideration when he is here.'

Mr. Wilson's remark that the government 'had no intention of changing their policy' at a moment when a powerful group within his cabinet had precisely this intention was unusual enough. But, in addition, his statement to the Commons that an announcement about the ban (presumably, in view of his earlier remarks, that it would be continued) had been postponed because of Mr. Brown's absence and his great 'concern with these matters' (which in the

[1] Mr. McNamara has publicly stated on several occasions that 'At no time did any Whip encourage us to draft our motion' (see e.g. *Sunday Times*, October 18, 1970). Nevertheless Mr. McNamara and Mr. Ellis, who put down the motion with him, would not deny (i) that the Whips did not ask them to delay its submission for 24 hours as they were entitled to do under PLP standing orders, and (ii) that, once the motion was on the Order Paper, the Whips encouraged backbenchers to sign it. 'People approached me to ask whether they should sign the motion or not and I did encourage them' (John Silkin, quoted in *Tribune*, October 16, 1970). Although Whips sometimes encouraged signatures for motions attacking aspects of opposition policy, it was unparalleled (according to the Labour M.P.s we have questioned on the subject) for them to interfere in a motion bearing on an issue under discussion within the cabinet. That the Whips did lobby on this occasion and that they did suggest that signatures would suit the Prime Minister, has been confirmed by too many M.P.s to be in serious doubt.

[2] *The Times*, December 14, 1967.

circumstances could only mean that he favoured the resumption of sales) was regarded by the press as a rebuke for Mr. Brown. By most of the cabinet Mr. Wilson's behaviour was seen as an extraordinary breach of collective responsibility.

In 1923, it is true, Mr. Bonar Law had written a letter to *The Times* stating his objections to a decision which his own cabinet had reached. But he did so after the discussion, under a pseudonym and without the personal tinge of Mr. Wilson's pronouncement. Mr. Brown was determined not to accept the Prime Minister's statement as a *fait accompli* and he had very strong support when the cabinet gathered the following morning. At the end of a long and acrimonious meeting there was no vote as the Prime Minister realised — so it was reported — that he might lose. Instead, a compromise was to be presented to the Commons on Monday, December 18. The ban was to continue for the time being, but the possibility of future sales was not to be excluded. As this was what the Defence and Overseas Committee had decided the previous week, the formula represented a considerable victory for Mr. Brown and the anti-Wilson 'Junta' (as it sometimes came to be called). Accounts of Mr. Wilson's come-uppance appeared in the weekend papers.

But the in-fighting was not over yet. Mr. Wilson refused to bear the humiliation. On Sunday night, at a late hour when the cabinet 'could not meet in groups' behind his back, Mr. Wilson summoned a further meeting for the following morning, shortly before he was due to make his announcement to parliament. He argued that his position would be intolerably undermined if he was forced to make a statement with which it was known that he disagreed. In the circumstances, he could not continue as Prime Minister. Confronted by this threat, the cabinet caved in. With the exception of Mr. Brown, Mr. Wilson's opponents were unwilling to carry through their objections to the point of making the split even wider. There were fears that the party would smash itself and it was considered necessary, regretfully, to rally behind him for survival's sake. At the eleventh hour Mr. Wilson thus changed what Mr. David Wood of *The Times* called 'a calculated devaluation of his own authority' at the Friday meeting into 'an almost effortless conquest' on the Monday morning. On Monday afternoon he was able to announce that the unconditional ban would be maintained. It may appear strange that Mr. Wilson's 'right-wing' opponents capitulated at the final cabinet meeting. There are three possible explanations: the first is that they were simply taken off guard and had not arranged for the possibility of co-ordinated resignations. The second is that the Gaitskellites had been effectively divided by the appointment of one of their most prominent members, Mr. Jenkins, to the Treasury. He was now in too good a position to spoil his future chances of the leadership by premature rebellion. Third, that the leaders of the Junta lacked the nerve to leave the government or to threaten convincingly to do so. Mr. Brown was a politician to whom the threat of resignation came much more easily than its fulfilment, and only in combination with his departure would that of the others be threatening. Besides, the resentment against Mr. Wilson which Mr. Brown and Mr. Callaghan shared did not outweigh their mutual distrust. Underlying all this, there was a more fundamental reason. Despite the failure of so many of Mr. Wilson's major policies, despite the distrust which he engendered among his colleagues, despite the unemployment and the low standing of Labour in the opinion polls, few doubted the jack-in-the-box qualities that made him the best leader available. At the back of people's minds there still lurked the feeling that, like it or not, Mr. Wilson had more chance than anyone else of rescuing the party from the predicament into which he had led it. This feeling saved him now and on the several occasions over the next eighteen months when there were moves against his authority. Mr. Wilson's instinct for self-preservation which encouraged him to offend some of his most senior ministers for the sake of securing the support of the left-wingers in the PLP was sound.[1] But the cost in terms of personal bitterness and distrust at the top was great. When Mr. Brown complained after his

[1] In the course of our interviewing, which was mostly carried out before the election, it was suggested by more than one cabinet minister that Mr. Wilson did not object to the sale of arms to South Africa on moral grounds but was motivated by the need to secure his support in the Parliamentary Labour Party at a time he greatly needed it. This uncharitable view is confirmed by Mr. Brown in his memoirs when he suggests that Mr. Wilson was 'taking a different view' after the 'great row . . . in the Parliamentary Labour Party' from his previous acquiescence in the preliminary negotiations (*Sunday Times*, October 11, 1970). Lord Longford has maintained, however, that the Prime Minister was opposed to the resumption of arms sales from the outset (*Sunday Times*, October 18, 1970). There are plausible arguments on both sides. On the one hand, there is little doubt Mr. Wilson had always been deeply and publicly opposed to *apartheid*. On the other hand, he clearly allowed the South African application to be given very serious consideration by officials and cabinet committees. He did not attempt to kill the proposal at the beginning in the way that he quashed the U.S. request for British troops in Vietnam without going to

resignation in March 1968 of 'the way this Government is run and the manner in which we reach our decisions', it was to the South African arms affairs that he was primarily referring.

A useful side effect of the controversy in December was that it slightly eased the passage of the cuts in public expenditure announced on January 16, 1968.[1] The main items affected were defence, education and health. The withdrawal from Asia was to be hastened and orders for the American F-111 strike aircraft cancelled; a charge of 2*s*. 6*d*. was to be made for doctors' prescriptions and the raising of the school-leaving age was postponed. However, despite the drastic nature of some of these cuts, they had relatively little effect on the upward trend of government expenditure. In fact the term 'cuts' was a misnomer as there was to be little actual reduction in expenditure, only in its projected rate of growth.[2]

It may reasonably be asked why the government permitted cuts at politically sensitive points while leaving some of the largest growth areas unaffected. It was partly because Whitehall departments were becoming more adept at resisting attempts to prune their spending and purposely put at the top of their lists the most awkward items; it was also because the sacrifice of a small, ideologically loaded service like free prescriptions enabled the government conveniently to convince the international financiers that it meant business and thereby avoided the need for deeper, if less symbolic stringencies.

Before the next instalment of the post-devaluation measures in the Budget of March 19, there was a dangerous international currency crisis. The rapid increase in the volume of world trade had for several years been leading to a liquidity shortage. The devaluation of sterling put pressure on the dollar which it was in

---

cabinet and without even telling the Defence Minister. Besides, the Labour government, before and after the controversy, allowed a very liberal interpretation of the 'ban'. Joint military exercises continued to be held with the South Africans and even Buccaneer aircraft were provided under existing contracts. It seems reasonable to conclude that in December 1967, unlike November, political and moral considerations both led Mr. Wilson to the same conclusion.

[1] It did not, however, eliminate the growing discontent. See David Wood 'Where should an M.P.'s loyalty lie?' *The Times*, January 22, 1968; Sir Dingle Foot's article on the 'permissive whipping' during John Silkin's period as Chief Whip, *Observer*, February 11, 1968, and Anthony King's discussion, *Spectator*, February 9, 1968. See also two later articles by Douglas Houghton, 'Labour's Discipline in Party and in Government', *The Times*, November 6, 1968, and 'The Labour Backbencher', *Political Quarterly*, October/December 1969.

[2] See table on p. 24.

no shape to bear because of the adverse United States balance of payments. The weakness of the hard currencies led to an increased demand for gold, fostered by the French government, which held large stocks and stood to benefit greatly from an increase in its price. The crisis came to a head on March 14. The demand for gold was now so great that it was becoming impossible for the Gold Pool countries to continue supporting the market at the existing price of $35 an ounce. A bank holiday was declared in the Gold Pool countries to allow a discussion of the future of the international currencies at a conference in Washington. Although arrangements were successfully made in Washington to protect gold at its existing price, international currency crises recurred during 1968 and 1969 and made sterling's position parlous. There was an undertone of rumours that the pound would have to be devalued once again. Although the public did not begin to understand the technicalities of high finance, an atmosphere of uncertainty filtered through. A casualty of the March gold crisis was George Brown, who resigned from the government on the ground that he had not been called to the Privy Council late on the night of March 14 when the emergency measures were decided. The explanation that he had been looked for but not found gave rise to some ribald interpretations. It was a relief to Mr. Wilson that Mr. Brown's resignation should ultimately have concerned such a comparatively trivial issue.[1] On March 19 Mr. Jenkins' Budget contained very large tax increases including a levy on high incomes; 2*d.* on 20 cigarettes; 2*s.* 6*d.* a bottle on spirits; 4*d.* a gallon on petrol; general increases in purchase tax and an extra £7 10*s.* 0*d.* a year on car licences.[2]

By now, the government's political stock had fallen dangerously. On September 21, 1967, the Conservatives made by-election gains in Cambridge and Walthamstow West. On November 2 Labour lost at Leicester S.W. to the Conservatives and at Hamilton to Mrs. Ewing, a Scottish Nationalist. On November 23 Labour fell into third place behind the Liberals at West Derbyshire and on March 28, 1968, lost three seats to the Conservatives at Meriden,

[1] Mr. Brown's account of his resignation appears in the *Sunday Times*, October 11, 1970. While there is good reason to accept that he was in a fit condition on the evening concerned, he was damaged by rumours to the contrary. The impact of his resignation was also lessened by the 'fit of pique' he displayed. See Richard Clements, 'What George Brown forgot'. *Tribune*, October 16, 1970.

[2] Although they totalled a huge £923 million, some of the measures of which this sum was composed had little effect on consumer demand. The Budget was not as severely deflationary as was often supposed.

Acton and Dudley. In each case there were huge swings from Labour to Conservatives averaging over 18%, which would bring a disaster of 1931 proportions if repeated at the general election. The municipal elections in May 1968 gave a grisly preview to this possible massacre: Labour held on to only 450 seats, compared to an average of 1,200 in all other post-war years and a previous low point of 846. In Scotland one seat in four went to a Scottish Nationalist, most of them gains from Labour. At the same time Labour's lag in the polls increased to a record 28%. Even the Conservatives in 1963 had never been more than 16½% behind.

Another blow was the victory of Hugh Scanlon over John Boyd as President of the AEF. Mr. Boyd had been the nominee of the retiring President, Sir William Carron, and an active supporter of the prices and incomes policy; his defeat meant that two of the three largest unions — the TGWU and the AEF — were in left-wing hands.[1]

Many of these difficulties were given full prominence in the press, whose working relationship with the Prime Minister had been gradually deteriorating since the summer of 1966 and which now reached a state of mutual hostility. Since becoming leader of the Labour party, Mr. Wilson had given his time generously to journalists and talked freely about his intentions. He understood their desire for interesting copy and provided it in profusion. At the outset he therefore received an excellent press. As time went on, lobby correspondents learned to treat Mr. Wilson's statements with suspicion, which grew rapidly after the decline in the government's fortunes in the autumn of 1967. Mr. Wilson made matters worse by his angry criticism and his handling of the 'D-Notice affair' which followed an article in the *Daily Express* of February 21, 1967, alleging that foreign diplomatic cables were being 'vetted'.[2] Mr. Wilson for a period almost ceased giving lobby briefings, confining his attentions to a smaller group which was dubbed 'The White Commonwealth'. In 1969, he was to complain that he had been subjected to more vilification from the press than any Prime Minister since Lloyd George. In the period preceding the 1970 election there was some relaxation of the hostility but the early love affair was never resumed.

[1] Other difficulties in Spring 1968 were provided by the Commonwealth Immigrants Bill and the Race Relations Bill. As they had a deeper impact on relationships within the Conservative party, they are considered in Chapter 3.

[2] See P. Hedley and C. Aynsley, *The D-Notice Affair* (Michael Joseph, 1967).

For some time, Mr. Wilson could not even rely on favourable coverage from the *Daily Mirror*. On May 10 Cecil King, the chairman of its parent company, the International Publishing Corporation, called for the establishment of a coalition government and raised fears about the possibility of a second devaluation, which could not be totally ignored as Mr. King was a director of the Bank of England. Mr. King's considerable nuisance value to the Prime Minister was reduced when the IPC board ousted him on May 30 from the post of chairman and voted Hugh Cudlipp into his place.

On April 5, 1968 there was a ministerial reshuffle aimed at giving the cabinet a facelift. The most important change in the 'Cabinet Mark II' (a phrase suggested by Mr. Crossman) was the substitution of Barbara Castle for Ray Gunter at the Ministry of Labour. At the same time the Ministry took over responsibility for prices and incomes policy from the DEA, and became the Department of Employment and Productivity (DEP). In addition a new 'Parliamentary Committee' was to function as an inner cabinet, supposedly to give the Ministry a greater consciousness of its overall political objectives which had often been submerged in departmental preoccupations.[1]

The 'Mark II' Cabinet did little to purge the atmosphere of failure or to end the sniping at Mr. Wilson from the Labour ranks. The most open attempt against him came from Ray Gunter, who made a scathing attack on the Prime Minister's leadership when he resigned from the government on July 1 after a short and unhappy spell as Minister of Power.

This was followed by rumblings of revolt and even some wild talk about 'going National' in line with the precedent of 1931. In retrospect, some spoke of this as having been 'Wilson's moment of greatest danger'. But any moves against him were too clumsy to present a real threat, even if the stories of them fanned the prevailing atmosphere of discontent.

In these circumstances, heavy fire was directed at Barbara Castle's bill to continue the Prices and Incomes Act for yet a further period and with stiffened delaying powers under Part II; 34 Labour M.P.s abstained on its second reading in May and 23 voted with the Conservatives on the third reading in July. In view

[1] For a favourable account of the Parliamentary Committee see John Mackintosh, 'Mr. Wilson's revised Cabinet System', *The Times*, June 21, 1968; for a more sceptical view see Patrick Gordon Walker, *The Cabinet* (Cape, 1970), p. 47.

of the widespread feeling within the PLP against the bill, no disciplinary action was taken against the rebels. To the government it must slowly have become evident that while the need for an effective incomes policy was constantly increasing, the chances of its being effective were lessening and the political difficulties involved in imposing it were becoming ever more serious.

Before the summer recess there were two other events which were to have important consequences in the autumn. In May, left-wing students and workers in Paris succeeded in producing a state of insurrection against the Gaullist regime. Although the General managed to reimpose his authority, the economy was damaged by the widespread stoppages during May and by the large wage increases which had been promised to conciliate the workers. On the home front the Royal Commission on Trade Unions and Employers Associations under Lord Donovan produced its report in June. It had been set up in 1965 following a decision in a court case (*Rookes* v. *Barnard*) which endangered the immunity given to unions by the 1906 Trade Disputes Act from actions for tort or representations for their activities in industrial disputes. The Donovan Report made a large number of proposals for the long-term, voluntary reform of collective bargaining procedures, and especially for the replacement of the existing system, under which workers in the same factory belonged to different unions which negotiated separately on their behalf, by a system of wage-bargaining on a factory-wide basis. After a welter of discussion and editorial comment its proposals seemed likely to suffer the genteel oblivion so common to Royal Commission findings.

August 1968 was marked by the violence at the Democratic Convention in Chicago and by the Russian invasion of Czechoslovakia. To the Labour government, it brought welcome respite. As nothing seemed to have gone right during the previous year, the period of summer inactivity in Britain could hardly fail to provide a turn for the better. The frailty of the Conservative hold on the voters' allegiance was shown by Labour's improvement in the polls from an average deficit of 20% in June to an average of 8½% in October. 'We are peaking too soon,' commented one cabinet minister, only half-frivolously during the Labour Party Conference. But later in the autumn, the government's wounds were reopened and deepened. The balance of payments problem remained unsolved and threatened the economy, the state of which continued to be very worrying despite the Chancellor's severity in the Budget. The chances of improvement were handicapped by a series of strikes which did much to undermine the incomes policy. In October the engineering unions threatened an official strike which was averted only by the offer of large increases in minimum rates of pay. This dispute was the latest of a long series which had already earned 1968 the headline 'YEAR OF THE STRIKE'. Whereas in the five previous years, 1963–67, there had never been as many as three million days lost in strikes, three and a half million had been lost in the first eight months of 1968.[1]

Industrial unrest was widely attributed to two general causes: the surge in the cost of living since devaluation, and the incomes policy (which sought to limit wage demands made in response to inflation). The government was faced by a difficult dilemma. Not only was the incomes policy becoming ever less popular with the PLP, the Labour party and the trade unions (it was voted down at both the TUC and Labour Party Conferences); it was also causing industrial disputes and possibly even stimulating the inflation it sought to stem. The incomes policy, it could be argued, was actually aggravating the serious balance of payments situation. But the government could not afford to abandon it without substituting something else; if it had no other use the Prices and Incomes Act at least reassured the international banking community — without whose support a second devaluation might have occurred — that the government was taking inflation seriously. What substitute could be found? In November, Michael Shanks argued that the government should 'press on with the modernisation of Britain, at whatever short-term inconvenience', and that it should offer to end the pay pause in return for acquiescence in trade union reform.[2]

Throughout the late summer and autumn, preparations for the legislation based on the Donovan Report, which in normal circumstances would probably have remained leisurely and of little strategic importance, became more urgent and assumed far greater significance in relationship to the government's activities as a whole. As Mrs. Castle became more and more bogged down by the incomes policy and ever more exasperated by many of the union leaders with whom she was coming into contact, she became more

[1] Cf. Rodney Cowton, 'Year of the Strike', *The Times*, October 10, 1968.
[2] 'Getting the Priorities Right', *The Times*, November 11, 1968.

inclined to accept some of the arguments put forward by her senior civil servants that Donovan had not gone nearly far enough and that it was necessary to put her teeth into her Industrial Relations Bill. The Prime Minister's mind was moving in the same direction. He shared Mrs. Castle's keenness to 'get things done', and once he had turned his mind to union problems, this naturally led him to think in terms of a tough bill. He was also influenced by the strong tide of public opinion against trade union irresponsibility: polls indicated that many Labour voters and trade unionists were as critical as the Conservatives of strikes and wildcat walkouts.

It is difficult to pinpoint the moment when Mrs. Castle and the Prime Minister became committed to 'penal' legislation or to determine whether Mrs. Castle or Mr. Wilson was the moving force. The balance of evidence strongly indicates that they were coming separately to the same conclusions, but that it was Mrs. Castle who took the initiative.[1] From November 9 to 11 there was a weekend meeting at the old Civil Defence College at Sunningdale between Mrs. Castle, with her officials, and a few industrial relations experts, employers and union leaders. Although most of the discussion supported the voluntary approach put forward in the Donovan Report, at the end Mrs. Castle seems to have instructed her civil servants to include penal sanctions in the draft White Paper which was to be presented as the first step towards legislation. In the following weeks her resolve was stiffened by the worsening economic and industrial situation. The debilitating events in France during May and June led to an autumn run against the franc and to speculation that the German mark would be revalued; both developments endangered the pound. On November 12 the French government announced an emergency package of credit restrictions which failed, however, to put an end to the speculation. A few days later crisis talks were held in Bonn between members of the Group of Ten which proposed to give financial assistance to the French in return for a 10% devaluation. The General refused,

[1] For an admirable account of the controversy over the Industrial Relations Bill, see Peter Jenkins, *The Battle of Downing Street* (Charles Knight, 1970). However, in a few respects his story is incomplete and it should be read in conjunction with Roy Hattersley's review in the *New Statesman*, September 4, 1970, and W. E. J. McCarthy's in the *Guardian*, September 3, 1970. See also John P. Mackintosh, *The Government and Politics of Great Britain* (Hutchinson, 1970). For a discussion of relationships between the government, PLP and the unions in the months after the abandonment of the Industrial Relations Bill see Francis Boyd 'Saying Blow You to Jack', *Guardian*, December 6, 1969.

preferring to impose a further dose of deflation. To meet the resulting pressure on sterling an autumn Budget was introduced by Mr. Jenkins on November 22, 1968, consisting of higher purchase taxes and more stringent restrictions on imports. It was calculated to reduce demand by £200 million a year. While nerves were being frayed by these financial problems, a 'who-does-what' strike broke out in early November in the Girling brake factory in Cheshire following ten months of industrial unrest at the plant. It started when twenty-two machine setters downed tools after a dispute which had begun when a member of one union had turned on an oil valve which another union claimed as its function. The stoppage affected over 5,000 car workers and underlined the need for legislation to provide a compulsory conciliation pause. This was inserted into the draft White Paper which was published on January 17, 1969, with the title *In Place of Strife*. Indeed, all three penal clauses (strike ballots, fines and conciliation pauses) could be directly attributed to the government's recent experiences with disputes.

From the outset it was plain that Mr. Callaghan, who saw himself as defender of traditional trade union interests, was opposed to the measures contained in the White Paper. For this reason it went directly from a small committee of experts to the full cabinet, bypassing the cabinet committee on industrial relations of which he was a member. Nevertheless, it seemed that he would be a relatively isolated opponent. The deep feelings that the proposals were later to release were not anticipated within the higher reaches of the government. George Woodcock, General Secretary of the TUC, gave his private opinion: 'I don't think there is anything in this to which the unions can fundamentally object.'[1] Public opinion was not unfavourable nor were many local Labour parties nor, as it first seemed, the mass of the PLP. It is an indication of the deep effects on the Labour party of two and a half years of almost non-stop crisis, and of the keen desire to get the balance of payments right by any means, that a Labour government was prepared to reintroduce penal sanctions against trade unionists in general for the first time in a century — and to do so with hardly a thought about the ideological implications of its action.

The bill might have had a different fate but for two things which Mr. Wilson could hardly have foreseen in early January. A few days after the publication of *In Place of Strife*, George Woodcock

[1] *The Battle of Downing Street*, p. 47.

had a heart attack; during his illness (he did not reach retiring age till October 1969) his place was taken by Vic Feather, who proved tougher than his predecessor. Soon afterwards, the Parliament (No. 2) Bill providing a scheme of reform for the House of Lords was debated in the House of Commons.[1] In essence, the measures before the House were those which had been agreed at a series of meetings between leading members of the government and the opposition. They did not have the active support of the shadow cabinet, however, as Mr. Wilson had formally ended the consultations the previous summer (when they were virtually complete) in retaliation for the action of Conservative peers in blocking a government order to extend mandatory sanctions against Rhodesia. Conservative backbenchers, intent on stopping the bill on the grounds that it reduced the power of the Lords, were now joined by a considerable number of Labour backbenchers who opposed it because it did not abolish the second chamber altogether and by others who resented the patronage it would place at the Prime Minister's disposal. Enoch Powell was brought into uncharacteristic alliance with Michael Foot. On February 18, Robert Sheldon filibustered for over two hours, the longest speech for fifteen years. The government was faced with the choice of letting the debate continue interminably on the floor of the House, or guillotining the discussion. But there was every sign that if it attempted to pass a procedural motion to cut short the debate sufficient Labour members would join the Conservatives in opposition to ensure its defeat. By the Easter recess ten days had already been spent discussing the first five clauses. Faced with total dislocation of the parliamentary programme, the government was under great pressure to abandon the bill.

During the spring there were other difficulties. The balance of payments continued to be adverse; there was a very serious dispute at Fords; and motions against *In Place of Strife* started arriving from the unions and constituency parties at an alarming rate.[2] To

[1] PLP reactions to the proposals are outlined by David Wood in *The Times* of July 4, 1968, and November 14, 1968.

[2] On March 26 the NEC passed a motion expressing its opposition to legislation based on all the proposals in *In Place of Strife*. Mr. Callaghan had voted for the anti-government motion, in a move widely regarded as a challenge to Mr. Wilson's leadership. A few days later, Mr. Wilson let it be known that he had reprimanded Mr. Callaghan during a cabinet meeting.

Mr. Wilson was not present at the NEC meeting because he was on his way to Nigeria in an attempt to mediate in the Nigerian civil war. It is incidentally interesting that the exceptionally deep feeling aroused for and against the Biafran

reimpose its authority, the government therefore decided to bring in a short Industrial Relations Bill before the summer recess instead of waiting as previously intended until the 1969–70 session. On April 15, Roy Jenkins announced in his Budget statement that statutory wage control legislation would not be renewed — but in its place an Industrial Relations Bill would be immediately introduced (parliamentary time being conveniently found by shelving House of Lords reform).

So far from halting the growing criticism within the PLP in its early stages as the cabinet hoped, this announcement stimulated a dangerous mood of revolt. To many Labour M.P.s the government had declared war on the unions which had given the party its birth. On April 29 Mr. Wilson, sensing the danger to his position, appointed Bob Mellish as Chief Whip in place of the 'permissive' Mr. Silkin. Mr. Mellish was M.P. for Bermondsey and a leading figure in the London Labour party where he had gained a reputation for his tough handling of left-wing militants. Mr. Wilson also appointed an 'inner cabinet' of six or seven senior ministers (Mr. Callaghan conspicuously not among them). The opponents of the bill, including members of all sections of the PLP, had already organised themselves into an 'action committee'. Eric Moonman, M.P. for Billericay, had summoned a meeting of the 113 Labour M.P.s who had either abstained or voted against the White Paper on March 3. Seventy of them attended and elected a committee[1] which continued taking soundings of backbench opinion during April and May. By the middle of May, they had the names of 61 M.P.s who were against the bill and a further 13 who would abstain. The figures were passed to the Whips and to the Chairman of the PLP, Mr. Houghton.

At the beginning of May, another much smaller group of M.P.s, who cared less about the Industrial Relations Bill in particular than about Mr. Wilson's general shortcomings, saw the crisis as an opportunity to force him from the leadership. They aimed to collect enough names to make Mr. Houghton call a special meeting of the PLP to consider the leadership question. Although they apparently succeeded in collecting the names of 95 M.P.s, word of

cause cut across party lines; the opposition never exploited the government's embarrassment over the supply of arms to the Federal government of Nigeria.

[1] Eric Moonman was chairman, and Joe Ashton, Roy Dobson, Roy Hughes and Trevor Park were officers. Of these only Trevor Park was associated with the left-wing *Tribune* group.

the attempted coup leaked too early for it to stand a chance of success and it was abandoned.

Mr. Houghton refused to support these moves against Mr. Wilson. But he gave backing to the 'action group' against the Industrial Relations Bill, warning the government at the PLP meeting on May 7 that it risked the 'disintegration' of the Labour party if it persisted with its contentious legislation. It was perhaps symptomatic of the demoralised condition of the government that on May 5 Mr. Crossman, the minister in charge of the social services and an acknowledged expert on psychological warfare, announced, three days before the borough elections, that charges for National Health Service spectacles were to be increased as an economy measure. Matters were not improved by his public admission of error and the assurance to the party activists who had sent in complaints that any future unpopular statements would be delayed until after elections were held. On May 8, Labour lost 639 seats in the municipal elections. The trade figures for April, announced on May 13, showed a deficit of £59 million and Mr. Lever, Financial Secretary to the Treasury, felt it necessary to make a statement denying that the International Monetary Fund was about to insist on a tight squeeze on the British economy.

Undeterred by these pressures, Mr. Wilson appeared to keep increasing his stake in the bill, declaring on April 17, for example, that its passage was 'essential to the government's continuance in office', and on May 21 that 'the question at issue is really whether this Labour government can continue'. But he carefully left open the door for negotiations with the Trade Union Congress, indicating all along that he would be willing to withdraw the penal proposals if the unions produced 'an alternative plan which was equally as urgent and equally as effective as the government's would be'.[1]

On May 12, the TUC General Council approved a document, *Programme for Action*, setting out its counter proposals which were to be debated at a special conference of the TUC at Croydon on June 5. Mr. Wilson welcomed *Programme for Action* as a 'determined effort' but doubted whether the proposals for dealing with unconstitutional strikes provided a viable alternative. And Mrs. Castle warned that unless the TUC General Council clarified what influence it could use to ensure that their members stayed at work during negotiations, the proposal 'could at best be regarded

[1] *TUC Annual Report*, 1969, para. 113.

as a pious hope'. Mr. Feather replied that the major fallacy of the government's thinking was the belief that the imposition of automatic sanctions would solve disputes.

Meetings between the government and the TUC General Council continued throughout May and the beginning of June, the TUC being kept informed by sympathetic members of the cabinet of the government's intentions and by trade unionist M.P.s of the rising opposition to the penal clauses in the PLP. At its special conference on June 5 the TUC overwhelmingly approved *Programme for Action*. The Prime Minister reiterated his 'considerable reservations', declaring that the government would proceed with its legislation unless the Congress Rule 11 was altered to give the General Council more effective powers to deal with unconstitutional union stoppages. But the General Council refused.

At the crucial cabinet meeting on Tuesday, June 17, Mr. Wilson 'gave it as his judgment that the credibility of the Government required it to legislate if the TUC would not legislate through its own rules'.[1] Mrs. Castle was in total support. But Mr. Mellish began with words to this effect: there was not a hope of the measure passing; the party would not stand for it; the loyalists were in revolt; there was hardly a supporter left for the penal clauses. He could not get a bill upstairs to the Committee; he could take no responsibility for what might happen if it was taken on the floor of the House like the Parliament Bill. Minister after minister expressed opposition to the penal clauses. 'At the end Wilson and Castle were virtually isolated.'[2]

On the next day, June 18, when the Prime Minister met the General Council and reiterated his demand for a change in Rule 11, the union spokesmen were aware of his weak position. Once again, Mr. Feather refused to budge. After lunch, Mr. Wilson agreed that, in lieu of a change in rules, he would accept a 'declaration of intent' from the General Council. An agreed statement was later issued on behalf of the government and the General Council:

> 'The General Council have agreed unanimously to a solemn and binding undertaking . . . [which] will forthwith govern the operation . . . of Congress Rule 11. . . .'

[1] *The Battle of Downing Street*, p. 152 ff.
[2] Ibid., p. 154.

This face-saving formulation and the Prime Minister's later declarations that the unions had, under the threat of the industrial relations legislation, moved further in a few weeks than in the previous forty years, did little to disguise the defeat.

[*Daily Telegraph*, June 19, 1969

Three years and two months after his victory in the 1966 election, Mr. Wilson had an unenviable record of disaster. He had been forced to withdraw two major bills in one parliamentary session. He had been compelled to devalue the pound and to announce, against his original hopes, British withdrawal from East of Suez. Despite its severely restrictive measures, his government had built up a deficit on the balance of payments, over the first three years of the parliament, of £502 million. There was still no prospect of British entry into Europe. Several of his policies had been voted down by Labour Party Conferences and he had survived more than one attempt on his leadership. Labour was left with fewer councillors than for a generation; it had suffered more than double the number of by-election defeats of any post-war government; and it had broken all records for trailing in the opinion polls.

But all was not lost. Leading Conservatives privately admitted that the election would be much more closely fought than the short term situation suggested and at least one of them — Enoch Powell — gave signs of basing his activities on the assumption of another Labour victory. There was much evidence that Labour's deficit in the polls was due almost entirely to dissatisfaction with the government: lasting conversions to the Conservative cause had been relatively few. Mr. Heath showed little popular appeal and few doubted that Mr. Wilson, if he could extricate himself from his immediate difficulties, could still outsmart him. During the final agony of the struggle over the Industrial Relations Bill, almost unnoticed, the May trade figures were published, showing a deficit which had fallen from £52 million in March and £59 million in April to a mere £14 million. Many experts predicted that the government's economic policy was beginning at long last to pay off. Mr. Wilson's humiliation over the Industrial Relations Bill brought its compensations. The Labour party, like someone who has just taken off a tight shoe, was doubly aware of its new-found comfort. When Mr. Callaghan announced before the summer recess that the recommendations of the Boundary Commission would not be introduced before the election, he had the support of almost all the parliamentary party; the indignation of the Conservatives, who accused the Labour party of unconstitutional gerrymandering, increased the feeling of unity and determination in the government ranks.[1]

In the next session — probably the last before the election — there would be little legislation to which the PLP could object. From now on, all would be geared to the election; ranks would be closed for the battle for survival. There were few who doubted that Labour was capable of making some recovery. The open question was whether they were too far behind: could the wounds of government be healed in the time that remained?

[1] The Boundary Commission's proposals meant, according to various estimates, a gain of between 5 and 20 seats for the Conservatives. The Home Secretary, introducing a bill to free himself from any legal obligation to present the proposals to parliament, argued that they should wait until the Redcliffe-Maud Report with all its transformation of local boundaries had been implemented. On July 21 the House of Lords threw out the bill and so in November the House of Commons went through the charade of Mr. Callaghan presenting the Commissioners' proposals and asking his party to vote them down. For the effect that the new boundaries would have had on the 1970 election, see pp. 414–15.

## CHAPTER II

# TRANSPORT HOUSE: THE RUSTY PENNY FARTHING

IF Labour was to win the 1970 general election, it would not be because of improvements in party organisation. The period from 1966 until the end of 1968 saw a steady decline from a level that was already dangerously low. There was then insufficient time to improve matters before the end of the parliament.

Mr. Wilson and some of his cabinet colleagues were not unduly worried about this state of affairs; a powerful organisation could be more trouble than it was worth. Mr. Wilson had a very simple view of the electorate. It was subject to tendencies and moods, which were more important in determining its voting disposition than were specific governmental or organisational actions. If, for example, a survey showed that the public was more confident than it had been a month before that Labour could handle a particular issue (such as education), this did not mean that there had been some action on the government's part to cause the improvement. *A fortiori*, it was not likely to be due to some sudden propaganda activity from the party headquarters. As likely as not it was the consequence of an irrational change of general mood, and subject to a number of imponderables beyond political control. A violent street demonstration, for example, or a strike, might bring a sharp movement to the right, out of all proportion to its intrinsic importance. And then there was the weather. Mr. Wilson was fond of quoting a remark allegedly made by Mr. Maudling: 'When the weather is good how can anyone really be dissatisfied?' Perhaps the most basic influence of all was the sound of 'half-crowns jingling in pockets'. In so far as these could be influenced by the government, it had to be by the Prime Minister and a few of his senior colleagues. It was their function to nurture the delicate plant of public opinion. Some silly action or interference by the party organisation could easily spoil their efforts. If, for instance, it insisted on including a penal proposal such as a wealth tax in the election manifesto, it would damage the Prime Minister's chances of reassuring the floating voter. Mr. Wilson was therefore not over-anxious to make 'the bloody machine' any more powerful than necessary. This attitude did not go unnoticed at the party headquarters: 'he thinks we are punks, and we know it'.

A further difficulty facing Transport House was the old-fashioned, puritanical approach of many trade unionists and leading members of the Labour movement. They were so used to regarding the Labour party as a poor, if worthy, workhorse that they were slow to accept the suggestions for making it richer and more efficient that were presented by some of the younger elements. Typical was the insistence on hoarding money which could more usefully be employed in building the organisation and in fighting the general election. For years the General Secretary of the party and the National Agent seemed to share and contribute to this deadening state of mind. On top of all this, it became harder to recruit members and activists as the popularity of the Labour government plunged from 1967 onwards.

Before the 1966 election, there had already been a spate of complaints about the condition of the organisation. *Socialist Commentary* devoted its October 1965 issue to an exposé of 'Our Penny-Farthing Machine'. The title was itself a reproach to the Prime Minister and the Transport House establishment, for it had been the phrase used in a scathing report on party organisation by a committee under Mr. Wilson's chairmanship after the election of 1955, and it suggested that nothing had been done in the interim. Soon afterwards the Plan for an Efficient Party campaign (p.e.p.) was established with Jim Northcott, a former Transport House officer and chairman of its staff council, as its organiser. It won editorial support from the most influential Labour publications, the *New Statesman*, *Tribune* and *Socialist Commentary*, and, in response to its requests, 36 motions on organisation were submitted by local parties to the Annual Conference held at Brighton in October 1966. A p.e.p. manifesto demanded: (1) A constitutional commission of high calibre, (2) A national agency scheme, (3) A new style Transport House, (4) A fund-raising unit.

These proposals, especially the demand for changes at the centre, implied criticism of the General Secretary of the Labour party, Len Williams. As Gerald Kaufman had pointed out in an earlier article,[1] Mr. Williams and Miss Sara Barker, the National Agent, were both due to reach retirement age in 1969 and their departure would be a good opportunity to consider modernising

[1] 'Does Labour's Machine Need a Shake-Up?', *New Statesman*, May 7, 1965.

the headquarters. Mr. Williams did not welcome the idea of an inquest into his stewardship. But the proposal was supported by several members of the National Executive Committee, including Anthony Wedgwood Benn and Ian Mikardo. It was difficult to reject it outright as it was likely to command wide constituency support when it came before the Conference in a motion from Ayr CLP. The NEC agreed by 14–13 (with Mr. Wilson abstaining) to an enquiry. It was, however, to be conducted by members of the National Executive itself. As it worked out (and perhaps as some intended), the Committee of Enquiry[1] did not finish its work for many months, and acted as a convenient method of defusing the pressures for reform. An interim report came to the 1967 Party Conference and the final report in 1968. The detailed recommendations then had to be considered over several months by the NEC 'in light of the debate at Conference'. This meant that most of the consequential decisions were taken only in 1969.[2]

While reorganisation was postponed pending the Simpson Committee recommendations, relationships deteriorated between the Research Department at Transport House and the government. Before the 1966 election there had been a prolonged tussle over the drafting of the manifesto 'Time for Decision'. Under its secretary Terry Pitt, the Department resented government pressure to tone down the socialist policies to which the party was committed. It now sought to prevent Mr. Wilson from forsaking them further. In evidence which it presented in January 1967 on

[1] The members of the Committee were Miss A. Bacon (M.P. for Leeds East and Chairman of the Publicity sub-committee of the NEC), Mr. R. H. S. Crossman (M.P. for Coventry East and Lord President of the Council), Mr. J. Gormley (Assistant General Secretary of the National Union of Mineworkers and Chairman of the Organisation Sub-Committee of the NEC), Mr. J. Jones (Assistant General Secretary of the Transport and General Workers Union) and Mr. W. Simpson (Assistant General Secretary of the Amalgamated Union of Foundry Workers). Mr. Simpson was elected Chairman. Presumably this was partly because he was one of the only members who had sufficient time. In October 1967 Mr. Crossman and Mr. Jones came off the NEC and their places on the Simpson Committee were taken by Mr. F. Allaun (M.P. for Salford East) and Mr. H. Nicholas (Assistant General Secretary of the Transport and General Workers Union). The Committee met 25 times during the first year and 15 times during the second. There were three working parties in the first year (dealing with the National Agency Scheme, Political Education and Regional Organisation for Greater London) and three during the second (on Regional Organisation, Labour Women's Movement and Young Socialists).

The membership of these and other standing and *ad hoc* committees of the NEC are recorded in the *Annual Reports* of the Labour Party.

[2] For a critique of the Simpson Committee proposals, see R. L. Leonard, 'That Old Penny Farthing Again', *Socialist Commentary*, November 1968.

behalf of the Labour party, to the Fulton Committee on the civil service,[1] the Research Department criticised the excessive secrecy in Whitehall and

> 'the amount of information which, in some departments at least, is kept from the Minister. . . . It is this secrecy that makes some Ministers tools of their departments a good deal of the time.'[2]

The implication that members of his cabinet were being twisted into abandoning their socialism did not please the Prime Minister, who declared the following day that none of his ministers were ruled by their civil servants and that he would dismiss them if they were.

There was further disagreement over the party's proposal to set up a National Hydrocarbons Corporation. At the 1966 Conference, the National Executive Committee accepted a resolution from the National Union of Mineworkers which called on it

> 'To examine and report on the advisability of taking into public ownership all operations concerning the production of natural gas and oil in Britain or on the British section of the Continental Shelf.'

This referred to the large finds of North Sea gas which private oil

[1] Formally, the Research Department acted under the instructions of the National Executive Committee. The NEC in the earlier part of the parliament played the role described in R. T. McKenzie's *British Political Parties* of supporting the government against the left-wing demands of backbenchers, constituency parties and Transport House. This was because it included several members of the government, elected under both constituency and trades unions' sections or appointed as PLP officers. In 1966–67 it included seven cabinet members — (Messrs. Wilson, Brown, Callaghan, Benn, Crossman, Greenwood and Mrs. Castle) — and seven ministers — (Messrs. Mulley, Padley and Skeffington, Mrs. White and Miss Lee, Miss Herbison and Miss Bacon) and members of trade unions (elected under the large trade unions' section) opposed to left-wing aims. As the parliament proceeded there were two developments: firstly some of the ministerial members became less reliable — Mr. Callaghan for example — and the overlap was reduced by the departure of Mr. Brown from the government and Mr. Crossman from the NEC; secondly the trade unions moved leftwards, especially after the election of Mr. Scanlon as General Secretary of the AEF, and the 'rightist' unions opposed the government's industrial relations policy. The combination of ministerial and trade union dissidents with left-wingers elected by the constituency section often just tipped the balance in their favour.

Two exceptions must be made to this general analysis. In the earlier period, the brevity of the proceedings and the inertia of some of the members made it possible for departments in Transport House to sell proposals potentially embarrassing to the government — as in the case of the North Sea Study Group. On the other hand, it was still possible in the later period for the Prime Minister to get his way on some occasions — albeit with greater difficulty — as there was increasing reluctance as the campaign approached to take decisions that might split the party.

[2] The Fulton Committee on the Civil Service. *Labour Party Evidence* (published by the Labour Party, January 1967), pp. 7–8.

companies were starting to exploit. To the Research Department, the resolution presented a good chance to press the government leftwards. With the agreement of the NEC, a North Sea Study Group was formed. Its report was published in August 1967 and presented to the 1967 Party Conference, which endorsed the doctrine that 'the public sector should advance where it was most needed — at the growing points of the British economy and in the new industries based on science. The Labour party believes that the North Sea provides the opportunity for such an advance and for a valuable experiment in a new form of social ownership.' In view of some 'unresolved issues' (i.e. private ministerial objections) the NEC reconstituted the Study Group. The main differences concerned the relationship of the proposed National Hydrocarbons Corporation with the existing Gas Council. In July 1968 the NEC, disregarding government objections, approved the proposals in the final report of the Study Group. The refusal of successive Ministers of Power to accept the party plans in view of objections from their civil servants led to considerable ill-feeling in Transport House. Mr. Wilson eventually formed an *ad hoc* cabinet committee under his own chairmanship to consider the question. Here, some minor concessions were made to the North Sea Study Group's views.

The state of suspended animation pending the departure of Mr. Williams ended in Spring 1968 when he was appointed Governor-General of Mauritius. The party officers met on April 2 and presented recommendations to the NEC on April 19 about the procedure for choosing a successor. Applications were to be considered by a sub-committee consisting of the officers and four others.[1] The vacancy was advertised and 37 applications were received including several 'Transport House' names. As none of the eight short-listed candidates were considered of sufficient public standing by the NEC at its June meeting, it referred the matter back to the sub-committee with instructions to approach a number of suitably senior figures. In effect, this was an invitation to Mr. Wilson on the one hand, Mr. Brown and Mr. Callaghan on the other, to push for candidates amenable to their purposes. Mr.

[1] Besides Jennie Lee (M.P. for Cannock) and Eirene White (M.P. for Flint, East) the chairman and vice-chairman, respectively, the other officers entitled to attend were Mr. Wilson, in his capacity as leader of the PLP, Mr. Brown, who remained deputy leader of the PLP despite his resignation from the government two weeks earlier, and Mr. Callaghan.

Wilson's first choice was Fred Hayday, Chairman of the TUC. As he proved unavailable Mr. Wilson then forwarded the claims of Anthony Greenwood, the loyal if undistinguished Minister of Housing and Local Government. Mr. Callaghan tried to persuade Mr. Prentice, M.P. for East Ham North and Minister for Overseas Development, to allow his name to go forward. He argued to Mr. Prentice that the party was likely in two years' time to find itself in opposition and he would be more important as General Secretary than as an M.P. Mr. Prentice declined. After other attempts including invitations to Alf Allen, General Secretary of USDAW, and to Merlyn Rees, M.P. for Leeds South, had failed, Mr. Nicholas was finally approached. He had long been second in command at the Transport and General Workers Union under Frank Cousins and had served on the NEC including a period as the Party Treasurer. He did not think he had a chance against Mr. Greenwood whose nomination he indeed had personally supported and it required considerable argument to persuade him to let his name go forward. The tactics for the special meeting of the NEC on July 24 were conspiratorially coordinated. Mr. Callaghan's secretary arranged for Mr. Nicholas to be in London for the meeting. Care was taken to ensure a secret ballot so that members of the NEC who were also government ministers would not be inhibited from opposing Mr. Wilson's choice. When Mr. Greenwood had been proposed, Mr. Brown himself moved the name of Mr. Nicholas. His motion had wide trade union support, the backing of Mr. Callaghan and Mrs. White. This was sufficient to defeat Mr. Greenwood by 14 votes to 12. In view of the fact that Mr. Greenwood's name had been unanimously proposed by the subcommittee of which Mr. Nicholas was a member, Mr. Wilson had reason to be aggrieved by the conspiracy. He consoled himself with the thought that organisation was of little consequence and that 'at the end of the day, it would be the government that would count'.[1]

In accordance with a recommendation of the Simpson Committee, which desired to make the post of General Secretary more weighty than under Mr. Williams' tenure, an Assistant General

[1] For press accounts of the manoeuvres leading to Mr. Nicholas's appointment, see David Wood, 'Who will ride Labour's Penny Farthing?', *The Times*, June 19, 1967, and 'Search for Labour's Chief Executive', *The Times*, April 22, 1968, John Bourne, 'Choosing Labour's General Secretary', *Financial Times*, July 5, 1968, and Nora Beloff, 'Things are looking up for Mr. Wilson', *Observer*, July 28, 1968.

Secretaryship was created, although the specific duties were undefined. On January 22, 1969, Gwyn Morgan, the 37-year-old head of the International Department at Transport House, was appointed by the NEC out of 16 applicants who included most of the senior members of the headquarters' staff. About the same time, Ron Hayward, the Southern Regional Organiser, became the National Agent in succession to Miss Barker. This too was an intentional interruption of 'Buggins' turn'. Mr. Nicholas's appointment was only a partial success. While he threw himself with much enthusiasm into his duties and had a mind open to new ideas, he did perhaps lack some of the intellectual qualities and the tactical experience of his opposite numbers at Conservative Central Office. He was at times criticised by his staff for being too suggestible, agreeing eagerly with some plan and abandoning it ten minutes later when counter-arguments had been presented. Considering the circumstances of his appointment it was only to be expected that his dealings with Number 10 were difficult, the Prime Minister complaining of his 'bureaucratic' tendencies. To his credit, Mr. Nicholas did much in his regional visits to key party workers to promote informality and enthusiasm. His activity provided a much needed antidote to flagging morale. As he was already in his sixties, his appointment was bound to be regarded as provisional and there was continued gamesmanship within the office as advocates of Mr. Morgan's and Mr. Hayward's (and sometimes Mr. Pitt's) future claims manoeuvred on their behalf.

These domestic divisions subtracted to only a limited extent from the greatly improved atmosphere under the new regime. The main difficulty was lack of time. There was an awkward interregnum between Mr. Williams' departure in April 1968 and November 1968 when Mr. Nicholas took up his duties. Mr. Morgan started in his new post in February 1969. The next months were then clouded by the controversy over the Industrial Relations Bill. During the early months of 1969, the NEC and the senior officials spent much of their time considering the Simpson Committee's recommendations, most of which they accepted. At last, steps were taken to introduce the National Agency Scheme advocated years previously by the Plan for an Efficient Party campaign. It had been included in the interim proposals of the Simpson Committee, which were accepted by the 1967 Conference, and was endorsed by the NEC in January 1968, but it was brought into operation only in July 1969, a high proportion of the appointments not being made until 1970 by which time the number of full-time constituency agents had declined from 204 in 1966 to 146. 1966–69 saw an equally serious decline in party membership. The number of constituency parties with over 2,000 members fell from 68 in 1966 to 23 in 1969. Here again, the Simpson recommendations for recruitment came much too late for the 1970 election. By Spring 1970, the National Agent guessed that there were only 300,000 party members.[1] A special drive was made to improve efficiency in marginal seats during the winter of 1969–70 and by May 135 'consultations' had been held by Transport House officials who visited the constituencies to survey efficiency and make suggestions.[2]

The least serious of Labour's problems was finance. But it tended to be used as a scapegoat for organisational inactivity. Underlying the cry of poverty and the reluctance of some senior members of the party to do anything about it was a lack of conviction that the purposes to which extra money would be devoted — better staff conditions, more advertising, more survey research, and — more expensive filming — were useful or indeed worthy.

The Simpson Committee included several suggestions about fund-raising in its report, some of which were adopted. A limited company (Labour Party Nominees Limited) was formed under Dr. Colin Phipps to advise constituency parties on methods of utilising their properties to greater advantage. In the long run, the Property Company promised to become a very useful innovation for the local parties concerned. But as the Labour party had not yet worked out a method equivalent to the quota scheme operated by Conservative Central Office of taxing the richer constituency parties, Transport House would derive little benefit from their enrichment. The possibility of a quota scheme was considered by the Simpson Committee, but it was rejected as constituency parties were 'not likely to be enthusiastic about any

[1] Our own estimate, compiled independently, comes close to this figure. See pp. 263–7.

[2] 'In every case these consultations confirmed how badly the constituency organisation had been hit by events of the last two or three years. In most cases the recovery had started. . . . Many of the plans required the summer months [of 1970] to obtain full advantage from organisational and publicity matters.' Report of the NEC of the 1970 Labour Party Conference, p. 9.

Critical assessments of the state of the organisation are made by John Cartwright, *Socialist Commentary*, May 1969, and Alan Lee Williams, *Socialist Commentary*, October 1969. The most detailed and in many respects the most informative accounts of Labour party organisation appear in the Labour Party Annual Conference Reports.

scheme under which the National Executive Committee would expect a much larger share of the contributions collected locally'. The Committee did suggest, however, that individual subscriptions should be graduated according to the personal income of the member. This was rejected by the NEC. The proposal to increase trade union affiliations was more successful. Early in 1969 the unions agreed to raise their affiliation fees from 1*s.* to 1*s.* 6*d.* per member. That this was agreed during the most bitter battle with the government on the Industrial Relations Bill is a tribute to the ability of Mr. Nicholas and Mr. Callaghan and to the basic loyalties of the union leaders. Perhaps it was also the reward for Mr. Callaghan's opposition to the ill-fated bill. In a full year the higher affiliation would add almost 50% to Labour's income, provided that the unions did not reduce the numbers on which they paid affiliation fees.

The main mistake made by members of the NEC, especially the trade unionists, was to cut the party's coat according to its cloth. Unlike the Conservatives, who based their targets largely (though not entirely) on what they thought they needed, Labour designed its activities according to the funds available.[1] The impetus to raise more was therefore missing. Excessive caution was caused partly by the fear of an inconclusive result followed at short notice by a second general election. The argument that there was no stimulus for contributions equal to an emergency, or that the party could simply go into debt (a process that seems natural to parties in the United States and that has been followed in Britain by the Liberals) did not impress the more conservative elements. The decision in January 1968 to allot £150,000 from the campaign fund to the National Agency Scheme increased the reluctance of the NEC to agree to the requests made in 1968 by the Publicity Advisory Committee for extra funds for party political broadcasts and private survey research. It was late in 1968 that permission was obtained to spend £15,000 between then and the general election on surveys. Early in 1969 the annual budget for producing party political broadcasts on TV was still £2,500. In summer 1969, £200,000 was allowed for advertising campaigns.

[1] According to the *Labour Annual Report, 1970*, central expenses in 1969 amounted to £504,545, including £235,679 on Transport House and £144,039 on the regional offices. Income was £366,620, of which £272,145 came in trade union affiliation fees and £33,729 from local Labour parties. At the end of the year, assets were down to £519,466.

The Publicity Advisory Committee[1] unofficially set to work shortly after the 1966 election. It had the same membership as before. Percy Clark, the Transport House Director of Publicity, three professional volunteers ('The three wise men'), and sometimes Mark Abrams, whose market research company, London Press Exchange, had previously carried out private polls for the Labour party. The professionals were David Kingsley, a director of the advertising firm KMP, Peter Davies of Central Press Features (a magazine agency) and Dennis Lyons, then of Infoscan, a public relations organisation. At first, the group gave general advice to ministers, particularly Mr. Wilson, on government publicity. After the misfiring of his 'pound in the pocket' statement in November 1967, Mr. Wilson called for their advice on the presentation of the public expenditure cuts in January 1968. Throughout 1968, the Publicity Advisory Committee acted as a pressure group for forward thinking about the election. The NEC, concerned with the problems of the interregnum and the increasing difficulties of the government's prices and incomes policy, was in no mood to start planning the campaign, especially if it involved expenditure. In October 1968, it finally accepted the argument that some private surveys had to be made, persuaded by the reminder that similar work had been commissioned in quantity before 1964. The Advisory Group considered its first priority was to stiffen the flagging morale of the faithful. If party workers were not influenced to canvass, and if their faith in the achievements and prospects of their government was not restored, they could hardly expect to persuade the doubtful. With a view to a publicity campaign based on its results, a survey in depth was commissioned to examine the feelings and motives of party activists and how they might be persuaded to return to the fold. The work was entrusted to an American survey expert, Mr. Conrad Jamieson. 1,200 interviews were carried out in Labour-held constituencies and a large amount of useful information obtained. Unfortunately Mr. Jamieson talked to the press and an article appeared in the *Sunday Times* on January 28, 1968 revealing that he was engaged in 'wide-ranging . . . motivational research'. This, together with Mr. Jamieson's eager claims about the possible value of such work (he was quoted as saying that it would 'break new ground in social

[1] It was sometimes known as the Voluntary Publicity Group. See Ludovic Kennedy 'Putting their life and soul into making Britain great again', *Daily Telegraph Magazine*, January 30, 1970.

research' and that its potential was 'enormous'), was doubly unfortunate: to the public it possibly suggested that Labour's position was so precarious that it needed to be bolstered by such new-fangled, suspect methods; more importantly, it confirmed the fears of the party faithful — particularly those on the NEC who had been reluctant to grant funds for the research in the first place — about the morality and value of the exercise. The party therefore returned to the company it had used before, the London Press Exchange, though Mr. Abrams was not personally so closely involved as in the early 1960s. Following the Jamieson leak, Mr. Wilson persuaded Mr. Nicholas to restrict the circulation of future polls to himself, Mr. Nicholas and Mr. Morgan. Ministers and members of Transport House staff would be briefed on the findings but would not be permitted to take notes. It was afterwards maintained by one of the pollsters that the aura of secrecy actually increased interest within the party in their work. This is arguable. But it certainly gave Mr. Wilson extra knowledge and an extra lever against his colleagues and some members of Transport House staff.

There was a survey on young voters in the summer of 1969. The lowering of the voting age to 18 would greatly increase their numbers, and they were potentially a fertile market for Labour propaganda as a majority had been brought up in Labour homes, unlike older generations, and were likely to be more sympathetic. The survey indicated, however, that their concerns and reactions to issues and personalities were not sufficiently distinct to make it worth while to direct publicity or organisational efforts specifically towards them.

In the spring of 1969, the Publicity Advisory Committee also started briefing Assistant Regional Organisers and party workers in interviewing techniques so that they could carry out (at minimal cost) the fieldwork for professionally designed surveys. There were several regional surveys by these 'Feedback' teams before the election, but only one national survey, at the start of the campaign.[1]

In August 1969 a Campaign Committee of twelve was formed at last, consisting mainly of NEC committee chairmen, to which the Prime Minister added three nominees so that government interests would not be ignored. It was necessary, in any case, to include several weighty members of the NEC so that decisions of

[1] See pp. 189–90.

the Campaign Committee were approved without trouble by the Publicity sub-committee of the NEC and by the full Executive.[1] The Campaign Committee was consequently an unwieldy body. Its first meeting was on August 11, 1969, and it met twelve times before the opening of the campaign, when it ceased to function. The Campaign Committee's first important decision was to sanction the short advertising campaign planned by the Publicity Advisory Committee for the autumn. The most important work of the Campaign Committee continued to concern publicity. Although Mr. Wilson regularly attended the meetings, he gave no indication of his thinking about the election date beyond giving instructions for plans to be made in such a manner that all options were left open. Mr. Hayward accordingly kept two 'war books' of campaign arrangements, one on the assumption of an early poll, the other on the assumption of a delay. The Publicity Group planned several short bursts of advertising; the number was to depend on the election date. At the back of most minds, however, there was the expectation that it would be in October 1970.

Besides publicity, there was not much that the Campaign Committee could discuss. The style of the Prime Minister's campaign would be very much his own and would not depend on the Committee's decision. The various technical arrangements — for the press conferences, ministerial tours, daily committees at Transport House, etc. — would be the same as before. As for the problems of aid to marginal seats and the concentration of helpers in key areas, it was too late to start anything fundamental; beyond arranging grants to cover election expenses in needy or important constituencies, little else could be done.

Meanwhile, the conflicts over policy remained unsettled. A 'mid-term manifesto', *Britain: Progress and Change*, was presented to the Party Conference in October 1968. It was the first major attempt by the Research Department to lead the party to a radical position in the future election manifesto. While its language was as yet tentative, its lines of thought were clear. It

[1] The nine members of the Campaign Committee nominated by the NEC were, besides Mr. Wilson as Chairman, three NEC officers, Mrs. Eirene White (Chairman), James Callaghan (Treasurer) and Harry Nicholas (Secretary), and four chairmen of sub-committees, George Brown (Home Affairs), Miss Alice Bacon (Publicity), Joe Gormley (Organisation) and Miss Joan Lestor (Youth), with William Simpson serving *ad hominem*. Mr. Wilson nominated three ministers to the Committee; Anthony Wedgwood Benn, Denis Healey and Robert Mellish. In October 1969 Peter Shore was coopted to the committee.

justified high taxation (with the possibility of even higher rates in the future) by the social benefits it enabled the government to bestow: 'The need to spend more on social services has meant that none of us can have this money in our pockets *as well.* Restraint in this direction is the inevitable price we are paying for progress on the social front.' It then started to explore methods of using taxation to reduce 'glaring *and unacceptable* inequalities in income and wealth', hinting at a wealth tax: 'We therefore propose to look again at the possibilities of taxing wealth . . . Large accumulations of unearned wealth must make their contributions to a fair society.'

Mr. Wilson could not have welcomed these sentences, but he was already in difficulties with the Conference over the prices and incomes policy and preferred to lighten his burdens by leaving the issues raised in the tentative manifesto for the time being. After the Conference, the Research Department set about consolidating its position. With the agreement of the Home Policy sub-committee of the NEC, it was to treat *Britain: Progress and Change* as 'the basis of . . . policy planning towards the next General Election Manifesto.' Detailed papers were to come more often from the Research Department directly, rather than through working groups as before. In February 1969 a small group on Economic Strategy was established, consisting of members of the NEC and Research Department. This group, of which Tom Bradley, M.P. for Leicester North-east, and Roy Jenkins' PPS, was an active member, forwarded the wealth tax proposal (which also had TUC backing). In late spring, two major papers on *Labour's Economic Strategy* and *Labour's Social Strategy* passed the Home Policy sub-committee and the NEC, which agreed to publish them as 'discussion documents' in August. These contained the major leftist proposals, most of which then passed through a further hoop when they were included in an 'NEC statement' presented to the 1969 Party Conference and entitled *Agenda for a Generation.* If it was not intended for a whole generation, it was certainly intended by Research Department for the manifesto despite the disclaimer in the introduction that it was 'not a Manifesto' but merely the commendation of 'the main guidelines of Labour party policy work as the election approaches'. In private, members of the Research Department were confident that the main proposals could not be omitted at this late stage from the manifesto.

The Prime Minister had other ideas. From the beginning, he

realised there were internal battles ahead. He regretted that the Labour party constitution, designed for an opposition grouping, denied him the freedom in making party policy enjoyed by his Conservative counterpart. Matters were not made any easier for him by the arrogant behaviour of some ministers (Mr. Marsh's name was occasionally mentioned in this context) towards Transport House. A Coordinating Committee was therefore established in December 1968 to ease conflicts between forward thinking in Transport House and in the various government departments. The Coordinating Committee was organised by Judith Hart, the Paymaster General, and consisted of 6 Ministers (5 in the Cabinet) on the one hand and on the other 11 NEC representatives (including two further cabinet members, Mr. Callaghan and Mr. Greenwood, and Transport House officials[1]). The Committee was intended by the Prime Minister to soothe rather than to decide. Mrs. Hart was extremely pleasant and suitably left-wing but she did not have the political weight to be very effective either in the NEC or among her ministerial colleagues. When the Campaign Committee was formed, she did not become a member and she was dropped from the cabinet in the October 1969 reshuffle. The Coordinating Committee met twelve times between December 1968 and April 1970, usually in Mrs. Hart's room at the House of Commons. Its limited scope is perhaps indicated by the fact that industrial relations were not mentioned in any of its meetings during the great controversy over the 'penal clauses'. However, when members of the NEC objected to clauses in the Post Office Bill which prevented the GPO from undertaking any manufacturing, clause 13 of the bill was removed as a token of the government's responsiveness to party pressures. The National Hydrocarbons Corporation was again discussed, and there were requests (partly a reflection of the survey material on young voters) to the government to maintain its housebuilding programme. These led to the allocation by the government of £100 million to be given in mortgages by local authorities. In response to complaints expressed at the Coordinating Committee about minor patronage appointments — to regional hospital boards, boards of prison

[1] The membership was: *For the cabinet*: Mrs. Hart, Mr. Jenkins, Mr. Stewart, Mr. Shore, Mr. Mulley, Mr. Crossman. *For the NEC*: Mr. Nicholas, Mr. Brown, Mr. Padley, Mr. Callaghan, Mr. Greenwood, Mr. Simpson, Mr. Chalmers, Mr. Lane, Mr. Morgan, Mr. Pitt and Mr. McNally (head of the International Department).

visitors, Justiceships of the Peace and such like, there was a concerted effort to channel them to nominees of constituency Labour parties. A great many positions went to defeated Labour councillors.

The Coordinating Committee was also a forum where Ministers could report their concern about drafts of *Labour's Economic Strategy*, *Labour's Social Strategy* and *Agenda for a Generation*. Mr. Jenkins reluctantly said that he 'could live with' the proposed wealth tax, possibly because the Prime Minister had assured him that there would still be opportunities to ditch it nearer the election. Nevertheless, he resented Transport House officials who seemed more concerned with their professional position than with the wider interests of the party. Mrs. Castle, who was still suffering from her Industrial Relations Bill experience, made a greater fuss and insisted on a passage reaffirming the 'vital importance of an effective prices and incomes policy'.

As the campaign approached, the major difficulties remained: lack of members, lack of agents, lack of preparation, divisions on policy and personal distrust between Transport House and No. 10. The Research Department ignored the Prime Minister's request at the beginning of 1970 to 'get on with the *Speaker's Handbook* and to cut out the policy stuff', insisting on continuing its preparations for the manifesto. For the only time since the war, apart from the election of 1966 which had followed very closely on the previous one, no *Handbook* was produced. There were continual complaints from senior Transport House officials that Mr. Wilson did not take them into his confidence, but he felt they did not 'get things done' and leaked any information he gave them into the gossip columns. During the spring, while Mr. Wilson's mind was moving towards the decision to go to the country in June, Transport House remained completely in the dark and proceeded to arrange a summer advertising campaign. As the Prime Minister was apparently not informed of the plans until they were presented to the Campaign Committee in April, and as he dared not indicate the possibility of an early election in case it leaked, he did not warn them against it. The state of the organisation was summed up by Mr. Hayward who presented a progress report to the joint meeting of the NEC and the government at Downing Street on May 17, 1970, the day before the election date was announced. The report warned that if there was a June election 'it will be very much a "Do-It-Yourself" campaign'.

## CHAPTER III

# A TROUBLED OPPOSITION

CONSIDERING the many difficulties confronting Labour, it is easy to suppose that the years out of office were simple for the Conservatives. This is far from the case. They were uncertain and troubled. Internal strains were never absent and it required wise party management to prevent them from developing into seriously damaging quarrels.

Mr. Wilson's moderate pragmatism made it hard for the Conservatives to find good targets. His defence of the $2.80 parity was in line with Conservative thinking; the incomes policy had been inaugurated under Mr. Macmillan; the credit squeeze was a Treasury method used equally under both parties. As Mr. Maudling, the Conservative Chancellor from 1962 to 1964, rather embarrassingly pointed out, Labour inherited 'our problems, and our remedies'.[1] Nor did the advent of a Labour administration usher in a period of retrenchment in foreign affairs. Until the summer of 1967, it was the shadow Defence Minister, Mr. Powell, who was the leading advocate of a withdrawal from East of Suez. The Labour flirtation with unilateral nuclear disarmament, which Sir Alec Douglas-Home had vigorously attacked during the 1964 election, disappeared without trace. British relationships with the United States were as good as under Mr. Macmillan and Sir Alec. The distinctive feature of Conservative foreign policy, its attachment to European union, was taken away in 1967. Rhodesia gave little scope for attack as Mr. Wilson was very nearly as accommodating in his dealings with Mr. Smith as the opposition. Successive Labour education ministers were very patient and flexible in introducing comprehensive schemes of secondary education; Mr.

[1] Mr. Maudling was, of course, referring specifically to the measures such as the import surcharge which were prepared by the outgoing Conservative government and adopted by Labour.

Gordon Walker's high-handed treatment of the Enfield Education Committee gave rise to the only controversial episode.

Apart from steel, Labour refrained from further major nationalisation. It introduced the Land Commission, the 'betterment levy', a huge Transport Bill and at the very end the Docks Nationalisation Bill; but, however important they were, these measures seemed highly technical and lacked the dramatic doctrinal impact of, for example, coal or rail nationalisation during Mr. Attlee's Labour government. It was not surprising that a senior member of the Conservative Research Department complained 'it was much easier in 1945–51 when we at least had some socialism to attack'.

If the opportunity to condemn Labour's policies was limited, the scope for casting doubts on its ability to carry them out was much greater. Mr. Heath, it would seem, had merely to convince the public that he would dispense the same moderate package less disastrously than Mr. Wilson. Yet, even when Labour lagged by more than 20% in the polls, this was a tricky task. The public attitude to the government's failures appeared not only to reflect disappointment with the Labour party but cynicism with politicians as a whole. Memories of the decline during the final years of the Conservative administration persisted, and aggressive Conservative attacks risked making people think 'politicians are all the same'.

Another Conservative handicap was Mr. Heath, who did not inspire confidence among the electorate or the party faithful. The circumstances in which he had come to the Conservative leadership in July 1965 were inauspicious. The party still smarted from the blows received in the final Macmillan years and during Sir Alec Douglas-Home's brief, unsatisfactory tenure. Mr. Heath was the third leader in as many years. As bad luck would have it, his first months coincided with Labour's recovery in the polls and with a bruising battle between Conservative factions over Rhodesian policy. In April 1966 he found himself in the unprecedented position of holding the Conservative leadership without previously having been Prime Minister, and having taken the party to an electoral defeat. In this difficult situation he performed with a hesitant prickly style. This caused initial public disappointment and contributed, in turn, to his continued tenseness and apparent lack of self-confidence. The vulnerability of the Conservative position, however, was not without its advantages to Mr. Heath.

The party, which had recently edged two leaders towards resignation, was unlikely to force a third change; the instinct for self-preservation was too strong. He could therefore count on its loyalty, if not on its enthusiasm. While there were no serious moves to displace him, the undercurrents of dissatisfaction were not eliminated at any time before June 18, 1970.

Mr. Heath's poor standing was reflected in the opinion polls. An awkward contrast emerged in 1967 between the Conservative party's lead over Labour and his personal lag behind Mr. Wilson.

*Support for leaders and support for parties 1966–1970*

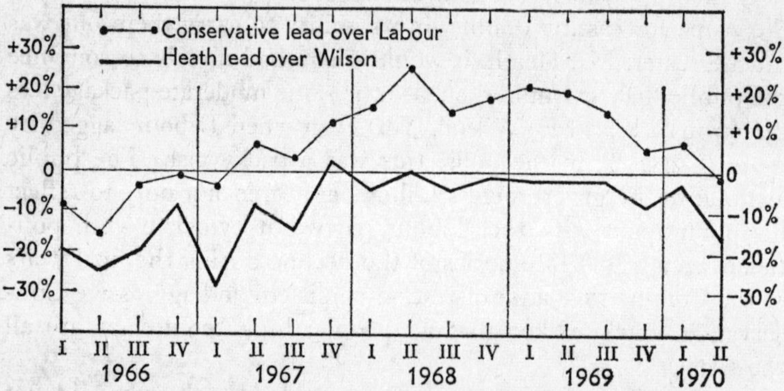


(Gallup findings (quarterly averages) on (i) percentage intending to vote Conservative minus percentage intending to vote Labour and (ii) percentage satisfied with Mr. Heath as Leader of the Opposition, minus percentage satisfied with Mr. Wilson as Prime Minister.)

Official explanations of his lack of impact went through three phases. At first, it was attributed to the Labour lead in the polls. When this disappeared, Mr. Heath's public acceptance was thought to be 'just round the corner' and was fostered by publicity showing him in happy family situations. Gradually, it was accepted that the 'new Mr. Heath' was not emerging and never would until the party won power. This revealing interview appeared in the North Somerset constituency magazine in 1969. It is typical of the language then current in Conservative circles:

'*Party activist*: People wonder why Ted Heath's undoubted qualities of leadership haven't come across as well as they should.

*Paul Dean M.P.*: . . . My guess is that he will inspire the country when he becomes Prime Minister and that he will break through much more effectively than as Leader of the Opposition.'

Irrespective of Mr. Heath's position, however, there were worries in several sections of the Conservative party that a renewed mandate would not be obtained unless it presented distinctive 'right-wing' policies. According to this view, the last years of Conservative rule in the early sixties had failed because pale pink ideas had been adopted. The Rhodesian issue stimulated the die-hard Conservative M.P.s and their allies, who had been active in the 1950s as members of the imperialist 'Suez Group' and in the early 1960s in the 'Katanga lobby'. The Monday Club, founded in 1961, provided a focus for their activities, which centred on colonial and foreign affairs.[1] A separate loose grouping demanded greater economic radicalism — particularly the reduction of government interference in industry and private welfare. Ideas of *laissez-faire* liberalism were fed into the discussion by such bodies as the Institute of Economic Affairs. In addition there was a constant, if less coherent, demand from the constituency parties — and occasionally from the Conservative backbenches — for tougher opposition. It sometimes took the form of pressure on a particular policy (the maintenance of grammar schools, for example), and sometimes of general obstructionism.

Mr. Heath, like Mr. Wilson, was therefore faced by the conflict between arguments of electoral prudence, which urged him to play for the centre, and the pressure of elements in his party, which demanded that he abandon it. In addition, he had to balance the dangers of leaving the party without any fresh policies against those involving working out and prematurely disclosing new proposals. Winston Churchill, who had been in a similar position after the Conservative defeat in 1945, had very clear attitudes about the demands of opposition. It was unnecessary and dangerous, he thought, for a Conservative opposition to prepare policies or to

[1] The Monday Club held monthly meetings and dinners. In addition it ran study groups and established branches in universities and in the constituencies. In 1968, the Club claimed 1,000 national and 3,000 local members. It existed to combat the influence of 'left-wing' Conservative organisations such as the Bow Group. According to its published statement of aims: 'In the 1950s and the early 1960s the left-wing of the party gained a predominant influence over policy. . . . The Monday Club aims to rectify this imbalance.' Largely as a reaction to the Monday Club, another 'left-wing' Conservative organisation was formed with branches in the universities under the name of PEST (Pressure for Economic and Social Toryism).

run a system of 'shadow ministries' as if it were a government in exile. His job was, first and last, to attack the government and, in R. A. Butler's caricature, to 'trot out the Bolshevik bogey'.[1]

As Mr. Heath once explained, his own notions were very different:

> 'In 1945, after great urging from his colleagues, Sir Winston Churchill said that Conservative policy was "to respect the monarchy, to maintain the constitution and to be a God-fearing party". This would hardly satisfy those modern commentators who are obsessed by the management of the economy. As well as the broad approach, there is the detailed policy approach . . . This is criticised on the grounds that detailed policy suggestions are ignored by the mass of voters and become an embarrassment at a General Election.
>
> There is probably a place for both the main themes and for detailed policies. The argument for detail is this: people today are so cynical and sceptical about the whole machinery of government that detail is needed to convince them that you really intend to carry out your promises.'

Mr. Heath devoted a great deal of energy and attributed much importance to a set of policy groups established to examine specific problems in depth. These groups had been originally established after the 1964 election and were composed of shadow ministers, M.P.s and outside experts. They worked in private and, in deference to the wishes of some of the outsiders, their membership was not disclosed.

Mr. Heath had succeeded R. A. Butler at the end of 1964 as Chairman of the Advisory Committee on Policy and in this capacity became responsible for the policy groups. He was ideally suited to the work and it was natural that he should extend their operation when he took over the party leadership. He saw several weighty political advantages in the policy group method. It avoided the further debasement of politics into a slanging match. It showed that the Conservatives were capable of managing the country and its economy. It therefore solved the problem inherited from the later Macmillan and Home years when the electorate suspected that 'the Conservatives can't even run a fish and chip shop let alone a government'. He thought that people did not necessarily require the details of the policies, but they demanded to know that they existed. It was also an insurance against

[1] Harold Nicolson *Diaries and Letters*, Vol. IV (Collins, 1968).

obstruction by civil servants when a future Conservative administration came into office. And, presumably, it brought numbers of academics into the Conservative orbit and thereby combated the hostility to the party in the early sixties among the opinion-forming elite. Finally, the study method, together with the parallel organisation of teams of spokesmen in parliament to oppose specific bills, involved more M.P.s and party figures in the policy-making process, thereby lessening the dangers of internal divisions.[1]

Before the 1966 election there were 23 policy groups with a combined membership of 181 M.P.s and peers and 118[2] outside experts. Ten groups were then disbanded and others were created. Altogether there were 29 groups between 1966 and 1970 with a combined membership of 191 M.P.s and peers and 190 outside experts.

The groups, which were normally chaired by shadow ministers, varied greatly in their size, composition and importance. The Law Reform Group, for example, consisted exclusively of members of parliament whereas those on the Position of Women, Balance of payments and Building Land each had only one or two. There were also differences in the frequency of their meetings and the thoroughness of their findings, depending generally on the keenness of the shadow minister and the availability of the Research Department officer who acted as secretary.

The overall management of the exercise was the responsibility

[1] Mr. Heath's leadership is considered in three articles by Ian Trethowan in *The Times* (July 22, 23, 24, 1968). See also an interview with Mr. Heath by David Butler, *Listener*, July 20 and 27, 1967). Interesting articles on Conservative policy-making in opposition include David Watt, *Financial Times*, October 20, 1967, an anonymous article 'Tories still searching for some new clothes', *The Times*, June 11, 1968 and Peter Jenkins 'It's only make believe' and 'The real right road', *Guardian*, February 3 and 20, 1970.

[2] These figures overstate the total numbers involved as several served on more than one group. They were labelled Economic Policy, Education, National Insurance and Health, Housing, Trade Union Law and Practice, Law Reform, Machinery of Government, Overseas Development, Public Service Pensions, Regional Government, Science and Technology, and Transport (all these were established before the 1966 election). Also, the Arts, Balance of Payments, Building Law, Furnished Lettings, Nationalised Industries, Power, Regional Development, Savings, Social Security, Voluntary Emergency Services, Position of Women under the Law and regional groups for London, Wales and Monmouthshire, the East of England and the West Country. Separate Scottish policy groups were run from Edinburgh.

The groups disbanded in 1966 had been those on Agriculture, Consumer Problems, Crime, Defence, Fixed Income Groups, Foreign Affairs, Immigration, Leisure, Rating, and Problem Family and Child.

of a senior Research Department officer and the Chairman of the Advisory Committee on Policy.[1] Reports went first to the Advisory Committee on Policy and then to the shadow cabinet. Throughout the process, Mr. Heath kept in very close contact and often dropped into the Research Department for impromptu policy seminars. It was initially intended to draw the work of the groups together into a document on economic policy for the 1967 party conference and to produce a mid-term report in 1968. Delays in the work of the groups concerned with economic policy prevented the former, but a major document, *Make Life Better*, was presented to the party conference in 1968.

Despite its suitability to his style, and its considerable practical advantages, the policy exercise did not solve all the political problems facing the Conservative leader. It seems that he tackled these in three ways: (1) By careful statements on aspects of colonial policy and immigration he eased some of the potential difficulties with the 'right-wing' over economic policy; it was particularly useful to have Sir Alec Douglas-Home, in the words of an aide, 'as a card to shut up the right'. (2) He used language which exaggerated his ideological differences with Labour; he was thereby able to suggest a distinctive approach without committing himself to specific policies likely to offend the floating voter. (3) He concentrated many of his policy enquiries on improving the methods and structure of government activity; he thereby aimed at lessening the scope of public interference without reducing its benefits.

His priorities and the difficulties they involved are best illustrated by the attempts to formulate economic policy. Spring 1965 had found Mr. Heath as shadow Chancellor in Sir Alec Douglas-Home's opposition. It fell to him to attack the corporation tax contained in the Budget. His performance was a model of the

[1] James Douglas coordinated the policy groups until summer 1968, when he went on sabbatical leave in America and Barney Hayhoe took his place. As Mr. Heath remained Chairman of the Advisory Committee on Policy until November 1968 the Deputy Chairman, Sir Edward Boyle, had general charge during this period. Mr. Maudling then became Chairman of the Advisory Committee on Policy. Neither Sir Edward nor Mr. Maudling shared Mr. Heath's energetic enthusiasm for the policy exercise.

The membership of the Advisory Committee on Policy consisted of seven representatives of the Conservative M.P.s and peers, eight representatives of the National Union Executive Committee, the party chairman, deputy chairman, CPC Director, the Director of the Research Department and four co-opted members.

'governmental' style of opposition. He divided the Labour proposals clause by clause between a team of frontbenchers who received detailed briefs from the Conservative Research Department which was, in its turn, in touch with various affected interest groups. During the debates on the 1965 Finance Bill, which took 22½ days — 217 hours — of parliamentary time, Conservative spokesmen proposed 680 amendments.[1]

In the course of this work, Mr. Heath investigated alternative tax systems. He was aided by the Economic Policy Group and by a comparative study of foreign taxation commissioned by the Conservative Research Department from the Economist Intelligence Unit. He believed one of the main faults in the existing economic structure was that it imposed penalties on the salaried managers and entrepreneurs — the pacemakers — the very people on whom growth depended; by contrast, holders of accumulated wealth on the one hand and some of the lower brackets of wage-earners on the other escaped too lightly. A key to economic success lay in removing the barriers to managerial incentive imposed by the tax system and in reforming the obsolete structure of industry and the trade unions. These ideas were outlined in *Putting Britain Right Ahead*, the policy statement published shortly after Mr. Heath became party leader, which was presented to the 1965 Party Conference.

In the winter of 1965–66 there was a major public controversy between Mr. Powell and Mr. Maudling, the former Conservative Chancellor of the Exchequer. Mr. Powell, in a sustained rhetorical offensive against incomes policy, was no less critical of the Conservative attempts at 'indicative planning' in the early sixties than those of the Labour government. He referred to the superstition 'which seems to underpin non-Socialist support for an incomes and prices policy. . . . This superstition is so pitted and hedged around with absurdity that one would be tempted to apply to it the Duke of Wellington's famous remark about believing anything.'[2] Mr. Powell and his fellow 'free marketeers' attributed the country's economic difficulties to the oversized governmental sector and to central interference with market forces. They favoured drastic decreases in taxation, and large-scale denationalisation,

[1] See *Notes on Current Politics*, pp. 486–7 (Conservative Research Department, September 20, 1965).
[2] Speech to the Manchester Statistical Society, January 12, 1966.

although these would necessitate a reduction in welfare benefits.[1]

Mr. Maudling upheld the previous Conservative experiments in indicative planning against Mr. Powell's charges and also defended his record against Labour charges that he had encouraged a pre-election boom. He suggested that the so-called 'crisis' inherited by the incoming Labour government had been the result of its own alarmism. Had it supported a continuing policy of growth, there would have been no speculation against sterling. It followed that it was unnecessary for the Conservative opposition to concoct new measures. In any case, policy making in opposition and without civil service assistance was pointless and likely to produce only useless generalities.

Although Mr. Heath agreed with the interventionists on the one hand that there was a continuing need for a voluntary incomes policy and, on the other hand, with the free marketeers that individual enterprise was being stifled and industry harmed by 'over-government', he had comparatively little interest in their controversies. For he looked for the solution to the problems of the economy in a different direction which can conveniently (if inadequately) be termed 'technocratic'. Like the advocates of *laissez-faire*, he wished to allow individual enterprise to flourish; but unlike them, he did not see drastic reductions of governmental activities as the best way of doing this. He saw in structural reforms a way of cutting the area of public interference without significantly reducing the overall level of services provided. If the form (rather than the total amount) of taxation was changed, if the machinery of government and industrial relations was improved, if industrial re-training was encouraged, and if public expenditure was cut at the points where its costs grossly outweighed its benefits, it would be possible to break out of the vicious circle in which the economy was placed without major — and politically unpopular — reductions in welfare benefits.

By spring 1966 the beginnings of a 'technocratic' economic policy had already been formed. Proposals had been drawn up for the reform of industrial relations and cuts in public spending

[1] In a speech at Morecambe during the 1968 Conservative Party Conference, Mr. Powell produced a set of proposals which would enable income tax to come down to 4*s*. 3*d*. in the pound without any reduction in the social services. It was widely accepted, however, that this could not be achieved. The 'free marketeers' generally acknowledged that they aimed to reduce spending on the social services though not in the areas of greatest need.

suggested, the most important of them being the abolition of agricultural subsidies and the concentration of subsidies for council housing in the 'worst areas'. These two measures would save £300–£400 million a year. In addition, a 'war on waste' in Whitehall was advocated. The 1966 Conservative manifesto optimistically suggested that this might lead to a 5% saving — another £400 million a year. These proposals did not touch the main areas of government spending: defence, education, the National Health Service and pensions.

Defence provided little scope for savings. Expenditure in this sector was fast decreasing if measured as a proportion of GNP, and there would, in any case, be strong objections to further reductions from important sections of the party. Indeed, there were pressures to increase defence commitments, and some of these were agreed in the course of the parliament. If there were to be any large savings they would have to fall on the social services. But these too were strongly resisted by Mr. Heath and his most senior colleagues. He regarded with particular contempt the proposal for a voucher scheme in education which was repeatedly put forward by the *Daily Telegraph*. Under the scheme, parents would be encouraged to send their children to private schools by the grant of vouchers equivalent to the cost to the government of their education at a state school. After an examination by the Research Department, the idea was firmly rejected by the shadow cabinet on practical grounds but also because it was unwilling to envisage what Mr. Heath saw as a 'return to 1870'. Besides, as a senior official later commented, 'even a suspicion that the Tories were thinking of abolishing free education and the like would have been politically disastrous'.

Far from economising on public education, the shadow cabinet adopted policies extending its scope and cost. The 11-plus examination was to be abolished (according to a shadow cabinet decision of 1967), and local authorities were to be allowed to choose between comprehensive and selective systems of secondary education. More attention was to be given to primary schooling and there would be no cuts in the *per capita* cost of secondary education (which would therefore rise because of the increased school population). Further education would grow even faster: ever larger numbers would reach A-level standard and they would proceed to the universities and technical colleges unless entry standards were raised or government grants to students lowered; and the Conservatives were willing to allow neither of these expedients. These policies were closely identified with Sir Edward Boyle, the shadow Minister for Education, and the butt of the Conservative 'right'. The plans for secondary education came under continual fire from constituency activists. Mr. Heath went out of his way to identify himself publicly with Sir Edward's policies, protecting him for three years 'while the party was shrieking against him'.[1]

Pensions and health remained subjects of internal controversy until the end. Mr. Heath and his senior allies were willing to accept limited reductions but would not countenance any major interference with the principle of universal benefits which had been accepted by the party in the late 1940s. As Sir Michael Fraser once retorted when he was confronted by a radical proposal at a conference attended by policy group members, 'You can't shoot Santa Claus'; he was referring to the electoral unpopularity (revealed in private Conservative surveys and in public opinion polls) of any major restrictions upon National Health Service benefits.

If there was to be relatively little change in the scope of governmental activity there would be no opportunity of reducing the tax burden. Changes would have to concentrate on the form rather than the amount of taxation. Mr. Macleod admitted this in an article entitled 'Taxation: Planning for Office' which appeared in the *Banker* in April 1969:

> 'In order to achieve a vital economy, taxation must be cut. But let us be clear what this does and does not mean. It does not mean that by international standards, the proportion of income taken in the U.K. is above average. On the contrary, if anything, it is below average. It does mean that we tax the wrong things in the wrong way.'[2]

In private, he was even more explicit:

> 'It is an illusion to think that there are vast savings to be made. . . . It is the tax system itself which is wrong and not the total tax burden.'

[1] Despite the criticisms from constituency parties, Sir Edward was able to point out to his colleagues that many Conservative-controlled councils were themselves introducing comprehensive schemes and had started to do so even before the return of the Labour government.

[2] Although this article appeared in 1969, it was probably written earlier and represents, as senior Conservatives assure us, his views in the earlier parts of the parliament. Nearer the election there was a shift in the emphasis. This is described later in this Chapter and in Chapter 6, pp. 126, 129–30.

See also *Britain's Taxes: Some International Comparisons* (Old Queen Street Paper 3, Conservative Research Department, September 25, 1967).

The first objective of the Economic Policy Group was to reduce income tax. Comparative studies had shown that it was in this sector that the burden was much heavier in Britain than abroad. As it penalised successful salary earners, it was thought to be particularly harmful. The most obvious alternative was to increase the conventional indirect taxes, but this was difficult as purchase tax was already high and petrol, alcohol and tobacco taxes in particular were near the point of diminishing returns. It was therefore necessary to look for new forms of levy. One of the early suggestions of a working party (in which Arthur Cockfield, a Director of Boots and a former Inland Revenue official, was one of the most active members) was to reduce Estate Duty (which was so widely avoided that it had become a 'voluntary' tax), to reform company taxes (including corporation tax), to reduce income taxes at their highest levels and to substitute, among other things, a wealth tax. There was such opposition when the idea was floated in party circles that it was not pursued. However, the possibility of adopting a single 'graduated tax on capital' (i.e. the wealth tax in ideologically acceptable language) continued to be discussed.

In his post-election Budget on May 5, 1966, Mr. Callaghan introduced a new tax — the Selective Employment Tax (SET).[1] This was strongly opposed by Conservative spokesmen, mainly on the ground that it was intended as a means of disguising the rise in taxation which the Labour party had promised not to make during the campaign. Nevertheless, whatever the motives for its introduction, and whatever its defects in detail, it offered a useful addition for the Exchequer and broadened the tax base in a manner the Conservatives were themselves considering. The Conservative pledge to abolish the tax when they returned to office, made almost immediately after the Budget by Mr. Macleod, was to restrict the party's room for manoeuvre and to cause serious difficulties with its own activists. For the undertaking was ambiguous; it meant either that the Conservatives would abolish the selective element in the SET but continue with another form of employment or payroll tax, or that it would shun all employment taxes. In higher party circles, it was interpreted in its narrow form, since Mr. Macleod thought that a payroll tax was 'inevitable'. To the party activists and the public, however, the propaganda against SET suggested the wider interpretation. As the yield pro-

[1] See p. 7.

duced by the SET increased from about £300 million in 1966–67 to over £600 million in 1970–71, its abolition became more difficult and it was later mentioned by some members of the shadow cabinet as an object lesson against making firm policy commitments in opposition.

In 1966–67, the Conservative policy-makers envisaged a package based on two new measures: a payroll tax and a Value-added Tax.[1] Mr. Heath remained chairman of the Economic Policy Group, which enabled him to retain close control over the discussion and avoided the need to pass the chairmanship to either Mr. Macleod or Mr. Maudling. Mr. Heath generally used his position to protect Mr. Macleod's proposals against the conventional objections of the former Chancellor. The package included 1*s.* off the income tax, a reduction of surtax so that no one paid more than 10*s.* in the pound of his total income, elimination of the differential rates of tax on 'earned' and 'unearned' income, a reduction in corporation tax and the abolition of SET. These would be replaced by a 5% payroll tax and Value-added Tax.

To these ideas there were three main objections: that it was impossible to plan changes of this magnitude without the advice of the civil service; that they would reduce income tax at the cost of unpopular rises in consumer prices; and that they missed the point by concentrating on structural changes in taxation, thereby ignoring fundamental economic problems, which demanded a change in the parity of sterling. These views were probably supported by Mr. Maudling and were expressed by several economists at a seminar organised by the Conservative Research Department at Church House on July 20, 1967. As the seminar was attended by most of the economic experts advising the opposition, their stand on devaluation was awkward. Mr. Heath was particularly anxious to avoid an open discussion on sterling within the party. He did not accept the arguments for change and wished for tactical purposes to avoid statements that would inhibit Conservative opposition to a future Labour devaluation.[2]

[1] The tax measures planned by the Economic Policy Group remained indefinite and the shadow cabinet did not at any time commit itself, even tentatively. Nevertheless, Mr. Macleod and the other front bench economic spokesmen clearly thought in terms of reasonably precise tax 'packages', though their contents naturally altered during the course of the parliament.

[2] See *Verbatim Report of an Economic Seminar* (Old Queen Street Paper 2, Conservative Research Department, 1967). See also S. Brittan, *Left or Right: the bogus dilemma*, pp. 124–5 (Secker & Warburg, 1968) and his 'Thoughts on

When devaluation occurred on November 18, 1967, the incipient controversy among the Conservatives about its desirability was at an end;[1] but the other doubts about the proposed tax package remained unresolved. In the next few months, however, there were immediate, less technical problems to face.

During 1967 there was growing restlessness among Conservative M.P.s and in the constituency parties. It became apparent during the education debate at the party conference in October 1967, when delegates criticised 'a non-motion advocating a non-policy' and stated their dissatisfaction with the apparent woolliness of Sir Edward Boyle and Mr. Heath on comprehensive schools. In the vote following Sir Edward's conciliatory summing-up, there was a large show of hands against the resolution and a ballot was demanded — the first since the 1950 Conference. The platform carried the day by only 1,302 to 816. A few weeks later, right-wing M.P.s quietly arranged to crowd the meeting of the Conservative backbench committee on education at which the vice-chairman was to be elected (Sir Edward, as shadow minister, was automatically chairman). They succeeded in replacing Richard Hornby, a progressive, by Ronald Bell, a leading Monday Club member, unsympathetic to official party policy on education. The move was calculated to cause considerable awkwardness as it was current practice for vice-chairmen of backbench committees to speak from the front bench in support of the shadow minister. Mr. Heath only grudgingly (and at Sir Edward's request) granted Mr. Bell this perquisite.

In the months following devaluation, the decline in Labour's position led to growing militancy on the Conservative backbenches. There were demands in the 1922 Committee (the backbench forum) for an all-out attack on the government's management of the economy, especially on its incomes policy. There was also a campaign, fostered by a former Conservative Commonwealth Relations Secretary, Duncan Sandys, to halt the inflow of Asians from Kenya. Their entry was not controlled by the Commonwealth Immigrants Act as they had been given British citizen-

the Conservative Opposition', *Political Quarterly*, April/June 1968, and a reply by J. Bruce-Gardyne M.P., 'The Strains of Opposition', *Spectator*, September 13, 1968.

[1] It did not, however, end the controversy about 'floating' rates. This was discussed by a policy group on the balance of payments set up under Sir Keith Joseph's chairmanship in 1969.

ship when the East African territories became independent in the early sixties. They were now coming to Britain in large numbers as their lives were being made difficult by the Kenya government's 'Africanisation' policy. In Britain, sympathy for their plight and a feeling of guilt at breaking a solemn pledge were outweighed in many minds by the fear of racial tension. On February 22, 1968, Mr. Callaghan announced that a bill would be introduced to restrict their entry. The shadow cabinet reluctantly gave its support, but fifteen Conservatives voted against the second reading of the bill on February 27 and a number of others abstained. They were mostly on the progressive wing, but included several others, among them Iain Macleod and Patrick Wall, a leading imperialist who considered the proposal a breach of good faith and colonial responsibility. Nevertheless, it was widely regarded as a victory for the right wing and strengthened pressures within the party to oppose another measure, the Race Relations Bill, which was shortly due to come before the House.

Counter preparations on the Conservative left[1] raised the possibility of the situation Mr. Heath most feared — an open split. As a former Chief Whip, he was almost obsessively concerned with internal unity and was determined to avoid the troubles following the defeats of 1906 and 1929, when the party had, in his own words, 'torn itself asunder'. A sub-committee of the shadow cabinet was set up to draft a 'reasoned amendment' to the Race Relations Bill to gain the widest possible Conservative support. Mr. Heath presumably aimed at placating the right wing by refusing to vote with the government and by declaring publicly that the party was committed to 'drastic' immigration controls. At the same time, he hoped to conciliate moderate opinion by not opposing the bill directly, by criticising its methods rather than its intentions and by permitting left-wingers to vote with the Labour party if they insisted, without the threat of disciplinary action.

On Saturday, April 20, three days before the Commons debate, Mr. Powell made a speech at Birmingham which, in later months, he was to call 'the earthquake':

'Those whom the gods wish to destroy, they first make mad. We

[1] It is often misleading to describe party factions in 'left/right' terms. The words have been used in this case as the members of the groups concerned tended to think of themselves in this way, though some 'right-wingers' preferred the name 'Conservative' or 'real Conservative', while 'left-wingers' sometimes used the words 'moderate' or 'progressive'.

must be mad, literally mad, as a nation to be permitting the annual inflow of some 50,000 dependents, who are for the most part the material of the future growth of the immigrant-descended population. It is like watching a nation busily engaged in heaping up its own funeral pyre. So insane are we that we actually permit unmarried persons to immigrate for the purpose of founding a family with spouses and fiancés whom they have never seen. . . . As I look ahead, I am filled with foreboding. Like the Roman, I seem to see "the River Tiber foaming with much blood". That tragic and intractable phenomenon which we watch with horror on the other side of the Atlantic but which there is interwoven with the history and the existence of the States itself, is coming upon us here by our own volition and our own neglect.'

The following day Mr. Heath dismissed Mr. Powell from the shadow cabinet and received in reply a letter which accused him of 'playing down and unsaying policies which you hold and believe to be right'. In the next week, left-wing Conservative M.P.s caucused and 24 of them abstained when the Conservative amendment to the second reading of the Race Relations Bill was debated on April 23, 1968; dockworkers marched to the Houses of Parliament to support Mr. Powell; and students marched in protest through several universities. He received tens of thousands of congratulatory letters, and a few threats; Mr. Heath's and Mr. Powell's homes were placed under police guard. Mr. Powell protested that he had been unjustly treated, that his speech was in accordance with agreed policy and was not intended to be inflammatory. This view gained surface plausibility from Mr. Heath's diplomatic assurances to the party faithful that the difference with his former colleague was a matter of 'tone' and not of substance. In truth, it involved a much deeper issue than the niceties of rhetoric. For several years Mr. Powell had refused to 'play the game'. He subscribed to the convenient constitutional theory that there was no single 'opposition', only 'men in opposition'. Consequently he considered that his position as a shadow minister did not stop him from publicly opposing policies advocated by his colleagues or carried out by previous Conservative governments to some of which he had belonged.

Ever since 1963–64, when he delivered speeches throughout the country as an ex-minister, having refused to join Sir Alec Douglas-Home's government, he had felt 'the Egerian stream forcing itself up' within him, enabling him to exploit a new medium — the massive presentation of an argument, combining the form of a platform speech with the content of a treatise. The power of his tongue and the richness of his pen gave him a new status and encouraged the 'honourable ambition' of gaining the party leadership. Unfortunately for Mr. Powell that position went in 1965 to a man four years his junior. Without openly opposing Mr. Heath, he constantly prodded, pressured and thwarted him, while carefully promoting his own personality among the party activists and expressing his distinctive philosophy of government non-interference with market forces. There is strong evidence that the Birmingham speech was intended to break the fragile unity that Mr. Heath was so anxious to preserve. But even Mr. Powell could not have foreseen its full consequences.

On April 23 Quintin Hogg, the shadow Home Secretary, sprang to an emotional defence of Mr. Heath's prompt action declaring that he would have resigned had Mr. Powell been allowed to stay in the shadow cabinet. But, in the 1922 Committee there were moves against Sir Edward Boyle on the ground that he had joined the 'left-wingers' who voted for the Race Relations Bill and was therefore more deserving of expulsion from his shadow ministry than Mr. Powell, who had kept to the letter of party policy. Luckily for the party managers the motion against Sir Edward was proposed by Sir Gerald Nabarro in a distasteful manner which alienated support. In the weeks that followed, several moderate M.P.s (including Sir Edward) came under fire from Powellites within their local party organisations. In June, the obstructionist temper spread to the House of Lords where the Conservative peers insisted, to the chagrin of their leader, Lord Carrington, in voting down the Mandatory Sanctions Order against Rhodesia which was due for renewal. This vote had one far-reaching but unanticipated side-effect: namely that Mr. Wilson abruptly ended private talks with Conservative representatives about the reform of the House of Lords.

With the summer recess, the divisions in the party became less acute. By autumn 1968, the parliament was entering its second half; the difficulties of changing the leader were greater, and the shock of Mr. Powell's Birmingham speech was diminishing. But Mr. Powell was still capable of provoking new tremors that reverberated from time to time throughout the Conservative ranks and indeed the country at large. His main speeches were usually timed to coincide with the periods when motions were being prepared by

'Go away!'

[*Tribune*, April 26, 1968

constituency associations for the party conference or with local elections. Handouts were carefully prepared for the press. Mr. Powell obtained with great ease the public attention Mr. Heath found it so hard to attract. He continued to receive many invitations from local Conservative parties and from other organisations. He had a huge postbag. In the House of Commons, he spoke rarely; among many Conservative activists he was a prophet; to the public, whether they trusted or hated him, he was a celebrity.

At no time was Mr. Heath in direct danger of losing his position. The major risk was of backbiting which would give the public a picture of a party divided and incapable of governing. If Mr. Heath failed to unite the different factions and consequently lost the coming election, the Powellites would then be in a much stronger position to make a frontal attack. Therefore he had not only to maintain his immediate control over the party at all levels, which was easy, but also to keep the dissident groups relatively satisfied. This was less simple.

Mr. Heath responded to the challenge with shrewd forbearance. While he refused to make any policy concessions, he made a series of well-publicised speeches (at the urging of the Chief Whip and the party chairman) in which he emphasised the severe restrictions to which the Conservative party was already committed. He also held several meetings with local party leaders, especially in the Midlands. In public he continued to minimise the breach with Mr. Powell. Conservative Central Office was permitted to process Mr. Powell's engagements in the constituencies and to distribute most of his speeches to the press. In parliament, morale among Conservative M.P.s improved; much of the credit for this lay with the sure intelligence and the tolerance of the Chief Whip, Willie Whitelaw. Although there were still occasional meetings of left- and right-wing groups, the organised factionalism which had been a growing danger during the spring declined. Mr. Powell had very few personal followers — probably less than a dozen — and their influence as an economic pressure group lessened as Powellism became associated in the public mind with race rather than *laissez-faire*. He remained an embarrassment — a very serious embarrassment — but the situation within the party was relatively stable and there was no longer a risk of a major break-up.[1]

While the immigration controversy continued, a small steering Committee prepared the mid-term manifesto *Make Life Better* for presentation in October 1968 to the Party Conference at Blackpool. The drafts were prepared by an Official Group which met sixteen times between November 1967 and July 1968.[2]

These drafts were discussed at six meetings of the Steering

[1] There is an interesting series of articles on the internal strains over race relations by David Wood in *The Times* during July 1968.

[2] The Official Group responsible for *Make Life Better* also prepared the election manifesto. It met eleven times between November 1969 and February 1970. The Steering Committee eight times between October 1969 and May 19, 1970. Its members were Sir Michael Fraser (Chairman), Brendon Sewill, James Douglas, Tony Newton and Barney Hayhoe (all of the Research Department), David Clarke (Principal of Swinton Conservative College), Tim Rathbone until May 1968 and then Geoffrey Tucker (Directors of Publicity) and Michael Wolff (Mr. Heath's private office).

Committee and finally at the full shadow cabinet and the Advisory Committee on Policy. The Steering Committee had a moderate bias, consisting of Mr. Heath, Mr. Maudling, Mr. Macleod, Sir Edward Boyle, Mr. Barber, Lord Carrington, Mr. Whitelaw and Sir Michael Fraser, with Mr. Sewill and Mr. Douglas of the Research Department as joint secretaries. A similar Steering Committee also prepared the election manifesto except that Sir Alec Douglas-Home replaced Sir Edward Boyle. Its first meeting was on October 21, 1969.

*Make Life Better* was satisfactorily received within the party but made little general impact. Its main objective was to satisfy the demands of Conservative activists for a general statement of policy. Senior party officials found that the clamour for a general statement of policy disappeared entirely after its publication and did not stir again before the election. However, it did not succeed in bringing to the notice of the wider public the new Conservative policies. One of the troubles with *Make Life Better* was perhaps that it lacked interest, being neither the statement of basic Conservative principles and distinctive policies that some members of the Official Group recommended, nor a comprehensive review of the ideas which were emerging from the policy groups. In some cases this was because final decisions had not yet been reached, and in others because it appeared unwise to publish them prematurely.

During 1968, as most of the policy groups completed their work and disbanded, the policy exercise entered its final phase. The emphasis turned increasingly to research projects designed to elucidate and define the details of specific aspects.

They were carried out within the Conservative Research Department or by professional consultants. Some of the studies were published, such as Barney Hayhoe's on family poverty, which culminated in the CPC pamphlet *Must the Children Suffer?* Others were prepared for consideration by the shadow cabinet or for particular shadow ministers. These included research papers on abuses of the social services and their disincentive effects, on the practicability of a negative income tax, on international treaty obligations which would need to be renegotiated if the party's agricultural policy was to be introduced and on the military and financial implications of the commitment to maintain forces East of Suez. Subjects investigated by outside units included labour relations in the London docks, and the government of Scotland (prior to the appointment of a constitutional commission under Sir Alec Douglas-Home). Several projects were carried out by two independent units, the Conservative Public Sector Research Unit and the Conservative Systems Research Centre.

While these preparations continued, a fundamental problem remained; the 'tax package' was not yet settled. Indeed, it became more difficult for three reasons: first of all, the benefits of the cuts in public spending which the party had already put forward were partially balanced by its extra commitments, particularly on defence. Conservative spokesmen emphasised that the cost of remaining East of Suez had been very carefully calculated and was much less than the £300 million per annum quoted by the Labour party. Nevertheless, even £100 million a year would vitiate the savings likely to accrue from the proposed restrictions on housing subsidies. Secondly, the proportion of the gross national product consumed by public expenditure was increasing sharply and tax rates were rising in consequence. After the Budgets of 1968 and 1969 it could no longer be claimed that the total tax burden as a proportion of gross national product was no higher in Britain than in most other developed Western countries. The tax reforms successively proposed by the Economic Policy Group were therefore out of date within a few months; reductions in direct taxation to the intended low level required ever more drastic measures; and the cost of abolishing SET was becoming much larger. Thirdly, it was becoming impossible to escape gracefully from the SET pledge by substituting a payroll tax. When this was suggested early in 1969 to the Advisory Committee on Policy and to the National Union Executive, there were very strong protests. The Area Chairmen, who had been loyally visiting the constituency parties spreading word of the heinousness of the SET and emphasising the need for honest government, warned that the party workers would feel cheated if they learned that SET was to be replaced by another tax which differed more in its name than in its effects. Possibly, it was not irrelevant that many of the Area Chairmen and the active members of the National Union Executive were businessmen who stood to lose by a payroll tax and tended to be conscious of the probable reactions of their commercial colleagues.

The abandonment of the payroll tax placed an extra burden on the Value-added Tax, which now became the only major substitute for the proposed cuts in direct taxation. This meant that it would have to be imposed at a higher rate than had previously been envisaged and would consequently lead to a greater rise in the cost of living. As it would be impossible to introduce the VAT immediately, it would be necessary to delay the removal of SET. This would be abolished 'in the course of the parliament'. It also became all the more important to give assurances that the burdens of the VAT would not fall disproportionately on lower-income groups. To this end, a detailed investigation was undertaken of the consumption patterns of twenty-eight families and the likely effects of different tax packages on their standard of living.[1] This was carried out by the Conservative Systems Research Centre, a unit under Miss Mervyn Pike, M.P. for Melton, and organised by Michael Spicer and several trained systems analysts. Mr. Macleod wrote that the study of taxation in opposition was carried out 'in a more detailed way than has ever been done before by an Opposition, or indeed by a Government'.[2] Despite some lack of communication between the Systems Research Centre and the Research Department, this was probably a fair claim, at least as far as oppositions were concerned.[3]

Nevertheless, however sophisticated the formulations for excluding some important categories (such as food) from the VAT and for varying the rates on others so that the burden was fairly apportioned, severe troubles were unavoidable unless the total yield of the proposed tax was lessened. As the election approached, the policy groups and the shadow cabinet therefore intensified their enquiry into further ways of reducing government expenditure. They concentrated as before on identifying the areas of wasteful government spending which could be eliminated relatively painlessly, and in advancing schemes for improving the structure of government and industry.

Some of the most important research and the most far-reaching decisions concerned industrial relations. The proposals were well advanced by 1966 and some of them were included in the election manifesto. In April 1968 — two months before the publication of the Donovan Report — Conservative plans appeared in a detailed

[1] See *Conservative Conference Report*, 1968, p. 64. [2] *Banker*, April 1967.

[3] An eminent authority on tax law, Professor G. S. A. Wheatcroft, worked half-time on Conservative tax-planning over the last eighteen months of the parliament.

pamphlet, *Fair Deal at Work*. Five earlier pledges were re-affirmed: (i) to make collective agreements legally enforceable, (ii) to set up a registrar of trade unions, (iii) to ensure a corporate legal status for registered trade unions, (iv) to establish a new system of industrial courts, and (v) to set up a code of good industrial relations practice. In addition, *Fair Deal at Work* added three new proposals: (i) to redefine trade disputes to exclude sympathetic strikes, inter-union disputes and action to enforce a 'closed shop', (ii) to enforce a 'cooling-off period' and a secret ballot, and (iii) to protect individual workers against the 'closed shop'. In a speech to the Party Conference in October 1969, Robert Carr, the shadow Minister of Employment, put forward eight other proposals as a basis for discussion and consultation.

The policy was based on the assumption that industrial progress was being thwarted by restrictive practices and unofficial strikes and that it was consequently worth while to risk the conflict with the unions that would accompany the introduction of legislation. It was backed by evidence in surveys that the public favoured trade union reforms. The policy group on Industrial Relations included three former Ministers of Labour and met frequently. Conservative officials claimed that its work was as detailed as that of the Royal Commission on Trade Unions which was preparing its report at the same time.

When *Fair Deal at Work* was accepted as Conservative policy, a committee was established to put the proposals in the form of 'instructions to parliamentary draftsmen' so that legislation could be introduced in the first session of a new ministry. Despite these preparations, it was impossible to predict how well the bill would work. It would not tackle the problem of the official strike and the periodical 'wage round'. Senior Conservatives admitted that its effectiveness would depend on the mood which it engendered. It was hoped that the introduction of trade union legislation together with the other Conservative economic measures would destroy the feeling that inflation was an inevitable fact of life and create a mood in which wage claims were no longer made in the expectation that they would be eroded by price rises.

While restrictive practices in industry would, it was hoped be removed by trade union legislation, inefficiency in government required direct surgery. A policy group on the machinery of government presented its report early in the parliament. It proposed a drastic reduction in the number of ministries and the reform of Whitehall to ensure more efficient management on business lines. The work of the policy group was continued by a small committee on the structure of government, which operated directly under Mr. Heath, and by the Conservative Public Sector Research Unit. This was set up in April 1967 under Mr. Marples. The main impetus was provided by David Howell, M.P. for Guildford and formerly director of the Conservative Political Centre, and Mark Schreiber, who was seconded from the Research Department. Both men were close to Mr. Heath and shared his concern to find new ways of eliminating waste in government activities. They were both influenced by American methods in business and public administration, making annual pilgrimages to the United States in search of ideas.

The main work of the Public Sector Research Unit consisted of commissioning research by outside consultants on specific aspects of governmental activity.[1] These included studies on the Rotterdam Europoort, the railways modernisation plan of 1954, the U.K. nuclear power programme, London Airport, the Channel Tunnel, government procurement procedures, government advisory services to industry and agriculture and many others. These studies suggested, as had been hoped, that considerable savings could be made by the introduction of more businesslike management into several sectors of the public service. As David Howell wrote in a pamphlet on *A New Style of Government* (a title which was to become the key phrase in the Conservative election manifesto):

> 'Research and enquiry shows it to be generally the position in central government today that the objectives, goals or targets of activities carried on in the name of the state are too often imprecise or go undefined altogether . . . to take a random example, if the annual budget of a body such as the Forestry Commission were subjected to an analysis in terms of the "output" of that body, an immediate question would arise as to whether it was worth subsidising the Commission annually to the tune of £17 m.'

It was proposed that a Conservative government should examine the 'outputs' of particular government activities, abandoning any which did not justify their cost, and reorganising many of the others into 'projects' under the direct responsibility of managers,

[1] An indication of the scope of these studies is indicated by the fact that they comprised a total of 7 man-years of work; the equivalent of 2–3 full time consultants. This allowed a few weeks for each project, hardly adequate by civil service standards, but very generous for opposition studies.

some of them seconded from industry. The most celebrated example of the 'management by objectives' which the Unit hoped to introduce was the reform of the Pentagon after 1961 by the U.S. Secretary for Defence, Mr. McNamara, a former President of Ford Motors. These ideas appeared in *Make Life Better*, which committed the party to reducing the number of ministries and sorting out their structure, improving methods of public purchasing, organising many of the tasks of government on a 'project' basis by teams under project managers and setting up under the Prime Minister a small central administrative unit to ensure that the latest techniques of business management were introduced throughout the public sector.

The next stage was to gather a group of businessmen prepared to help with planning to introduce the new techniques of project management if a Conservative government came to power. It was considered essential to brief them fully before the election as it was feared that they would be prey to civil service intransigence if they came into their posts unprepared. Two firms of consultants (P.A. and Booz-Allen) were employed to recruit them and to arrange a two-week briefing in August 1969 at Sundridge Park (in Kent). This prolonged meeting was attended by twenty-eight businessmen and eleven Conservative M.P.s marked out by Mr. Heath for positions in his government; members of the shadow cabinet came down in succession and outlined their intended policies. After the Sundridge Park meeting the fourteen businessmen who were still interested and able to participate started detailed work on the projects in which they would be involved. 'Action groups' were formed and were coordinated by a committee consisting of Lord Carrington, Sir Keith Joseph, Robert Carr, Richard Meyjes (the chief businessman in the exercise) and Mark Schreiber. Some of the 'action groups' found it difficult to determine their functions as a number of the shadow ministers had still not worked out their intentions in sufficient detail. Greater emphasis was therefore given to the small central administrative unit envisaged in *Make Life Better* to ensure that the 'thrusting and questioning analytic capability' was not dissipated through the lack of precision in some areas of Conservative policy planning.[1]

[1] See David Watt 'The Tories want more whizz kids in Whitehall', the *Financial Times*, November 4, 1969. See also John McGregor 'Tories bring in scholars, lawyers and businessmen', *Glasgow Herald*, May 12, 1970, and Robert Jones, 'Towards a businesslike government', *The Times*, August 3, 1970.

Alongside these attempts to improve the machinery of government, the search for specific cuts in public spending continued. Proposals were repeatedly made (especially by Maurice Macmillan's policy group on Health) for the introduction of selective welfare benefits. The shadow cabinet refused to accept them on both political and technical grounds. More progress was made on regional and industrial policy. It was decided to discontinue after 1974 the Regional Employment Premium introduced by the Labour government and to replace the investment grants under the Industrial Development Act by the more flexible provisions of the Local Employment Acts.

The depressed regions and the 'grey' areas surrounding them were to be aided by improving their economic infrastructure — their roads, airports and housing and by providing better facilities for industrial re-training.[1] It was argued that this would help them more effectively and at a much lower cost per job than the existing system of capital grants which subsidised companies in the development areas indiscriminately and which provided on average only one extra job for every £20,000 of public money consumed.

In the long run, there were likely to be very considerable savings from these changes, though they would not amount to the 'several hundred million' pounds that was sometimes quoted, as a large proportion of the savings in investment grants and REP would be consumed by the suggested improvements in regional infrastructure. In the short run, the savings would be smaller, as investment grants had been guaranteed for periods of several years. Consequently the full economies would not be realised in the first term of a new Conservative government.

The proposals had a further limitation. As any savings would be made at the expense of companies, it became more difficult to cut the other grants they were receiving under the Labour government. The shadow cabinet therefore refrained from committing itself to winding up the Industrial Reorganisation Corporation. Radical suggestions for pruning public expenditure on the nationalised industries were made late in the parliament by a group organised by Sir John Eden and Nicholas Ridley, who tended to sympathise with Powellite economics. Others came from Sir Keith Joseph, one of the shadow ministers most actively concerned in

[1] Grants were also to be given selectively under the Local Employment Acts to companies in development areas.

policy formulation. From late January 1970, Sir Keith gave a series of speeches in which he outlined his philosophy of 'civilised capitalism' and gave a number of hints about possible public expenditure cuts. But he revealed little precise information about Conservative plans. This was partly for tactical reasons as this extract from an interview with Sir Keith Joseph indicates:

> '*Watt*: You do talk about a rollback of the public sector. Now I'm not clear from this ——
> *Joseph*: You're not meant to be ——
> *Watt*: How far you think this is really feasible?
> *Joseph*: We obviously want to leave our options open.'[1]

But a further reason for the opposition's coyness was that its search for cuts in the public sector still continued. Even after the weekend conference of shadow ministers at Selsdon Park at the end of January 1970,[2] the Research Department was asked to examine schemes for further savings. The exercise was still in progress when Mr. Wilson announced the election.

At the time of the election there was disagreement about the depth of Conservative preparations for office. Some members of policy groups likened their activities to a genial seminar every few weeks, but some made far more ambitious claims; others acknowledged that work had been extremely thorough in certain fields but regretted that the gaps were so many that it had been impossible to coordinate the proposals into a coherent programme. There was similar disagreement about the political direction of the policy exercise. The *Economist*, on the one hand, described the economic plans as 'dramatic' and constituting a 'real change of mood in Whitehall'. On the other hand, there were grumbles by numbers of Conservatives who were 'in the know' that every radical alternative had been rejected.

There can be few doubts about the assertions that the researches were larger than any previously undertaken by a party in opposition, if only because other exercises had been so thin. There is

[1] Colin Jones and David Watt, 'The object is a middle-income society, with more aid for [the] poor', the *Financial Times*, March 17, 1970. Other useful articles on Sir Keith Joseph's speeches are by Maurice Corina, 'Setting Industry Free', *The Times*, March 9, 1970, and Nicholas Faith, 'The 20 steps to civilised capitalism', the *Sunday Times*, March 8, 1970. One of the fullest published accounts of Conservative tax proposals is 'The Tory way with taxes', *Economist*, June 13, 1970.

[2] See pp. 129–131.

more room for uncertainty about official claims that they were sufficiently thorough to justify the important conclusions that were sometimes drawn from them. The opposition was handicapped by lack of the kind of information available to the government and by lack of staff.[1] The establishment of officers at the Conservative Research Department increased from 23 when the Conservative government was still in office in 1964 to 35 by the beginning of 1967. By 1968, when the policy exercise was still at its height, the number had dropped to 27,[2] due to a restriction on recruiting imposed for financial reasons in the autumn of 1967. A management survey showed officers spent only 25% of their time on long-term research, the rest being required for parliamentary briefings and administration. The outside consultants relieved these problems only to a limited degree. In consequence, the Research Department often aided the policy groups, in the words of a junior official, 'mostly as mere minute takers and notice despatchers'. This sometimes meant that the high-powered outside experts often met with nothing concrete to discuss or decide on.

It was no coincidence that two of the groups which worked most thoroughly had the services of a full-time Research Department official, Stephen Abbott (Industrial Relations) and Brian Reading (Economic Policy). Some of the most useful policy papers went directly from the Research Department to Mr. Heath and to the shadow cabinet.[3]

Much also depended on the initiative of the shadow minister in

[1] Senior civil servants commented privately during early 1970 on how little the opposition had sought to consult them. It was even said that no incoming ministry had shown such ignorance or distrust of the civil service for many years.

[2] This figure includes three officers seconded to the Public Sector Research Unit.

[3] Someone closely associated with the policy exercise wrote to us:

> 'Most groups experienced [difficulty in] finding mutually convenient meeting times, and sufficiently long sessions to get down to work thoroughly. . . . A group was most effective when it limited its aims and tackled one really specific point. . . . But some Policy Groups . . . really did throw up terribly perfunctory and useless reports.'

Another wrote of:

> . . . 'the excitement which was, I believe, widely felt by those involved of working in one of the two great periods of fundamental re-thinking of our political and social institutions of the last thirty years.'

A third told us:

> 'I have been saying for years that we have been making too much policy. We have come out with a glorious set of platitudes and have avoided having a detailed set of economic policies.'

charge of the group. Here also there were difficulties as most of them were unable to live on their parliamentary salaries and had to find other employment. The combined demands of attendance at parliament, constituency engagements and private employment left the majority little time or energy for other things. The same considerations hindered effective coordination by the shadow cabinet. It usually met twice a week, on Monday and Wednesday. According to several members, a disproportionate amount of time was consumed by discussions on parliamentary tactics and on the subjects to be chosen for Supply Day debates. It was not a useful forum for decisions about the future Conservative programme. The momentum of the policy exercise therefore depended to a large extent on Mr. Heath himself and a handful of colleagues, notably Mr. Macleod, Sir Keith Joseph and Mr. Carr. The product bore the stamp of Mr. Heath's personal priorities.

One of the reasons Mr. Heath was so anxious to establish the credentials of the policy exercise was to enable him to show that, in lieu of fundamental ideological changes, he could run the government more efficiently than the Labour party. Or, to put it in different terms, efficiency became an ideological aim in itself, Mr. Heath believing that structural changes in government activities would lead to greater economic growth and personal initiative and that it would therefore be possible to introduce a distinctive 'style of government' without any radical interference in the welfare state. It was for this reason that institutional reforms played such an important part in his programme: even at the end of the parliament, when the search for economies in public expenditure was becoming more pressing, the total amount of taxation would remain, according to the plans, relatively unchanged, but the type of taxation would alter; the framework of industrial relations would be changed; the structure of ministries would be sorted out; government aid would continue to flow into the development areas, but, it was hoped, through more efficient channels. In short, structural reforms would make ideological measures unnecessary.[1]

It can be maintained that in concentrating on ways of eliminat-

[1] It was no mean achievement that he managed to persuade his colleagues to adopt in most essentials the policies that he personally wanted. Those close to him claim that he was almost never forced to accept any policy that he did not like for the sake of internal party peace. 'He got his own way in policy and he got his own men where he wanted them,' was one verdict.

ing waste in government and in looking for means of reforming stagnant institutions, Mr. Heath was tackling the most important problems facing the country. From an electoral viewpoint, however, it was difficult for him to acknowledge to his right-wing supporters or to the electorate that his disagreement with Labour was limited to these technical matters. It was much easier to explain that taxation was too high than to argue that it was of the wrong sort. That the substitution of one measure for another would promote growth and would, thereby, ultimately lessen the proportion of personal incomes levied by the government was likely to seem too complex.[1] Shadow cabinet spokesmen therefore tended to use rhetoric far simpler than their proposals and compensated for rejecting the views of *laissez-faire* radicals by using their language. Mr. Heath sometimes talked of a 'great divide', or the choice between a

> 'Labour Government pledged and committed to more and more taxation . . . [and] a Conservative Government which will reduce it . . ., [between] a Labour Government pledged to ever increasing interference in industry . . . [and] a Conservative Government which will give new opportunity to industry . . . [between] Labour equality, or Conservative opportunity. Labour increasing the growing power of the state, or Conservative seeking still larger freedom for the individual.'[2]

Or, in Mr. Macleod's words:

> 'I only mention . . . in headline form, the main points of difference between our two parties so that you can see how different they are. . . . First, we stand and we have always stood for policies of lower personal taxation. They do not. Secondly, we stand for the minimum of government intervention, and they do not. Thirdly we stand for a reduction in the percentage taken of our gross national product by public expenditure, and they do not. We stand for the commercial efficiency of the nationalised industries, and they do not. We stand for increased selectivity in the social services, and they do not. We stand for trade union law reform. . . . It follows then that there are great differences between our economic policy and that of the Socialists.'[3]

Conservative pronouncements thus attacked Labour at two very different levels — with highly detailed proposals (or with hints of them) and with statements of abstract principle: the former too intricate to be fully comprehensible to the electorate, the latter

[1] See the special issue of *Political Quarterly* (January–March, 1971) on Taxation Policy, *passim*.
[2] *Conservative Campaign Guide*, 1970, p. 1.
[3] *Conservative Conference Report*, *1967*, p. 82.

too general to be convincing. The gap in the Conservative alternatives was at the intermediate level of issues. Almost every potential issue was avoided or underplayed. As has already been suggested this was largely because the Labour party adopted so many Conservative policies that it left Mr. Heath little room for manoeuvre if he did not wish to break the consensus by moving to the right. The electorate was denied a direct choice between grammar schools and comprehensive schools, between going in or staying out of the Common Market, between lower taxes and fewer social services on the one hand and higher taxes and benefits on the other, between neutrality and British membership of the Western Alliance, between large-scale immigration and restriction, between retention and abolition of capital punishment and even between British support for Nigeria or for Biafra. In these circumstances, the lack of interest in the new Conservative policies was hardly surprising.

While the Conservative programme suffered from dullness, it avoided the graver disadvantage that would have accompanied a more forthright or extreme set of proposals. For though Mr. Heath would undoubtedly have held public interest more fully by abandoning his moderate stance on several issues and by initiating a national debate, he would probably have forfeited support. If the policies presented in *Make Life Better* and *A Better Tomorrow* did not compel attention or convert the doubtful, they had the negative virtue — none the less important — of not actually repelling them.

In his handling of the Conservative party and the public, Mr. Heath scored the same negative success. Although he failed to inspire confidence or affection among most Conservative activists and M.P.s, he managed to keep them united, despite Mr. Powell's disruptive efforts and the other fissiparous tendencies to which they were subject.

In the words of a senior colleague:

> 'Things didn't go easily in Opposition. Ted was often worsted on the front bench, and this was a serious matter for the leader of a party which is far too inclined to demand that its leaders should always be bringing home the bacon. But Ted stuck to the themes that he cared about. . . . On balance, and despite everything, he deserves pretty high marks.'

One of the most substantial achievements of the Conservative party under Mr. Heath's leadership was the maintenance of its organisation. This possibly tipped the balance in the election. It is to a consideration of developments at Central Office that the story now turns.

## CHAPTER IV

# QUIET REVOLUTION AT CENTRAL OFFICE?

MAJOR Conservative electoral defeats have been followed, with a single exception, by inquests into the state of party organisation. The formation of the Central Office itself was largely a response to the Liberal victory of 1868. In 1880, there was a high-powered committee under W. H. Smith. In 1906 (the exception) divisions between free trade and tariff reform factions were so bitter that it was impossible to maintain, let alone to consider, ways of improving the machine. Major reforms were introduced in 1911 by a committee including Arthur Steel-Maitland. After the 1929 election, Neville Chamberlain established a 'Committee of Investigation' and the celebrated Maxwell-Fyfe Committee sat after the Conservative defeat of 1945. In eschewing the idea of a major commission of investigation after 1964, and again after 1966, it would appear that the Conservative leaders were flying in the face of precedent. In fact, they sponsored changes that were potentially as radical as any that had followed previous inquests. The 'quiet revolution', a phrase often used after 1966, fairly summed up the intentions of the party managers, though it overstated their success in achieving them.

The narrow Labour victory in 1964 had left the Conservatives tired and dispirited, and their organisation in decline (though still far superior to Labour's). Some improvements were discussed and introduced in the months that followed, but the possibility of a snap election excluded long-term changes. These mostly came after the 1966 election, which gave the party both the time and the incentive to introduce them.

The most damaging bequests of the Macmillan and Home years were probably the gulfs which, as the long period of Conservative office went on, had developed between the parliamentary leadership and the backbenchers, between the parliamentary party and the constituency associations, and between the local activists and the electorate. Mr. Heath, as the new party leader, was concerned above all to ease the dangerous 'gap and conflict' between the different branches of the party. It was widely recognised that this meant the party would need to become more representative in its social make-up.

A second major problem was finance. The prolonged publicity campaign preceding the 1964 election had been exceptionally expensive. Post-election business contributions had been smaller than expected, preventing the party from saving its funds for the period of electoral peace, when income usually fell short of expenditure. Although the 1966 campaign was short and relatively cheap, it left reserves of barely £1 million and a growing annual deficit which reached the rate of £400,000 by 1967.

Thirdly, the Conservatives had failed fully to harness modern electioneering techniques and, indeed, had fallen behind Labour before the 1964 campaign in the use of private market research.

From 1965 onwards a series of measures was brought in to deal with these problems. The separate projects and changes are outlined below in order to show their combined role in Central Office strategy and there is then a brief assessment of their effects. A more detailed description of their individual effects is given in Chapter Eight and Chapter Eleven.

Soon after the 1964 defeat, there were significant *internal reforms* at Central Office. In late October 1964, Sir Michael Fraser, the Director of the Conservative Research Department and by far the most influential Conservative official, was appointed to the new post of Deputy Party Chairman.[1] In January 1965, six months before Mr. Heath was elected party leader, Edward du Cann became Party Chairman. Both of these appointments indicated a desire to modernise the organisation. Mr. du Cann was a highly successful businessman who would bring the advantages of his administrative expertise.

Sir Michael's presence was calculated to integrate the work of the Research and Publicity Departments which had lived, according to a senior official, 'in too great isolation from each other'. When the General Director of the Central Office was a career agent there was a tendency to give too little emphasis to policy and sophisticated publicity and advertising methods. Almost immediately after the 1966 campaign, the General Director and the Chief Organisation Officer (the senior professional agents) left, and their posts were abolished. The increased importance of research, political educa-

[1] There had been Deputy Chairmen on three previous occasions. But, unlike Sir Michael, they were not full-time professionals.

tion and publicity was recognised in the overhaul of Central Office, with the organisation sections reconstituted on a par with the others. Henceforth there were four departmental directors of equal status.

*Finance* was a priority of the new regime. Urgent steps were taken to increase Central Office income and to bring its expenditure under strict control. A leading firm of management consultants, P.E. Consulting Groups, spent two months in Central Office in 1966 and made some suggestions for streamlining, and 'provided a useful weapon for the pruners', enabling them to cite independent support for cuts they had urged beforehand. A thorough internal budgeting system was introduced for the first time and departmental heads were required to frame and justify annual estimates.[1] The CPC was instructed that it should in all normal cases refuse to publish pamphlets unless they were likely to break even. There were large reductions in the number of secretaries, and duties previously carried out in the eleven area offices by separate publicity officers, trade union organisers and CPC officers were assigned to a single person with the title of Deputy Area Agent. This generally produced a net reduction of two officials per area. Displaced APOs, TU organisers and CPC officers became deputy area agents, constituency agents or left the organisation. A few were appointed to other posts at Central Office. At the constituency level the employment, at Central Office expense, of paid canvassers ('missioners') was discontinued. These economies saved about £200,000 a year.

The problem of fund raising was aggravated by the Labour government's decision to include a provision in the Companies Act to force disclosure of contributions by firms to political parties. Although it was confidently stated by some Conservative spokesmen that this would lead to increased support, its effects were inevitably uncertain and it was unwise to exclude the possibility of a drop in large business donations. When it was decided to organise a major appeal on the lines of Lord Woolton's successful campaign to raise £1 million before the 1950 election, it was clear that a considerable proportion would have to be raised by the constituency associations.

[1] Mr. du Cann instituted an internal Finance Committee consisting of the Treasurers, the Director of Organisation and himself, with a member of the Treasurers' Department as Secretary.

The imminent disclosure of company contributions, and the increasing reliance on small contributors in the local parties who were naturally curious how their money was being spent, finally persuaded the party managers to agree to the publication of the accounts.[1] This was announced by Mr. du Cann in June 1967, and some figures were given by Lord Carrington when he introduced the National Appeal to the Party Conference in October 1967. Mr. du Cann had previously persuaded the National Union to agree to the publication of 'quota' contributions from individual constituencies in the Conference Handbook as a means of putting moral pressure on dilatory associations. These were included from 1967 onwards.

Plans for the appeal were carefully made, advice being sought from the fund-raising consultants Hooker, Craigmyle. There were differences of opinion about the amount that could be reached. During somewhat diffuse discussions, Mr. du Cann apparently favoured a higher sum and officials in the Treasurers' Department favoured a lower one than the £2 million that was eventually adopted as a target.[2] For eighteen months between the autumn of 1967 and early 1969, Lord Carrington and regional teams of helpers (such as Selwyn Lloyd in the North-western counties) devoted their time to visiting constituencies and lunching with potential contributors — 'eighteen months of eating for the party' as one of them later described it.

The Conservative agency service presented similar (though less acute) problems to Labour's. In 1965 there was a wide-ranging enquiry into all aspects of the agents' profession by a committee under Lord Chelmer. There were salary reviews in 1965 and again in 1969. Recommended starting salaries rose from £700 to £900 in 1965 and to £1,080 in 1969. Maximum salaries rose from £1,250 to £2,000 in 1965 and to £2,400 in 1969.

[1] Publication of the accounts had been intermittently discussed since its recommendation by the Maxwell-Fyfe Committee in 1948 which was never implemented, for reasons, some of which were summarised by Sir Stephen Pierssénè in *Parliamentary Affairs*, Autumn 1948. As our interviews revealed no one of consequence who admitted to having been opposed to disclosure, it is difficult to see why the decision was so delayed. It appears likely, however, that an important influence for the change was Lord Chelmer, one of the party treasurers. Mr. Heath also took a close personal interest in the problems of finance and supported publication, feeling it important that a party which proposed to cut public expenditure should be seen to be keeping its own under firm control.

[2] The £2 million was to relate not to the extra amounts raised by special efforts, but to the total income (including normal contributions) during the Appeal period.

In 1965, Central Office started to commission regular *private polls* and their use was extended after April 1966. From 1966 to 1970 annual expenditure on these polls averaged about £30,000. Besides their value in symbolising the hierarchy's willingness to explore modern methods of electioneering, they had several specific uses, discussed in detail in Chapter VIII.

A campaign directly resulting from a Conservative survey was 'Project '67'. A private poll carried out shortly after March 1966 examined the social background of Conservative party members, revealing that they were mostly self employed (many from the traditional Conservative upper middle class but most from the ranks of the small traders); that women predominated over men and that retired people outnumbered the Young Conservatives. There followed an effort in which Miss Susan Walker, one of the vice-chairmen of the party, was actively involved, to encourage the participation of people from backgrounds which were under-represented on local committees. Associations were first of all given information analysed by Central Office from the 1961 Census about the demographic structure of their constituencies. This was intended to demonstrate to many of them how unrepresentative they were — perhaps to show to the farmers or retired servicemen who formed the Committee of a Conservative Association in a supposedly agricultural constituency that farming was no longer the major source of employment. They were then urged to engage in a survey canvass for new members of backgrounds that had previously been ignored. Time-honoured methods of doorstep canvassing were to be replaced by a more vigorous five-item questionnaire, providing more solid information and greater interest and status for the volunteers administering the survey than an ordinary canvass. 'Project '67' was launched at the 1966 Party Conference and pursued intermittently until the general election.

Alongside 'Project '67', another campaign also aimed at widening the party's social base was presented to the 1966 Conference. It was a full-scale *Young Conservatives* membership campaign, entitled 'Action '67'. By the 1960s the YCs were in decline, no longer providing a gateway into the Conservative party for hundreds of thousands of young people, many from non-Conservative backgrounds, as in their heyday in the late 1940s. As a committee under Mr. Macleod reported in 1965:

'Young people today are marrying and having families earlier and an increasing proportion of them are buying their homes. To those who do so, the home is the natural centre of their lives and there they entertain their friends.'[1]

The campaign was preceded by careful research and preparation and the publicity was drawn up in the light of a survey on the image of the YCs. It lasted until Spring 1967.

In addition, there were continuing efforts to create clubs (sometimes called 'new groups') for couples too old for the YCs and too young for the senior associations. Organisers were employed by some area offices to create these groups.

The attempt at democratisation also embraced the selection of *parliamentary candidates*. In May 1965, Mr. du Cann announced that the Central Office list of parliamentary candidates would be redrawn. In itself this was nothing unusual as the list was amended after every general election. In any case, it contained so many names that inclusion was not a significant step in the search for a seat in parliament and, conversely, exclusion did not always mean the end of an aspirant's chances as local associations sometimes chose candidates who were not on the Smith Square roster. Nevertheless, Mr. du Cann let it be known that the shake-up would be larger than usual as he was determined to attract 'a younger, more broadly based and more widely representative list of candidates'. In the words of the *Yorkshire Post* 'Once and for all, party leaders are determined to lay the old school tie and family background look'.[2] Local associations were encouraged to delay selections until the new list was completed; letters were written to defeated M.P.s asking them to reconsider their position, bearing in mind their age; others on the list were invited to re-apply and come again for interview.[3] Advice on vetting methods was obtained from Management Selection Limited.

The 'Contact' programme of the Conservative Political Centre (known as the 'three way movement of ideas') also comprised a 'conscious effort by party leaders to wean constituency associations away from the old routine and to encourage more genuine political activity'. As David Howell, who had until four months

[1] *The Macleod Report*, 1965, p. 6.
[2] Gordon Leak, 'Tories seek new reality — candidates' list to be slashed to less than 400', *Yorkshire Post*, May 9, 1966.
[3] See Chapter XII for a fuller discussion of candidate selection.

earlier been Director of the CPC, claimed in the *Spectator* in January 1967:

> 'More energy is beginning to be spent on contact with the world outside the association membership, less on tea and jumble sales.
>
> Formally this switch of emphasis was signalled by the decision in March 1965 to change the status of the political education wing of the party.'[1]

The Contact Programme involved a set of topics sent monthly to constituency discussion groups which returned reports to Central Office, when the results were collated and passed to the party leaders.

In the early 1960s the problems of social narrowness and lack of efficiency were most evident in some of the Conservative organisations in the large cities and in Scotland. As the *city associations* were able to tap large contributions from local businessmen, they had little incentive to recruit members, form ward branches and run fund-raising events. As a result they tended to become over-centralised and not very efficient as electioneering organisations. After the particularly heavy Conservative losses in the cities in the 1964 and 1966 elections, a committee was set up in 1966 under Lord Brooke of Cumnor to consider possible improvements.

The *Scottish Conservative party* had always maintained its administrative independence, with its own Central Office and a separate party conference. Besides being inconvenient, this arrangement had political disadvantages which were emphasised by the poor Scottish results in the 1964 election. This led to an internal reorganisation in 1965 of the regional structure north of the Border. This did little to solve the basic difficulties. After 1966, when four more Scottish seats were lost, serious consideration was given in London to the possibility of integrating the Edinburgh office into the London Central Office machine. As a senior Central Office official complained, constituency organisation in Scotland was 'all terribly feudal'. Agents were 'treated [by the voluntary workers] as though they shouldn't even come through the kitchen door' and the Scottish Central Office was 'very independently minded'. Indeed there was much evidence that constituency associations were more poorly run than their English

[1] David Howell, 'The Change at the Grass Roots', *Spectator*, January 6, 1967. See also his articles 'What's Wrong with Central Office?' and 'The Most Urgent Reform of all', *Spectator*, January 13 and 20, 1967.

counterparts and that in many places this was a consequence of their limited social composition. They employed fewer agents, recruited members less keenly and raised less money. Numbers of diplomatic efforts by officials and by the party leader himself were made from 1966 onwards to improve the situation.

Realising that elections are won and lost in the marginal constituencies, and fully aware of the limited financial resources at their disposal, the party managers took a major decision soon after March 1966, to concentrate their efforts on the seats that needed to be won if there was to be a working parliamentary majority of about 50 seats. To emphasise their importance, the 70 or so constituencies concerned were named '*critical seats*'.[1] Previous experience showed that financial grants from Central Office failed to stimulate local activity as they dulled initiative and were a disincentive to local fund-raising efforts. The aid given to critical seats was therefore in the form of centrally paid press and post advertising, direct mailing, survey research and the provision of front bench speakers for constituency functions — additions, not substitutes, for normal association activities.

Individually, all these varied measures concerned the technical details of organisation. In total, they formed a more ambitious, unified programme than was generally realised. They reflected the determination within Central Office to make the machine more efficient and modern, and the realisation that this meant that it had also to become more representative. The fact that the overall programme failed to achieve its full objectives ought not to obscure the considerable advances that were made in a few directions, for the machine was maintained and, in a few respects improved, at a time when Labour's was in decay.

Some of the schemes resulted in almost total failure. Within a few months of 'Action '67' YC membership declined to its previous level. 'Project '67' was not much more successful, as few constituencies persevered with 'survey canvassing' and there was no marked change in the social composition of constituency officers; as it was later remarked at Central Office: 'In the constituencies in which the leaders were already representative, the campaign was unnecessary; where they were unrepresentative,

[1] The exact number varied as some constituencies were removed from the list after they were captured at by-elections. Details are given on p. 288.

they dug their heels in.' The CPC 'three-way movement of ideas' regularly attracted responses from 300–400 study groups a month (consisting of about 10 members each), but stubbornly failed to expand beyond this number and made little impact on party or public thinking. The attempts to modernise organisation in the cities and in Scotland met with firm local resistance. They were therefore abandoned as the party leaders considered that any gains in efficiency that would result from organisational reforms would be vitiated by the friction generated by their heavy-handed imposition. In particular, the emergence of Scottish nationalism provided an extra argument against reducing the independence of the Edinburgh Central Office.

The effects of the reformulation of the candidates' list were hardly greater. Some of the older, less qualified aspirants whom it was sought to exclude were among the most active constituency figures. The ending of their parliamentary hopes risked turning them into troublemakers. These diplomatic considerations prevented a drastic reshuffle, though the new list was probably marginally more representative and better qualified than its predecessor.

The National Appeal, the improvements in the agency service and the critical seats exercise were more productive, though even here, the success was not complete. The National Appeal, which lasted from autumn 1967 until Spring 1969 raised £2¼ million, over £¾ million of it from local associations. But as £800,000 or so would have been raised during the same period had there been no Appeal, the net gain was about £1½ million. And as many companies and individuals made extra large donations, there was likely to be a drop in income in the succeeding years. On the brighter side, the contacts gained during the appeal won new contributors and imposed higher standards on the local parties. This increased the income that could be expected in an ordinary (non-election) year from £600,000 to £850,000 or more. But this was still well short of expenditure, which topped £1 million a year, even after the economies.

In October 1967, Conservative funds amounted to about £700,000. During the next eighteen months, expenditure totalled about £1½ million as against income from the Appeal of £2¾ million, leaving about £1½ million in Spring 1969. This had to cover the running deficit, and the expenses of a possibly lengthy campaign; it was also considered necessary to leave enough in reserve to provide for a lean post-election period. While the success of the Appeal eased the immediate economic difficulties, it did not provide for campaign expenditure on the larger scale of 1963–64.

An important side effect of the National Appeal was to accustom constituency associations to raising larger sums. This usually involved an extension of social fund-raising functions. These, in their turn, were useful ways of drawing extra helpers into the local party orbit. The increased fund-raising capacities of the local associations also made them more willing to pay increased salaries to their agents. Edward du Cann, speaking to the National Society of Conservative Agents before the Party Conference in October 1966, claimed that he knew of thirty agents who were being paid over £2,000 a year and many others who were receiving nearly that amount. From 1967 to 1969, salaries in most constituencies more than kept pace with the increased cost of living. Nevertheless, it remained difficult to attract suitable new recruits, and it was a considerable achievement that the overall number of agents in 1970 was on a level with 1966. Had agents' pay and conditions not improved, there would undoubtedly have been a considerable drop.

Inside Central Office itself, the appointment of Sir Michael Fraser as 'chief of staff' greatly aided forward planning and co-ordination between the different departments, thereby avoiding tangles and last minute rushes, such as those which continued to bother Transport House.[1]

[1] The general oversight of affairs was essentially carried out in two committees that met weekly:

(*a*) The Policy Initiatives and Methods Committee met weekly on Tuesday at 10.30 a.m. In May 1970 its membership was Sir Michael Fraser (Chairman), Mrs. Maurice Macmillan and Richard Sharples (Party Vice-Chairmen), Richard Webster (Organisation), Brendon Sewill (Research), Geoffrey Tucker, Gerald O'Brien and Edward Rayner (Publicity), Russell Lewis (CPC), Tommy Thompson (ORC), Douglas Hurd and Michael Wolff (Mr. Heath's office, though officially Michael Wolff was a member of the Research Department), John Cope (Mr. Barber's office).

(*b*) The Party Chairman's Wednesday Meeting had as its members in May 1970: Anthony Barber (Chairman), Sir Michael Fraser (Deputy Chairman), William Whitelaw (Chief Whip), Earl St. Aldwyn (Chief Whip, House of Lords), Sir Arthur Vere Harvey (1922 Committee), Mrs. Maurice Macmillan, Richard Sharples and Geoffrey Johnson-Smith (Party Vice-Chairmen), Anthony Kershaw, James Prior (Mr. Heath's PPS), Douglas Hurd and Michael Wolff (Mr. Heath's office), George Younger (Scottish Party), Richard Webster (Organization), Geoffrey Tucker, Gerald O'Brien, Edward Rayner (Publicity), Russell Lewis (CPC), Tommy Thompson (ORC), John Cope (Mr. Barber's office), David Dear (Secretary).

By the time Mr. du Cann left the Party Chairmanship in September 1967, basic preparations for the campaign, which was expected to be held in October 1970, had already been made. Despite his public declarations that he was leaving because of the pressure of his business responsibilities, he almost certainly wished to remain at Central Office to carry his plans into operation. But his relationship with Mr. Heath had seriously deteriorated.

The months between April 1966 and September 1967 saw several minor irritations at Central Office. Although, for example, there was general agreement in the hierarchy that the positions of 'General Director' and 'Chief Organisation Officer' needed to be abolished, some thought that the retirements of Sir William Urton and Rex Bagnall in May 1966 were badly timed and brusquely managed. It was rumoured that there were disagreements over senior staff appointments. Furthermore, the allocation of responsibility between Mr. Webster, the Director of Organisation, and Miss Walker, who survived the old regime and remained until 1968 as Vice-Chairman (and officially Mr. Webster's superior), was unclear. The most serious internal difficulty concerned the Publicity Department. It had proved impossible for several years to obtain a specialist in public relations or advertising on a permanent basis and there had been a rapid turnover of Directors of Publicity. During the 1966 election, Mr. Gerald O'Brien, the main permanent official in the Publicity Department, had temporarily filled the post, but soon afterwards the party again looked for an outside director.

This naturally caused some friction and the directorship was aptly described by a former head of publicity, George Hutchinson, as a 'rather delicate — and latterly troublesome — appointment'.[1] In November 1966, Mr. J. R. Rathbone was recruited from the New York public relations firm, Ogilvy & Mather, to head the Publicity Department. The arrangement did not work out very well. In April 1968, Mr. Geoffrey Tucker, who in the 1950s worked with Colman, Prentis and Varley (the company which acted from 1957 to 1968 as advertising agents for the Conservative party) became Director of Publicity with Mr. O'Brien as Deputy Director and the line of command was cleared.

Mr. du Cann's manner also annoyed some people. In May 1966, the *Sunday Telegraph* reported that his pessimistic account of the

[1] *Spectator*, April 19, 1968.

state of party finances at a meeting of the 1922 Committee had offended a number of M.P.s as it implied criticism of the former Treasurers, Mr. Robert Allan and Mr. Richard Stanley.[1] The redrawing of the candidates' list led to further resentments. James Margach referred to the letters sent to those on the old list in an article entitled 'Velvet touch was absent':

> 'To invite more than 300 men and women to . . . sacrifice their personal ambitions, often after a lifetime of dedicated service to the party, requires above all the velvet touch. This approach has been conspicuously lacking . . .
>
> Of course an excellent case can be established for cutting out the dead wood, but surely a more diplomatic, warm and understanding approach, even sympathetic interviews — and time is not in short supply — might have been tried, instead of the cold, impersonal, cyclostyled epistles of doom.'[2]

At its worst, the charge against Mr. du Cann was that he concentrated on the bureaucratic aspects of organisation at the expense of the human. Mr. Heath was disturbed by reports that the area chairmen — the representatives of the constituency chairmen — felt they were being denied access to him. These fears were probably exaggerated. The affection for Mr. du Cann among the constituency leaders was demonstrated by the statements of the Chairman of the National Union, Sir Dan Mason, and the Chairman of the Executive Committee, Sir Clyde Hewlett, who sprang warmly to his defence on the eve of the 1966 Party Conference when it was rumoured that his resignation was about to be announced. When Mr. du Cann finally went, the tributes from the National Union and from the National Society of Conservative Agents went far beyond the requirements of good form.

Nevertheless, there were some who suspected that Mr. du Cann was using the Party Chairmanship as a private weapon on his own behalf. Mr. Heath was apparently aware of his support for Mr. Maudling during the leadership contest in 1965 and had heard reports of his reaction to the result, when he allegedly exclaimed 'this will be awkward for me'. To some, though not all, of the senior party managers he was equally suspect on the ground that his tendency to be 'all things to all men' made him a bad administrator and an unreliable colleague. In particular it was sometimes felt that he did not delegate enough. In his defence, it

[1] *Sunday Telegraph*, May 22, 1966.
[2] *Sunday Times*, May 15, 1966.

can be justly claimed that most of the major developments at Central Office were initiated under his Chairmanship.

Mr. Heath seems to have intended to appoint a new Party Chairman in October 1966 but was effectively prevented from doing so by an embarrassing report in the *Daily Mail* that he was about to dismiss Mr. du Cann. This report had to be speedily denied. It was widely rumoured among Mr. Heath's advisers that the story had been planted and it was said that the same tactic was used the following year. This time, public awkwardness or no, Mr. Heath was determined to instal a Chairman more congenial to himself.

Mr. Barber enjoyed Mr. Heath's full confidence and his style of chairmanship contrasted with Mr. du Cann's. He gave less attention to the reforms which had been initiated, concentrating on improving cohesion between the shadow cabinet, the Central Office, the parliamentary party and the constituencies. No further efforts were made, for example, to implement the recommendations of the Brooke Report on city associations; there were apparently doubts about publishing the accounts (though it was eventually decided to do so because of Mr. du Cann's preliminary announcement in June 1967 and the imminence of the Party Conference). 'Project '67' petered out. Mr. Barber devoted himself to 'talking party in the constituencies, party in parliament and party in the shadow cabinet'. He took great trouble to tour local associations, particularly in critical constituencies, to explain the policies proposed by the shadow cabinet and to listen patiently to criticisms. On each visit to a critical seat, he had a lengthy private meeting with the chairman, candidate and agent. Fully sensitive to the criticism that Mr. du Cann had mishandled the area chairmen, he paid careful attention to their views and assiduously passed their constituency reports to Mr. Heath, even when they were critical of him. It is indicative of the importance he attached to their role that when he returned to Central Office with Mr. Heath on the day after the election he corrected a BBC commentator who announced that they were returning to thank the headquarters staff, insistently adding that they were also coming to thank the area chairmen.

In the shadow cabinet, he spoke as the representative of the constituency parties warning his colleagues against potentially divisive policies and urging them to choose subjects of general concern to the party for Supply Day Motions.

Having sorted out the internal tangles at Central Office and defined the responsibilities to the departmental directors, Mr. Barber was content to hive off most of the administrative decisions and the committee work at Central Office to Sir Michael Fraser, leaving himself to carry out the functions which needed to be performed by the public figurehead of the party. The pay-off for his efforts came during 'the difficult situation with Enoch', when the area chairmen, despite the Powellite sympathies which some of them shared, remained understanding and loyal, and spoke to the constituency parties in Mr. Heath's defence. It was considered of immense importance by Mr. Heath and Mr. Barber that the National Union side of the party did not 'kick over the traces' during the troubles and a source of great satisfaction that the consultative machinery worked so smoothly.

By Spring 1969 it was possible to make detailed plans for the run-up and for the campaign. In this task, the party managers faced two major problems — timing and finance. Although the huge Labour deficit in the opinion polls made an early election very unlikely, the volatility of the polls suggested that the situation could change in a matter of weeks and Mr. Wilson might later be tempted to dissolve parliament at short notice. Over the summer of 1968, Labour had cut into the Conservatives' lead by 20% in five months, and the same could easily happen again. This made it desirable to start the pre-election advertising campaign without delay. For, even if there was not to be an early contest, it had been shown that political advertising was most effective if continued over a long period.

The financial situation, however, excluded a prolonged publicity drive on the lines of 1957–59 and 1963–64. The party managers were determined to insure against the dangerous position in which the finances had been placed by the elections of 1964 and 1966. This excluded the possibility of spending money on a large scale, for this would risk leaving the party without sufficient reserves if there was a long campaign, followed at a short interval by a second election. One method of covering the possibilities of both early and late campaigns was to plan advertising in short bursts. In practice, elections can be held only at certain times of the year — winter weather, spring elections and summer holidays have to be avoided. It was therefore possible to restrict national advertising to the other months. Central Office was unwilling to do this as it was considered that continuous publicity was more efficient even if it had to be on a smaller scale. Room for manoeuvre was somewhat increased by the decision which had been taken after the 1966 election to concentrate advertising on the 'target voters' (C2s under 35, particularly women) in the critical seats. Although this resulted in the greater use of advertising in local papers, it was not possible to eliminate the far more costly national advertising altogether as some of the critical seats were badly served by local journals. But the shift of emphasis did permit sufficient economies to allow a longer run-up campaign than would otherwise have been possible.

It was decided to launch in the summer of 1969 (the date was later put back to September) a publicity drive consisting of: (*a*) advertisements in the national newspapers with the highest proportion of target voters among their readership (these were the *Sunday Mirror*, the *People* and the *News of the World*); (*b*) weekly advertisements in local newspapers serving 'critical seats'; (for constituencies in cities or suburbs, this often meant using regional papers, while the most efficient way of reaching the London 'criticals', for example, was to place advertisements in the *Evening News* and the *Evening Standard*). There was to be a weekly column in each of the papers used, in the form of a leading article, which was to continue until the general election;[1] (*c*) poster sites were to be hired in the 'criticals' as they became available and were to be retained until the election.

Even if the election was delayed until the last possible moment — May 1971 — the publicity drive would not cost more than £½ million, compared with the £1 million or so spent in 1963–64. The money would, however, be used far more selectively and scientifically. The placing of advertisements, for example, was largely based on the revealing information about newspaper readership derived from surveys carried out in each critical seat.

Technical expertise was also brought to bear on the party political broadcasts. As radio and television time was assigned to the major parties free of charge, there had been a tendency to underestimate its crucial importance and to provide sparing pro-

[1] In view of legal ambiguities, left unsettled by the Tronoh-Malayan decision of 1952 (see *The British General Election of 1951*, pp. 32–4), advertising was discontinued during the Spring 1970 local elections.

duction budgets. Realising that their broadcasting time was worth hundreds of thousands of pounds, Central Office decided to carry out market research to find out which type of broadcasts had the greatest impact and then to employ the best producers available to make them. As the research suggested that the public tended to suspect and be bored by straight-to-camera talk from politicians, a snappy, 'newsreel' style, which had been used to good effect in short political advertisements in the United States, was introduced. Production was carried out by James Garrett (of James Garrett and Partners) and the broadcasts were supervised by a Central Office committee which held a preliminary meeting in July 1968 and met regularly from July 1969 onwards.[1]

If the activity at Central Office from 1966 to 1970 is to be summed up in a phrase, it must be the same as for Mr. Heath's handling of the party as a whole: it was a negative success. There was no resurgence of widespread constituency support for party activities as in the heyday of Conservative organisation in the late 1940s. Despite the marginal advances made towards the goal of greater representativeness, the party remained basically unaltered and the various campaigns and measures organised in the early parts of the parliament did not achieve a quiet revolution. This was probably not the fault of the party managers, but reflected the comparative lack of interest in party politics among the electorate at large. No Conservative battle-cry in the late 1960s brought the immediate emotional impact of 'Set the people free' amid the austerity of the late 1940s. Nor did the local parties continue to play the important social role as in the post-war years for the middle and lower middle class reintegrating themselves in civilian society.

Nevertheless, while large resources — in terms of members, agents or finances — were not built up, steps were successfully taken to prevent them from running down and they were used with greater efficiency. The best example of this negative success is probably the Carrington Appeal. This managed to remedy a

[1] The members of the Television Broadcasting Committee, which also handled sound broadcasts, were: Mr. Barber (Chairman), Mr. Whitelaw (Chief Whip and responsible for the political coordination of broadcasting during the campaign), Sir Michael Fraser (Deputy Chairman), Mr. Garrett, Mr. Tucker (Director of Publicity), Mr. Sewill (Director of the Research Department), Mr. Johnson-Smith (Vice-Chairman), Mr. John Lindsey (Head of the Broadcasting Section of the Publicity Department).

See H. B. Boyne, 'How much politics on TV?', *Daily Telegraph*, December 5, 1968.

potentially dangerous situation but did not raise sufficient funds to permit spending on previous scales. It was in these circumstances that staff work at Central Office made its contribution, ensuring that the budget was managed to best advantage. A further success was the effective way in which the channels of intra-party communications were used. This prevented the outbreak of damaging disputes.

As the election approached, Mr. Heath realised that Central Office had still not managed to bring constituency organisation to the level of efficiency that could optimistically have been expected, but he could count on clear organisational advantages over his opponent; in Central Office and the National Union, the unity of purpose which had been maintained throughout contrasted sharply with the situation in the Labour movement, over much of the period, and the net improvements in the Conservative organisation meant that the difference between Conservative and Labour machines was even larger than before. When Mr. Wilson decided at short notice in May 1970 to go to the country it was Transport House rather than Central Office that was taken off guard.

The Prime Minister and members of his Cabinet: *l. to r.* Richard Crossman, Roy Mason, Fred Peart, Denis Healey, Roy Jenkins, Barbara Castle, Lord Gardiner, Anthony Wedgwood Benn (*Labour Party advertisement in national newspapers, autumn 1969*)

Mr. Brown 'unresigns', July 20, 1966

Mr. Wilson, General de Gaulle and Mr. Bro
at the Élysée, January 22, 1967

Mr. Wilson and Mr. Smith on HMS *Fearless*,
October 9, 1968

Mr. Wilson explains devaluation,
November 19, 1967

Mr. Feather, Mr. Wilson and Mrs. Castle,
June 18, 1969

Mr. Whitelaw, Mr. Heath and Mr. Maudling
at Selsdon Park, January 31, 1970

# BEHIND THE SCENES

## *Labour*

Williams, General
retary 1961–68

Sara Barker, National Agent 1961–68

Harry Nicholas, General Secretary 1968–

Gwyn Morgan, Assist. General Secretary 1969–

Ron Hayward, National Agent 1969–

Gerald Kaufmann, Mr. Wilson's Press Adviser 1965–70

y Clarke, Press
fficer 1960–

Terry Pitt, Research Secretary 1965–

## *Conservative*

Edward du Cann, Party Chairman 1965–67

Sir Michael Fraser, Deputy Chairman 1964–

Richard Webster, Director of Organisation 1966–

Humphrey Taylor, Opinion Research Centre Ltd. 1965–

Douglas Hurd, Private Secretary to Mr. Heath 1968–

Geoffrey Tucker, Director of Publicity 1968–70

Brendon Sewill, Director of Research 1965–70

# CAMPAIGN POSTERS

Clip from Conservative party political broadcast

CHAPTER V

# A VACUUM UNFILLED: THE OTHER PARTIES

THE political situation after 1966 offered a fertile climate for minor parties and fringe groups to flourish in. The government was in trouble; the party of change, the party of the left, the party of the working class was not delivering to its traditional supporters or to its new recruits what they expected — neither revolutionary measures nor rapid increases in material prosperity. At its nadir in 1968 polls found that Labour support had slumped from the 47% of 1966 to a mere 26% of the electorate. Where were these disillusioned voters to go? The Conservatives were led by a man who had a low rating in the polls and their policies were little known or understood: it is clear that the great bulk of Conservative gains in this period were due to repulsion from Labour rather than to their own attractions. Why did no one else step in to gather this harvest of discontent? While the failure of the Liberals to make any headway is plainly the central problem, the failure of more extreme or eccentric groups also demands explanation.

Only in Scotland and Wales did voters turn to fresh solutions. In Appendix V James Kellas has explored the rise of the Scottish National party; a similar if less spectacular story could be told of Plaid Cymru.[1] Scotland and Wales were traditional Labour strongholds and they contain substantial areas that had not shared equally in the growth of affluence. The failure of a Labour government

[1] Plaid Cymru, which had 300 branches and a nominal membership that reached 42,000, fielded candidates in each of the thirty-six Welsh constituencies. It had a strong backing among teachers and professionals and traditional religious groups. For the first time it effectively extended its appeal beyond the Welsh-speaking quarter of the population. But in a law-abiding community it suffered from the violent activities of the militant Welsh Language Society and from the still more violent activities of a few extremists who used explosives. The ambivalent or hostile attitude of Plaid Cymru towards Prince Charles during his successful studies in Aberystwyth and his Investiture at Caernarvon in the summer of 1969 also damaged the party's standing. Moreover, the geographic, linguistic and other divisions of Wales made it even harder than in Scotland for a single nationalist party to move towards majority support. Even after its president Gwynfor Evans had won the Carmarthen by-election in July 1966, Plaid Cymru made little headway in local government elections. See Alan Butt Philip, *New Society*, January 9, 1969; see also E. Hudson Davies 'Welsh Nationalism', *Political Quarterly*, July/September 1968, and W. P. Grant and R. J. C. Preece, 'Welsh and Scottish Nationalism', *Parliamentary Affairs*, Summer 1968.

with a comfortable majority to remedy their distress provided perfect ammunition for parties which had so long argued that London could never understand or satisfy their national needs. Before 1966 scarcely any nationalists had even saved their deposits in by-elections.

*Nationalist support in by-elections, 1966–70*

| *Scotland* | | | *Wales* | | |
|---|---|---|---|---|---|
| Mar. 9, 67 | Glasgow Pollok | 28% | July 14, 66 | Carmarthen | 39% |
| Nov. 2, 67 | Hamilton | 46% | Mar. 9, 67 | Rhondda West | 40% |
| Oct. 30, 69 | Glasgow Gorbals | 25% | July 18, 68 | Caerphilly | 40% |
| Mar. 19, 70 | Ayrshire South | 20% | | | |

The nationalist vote showed how ready people had suddenly become to jump at a plausible alternative. But nothing comparable happened in England. Efforts were made but none found a response. The Communist party continued to put up candidates at occasional local and by-elections but there was no growth in its vote. Although its industrial strength had probably increased, its political appeal remained obstinately negligible. The failure of those other traditional spokesmen of the left, the Independent Labour party and the Socialist Party of Great Britain, was still more complete. The New Left largely ignored the challenge of democratic vote-getting. Suggestions of Maoist or simply anti-political candidatures were scarcely heard.

At the other extreme, racialist or other dissident right-wing groups also made a negligible impact. In one or two local government contests National Front and British National party candidates won up to 10% of the vote but nowhere was their activity on a scale to give serious concern to the major parties. In the end ten National Front candidates stood but showed little evidence of being able to mount a fully organised constituency campaign.

The one publicised attempt to launch an alternative party nearer the centre was not taken seriously either. Mr. Desmond Donnelly, Labour M.P. for Pembroke since 1950, resigned the party Whip in June 1968 and was expelled from the party in March.[1] In April

[1] Party activity is seldom a matter for litigation in Britain. But Mr Donnelly's battle over who controlled the assets of the Pembroke Labour party (finally decided against him in the High Court on October 18, 1968) is a classic exception.

1969 he launched his National Democratic party, with a relatively right-wing programme of national regeneration. But his promised 40 candidates dwindled to 5. At its first test in the Louth by-election, Sir George Fitzgerald won only 4% of the vote and when the election came it was only Mr. Donnelly's highly independent efforts to retain his seat in Pembroke that attracted any attention.

Indeed the greatest electoral success of a minor party candidate in England was the meagre triumph of Mr. Creasey, the crime novelist, whose demands for an all party coalition won him 13% of the vote in Oldham West in 1968 — only the fourth independent to save his deposit in an English by-election since the war.

But if the voters were unwilling in their disillusion to move to extremes or new groups, it remains strange that they did not turn, as they had done in the early 1960s, to the Liberals, inheritors of a proud and moderate tradition, and still regarded with general goodwill. The Liberal party started the 1966 parliament with 12 M.P.s, more than at any time since the war. Almost two and a half million people had voted for them and polls showed that up to 52% of electors were still ready to say that they would consider voting Liberal if they thought the party had a chance.

But the Liberals were in a dilemma. Jo Grimond had some years previously said that the party must get on or get out. The revival which he needed reached its peak at the Orpington by-election in March 1962, with Mr. Lubbock's victory in one of the safest of Conservative seats. Although that heady peak had not been maintained, in 1964 the party had, for the first time since 1929, increased its representation and won over three million votes. But the 1964 parliament had proved a disappointment. Despite his majority of only three, Mr. Wilson had not sought to come to terms with the Liberals. Moreover, the party's general stance as a radical, non-socialist alternative to the Conservatives was undercut by Mr. Wilson's play for the middle ground of moderation. The Liberal strategy that was based on the assumption that Labour could never achieve success on its own came finally to grief with the 1966 election.

The party had to start again and Mr. Grimond decided that it should be under someone else. Although immeasurably the best-known figure in the party and unchallenged by his followers, he resigned the leadership on January 17, 1967. In the election that followed the 12 Liberal M.P.s gave six votes to Mr. Thorpe three to Mr. Hooson and three to Mr. Lubbock. Mr. Thorpe, like his predecessor a fluent, idiosyncratic Etonian on the left of the parliamentary party, differed from Mr. Grimond in being more interested in the routines of politics and less in the world of ideas. He had wit rather than weight. Before long his alleged capriciousness led to murmurings within the party and in May 1968 there was a major revolt against his leadership which was clumsily launched and skilfully contained. But his was no easy task. Even the parliamentary party was divided between a traditional, if anti-Tory right, a pragmatic centre and a more doctrinaire left. In the country the established loyalists had less and less sympathy with the increasingly radical (some would even say Maoist) activities of the Young Liberals, which earned more headlines than anything else done under the name of the party.[1] The lack of intellectual leadership or direction weakened the party's efforts to offer a coherent appeal to the public or to set its house in order organisationally.

In the hopeful days of the early 1960s the party machine had expanded far more than the party's means. Expensive premises were taken in Smith Square and headquarters staff expanded and, with wealthy Liberals acting as guarantors, a huge bank overdraft was deliberately allowed to accumulate: after 1966, it never fell below £50,000 and, after touching £93,000 in the autumn of 1969, was still £70,000 on the eve of the election. One fund-raising expedient after another was tried and failed. An appeal for £1 million launched in 1967 raised only a few thousand. Ever more drastic economies had to be made. In 1968 the headquarters were moved to much cheaper but less convenient premises off the Strand — the rent bill fell from £19,000 to £9,000. In 1969 the party's very able director, Pratap Chitnis, resigned in protest against the high command's reluctance to wield the financial axe more ruthlessly. Even so the headquarters staff had been almost halved since the 1966 election and the decline in quality was more than proportionate.

After the departure of Mr. Chitnis, the Liberals turned for a campaign manager to Mrs. Doreen Gorsky, a senior television executive who had stood for the party in the 1950s. Under the

[1] The Young Liberals most definite achievement lay in their leading role in the 'Stop the Seventy Tour' Campaign against the Springbok visit. (See pp. 139–141.)

perennial Lord Byers, she took over, unpaid, the management of affairs until the election. She looked to the nuts and bolts of the organisation but she was handicapped by the desperate financial position from which the party was only rescued on the very eve of the election when Mr. Thorpe suddenly announced that they were out of the red — the bank overdraft had been paid off and there was enough to give small grants to seats where it would make a difference to their entering the contest or not. But for this windfall, the number of candidates would probably have been around 300, or even less, rather than the 332 finally nominated.[1]

The size of their battlefront had been a perennial problem for the Liberals. Some wished to contest every seat — in 1968 the Party Council endorsed the target of 500 candidates — and some wished to focus all their resources on a relatively few winnable seats. Neither strategy was realistic. Against the comprehensive assault lay the brutal fact that in a voluntary party it was not possible to force local associations to fight and in many seats there was not even any semblance of a local organisation: a great deal of money from the centre would be needed if anything was to be done in such seats. The autonomy of local parties stood equally in the way of the narrow front; many would insist on fighting anyway and most were too distant geographically to be able to send workers to help in winnable seats.[2] Moreover, the Liberals needed to fight a substantial number of seats if they were to hang on to their biggest asset — an established claim to a substantial amount of television time during the election campaign. Their ration, agreed in 1963, was always liable to challenge if the evidence of party decline became too apparent.

In fact there were plenty of signs of retrenchment, not only at

[1] The source of these funds is not clear. The Liberals reveal less of their accounts than the Conservative or Labour parties. Some of the money came in after a party political broadcast had been used for a financial appeal and some from a number of rich individuals. But it was widely rumoured that the bulk had come from a single donor. *The Times*, August 31, 1970, suggested that it was Mr. Hayward, a Barbados millionaire who in 1968 had, after Mr. Thorpe's intervention, bought Lundy Island.

A revealing article by the Party Treasurer, Sir Frank Medlicott, in the *Liberal News*, July 9, 1970, named a number of major donors, among them Lord Beaumont, who had turned a loan of £10,000 into a gift. He referred to five donations of exceptional size being received shortly before the election and he pointed out that 85% of the money subscribed in the last eight months had been given by less than 25 people.

[2] The party did in fact designate 26 seats (later raised to 35) as special seats or as winnable seats and put extra money and effort into them.

the centre, but also in the constituencies. The number of constituencies with full-time agents fell from 20 in May 1966 to 17 in April 1969. Local membership fell too and there was a sharp decline in the number of really active associations. Attendance at the party Assembly went down from 1,400 at Brighton in September 1966 to 900 at Brighton in September 1969.

Opinion polls found popular support fairly stable. It was seldom recorded as less than 7% or more than 11%. But by-elections offered little encouragement. Deposits were lost in 12 of the 28 seats fought. Moreover, there was anxiety about the nationalists making serious inroads into Liberal support in Wales and Scotland. In Scotland Mr. Grimond and others urged some alliance with the SNP; but this aroused strong opposition from other leading Liberals and, in any case, met little response from the nationalists, riding the crest of their wave and eager to fight every seat themselves.

Much of the Liberal advance in the early 1960s had had a growing base in local government. After 1965 — when those elected in the floodtide of 1962 ended their terms — the number of Liberal councillors declined. But there were isolated advances — with energetic local initiatives, new and firm Liberal bases were established in one or two wards of Leeds and of Liverpool as well as in some lesser authorities, while in Birmingham Mr. Wallace Lawler's efforts as a well publicised local ombudsman reaped rich rewards. In the Ladywood by-election of 1969 he became the first Liberal to represent Birmingham at Westminster since 1886. But this success (in a Labour stronghold which happened to be the most depopulated constituency in Britain) was not the harbinger of other triumphs. Mr. Lawler was recognised as unique and indeed his alleged stand on immigration and other matters excited some consternation among the more left-wing members of the party.

In its unpromising situation, the party became more inward-looking. It engaged in elaborate scrutiny of its own complex constitution; some of those who felt dissatisfied with the conduct of the party's affairs lapsed into inactivity. The Young Liberals apart, little that was new or challenging seemed to emerge although David Steel's private member's bill to legalise abortion did attract a lot of attention and Liberal M.P.s took a well-publicised stand against the Kenya Asians Bill in 1968. Of the most distinctively

Liberal policies, co-ownership remained but stirred little public interest. The flag of devolution was being waved much more vigorously by the nationalists and that of Europe by the Labour government. The Liberal M.P.s, with Lord Byers, Lord Beaumont and others in the Lords, took up various causes but at no point seemed to engage the attention of the nation.[1]

In the end much of the failure of the Liberal party during the later 1960s has to be ascribed in part at least to a lack of 'weight' among its leaders, who never found words to harness the disillusion or apathy of the moderate mass of the British electorate. It is, of course, true that the attitudes of the mass media and the ineluctable harshness of the electoral system hindered the Liberals and still more the lesser groups from making progress. Yet the impact made by the nationalists in 1966–68 and by Mr. Powell in 1968–70 shows that it would not have been impossible for those who could find the key to have unlocked a large hoard of public support for a plausible alternative to the two main parties.

[1] The best source of material on the Liberal party is *New Outlook* (monthly up to 1968, bi-monthly in 1969 and 1970) which contains many articles on the role and tactics of the party. See e.g. John Pardoe, 'Should Liberal M.P.s opt out of Parliament?', September 1966; the critique of Jeremy Thorpe's leadership, September 1969; and Pratap Chitnis, 'The Ladywood by-election', September 1969. Francis Boyd's coverage of Liberal Assemblies in the *Guardian* are particularly helpful. See also his article on Liberal organisation, *Guardian*, October 24, 1969.

CHAPTER VI

# HEALING THE SCAR TISSUE 1969–1970

APPROPRIATELY, Roy Jenkins had just opened the Export Services Exhibition at Earl's Court on September 8, 1969, when the export figures for August arrived from the Treasury. He had been hoping for, and had reasons to expect, some improvement. In his speech he had claimed that 'The trend of our balance of payments statistics is very favourable . . . and all the signs are that we are moving into substantial surplus.'[1] But his surprise was as great as his delight at the full extent of the good tidings. The seasonally adjusted figures indicated a huge rise in exports from £602 million in July to £662 million in August — far too large to be dismissed as a chance freak. At long last the pound was in the black.

In a single stroke the political situation was transformed.[2] Month by month the trade figures had been like raucous jesters mocking Labour's pretensions to responsibility and competence, giving a hollow sound to its claims that it was sacrificing short-term advantages to get the pound on its feet 'in the end'. In the long run, as Keynes once pointed out, we are all dead. But now these statements took on a new meaning. The appeals to patience or the spirit of Dunkirk made over the last three years — particularly by Mr. Wilson — which had seemed such lame excuses for failure at the time, now appeared statesmanlike in retrospect. The prominence given to the government's economic difficulties by Tory propaganda was in danger of backfiring.

The reversal of fortunes became apparent three days later, on

[1] *The Times*, September 9, 1969.

[2] It is hard for those outside Whitehall to appreciate how sudden changes in the economic situation appear, even to those at the centre of events. A few percentage points in the exports and imports, or in capital movements, can mean all the difference between success and abject failure. Despite the development of highly sophisticated methods of forecasting, it is not always possible to make predictions of the necessary accuracy. Mr. Maudling has described how rapidly the forecasts were changing over the summer of 1964 in the *Sunday Times*, October 25, 1964. S. Brittan gives a detailed assessment in his section on 'Forecasting' in Chapter 3 of the first edition of *Steering the Economy* (Secker & Warburg, 1969).

Our interviews with members of the government in September 1969 showed a striking improvement in morale from the low point in June.

September 11, when the revised trade figures for the second quarter of 1969 (April to June) were released, showing a handsome overall surplus. Writing under the headline 'Britain builds up surplus of £100 million', Hugh Stephenson of *The Times* referred to the 'scarcely restrained optimism' that had been running through the Prime Minister's recent public statements. A smaller article lower on the page ('Heath gives cautious verdict on results') quoted the Conservative leader as saying 'Perhaps we had better see the year as a whole before we conclude that all is well. The second quarter is always a good quarter. The quarter we are in at the moment is always a difficult quarter of the year.'[1] This was to become the pattern over the following months: good news from the Treasury, eliciting grudging acknowledgement from the Conservatives, combined with predictions of worse to follow ('. . . of course we are pleased, but . . .'). But the Conservative warnings were to boomerang as they were not fulfilled. The improvement continued through the third and fourth quarters of 1969 and the first quarter of 1970. The balance of payments in 1969, including the bad first quarter, showed a surplus of £387 million as against the deficits of £398 million in 1968 and £461 million in 1967.

The government also benefited from its firm but understanding handling of the violence which broke out again in Northern Ireland. The situation had deteriorated in 1968, when Terence O'Neill, the moderate Prime Minister, came under attack from Protestant hardliners within his own Unionist party as well as from the militant Catholics who regarded his progressive policies as 'too little and too late'. A revolt against his progressive policies by 12 Unionist M.P.s in the Stormont parliament forced him to dissolve parliament and hold new elections in February 1969. Although his Unionist party scored its inevitable victory, with voting still polarised on sectarian lines, Captain O'Neill was unable to prevent the readoption of most of the rebels by their local Unionist associations. His authority was also gravely impaired by the Reverend Ian Paisley, an uncompromising Protestant Unionist, who obtained almost 40% of the vote standing as an Independent in Captain O'Neill's own constituency. On April 17, the Ulster Unionist candidate in a by-election for the Westminster parliament was defeated by a 21-year-old student, Bernadette Devlin. Standing under a Civil Rights banner, Miss

[1] *The Times*, September 12, 1969.

Devlin, trumping her electoral success with a remarkable maiden speech in the House of Commons further focused the attention of the British public on Ulster. On April 28, 1969, Captain O'Neill resigned as Prime Minister of Northern Ireland and was succeeded by Major James Chichester-Clark, a moderate cabinet member not too unacceptable to the anti-O'Neill Unionists.

For some weeks there was uneasy calm. This was broken on August 12 when fighting broke out between Catholics and Protestants in the Catholic Bogside area of Londonderry during the annual march of the Protestant Apprentice Boys of Derry. The police were unable to handle the rioters and were driven out of the Bogside. Shooting incidents and petrol bomb attacks soon spread to Belfast, where hundreds of houses (most of them occupied by Catholics) were burned. The Northern Ireland cabinet met in emergency session on August 14 and appealed for troops from the United Kingdom government. Within hours soldiers moved into the Bogside and, on August 15, took over from the local police in the Catholic area, of Belfast. In return for his government's assistance, Mr. Wilson insisted that Major Chichester-Clark should agree to the phasing out of the Protestant auxiliary police force, the 'B-Specials', and continue with the promised introduction of full civil rights for the Catholic minority. On August 27 the Home Secretary, Mr. Callaghan, arrived in Northern Ireland for a three-day visit. He toured the damaged areas, spoke to representatives of all groups and did much to reassure the public both in Northern Ireland and in Britain that the violence could be brought under control.

The success of the government's actions in Northern Ireland came at an opportune time. In the spring, Mr. Callaghan had been publicly identified as the Prime Minister's main opponent during the crisis over the Industrial Relations Bill. Now the two men were working in harness. They managed to re-establish law and order and simultaneously to demonstrate their concern with the deep human problems caused by the long-standing religious cleavage in Ulster society — a heritage in which Labour was not slow to implicate the Conservative party. Northern Ireland appeared as a working example of Labour's claim that it was more than a match for the Conservatives in terms of its responsibility and still more its humanity.

An emphasis on Labour's ideals was also the keynote of a

£100,000 publicity campaign launched by Transport House at the end of August. The key slogan 'Labour's got life *and* soul' was intended to appeal to the Labour activists who had been discouraged by the government's poor record but might now be persuaded to return to the fold. Advertisements were placed in newspapers read by the activists (including the *Guardian* and *The Times*) rather than those read by ordinary Labour voters. The campaign theme caused some controversy within the Labour party. The Prime Minister and his advisers had their doubts, and the plans were finally approved at an NEC meeting from which he was absent. It was perhaps lucky that the campaign coincided with the upswing in Labour's fortunes. Those who advocated it (mainly the Voluntary Publicity Group) quoted later market research showing it had made a considerable impact. The 'boardroom' advertisement (see the illustration facing page 124) received the highest 'reading and noting' score of any advertisement in *The Times* during 1969. However, a later private study commissioned through Mark Abrams offered a much more depressing verdict.

The party conferences were both due to be held in Brighton, Labour's at the end of September and the Conservatives' a week later. Mr. Wilson and his colleagues looked forward to the opportunity to communicate their new-found optimism to the party faithful. Not only were the economic indicators becoming even more favourable, but the opinion polls showed that the public was responding. The Conservative lead which had averaged over 19% in July was down to 12½% in September, with NOP, Gallup and ORC showing leads of 11% or less. The Labour leaders, confident that they had at last 'put the economy right', prepared to present to the delegates their vision of a prosperous technocratic Britain, a society in which material progress went hand in hand with humanity and social justice. By-passing the conventional socialist measures contained in the NEC document *Agenda for a Generation*, they decided to hint at economic policies which could be developed as the campaign approached and which, in language suitable to the Labour movement, effectively stole the Tories' clothes. George Brown mentioned to the delegates the need to widen the tax base:

> 'It may be that we should be thinking very hard about how to relate what folk have to pay more to what they spend than to what they earn; that may be part of the answer to the complaints we

meet . . . we must not be frightened off making a high priority of continuing tax reform. . . .'[1]

He was referring to the complaints received by ministers and by the Chief Whip when, for the first time in years, they toured the regions to rally the party workers. They found that even active Labour supporters were complaining that their income tax was too high. It was therefore decided that assurances had to be given that Labour was no longer the party of high taxation, particularly high direct taxation. In the new year this tactic was to be reversed as it then appeared that there was more mileage to be gained from attacking than assimilating Conservative tax policies. For the time being, however, senior cabinet ministers talked (as Ronald Butt pointed out in *The Times*) in language reminiscent of Sir Anthony Eden's 'property-owning democracy'.[2] Roy Jenkins, who had just flown back from the meeting of the International Monetary Fund in Washington, reported that the current account surplus in the balance of payments was running 'at an annual rate which cannot be significantly below £450 million and might well be in excess of £500 million'.[3] He ended an extremely optimistic speech with a broad conclusion about the 1970s:

> 'We should look forward to expanding public services — certainly they are vitally necessary — but expanding them roughly in line with, and not ahead of, the growth in national income . . . we certainly ought not to be a party of taxation for taxation's sake or a party which is instinctively hostile to private consumption.
>
> One of the central purposes of democratic socialism is to extend throughout the community the freedom of choice which was previously the prerogative of the few.'[4]

In an address to the annual *Socialist Commentary* tea meeting, Denis Healey also concerned himself 'with the way affluence has affected the political context in which the Labour Party has to work in Britain'. He described how it had eroded class consciousness:

> 'Two things have struck me as a Leeds M.P. Eight of the Labour Clubs in my constituency have recently acquired new premises of

[1] *Labour Conference Report 1969*, p. 233. Formally, Mr. Brown was speaking as Chairman of the Home Policy Sub-Committee of the NEC. He still continued to speak partially with the air of a member of the government and there was some talk that he would rejoin the cabinet as Lord Privy Seal to coordinate between government and the party in the run-up to the campaign.

[2] 'Change of Theme', *The Times*, October 2, 1969.

[3] *Labour Conference Report 1969*, p. 253.

[4] Ibid., p. 255.

> palatial splendour — their only defect is a lack of parking space. When I go into these clubs on a Saturday night, four out of five complaints are that income tax is too high and that we should not pay out so much in family allowances.'

He concluded (echoing, perhaps unconsciously, a common Conservative line) that the state should concern itself with the remaining 'pockets of distress', leaving the majority free to enjoy, presumably by reduced taxation, their extra earnings.[1]

The highlights of the Conference were two sparkling, throw-away speeches by Mr. Wilson. On the Tuesday his theme was excitement: [2]

> 'We are creating a Britain of which we can be proud. And the world knows it. The world's tourists are coming here in their millions. . . . They are coming here to buy because they get better value for money in our shops than anywhere else in Europe. But they are coming, above all, because the new Britain is exciting.
>
> Last year, nearly five million tourists came to Britain. . . . It is not just the Tower of London, not just the Beefeaters they want to see either, nor even the King's Road. . . . It is Britain.
>
> Month after month, the Tories have been painting the picture of a Britain down in the dumps. . . . But it isn't the Britain that really exists. It isn't the Britain that these hundreds of thousands of tourists have been coming here to look at. They have been coming here because to them Britain — yes, Britain with a Labour Government — is an exciting place.
>
> Many of our visitors come to look at what British industry has done. . . . In nuclear energy — our prototype fast reactor now going ahead at Dounreay is 3 or 4 years ahead of anything else in operation or planned in any part of the Western world, including America. . . . So are the aluminium smelters now being built by private industry with Government encouragement; in three development areas, Northumberland, Invergordon, Anglesey. . . . We lead the world in vertical and short take-off aircraft. The Rolls-Royce engine R-B 211, which won from America the biggest order in the history of British aviation . . .
>
> The hovercraft . . .
>
> The Cephalosporin antibiotic . . . Cephalosporin, now earning millions of dollars from its American royalties alone, and making a profit for the British taxpayer. . . .
>
> Then there is spray steel making;
> satellite communications stations;
> pulse code modulation;

[1] *Socialist Commentary*, November 1969.
[2] September 30; *Labour Conference Report 1969*, pp. 199–206.

Dracone barges;
the new aviation navigational aids;
the ammonia steam-naphtha process;
the electron-probe analyser and the rest.

And still newer developments.

Carbon fibres. . . . This is a new British achievement, a product of work in a Government research establishment developed by public enterprise under Labour Government legislation in collaboration with industry. And American private enterprise is falling over itself to buy the right to use this product of British public enterprise. . . .'

Then he turned to the Tories:

'We all recall how Her Majesty's Opposition were dining out on the prospects of our failing to get the balance of payment into surplus. The champagne corks popping. Now, as Britain moves from long years of deficit into surplus, their champagne is turning into gripe-water. . . . I believe they are getting rather worried about the image they will be presenting in this hall next week. . . . I have gone to the trouble of working out a motto for them — *Bonum patriae Conservatoribus pessimum*, which being translated, broadly indicates that what is good for the country is bad for the Tories.'

On the Friday,[1] the *chutzpah* went even further:

'On Tuesday, I gave some helpful advice to those who will occupy this hall next week. (Laughter)

Even now their back-room boys are reading through every one of the 150,000 words and more that have been spoken at this conference, trying to find a word here, a phrase there, a neat little piece for extra-contextual selection. (Laughter)

I believe they have already taken their big decision. They have decided that they will have to admit that Britain not only can pay her way, but is paying her way under a Labour Government. (Applause) So now the line will be dramatically switched to a calculation of the debts that have got to be paid back. . . .

Well, I have thought a good deal about this and with every sympathy — reverend sympathy! — I offer them this constructive way out of their dilemma. Cut out the speech altogether and stage a forty-minute ovation.' (Laughter and applause)

These speeches, typically, made little mention of detailed policy. Mr. Wilson's aim was to heal the wounds of the past years, to re-instil into the party self respect and the will to win. Realising that his impact depended less on the substance of his text than on the manner in which he delivered it, he radiated a jaunty good humour and used laughter as the key to confidence. The extracts above

[1] October 3; *Labour Conference Report 1969*, pp. 356–7.

have been quoted not only to give some impression of his favourite themes of technological socialism and technological patriotism which had influenced his actions in government but also to illustrate both the condescending mockery of the Tories and the

'You name it — I'll be it!'
[*Daily Express*, June 1, 1970

absence of any specific details of what a Labour ministry would do when re-elected that were increasingly characteristic of his orations. With hindsight, it could be argued that the hearty successes at Brighton and in the attacking speeches he delivered in the new year served him ill, as they encouraged him to adopt the same style in the campaign and to ignore the development of a more positive statement of his case which (it seems) the electorate finally demanded in June 1970.

In the short run, Labour was making all the running. When Mr. Barber rose to address the Conservative conference the next Wednesday, he bore not only the burden of Mr. Wilson's scorn but the knowledge that the latest ORC poll which would appear on the Brighton newstands hours later showed the Conservative lead down to 4%. Ronald Butt caught the atmosphere of uncertainty in an article titled 'Tories Losing Advantage':[1]

'Though this year's conference is far from pessimistic, the mood I sense at Brighton is one of "if we win", rather than "when we

[1] *The Times*, October 9, 1969.

win". The contrast with the atmosphere of the Labour pre-election conference in 1963, when victory was regarded as inevitable, is very noticeable. . . .

It is now at least conceivable that if the Conservatives were to lose again the consequences for their own party might be nearly as shattering as those that Labour would have faced had they lost decisively in 1964 . . . the Conservative Party, which has provided the norm of British politics for so many decades, might become the usual minority party. . . .

The Conservative Party . . . is now paying for the success it had in educating the Labour Party out of socialism and forcing it to operate in the mixed economy of the twentieth century.'

The narrowing of the gap between the parties and the signs that Labour was preparing to absorb some of the basic elements of the Conservative tax package put the Conservative strategists in a tactical dilemma which was never satisfactorily resolved. If they refused to reveal details of their plans, not only would their credibility be damaged, but Labour's task of taking over their distinctive policies would be eased. But if they showed their hand, they risked attracting attention to the new taxes they would in some measure have to introduce and away from the tax cuts they were proposing;[1] they would lose their freedom of action in relation to civil servants on entering government; and they would risk enabling the Labour government to state that its official information showed their proposals to be unworkable. In his Conference speech, Mr. Macleod nevertheless went into considerable detail about a possible Value-added Tax, adding that the party was not finally committed to it. Mr. Carr gave more details of the proposed industrial relations reforms. This was probably the high point of detailed declaration. Although some new policies were announced nearer the election, spokesmen generally became more cagey and those who expected a formal commitment to the Value-added Tax before the election were disappointed.[2]

[1] They feared they would inevitably have to specify exact economies in public expenditure, but still leave vague the reductions in taxation. They considered it impossible to promise in advance to take a specific amount off income tax.

[2] There appear to have been substantive reasons for giving less emphasis to the switch to indirect taxation in early 1970 than before. The Economic Policy Group's calculations now showed that the measures it had been hoped to include in the package would have the combined effect of boosting demand by £500 million. Consequently it would be necessary to impose a Value-added Tax at a higher rate than had been envisaged or there would have to be a shift of emphasis in the party's planning onto reductions in the growth of public expenditure. But meanwhile it would be imprudent and very difficult to present a specific tax package to the electorate.

Mr. Heath's speech at the end of the Conference, a mixture of slightly laboured fun (in reply to Mr. Wilson) with a description of the Conservative programme, was very well received both by the representatives and by the press. But, as *Private Eye* showed with a series of cuttings about his performances at previous conferences, headlines saying that he had 'broken through at last' had been appearing for years, their very repetition showing that his standing remained uncertain. There could be little doubt that Mr. Wilson was now the happier of the two. Although the Labour recovery was coming just too late to permit an autumn election and bad weather excluded winter campaigns, all would be set for spring if the by-elections due to be held at the end of October confirmed the movement of the opinion polls.[1]

In the circumstances, the five by-elections were very disappointing for Labour. Although the swings to the Conservatives from the 1966 results were smaller than in the spring by-elections, they still averaged 10½%. This was equivalent to a Conservative lead in the polls of about 15%. The polls, however, suggested that Labour was consolidating its position — the average Conservative lead coming down to 7% in November and 7½% in December. Ministers were urged to complete any contentious business before Christmas. Mr. Callaghan introduced a measure abolishing capital punishment, despite the fact that the five-year trial period of abolition had not quite ended. Although there were some Conservative objections, there was considerable relief that this sensitive question, which had in the past caused much ill feeling between some Conservative M.P.s and their constituency parties and which threatened to do so again, was so conveniently removed.[2] After much cajoling from Mr. Mellish, Labour M.P.s reluctantly accepted the reactivation

[1] As a subsidiary annoyance during the Conference, a demand for the restoration of capital punishment for murder was put forward as an amendment to a law and order motion. There was some confusion when the ballot was taken. So unusual were formal conference votes that the Chairman was unsure of the correct procedure. The hardline amendment was carried, against the platform, by 1,117 votes to 958. Two further ballots were demanded by right wingers against British entry into the Common Market and against Conservative immigration policy. The Common Market was approved by 1,452 to 475 but a hefty minority (954 to 1,349) favoured even tougher control of immigration.

[2] The vote was (including tellers):

| | Conservative | Labour | Liberal | Other | Total |
|---|---|---|---|---|---|
| For abolition | 53 | 278 | 11 | 3 | 345 |
| Against | 181 | 3 | 2 | 1 | 187 |

Among the 50 Conservative abolitionists were Mr. Heath, Mr. Macleod and Mr. Powell.

of Part II of the Prices and Incomes Act demanded by Barbara Castle. Ill-feeling within the Parliamentary Labour Party was lessened by the knowledge that this was the last bitter pill it would have to swallow, and also by the imminence of Christmas.

Over the Christmas recess, Mr. Heath flew to Australia to skipper his yacht *Morning Cloud* in the Sydney–Hobart race. He was a comparatively inexperienced yachtsman and it was sometimes suggested (certainly wrongly) that he had taken up the activity at the request of his publicity advisers at Central Office. His victory in this major event was therefore a great sporting triumph and much commented on, generally (but not always) favourably. More important, it refreshed his spirits and according to close associates did much to carry him through the difficulties of the campaign with such dogged optimism. In January and February 1970, he was given further relief by the polls which started, unexpectedly, to swing back to the Conservatives, showing an average 10½% Conservative lead in January and again in February. The second burst of Labour publicity, tentatively planned for early spring, was postponed.

The continued delay in the response of the polls narrowed Mr. Wilson's room for manoeuvre. It was widely (and probably rightly) thought among strategists in both parties that the result of the election would depend on the timing of the trade cycle and the public opinion cycle which was largely dependent on it. Economic expansion brought increased wages and shortly afterwards increased prices. These soon reduced the benefits of higher incomes and eventually prejudiced the balance of payments. Economic expansion also brought, with a few months lag, a large movement of opinion in the government's favour. The relative speeds of these movements remained uncertain, and they were crucial. For if the public opinion cycle moved faster than the economic cycle (i.e. if Labour moved into the lead before the economic crisis and preferably during the time when higher wages had not yet been eroded by inflation), it would win. If, however, it had not gained the lead by the time inflation was getting out of hand (which in the early part of 1970 it seemed would happen in the autumn or winter), then the government would have either to go to the country while it still trailed, or to wait over the summer despite the risk of runaway inflation. The only way the government could prolong the economic cycle was by slowing the rate of expansion, holding back tax cuts and firmly resisting public sector wage demands. The *Bank of England Quarterly Review* advised this policy in its December 1969 issue, warning that increased wages would put up industrial costs to the detriment of the balance of payments, and asserting that 'the scope for expansion of domestic [consumer] demand — whether from the private or public sector — can be only modest.' But if Labour accepted this advice it would also be prejudicing its public standing: what was the point of a balance of payments surplus if it did not permit any domestic relaxations?

In an effort to stimulate further recovery in the polls and, if this succeeded, to lay the ground for a late spring election, Mr. Wilson made a series of campaigning speeches starting in Swansea on January 10, 1970.

More significantly, he made little attempt to slow the rise in wages which was becoming exceptionally severe by January and February. Many of the largest wage awards were in the public sector and included nurses, Post Office workers, civil service staffs, railwaymen, teachers, dustmen and busmen. These settlements averaged 12%.

At the end of January, the shadow cabinet gathered for the weekend at the Selsdon Park Hotel in Surrey. Although it had regularly considered separate policy papers there was little opportunity within the normal busy routine to consider as a whole the plans being prepared under the responsibility of the different shadow ministers. In times past, informal gatherings at country houses had provided an opportunity for colleagues to find out about each others' work. In lieu of these, Mr. Heath proposed a meeting to last a whole weekend at which the various proposals could be seen in combination and the shadow ministers could get accustomed to each others' working methods. Publicity was not the object of the exercise; indeed, it seems that it was only the impossibility of keeping the meeting secret that led to the decision to announce it to the press in advance and to arrange for lobby briefings to be given. In the event Selsdon was a huge publicity success. With the approach of the campaign, the papers were at last becoming interested in Mr. Heath and his team and there was very heavy coverage over the weekend and on the Monday. The policies outlined to the press were not new, most of them having been adopted as early as 1965.[1] But this was the first time that they

[1] See David Wood, *The Times*, February 2, 1970.

started to enter the consciousness of the general public. The Selsdon meeting also performed its original function, that of educating the shadow cabinet and of making its policies 'gel'. The confrontation between different policy papers revealed conflicts in certain cases, as a result of which some were abandoned and others returned to the Conservative Research Department or to policy groups for further consideration.[1] According to some reports, it again proved impossible to evolve a satisfactory policy on health, and technical difficulties were revealed in the projected housing subsidies. This latter problem was one of the factors which dissuaded the shadow cabinet from revealing, even in outline, a 'tax package' before the election. For there were good electoral reasons to delay announcing proposals for the move from direct to indirect taxation until those for measures such as housing subsidies were also ready. The substitution of taxes on consumption for taxes on income would put those in medium and low wage brackets (many of them target C2s) at a disadvantage which they would recoup from selective benefits, possibly including a housing subsidy. But even if these technical problems had permitted the publication of a 'package', the shadow cabinet would probably have been reluctant to commit itself. Even before Selsdon it had decided not to decide between a Value-added Tax and other taxes on consumption, limiting itself to the general resolve to increase one of several alternative forms of indirect tax.[2]

If Mr. Heath was delighted by Selsdon, so was Mr. Wilson, after some initial anxiety about the publicity it had gained. Whereas Mr. Heath preferred a 'governmental' style of opposition, Mr. Wilson felt in his element when he was on the attack. Now that Conservative policies were at last entering public awareness, he could deal with them to his advantage. He singled out two parts of the Selsdon programme for special attention: the Conservative industrial relations reforms (which, he said, spelt a return not to the Conservatism of the 1940s but to an even more reactionary pre-war brand) and the projected stiffening of the law of trespass against squatters and demonstrators.[3] To Mr. Wilson, these were demon-

[1] Several of the policy groups had by now produced their reports and dissolved. Others, including the Economic Policy Group, remained in existence.
[2] See pp. 82–3.
[3] It was later claimed by some senior Conservatives that the newspapers had paid undue attention to the Law and Order proposals, which formed only one element in the 'Selsdon programme'; also, that the programme announced to

strations of atavistic Conservative instincts, which he summed up in a phrase he repeated time and again: 'Selsdon man'.[1]

While these skirmishes were taking place, preparations were being made for the Budget with the usual official secrecy and public curiosity. During February and March it was suggested in press reports that Mr. Wilson was pressing for a 'give-away' budget, while Mr. Jenkins, whose political career would suffer less than Mr. Wilson's from a Labour defeat in the general election, was putting the case for a 'responsible' one.[2] Parallels were drawn with 1950 when it was alleged Mr. Attlee's inability to persuade Sir Stafford Cripps to agree to a lenient Budget had had some influence on his decision to go to the country in February rather than in the late spring.[3]

The triennial county elections took place between April 6 and 11, the week before Budget day (April 14). They offered little comfort for Labour. There was practically no change in English and Welsh counties from the 1967 results, when the Conservatives had made large gains.[4] According to Peter Pulzer's estimate[5] this was the equivalent to a 9–10% swing to the Conservatives since

---

the journalists bore little relation to the matters still under discussion at the weekend meeting. Possibly, it was the fact that the other measures were not new that brought those on Law and Order into the headlines; also, the prolonged occupation by a group of long-haired youths of No. 144 Piccadilly, a mansion awaiting demolition, had recently focused interest on the problem.

[1] After the election, Mr. Wilson and Mr. Heath both continued to think they had come best out of Selsdon. In psychological terms, it undoubtedly gave them, in their different ways, intense satisfaction. Objectively, honours were probably even. To the Conservative advantage were (*a*) widespread publicity, (*b*) the fact that 'Selsdon man' was meaningless to most people, and (*c*) the Conservative policies on industrial relations and law and order to which Mr. Wilson was drawing attention were, as surveys showed, favoured by a majority of the electorate.

On the Labour side: (*a*) Labour now had a target: Mr. Wilson an essentially combative politician, had a whole set of policies to attack; (*b*) even if people didn't know exactly what 'Selsdon man' referred to, they accepted it as a brilliant insult; (*c*) it gave great encouragement to active Labour supporters; (*d*) it put Mr. Heath on the defensive, making him excessively reticent about explaining policy, notably at the manifesto-launching press conference in May and during the early days of the campaign.

[2] 'Roy Jenkins . . . was under considerable pressure to give a large hand-out. . . . He stoutly resisted these pressures.' S. Brittan, *Steering the Economy* (Penguin, 1971), p. 407.

[3] The Treasury appears to have favoured caution, though it was content to recommend a set of neutral, rather than deflationary measures. The £179 million give-away by Mr. Jenkins was thus within the limits advised by the Treasury, though it is probably fair to say that it would have ideally have preferred a smaller figure.

[4] See 'Swinging London is not much use to Mr. Wilson on its own', *Economist*, April 18, 1970, from which the table on p. 132 is drawn.

[5] 'ILEA win a boost for Labour', *The Times*, April 11, 1970.

the 1966 election, which amounted (even when taking account of differential turnout estimated at 5% in the Conservatives' favour) to a 7% Conservative lead in the opinion polls. Labour could draw some comfort from the results of the Greater London Council elections in which it captured 16 seats from the Conservatives, polling particularly well in the areas of inner London which formed the Inner London Education Authority. This body was narrowly captured by Labour. Besides its psychological value, it was a hopeful sign of a large pro-Labour swing in the borough elections which were due to take place in May.

*1970 County Elections*

| | Pro-Conservative swing since | |
|---|---|---|
| | 1964 | 1967 |
| ILEA . . . . . . . | +6·7% | −7·6% |
| Outer London . . . . . . | +9·9% | −2·8% |
| Counties . . . . . . . | +12·8% | +0·3% |

On April 14, Roy Jenkins presented in a cautious, moderate speech a Budget containing none of the big concessions that had been expected. In David Wood's words it was 'an economist's Budget, not a politician's or party manager's'. To Peter Jay, the Economics Editor of *The Times*,[1] its economies 'were in fact about as pure and proper as anyone could have wished'. He referred in particular to the Chancellor's announced intention of limiting any increase in the domestic money supply to 5% 'wholly in accordance with the best Chicago tradition of setting a neutral "transcyclical" course in line with the economy's long-term growth potential'. The *Economist* was more cynical. While its editorial praised the Chancellor's resolve to limit the growth of the money supply, it pointed out that this would not be possible, in view of the 'present roaring 10% wage inflation', unless the Chancellor took deflationary measures in the next few months, but political pressures over the summer would make this very difficult. The Budget was therefore to be interpreted as an irresponsible escape from the task of tackling wage inflation under the guise of reflective moderation:[1]

'It had been assumed for some time that the Treasury civil servants

[1] *The Times*, April 15, 1970.

had told Mr. Jenkins that he should not give away more than £200 million, or ½ per cent of gross national product; and he has stuck more than rigidly within that formula (£179 million of loss of tax revenue in 1970–71). Oddly, however, this does not mean that he is being more responsible than his Tory predecessors at election time. Although few people seem to have realised it, his own Treasury figures suggest that he is aiming for a bigger pre-election consumer boom than did Mr. Maudling in 1964.'

These worries were not shared by the public. The Budget was the signal for the further movement to Labour which had started in the autumn of 1969 but had failed to gather momentum during the winter and spring. From April 14 it seemed that little could go wrong for the government. All was set for October, or, as people now seriously began to suggest, June. It was later claimed that it was on April 13 that Mr. Wilson made his broad decision to go in the summer.

On the morning of Budget day, a series of models were smuggled into Mr. Wilson's room in the House of Commons and unveiled before the Campaign Committee with electrifying effect. They showed members of the shadow cabinet in lurid colours and with down-in-the-mouth expressions. 'Yesterday's Men' was to be the theme of a £60,000 publicity campaign due to start on May 15 (after the local elections) and to continue over the summer in expectation of an October campaign.[1]

Two weeks later, as Mr. Wilson stopped at a Glasgow hotel on his way to address the Scottish TUC meeting in Oban, he was shown the *Scottish Daily Express* with its headline 'GOOD

[1] There was considerable criticism from the constituency parties when the 'Yesterday's Men' campaign opened on the ground that it degraded politics by its tough portrayal of the Conservative leaders. The campaign never established itself as it was overtaken by the announcement of the general election. It could be argued that it showed more flair than any other political publicity during 1966–70 with the exception of the 'frozen wage packet' and the 'vanishing pound' in the Conservative party political broadcasts.

The campaign was conceived by Dennis Lyons and other members of the Voluntary Publicity Group. They argued that Conservative mass advertising had contained 75% 'knocking copy' whereas Labour had mistakenly avoided 'this knockabout stuff'. It was therefore necessary to 'accentuate the negative' by attacking the Tory leaders. They maintained further that 'a General Election has a considerable affinity with a major take-over bid in industry', and 'the people who are proposing the take-over are basically the same board of management who previously ran the firm to the point of bankruptcy'. The campaign sign would therefore start by 'highlighting the incompetence of the men who, having visibly failed before, are now getting themselves put forward as prospective management'. In its second phase the Labour team would be shown in favourable contrast. 'Labour's Winning Team'. However, the election came too soon for the second stage.

MORNING MR WILSON. LABOUR TAKES THE LEAD'. It was the first time since March 1967 that any national poll had shown Labour ahead. The next day the findings of the *Daily Express* Harris poll were confirmed by Marplan which reported an 0·8% Labour lead. Speculation about an early election started in earnest. It was announced that a joint meeting of the NEC and the government would be held at Number 10 Downing Street on Sunday, May 17. It had been planned in March for liaison purposes, possibly to encourage summer activity in the constituencies in preparation for an October election; but it would equally serve as a useful curtain-raiser for the dissolution of parliament in time for a June poll. On April 30, Mr. Wilson happened to be guest on the popular BBC programme *Sportsnight with Coleman* (blanketing Mr. Heath's simultaneous interview on Granada's *This Week*). Although he could only assume the guise of football fan, his appearance balanced that of Mr. Heath quizzed in January on his yachting triumph. 'When Harold took the option to go on *Sportsnight*, I knew we were in for a summer dissolution,' commented one senior Conservative.

The municipal elections started at the beginning of May, most of them being held on Thursday, May 8. On Friday morning, May 9, the Prime Minister was 'purring like a Persian cat' at the results which indicated an overall Labour majority of 50 in a general election. According to an analysis in the *Economist*:

> 'the swing (to Labour) between 1969 and 1970 was one of the largest ever recorded in local elections over a twelve month period. Seldom much below 10% in most of the big cities, and ranging up to 23 per cent in Preston and an astonishing 27 per cent in Hull . . . Labour's recovery has taken the party almost back to 1966.'[1]

Conservative Central Office did not delay in issuing figures showing that in the marginal constituencies, the total votes cast for Conservative candidates exceeded those for their Labour opponents. These figures gave an over-optimistic picture from the Conservative viewpoint as they ignored the effects of differential turnout. In local elections, turnout is much lower than in general elections, Labour voters abstaining in greater proportions than Conservatives. In May 1970, there were signs that differential abstention had favoured the Conservatives less than usual (less, in particular, than in 1969), thereby accounting for some of the swing

[1] *Economist*, May 16, 1970.

to Labour from 1969. Nevertheless, if local election figures were to be used as indicators of probable national results, precedent suggested that the Conservatives would fare worse in a general election, when turnout would be much higher and their differential turnout advantage would disappear.

The following Tuesday evening (May 12), Gallup showed a 7% Labour lead. The Prime Minister's mind was finally made up. He made a point of consulting his senior cabinet colleagues. Roy Jenkins advised that June or October would be equally good as far as the balance of payments was concerned; all the other senior ministers were agreeable to a summer campaign, including Mr. Crossman and Mrs. Castle, who had earlier expressed doubts as they wanted time to pass important pieces of legislation before the dissolution. A poll of M.P.s carried out by the government Chief Whip also revealed a predominant eagerness for an early election. If Mr. Wilson went to the country in June and lost, there would at least be few who could say 'I warned you'. But if he delayed until October and lost, there would possibly be severe pressure against his leadership.[1]

The Prime Minister was primarily influenced, however, by the thought that he could win in June, whereas, if he did not go to the country immediately, he would 'become a prisoner' unable to call an election until October. Although he did not expect major balance of payments troubles over the summer[2] there was the risk that the favourable, but treacherous tide of public opinion would turn against him. He seriously believed that the Conservatives were planning to spend £2 million on a summer advertising campaign and feared the influence of the Tory press over the months while parliament would be in recess. Other anxiety included the pos-

[1] See Peter Jenkins, *Guardian*, May 12, 1970. See also Ian Aitken, *Guardian*, May 13, 1970. 'As one Minister put it, "if he [Mr. Wilson] waited now and lost in October, he would never be forgiven by the party. But he would not be blamed for grasping the opportunity offered by the polls even if he turned out to be wrong."'

[2] The evidence suggests that Mr. Wilson was not seriously influenced by the prospect of a balance of payments crisis over the summer. During the week before May 18, we questioned several economists of standing including ones who were themselves, or who were close to, advisers of both government and opposition. Without exception they were of the opinion that there was little to choose between June and October from a balance of payments point of view. They also dismissed fears of a recession following the setbacks on Wall Street. But they almost all emphasised that a price explosion was imminent. Interviews held after the election suggest that this was also the advice tendered to Mr. Wilson.

sibility of a speculative *putsch* against sterling which Mr. Wilson appeared to think was being hatched by ill-disposed foreign bankers, and strikes at London Airport and the docks, which would badly hurt his party's image if they occurred during the holiday season. Confronted, as it seemed, by a choice between a small, but relatively assured majority in June and a large, but riskier majority in October, the Prime Minister chose the former.

Throughout the week following the local elections, broad hints were dropped to the press that the dissolution would be announced on May 18 and that the election would take place a month later; indeed most people outside Transport House and the Labour organisation seemed to be in the know. Even on May 17, when the NEC and the cabinet met at Downing Street, Mr. Wilson did not indicate that he would be visiting the Queen the following day.

Meanwhile, the Conservatives were facing up to the grim prospects that the polls had opened up. In the *Sunday Times* on May 17, James Margach reported:

> 'I have never seen a party plunged more suddenly and irrationally into such black despair as happened to the Conservatives the other night when the Gallup poll figures showed Labour ahead by an astonishing 7·5 per cent.
>
> Suddenly, groups of bewildered Tory M.P.s formed in the lobbies and elsewhere in the precincts, stunned and shaken by the news.'

The annual conference of the Scottish Conservatives was taking place from May 13 to May 16. Mr. Heath was due to speak on the Saturday (May 16). On Friday evening there was uneasy merriment at the conference ball. Sir Alec Douglas-Home circulated among the representatives: 'In Scotland swings are less than in England,' he said reassuringly 'so, at least, we won't do as badly up here.' And to another:

> 'In the Conservative party, we always do our best with our backs against the wall. And all I can say is that it's a damned great wall we're up against now.'

CHAPTER VII

# THE FINE WEATHER CAMPAIGN

THE party headquarters were in different degrees of readiness for the battle — if that is the way to phrase it. Elections are always described with the metaphors of war — headquarters, tactics, campaign and so on. This can lead to a fundamental misunderstanding of their nature. The headquarters have very little control over their volunteer armies; they cannot even coordinate very closely the salvoes fired by their big guns. The two sides seldom encounter each other on the field, either in routine constituency electioneering, or in the arguments launched in Smith Square or on the air. Each party tends to campaign on its self-chosen battleground against straw men of its own devising. There is no obligation to answer the challenges of the other side; the general view is that it is a strategic mistake ever to do so. Little evidence exists to show any link between the firing of campaign ammunition and the achievement of the strategic objective — more votes. In fact, in describing an election the metaphors of fashion shows or beauty contests might be quite as appropriate as those of battle. Certainly it is almost impossible to describe what happened in June 1970 using the analogies of assault and counter-attack, of tactics modified in response to the enemy's initiatives. If changes in what the parties did and said as the days went on represented a response to something, it was a response to the findings of the opinion polls. A chart on p. 143 maps the main features of the campaign, but few of them could have stood out as signal-flares to the voter. Most of what happened in the month preceding polling day involved, as so much of war does, sound and fury signifying nothing. The parties' search for support was important and seems to have switched more votes in 1970 than ever before, but to liken Mr. Wilson and Mr. Heath to army commanders involves a fundamental misconstruction of their role.

On the afternoon of May 18, the Prime Minister waited until the Queen had flown to London from Sandringham and then went to Buckingham Palace. At 5.45 p.m. a statement was issued from 10 Downing Street.

> 'The Prime Minister has asked Her Majesty the Queen to proclaim the dissolution of Parliament. Her Majesty has been graciously pleased to signify that she will comply with his request. In order to complete essential financial and other business, the Government have therefore requested Mr. Speaker to recall the House of Commons to meet on Tuesday, May 26th, and the House of Lords will also be asked to continue to sit that week. Parliament will be prorogued on Friday, May 29th. Dissolution will take place on the same day. Polling will take place on Thursday, June 18th. The new Parliament will be summoned on Monday, June 29th when the first business will be the election of the Speaker and the swearing in of Members. The new Parliament will be opened on Thursday, July 2nd.'

In giving 31 days' notice of the vote Mr. Wilson was not merely following his own precedent of 1966, but also conforming to an older pattern: since 1950 the announcement had always been made between 28 and 35 days before polling day. In the brief, formal style of the announcement, too, Mr. Wilson was following the procedure of 1966 although even he, apparently, did not foresee the sequel later that evening, when both party leaders appeared on television: Mr. Wilson basked comfortably in the garden of No. 10 before the B.B.C.'s respectful political editor while Mr. Heath was grilled toughly in the studios by Robin Day.[1]

The June election was unexpected, at least to judge by the commentaries of a few weeks earlier, but the Conservatives had for so long challenged the Labour party to come out and test the feelings of the voters that there could be no serious protest at a 'snap election'; as Mr. Heath had said that weekend at Perth, the Tories were 'rarin' to go'. There were, however, complaints from prospective holiday-makers, above all in the Potteries, where the five seats, all Labour, around Stoke-on-Trent were the only ones in which 'Wakes Weeks' coincided with the election. In fact, of course, the Conservatives were hit more by holidays than Labour both because the middle class are more prone to holiday away from home and because the elderly take advantage of the lower tariff in June.[2]

But if the date of the poll is traditionally announced four and a

[1] See p. 199.

[2] An ORC poll (*Sunday Times*, April 26, 1970) estimated that in mid-June 900,000 Conservatives would be away on holiday as against 650,000 Labour voters.

half weeks in advance, the formal campaign is confined to a mere three weeks. There is, indeed, arcane discussion on both sides of Smith Square about the dangers of peaking too early. Mr. Wilson remarked on May 18 that he did not think the British people wanted a campaign of more than three weeks; afterwards he was to be accused of running out of steam a week early.

Certainly there was a marked reluctance to use the first ten days after the announcement for much public electioneering. Mr. Heath did call together all Conservative candidates for a briefing at Church House on Friday, May 22, but Mr. Wilson, who had talked things over with his colleagues in the cabinet and the National Executive on May 17, then seemed to content himself with carrying on the work of government. But an eye was duly kept on the voter as the decks were cleared; in these ten days, a number of statements were accelerated through the administrative machine.

Mr. Crossman announced a £70 million a year increase in supplementary benefits and a £10 million a year increase in allowances for the disabled. Mr. Healey announced a £76 million development in Plymouth and Portsmouth dockyards. From the Ministry of Technology came a £10 million loan for Rolls-Royce and £8 million for Cammell Laird. There was also a forecast of £40 million expenditure on urban aid, while £8 million was to go to Scotland for the development of a second runway at Turnhouse Airport. At the same time it was announced that Mr. Greenwood was leaving politics to join the board of the Commonwealth Development Corporation, with a view to his becoming its Chairman. Labour's Chief Whip, Robert Mellish, leapt into a brief new prominence as Minister of Housing.

The newspapers in the week after the announcement of the election were dominated by two themes, neither of which was to matter much in the campaign. The lesser — merely from the British electoral point of view — came from America, where, following the reactions to President Nixon's Cambodian intervention, there was a sharp slide on Wall Street and anxieties were voiced about an international financial crisis which did not in fact materialise. It made this the most inward-turning election in the country's history: it was a reflection not just of the decline in Britain's international strength but also of the absence of outside stimulus in the crucial month.

In Britain the headlines were dominated by the manoeuvring

over the South African cricket tour. Anti-apartheid agitation had long been growing, and the question of the South African visit to Britain in 1970 had been a vexed one ever since 1968 when the South African rejection of the coloured Basil D'Oliveira as a member of the British team had led to the cancellation of that winter's tour. Led by a young South African expatriate, Peter Hain, there had been strident demonstrations against the Springbok Rugby Tour during the winter of 1969–70, avowedly as a rehearsal for wrecking the cricket tour. Fear of violence had led to the curtailment of the South Africans' programme and to elaborate defensive measures at the eight grounds where matches were to be played. At the same time, many reputable organisations, well away from the violent fringe of 'non-violence', had asked for the tour to be cancelled — among them the TUC, the Liberal party and the Labour party. Mr. Wilson and Mr. Callaghan had each won both applause and opprobrium for expressing dislike of the tour and welcoming peaceful demonstrations.

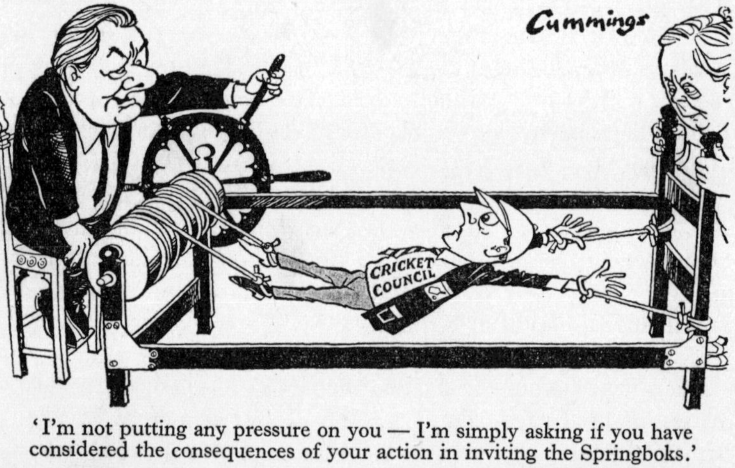


'I'm not putting any pressure on you — I'm simply asking if you have considered the consequences of your action in inviting the Springboks.'

[*Daily Express*, May 22, 1970

Increasing anxieties were voiced about the effect of the tour on community relations within England and about the danger of black African countries pulling out of the Commonwealth games (due to be held in Edinburgh in July). On May 19 the Police Federation expressed unhappiness about the strains the tour would impose on its members. The coming of the general election made the problem much more urgent, for the South Africans were scheduled to arrive on June 1 and to play their first match on June 6; June 18 was scheduled for the start of the First Test at Lord's. Nonetheless, despite an appeal by the Home Secretary, the Cricket Council announced on May 19 that they had decided 'by a substantial majority' that the tour should go on (although, departing from their stance about the separation of sport and politics, they said that no future team from South Africa would be welcome until cricket was played on a multi-racial basis). The Home Secretary seized neatly on a phrase in the announcement to the effect that the Council considered non-cricketing consequences of the tour 'to be the responsibility of the government who are best equipped to act upon and judge them'; he formally asked them to call the tour off; and on May 22 they reluctantly complied. The episode provoked a short-lived outburst of indignation about capitulating to violence and in the early speeches of the campaign many Conservatives made slighting references to the government's handling of the issue. Mr. Hogg summed it up:

> 'The whole operation is a classic example of the inability of this Government to preserve freedom in this country or to maintain law and order.'

Opinion polls suggested that a majority of the public was against the cancellation of the tour,[1] but there is no evidence that it continued to be a live issue during the campaign. In the final three weeks none of the many agents of all parties with whom we were in contact laid any stress on it, and in a ORC survey immediately after the election less than 1% of electors mentioned it. What is certain is that the election would have had a distinctly different flavour if the tour had gone on and demonstrations against it had been making headlines throughout the relatively newsless days of June: it seems likely that, despite all the reassuring skill of Mr. Callaghan, any such unrest could only have helped the Conservatives, as the press highlighted the activities of the wilder fringe of demonstrators.

Parliament was recalled on May 26 for three days to see to the completion of necessary, uncontroversial business. There were no obsequies for the three major pieces of legislation that had to be abandoned because of the dissolution, measures to nationalise the ports, to introduce a comprehensive graduated pension scheme and

[1] On May 3 ORC reported in the *Sunday Times* that only 30% of people wanted the tour called off, as against 59% who wanted it to go ahead.

to enforce comprehensive education on all local authorities. In the prevailing mood, it was assumed that the Labour government would deal with them after the election. The Conservatives deliberately forwent the propaganda opportunities offered by the meeting of the House. Since M.P.s wanted to be in their constituencies attendance in the Chamber was too thin for any set-piece dramas. The party point-scoring was restricted and attracted no more publicity than did the speedy passage of the Finance and Consolidated Fund Acts. More attention indeed was paid to the passing from the House of Commons of old stalwarts, most notably Emanuel Shinwell who had served, on and off, since 1922.

Meanwhile, the parties were busy with their preparations. In part it was a matter of checking established plans, seeing whether the right halls were available on the right days, finding substitutes for candidates who withdrew at the last moment, modifying arrangements to meet the broadcasters' schedules and, in some measure, arguing afresh what the campaign strategy should be. The Conservatives' plans were thorough. As in previous elections a detailed memorandum defined roles and laid down individual responsibilities. There was an elaborate structure of office meetings to coordinate campaign activities. The first important one was a 9.45 News Conference Briefing, chaired by Sir Michael Fraser; half of those present went on at 10 a.m. to talk with Mr. Heath.[1] (A few minutes before he faced the press at 11 a.m., word would be brought in of what had transpired at the Labour news conference.) There was also a daily committee at the Research Department, chaired by Lord Carrington, to discuss questions of policy that arose from the constituencies.[2] A daily working lunch at St. Stephen's Club was intended to gather together the threads, with reports on private polls and on organisation. Attendance varied but closely overlapped with the full News Conference Briefing group; others came from time to time including Mr. Barber and Mr. Whitelaw as well as Mr. Allan and Mr. Hurd from Mr. Heath's

[1] Normally present were Sir Michael Fraser,* Tommy Thompson* and Humphrey Taylor (both ORC), Richard Webster (Director of Organisation), Brendon Sewill* (Director of Research Department), Geoffrey Tucker* (Director of Publicity), Gerald O'Brien (in charge of the Press), Michael Wolff*, and Cyril Townsend (both working with Mr. Heath). Those starred normally went on to Mr. Heath's 10 a.m. briefing.

[2] It was known as the Questions of Policy Committee and its members were Lord Carrington, Earl Jellicoe, Lord Chelmer, Lord Drumalbyn, Mrs. Charles Doughty, Richard Sharples and David Dear, with David Clarke (Principal of Swinton Conservative College) as Secretary.

# THEY ALSO RAN

Enoch Powell, Conservative

Jeremy Thorpe, Liberal

ynfor Evans, Plaid Cymru

Ian Paisley, Protestant Unionist

Bernadette Devlin, Unity

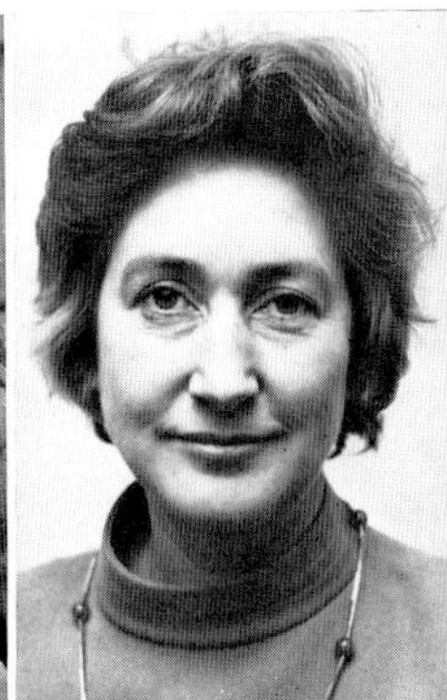

Winifred Ewing, Scottish National Party

# THE LABOUR CAMPAIGN

Mr. Healey, Mr. Wilson and Mr Nicholas at the press conference

Whistlestop

George Brown at Watford

James Callaghan at Ninian Park

Roy Jenkins at Birmingham

# THE CONSERVATIVE CAMPAIGN

Mr. Heath at his press conference

'. . . Out and back by plane'

Anthony Barber at Hampstead

Iain Macleod at Romford

Sir Alec Douglas-Home at Reading

JUNE 19, 1970

James Prior
(PPS)

Lord Carrington
(Leader in the Lords)

Michael Wolff
(Speechwriter)

| | Events | Main public appearance: Mr. Wilson | Main public appearance: Mr. Heath | Main TV appearance | Labour poll lead | London: Max. temp. °F | London: Hours of sunshine |
|---|---|---|---|---|---|---|---|
| May | | | | | | | |
| M 18 | Announcement | | | All leaders | | 72 | 8 |
| T 19 | S.A. tour confirmed | | | | M. 2·7% | 71 | 3 |
| W 20 | | | | | H. 2% | 68 | 11 |
| T 21 | | | | | G. 7% O. 1% | 61 | 9 |
| F 22 | S.A. tour cancelled | | Westminster | | | 60 | 11 |
| S 23 | | | | | | 66 | 3 |
| S 24 | | | | | | 71 | 1 |
| M 25 | | | | | | 70 | 9 |
| T 26 | Con. Manifesto | | | Thorpe (BBC forum) | | 73 | 11 |
| W 27 | Lab. Manifesto | | | Heath (BBC forum) | | 70 | 9 |
| T 28 | Lib. Manifesto | | | Wilson (BBC forum) | O. 2% | 73 | 7 |
| F 29 | Dissolution | Cardiff | Bexley | | N. 3·2% G. 2% | 64 | 2 |
| S 30 | | Eltham | Bexley | | | 72 | 9 |
| S 31 | | Yorkshire | | | G. 5½% O. −2% | 70 | 3 |
| June | | | | | | | |
| M 1 | Press Conferences begin | London | Westminster | Wilson | | 68 | 4 |
| T 2 | | East Anglia | Cardiff | Heath | M. 3·7% | 72 | 7 |
| W 3 | Benn on Powell | Birmingham | Leicester | Thorpe | H. 5% | 70 | 11 |
| T 4 | Doctors' Pay | Liverpool/London | Birmingham | Callaghan | N. 5·4% O. 4½% | 68 | 14 |
| F 5 | | Beds./Herts. | Portsmouth | Maudling | | 70 | 14 |
| S 6 | | Glasgow | Chatham | | | 70 | 14 |
| S 7 | | North-East | (Albany consultation) | | G. 5½% O. 2% | 77 | 9 |
| M 8 | Nominations close | East Midlands | Bristol | Macleod | | 81 | 14 |
| T 9 | Quarterly payments figures | Essex/London | Newcastle | Short | | 85 | 11 |
| W 10 | Press strike in effect | Southampton | Glasgow | Grimond | | 85 | 12 |
| T 11 | Powell on race | Exeter | Norwich | Macleod | H. 7% O. 7% | 82 | 11 |
| F 12 | | Merseyside | Manchester | Jenkins | | 77 | 4 |
| S 13 | Press strike ends | Lancashire | Orpington | Thorpe | N. 12·4% | 73 | 12 |
| S 14 | World Cup exit | Bristol | | | G. 2½% | 64 | 8 |
| M 15 | Monthly trade figures | Hammersmith | West London | Heath | | 69 | 13 |
| T 16 | | Oldham | Bradford | Wilson | | 62 | 4 |
| W 17 | | Liverpool | Bexley | | M. 8·7% H. 2% | 70 | 1 |
| T 18 | Polling day | | | | G. 7% N. 4·1%<br>O. −1% | 80 | 11 |

Polls G. = Gallup, H. = Harns, M. = Marplan, N. = National Opinion Poll, O = Opinion Research Centre (see p. 178).

entourage. Broadcasting problems were naturally discussed at this lunch but they were to some extent dealt with separately in meetings at the private studios. There the programmes were prepared under the general supervision of Mr. Tucker but with Mr. Whitelaw in overall charge of political co-ordination. Since Mr. Barber, although far from inactive as Chairman, was away campaigning for much of the time, a central role fell on Sir Michael Fraser, the Deputy Chairman. In so far as strategic matters were settled by staff work, the St. Stephen's Club lunches provided the main forum for argument. However, the most influential advice to Mr. Heath probably came in discussions with his senior colleagues at Albany or, more often, by phone.

On the whole the machine worked smoothly, but it would be wrong to picture the campaign going according to plan. Initially, the Conservatives envisaged that the pattern would follow 1966, when the party won good coverage for the different initiatives launched each day in press conferences and speeches. This time the response was much more sluggish. While the pre-eminence of the economic theme was deliberate, it was in part reinforced by the failure of other themes to evoke a response from the press, let alone the public.

The only specific deviation from prior plans was when Mr. Heath called a meeting for May 22 at Church House, at which he was to brief all candidates; and on June 1 when the death of Mr. Macleod's mother led to his withdrawal from the campaign for five days and to a re-scheduling of one or two broadcasts. In so far as there were fundamental dislocations to the Conservatives' planned campaign, they came from the need to reassess tactics because the campaign atmosphere proved so tranquil, apart from the dramatic incursions of Mr. Powell and from the impact of the opinion polls.

Labour's efforts, however, were much more a matter of improvisation — the 'do-it-yourself affair' of which the National Agent had spoken. The campaign committee had dealt with publicity but had done very little to plan the campaign: they did not meet again after the election was announced. The party officials had prepared a 'war book' which dealt largely with matters of routine but also laid down a daily committee structure comparable to the Conservatives'. The office meetings began at 7.45 with the publicity or planning group, with Mr. Nicholas in the chair; it involved an exchange of ideas that does not seem to have been very influential.[1] At 8.15 the 'Today' meeting followed, with Tom McNally and members of the Research Department preparing plans for the next issue of the daily information bulletin *Today*, sent to all candidates. At 9 a.m. the main daily meeting began, chaired by Mr. Nicholas.[2] It often included telephone conferences with Mr. Callaghan or Mr. Brown. Mr. Wilson usually arrived about 9.30 to be briefed on any new developments and to make suggestions about the future lines to be pursued, as well as to approve the handouts for the press conference to which he went at 10 a.m. Despite all their staff work, they had to await the Prime Minister's lead for broad guidance on the direction of the campaign. (It was characteristic that Mr. Wilson kept his own counsel about his 'walkabout' plans virtually to the last moment.) Transport House advice probably mattered much less than the suggestions from his personal entourage in 10 Downing Street and from one or two of his most senior colleagues.

At the start, both parties were worried about the possibility of violence frustrating their plans. In 1966 there had been a growth of violent heckling, fostered perhaps by television coverage. Since then, in Britain and elsewhere, street violence had increased and, particularly in universities, politicians had been denied a hearing in a manner unknown since before the war. The party managers felt concern not only for the physical safety of the leaders but also for their semblance of authority. The damage done to Sir Alec Douglas-Home's image by the way he was shouted down during the 1964 election was often cited.

In their initial planning the parties approached the problem differently. Mr. Heath was to appear on the home ground of his

[1] Those present usually included Mr. Nicholas, Gwyn Morgan (Assistant General Secretary), Ron Hayward (National Agent), Percy Clark (Press Officer), Doreen Stainforth (Broadcasting), Tom McNally (Acting Research Secretary), David Kingsley, Dennis Lyons, Peter Davies (publicity advisers) and Robert Worcester (polling adviser). Mr. Wedgwood Benn and others occasionally attended.

[2] Those present usually included Gwyn Morgan, Percy Clark and Tom McNally but oddly enough not Ron Hayward, the National Agent. Mr. Healey was normally present and Mr. Callaghan and Mr. Wedgwood Benn attended if they were in London. Mr. Wilson would normally bring with him from his own entourage John Allen and Will Camp (who had taken leave from his job as Director of Information Services at the British Steel Corporation, in order to help and travel with Mr. Wilson). Tom McNally, the head of the International Department, took charge of the Research Department in the absence of Terry Pitt who was selected as the candidate for Lichfield and Tamworth on May 21. Mr. Pitt's absence added to the general confusion and the interdepartmental rivalries at Transport House.

press conference and in ticket-only, question-free meetings. Mr. Wilson was to go out to meet the party workers and the people — but secretly and without advance publicity so as to obviate organised trouble-making.

Gradually it became plain that fears had been exaggerated. The television authorities may have been more cautious in publicising rowdiness — but there was not much to publicise. In the course of the campaign 14 eggs were thrown at Mr. Wilson. Both party leaders experienced mild jostling by demonstrators. But in general the heckling was of the sort that any experienced politician revels in. Mr. Wilson's travels were increasingly announced in advance and he increasingly met with organised but moderate Tory demonstrations. 'You come to see me because your own leader won't come to see you', was Mr. Wilson's most frequent scoring point. Mr. Heath's meetings were opened up more and more; tickets were sent to students and a proportion of places were reserved for passers-by. He too thrived on the heckling and had to stop over-zealous stewards from ejecting the very interrupters who were giving life and zest to his performance. He also 'went walkabout' on a few occasions and by the end of the campaign at last seemed genuinely to be enjoying the experience of mixing with crowds.

To a greater degree than in any post-war election, both parties focused their campaigns on their leaders — the team was very little in evidence. Mr. Heath appeared at his early press conferences alone and acted as his own question master. His speeches at first were against a backdrop not of people but of a portable blue screen. His colleagues attracted little publicity and there was no evidence of any effort to promote the collective leadership of the party.

Outwardly Mr. Wilson was less pre-eminent. Apparently for the first time, the Labour party put out publicity leaflets about 'Labour's winning team' and not just about its leader. Mr. Wilson always had colleagues with him at the press conference and even on three occasions left the whole show to senior colleagues. He talked about the Labour government and often praised Mr. Jenkins and Mr. Callaghan. Nonetheless the Labour campaign centred even more exclusively around him than the Conservatives' did around Mr. Heath. Such tactical decisions, or non-decisions, as were made came from him without much of the infra-structure of staff work that characterised the Conservative efforts. There was a great willingness, even among those who were normally most critical of him, to trust in his campaign expertise and timing and to accept that he was Labour's greatest electioneering asset.

Mr. Heath's advisers were determined that he should not become too exhausted. After his press conference he normally waited till early or mid-afternoon before boarding his Dart aircraft to fly out to his evening engagement (pressmen were charged a total of £175 for the 19 trips). Mr. Wilson relied on British Rail but, although Inter-City trains allowed him to pay momentary visits to a number of marginal seats, he was in fact late several times, unlike Mr. Heath whose plane, in the fine weather, was always punctual.

Mr. George Brown, still the Labour party's Deputy Leader, went on a well reported nationwide speaking tour, neglecting his own marginal seat to address 98 meetings in two weeks. He drew big crowds and sympathetic press coverage, especially in photographs. But he spoke extempore and, though he had many cheerful exchanges with hecklers, his arguments were little quoted — and he made no gaffes. The main impact of his tour must have been local. His aide wrote later:

> [This] 'may well be the last of the old style campaigns in the true market place tradition, the reason being that there are very few politicians who have the almost mystical essential for drawing and holding a crowd. . . . In many, many cases the bantering to and fro between opposition and speaker avoided the issues, prevented reasoned debate and was a very long way from influencing a floating vote. . . . [Yet] the Labour party supporters gained cheer from the verbal battles.'[1]

The Liberal campaign attracted less attention than in the previous three elections, although the party fought on a wider basis than expected. On May 18 it had only 286 prospective candidates. But then Mr. Thorpe announced a sudden windfall of funds to the party.[2] The huge overdraft was paid off and modest subsidies were available to associations which were ready to put forward candidates: the final number — 332 — was a pleasant surprise to those who wanted to fight on a broad front. The opinion polls did not augur badly for the party. The 7%–10% they showed throughout the campaign was as great as in 1964 and 1966. But the party efforts made little splash in the media.

[1] Neil Vann, 'The George Brown Tour', *Labour Organiser*, July/August 1970, pp. 130–2.
[2] See p. 115.

As a leader Mr. Thorpe was perhaps less newsworthy than Mr. Grimond had been, although he fought an energetic campaign. Despite some frustrations due to the local sea-mists, his helicopter forays from North Devon were as extensive as Mr. Grimond's excursions from Orkney and Shetland in 1966. His comments lacked the grand sweep that Mr. Grimond sometimes achieved but they were still pungent and quotable. His general showmanship and his television skill were praised and his press coverage was almost universally sympathetic. The picture of the reasonable man, standing away from the negative battle of the party giants, had an obvious appeal which he exploited gracefully — but to little avail except in North Devon.

The real difference between the Liberal campaign in 1970 and former years was that the other parties took less notice of it. It was assumed that, by and large, the Liberals took votes equally from both sides; there was less angling for Liberal support and less attempt to refute Liberal stands. The Liberal manifesto *What a Life!* drew little reaction from the press or the other parties: even on what used to be its most distinctive policy — self-government for Wales and Scotland — the party's appeal was undercut by the broader nationalist challenge.

But the nationalists, too, made far less impact than had seemed likely even a few months earlier and the London-based press tended to write them off fairly cursorily.[1] As for the rest, the Communists with their 58 candidates got even less coverage than Mr. Donnelly with his four, while the National Front challenges in 10 constituencies and Independents in a hundred or so others were scarcely heard from except in their local press. The tinder-box situation in Northern Ireland did attract considerable attention as reporters waited for Miss Devlin and Mr. Paisley to spark off trouble — but the anticipated Ulster explosion never came.

The contrast between the parties' approaches was most evident in the launching of their manifestos. The Conservatives released *A Better Tomorrow* on Tuesday, May 26, as a well-produced pamphlet. The Selsdon draft of February had been modified and refined in the intervening months, although there were some remaining niggles and some passages which needed polishing when the final version came before the shadow cabinet on May 20. Mr. Heath added a new and more personal foreword:

[1] See pp. 446–62.

> 'Good government is not just a matter of the right policies. It also depends on the way government is run. This is something I have thought about deeply. Indeed it has been one of my main interests since I entered the House of Commons in 1950.
>
> During the last six years we have suffered not only from bad policies, but from a cheap and trivial style of government. Decisions have been dictated by a desire to catch tomorrow's headlines. . . . Government by gimmick has become the order of the day. . . .
>
> I am determined therefore that a Conservative Government shall introduce a new style of government. . . .'[1]

The Labour manifesto had a much more hasty and chaotic birth. The campaign committee had never decided what sort of a manifesto there should be. In the early months of 1970 Peter Shore, the Minister without Portfolio, had been charged with collecting from Ministers lists of departmental achievements and plans for the future. At the same time — but without adequate coordination — Terry Pitt, the Research Officer, had been assembling material for a manifesto. At the May 17 meeting between cabinet and National Executive, it was stressed that the final form of the manifesto was still quite open. To remedy a 1966 grievance, a drafting committee was set up that included representation from the parliamentary party and the cabinet as well as the NEC.[2] This committee met on May 18 and argued lengthily about how far the document should be a record of achievement and how far it should include specific promises for the future. Under the chairmanship of Mr. Shore a sub-committee of three senior Transport House officials — Gwyn Morgan, Terry Pitt and Tom McNally — was asked to produce a working draft. Although some of its members were consulted and sent in comments in writing, the full drafting committee did not meet again until May 26 when there was still a lot of polishing to do and some clear disagreements on substance; one or two of the wrangles were in some degree repeated on May 27 when the NEC met to approve the final document. Mr. Wilson, Mr. Jenkins and the majority of their colleagues were opposed to detailed commitments, while Mr. Brown, Mr. Mikardo, Mr. Pitt and others wanted

[1] The Conservative manifesto was printed in full in the *Guardian* of May 27, 1970. Most of the text was also reproduced in *The Times* and in the *Daily Telegraph*. For a discussion of the genesis of the manifesto see Chapter 3 *passim*.

[2] The Committee had 4 NEC members — Messrs. Brown, Mikardo, Padley and Bradley; 4 cabinet representatives — Messrs. Healey, Ross, Shore and Mellish — 2 with a foot in both camps — Mr. Callaghan and Mr. Benn, with Mr. Houghton from the parliamentary side and Mr. Nicholas from Transport House.

something more specific than the listing of past achievements and generalities about the future. The main argument was over the proposal, first set out in the 1969 *Agenda for a Generation*, for a wealth tax. Those opposed to mentioning so alarming a phrase prevailed although the compromise formula 'we shall ensure . . . that there is a greater contribution to the National Revenue from the rich' was included to pacify those who had fought for some commitment. It was probably inevitable that Mr. Wilson would get so much of his way. At this late stage, party unity was at its highest premium and in the last resort it would have been unthinkable — even to the most ardent left wingers — to impose policies which the party's main standard bearer was unwilling to accept; yet the readiness with which the recalcitrants on the sub-committee and the full NEC submitted was perhaps surprising.[1]

At the end of the afternoon on May 27 the press conference to launch *Now Britain's Strong — Let's make her great to live in* had to be delayed for half an hour while the final version was rolled off. Mr. Barber, the Conservative Chairman, commented:

> 'It's an intriguing side-light on Mr. Wilson's disclosure about planning the election four years ago and deciding on the date five weeks ago that when the moment came to launch his manifesto to the press of the world there wasn't even time to get it printed. Ah, well, that's purposive planning for you.'

Neither manifesto got a very warm reception. Mr. Heath answered journalists' questions rather abruptly, referring them to the document rather than providing quotable summaries of its message; he was teased above all about the manifesto's ambivalence on the much-heralded Value-added Tax. He offered this general defence:

> 'When you read the manifesto you will regard some of [the policies] as rather old friends and you will not find a large number of declarations in the document. . . . We're not going to fall into the trap which the Labour party fell into in 1964 of making commitments about particular changes before . . . the opportunity of discussing them with Whitehall. . . . Then in some cases we can take final decisions. . . . This, I believe, is the only responsible way in which an opposition can set out its policy.'

[1] The Labour manifesto was printed in full in the *Guardian* of May 28, 1970. Most of the text was also reproduced in *The Times* and in the *Daily Telegraph*. See 'Insight', *Sunday Times*, May 31, 1970, for a full, if not infallible, description of the drafting process.

The manifesto's appearance was somewhat blanketed in the mass media by the tribulations of Bobby Moore, the England football captain who had been arrested in Colombia. But in general it was seen as containing little that was new. The key points had been familiar since Selsdon and before, and there was little sign of public response to the 'new style of government' theme.

The Labour manifesto gave even less that was new to report. As Mr. Heath had been teased on the non-commitment to VAT, so Mr. Wilson was teased on the non-appearance of a wealth tax. The emphasis on past achievement as distinct from future promise was widely criticised and there was comment on the proportion and vehemence of its 'Tory-bashing'.

The manifestos and the grilling of the party leaders on BBC *Election Forum* were the main contributions to public electioneering in the run-up to the dissolution on May 29. That evening, Mr. Heath in Bexley and Mr. Wilson in Cardiff started to face the electorate, although the campaign was generally described as opening 'formally' on Monday, June 1, when the routine press conferences began.

These interrogations, first given prominence in the 1959 contest, were dominated by Mr. Heath and Mr. Wilson. At 10 o'clock each morning, in a rented church hall 5 minutes from Smith Square, Mr. Wilson, normally flanked by Mr. Healey, and with Mr. Nicholas the General Secretary acting as chairman, met the national press. In another church hall nearby, the Liberal spokesman, Lord Byers, was waiting at 10.30 to catch the journalists on their way to the 11 a.m. meeting with Mr. Heath at Conservative Headquarters in Smith Square. Transport House had nowhere large enough for the press and even the church hall was cramped. A minor furore was caused when, for reasons of space, overseas journalists were at first excluded from the main Labour press conference and offered a later meeting with Mr. Healey. Their protests, supported by their British colleagues, led to a quick climb-down and a more crowded gathering.

Both Mr. Wilson and Mr. Heath usually opened with a short prepared statement and then for nearly half-an-hour answered questions. At first they issued challenges to the other side. Mr. Heath asked Mr. Wilson four questions on the economy. Mr. Wilson asked Mr. Heath questions about his industrial relations policy. The journalists were on the whole reluctant to act as messengers for such challenges, although there plainly was an occasional planted question, sometimes friendly, sometimes hostile. However, Mr. Wilson did draw some blood with his enquiry about Conservative plans for union contracts. In his early press conferences, Mr. Heath was, as one senior Conservative put it, 'blown off the economic course' by a sustained quibbling about the meaning of 'enforceability'. Mr. Heath seemed rather strained and curt in these meetings, although he did produce one beautifully timed deadpan joke. Asked on June 2 about an egg — the first — that had hit the Prime Minister, he replied,

> 'The implications are really very serious . . . because this was a secret meeting on a secret tour which nobody was supposed to know about, and what it shows is that there are men walking the streets today, also women, with eggs in their pockets, just on the offchance that they'll meet the leader of the Labour party.'

Mr. Wilson counted on his morning press conference to provide the solid fare for the news bulletins during the day, while his afternoon and evening 'walkabouts' in marginal seats would expose him to more voters than he could meet in any other way and would enthuse party workers. As he said in West London on June 1:

> 'There's method in my madness. I want to get to a very large number of key constituencies. I want to meet the party workers. We've got a summer election. It's great to have a summer election. It's going to be a happy fight, an exciting fight. . . . I just want to wish you a happy campaign. . . . I'll allow you ten minutes off your canvassing so you can see me on TV at 10 o'clock tonight. . . . There's nobody here so shameless that he'd come to these committee rooms tonight and not every other night for the rest of the campaign. . . .'[1]

Mrs. Wilson normally accompanied her husband and the family role of Mr. Wilson was quietly underlined to point up his rival's bachelorhood. At first, to the great inconvenience of the press and even the local parties, his plans were kept secret. But, as the walkabout caught the fancy of the mass media and the public and there was little trouble, the secrecy was abandoned and, in due course, Mr. Heath paid him the compliment of imitation. Mr. Heath's decision to mingle with crowds was made about June 5. The change was partly due to Mr. Wilson's success, and partly due to the fact that those planning his tours had overestimated the interview demands of the

[1] Quoted by George Gale in *Evening Standard*, June 2, 1970.

local news media, leaving him with too much spare time between the arrival of his plane in each local centre and the beginning of his advertised meeting.

In practice, Mr. Wilson's morning remarks were seldom carried after the 6 o'clock bulletin and the main picture of him given to the television public was of an amiable man bustling through crowds or skilfully trading insults with hecklers in off-the-cuff speeches. Even when he gave a formal indoor speech, the TV cameras often neglected it. Mr. Heath was much more often seen against the carefully-lit setting of his public meeting, delivering his economic message. With hindsight it is easy to recognise the short-run success of Mr. Wilson's tactics and the cumulative effectiveness of Mr. Heath's. But at the time, perhaps because of the polls, there was no doubt about the verdict of the press. *The Times* correspondent who had followed him, after stressing the apparent snags and hazards of the walkabout approach, summarised the first week: 'My verdict is that the tour has been an unqualified success.' His colleague who had been following Mr. Heath wrote a matching piece which, after paying due tribute to the enthusiasm of the Conservative audiences, concluded, 'Something is missing and one suspects it is missing in Mr. Heath himself.' Other reporters, right to the end of the campaign, echoed these themes ever more forcefully. Whether it was blindness induced by the opinion polls or objective observation, there is no doubt that the general picture emerging from the campaign commentaries was of Mr. Wilson following a brilliant, effective strategy, and of Mr. Heath stumbling along courageously in the face of defeat.

It must be remembered that the election was taking place in the finest June for many years. Over most of the country no rain fell between May 18 and June 18, apart from a few thunderstorms on June 11.[1] The excitement of the World Cup contributed to the

[1] The official meteorological report for June for Oxford would broadly apply to most of the country.

'June was outstandingly warm both above and below ground with above average amounts of sunshine and less rain than normal. Pressure was higher than average giving frequent, and often persistent, haziness. The first week was completely dry, being the end of an 'official' drought of 17 days. After very slight rain on the 8th, the dry and increasingly warm weather lasted until the 11th. Up to this point the daily maxima had scarcely dropped below 70°F and had been in the lower eighties from the 8th. From the 11th to the 12th the maxima dropped 8°F, and fell a further 12°F on the 13th to usher in cooler more changeable weather that lasted to the end of the month. The break in the weather was marked by very heavy rain on the evening of the 11th.'

political summer mood.[1] Mr. Wilson was likened to a reassuring Baldwin, asking for a 'Doctor's Mandate', a man who wanted the electorate to be happy and not to worry, who was trying to reduce the election almost to a non-event. As David Watt remarked: 'The election is a struggle for the voter's peace of mind.' Mr. Heath, in his seemingly desperate position had to be a messenger of bad tidings, trying to awake the public to dangers which he claimed to see but which they did not want to hear about. The difficulty of his task was epitomised in his forlorn cry on June 13:

> 'I have to say to the British people "For heaven's sake, wake up". I want them to recognise what the real issues are, because Labour has pursued a policy of diversion with a bogus story of sham sunshine.'

Yet of course the campaign did have its events and its issues. One of the first disturbances to the general calm was the dispute over doctors' pay. Mr. Crossman, as Secretary of State for Health and Social Security, had wanted to hold up publication of the recommendations of Lord Kindersley's arbitration committee until after the election. The British Medical Association spokesmen protested, with threats of complete or partial withdrawal from the National Health Service; it was agreed on May 27 to publish the report and the government's decision on it on June 4. The government only granted to the more senior doctors half the recommended 30% rise, pending an enquiry by the Prices and Incomes Board. The doctors and the Conservatives cried out against this, as an attack on independent arbitration. Labour strategists argued that the public would have limited sympathy with £7,000 a year doctors, who were getting a pay rise of up to £3,000 a year; but the Conservatives' private polls on both June 3 and June 4 found 60% support for the doctors getting a rise. The issue put both sides in a dilemma. The Conservatives were pledged to check pay rises, especially in the public sector, yet here they seemed, after all their criticism of inflationary wage increases, to be supporting an unparalleled award to a middle-class group. The Labour party were

[1] The World Cup matches began in Mexico on May 31 between the last sixteen countries. England, trying to hold on to the title won in 1966, defeated Rumania 1–0 on June 2, lost to Brazil 1–0 on June 7 and defeated Czechoslovakia 1–0 on June 11, thus getting through to the quarter-final round, facing West Germany on June 14. All these matches were covered live on evening television and filled many columns in the press. An ORC poll found 20% of people, the majority of them Labour supporters, saying that they were more interested in the World Cup than in the election.

basing their campaign on Britain's economic recovery, yet here they were rejecting the decisions of an independent arbitration tribunal which, it had been agreed, could only be done 'very rarely, and for most obviously compelling reasons';[1] the allegation that Mr. Crossman had said to the doctors that the country was 'in extreme economic peril', flatly denied by him, was eagerly seized upon by the Conservatives.

In the first week the Conservatives found three other pieces of ammunition for their central assault on the credibility of Labour's economic claims. On May 30 the idiosyncratic Woodrow Wyatt referred to the need for a compulsory prices and incomes policy in the autumn. More seriously, on June 3 Mr. Callaghan remarked that after the election was over the government would have to give attention to the level of wage increases, and then, under questioning, refused to promise that there would not be a wage-freeze. But the most publicized contribution came in the BBC *Panorama* programme on June 1: Lord Cromer, who had been Governor of the Bank of England from 1961 to 1966, stated that 'there's no question that any government that comes into power is going to find a very much more difficult financial situation than the new government found in 1964'.[2] Lord Cromer's remarks, which he expanded in a *Times* article on June 8, were to come up time and again throughout the campaign and not surprisingly to provoke personal counter-attacks from Labour spokesmen about the judgement he had shown in 1964–66 and about his political partisanship since.

Mr. Heath was slow to seize on Lord Cromer's remarks. At his press conference on June 3 he merely commented that there were big problems ahead. In this failure to exploit fully and immediately what some saw as manna from heaven, signs can be traced of a division in Conservative strategy between those who wanted to portray the economic situation in the very bleakest terms and those who believed that too stark a presentation would be counter-productive. Even when the economic theme seemed to be making little impact most advisers rejected any ideas of switching the

[1] Royal Commission on Doctors and Dentists Remuneration Report, Cmnd. 939/1960.

[2] See p. 214. Lord Cromer's remarks gained extra weight from the fact that Lord Kearton, who was appearing with him as someone not unsympathetic to Labour, seemed to agree with his verdict.

emphasis to other subjects (though one or two voices seem to have been raised for such a course). But there were those who believed that really extreme language was needed to awake the public from its comfortable, hot-weather faith that Labour had at last got the economic situation right; and there were those who worried about seeming to be prophets of gloom and doom, or to be unpatriotically endangering economic confidence. The latter group seem to have prevailed in the initial reaction to the Cromer statement.[1]

At the end of the first week there was little sign that the Conservative campaign was getting across, and Mr. Heath invited the shadow cabinet and other senior advisers to drop in for coffee at Albany on Sunday, June 7. It is plain that they were mutually cheered by the reports from their travels about the country and their own constituencies. It is also plain that they encouraged Mr. Heath to press on still more vigorously with the economic theme. But privately many of them had the darkest forebodings about the outcome.

The Conservative campaign featured, jointly with their broader onslaught on the state of the national economy, a more homely alarm about the cost of living. The price index had made a record jump of 2·1 on May 19 and in his first press conference Mr. Heath referred to the probability, given Labour policies, of a 3*s*. loaf. He later began to reiterate a point first made by Mr. Macleod, that on present trends the 1964 £ would be worth only 10*s*. by 1974. On June 9 he suggested that it was to be a 'shopping basket election' and in the lobby of Conservative Central Office there was a changing

[1] It seems that Brendon Sewill and Tommy Thompson were among the most outspoken advocates of Mr. Heath's becoming a prophet of woe while Geoffrey Tucker and some of Mr. Heath's personal entourage were in favour of fighting 'on the high road'. But, it should be stressed, it would be wrong to paint what was a continuously evolving and quite amicable tactical discussion in too lurid a light. There is also a danger of exaggerating the importance of the Central Office advisers. Mr. Heath was in frequent telephone contact with Mr. Maudling, Mr. Macleod, Mr. Whitelaw, Mr. Barber and other senior colleagues. In so far as his tactical decisions were influenced by the views of others, such senior politicians plainly carried more weight with him than officials in Smith Square. Yet the officials were, of course, in independent touch with the politicians, above all with Mr. Barber, supplying them with poll and other information, and any advice from any quarter must in some degree have been an amalgam of backroom staff-work and politicians' judgements from the field. One who was close to the scene concluded: 'When it was a question of campaign tactics — like whether to go "walkabout" — then Central Office counted. But when it was a real gut question of politics — like how to deal with Enoch —, then it was for the big beasts of the jungle to talk to Ted.' It is plain that the 'big beasts of the jungle' who mattered most were Mr. Maudling, Mr. Macleod, Mr. Whitelaw, Mr. Barber and Sir Alec Douglas-Home.

exhibition showing the latest price rises. The penultimate Conservative television broadcast was given over to exemplifying the tribulations of the housewife.

Labour's main counter to all this was to point to rising prices in other countries and to argue that prices would rise still faster under the Conservatives with their fiscal irresponsibility and their Value-added Tax. Mr. Jenkins on June 2 explained how VAT would mean 20% extra on a vast range of goods and services — fares, fuel, clothing; 'Mr. Heath knows all this. And that is why, despite all this talk about prices, he is so silent about his plan for swingeing tax increases.' Mr. Diamond, the Chief Secretary to the Treasury, went to Bexley on June 9 to deliver an elaborate costing of the Conservative promises. He estimated that their proposals would increase government expenditure in every field but agriculture, by a total of between £750 million and £1,050 million per annum. With a saving of £350 million on agriculture that would mean ninepence on the income tax; and the Conservative agricultural policy would put twenty-one shillings on the average weekly food bill.

Mr. Jenkins, however, reserved himself more for the broad economic position, boasting naturally about the £606 million payments surplus for 1969–70, announced on June 9, and asserting repeatedly that nothing had happened since April to make him change the judgements on which his Budget was based. Mr. Wilson cited Mr. Jenkins' authority for saying that there was no economic reason why he should not have the election in October

'Abominable snowman? — just another Tory scare, Roy — I promise you!'
[*Daily Mail*, June 9, 1970

or June. And on June 9, in what the Conservative private polls rated as one of the very best of all the television broadcasts, Mr. Jenkins epitomised the cautious, responsible, successful image at which the Labour campaign seemed to be aimed.

As in every campaign, there were issues that created one brief ripple and were then largely forgotten. On May 23 Mr. Healey, the Minister of Defence, remarked 'For the next month the 18-year-olds will hear no more of the Tory pledge to send our young men to fight guerrilla wars in the Far East'; to the innuendo that the Conservatives would reintroduce conscription, Sir Alec Douglas-Home on May 25 pointed out that Britain had treaty commitments in the Far East whoever was in power and that, at that moment, troops were exercising in Malaysia on Mr. Healey's orders; there were currently more troops East of Suez than there would be under the Conservative proposals.

On May 31 Mr. Mellish, the newly-appointed Minister of Housing, annoyed his colleagues by promising to turn housing policy upside down and by endorsing a switch to more building of houses for sale. In late May too, after the cancellation of the South African cricket tour, the Conservatives challenged Mr. Wilson to say whether he would also embargo trade with South Africa, as Mr. Hain and other anti-apartheid campaigners were demanding. The law and order theme had a short airing at the same time but received little prominence thereafter. During June attempts were made to raise other issues — education, housing, unemployment — but none received much attention. Some headlines seized on Mr. Wilson's ban of Mr. Stewart's proposed appearance in *Panorama* on June 15 and others on Mr. Wilson's discussion of an invitation to visit Moscow in July, when the Russian Ambassador called at Downing Street on June 13.

On June 13 Mr. Wilson unexpectedly brought the Northern Ireland situation into the campaign, asking where the Conservatives stood on the issue and pointing out how dependent they were on Ulster Unionist votes in a tight parliamentary situation. Would Mr. Heath accept the support of Paisleyites? But the most astonishing thing about the Ulster situation was in fact that so little was heard of it.[1]

[1] However, the million Irish in Britain (the only non-Commonwealth residents to have a vote) undoubtedly felt more involved in the election than for many years past; they were to vote in unprecedented numbers and, it seems, overwhelmingly for Labour. See p. 408.

The most recurrent of the issues that never really received any limelight was the Common Market. In the *Election Forums* of May 26, 27 and 28 all party leaders, in reply to a concerted barrage of questions from the public, took a common line — in essence 'We must look at the terms but we should go in if the terms are right.' All of them on formal constitutional grounds rejected the idea of a referendum on the issue, and Mr. Wilson and Mr. Heath refused even to contemplate a free vote. Mr. Heath in particular had to face further questioning on the free vote issue, since Mr. Macleod in a speech on June 1 had seemed to endorse it. As the campaign wore on he seemed to move his position slightly, saying that any government would take account of parliamentary opinion and adding that back in 1963 he had never thought it practicable to go in unless a majority of the British people wanted it. The subject provoked Mr. Heath to one of his rare citations of the polls.[1] On June 2 he said:

> 'I think it is quite clear from the opinion polls that there is a large majority in favour of going into negotiations'.

Candidates in many areas, particularly rural ones, faced many questions on the Common Market and some made their hostility to it very plain [see p. 440] but it was not made into a general campaign issue except by the Scottish Nationalists and by Mr. Powell.

There is no doubt that the most conspicuous character in the election after Mr. Wilson and Mr. Heath was not Mr. Thorpe or Mr. Jenkins, Mr. Macleod or Mr. Brown, but the wholly unofficial figure of Mr. Powell. On May 30 his election address was published and its call to 'halt immigration now' made headlines in all the Sunday papers. It excited strong reaction from a wide range of Labour and Liberal speakers; Mr. Heath merely observed: 'It does not seem to me that Mr. Powell is saying anything that he has not said before.' The Labour party hierarchy was not keen to stir up the Powell issue but Mr. Wedgwood Benn on June 3 made an extraordinarily violent attack on Mr. Powell:

[1] The polls, as always, presented a dilemma for the party leaders which they, as always, met by a declared policy of not commenting on them, except of course when it suited them. Mr. Wilson at his press conference on June 2 produced this revealing passage:

> 'I never comment on the polls. . . . [One law I have learnt is that] during an election Labour gets a chance of putting its case better, whether in government or in opposition, than in other years. There is another law. Perhaps you can point to the last occasion on which a party won with its leader trailing behind the other leader in personal ratings — particularly if you find he was trailing nearly two-to-one behind the other leader. It is a good law.'

'The flag of racialism which has been hoisted in Wolverhampton is beginning to look like the one that fluttered 25 years ago over Dachau and Belsen.

If we do not speak up now against the filthy and obscene racialist propaganda . . . the forces of hatred will mark up their first success and mobilise for their next offensive.

. . . Enoch Powell has emerged as the real leader of the Conservative Party. He is a far stronger character than Mr. Heath. He speaks his mind; Heath does not.

The final proof of Powell's power is that Heath dare not attack him publicly even when he says things that disgust decent Conservatives.'

Mr. Powell was not eager at this stage to step up his campaign and he restricted his immediate riposte to:

'All that I will say is that in 1939 I voluntarily returned from Australia to this country to serve as a private soldier in the war against Germany and Nazism. I am the same man today.'

But Mr. Powell was headline news from then onwards even though press fire was at first directed towards Mr. Benn for using language as intemperate as that used by Mr. Powell in his famous speech of two years before. Although Transport House (which had seen the speech in advance and distributed it) let it be known that Mr. Benn had spoken out of turn, and that he had incurred Mr. Wilson's displeasure, the Conservatives did not spend much time attacking him. Both sides were anxious about Mr. Powell. The Labour party feared with good reason that he excited some sympathy among their normal supporters, especially in the Midlands. The Conservatives knew that the Powell issue could divide their party down the middle; in both personal and ideological terms, most of the leadership was implacably opposed to him, but among the rank-and-file there were all too many who would say that Mr. Powell was their favourite Conservative.

Mr. Powell had let it be known that he had some major speeches to deliver at the end of the campaign and these were awaited with most apprehension on the Conservative side of Smith Square. On Thursday, June 11, he returned to the immigration theme, attacking those in power for their presentation of the facts.

'Indeed, the figures which have become known in the last year, or year and a half, have in every case proved to be higher than I myself would have guessed. If I have been guilty on this score, it is *under*-statement that has been my offence. On this subject, so vital to their future, the people of this country have been misled, cruelly and persistently, till one begins to wonder if the Foreign Office was the only department of state into which enemies of this country were infiltrated.'

On June 13, in another speech that was not surprisingly stigmatised as McCarthyite, he made an onslaught on the 'enemy within', the small minority who were infiltrating and brainwashing decent people into accepting the collapse of law and order — as exemplified in Ulster and in the cancellation of the South African tour.[1] On June 15 he took up the theme of the Common Market, his onslaught being the one well-publicised speech on the subject heard during the election. On June 16 he made his final appeal to his constituents:

'In saying to you, and through you to the country: "Vote, and vote Tory", I have at least one accidental advantage. It is not such as anyone would go looking for; but having it, I claim the right to use it. I have no personal gain to expect from the outcome, other than that of any other citizen. I am not among those candidates at this election who can look forward with assurance, or at least with hope, to retaining or to achieving political office under the Crown according as the result of the election inclines one way or the other. Whatever might have been obscure or undefined about the policies of the Conservative Party, this at least has been made crystal clear, over and over again by the Leader of the Party, that if there is a Conservative Government after Thursday, I shall not be a member of it. The place to which I ask the electors of Wolverhampton South West to return me is that place, somewhere about the middle of the third bench above the gangway, which I have customarily occupied during more than half my twenty years in Parliament. The most I can hope is to be sitting there again — on one side of the House or the other. Nor have I received in the recent past from men who will form a Conservative Cabinet even the ordinary loyalties and courtesies that prevail generally between colleagues in the same cause. Not for them to repudiate attacks upon me which were unfounded, and which they knew to be unfounded. Nor for them to place my words and arguments the more favourable, or the most obvious, construction, or even to accept my own assertion of my own meaning. Not for them to protest when in the House of Commons language has been used about me, and insults have been cast, the obscenity of which has

[1] A Conservative snap poll on Monday, June 15, found that of the 48% who claimed to have heard or read the Saturday speech almost two-thirds thought Mr. Powell was talking sense in it, although four-fifths of them thought the speech would harm the Conservative party in the election. On June 16 their snap poll found 25% saying that Mr. Powell's speeches, as a whole, would help the party and 43% that they would harm it. But, after the election, when NOP asked people whether Mr. Powell had made them more or less likely to vote Conservative 37% said more and 23% said less. However see pp. 406–8.

lowered the dignity of Parliament itself. . . . [But] . . . On Thursday your vote is about a Britain that, with all its faults and failings, is still free, and great because it is free. On Thursday your vote decides whether that freedom shall survive or not. You dare not entrust it to any government but a Conservative government.'

Mr. Powell declares that his speeches, long planned and prepared, were designed to take the headlines away from Mr. Wilson when he put on the pressure in the last few days of the campaign: he had found in the last few years that he had an extraordinary power of communicating to his fellow countrymen and he was using it in the Conservative cause.

Neither the press nor the Conservative leadership put that construction on his speeches at the time. It was widely said that he had

'But what if this hurts me more than it hurts him?'

[*Daily Telegraph*, June 1, 1970

written off the chances of the Conservatives in the light of the polls and that he was making a crude bid for Mr. Heath's mantle in the holocaust that would follow. If that was his goal, he was setting about it in an odd way and others put a different interpretation on events. 'He is stark staring bonkers,' said Mr. Thorpe on June 15.[1] Certainly the consensus of views, both in press comment and in

[1] An echo, of course, of Mr. Hogg's 1964 characterisation of anyone who voted Labour. See *The British General Election of 1964*, p. 124.

opinion polls, was that Mr. Powell was making things more difficult for the Conservatives.

Mr. Heath had his most difficult press conferences on June 12 and 13. The journalists refused to be interested in any other subject than Enoch. Would Mr. Heath withdraw from Mr. Powell the status of an officially-endorsed Conservative candidate? Mr. Heath stressed the independence of local Conservative Associations and referred back to his earlier statements on Mr. Powell. Relentless pressmen forced him to admit that in 1950 the party had repudiated a candidate in Chorley who had expressed anti-Semitic views, but they did not drive Mr. Heath from his defensive position — plainly anti-Powell but unwilling explicitly to widen the breach. On June 14 Mr. Heath issued a statement

> 'The Conservative Party is the party of one nation. . . . My colleagues in the Shadow Cabinet and I will never use words or support actions which exploit or intensify divisions in our society. . . . The purpose of the next Conservative government will be to safeguard the unity of the nation through honest government and sound policies. That is the central issue and those who divert attention from it at this time do our country no service.'

On June 15 at his press conference he curtly referred to the statement and refused to answer any further questions. To the relief of his advisers, who had argued at length on whether journalists could be thus silenced, the tactic worked. After one further Powell question had been firmly snubbed, the subject was not pursued and the press conference ended before half the normal 30 minutes was over. If this effective assertion of authority by Mr. Heath was, as some argue, one of the factors which gave such a lift to his campaign in the last few days, Mr. Powell may have helped in an unexpected way.

Every election since 1959 has been bedevilled by at least one major strike story. In 1970, when there was increasing industrial militancy and when one of the major Conservative themes was a demand for a radical change in union law, it was inevitable that the government should feel especial anxiety on the subject. Jack Jones, the General Secretary of the TGWU, told a meeting attended by the Prime Minister on May 29 that the employers might foment strikes to embarrass the government during the election. There were indeed allegations of political motives behind the doctors' threatened withdrawal of labour, but there was in fact little exploitation of industrial trouble.[1] It is possible that the unhappy exchanges on the enforceability of contracts in Mr. Heath's first press conferences on June 1 and 2 deterred the Conservatives from developing what they had always regarded as one of their winning themes.

Yet one strike did play a prominent role in the election. After four days of razor-edge negotiations, the London-based press was shut down on June 10. Under Mr. Richard Briginshaw, SOGAT (the Society of Graphical and Allied Trades) demanded an interim wage increase of 25%. The proprietors pointed out that such an increase would cost more than the combined profits of all their papers and that it would lead to leapfrogging demands by the other printing unions. They maintained an unwontedly united front in insisting on a general agreement signed by all the unions concerned. First Mr. Feather of the TUC and then the Prime Minister intervened to find a procedural formula for bringing the two sides together; on June 11, indeed, Mr. Wilson cancelled his walkabouts in London marginals to continue negotiations. The dispute was finally settled on June 13 in time for abridged Sunday papers to come out. But it had meant that on four of the last eight days of the campaign there were no national morning or London evening papers.

The press, ever delicate about what they print on their own industrial disputes, did not exploit the implications of the stoppage and the political parties, too, were cautious in what they said. The Labour party feared that any industrial trouble would rebound on them electorally. Moreover the first day of silence effectively blanketed the triumphant Treasury announcement of a £606 million balance of payments surplus in 1969–70. The Conservatives were at first concerned because, if the polls were right, they needed the press to deploy the economic arguments with which, they believed, opinion could be shifted. However, when the press strike muffled the first of Mr. Powell's outbursts and Mr. Heath's embarrassed reaction, they found some consolation in the absence of newspapers.

[1] No one suggested that politics lay behind the threat of a strike by local government officers, publicly mooted on May 19 and called off only on June 2, even though it could have caused chaos in polling day administration and vote counting. A strike that may have had political consequences was that at Granada Television which meant that from May 26 to June 22 viewers in the North West could see only BBC TV, and that viewers throughout the nation were denied the twice-weekly reassurance of that most popular of all programmes *Coronation Street*.

After the event it is difficult to record how completely the astonishing Labour upsurge in the polls had swept most commentators and politicians off their feet and had had a massive effect on public expectations. Marplan's answers to the question 'which party do you think will win the general election?' summarise the transformation.

| | Con. % | Lab. % | Don't Know % | Majority believing Con. would win % |
|---|---|---|---|---|
| Jan. . . . | 57 | 27 | 16 | 30 |
| April . . | 47 | 36 | 17 | 11 |
| Mid-May . . | 21 | 64 | 15 | −33 |
| Mid-June . . | 14 | 67 | 19 | −53 |

But these poll findings do not do full justice to the change in expectation over the final month. Ladbrokes betting odds, advertised in the national press, moved from 13 to 8 on Labour and 11 to 10 against the Conservatives on June 1, to 12 to 1 on Labour and 6 to 1 against the Conservatives on June 15. At one moment the odds on Labour reached 20 to 1 and the bookmakers for a while refused to accept any more money.

In the day-to-day press comment the assumption of a Labour victory became more and more overwhelming. The Conservatives had gone into the election behind on every opinion poll, and apart from a slight check on Sunday May 31, the message of the polls became progressively worse for them until the very last days of the campaign. They could protest that reports from the constituencies were excellent and in flat conflict with the poll findings, but such assertions, although they may have comforted the faithful, convinced no one else. As the election advanced, one leading commentator after another wrote off the Conservatives' chances.[1]

> 'Both party leaders are now recognising that only a bolt from the blue . . . can save Harold Wilson from becoming the first Prime Minister in British history to win three general elections in a row.'
>
> Nora Beloff, *Observer*, June 7.

> 'Short of a miraculous turn-around in public opinion Mr. Wilson is headed straight back towards 10 Downing Street, probably with an increased majority.'
>
> Ronald Butt, *Sunday Times*, June 14.

[1] In presenting this catalogue the authors do not seek to embarrass unwary prophets (we could not claim to have been any wiser at the time) but only to chronicle how universal and publicised were the expectations of a Labour victory.

'It will be no surprise to anyone to learn that I think [Labour will win] by a majority of 40 or 50 seats.'

David Watt, *Financial Times*, June 15.

'What will become of the Tories after a third successive poll defeat? Why is the Labour party winning with such apparent ease?'

Peter Jenkins, *Guardian*, June 15.

'It is too late [for the Conservatives] to recover lost ground.'

David Wood, *The Times*, June 15.

'Unlike the O.R.C., I am registered as a "Do Know". The Tories will have some gains but, as I have kept saying, Labour will certainly win.'

Robert Carvel, *Evening Standard*, June 18.

Although the Conservatives kept a resolutely optimistic face to the world and gave no outward evidence of any crack in morale, politicians of the other parties voiced conclusions similar to the commentators. Mr. Wilson was speculating on June 14 whether he should have spent more time on seats Labour might gain rather than on those it was defending, and Mr. Thorpe commented on June 13: 'It is now clear nationally that Labour is romping home.' Yet at this very moment the situation was changing.

On Sunday, June 14, England was knocked out of the World Cup by Germany, after leading 2-0 at half-time. On Monday there was a slight break in the flaming June sunshine that had dominated the campaign; the weather continued good but the change, like the World Cup defeat, may have contributed to a switch in mood.[1] On Monday, too, Mr. Heath had his successful press conference and managed a generally acclaimed final appeal on television. But, above all, on Monday the monthly trade figures were announced, showing, after very good returns for nine months, a £31 million deficit for May. Mr. Heath immediately issued a statement.

'Today's trade figures are a warning even when special factors are taken into account. . . . It is becoming increasingly clear that we are over the best.'

Mr. Wilson countered by pointing to the fact that the £31 million included the exceptional purchase of two Jumbo-jets costing £18 million, and teased Mr. Heath with making, in his desperation, a jumbo-sized scare out of it.[2]

[1] The football-minded Mr. Wilson did not discount this misfortune but put on a brave face when challenged. 'I am not aware that any of my Cabinet colleagues were in the British team.'

[2] See p. 347 n. for an odd twist to these figures.

On the morning of June 16, the Conservative strategists found in their private polls not just that Mr. Heath's final broadcast had been very well received but also that there had been a continuing shift in attitudes on the economic situation.[1]

Two questions held the key:

'The Conservatives say that another economic crisis is coming, Labour say it is not. Who do you believe?'

| | 8 June | 11 June | 15 June | 16 June | (17 June) |
|---|---|---|---|---|---|
| Conservative | 44 | 48 | 50 | 49 | (44) |
| Labour | 35 | 32 | 28 | 25 | (31) |
| Neither/DK | 21 | 20 | 22 | 26 | (25) |

'If there is an economic crisis which would you want to handle it, a Labour government or a Conservative government?'

| | 8 June | 11 June | 16 June | (17 June) |
|---|---|---|---|---|
| A Labour government | 44 | 43 | 41 | (40) |
| A Conservative government | 39 | 43 | 45 | (49) |
| Same/DK | 17 | 14 | 14 | (11) |

Here, it seemed, was clear evidence that the Conservative central theme was getting across and, even if by the next day the sense of imminent crisis had abated, confidence in the Conservatives' economic competence continued to grow.

A further development of the economic issue came on June 16, which may have been for the Conservatives (like Mr. Wilson's 1964 indiscretion on the Hardy Spicer strike)[2] a snick through the slips that went to the boundary. A detailed economic brief had been handed out as a statement at the end of Mr. Heath's press conference: on its fourth page the argument mentioned in passing that, if policies of the sort Labour were following were pursued without check for some years, the country might be forced into another devaluation. This brief had been prepared as an answer to those who said that the inner logic and professional expertise behind the Conservative economic case was not getting across to the elite audience which alone could understand it. Since the brief was too technical for a speech or even as press conference material, it was rather casually handed out to the press at the end of the June

[1] The Conservatives took the unprecedented step of releasing their private poll findings to the press (see the back page of the *Daily Telegraph*, June 17, 1970) although they attracted little notice. Only their economic findings were released. The Conservatives did not reveal that the same poll had indicated that Mr. Powell was hurting the Conservatives (see p. 161).

[2] See *The British General Election of 1964*, p. 116.

16 briefing and only slowly exploited as the successive editions of the evening papers appeared.

Mr. Wilson jumped into the attack, suggesting that in their final panic the Conservatives were unpatriotically launching a run on the pound. The following day, while Mr. Wilson was in Lancashire, Mr. Callaghan took the Labour press conference in order to refute the 'devaluation smear'. Since it was Mr. Callaghan who had presided over devaluation in 1967, this was presumably likely to evoke in voters' minds that blackest moment in Labour's six years. Nothing in the way the Conservatives launched their off-hand reference to the possibilities of another devaluation could suggest that it was a deliberate scare, and it is in fact unquestionable that the initial reaction of the Conservative hierarchy to the furore was one of dismay. But it was handled in a way that can only have reinforced the anxieties that some of the electorate felt about the solidarity of the economic recovery on which Labour's campaign was so firmly based.

Other illustrations of the economic argument came up in the last week. The Conservatives made much of the high unemployment figures due to be published on polling day: the reference in the 6 p.m. news bulletins to the 'record number of jobless' could hardly have encouraged people to go out and vote Labour that evening. Labour could cite the trifling change in the price index announced on June 16. But it would be wrong to stress them or even the balance of payments figures to the exclusion of all else. The final appeals of the party leaders on television on June 15 and 16 may have reached more voters than the economic news. Mr. Heath's brief, personal, earnest, almost non-partisan, appeal won general applause. He referred to the man in Australia who had said, 'Everyone knows that tomorrow will be better than today.'

> 'Nobody in this country would say that. Not these days. And yet why not? . . . We may be a small island. We're not a small people. . . . For the last six years the Government of this country . . . have let us be treated as second rate. They even plan for us to stay second rate. Because that's what Labour policies mean. . . . Now I don't intend to stand by and see this happen. . . . Do you want a better tomorrow? . . . That's what I will work for with all my strength and with all my heart. I give you my word and I will keep my word.'

Mr. Wilson, for all his skill before the camera, seems to have been less successful. Even before polling day there was some dismayed comment at the complacency, at the negative Tory-bashing and at the absence of a sense of vision about the future.

> 'People everywhere . . . realise that no Prime Minister in this century has fought an election against such a background of economic strength as we have got today. The Conservatives thought they could win this election by giving the impression of sweeping, wide-ranging cuts in taxation while at the same time holding out promise after promise to spend more on everything they thought would gain them votes. . . . Their whole campaign is based on exploiting rising prices but everyone knows that the cost of living in Britain is lower than in any country in Europe or North America. . . . Conservative policies are deliberately designed to raise prices. . . . The socialism I believe in means above all using all our resources for making Britain a better place to live in. . . . A great country, tolerant and compassionate . . . admired and respected throughout the world because it combines stability with change. . . .'[1]

Yet as so often in the campaign it was the opinion polls rather than the party leaders or the economy that dominated the reporting in the last week. On Sunday the papers, appearing for the first time after the press strike, were much more under the influence of the 12·4% lead released by NOP late on Friday than of the 2½% lead reported by Gallup in the *Sunday Telegraph*. The *Sunday Times* and *Observer*, averaging all of the polls, yielded leads of 6·4% and 7·3% respectively, pointing to a 100-seat Labour majority. The whole tone of press comment then and up to polling day took for granted a Labour victory. But, with a 2½% Gallup lead, that was certainly not a forgone conclusion. On the Wednesday before the poll, Marplan in *The Times* reported what, on a basis comparable to the other polls, was a 9·6% Labour lead and this too seems to have had more influence than the Harris 2% lead reported in the *Express*. When Gallup, which until the Wednesday had offered the only Conservative comfort, reverted on polling day to a 7% lead all seemed to be over. NOP with 4·1% lead seemed to confirm that Labour was comfortably enough ahead. In all the press comment up to the morning of polling day, there can in retrospect be traced no hint of what was to come. It is true that the betting odds on a Labour victory dropped slightly, but only in the inner reaches of the Conservative party was there some real revival of spirits, fortified by the Harris poll and by the fact that the headlines seemed really to be putting over their economic case; and, at the very last

[1] For the snap reactions to these final appeals see p. 194 and p. 224.

gasp, there was also ORC's public prediction in Thursday evening's papers of a 1% Conservative lead. Yet it does seem probable that Mr. Heath was almost the only leading Conservative who, in private as well as in public, behaved as though he was unfalteringly convinced that his party was going to win.

CHAPTER VIII

# PUBLIC POLLS AND PRIVATE POLLS

THE public opinion polls had already claimed a major role in any account of the 1970 election even before they got the answer wrong. As the number of regularly published polls had increased in the later 1960s, so had the attention accorded them; their influence permeated all reports about the party battle. During the 1970 campaign there were in fact five national polls — and two of them were producing two sets of national findings. Although this number was not much more than during the 1966 campaign the impact was enormously enhanced because exclusive publication was abandoned. Gone were the attempts to prevent plagiarisation by rival journals or by the broadcasters; no paper held up its findings to its later editions or sent letters invoking the copyright laws. As each poll emerged it was reported in the news bulletins[1] and in the national papers — even in ones which were simultaneously publishing a poll of their own with a different answer. Poll stories dominated campaign reporting; in the extreme case, eight of the 23 issues of *The Times* published between May 18 and June 18 referred to them in their main fiont page headlines. In an election marked by few major events and few colourful incidents or phrases, these reports on the latest racing form had an especial appeal to the newsmakers.

One reason why the polls had such interest was because of the dramatic story they had told over the past few years — a story endorsed by local and by-election results. Labour had slumped from a 20% lead in May 1966 to a deficit of over 20% in May 1968 and, after an autumn recovery, to a similar abyss in the summer of 1969. Labour's autumn recovery in 1969, though more sustained than the previous year, had not lasted long and the party entered 1970 10% or so behind in voting intention. It was not

[1] The Harris Poll found in September that out of the 62% of the electorate who claimed to remember seeing polls during the campaign, 71% said that they had seen them on television; among the newspapers publishing polls the *Daily Express* (27%) and the *Daily Mail* (15%) were mentioned most often in accordance with their circulation level. But even in aggregate the press as a whole did not reach the level of television as a source of information to the electorate on polling figures.

until April that any opinion polls showed Labour ahead, but by the middle of May all were agreed in doing so. Some would see evidence of the power of the polls in Gallup's finding of a reversal from a 54% to 27% belief in a Conservative as against a Labour victory in March to a 56% to 26% belief in a Labour victory in May.[1] Although the county elections in April had shown a marked improvement for Labour and the municipal elections in May had been much more obviously encouraging, the polls can probably claim credit for Labour entering the election as strong favourites.

The 1966 election had in fact been one of the least successful for election forecasting. Throughout the campaign Labour was given a larger lead than it finally achieved and, though the final forecasts were less extreme, all the four national polls over-estimated Labour's lead (three by from 0·8% to 3·7% and the *Daily Express* by 9·9%), though all did agree that Labour would have a comfortable win. Two of the polls involved in the 1966 election were missing in 1970. The *Observer* no longer employed Dr. Mark Abrams and Research Services to do election forecasting; and the *Daily Express*'s own internal poll, often taken less than seriously (even by the paper itself), was finally allowed to lapse. But three new polls were on the national scene. The Opinion Research Centre started in 1967 a regular monthly political poll, syndicated in the *Evening Standard* and twenty or so provincial evening papers. In 1968 *The Times* arranged for Marplan, long established in market research, to provide a quarterly political survey. In 1969 the *Daily Express* asked Louis Harris, a very well-known American pollster, to set up, in conjunction with ORC, a new and independent poll. So, from September 1969 four different polls, Gallup, NOP, ORC, and Harris each reported on the nation's mood at least once a month, with Marplan supplying a quarterly analysis. In addition ORC provided *ad hoc* special surveys for the *Sunday Times*.

Over the period from 1966 the polls were broadly in agreement in their findings. On several occasions a gap of as much as 10% appeared in their estimates of the party lead but in most cases that could plausibly be explained by the inevitable variations due to sampling reinforced by movements of opinion between the dates at which the interviews were taken. Over the long run no poll

[1] In every election since 1950 the polls had found that the majority of the public expected victory for the side that did in fact win.

was systematically more or less favourable to either party.[1] NOP, Harris and Marplan used larger samples and the more academically approved random method of selecting respondents (drawing names from the electoral register), but their findings were not

*Nationwide Public Opinion Polls, 1970*

| | | Founded | First regular poll | Director | Normal sample |
|---|---|---|---|---|---|
| Gallup | *Daily Telegraph* | 1937 | 1938 | Geoffrey Faulder | 1000 quota (GB) |
| NOP | *Daily Mail* | 1957 | 1957 | Frank Teer | 2000 random (GB) |
| ORC | *Evening Standard* and others | 1965 | 1967 | Humphrey Taylor | 1000 quota (GB) |
| Marplan | *The Times* | 1959 | 1968 | Derek Radford | 1500 random (UK) |
| Harris | *Daily Express* | 1969 | 1969 | Peter Bartram | 2500 random (GB) |

significantly more stable or nearer the average than those of Gallup and ORC which followed the quicker and cheaper quota method (telling interviewers to choose an appropriate number of old and young, rich and poor, men and women).

But public opinion was behaving in new ways. Over the previous twenty years the electorate had shown itself extraordinarily stable in its voting intentions. 1946 and 1958 were the only two years between 1945 and 1965 during which the gap between the highest and the lowest party lead recorded in Gallup's monthly readings exceeded 10%. But in every year from 1965 onwards the difference between the highest and lowest figure was much greater.

*Variations in Conservative lead 1965–70 (Gallup)*

| | 1965 % | 1966 % | 1967 % | 1968 % | 1969 % | 1970 Jan–May % |
|---|---|---|---|---|---|---|
| Highest Con. lead | 9 | 2½ | 16 | 24 | 21 | 9 |
| Lowest Con. lead | −6½ | −15½ | −11 | 5½ | 3½ | −7 |
| Range | 15½ | 18 | 17 | 18½ | 17½ | 16 |

[1] There was, however, a disquieting period in 1966–67 when in all but one of the monthly readings NOP found a result more favourable to Labour than Gallup (in exact contrast to the situation in the last year of the Conservative government when NOP findings were more favourable to the Conservatives). In the latter half of 1966 NOP on average gave Labour on average a 10% greater lead than Gallup. But in the following years this systematic discrepancy gradually disappeared.

These fluctuations reflected a desertion of Labour more than an access of strength to the Conservatives. There was a lot of Labour switching to 'Don't know' or to minor parties and there was no great constancy about most of the converts to Conservative. Unpublished Conservative studies suggested that cross-switching was larger in volume and frequency than ever before. But it was not only the volatility that stood out in this period; it was also the extent to which the government fell behind. Of the thirteen years of Conservative rule there were only four in which the monthly Gallup figures ever showed the opposition as much as 10% ahead. The only time that the lead exceeded 13% was in 3 months in 1963 when the peak touched 15½%. But in the 20 months from December 1967 to July 1969 the Conservative lead only dropped below 15% in 3 months and was over 20% in 9 months and over 25% in two.

Moreover, there were signs that even when they were furthest ahead the Conservatives did not command great public confidence. As we show on p. 346, even at times when a comfortable majority were saying they would vote Conservative, there were still more people describing themselves as basically Labour. Mr. Heath's popularity ratings, apart from slight booms during the Annual Conference seasons, stayed obstinately low, and the Conservative party as a whole fared poorly in response to some questions. The contrast with 1963 is striking. When Labour was 10% ahead in voting intention in March 1964, 64% were satisfied with Mr. Wilson as Leader of the Opposition. In May 1968 when the Conservatives were 28% ahead in voting intention, only 31% were satisfied with Mr. Heath.

In a situation when the party leaders and the party performance of both government and opposition commanded such little enthusiasm and voters were switching support so casually, the pollsters should perhaps have been worried: the more volatile the electorate the greater their difficulty. Hot votes, like hot money, can vanish as easily as they come. But no one seems to have recognised that predicting the 1970 result might therefore pose new and difficult challenges. Relying on past success the pollsters faced the election with confidence.

Indeed the only questioning of the polls in this period was a tribute to their power if not their accuracy. The Speaker's Conference on Electoral Law in its report in June 1967 recommended that the publication of polls should be banned for 72 hours before polling day.[1] This proposal, which was not based on any evidence or research into 'bandwagon' or other effects of polls, received a hostile press reception. No sympathy was expressed for it from either front bench when most of the other points advocated by the Speaker's Conference were enacted in the Representation of the People Act of 1969.

Almost all the problems of public opinion polling that the 1970 election was to highlight were already in evidence during the 1966 parliament. To the public, which sometimes seemed unduly sceptical but more often unduly credulous, the poll findings were presented in an over-simplified form. Although the sample size and interview method were usually mentioned in press reports, it was often impossible for the reader to discover the number of 'don't knows', let alone refusals. The dates between which the interviews were taken were given only intermittently. It was seldom that any breakdown was offered of the findings by region, class, age or sex. The focus was overwhelmingly on voting intentions and upon ratings of leaders to the exclusion of opinions on issues. Most serious of all, the reports almost never referred to the possibility of sampling error. Headlines were often based on statistically insignificant changes of percentages.[2] Moreover, while newspapers certainly never interfered with the statistics supplied by the pollsters, there are grounds for supposing that the prominence and headlines given to the poll stories in some papers were at times affected by the degree to which the findings were congenial to the paper's editorial line.[3]

At the outset of the 1970 campaign the pollsters, conscious of their vulnerability, drew together despite some past quarrels; they exchanged friendly phone calls about their findings and even their working methods. On May 22, 1970, they announced a collective agreement:

[1] Cmnd. 3275.

[2] With irreproachably selected samples of one thousand, in a population divided 55–45 between two parties, the lead of the majority party recorded in successive surveys will vary by over 3% on at least one occasion out of two even if opinion is in fact totally static. See the *Sunday Times* of June 8, 1970, in which Ron Hall produced an elaborate discussion of the likelihood of sampling error.

[3] It should be stressed that NOP and Gallup provide much extra information to interested subscribers in regular monthly bulletins. Moreover they and all the other polling organisations have shown themselves very ready to supply fuller information, both technical and substantive, to outside enquirers.

> 'We recognise that the standards, techniques and presentation of opinion polls are matters of legitimate public concern. We believe it is in the public interest that the methods used by the polls should be open to public scrutiny.'

A four-point code of practice followed: (1) every poll report should mention sample size, method and timing; (2) sharp changes in 'don't knows' should always be recorded; (3) details of survey design and execution should be made available on demand; and (4) unpublished findings should be available to other media. The pollsters themselves were often irked by the difficulty of controlling the way their client newspapers presented their findings, above all in their headlines.

The attitudes of the newspaper industry towards polls had changed over the years. From circulation-building exclusive features to draw in readers, polls had developed into prestige possessions. Apart from the tabloids, the *Guardian* was the only national daily paper without its own poll. The findings of the polls were released early to the other papers and still more to the broadcasters as a form of advertising. This new logic was partly inspired by the higher cost of polls. A national quota sample of 1,000 interviews must cost a newspaper £1,000 and a national random sample of 2,500 at least £3,500. For perhaps 20 column inches of copy that is, by any newspaper standards, an expensive story. But by any advertising standards, it is by no means excessive for perhaps 20 mentions of the paper's name, on television and in rival papers.

The cost of polls may explain why there were fewer local ones than in 1966 or 1964. NOP and Harris carried out none on a constituency basis and Gallup and ORC only one each. ORC came close to the result in Oxford although the sample was described as too small to justify a forecast, and Gallup was only 0·6% out on the party lead in Orpington (though with 3·3% average error in the party estimates). Marplan conducted four surveys in the Midlands which gave the Conservatives great hopes of a local breakthrough; in practice, although very close to the result in two divergent Birmingham seats (All Saints and Perry Barr), Marplan overestimated the Conservative lead by 12½% in Dudley and 13% in Oldbury and Halesowen. Over the four surveys the average *over*estimate of the Conservative lead was 6% — a remarkable contrast to every other local or national polling effort. The Westminster Press group, using local reporters, sponsored polls in six widely scattered marginals; it got five results right, being within 3% of the actual lead in each of them, but in Brighton, Kemptown there was a 9% gap between forecast and reality: and the six surveys together, on average, underestimated the Conservative lead by 2%.

NOP fared less well in its attempts to disaggregate regional trends from its national findings. It reported very divergent trends in London and the South East in successive weeks and it consistently suggested a massive swing to Labour in Scotland which never materialised. Gallup conducted special surveys in 50 of the 100 most marginal Labour seats: the findings were in some contrast to the trends in their nationwide poll and because the sample was smaller they were given less prominence.[1] On June 18 Harris reported a special survey in marginals which cut 5% off the Labour lead its national survey was showing.

When the election was announced all the polls were not only showing Labour ahead but they were all showing a continuing trend away from the Conservatives which, unchecked, would yield a fantastic landslide on June 18. For one moment, at the start of the campaign, the polls offered sudden hope for the Conservatives. On Sunday May 31, a special *Sunday Times* quick poll showed a 2% Tory lead while Gallup in the *Sunday Telegraph* cut Labour's lead from 7% to 5½%. But it proved a false dawn. In all the other polls the pro-Labour trend continued to the last week. On Saturday June 13, NOP released the most startling figures of the election — a 12·4% Labour lead. The crushing effect that this could have had on Conservative morale was damped down, first by the absence of Saturday papers, and then by Gallup's finding next day of a Labour lead of only 2½%. If the polls could differ that much, many concluded, they could not be very trustworthy. In a wider context the episode showed how the sports of sampling could have a massive effect on morale. Obviously both the NOP and Gallup samples were freakishly out of line with their own time series of polls. If these chance deviations had not occurred or if one of them had been in the opposite direction, the way in which the party strategists and the commentators interpreted the campaign during the last few days might have been very different. But this was only a forerunner of more divergent

[1] See p. 179.

readings. On the eve of poll Marplan with an 8·7% lead (9·6% in GB) and Harris with 2% offered very conflicting messages. On voting day Gallup's 2½% Labour lead was raised to 7% and NOPs 12·4% Labour lead was cut to 4·1%. NOP's final poll was based, as in 1964 and 1966, on re-interviews with some of earlier samples to check on change. However, being convinced that there was something odd about their previous June survey (the 12·4% Labour lead) they excluded it from consideration and chose their

*Election polls*

| | Date of publication | Con. % | Lab. % | Lib. % | Other % | Labour lead % | Don't know (when published) % | Sample size |
|---|---|---|---|---|---|---|---|---|
| Gallup | May 21 | 42½ | 49½ | 6½ | 1½ | 7 | (11½) | |
| | 31 | 44½ | 50 | 4½ | 1 | 5½ | (8½) | 2,571 |
| | June 7 | 44 | 49½ | 5 | 1½ | 5½ | (7) | 2,312 |
| | 14 | 45½ | 48 | 5½ | 1 | 2½ | (9) | 2,336 |
| | 18 | 42 | 49 | 7½ | 1½ | 7 | (8) | 2,190 |
| Harris | May 20 | 46 | 48 | 6 | | 2 | | 2,559 |
| | June 3 | 43 | 48 | 7 | 2 | 5 | | 2,723 |
| | 12 | 42 | 49 | 8 | 1 | 7 | | |
| | 17 | 45 | 46 | 7 | 1 | 2 | | 2,661 |
| | 18 | 46 | 48 | 5 | 1 | 2 | | |
| Marplan | May 19 | 44·5 | 47·2 | 6·6 | 1·7 | 2·7 | (3·9) | 1,613 |
| | June 6 | 44·4 | 48·1 | 6·2 | 1·3 | 3·7 | | 1,480 |
| | 17 | 41·5 | 50·2 | 7·0 | 1·3 | 8·7 | (9·3) | 2,267 |
| NOP | May 14 | 44·4 | 47·6 | 6·7 | 1·3 | 3·2 | (8·2) | 2,054 |
| | 29 | 44·8 | 48·0 | 5·9 | 1·3 | 3·2 | | 2,511 |
| | June 4 | 44·0 | 49·5 | 4·8 | 1·3 | 5·1 | (9·4) | 2,487 |
| | 12 | 39·2 | 51·6 | 7·9 | 1·3 | 12·4 | (9·4) | 2,373 |
| | 18 | 44·0 | 48·1 | 6·4 | 1·3 | 4·1 | | 1,562 (re-interview) |
| ORC (*Evening Standard*) | May 21 | 44½ | 45½ | 7 | 3 | 1 | (9) | 1,090 |
| | 28 | 43 | 45 | 10 | 2 | 2 | | 1,047 |
| | June 4 | 43 | 47½ | 8 | 1½ | 4½ | | 1,083 |
| | 11 | 42 | 49 | 8 | 1 | 7 | | 965 |
| | 18 | 48½ | 45½ | 6½ | 1½ | −1 | | 1,583 + 257 |
| ORC (*Sunday Times*) | 31 | 47 | 45 | 5 | 1 | −2 | (10) | 1,640 |
| | 7 | 45 | 47 | 7 | 1 | 2 | (9) | 1,726 |

Special Gallup Poll surveys in (30) marginal seats (sample size just under 1,000) were reported on four occasions. These indicated on a basis comparable to the figures above the following Labour leads

| June 1 | 8 | 15 | 18 |
|---|---|---|---|
| 1% | 6½% | 10½% | 5½% |

*Average of previous week's polls (weighted by sample size)*

| | May 31 | June 7 | June 14 |
|---|---|---|---|
| *Observer* | 2·6 | 4·5 | 7·3 |
| *Sunday Times* | 3·5 | 4·1 | 6·4 |

re-interviews from their May 29 and June 4 polls only. NOP, Gallup and Marplan made no attempt to allow for differential turnout (although their surveys had found that Conservatives felt more certain that they would in fact go and vote) nor did they allow in their final forecasts for the continuance over the last few days of any trends they detected. Harris and ORC offered more complex predictions which they meticulously explained.

The Harris Poll, by merging a 4% Labour lead in its final national re-interview survey with a 1% Conservative lead in a special survey of marginals, found a 3% Labour lead; then, making allowance for differential turnout, it settled on a 2% overall forecast. ORC found a 4½% lead in its final national survey: but a late re-interview survey of 257 voters found clear evidence of last minute switching to Conservative and on this basis ORC concluded that the parties were level-pegging; however in view of the fact that Conservatives seemed more likely to turnout to vote, it decided on a 1% Conservative lead as its forecast.[1]

Thus it was plain, even before the votes were counted, that some pollster would be humbled. The range between a 9·6% Labour lead and a 1% Conservative lead could hardly be bridged; only if the result fell just midway between these extremes could all the polls claim that their forecast was within the normal sampling error. How the polls diverged from their early June con-

*Final Forecasts*

| | ORC % | Harris % | NOP % | Gallup % | Marplan (UK) % | Average of the 5 polls % | Actual result (GB) % |
|---|---|---|---|---|---|---|---|
| Conservative | 46½ | 46 | 44·0 | 42 | 41·5 | 44·0 | 46·2 |
| Labour | 45½ | 48 | 48·1 | 49 | 50·2 | 48·2 | 43·8 |
| Liberal | 6½ | 5 | 6·4 | 7½ | 7·0 | 6·7 | 7·6 |
| | 1½ | 1 | 1·3 | 1½ | 1·3 | 1·3 | 2·4 |
| Labour lead | −1 | 2 | 4·1 | 7 | 8·7 (9·6 GB) | 4·3 | −2·4 |
| Average error on 3 main parties share | 1·0 | 2·3 | 2·6 | 3·2 | 3·9 | 2·6 | — |
| Error on lead | 1·4 | 4·4 | 6·5 | 9·4 | 12·0 | 7·1 | — |

[1] The numbers involved were very small but since only 1 voter out of the 257 re-interviewed by ORC had switched from Conservative to Labour while 14 had switched from Labour to Conservative it seemed legitimate to deduce that a real tide was flowing in one direction. It is an ironic commentary on polls that if it had not been a final forecast and ORC had been following its normal routines, its headline on June 18 would have been 4½% Labour lead not 1% Conservative lead.

sensus in the last ten days of the campaign is shown by the chart on the opposite page.

In fact, of course, even the ORC forecast fell short of the actual Conservative lead in Great Britain by 1·4%.[1] What went wrong? To suggest dishonesty or conspiracy by the pollsters is absurd to anyone who knows the men themselves; moreover, apart from their own integrity, their commercial self-interest lay overwhelmingly in getting the answer right. There is no doubt that they exercised a high degree of care and professionalism in their work; this abrupt break in their record of accuracy came as a bolt from the blue.

A number of explanations are possible.

*Interviewing bias.* It is possible that some new element had entered the national scene or the techniques of polling which led polls consistently to exaggerate Labour strength. In the early days of their trade some pollsters found themselves regularly over-estimating the strength of the more middle-class parties — Republicans and Conservatives. (Certainly the error was in this direction in Gallup's first four predictions of US Presidential elections and also with their first four predictions of British general elections.) But the pollsters were aware of the problem and took steps to correct for this bias. It has not been in evidence over the last decade. Indeed in three out of the last four general elections in Britain (1955, 1959 and 1966) the pollsters' errors have been in Labour's favour. It is just possible that there has been over-correction.

Mark Abrams, a very experienced pollster, suggested that[2] the unprecedented publicity given to the polls and to the Labour lead could have affected interviewers in their style of interviewing as well as in their selection of respondents (in quota samples) and their call-back efforts (in random samples). The pollsters we have consulted can find no evidence for any such tendency. It is not easy to disprove interviewer bias; however if respondents selected were unrepresentative this should have become evident when their characteristics were tabulated and analysed.

*Sampling misfortunes.* It is theoretically possible for a sample

[1] It should be stressed that ORC's forecast was well within the margin of error that even the most sanguine of pollsters could set themselves. Only 6 of the 23 national forecasts made by British polls since 1945 come as close. But even Harris, the next best 1970 forecast, was more in error than Gallup or NOP had ever been in previous years.

[2] *Public Opinion Quarterly*, Fall 1970–1, pp. 317–24.

*Party leads in opinion polls, May–June 1970*

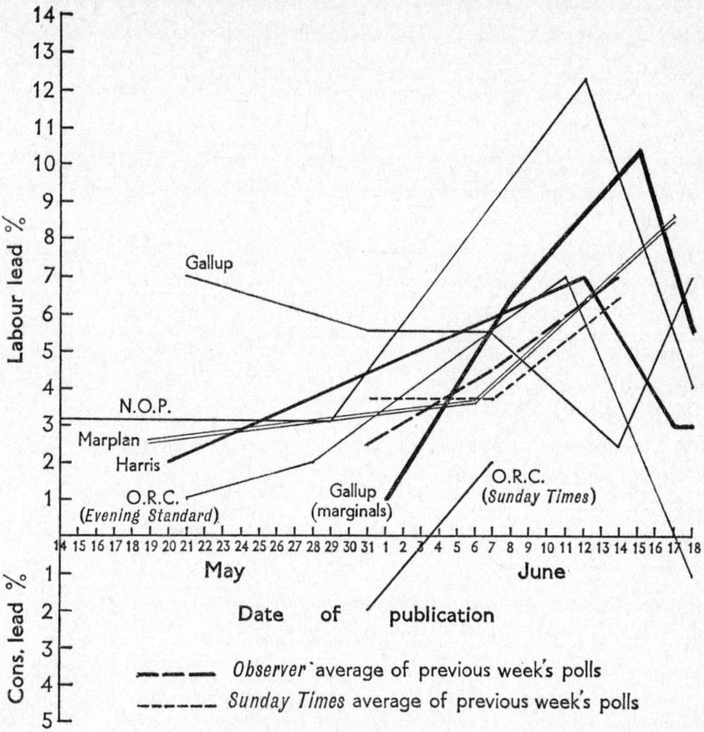


survey in an evenly balanced election to find 1,000 Labour supporters and not one Conservative. But with a poll every day for a million years, the chances against that happening, even once, are billions to one against. It is however quite likely that a single poll will, for sampling reasons alone, be 3% out in its estimate of each major party's strength and therefore 6% out in its estimate of the party lead. It is also conceivable that all of five polls will, through the chances of sampling, err simultaneously in the same direction — that is no more unlikely than five tossed pennies all coming down 'heads' (i.e. a 1 in 32 possibility). But the odds against them all having substantial errors in the same direction become fairly astronomical. The two polls most seriously in error were the two which offered the simple unadjusted figures of an ordinary national survey: if sampling were the sole source of polling error, the odds against an error as big as Gallup were tens of thousands to one — and even more against the Marplan finding. The odds against two such lopsided errors occurring simultaneously and against two other polls having substantial, if smaller, errors in the same direction are far outside any limits that need be taken seriously.[1]

At the most it can be argued that the chances of sampling went against Marplan and Gallup in their final polls, just as they had gone against NOP in their survey the previous week. But bad luck in sampling cannot be made the scapegoat for the disaster.[2]

*Non-contacts, Deceivers, and Don't knows.* Polling organisations seldom publish the rate of responses secured by their interviewers. In quota sampling a limited number, perhaps 10%, refuse to answer an interviewer's questions — but the interviewer has, of course, been free to avoid unhelpful-looking people; moreover, many voters may not often be in situations where an interviewer is likely to happen upon them. In random sampling, there is a similar proportion of refusals as well as a number of non-contacts — people on the electoral register who have gone away or who continue to be out on repeated call-back. The non-contacts, ranging from 10% to 25%, are a smaller source of error than their numbers would suggest since disproportionately many of them will also be non-voters and many of the rest will be unavailable for reasons completely uncorrelated with political choice.

During and after the election there were suggestions that the public was deliberately misleading the pollsters. Obviously there could be no organised conspiracy between the randomly selected electors who were interviewed, but if only four or five Conservatives in every hundred were capriciously to say they would vote Labour, or even if Conservatives had become more prone than Labour supporters to refuse to be interviewed, the polls could be

[1] It should however be stressed that the margin of error to be allowed for sampling is seldom accurately assessed. The simple formula for sampling error in a sample drawn completely at random $\left(\sigma = \sqrt{\frac{pq}{n}}\right)$ is not applicable to samples which, like all pollsters' samples, are in some degree stratified and quite heavily clustered. The formulae to calculate the error in a stratified cluster sample are much more complex: by and large, the likely error in the sample designs used by British pollsters is substantially greater than the error for the same sample size calculated on the simple formula given above.

[2] It has been suggested that in drawing their sample constituencies in which their interviewers operated, the polls were to some extent using out of date evidence, from the 1966 election or the 1966 or 1961 Censuses. But population movements over four years are, because of mutually cancelling effects, not on a scale to add very significantly to polling error.

utterly thrown out. But there is no convincing evidence that anything of this sort happened (and it is hard to see what motive a dedicated Conservative could have in helping the polls to findings which threatened to break his party's morale). Marplan did find more refusals in late May and early June just when the Labour lead was mounting, but the other polling organisations recorded no increase in refusals or in frivolous answers. Internal checks on

'There is also evidence of a teeny weeny swing against public opinion polls.'
[*Daily Mirror*, May 27, 1970

the responses to the questionnaires showed no trace of greater inconsistency or anything else that could give rise to suspicion. That a significant number of the public were consciously hoodwinking the pollsters is an assertion that can never be definitively disproved: but no informed person in the polling industry seems to give it any credence.

The 'don't knows' constitute a more serious problem. The polls were not consistent in reporting how many 'don't knows' they were finding. Those who did offered figures ranging from 7% to 11½%. But this reflects differences in interview practices. What is a 'don't know'? No polling organisation confines its percentages only to those (usually about 80% of respondents) who answer, straight off, the question 'How will you vote?'. They all include in their findings the answers to a follow up question put to those who hesitate: 'Which party are you more inclined towards?' Some give tougher instructions than others to their interviewers on how far to press for a definite answer. Nonetheless it is possible that one cause of the apparent 'late swing' was that the 'don't knows' came down quite disproportionately in favour of the Conservatives. There is some evidence that the behaviour of 'don't knows' played a major role in Gallup's disaster in the Truman–Dewey election of 1948 and in a number of periods in the 1950s and 1960s a percentage slump in the polls has been caused more by a switch to 'don't know' than by a transfer to the other side. However, NOP's post-election recall surveys found that the votes of those who were 'Don't know' or 'Won't say' in the pre-election interview almost exactly cancelled out.

*Selective turnout.* Early in the election all the polls found Labour supporters less determined to vote than Conservatives and more interested in the World Cup. On May 28 ORC argued that any forecast should knock about 4% off the apparent Labour lead to allow for greater Labour abstention: on June 1 Gallup suggested a reduction of 4½%. But by the end of the election the difference had greatly diminished. In their final predictions both ORC and Harris changed their lead figure by a mere 1% in the Conservatives' favour to allow for differential turnout. The actual voting figures certainly give no support to the idea that Labour abstention was the key factor in the results; for if it was, then Labour should have suffered most where turnout fell most. But detailed analysis shows[1] that there was a negligible correlation between the fall in turnout and swings to the Conservatives. Post-election surveys of admitted non-voters found almost as many who would have supported the Conservatives as would have supported

[1] See pp. 390–2.

Labour. NOP concluded from their recall interviews that if they had allowed correctly for the Conservatives' greater propensity to vote they would have cut their forecast Labour lead from 4·1% to 3·1%.

*Late swing.* The most plausible explanation for the 1970 failure of the polls (which is also the most convenient for the pollsters) must lie in a late swing back to the Conservatives. If we take the middle of the interviewing period for each of the final polls we get this picture:

| | June 12 | June 15 | June 15 | June 15 | June 17 | June 18 |
|---|---|---|---|---|---|---|
| Labour lead (GB) | 9·6% | 7% | 4·1% | 2% | −1% | −2·4% |
| | Marplan | Gallup | NOP | Harris | ORC | Actual result |

It is almost too neat a pattern. But there is some fairly substantial confirmation for it in the pollsters' post election surveys.[1] On the weekend of June 20, 6% of those who told ORC interviewers that they voted Conservative said that they had intended to vote Labour at the beginning of the campaign. Only 1% of Labour voters said they had switched from Conservative. Gallup, going back to 700 of its final sample, found something like a 3% net swing to the Conservatives among those who did not vote as they had said they would. Marplan, in a similar exercise with 664 of its final sample, found 4% switching to Conservative from Labour and between 1% and 2% from Liberal; the reverse movements were much smaller. (However, even with allowance for such late switches, the Marplan figures would still have left Labour in the lead.) NOP in the most elaborate of the re-interviewing exercises found a net gain in lead to the Conservatives of 4·3%.[2]

[1] For details of the post-election surveys see *Sunday Times*, June 28 (ORC); *Daily Telegraph*, July 10 (Gallup); and *The Times*, July 20 (Marplan). The *Daily Mail* did not publish the NOP findings. See also the Gallup Monthly Index for September which are reported in the NOP Bulletins of June/July, August and September. The text of all the post-mortem reports is given in R. Rose, *The Polls and the 1970 Election* (University of Strathclyde Survey Research Centre. Occasional Paper Number 7, 1970), which provides much the fullest assembly of facts about the polls, together with an important discussion of the likelihood of sampling error. See also M. Charlot, 'Les Sondages et les élections législatives britanniques', *Revue Française de Science Politique*, October 1970, pp. 951–63.

[2] NOP in its post-election survey asked people interviewed during the campaign how they had actually voted. They found this picture of change.

| | |
|---|---|
| Labour to Conservative switching | +2·9% |
| Movement to and from Liberals | +0·1% |
| Movement to and from other parties | +0·4% |
| Differential abstention | +1·0% |
| Actual votes of undecideds | −0·1% |
| Net change to Conservatives | +4·3% |

The survey found 8% of Labour voters believing that the Conservatives would

It is possible that awareness of the outcome slightly influenced the results of the post-election surveys and they cannot be taken as conclusive evidence. But there is independent support for the late swing theory in the findings of at least two of the three polls which based their forecast on re-interviews of electors contacted earlier in the campaign. ORC and Harris were both influenced to modify their forecast in a Conservative direction by the sharp trend among people seen only four days earlier. It is true that NOP, re-interviewing electors from their May 29 and June 4 surveys, found much less of a trend, but most of their re-interviewing was completed by June 14.[1]

There can be no final demonstration of how great the trend was; it cannot be definitively proved that it occurred at all. Only a small minority of Conservative agents reported noticing any last minute change. Lord Poole, among others, has flatly denied that the Conservatives were ever behind.[1] Those at Conservative headquarters who have studied the matter most closely would scarcely agree with him: the contrary evidence is too difficult to explain away. Yet in a sense he was right: even if a majority of voters were saying around June 10 that they would vote Labour, enough of them had the seed of doubt in them for massive conversions to take place in the final few days. Last minute switching on such an unprecedented scale does suppose that there was always a potential Conservative majority waiting to be harvested.

But, if late swing offers much the most plausible explanation of the failure of the polls, the foregoing argument leaves untouched the question of what the nature or the cause of the recovery was. It could have been due to a sudden, collective change of mind which no survey could have foreseen, a reaction to the trade figures, the Powell speeches and other unpredictable stimuli to which the electors were exposed between June 15 and 18. Or it could have been the realisation of an intention that was latent all the time but that was only brought to the surface by the imminence of polling day, when the solemn decision had to be made. In other words, it is entirely possible to explain the error of the polls without reaching the answer to one of the central mysteries about the

---

be more likely to solve the nation's economic problems but only 1% of Conservatives believing the opposite. It also found that among those who had intended to vote Labour but did not do so there was some slight indication that Mr. Powell had an effect.

[1] See *The Times*, August 3, 1970.

election.[1] On June 11 England was still in the World Cup, the weather was at its most perfect and the trade figures had not been announced; would a vote then have produced the same result as the vote on June 18? Alas, we do not know and never shall.

During the election the usual anxieties were expressed about the impact of polls on the electorate — though the critics were divided on whether any movement they created would be a band-wagon swing to the party that was ahead or an 'underdog' rally to the party that was behind, or indeed whether they would cause apathy among Labour supporters or defeatism among Conservatives. No real evidence was offered on any of these counts. However, the polls could no longer take refuge, as was once possible, behind public ignorance of their activities. Even as late as 1964 it could be shown that only a minority of voters followed the polls and that those who were most aware of their findings were the most partisan and least likely to change. But by 1970 the salience of the polls was appreciably greater. In their post-election poll NOP found that 56% of people claimed to have noticed polls during the election — and 92% of these recalled them as predicting a Labour win. There is still no indication that polls directly switched votes. Nevertheless, one can hardly doubt that they had a great effect on the attitudes of the active participants, both centrally and in the constituencies. If the Conservative recovery had been reported a week earlier it is inconceivable that party behaviour in the last week would have followed the same pattern — although the final outcome would not necessarily have been any different.

The 1970 débâcle for the polls may well be regarded as healthy both for pollsters and for the public, just as the 1948 débâcle was in the United States. The pollsters will be more cautious in future, they will be more zealous in checking on the possible effects of willingness to vote and of latent propensity towards switching and they will be more conscientious in conducting surveys up to the very last possible moment. They will also be more insistent on their press reports containing some reference to the range of

[1] The findings of the Conservatives' private polls throw ambiguous light on 'late swing'. The percentage believing on June 17 that 'another economic crisis is coming' (44%) is no larger than nine days previously. However, over the same period, the percentage preferring the Conservatives to handle a possible crisis increased from 39% to 49%.

sampling error.[1] The public — as well as the politicians and the professional observers — will be more cautious in accepting poll findings as final indicators. It is unlikely that the betting public will ever again allow the London bookmakers' odds on the party favoured to win to reach 20 to 1: the historical justification for backing the underdog will be too strong.

Yet to say this is not to forecast a decline in election polling. It remains the best available source of information. What else is there? Journalistic observation and intuition is unlikely to detect movements of one or two voters in a hundred. Inside information from the parties may be based on wider collection of evidence, but it is likely to be coloured, if not by deliberate propaganda motives, then by subconscious self-deception. In 1970 Conservatives claimed that their local evidence always conflicted with the poll findings — but they were saying the same in 1966 when the polls were much less far out. Moreover on the Labour side, there were virtually no indications that things were going wrong. The Conservative organisation is much more systematic and professional than Labour's — but there are some highly competent and experienced Labour officials and virtually none of them suspected that the polls were leading them into a fool's paradise. If the late swing had been in the other direction the Conservatives would probably have been little better at spotting it. It is in the nature of parties to be optimistic. When optimism happens to find justification, it does not necessarily mean that the optimism was based on good evidence.

In the future politicians and journalists will look more carefully at the evidence they gather themselves, but, fearful of selective observation and wishful thinking, they will still turn to opinion polls for confirmation. With all their faults the techniques of survey research offer the most objective and systematic way of assessing what people are thinking. But from now on everyone will be aware that polls are fallible and that, if a large mass of people

[1] However, one danger may be that the polls will introduce their own weighting devices for likelihood of voting or of switching, based on their experience in 1970 and on subsequent researching, but that these devices will be too technical to be explained to the mass public. In 1970 ORC produced a reasoned argument based on some very limited evidence about a series of adjustments to their figures: the success of their prediction may induce others to make guesses and introduce the sort of 'fudge factors' that were for so long the stock in trade of American election forecasters. It is to be hoped that British pollsters — and newspapers — will continue to be fully candid about any 'fudge factors' incorporated in forecasts.

change their minds on their way to vote, polls will once again get the answer wrong.

Public polls attracted vast publicity; private polls attracted none. But the advances in private polling, at least on the Conservative side of Smith Square, were of major significance.

The Labour party, which in the early sixties had been the first to make extensive use of private polls, did relatively little.[1] There was a pause after 1966 but in 1968 the party voted £15,000 for survey research between then and the general election. There followed the false start with Conrad Jamieson's study of party activists (see p. 56). The party then turned back to Mark Abrams who had done their pioneer work in the 1959 parliament[2] and he did some further work on party activists and then two substantial surveys. In October 1969 he carried out a study on youth which showed how close the new voters were to their parents' political attitudes and thus discouraged efforts to appeal to them separately. Another study on party advertising had indicated a very disappointing response to the 'Life and Soul' campaign. The results were not distributed in a way to create much impact: only the Prime Minister, the General Secretary and the Assistant General Secretary were allowed to keep copies, though the Campaign Committee were briefed orally about what had been found and some of the information was used in regional meetings with party activists. There were also some small-scale polls, mostly amateur, on a local basis, for example in connection with one or two by-elections and with the GLC elections.

In 1970 Mark Abrams withdrew from commercial polling and in March the party turned to Robert Worcester, the Director of Market Opinion Research International (a new firm owned jointly by NOP and the American Opinion Research Corporation — no connection of the British ORC). The elaborate and shrewd plans which he put forward were geared to an autumn election and had to be scrapped. He did however conduct two surveys after the election was announced. A random survey of 2,000 people, conducted between May 21 and 26, reached Transport House on May 29. It sought to identify changers and potential changers as

[1] After 1966 the Liberals lacked the resources to do any polling, though in 1968 a private gift of £1,500 had financed one special survey on the possibilities of winning over the industrial worker.

[2] See *The British General Election of 1964*, pp. 66–71.

well as the issues which were most important and best understood. Its essential conclusion was that younger women in the poorest classes, especially in the North, were the most prone to swing against Labour and that prices were their main worry. An incidental finding of the survey was that 30% of people were aware of the 'Yesterday's Men' advertisement and 69% of these knew they referred to the Conservatives. Of these 69% two-thirds thought the advertisements 'unfair'.

A second survey by MORI was a 540 quota sample on the week-end of May 31. It reported to Transport House a 1% Conservative lead (which was dismissed as a sampling accident). It touched on three subjects. One finding that caused some surprise and distress was that the public showed no sense that Mr. Wilson had been unfairly treated in *Election Forum* — a backlash of sympathy for his rough handling had been expected. Another finding showed that the bulk of voters did not appreciate that the real income of most people had in fact increased in recent years. The poll also showed that only 11% of respondents could recall any recent contact with Conservative canvassers and only 9% with Labour canvassers. MORI also helped with comment on 'Operation Feedback', a strictly amateur survey organised privately through Transport House, the findings of which were received in late May. This study stressed the balance of payments, industrial relations and the cost of living as the main issues. It concluded that the voting uncertainty of women who would normally be Labour was the party's weakest point.

There is no evidence that these surveys had any impact on Labour strategy. The party in fact seemed to lack the skill to commission polls that would be of much real use to it, still less to digest or give effect to their findings. The absence of expertise or rigorous thought about what polls could offer and the absence of trust over the dissemination and analysis of the reports that were received greatly diminished any return on the party's efforts in this field.

The Conservatives' efforts were much more far-reaching — but it was not just a matter of scale. Elaborate thought went into how most effectively to harness private polls to the diverse needs of the party and it is arguable that they got very good value for the money spent — which amounted to something like £30,000 a year from 1966 onwards. The party's basic acceptance of the potentiality of private polls had come after the 1964 election with the launching of a long term panel survey conducted by the British Market Research Bureau and the subsequent award of a general contract to ORC under Humphrey Taylor.

A great variety of polls were commissioned and their conclusions offered significant contributions to almost all aspects of Conservative activity: to policy and its presentation, to national campaigning and constituency organisation. Some of the techniques employed were based on those observed in the United States and Germany. They appear to have been at least as fully developed and as ingeniously applied as those used by political parties anywhere with the possible exception of Germany. Nevertheless the Conservative experience during the 1966 parliament showed that private surveys, despite their many uses, had distinct limitations. It would be hard to portray them as powerful instruments of some hidden persuaders. There were four general categories of polls: (1) long-term (2) medium-term (3) short-term and (4) campaign.

(1) *Long-term surveys*: Studies carried out in the United States suggested that the relative stability in the net figures for 'voting intention' possibly masked much larger gross movements. For example the information that Labour's public opinion poll lead had increased from 3% to 6% did not indicate whether there had been a single transfer of 1·5% of the electorate from Conservative to Labour, or whether there had been a large movement from Labour to Conservative counterbalanced by an even larger movement in the opposite direction, or, as seemed more likely, a complex series of switches from 'Conservative' to 'Don't know', 'Liberal' to 'Don't know', etc. Conventional public opinion polls also gave little indication about the motives which had influenced the switches.

It was therefore decided to set up a panel operation. Out of an original group of 4,500 electors interviewed in 1965, attempts were made to re-contact 700 or so each seven months with a view to detecting long-term changes in voting behaviour and party loyalty.[1] Re-interviews carried out after the 1966 election showed

[1] In some measure the inspiration for this approach can be traced to the long-term study of political attitudes launched at Nuffield College in 1963 and reported in 1969 in David Butler and Donald Stokes, *Political Change in Britain*. In its turn, this study was influenced by panel studies carried out at the University of Michigan for A. Campbell *et. al.*, *The American Voter* (New York, 1960).

that at least 30% of the electorate had changed their voting behaviour in some way or other between 1964 and 1966. These wobblers were disproportionately concentrated in the C2 (skilled manual) group, among under 35s and among women. These findings provided a warning against too narrow a definition of 'target voters' but enabled the party strategists to outline from an early date the sections of the population at which policy and propaganda should be aimed. In preparing its tax proposals, for example, the shadow cabinet and its advisers were continually aware of the dangers of offending the C2s. Advertising was concentrated in newspapers with the highest proportion of C2 readership; 'Project '67' and other organisational efforts were influenced by the knowledge that 'target voters' were under-represented and ignored by local parties.

The most important discovery of later panel studies was that even during the Conservative upsurges of 1968 and 1969, when the party was handsomely ahead in 'voting intention', Labour still led in 'party identification' (i.e. in answers to the question 'Generally speaking would you describe yourself as Conservative, Labour, Liberal or what?').[1] The warning implicit in this finding helped to keep some feet on the ground in Central Office when there was a danger of premature complacency. Even in the headiest moments most senior Conservative officials were indicating that a relatively small majority was the most likely result when the election came.

(2) *Medium-term surveys* included surveys designed to test public opinion about the images of the parties and of their leaders and surveys about specific issues. There were regular studies (usually monthly) which looked in some depth into a current issue, though each one would be covered only infrequently. In addition there was each year a more general issues survey. This dealt mainly with 'valence' issues (those where there is general agreement on the goal, such as stable prices, plentiful housing or industrial peace). It sought to measure the importance of the issue to the public, the manner in which it was perceived, and the party which was thought likely to handle it best. It also gave a measure of the relative importance of different issues in the public mind. Other medium-term surveys included investigations into newspaper readership and into political issues, and other matters, in the 'critical seats'.

[1] See p. 346 for the figures.

The surveys on specific issues influenced the work of some of the policy groups, whereas the general issues surveys helped in determining the prominence to be given to particular themes; the concentration on prices and taxation from the beginning of 1970 offers one clear example.[1] The fact that polls showed a heavy majority against educational selection at 11 plus was used to check those who wanted the party to come down too heavily against the move to comprehensive schools. The sale of council houses was stressed in the 1967 GLC election campaign because surveys showed it would be popular. Every one of the five main Selsdon Park themes was described as having support in private poll findings (though in fact there had been no poll research on 'law and order').[2]

(3) *Short-term surveys* took various forms. There were spot reaction polls the morning after party political broadcasts. There were publicity studies to test the comprehensibility and appeal of slogans and words, and to measure the impact of particular speeches. There were also by-election surveys.

(4) *Campaign surveys* in June 1970 were all high speed affairs, designed to be fed instantly into party strategy-making. There were three separate daily quota-sample polls with 500 or so respondents; the results were telephoned in and very rapidly processed. The lunch meetings of Conservative strategists at St. Stephen's Club received a report on the previous night's television. By 4 p.m. the findings on public reaction to issues were available. A third survey, on the impact of the mass media, reached Central Office by early evening. The television surveys (see p. 224) suffered from sample size; usually only 120–150 respondents had actually seen the party broadcast of the previous night. While the rating of

[1] Explaining his success in a different policy field, one shadow minister commented that he was greatly helped when 'a specially commissioned poll pointed very much my way.'

[2] An impression of the scope of the monthly ORC surveys is given by this listing of subjects for the year 1967–68:

| | |
|---|---|
| June 30, 67 | Education |
| July 17, 67 | Taxation |
| August 17, 67 | Old People |
| October 13, 67 | General Attitudes |
| November 27, 67 | Industrial Relations |
| January 29, 68 | Economic Situation |
| February 22, 68 | General Issues |
| March 21, 68 | Nationalised Industries |
| April 11, 68 | Women's Interests |
| June 18, 68 | Social Services |

the broadcasts varied appreciably, on average there was little Conservative advantage. However, the polls did give comforting evidence that Mr. Heath had more than matched Mr. Wilson in the *Election Forums*, and in the opening and the closing appeals. Above all there was great delight in the fact that, excluding Mr. Thorpe's, Mr. Heath's final broadcast got the best rating and Mr. Wilson's the worst rating of all the broadcasts in answer to the question, 'Do you think that viewers will have come away thinking Mr. —— was more honest or less honest than they thought before?'. The issue surveys were mainly important for showing that the economic theme was having some impact even during the unhappy second week and far more on June 15 and 16 (see p. 167). The media surveys were fairly depressing: they often suggested that the Labour case was getting across best; however, the findings appear to have been shown to very few people.

It is ironic that the last report from ORC on June 17 should have concluded:

> 'What emerges from the final issue survey is the following sad truth: the Conservatives and Mr. Heath are seen to be more efficient, more straightforward, more honest, and more correct in their economic forecast than the Labour party and Mr. Wilson. In spite of this they have communicated less well than Labour and for some reason which has nothing to do with logic they have been less convincing.'

The experience of the political parties, especially the Conservatives, with private surveys before the 1970 election illustrates the difficulties inherent in their use. First of all, there tends to be a large barrier between the pollsters and their political clients, who are often incapable of grasping their most relevant findings and are naturally inclined to interpret them in accordance with their preconceptions. Sometimes a convenient result based on a small sample has more impact than it warrants. For instance, it may well have been chances of sampling that in May 1969 temporarily promoted taxation to top place, above the cost of living, in the Conservatives' special index showing the importance of various issues and, by doing so, significantly increased the emphasis placed upon it. Another hazard is that, as the possession of private survey material may give evidence to one side or other in an internal dispute, it may become the subject of office politics. The distrust within the top echelons of the Labour party organisation was reflected in the excessive secrecy with which private polls were treated at Transport House, which did much to sabotage the application of their findings. In the Conservative party, liaison between the pollsters and the party managers was much better: polls had a circulation list of about 50 and there were regular presentations. Even so, internal communications had their limitations. When we asked one senior shadow minister what he thought of the polls produced by Humphrey Taylor (by then four years the party's pollster), he replied, genuinely baffled, 'Who is he?'.

A second difficulty is that, to quote one of those most concerned with Conservative policy, 'in eight cases out of ten, you know already what the poll is showing, or if you don't there is still absolutely nothing to be done as a result of them'. This applies notably to image polls. The discovery that Mr. Heath was considered 'weak' by a large section of the population did not indicate what ought to be done about it. On the one hand, it could be concluded that the image ought to be combatted by showing him in poses suggesting strength. On the other hand, it could be concluded that publicity ought to concentrate on his better points, or indeed, that publicity ought to play down the leadership altogether and emphasise policies.

A similar problem arises when efforts are made to direct advertising towards 'target voters'. Vote switching may be a little more common among younger people, among women and among those on the margin between the middle and working class. But any tendency apparent among these groups is likely to be found among almost every other group. Nor, even if a 'target voter' is decided upon, is it easy to direct propaganda selectively at him — it is bound to reach much of the rest of the population as well. There is, as we show on pp. 342–3, little evidence that the younger working class women, spotted by pollsters on both sides as particularly vulnerable, behaved differently from other people.

Thirdly, there is the not inconsiderable danger of a misleading conclusion resulting from poor wording in the poll itself or from precipitate interpretation. Before the election, both the Conservatives and Labour investigated the type of election broadcast preferred by the public. Labour concluded that 'straight-to-camera' was more popular, while the Conservatives using different questions and interviewing immediately after their routine party political broadcasts found the opposite.[1] As the Conservatives were prepared to spend handsomely on producing 'newsreel' type broadcasts while Labour was not, these results were convenient all round. The dangers of 'precipitate interpretation' are illustrated by the Labour slogan in 1964 and 1966 'Thirteen wasted years'. At the beginning, few realised what it referred to, and had it been market researched it would probably have been abandoned in 1964. But by 1966 it seems to have entered quite deeply into public consciousness. As public opinion is constantly developing, it is always difficult to extrapolate from the present to the future.

Fourthly, it is often impossible, for technical and financial reasons, to carry out polls when they are most required. For example, the Conservatives made inclusive contracts for polls to be done according to a fixed schedule and the polling organisations it employed could not lay on extra teams of interviewers at short notice at prices which the party could afford. Thus, in April and May 1970, when a further panel study in the long-term series would have been very useful in determining who the converts to Labour were, there had been no survey for months and the next 'wave' was not due until early summer.

Fifthly, there is the moral danger of tailoring policy to the quirks of public opinion. Although politicians do at times develop a healthy awareness of Burke's dicta about the duties of a representative to exercise his own unfettered judgement, and although it would be hard to cite examples of craven fawning before opinion poll verdicts, the dangers and the temptations are obvious.

Sixthly, much of the information contained in private surveys is already available far more cheaply in public opinion polls. At times indeed all parties did purchase detailed breakdowns of their findings from the commercial polls.

These problems are balanced (partially, at least) by substantial benefits. For, while the private survey may have little use in eight cases out of ten, it is a useful instrument in the remaining two. Despite the ambiguous implications of image surveys about the party leader, for instance, the knowledge that one member of his (shadow) cabinet is more successful as a broadcaster than another can be very useful. The retention of Iain Macleod for the

[1] The Liberals, impressed by the academic research of J. D. Halloran at Leicester University, were, like Labour, believers in the straight-to-camera talk.

fourth Conservative election broadcast was a logical result of his excellent showing (revealed in a private poll) in the third. And, although the Conservative surveys in the 'critical seats' gave little useful information about local issues according to most local agents, they did save some of them from worrying too much about matters they had thought important, but which had little resonance with the public; moreover, the surveys were plainly justified by their findings about the readership of local newspapers, and possibly in other ways.

Worries about the effects of polls on the democratic process are perhaps not without some theoretical justification. In practice they were not fulfilled during 1966–70. Conservative polls on issues found heavy majorities in favour of wholly contradictory policies. Their effect was generally to release the Conservative leaders from the constraints provided by their previous impressions of public opinion (sometimes provided by party activists) against policies which they wished to pursue.

Above all, private polls have a value in warning the politicians of total public ignorance or indifference about issues that they regard as key. One of those involved in Conservative polling remarked that, thanks to their private surveys, they were able to say to Conservatives

> 'Remember that for every one of the people who have the sort of attitudes and interests of those whom you met at the constituency's annual garden party, or whose views you read in the *Daily Telegraph* there are ten people whose votes you need, and in many cases whose votes you got at the last election, who have quite different interests and views and who look at party politics in a quite different way.'

In a broader strategic way it could be argued that just as the Mark Abrams private polls of the early 1960s played a major part in Labour's escape from its cloth-cap image, so in the later 60s the whole message of Conservative speeches was concerned with Labour's failure to satisfy the needs of its own sort of people. Conscious that more people still identified themselves with Labour than with the Conservatives and that the long-term forces of demography were working in Labour's direction, influential people at the centre of the party were persuaded more than ever before to gear their appeal not to their own ilk but to the mass of ordinary people who might naturally be expected to vote Labour It did not need polls to devise this strategy but the evidence of polls gave powerful encouragement to stick strictly to it. A senior Conservative wrote 'The fact that we did as much and as thorough research was of immense help in resisting temptations to change the line, which always arises in the middle of the battle.'

CHAPTER IX

# BROADCASTING

By Martin Harrison

Eight p.m., May 18, 1970. The election had just been announced: on BBC-1 *Panorama* was showing Mr. Wilson, Mr. Heath and Mr. Thorpe in turn giving a first airing to phrases which were to be daily fare during the month ahead; and on ITV the same three were facing different inquisitors in different order, but answering almost identical questions in almost identical words. Here was a demonstration both of the place that television had taken in 'traditional' election ritual and a vignette of its place in the campaign ahead — the parallel behaviour of the two networks, the conventional questioning, the absence of direct discussion between the politicians and the implicit evidence of uneasy relations between the broadcasters and the parties. For while Mr. Heath and Mr. Thorpe were interrogated sternly in the antiseptic decor of the studios, Mr. Wilson had been recorded amiably puffing his pipe amid the sunshine and flowers of his Downing Street garden. Whether from pressure of work or painful memories of his rough handling at the comparable stage in 1966, Mr. Wilson had made it known that he would be available for interview at Number 10 by 'accredited political correspondents' only, which in the event meant the unfailingly courteous Peter Hardiman Scott for the BBC, and George Ffitch for ITN. Had the BBC lost its nerve after what it felt was the bullying of recent years and cravenly conceded a soft interview? Or had Mr. Wilson simply used his skill at manipulating the media again? Or was it simply one of those accidents for which the suspicious so rarely allow? Characteristically, the ensuing press speculation touched on the underlying tensions without illuminating or penetrating them.

*The framework.* Tension between broadcasters and politicians may well be inevitable, and can even be creative. But there was nothing creative in the attitudes which built up before the 1970 election. Antagonism towards the BBC had been deepening among Mr. Wilson and some of his lieutenants since at least 1964. It had flared briefly and acrimoniously during and after the 1966 campaign,[1] and although the hatchet was then officially buried, the residue of mutual suspicion was never dissipated. Instead, a trickle of disagreements and misunderstandings over 'balance', 'fairness', 'trivialisation' and the selection of participants for discussions helped sustain a mild paranoia on both sides. Downing Street was increasingly convinced of the BBC's bias and irresponsibility, while fears grew among the broadcasters that some politicians were set on crushing their independence. And though the Prime Minister's sense of grievance remained unabated, the Conservatives in turn became increasingly disposed to complain. Mr. Macleod, Mr. Eldon Griffiths and Mr. Ian Gilmour all launched attacks reminiscent of the onslaughts on 'leftists' at the BBC familiar in the fifties. Mr. Gilmour even suggested that Mr. Wilson's anger was really a smokescreen to divert attention from the Corporation's left-wing bias.[2] Much of this new criticism was related to the campaign for local commercial radio, but some reflected an unsentimental assessment that Mr. Wilson's attempts to intimidate the BBC had succeeded sufficiently to justify counter-intimidation.

If some attacks were cynical and others self-seeking, many politicians genuinely regarded television with a 'mixture of contempt and fear'.[3] This was clear both in the 1966 and 1969 debates on televising the Commons, which foundered chiefly on lack of trust; it also emerged in much-discussed speeches by Mr. Benn and Mr. Crossman in 1968, assailing the insufficiency and triviality of much current affairs broadcasting. For many politicians televised politics was beset by 'trendiness' and superficiality, preoccupied with gladiatorial clashes rather than serious exploration of the issues. Though much of the discussion following the Benn and Crossman speeches was itself superficial, ironically some of the most frequently criticised broadcasters were also the most ready to agree that TV's treatment of politics was unsatisfactory.[4] How-

[1] See *The British General Election of 1966*, Chapter VII.

[2] *Sunday Express*, May 31, 1970.

[3] The phrase is used by Mr. John Grist, Head of BBC-TV's Current Affairs Group, in a refreshingly thoughtful and self-critical review of the campaign in *Listener*, July 2, 1970.

[4] See articles by Robin Day (*Encounter*, May 1970), and Jeremy Isaacs (*Encounter*, March 1968 and *Listener*, June 18, 1970); also John Grist's article, already mentioned, and John Whale's *The Half-Shut Eye* (London, 1969). For the Benn and Crossman criticisms see the national press for October 19 and 22, 1968. The most notable academic contributions have been J. G. Blumler and D. McQuail, *Television in Politics* (London, 1968) and articles by Blumler

ever, although Mr. Crossman might accept that more serious current affairs programming would also be more searching, some of the other critics seemed really to be asking for television to provide a passive channel for party views rather than a creative forum. In summarising such a complex controversy it is easy to depict the issues and alignments too starkly; the battle-lines were never in fact rigidly drawn between 'broadcasters' and 'politicians'. Mr. Wilson's attacks on the BBC provoked sharp reaction from within the Labour ranks; while some broadcasters thought privately that the BBC had made mistakes which laid it open to criticism, and that if ITV had been watched by politicians as intensively as the BBC it would not have escaped so unscathed. Nevertheless, the absence of confidence between some politicians and some broadcasters cast its shadow over the campaign.

However, some minor obstacles had been removed. The new Representation of the People Act granted ITV and the BBC the same standing in certain aspects of campaign coverage as the written press, made clear their freedom to include candidates in any items which were not 'about the constituency or electoral area' and allowed candidates who did not intend to appear in a 'constituency item' to consent to the programme continuing without them.[1] Although the ITA interpreted the new provisions rather more restrictively than the BBC, the broadcasters had nevertheless won a little greater freedom.

Arrangements for the 1970 campaign were reviewed by the Committee on Political Broadcasting at a hastily convened meeting on May 19. In addition to the customary august representation of the BBC, ITV and the main parties, party broadcasting officers attended for the first time; the BBC and ITV delegations, however, included no comparable infusion of people directly concerned in programme production. Details of party broadcasts were settled fairly easily: there were again to be thirteen on television, shared 5 : 5 : 3, and all were to run ten minutes. (In 1966 all parties had found fifteen minutes too long; some Conservatives would have welcomed five-minute programmes, but this had little support elsewhere.) The BBC–ITV decision to shift the broad-

in P. Halmos (ed.), *The Sociology of Mass Media Communicators*, and *Listener*, June 25, 1970.

[1] By withholding consent recalcitrant candidates could still prevent their rivals from appearing — and did so in at least two cases.

casts to 10 p.m. (from 9.10 p.m.) to facilitate joint scheduling was accepted without enthusiasm, for it meant smaller audiences. On radio the big parties were allocated four ten-minute periods, at 5.40 p.m., on Radio 4 (primarily a speech channel in the revised radio structure), and three five-minute periods, at 8.01 p.m., on Radios 1 and 2 combined (the pop and light music outlets). The Liberals received two on each channel.

The rest of the committee's proceedings were confused and contentious. Ostensibly the broadcasters outlined their plans and the parties commented — that is, indicated on what terms they would cooperate. Whether any firm agreements were made was a matter of dispute; and even the official minutes were neither wholly clear nor universally accepted as a complete record. As a result some politicians believed there was a gentleman's agreement not to use the time liberated by shorter party broadcasts to extend other political programming — but this was not the broadcasters' recollection. And a senior politician considered it settled that there were to be no frontbench confrontations, though the minutes were silent on this. Uncertainty increased as incomplete versions of the confidential proceedings filtered down, and producers who had no direct knowledge of the deliberations negotiated with party officials who invoked committee 'decisions' against them.[1] Moreover, the suddenness of the election caught the broadcasters with their plans incomplete, particularly for new types of programme, which were naturally the most likely to rouse the politicians' anxieties. Tangled communications exacerbated a situation already lacking in goodwill. The committee might have functioned better had it included some working producers, but if it had been clearer and more businesslike it would probably also have been more restrictive. As it was, producers who officially knew nothing about the 'decisions' were free to use their ingenuity in mounting programmes which bent the rules the parties sought to impose.

Formally these conditions had altered little: no live audiences, no Sunday programmes and full consultation over both invitations to speakers and choice of constituencies for survey. In practice, the 'rules' were invoked more rigidly and restrictively. Plans by

[1] I understand that, formally, the committee decided nothing, but simply 'took note' of a series of arrangements and statements. In particular, the minutes contained no agreement to bar political broadcasts on Sundays and the eve-of-poll, despite the clear implication that this was so in its communiqué of May 19 which, however, was cleared with all sides before release.

several of the BBC's new local radio stations to run recorded election programmes on Sundays were vetoed by party headquarters. BBC-2's proposals for two long Sunday evening debates also fell foul of objections to increasing the volume of 'non-party' programming and to having a live audience. The 'live audience' BBC-2 was proposing would have comprised barristers, academics, union leaders and city men, and the BBC was prepared to guarantee responsible behaviour. But memories of Mr. Lloyd's and Mrs. Castle's unhappy encounter with a rowdy audience in 1959 had still not faded. Led by the Liberals, the parties were united in opposing anything which could be construed as a live audience. This put paid to the hopes of two local radio stations of getting local candidates to answer voters' questions, and to Radio Sheffield's plans to use a panel of young voters — who were ruled out as both 'live' and 'unrepresentative of the electorate'. *This Week* was unable to persuade the party leaders to agree to be questioned by a panel of voters and had the greatest difficulty in mounting a programme with party spokesmen facing a youth panel of six, while Labour had to be pressured into appearing in Thames' *Hook-Up*, which featured 'live' — though physically remote — individual questioners. At bottom, the parties often lacked any confidence that producers would provide representative rational panels, while producers increasingly suspected the politicians of using the live audience objection to insulate themselves completely from questioning by anyone but professional interviewers and journalists. But here and there, where relations were more relaxed, some of the ITV companies and local radio stations did manage to run successful panel programmes with young voters, farmers or housewives.

'Confrontations' between leaders had been once more ruled out by Mr. Wilson early in 1970, and his dislike of lower-level encounters was well known within the party. The Conservatives were equally cool. During the campaign programmes like *Panorama* and *Campaign Report* were to be bedevilled by uncertainties over whether ministers and shadow ministers would agree to direct discussion. Although a few such confrontations did take place, more typically one saw Mr. Robin Day valiantly ferrying between Mr. Jenkins on one monitor in a distant studio and Mr. Maudling on another in the hope of provoking a dialogue, while each man studiously ignored the other's arguments and referred to him only in the third person. After three elections with a steady increase in discussion between the parties, 1970 brought a clear decline. Ultimately the parties' attitudes proved an irritant rather than a major constraint on producers, but though the broadcasters usually found a way of doing what they intended, it was often only after an outlay of time and energy which left its mark on the programmes themselves.

*Minor parties.* Minor party arrangements were as controversial as ever. Plaid Cymru and the Scottish National Party had jointly asked for membership of the Committee on Political Broadcasting and for the review of arrangements for minor party election broadcasts recommended by the conference on Electoral Law. Neither request had been met. The committee announced without any consultation that the nationalists would receive one five-minute broadcast on their national transmitters on both radio and television, with the same allocation at United Kingdom level for parties 'nominating on a national basis fifty candidates on nomination day'. Nor was there consultation over times; these were apparently settled by the BBC and ITA national controllers for Wales and Scotland and, for the Communists, by the BBC and ITA in London. The Communists were particularly angry at being given 6.30 p.m. (and no showing on BBC-2), and at the alleged refusal of the BBC to tell them when their broadcast would go out until 33 hours before air time, even though they cleared the fifty-candidate hurdle well before nomination day. The broadcasting authorities must have known that by assigning the party so unfavourable a time and robbing it of listings in the programme weeklies they were cutting its audience.[1] After accommodating thirteen major programmes it was natural for them to dislike having to find more time for minor parties. But even someone with no sympathy for the smaller parties could feel that they were treated less than courteously and fairly.

The smaller parties also complained of unfairness in other programmes. The argument turned on whether coverage should reflect 'news value', number of nominations or past election per-

[1] How seriously the off-peak times allocated to small parties cut their audiences depends on which ratings data one follows (below, p. 227), but there is no question that the Communists suffered.

Plaid Cymru complained that 10% of the Welsh received TV only from English-based transmitters not carrying their programmes, while the SNP contended that their 65 candidates entitled them to put their case to the whole United Kingdom.

formance. No single yardstick was universally acceptable, and the broadcasters were under pressure from the big parties, who argued that nationalist strength had been bolstered by excessive attention from the media. In practice the coverage of the minor parties ranged from nothing at all to full equality. In constituency items all contenders were on a par, and in Wales and Scotland the nationalists and Communists had equal status in discussions. (There was some relief when the Paisleyites failed to qualify in Ulster.) But the small parties argued that while regional programmes provided a modicum of exposure, they made only rare, fleeting appearances in the dominant nationally-networked programmes. The thinly-scattered Communists had the leanest time: here and there they featured on local radio, and they won time on Thames' *Hook-Up* after a demonstration at the studios, but they had almost no national coverage apart from brief reports of their manifesto. The SNP turned to the courts, but their attempt to obtain an injunction over their exclusion from the *Election Forum* series was unsuccessful.[1]

*Reporting the campaign.* The abrupt announcement of the election caught the broadcasters with schedules long-fixed for saturation coverage of the World Cup. Because of this ITN could not hope to repeat its 1964 and 1966 success with late-evening election specials. Its whole coverage had to fall on *News at Ten*, becoming lighter and more popular in consequence. *News at Ten*, hemmed in by party broadcasts and World Cup programmes, had only from two to five minutes extra each evening to cover the election and meet an exceptionally determined BBC challenge. BBC–TV brought its News and Current Affairs Group together in the Television Centre's largest studio to provide, under unified editorial control, material for both the regular news bulletins and the special *24 Hours Campaign Report*. This temporary marriage was to bring to bulletins both presenters and a style of presentation more customarily found in programmes like *24 Hours*.

All channels sought to establish a distinctive election format. Radio had its special studio feeding inserts into its bulletins and producing a nightly campaign round-up at 10.10 p.m. ITN used Alastair Burnett as election anchor-man, emphasising this with the caption, 'The June Election — Day 1', and so on up to polling day. BBC-1 was even more determined that viewers should

[1] *The Times*, May 27, 1970.

grasp that a major operation was under way: their anchor-man-of-the-day sat in their cavernous studio backed by 'V-Day Minus 18' (counting down daily), or huge pictures of the party leaders, together with the other familiar accoutrements of great TV occasions — flickering monitors, cluttered desks and minions wandering apparently aimlessly across the shot or slumped in moribund contemplation of the monitors.

Coverage began in a minor key; it picked up after the dissolution, but it was only in the final week that the election consistently led the bulletins.[1] Yet the story always had substantial play: of more than one hundred bulletins analysed, all carried something on the election; together the 8.50 BBC-1 news and *News at Ten* alone totalled almost seven hours of election reporting. The broadcasters could scarcely have done more without neglecting the other news — and yet a nightly ten to fifteen minutes is little enough to cover the campaigning of even the two front benches, let alone the activities of the 1,837 candidates in the country as a whole.

Achieving a balanced coverage of the campaign was at one level simple. As a matter of routine all channels ensured that the big parties emerged with roughly equal exposure (a slight Conservative lead being chiefly due to the 'Powell effect'). It was harder to give the Liberals a good showing. Most of their best-known figures were fighting constituency campaigns in peripheral areas, while Mr. Thorpe's helicopter forays in search of national exposure were dogged by sea mists. Newsmen sometimes tried hard to redress the balance: Lord Byers reported that he was once offered film coverage providing he would speak from a rubbish dump — which he duly did. Nevertheless, much less was seen of the Liberals than in the two previous elections.

[1] Throughout, my comments and calculations relate primarily to radio news at 8 a.m., 1 p.m. and 6 p.m.; on BBC-1's 8.50 p.m. bulletin and on *News at Ten*, May 31–June 17 inclusive. There was also spot news on radio and longer evening bulletins, the lunchtime and early evening television bulletins, and BBC-2's long 7·30 p.m. bulletin and late summary. These greatly increased the volume of the coverage but added little to its variety.

The 8 a.m. radio news gave 20% of available time to the election, the 1 p.m. bulletin 40% and the 6 p.m. bulletin 28%. The 8·50 p.m. BBC-1 news (backed later by *24 Hours Campaign Report*) gave 46% of its time to the election. So did *News at Ten*, which ran longer but took the full burden of ITN coverage.

During the Fleet Street strike some BBC bulletins were extended, and there were extra breakfast-time programmes in which displaced journalists commented on the news and said what would have been in the papers had they appeared. These were an unhappy mixture of genres which added little to election reporting. ITN ran no additional programmes during the strike.

TABLE I

*Party shares of news coverage 1970 (1966 and 1964 in brackets)*

| | Conservative % | Labour % | Liberal % | Other % |
|---|---|---|---|---|
| BBC-1 | 46 (39/42) | 42 (42/41) | 10 (16/17) | 1 (2/...) |
| ITN | 45 (43/44) | 43 (40/40) | 11 (16/16) | 1 (1/...) |
| Radio | 43 (36/41) | 41 (46/39) | 16 (17/20) | ... (.../...) |

Striking a proper balance over men and issues proved more difficult. As in 1966 the bulletins were dominated by the two main party leaders, whose tours, speeches and morning press conferences took up 53% of all the news coverage of politicians. (Mr. Wilson receiving 56% of his party's coverage, and Mr. Heath 60% of his.) But although they received roughly equal attention, the qualitative balance between such different approaches to campaigning proved more elusive. For while Mr. Heath was usually seen hammering away earnestly at an issue, the prevailing picture of Mr. Wilson was of 'walkabouts' in which he greeted the faithful, paused to jibe at his opponents but said little about issues. Coverage of this rather incoherent tourism continued well after it had become boring and repetitive because bulletin editors felt compelled to run it both to reflect his campaign and to provide balance to their footage on Mr. Heath — rather than for its intrinsic news value.[1] This insistent preoccupation with leaders was due partly to technical and financial considerations, but there were also signs that radio and television journalists saw a 'presidentialised' approach as the most significant way of presenting the campaign. But concentration on leaders was inevitably at their lieutenants' expense: only forty-four people achieved national news recognition during the campaign. While the cameras frequently caught the pugnacious debating of Mr. Barber, the graver admoni-

[1] Some Labour supporters saw this dull coverage as proof of anti-Labour bias, while some Conservatives thought it showed the BBC to be so biased towards Labour that it showed Mr. Wilson even when he was only puffing his pipe. In fact equal coverage was rendered more difficult because, while Mr. Heath's itinerary was planned with scrupulous attention to optimum conditions for filming and the timing of bulletins, Mr. Wilson was much more casual about deadlines than in 1966. Since he often spoke too late for the 8.50 p.m. bulletin it contained more 'walkabout' material than *News at Ten*. Radio gave much less attention to 'walkabouts' because they tended to produce incoherent soundtracks. Mr. Wilson's coverage was also affected by the tendency of all channels to drop material from the morning news conferences before the main evening bulletins.

tions of Mr. Jenkins and the colourful barnstorming of Mr. Brown, senior figures like Mr. Stewart, Mr. Short and Sir Keith Joseph went almost unnoticed. Backbenchers and dissidents featured even less — with one exception. Quoted more often than

TABLE 2

*Politicians quoted in news coverage 1970*

| | Times quoted | | | | Times quoted | | |
|---|---|---|---|---|---|---|---|
| | BBC-1 | ITN | Radio | | BBC-1 | ITN | Radio |
| Wilson | 33 | 32 | 57 | Heath | 32 | 31 | 72 |
| Jenkins | 3 | 8 | 9 | Powell | 10 | 11 | 9 |
| Brown | 5 | 5 | 7 | Maudling | 4 | 7 | 7 |
| Callaghan | 7 | 5 | 6 | Barber | 5 | 4 | 5 |
| Benn | 3 | 5 | 2 | Macleod | 3 | 2 | 6 |
| Healey | 2 | 2 | 3 | Hogg | 3 | 2 | 2 |
| Mellish | 1 | 3 | 1 | Home | 2 | 2 | 1 |
| Crossman | 1 | 2 | 0 | 6 other Conservatives | 5 | 3 | 2 |
| 11 other Labour | 3 | 2 | 8 | Thorpe | 9 | 15 | 18 |
| | | | | Byers | 6 | 6 | 28 |
| 5 others | 3 | 3 | 2 | 5 other Liberals | 3 | 5 | 8 |

anyone but the three party leaders, Mr. Powell actually received slightly longer attention than Mr. Thorpe (7% of all coverage of politicians, and 15% of that given to Conservatives).

The 'Powell issue' was the biggest single problem in handling the election. Irrespective of their personal views newsmen felt that they had to play the story hard. Mr. Powell's own views and the resulting reverberations took about one-fifth of all election coverage. Mr. Powell himself filled only a fraction of this time; it was the comments of Messrs. Benn, Callaghan, Heath and others which forced the question into pre-eminence on all channels. From the publication of his election address right through to Mr. Powell's complaint about his colleagues' treatment of him, his name was rarely out of the bulletins. BBC and ITN treatment ran closely parallel: both succinctly reported his election address, splashed the Benn–Powell affair, noted Mr. Powell's disavowal of racism and gave full play to his speeches on immigration, violence and 'the enemy within'. Both also reported him on less explosive issues. At the end many broadcasters felt uneasy at the emphasis the story had received — though Mr. Powell's appearances produced the most dramatic and compulsive viewing of an otherwise grey campaign.[1] Was he given too much attention? There could be

[1] The Liberals complained that both networks reported Mr. Powell's speech on immigration in his constituency and interviewed him there, infringing the Representation of the People Act's provisions on coverage of 'constituency

no objective yardstick and no conclusive answer. Yet since news time is inelastic, concentration on this issue meant automatically giving less attention to others. This could be one explanation of the 'forgotten issues' like education, foreign affairs and the social services, of which little or nothing was heard. At such a price it was perhaps unwise to play something as essentially peripheral as the Powell issue quite so hard, and particularly to let it dominate the bulletins so heavily on specific days, two of which fell during the period when the country was unusually dependent on broadcasting for news.[1]

The parties had announced an economic election and, despite the prominence of the Powell affair, the various facets of the economic debate collectively loomed larger still, with almost 30% of the coverage of issues. The arguments on prices and incomes, the balance of payments, taxation and industrial relations formed a major running story on all channels, which also reported each fresh portent about the general health of the economy. The prominence given towards the close of the campaign to reports and statistics conflicting with the official euphoria understandably became a major irritant to Labour. But it seems hard to substantiate the Labour belief that the reporting of their compaign was particularly unfavourable; in fact the BBC and ITN ran closely parallel in both their assessment of news value and in their handling of the signs of a weakening in the economic position.

Not all the coverage related specifically to issues: there were extensive nightly travelogues about the leaders' tours, a sprinkling of constituency surveys and the usual crop of campaign 'incidents' including film of the rumbustious campaigning of Mr. Brown and Mr. Hogg, and succinct reporting of the egg-throwing incidents. The only ugly moments were the jostling of the Wilsons and of Mr. Heath, while twice there were minor disturbances at Mr. Powell's meetings. But these were scarcely on a scale to justify his allegation that television was being used to 'cast a mantle over disorder'. In fact less overtly disruptive behaviour was seen and heard than in either 1964 or 1966, partly because the broadcasters had

---

issues'. The broadcasters felt that immigration and alleged infiltration of the civil service were not constituency issues alone, and that to ban reporting of the story would be an intolerable curtailment of journalistic freedom.

[1] On June 11 the immigration speech and reactions to it made up about 50% of BBC-1's 8.50 p.m. election coverage, 75% of *News at Ten*'s, and all of *24 Hours Campaign Reports*.

TABLE 3

*Ranking of subjects in news and party broadcasts*

| | BBC-1 | ITN | Radio | Party broad-casts* | | BBC-1 | ITN | Radio | Party broad-casts* |
|---|---|---|---|---|---|---|---|---|---|
| 'Powell'† | 1 | 1 | 1 | — | Bal. of payments | 9 | 7 | 5 | 8= |
| Politicians' tours‡ | 2 | 2 | 9= | ... | Law and order | 10 | 11= | 9= | ... |
| State of economy§ | 3 | 3 | 4 | 2 | Ulster | 11 | 9 | 8 | ... |
| Campaign incidents | 4= | 8 | 7 | — | Housing | ... | 10 | ... | 10 |
| Prices and wages | 4= | 6 | 6 | 1 | Education | — | — | — | 4 |
| Polls | 6 | 4= | 3 | ... | Social services | ... | — | — | 5= |
| Invective | 7 | 11= | 11 | 3 | Taxation | ... | ... | ... | 5= |
| Ind. relations‖ | 8 | 4= | 2 | 7 | Leisure, culture | — | — | — | 8= |

* All major party boardcasts, radio and TV.
† Includes both Mr. Powell's own views and those of others on him or his critics. His views alone would have ranked 4, 4, 9 and —.
‡ Excluding all 'incidents' and classifiable issue content.
§ Includes general remarks also relating to prices and wages, industrial relations, balance of payments and taxation.
‖ Includes directly political aspects of the press and doctors' pay disputes.

decided on a low-keyed approach, but chiefly because the election proved far quieter than had once been feared.

Two major differences from earlier campaigns were the increased attention to the polls and the development of more analytical presentation. Formerly polls had usually been reported only after publication; now they were picked up from the early editions before these had reached their readers, or published only over the air because of the press strike. Both channels played them heavily: BBC-1 led its 8.50 p.m. election segments seven times on the latest poll, and ITN did so six times. The tendency towards more explanatory reporting was viewed with some disquiet by the parties. Without a certain amount of linking material, bulletins would have simply been successions of snippety excerpts which ordinary viewers would have found quite unacceptably confusing. For the most part this presentation was limited to a discreet linking of the day's clips from speeches or circumspect weekend campaign retrospects, but at times presenters lapsed into somewhat glib and cavalier resumés of the day's events (drawing a handful of minor incidents together as 'aggro day'). Sometimes presentation of the polls encouraged a horse-race view of the election; and it was surely wrong to take the outcome almost for granted and to depict Mr. Powell's activities as the opening skirmish in the coming struggle to succeed Mr. Heath.

During and after the campaign the parties were charged with avoiding the real issues. But Mr. Hogg and Mr. Healey (among others) vigorously objected that they frequently talked on Vietnam, EEC, pollution and education, but the media showed little attention. Though it was hard to see where justice lay, it was clear enough that television's election was increasingly taken for 'the' election, at least in the sense of being a faithful microcosm. Yet the drastic selectivity time imposes on newsmen, enhanced by technical, financial and political restraints, means that television is always liable to be holding a distorting mirror to reality. And broadcasters and parties live in a symbiotic relationship. If some issues were splashed and others forgotten, this was partly because of the way the politicians signalled which speeches they thought routine and which important. Criticisms of the 1970 campaign perhaps centred too much on what was visible in the media — the tip of the iceberg. What lay beneath may have been rather different.

Somewhere between 'news' and 'current affairs' came *24 Hours Campaign Report*, which ran on BBC-1 against *News at Ten*. Though suffering initially from the BBC's preoccupation with beating ITN with the main news, it later developed into a varied nightly election magazine. Some of the items were traditional: the discussions with lobby correspondents, the round-table of foreign journalists, the Marxian critique by a Soviet newsman. But the programme tried hard to cast its net wider, despite the parties' dislike of direct discussion. It featured less frequently exposed figures like Mr. Rippon, Mr. Patrick Jenkin, Mr. Diamond and Lord Balniel, and included two extended explorations of the economy with Mr. Maudling and Mr. Jenkins, as well as discussions of under-aired issues like housing and social welfare.[1]

In its attempts to be enterprising *24 Hours Campaign Report* became itself a subject of controversy. Lord Byers complained that between June 4 and 11 no Liberals appeared, apart from stylised constituency reports. Overall they had only about 4% of its time — much less than on any other programme. Labour was particularly angry about two items. The first was on direct grant schools in Bristol. Considering education among their 'strong' issues, Labour felt it unfair to select a small aspect where comment would be largely hostile. (This imbalance was in fact an accidental consequence of the collapse of a proposed general discussion of education.) The second tried to settle the cost-of-living argument through a clumsily-executed 'case study' of a postal worker's wife, which several Labour leaders branded as a 'Conservative party political'. Its weaknesses were not denied in retrospect. But there were other items (such as discussion of Mr. Heath's future after defeat) to which Conservatives could have taken equal exception, and also 'non-partisan' errors like a misleading piece on the pollster's methods. The ability of the programme to offend all sides was no proof of objectivity, but its faults seemed due to lax editing rather than to wilful party bias. In the hectic pace of the election *24 Hours Campaign Report* was sadly lacking in the extended reporting which can be the saving grace of its normal programmes (though a visiting American's

[1] *24 Hours Campaign Report* gave most time to 'the state of the economy', with the Powell issue second, followed by constituency surveys, discussions among journalists, industrial relations, polls, prices and incomes, housing and the social services.

light, wry personal view of the campaign stood out as almost the only notable reportage seen anywhere during the election). But at its best it was varied and enterprising, successes outnumbering failures — even if they could not outweigh them in the eyes of tensely electioneering politicians.

*Current affairs programmes.* In the now established ritual of current affairs coverage the BBC opened with *Election Forum.* On successive evenings at the start of the campaign the party leaders answered questions from some 15,000 postcards submitted by viewers and put by a three-man team.[1] Mr. Wilson had far the roughest passage, partly because of the virulence of many of the postcards directed to him as leader of the governing party ('In view of your past record of lies and broken promises do you really expect the electorate to place any reliance on your word?'), and partly too from a desire among the panel to balance the unduly easy interview he had contrived on the evening of the election announcement. Overall, the series confirmed its established qualities: hasty questioning over a wide range of topics, but a chance for the leaders to respond directly to the preoccupations of ordinary voters rather than the usual circle of professional interviewers.

The party leaders also featured in three of *This Week*'s four election editions.[2] In Mr. Robert Kee they had a usually gentle if prosy interviewer doing his best to be tough. Unfortunately, an over-aggressive or ill-prepared questioner can divert interest from the subject's ideas to whether he can keep his composure. And Mr. Kee, giving Mr. Wilson the roughest ride again, jolted him into saying he had been more civilly handled by the BBC, and then inflicted a technical knockout on himself while attempting to floor Mr. Wilson with an incomplete quotation. There was little real illumination either there or in the remaining edition of *This Week*, featuring an encounter between Sir Peter Rawlinson, Mr. Crossman and six young voters. Their noisy, intolerant onslaught drove the politicians into a joint defence of politics but produced

[1] Though planned originally to run 45 minutes (with 30 for Mr. Thorpe), the programmes were cut to 35 (25) because Mr. Wilson decreed that more would bore the viewers — a curious view of the first occasion for four years when senior politicians had answered ordinary citizens' questions on television.

[2] *This Week* had a particularly difficult time negotiating with the parties, and the programmes eventually presented differed considerably from its original plans. ITV's other nationally networked current affairs programme, *World in Action*, was blacked out by the Granada strike, which put many North-west viewers back under a BBC monopoly from May 26 until after polling day.

no real dialogue. It was 'good television' but it understandably deepened the politicians' mistrust of live audiences still further.

The most sustained attempt to illuminate the issues came as usual from *Panorama*, with editions on the economy, foreign affairs and industrial relations. These were notable for ensuring that the election programmes should not be monopolised by the politicians. Though far too much of the producers' energies were drained by protracted negotiations with the parties, the industrial relations edition was notable for its attempt to explain the parties' proposals and open them to critical discussion by both sides of industry, in addition to providing one of the rare 'confrontations', between Mrs. Castle and Mr. Carr. The economic edition also supplemented its conventional interviews with Mr. Jenkins and Mr. Maudling with a sceptical survey of recent economic performance by Nicholas Harman which could have pleased neither big party, and the famous discussion with Lords Cromer and Kearton (though the militant Tory and the muted Labour sympathiser proved an ill-balanced pair).[1] A special edition of *The Money Programme* went even further. After the parties refused to participate with a 'live audience' of eminent figures like Lord Beeching and Mr. Feather the programme went ahead without them. With the aid of Labour and Conservative economists and pairs of city men, industrialists, union leaders and a shop steward, an insurance broker, a bank manager and two managing directors, they provided a useful if slightly pedestrian seventy-minute scrutiny of the economy and the parties' proposals which suggested that the politicians had little to fear except more searching discussion of their policies. Spacious and serious, the programme was a precedent for the politicians to ponder.

The one other nationally networked programme was *The Question Why*, which escaped the ban on Sunday broadcasts since it appeared under the auspices of the Religious Broadcasting Department. Featuring Mr. Malcolm Muggeridge, Mr. Hogg and Mr. Healey among a panel of discussants which would have been vetoed as a 'live audience' anywhere else, this dealt with some of the moral aspects of participating in the democratic process. The change of setting brought a striking transformation: with its reasoned and courteous tone this was one of the few programmes

[1] Cf. above, p. 155.

from which the viewer was likely to emerge with a more sympathetic understanding of politics and politicians.

Regional programmes ran along established lines, and were almost always screened either before 7 p.m. or after 10.45 p.m. The most favoured format was the panel of party representatives questioned by journalists. This was the pattern of the BBC's customary regional contribution, *Question Time*. Worthy and useful, such programmes often suffered from spokesmen nominated for reasons unrelated to television skills and from the unfamiliarity of newspapermen with television questioning.[1] The boldest of the regional contributions was *Hook-Up* broadcast by Thames three times for $1\frac{3}{4}$ hours, with Mr. Richard Marsh and Mr. Maudling answering questions telephoned by viewers who had sent postcards to the studios, and briefer interventions by a Liberal and a Communist. Despite intrusive technical difficulties the programmes were relaxed, informative and courteous. It was an innovation which deserved something better than the tiny audiences of midday television.

While some ITV companies took their public service responsibilities lightly, others with a more settled regional identity did better. Anglia's programme on agriculture dealt usefully with a major regional interest which metropolitan coverage ignored. Tyne-Tees showed enterprise in mounting locally-oriented programmes without falling foul of the parties' restrictions. And STV, Grampian and Border ran more local news and constituency features than most of the English regions. BBC Scotland also offered nightly Scottish coverage and even its own *Scottish Viewpoint* in place of London's *The Question Why*, because the religious and political balance were thought inappropriate to Scotland. Though the nationalists still complained of London domination, Scottish viewers had access to considerably more home-grown programmes than those in England. The same was true in Ulster, where it at one time seemed doubtful whether any discussions could be mounted. In the event Ulster TV ran six rather conventional *Campaign Ulster* programmes, and the BBC ambitiously covered every seat in the province and ended with a two-hour *tour de force* with thirteen candidates from four seats answering viewers' questions. Party obstructiveness proved sur-

[1] *Question Time* was one of the few programmes to which the parties nominated spokesmen; the precedent was not encouraging.

prisingly little hindrance, and although some programmes too resolutely avoided awkward issues while others talked about nothing but the Border or otherwise raised more heat than light, there was far broader and more coherent discussion of the province's problems than could fairly have been hoped.

Ulster is about the only television area which can be covered comprehensively. For this reason a major innovation in 1970 was the contribution by the new BBC local radio stations at Brighton, Durham, Leeds, Leicester, Liverpool, Nottingham, Sheffield and Stoke-on-Trent. In covering their first general election they met a number of frustrations, whether from the hostility of national party headquarters to Sunday broadcasts or live audiences or from candidates who, as one station manager put it, seemed to have an inbuilt dread of confronting an ordinary voter. But most candidates welcomed this fresh outlet, and all the local stations made a major effort for the election. All succeeded in injecting a degree of discussion between the parties which would usually have been completely absent without them. The programmes were mostly along familiar lines: lengthy news coverage, constituency surveys, and local *Election Forums* or *Question Times*. Though the audiences were often modest, cumulatively the extension of coverage was noteworthy. Thus Radio Stoke ran some nine hours of election programmes, giving candidates who were totally ignored by the national media some forty minutes each over their home station. Limited though local radio's scope was, it stood notably counter to the trend towards nationalised or 'presidential' presentation.

*Party broadcasts.* Within their uniform ten-minute span the party broadcasts showed markedly contrasting approaches. Labour's strategy was in the hands of its Campaign Committee, advised by the Technical Committee of specialists in various media. Determined to remain flexible, and remembering the large sums spent on film that was never used in 1964, their basic plan was not to plan. Broadcasts would be decided on a day-to-day basis, though from the beginning it was agreed that the Prime Minister would open and close the television series, and that in an 'economic election' a place must obviously be reserved for Mr. Jenkins. But the Labour series was never conceived as a whole nor built around any fully elaborated theme.

Mostly Labour's programmes adopted a conventional style, and

## LABOUR TELEVISION BROADCASTS

I. Wilson at cluttered 'Downing St.' desk, shot closing to head-and-shoulders. One of strongest economies in world, yet had maintained tolerance, compassion, stability. Britain now more compassionate: widows, aged, ending eleven-plus. From economic strength could now improve social services, pensions, housing, roads, modernise towns, tackle pollution, help other countries. Tories had exploited weakness, rejoiced in setbacks, would fritter away surplus. Proposals to raise expenditure while cutting taxes were irresponsible. Law and order being made political football — but look at Ulster where Tories ruled. Must judge on responsibility, on men, on purposes, on ideals, decide whom to trust in guiding Britain in changing world.

II. Fanfare. Welsh voice introduces to Callaghan at Cardiff rally, beside platform among loose group of questioners, camera cutting from C. to questioners to group. C. answers questions on problems ahead, work-shy, age of majority, conscription, mortgage rates, law and order, achievements in Wales. Fanfare. 'Now Britain's strong — let's make it great to live in.'

III. Building blocks marked 'homes'; 'hospitals', etc., being piled: stack falls as 'tax' block removed. Children screech. Cut to young mothers in classroom on opportunity in education, noises off of playing children. Cut to children working in class: voice over, you're voting for their future. Cut to Short at desk to camera, closing to head-and-shoulders. Attacks Con. on selectivity, praises comprehensives, wants smaller classes, more buildings, teachers. Cut to film of school child, with S. over on plans for higher education and pre-school years. Shots of winsome children. S. to camera: election about your children, their future, country's future. Child making up jigsaw, voice over listing Lab. education achievements. Woman's voice over 'roads', 'hospitals' — and taxes — bricks. Flute music, Lab. slogan.

IV. Jenkins to camera at desk, closing to head-and-shoulders. Things neither perfect nor near-catastrophic: paying way; pound strong; debts melting. Success story though prices not solved. Tory proposals inflationary. Must give prices attention gave to paying our way. Voluntary wages policy, fair taxation, investigate price exploiters. Use economic strength for more regional employment, old, disabled, widows. Can't tolerate poverty here; mustn't forget it abroad. Must produce wealth, but also civilise. Position of strength: only you can maintain advance. Relief map of UK Voice over: Lab. slogan, June 18th Vote Labour (caption).

V. Children wave, cheer Mr. and Mrs. Wilson. Voice over: this was their reception. Bond with people built over 5 years, gatherings symbolise trust. W. amid crowds, fading to W. at desk, to camera, closing to head-and-shoulders. Been like this all over country. No PM this century had fought from such economic strength. Tories tried issue after issue. Had tried proposals to spend more, tax less, but reckoned without common sense of British. Con. proposals would raise prices. Lab. modernised industry; Con. would cut back. Socialism meant using resources to make Britain better to live in: strengthening social services, freedom and opportunity for young, concern for minorities. Make great, compassionate country. Must decide whether to build on or squander achievements. Too vital choice to stand aside. Fade.

the message was simple: that of a governing party looking back with pride and forward with diffuse optimism, finding its opponents sadly unsuited to office. Mr. Wilson's opening talk to camera told again how the country had been brought from perilous straits and was now poised for advance. The next programme was assigned to Mr. Callaghan, who chose the format on the favourable memory of an earlier televised question and answer session with workers. It was filmed at short notice, forgoing colour, after one of his Cardiff rallies. A simple programme, shot in a single take with a group of twenty or so questioners, it made rather uneven viewing. Even as seasoned a campaigner as Mr. Callaghan found it hard to wring political advantage when asked about the work-shy or how to define law and order. Though the programme was scorned by the critics, its appeal lay in the fact that Mr. Callaghan was answering questions with visibly 'real' people with whom viewers might identify, rather than lecturing one through the camera. Ironically such an encounter with a 'live audience' was acceptable only within the secure confines of a party broadcast.

The Conservatives were to bid for the women's vote over the cost of living; Labour chose to appeal to them through their children. More women may be struggling with housekeeping than are currently rearing children, but education was a Labour success story, while on prices they would have been forced on to the defensive. In the third programme Mr. Short was seen only briefly as he recalled Labour's educational and social welfare record; additional visual and emotional appeal was sought by illustrating his talk with engaging film of children at work in a Streatham pre-school play group. There was also an attempt to make visually the point that Conservative proposals to cut taxation would undermine social welfare: a tower of blocks labelled 'schools', 'hospitals', 'pensions' and so on toppled over when the 'taxes' block was removed — but this was too clumsily staged to be effective. That was Labour's most ambitious effort. Mr. Jenkins' programme was a conventional talk to camera with one of the familiar study sets, outlining the economic record and prospects in noticeably more prudent terms than Mr. Wilson had. Then as usual the Prime Minister closed the series. He was heralded by a montage of film clips demonstrating his (and Mrs. Wilson's) warm reception during his tours, and his ability to mix with ordinary people. Some on the Labour side were to feel the build-up had been a trifle too fulsome for a rather tired Prime Minister who had little new to say. He reiterated the health of the economy more ebulliently than ever, slated the wretchedness of the opposition and then closed on the obligatory note of uplift in looking to a bright if quite unspecific future.

The Liberal series also adopted a conventional format. If simplicity was partly dictated by lack of resources, the highly experienced Mrs. Doreen Gorsky who was responsible for their programmes was also a strong believer in the head-and-shoulders approach which was adopted in all three broadcasts. The first and third (which was done as an outside broadcast from Bideford) were assigned to Mr. Thorpe both because he was the leader and needed putting across, and because he was thought a good performer. The second, recorded in the BBC's Glasgow studios, went

LIBERAL TELEVISION BROADCASTS

I. Thorpe at desk in study, shot closing slowly to head and shoulders. Commenting on big party polemics, proposes to focus on agreed facts: balance of payments surplus; more wealth needed to pay for welfare; sluggish growth; Con., Lab. difficulty in controlling inflation. Big parties = stop-go, wage freezes. Lib. answer: national minimum earnings £15 p.w., works councils, tax incentives for profit sharing, plant productivity bargaining. Cf. Donovan and PIB. Criticises Con., Lab. proposals. Libs. right on Europe, E. of Suez, right again on partnership in industry, wage structure, efficiency audits in nationalised industry, Scots and Welsh parliaments and English regional assemblies. Need large Lib. vote, group to knock sense into giants. Caption read by woman, man: 'Show them you care — VOTE LIBERAL'.

II. Grimond at desk to camera, moving slowly to head and shoulders shot. Tories going to lose — men with yesterday's ideas. New parliament needs new men, ideas: decentralisation. Libs. pioneered regionalism. Don't want remote rule. Reduce gap between boardroom and shop floor with works councils. Lab. = devaluation, inflation. Con., Lab. unable to reduce friction in industry. Bring wage negotiations nearer people, reform methods of government. Special committees to improve efficiency. More public-, private-sector competition. Need more skilful, humane country with more involvement. Increased Lib. representation promotes good sense, humanity, decentralisation, less and better government, more freedom.

III. Thorpe at desk to camera, shot closing to head and shoulders. Thinks voters decided to return Lab., not because Lab. deserve to win, but Con. deserve to lose. Still question of opposition, vital in democracy. If Tories lose, danger of party civil war. More Libs. needed for constructive opposition. Cites Lib. policy on industry, taxes, Ulster, immigration, housing, nationalised industries, bureaucracy, national parliaments and regional assemblies. Few more or less Lab. or Con. unimportant, but 20–30 Libs. vital. Problem of government settled: see there's effective opposition. Voting Lib. good for you, parliament, country.

to Mr. Grimond who had been particularly successful in past election broadcasts. In the event he seemed older, with less of the freshness and vigour of earlier campaigns, and his script was noticeably thin. Though Mr. Thorpe was slightly funereal he brought an air of quiet reasonableness to both his broadcasts. Both he and Mr. Grimond saw the basic task as putting across the distinctive Liberal policies on issues like industrial relations and regionalism and in making the case for a solid nucleus of Liberal M.P.s. Mr. Thorpe was a trifle unfortunate in the timing of his closing broadcast, which was pegged to the prevailing belief in a Labour victory and argued that the chief remaining issue was the nature of the opposition: the preceding BBC news and the ITN bulletin which followed his recorded broadcast both reported Gallup's sharp cutback in Labour's lead.

For theii single broadcast the Communists fielded their General Secretary, Mr. Gollan, in a straight talk to camera. With notable economy of words he used the opportunity to indicate his party's position on wages, taxation, the state of the economy, the Common Market and Cambodia, ending with a special appeal to young voters — and all in five minutes.

Conservative preparations began over a year before the election with the formation of their Thursday Group on broadcasting aspects of the campaign,[1] with Mr. Barber, Mr. Whitelaw, Central Office staff, advertising men, and Mr. Geoffrey Johnson-Smith. The problem was to use effectively about one hour of television time, divided into five segments and transmitted at around nine in the evening. A unified series suggested using an anchor man, but there would be political difficulties over the dominance of a single anchor man. It was decided to use two anchor men, who could in any case put material over in a more rapid-fire way than one. Gradually thinking moved towards a format strongly resembling that of *News at Ten*, though this was settled before it was known that the party broadcasts would be transmitted at ten o'clock. This fast-moving, complex formula could scarcely have worked as smoothly without the great professionalism of Johnson-Smith and Chataway. As it was the programmes were to be the most striking attempt yet seen in a series of party broadcasts to reach the television audience through the verbal and visual idiom to which it has become accustomed,

[1] Cf. above, pp. 108-9.

particularly on ITV. The set itself bore a family resemblance to *News at Ten*'s; Ken Jones' theme music again seemed vaguely familiar while cunningly following the rhythm of 'A Better Tomorrow'; there were even explicit breaks for 'commercials'. One showed Mr. Wilson unresponsive to a bombardment of questions, another the wastebasket full of Labour promises used in the press campaign and a third a pound note being steadily snipped away as a commentator recorded its declining value. This 'ten bob pound' clip was in twenty seconds visually the most telling single moment of the campaign — it even stung a rejoinder from Mr. Jenkins.

The series also drew extensively on short film cuts of street interviews, party broadcasts over the previous two years having shown that some points could be made more acceptably and believably through ordinary people than by politicians. This vox pop material was skilfully used to strike the hardest and lowest blows:

> 'Voice 6: My pay over the last twelve years has doubled, but my standard of living has gone down by half.
>
> Voice 7: Oh, you take a pound note — it's gone. You take a five pound note and that's gone. It's terrible.
>
> Voice 8: Bloody disgraceful.
>
> Voice 9: Terrible.
>
> Voice 10: Shocking.
>
> Voice 11: It's disgraceful. Everything's gone up. Toothpaste, baby clothes, baby food, everything you go for.'

Had politicians voiced the abuse of the 'vox pop' material there would have been uproar. The Johnson-Smith/Chataway dialogues which opened four programmes were also used to hit the government with hard-hitting topical jibes, but without overt abuse. The senior politicians were thus left free for a more positive approach in their brief statements to camera.

The primary brief, agreed in 1969, was to stress prices, taxes and broken promises, presenting the Conservatives as the party of choice and freedom who would keep their promises — few of which were offered in specific terms. The need to re-establish trust was a major theme in Mr. Heath's opening broadcast. With the second there was a temporary diversion to nail the 'Labour lie' that the Conservatives lacked compassion, with an unhappy and wooden Lord Balniel discoursing on Labour's arrogance while walking in the park, and Mr. Maudling arguing that only the Conservatives were competent enough to make their com-

## CONSERVATIVE TELEVISION BROADCASTS

I. Woman, vox-pop: wouldn't vote for either party. Johnson-Smith, Chataway in *News at Ten* set. Crosstalk dialogue recalls Lab. pledges on taxes, unemployment, freeze, living standards (quotes on back-projected slides). Party motif. Clip of wastebasket filling with scrapped promises. Pound note being snipped, voice over recalls 'pound in pocket', inflation record: 'The ten bob pound. Only you can stop him'. Wastebasket, voice over reading tax pledge and taxation record (also superimposed). Ten vox-pops of grumblers on promises, taxes, homes, jobs. Cut to Heath at desk to camera, moving in to head and shoulders. Understood why people felt let down. Politicians not all same. Does matter who wins. Cons. for freedom — to live in own home, be better off, spend own money, have real say, be individual. Opportunity for youth. Old to have help they needed. Promises to do best to secure better tomorrow.

II. H. rises to speak amid applause. Cut to S. and C. in *News at Ten* set. C.: care and compassion tonight's theme. Music. S.: much heard of compassion, but what does Wilson care. Introduces Balniel on suffering old and poor, arrogance Lab. claim to monopolise compassion. C. introduces break. Theme. Still sequence old faces, voice over on plight of aged. Commentator on misery of Lab. compassionate society. Ten bob pound clip. Still of Wilson's face, closing in on mouth as irate voices question. Commentator: why can't W. answer? Vox pops on hardships. Maudling to camera: Lab. had let people down. Must return to growth so as to help needy, old chronic sick, large poor families. Needs party with both compassion, competence. Theme. Vote Con. on June 18.

III. Hand draws object from frig. Voice over: frozen wage packet — Vote Lab. and get family-size. S. and C. crosstalk on strength of economy, quoting Cromer, Kearton, Callaghan *et al.*: four years freeze, four months sunshine. Clip of grocer in shop mentioning price rises. C. warns of long cold winter. Ten bob pound clip. Still of Wilson, closing in to mouth, volley of queries — W. silent. Theme. Party motif. Twelve vox pop clips on taxes, prices. Cut to Macleod to camera: Con. kept promises, contrasts Lab. promise and performance on housing, prices. Con. would cut expenditure, boost savings, expand output, reform and simplify taxes. Choose us for both freedom and choice. Theme. Motif. Vote Con. on June 18.

IV. Wedding bells, wedding photo closing in to the woman. Women's voices over, jaundiced about politicians. S.: election may be decided by hidden majority — housewives. Motif. Theme. S. and C. crosstalk on housewives' problem. Introduce Sylvia in still and film, entering home, shopping while her voice over talks of wants, making ends meet. Full face: won't vote Lab. again. Over clip of children in playground complains of strikes. Con. couldn't be worse than Lab. Full face: thinks husband still Lab., but she'll vote Con. Macleod to camera: she's right. Can you afford ten bob pound, frozen wage packet? Socialism = high prices and taxes. Throw them out, they just don't care. S.: what does better tomorrow mean to Sylvia? She over clip of child in park: hope. Theme. Motif. Vot Con. Still of ballot. Voice over: wrong decision could be expensive.

V. Clips of Heath touring. C. (over): H. enjoyed himself, had come to life, could be trusted; well prepared for office. Stills of H. as schoolboy, in uniform; film of Glasgow arrival. C.: best equipped PM ever. Clips H. addressing crowds, signing autographs, calling for change, drinking beer, mingling. C (over): people have been seeing real man. Clips of H. victory drink after Sydney–Hobart, campaigning, at desk, amid crowds. C.: H.'s message getting through. Audience rises to H., who blows kisses. C.: not easy man to know, but man to trust. S. introduces H. at desk to camera. H. recalls Sydney–Hobart origins of 'better tomorrow'. Lab. expected people to be dismal, encouraged country to be second-rate. We should enter race to win. Virtues of prosperity, freedom. Duty of government to let people be proud, free. Do you want worry of last 5 years or better tomorrow? Promises will work for better tomorrow — 'and I keep my word'. Theme. Motif. Ballot form. Voice: wrong decision could be costly. Theme. Vote Con.

passion effective. Some party loyalists thought Mr. Maudling too gentlemanly. They preferred the more robust verdict of Mr. Macleod in the third programme: 'They (Labour) just don't care.' The popularity of Mr. Macleod's destruction of the government's economic record resulted in his being brought in again for the fourth programme, which some in the party considered a landmark in political television. This was the bid for the women's vote, returning to the long-standing Conservative conviction that women are more likely changers than men if only they will 'vote for themselves'. The leading figure was Sylvia, a twenty-two-year-old working housewife from Wandsworth who had featured in a vox-pop clip in an earlier party broadcast, and was remembered for unaffectedly personifying the target voter. She was now filmed going about her daily chores and commenting on the difficulty of making ends meet, her disillusion with Labour and her intention of giving the Tories a trial. Even in the heavily-edited version shown her genuineness was transparent, if only from the torrent of 'you knows', and film of her child playing and a shopping expedition provided plenty for women to identify with. Yet if she struck a chord with younger women, in the domestic detail there was much to make older women doubt just how good a 'manager' Sylvia was. In some respects Sylvia resembled rather too closely television's familiar slightly feckless housewife whose life is transformed by discovering some new detergent.

Mr. Heath appeared for ten of his party's fifty minutes (against Mr. Wilson's twenty). His second appearance was preceded by a fulsome montage of film and stills, more complex than the introduction to Mr. Wilson's closing broadcast. This sought to convey his honesty, magnetism and experience and instil a brave air of optimism when most of the faithful saw defeat only seventy-two hours ahead. Mr. Heath moved skilfully from shots of his Sydney–Hobart race to recalling how 'a better tomorrow' arose from a conversation in Sydney harbour, and offering to work for a 'better tomorrow' for Britain in contrast with the worries of the past five years. Though less impressive than in his final 1966 broadcasts, what he said seemed more suited to his personality than much of what he had earlier been persuaded to utter.

Overall, the Conservative series had a professional polish never previously achieved in party election broadcasts. The team of writers, producers and technical staff assembled by Mr. Geoffrey Tucker was experienced in the highly specialised genre of party broadcasts and used to working with the politicians. The party also called on professional producers, Mr. Bryan Forbes, Mr. Dick Clement and Mr. Terence Donovan, specialists in TV commercials, and a free-lance TV director, Mr. Gordon Reece. The programmes were taped in the London studios of TVR Ltd. Though sometimes visuals were jumpy and the pace too hectic, the careful consideration to detail was evident. Yet the test of such broadcasts does not lie with the verdict of professionals or critics, but in the ballot boxes, and the limited evidence collected by the Conservatives and BBC Audience Research about the effectiveness of the programmes was inconclusive.[1] It suggested, though, that while straight talks to camera may bore producers, they are as likely to be effective as more elaborate productions. Thus Mr. Jenkins seems to have been better received than some of the Conservative 'glossies'. And if Mr. Wilson's final programme was indeed a failure and Mr. Heath's a success, the explanation seems unlikely to lie in the packaging.

Despite very differing approaches, all three parties were attempt-

[1] The Conservatives had daily 'morning after' polls done by ORC, with a 500 sample, but the ratings calculated for effectiveness depended on the 100–150 who had actually seen the programme. The BBC used a daily quota sample of 2,250, and calculated 'reaction indexes' for each programme. BBC data suggested that viewers were less enthusiastic about the party broadcasts generally than in 1966, with little to choose between the Labour and Conservative TV. The two series of data agreed in assessing Mr. Jenkins highly as well as Mr. Heath's closing broadcast (which scored heavily over Mr. Wilson's), and also both gave Mr. Thorpe a high rating. Conservatives laid a great emphasis on Mr. Heath's 'honesty rating' for his final broadcast, but this was no higher than Mr. Callaghan's or Mr. Grimond's.

ing to foster impressions and attitudes than to engage in direct argument on issues. The Conservatives were intent on hammering home ideas about honesty and performance, while Labour sought to project itself as a party of courage and decency. By themselves the party broadcasts would have given an odd idea of what the parties stood for, and what they might achieve in office. It needed the autonomous current affairs programmes to tackle the unstated issues and to fill in the vacuum in the parties' discussion of the future; but the parties by using their time to convey a different range of themes from those explored by the other programmes, could claim that their broadcasts complemented rather than duplicated the rest of the television campaign.

Radio was secondary. It had been reorganised since 1966 and the parties seemed unsure what conclusions to draw from the changes. The Liberals saw the Radio 1 and 2 audience as young and trendy, using both their programmes for a dialogue between the Young Liberals' Political Vice-Chairman and a pop-group drummer. Labour also saw a relatively unpolitical audience, and used Andrew Faulds on culture and leisure, and Denis Howell on sport and leisure, both being only minimally partisan. Then Miss Joan Lestor, interviewed by John Hatch, emphasising leisure yet again, also appealed to the idealism of the young with references to development aid and the South African arms embargo. But the Conservatives saw the Radio 1 and 2 audience as older and more receptive to politics. Mr. Maudling attacked the Labour economic record and promised to set the country moving, and Mr. Heath looked back to an earlier Battle of Britain to argue that 1970 was another national turning point. Finally Mr. Bryan Forbes also dipped into nostalgia, as one who had voted Labour and had now discovered that 'the plasticine wasn't only in that puerile schoolboy campaign, but in the souls of men who begged to lead them to a better world'.

On Radio 4 this tone was sustained by Mr. Ronald Millar, the playwright, who had general responsibility for scripting the radio series. This was another angry onslaught from a disillusioned Labour voter, who saw Mr. Wilson as 'the man who was always wrong', 'who shrank in his job in order to keep it'. To its surprise Central Office received a more intense reaction to this broadcast than to any since Dr. Charles Hill's celebrated attack on the Attlee government in 1950. As in the television series the Conservatives used vox-pop material for the more outspoken attacks, though in another Radio 4 programme Mrs. Lynda Chalker and Sir Edwin Leather coupled a direct lashing of Labour with extended praise of Mr. Heath. Finally, speakers from England, Scotland and Wales assailed the economic record from the angle of the regions and the housewife.

In Labour's Radio 4 programmes Mrs. Castle attacked on prices and incomes; Mr. Benn defended the record and looked forward with equal idealism and imprecision; Mr. Jenkins reviewed the economic situation, and the Prime Minister once more demonstrated Labour's statesmanship and found the Conservatives wanting. The Liberals used both Radio 4 programmes to emphasise their regional policies and put the case, through Mr. Russell Johnston, for a small party at the side of the giants. For the Communists Mr. Solly Kaye concentrated in his five minutes on prices and incomes policy.

Apart from a few highly polemical contributions, the appeals on radio were more sober and reasoned than on television. Wherever both covered similar matters, facts and figures were thicker on radio. Some in the parties were tempted to deduce from 1970 experience that radio series should be cast in the same brand image as those on television. But perhaps the real lesson was that television often underrates its audience.[1]

*Audiences*. The 1970 campaign was short; four years had elapsed since an election, compared with the almost continuous politicking of 1963–66, and television was in fact less obtrusive. Apart from *Panorama*, *This Week* and the main 8.50 BBC-1 news, there was little politics in peak viewing hours. By the time the party broadcasts came on, followed by *Campaign Report* and *News at Ten* many people were going to bed or could switch off without feeling robbed of an evening's entertainment. With BBC-2 entirely apolitical apart from news and *The Money Programme*, viewers in three-channel areas had only ten minutes a night on thirteen evenings when the choice was politics, politics or politics.

Comparing audiences with 1966 is exceptionally hazardous owing

[1] Radio 4 broadcasts averaged 450,000 listeners; those on Radios 1 and 2 about 250,000. These figures cannot usefully be compared with 1966. BBC Audience Research data shows Mr. Heath's broadcast receiving the most favourable reaction, closely followed by the polemics by Messrs. Millar and Forbes. Though the parties appealed roughly equally to their own sympathisers, the Conservative broadcasts were better received among the uncommitted. The Liberals' 'youth dialogues' were particularly poorly received.

to changes in season, schedules and broadcasting structure, and to the distortions arising from the World Cup coverage. Thus viewing of party broadcasts fell sharply, but it was unquestionably depressed by the switch from 9.10 p.m. to 10 p.m. and the Granada

TABLE 4

*Audiences for party television broadcasts*

| | % of population aged five or over (BBC) | % of sets in use (JICTAR)* | | % of population aged five or over (BBC) | % of sets in use (JICTAR)* |
|---|---|---|---|---|---|
| Conservative | | | Labour | | |
| June 2 | 19·3 | 58 | June 1 | 19·3 | 52 |
| June 5 | 20·7 | 55 | June 4 | 18·9 | 51 |
| June 8 | 17·6 | 50 | June 9 | 19·9 | 45 |
| June 11 | 21·0 | 59 | June 12 | 19·4 | 53 |
| June 15 | 21·5 | 53 | June 16 | 24·6 | 45 |
| Average | 20·0 | 55 | Average | 20·4 | 49 |
| Liberal | | | Communist | | |
| June 3 | 19·5 | 56 | June 10 | 7·4 | 44 |
| June 10 | 16·3 | 48 | Scot. Nat.† | | |
| June 13 | 19·2 | 54 | June 12 | 16·0 (est) | 52 |
| Average | 18·3 | 53 | Plaid Cymru† | | |
| | | | June 10 | 14·4 (est) | N/A |

* BBC-2 excluded.
† Shown on Welsh or Scottish transmitters only.

strike, and doubtless it also suffered from the pull of the light, fine evenings.[1] But whatever the reason, audiences for almost all the political programmes were down on 1966,[2] and although fewer public complaints were heard of 'too much politics' on the air than in 1964 or 1966, there was evidence that few viewers

[1] Audience data is published with grateful acknowledgement to the BBC and JICTAR (Joint Industry Committee for Television Advertising Research). BBC Audience Research figures derive from interviews with a daily quota sample of 2,250 people aged 5 and over. Audience reaction is gathered from voluntary panels of listeners and viewers. A further post survey was conducted just after polling day with an effective sample of about 1,750. JICTAR ratings show the percentage of sets in a sample of 2,650 homes receiving both BBC-1 and ITV which were switched on during a broadcast, on the basis of minute-by-minute metered records. The two series are not comparable.

[2] On the BBC's calculation audiences for some of the principal programmes were: *Election Forum*; Mr. Thorpe 4·7 million (Mr. Grimond, 1966, 7·1 million), Mr. Heath 5·5 million (8·15 million), Mr. Wilson 8·5 million (10·3 million). *24 Hours Campaign Report* averaged 4·4 million; *Question Time* had 3·4 million and 4·0 million on television, and 250,000 and 200,000 on radio. *Panorama*'s election editions had audiences of 4·35 million, 4·2 million and 4·6 million. JICTAR ratings for *This Week* (depressed by the Granada strike) ranged from 4·13 million homes to 4·68 million, and for *News at Ten* their average rating was 4·17 million homes.

would have wanted more political programming and very many would have preferred less.[1] Whether this was a verdict on television itself or on the parties and politicians could not readily be determined. Smaller and less enthusiastic though the audience was, even the least popular major party broadcast was seen by some 8·5 million people, and the average nightly audiences for the main TV bulletins were 7·5 million on BBC-1 and 5·25 million (on the BBC's reckoning) for *News at Ten.* Fewer than one person in ten did not see or hear at least one programme about the election each day during the campaign.

Striking though such figures are, they really tell nothing about the 'effects' of broadcasting in the 1970 campaign. But some people believed that they knew only too well what effect television had. Labour anger about 'BBC bias' flared afresh, even though Mr. Wilson had said just before polling day that he had no complaints. However, as in 1966, the party offered no detailed substantiation of its charges of deliberate unfairness. From the varying piecemeal accounts which emerged semi-officially it appeared that some of the Labour leaders had become so deeply suspicious by the time of the election that every minor incident was automatically seen as confirmation of the Corporation's bias. Some of the party's anger seems also to have been an oblique expression of frustration at the way in which signs that all was not well with the economy figured, legitimately, so prominently in both networks' coverage towards the end of the campaign (quite conventional reports of the trade figures and the views of the Bank of International Settlements causing particular offence). Of the known grievances, some were too general to verify, others were trivial or factually inaccurate, and others were things on which reasonable men might differ; only a handful had any real substance. But in leaping from these to a conclusion of 'bias', Labour overlooked the unflattering material never screened, the mistakes which were made in its favour and the fact that the Conservatives, Liberals and minor parties in turn felt they had reasons for complaint. And uncommitted viewers could have objected as reasonably to the extraordinarily complais-

[1] The BBC's post-election survey found 47% saying too much time had been given to the election, 45% thinking it about right and only 3% saying there was not enough. Even among the most politically interested only 9% wanted more election programmes. A depressing 25% were prepared to agree that the campaign reports in news bulletins were 'completely unnecessary', and 40% thought they were 'a good idea but went on too long'; 26% thought they were 'absolutely right for me'.

ant interviews with the party leaders which both networks ran in their eve-of-poll bulletins, or the assumption of some political programmes that elections are for the politicians rather than for the voters. After watching or hearing well over a hundred election bulletins as well as every major current affairs programme during the campaign, I found a number of errors of judgement on all channels but nothing which could reasonably be categorised as bias for or against any of the major parties. However, Labour's own behaviour in a number of incidents had serious implications. There was the attempt to make *Panorama* drop a proposed discussion of international affairs with Mr. Stewart for one involving defence and featuring Mr. Healey, in which the Prime Minister apparently claimed a right to decide the programme's choice of subject and participant. Even more serious was a major outburst of indignation about the Corporation's partiality, particularly in its handling of eve-of-poll television news coverage.[1] Labour had legitimate enough viewpoints to defend, but chose to do this in ways which contained serious threats to the broadcasters' autonomy.

For the moment at least, then, hostility to the BBC was once more entrenched in the highest reaches of the Labour party, distracting attention from the overdue discussion of the adequacy of both BBC and ITV handling of politics which many broadcasters would have welcomed. It would be disingenuous to cast the politicians as the sole villains of the piece; as the Head of BBC-TV's Current Affairs Group recognised, the broadcasters must also accept some responsibility for the deterioration of relationships and the anxieties of politicians generally. Nevertheless, the greatest immediate danger was probably the threat to their independence. Conceivably this would take the form of fresh machinery of supervision and control, but it was clear that much of the backstage pressure on the BBC's senior administrators was aimed at making the broadcasters themselves emasculate their political coverage in the hope of appeasing the critics. In such a situation it could become all too easy to forget that political broadcasting does not exist for producers or politicians but for the ordinary citizen.

[1] Both incidents were poorly reported, but a circumstantial account of the week-long wrangle over *Panorama* was given in *The Times* (June 18), and it includes the firm reminder to Mr. Wilson by Lord Hill and Mr. Curran that his statements ran counter to the understandings between parties and broadcasters on the Committee on Political Broadcasting.

It seemed clear that in the years before the next election the broadcasters had to grapple with the delicate task of improving relations with the politicians but without in the process eroding their hard-won traditions of independence.

CHAPTER X

# FLEET STREET

BY COLIN SEYMOUR-URE[1]

IN 1970 a voter who sought to follow the election in the national press would have found himself quite well served with the usual mixture of description, analysis and partisan comment. But the papers did not seem to enjoy the election much. They announced their plans with a show of enthusiasm (almost as if the election were between themselves). They watched the cricket tour controversy as a promising warm-up. They accepted the manifestos as important preliminaries; and braced themselves after the spring Bank Holiday for the big fight.

It did not come. Mr. Wilson wanted a 'quiet' election and started his walkabouts. Mr. Heath aroused respect and sympathy but was dull. 'Covering Heath,' one journalist was reported to say, 'is like covering El Salvador in the World Cup.' By the end of the first week the leader writers were complaining of the depressing tone and triviality of the election. Then, just as Enoch Powell began to emerge, the polls to liven up and the journalists to assume a Conservative defeat, the strike of SOGAT members stopped publication of national newspapers for the four days June 10 to June 13. This upset the schedules for press coverage — constituency reports, for instance — probably much more than it upset the public. The strike was quickly buried, with scant attention to the democratic implications of such an event at election time.[2] The daily papers reappeared on the Monday before polling day; and for the first time the election really seemed to come to life in their columns, as they seized on the topic of Enoch Powell. This and the economy engrossed them for the last few days.

Quite likely the reality of British elections never lives up to Fleet Street's expectations (though the *Observer* did view the parties as 'engaged in a courtship display'). But if 1970 seemed

[1] The author is grateful to Roger Fenton and Richard Warner for their analysis of the newspapers (specially for Tables 1 and 2) and for their general suggestions and comments.

[2] See p. 164

## TABLE I

| Name of paper<br>Proprietors<br>Editor<br>Preferred result on June 18 | Circulation[1] (1966 in brackets) '000 | Readership[2] '000 | % of its readers in social class:[3] | | | | Mean number of pages May 27 to June 18 (1966 in brackets) | Number of lead stories on election May 27 to June 18 | Number of leading articles on election May 27 to June 18[4] | Numb of con stituen report May 2 to June 1 (1966 bracket |
|---|---|---|---|---|---|---|---|---|---|---|
| | | | AB | C1 | C2 | DE | | | | |
| *Daily Mirror*<br>Reed/International Publishing Co. (Don Ryder)<br>Lee Howard<br>Labour win | 4,850<br>(5,019) | 15,150 | 5 | 18 | 40 | 37 | 27<br>(29) | 3 | 9 | 0<br>(0) |
| *Daily Express*<br>Beaverbrook Newspapers (Sir Max Aitken)<br>Derek Marks<br>Conservative win | 3,670<br>(3,987) | 10,204 | 14 | 28 | 30 | 28 | 16<br>(20) | 10 | 13 | 4<br>(36) |
| *Daily Mail*<br>Associated Newspapers (Lord Rothermere)<br>Arthur Brittenden<br>Conservative win | 1,938<br>(2,464) | 5,144 | 18 | 31 | 25 | 26 | 14<br>(16) | 9 | 11 | 0<br>(7) |
| *Sun*<br>News of the World Ltd (Rupert Murdoch)<br>Larry Lamb<br>Labour win | 1,509<br>(1,274) | 5,512 | 4 | 16 | 41 | 39 | 27<br>(15)* | 6 | 11 | 2<br>(11) |
| *Daily Telegraph*<br>Telegraph Newspapers (Lord Hartwell)<br>Maurice Green<br>Conservative win | 1,391<br>(1,337) | 3,472 | 40 | 37 | 13 | 9 | 31<br>(29) | 14 | 15 | 62<br>(72) |
| *Daily Sketch*<br>Associated Newspapers (Lord Rothermere)<br>David English<br>Conservative win | 839<br>(844) | 3,085 | 7 | 18 | 37 | 37 | 25<br>(22) | 5 | 11 | 5<br>(0) |
| *The Times*<br>Thomson Newspapers (Lord Thomson)<br>William Rees-Mogg<br>Conservative win; more Liberals | 414<br>(254) | 1,318 | 46 | 32 | 13 | 8 | 30<br>(21) | 14 | 13 | 40<br>(69) |
| *Guardian*<br>Scott Trust (Laurence P. Scott)<br>Alastair Hetherington<br>Labour win; more Liberals | 297<br>(270) | 884 | 46 | 36 | 13 | 6 | 22<br>(20) | 10 | 11 | 44<br>(87) |

*Notes:*

[1] Average of ABC figures for July–December 1969 and January–June 1970, except for the *Sun*, which is for Janua June 1970 only.

[2] Joint Industry Committee for National Readership Surveys, July 1969–June 1970 average, except for the *Sun*, wh is for January–June 1970 only

[3] JICNARS definition classifies estimated population 15 and over as follows:
AB — 13%, C1 — 23%; C2 — 31%; DE — 33%.

| Opinion polls | % of election coverage (column inches in brackets) given from May 27 to June 18 to: Speeches, Conferences, Handouts, Manifestos, etc. Con. | Lab. | Lib. | Other | By and about Powell [6] | TV programmes (1966 in italics) [7] | Constituency [5] reports and polls (1966 in) italics) [7] | Leading articles [8] | Other: features, notebooks, 'personalities', etc. |
|---|---|---|---|---|---|---|---|---|---|
| o | 16 (506) | 27 (854) | 3 (106) | 1 (18) | 5 (141) | 2 (54)<br>*4*<br>*(169)* | 2 (62)<br>*4*<br>*(154)* | 26 (814) | 24 (761) |
| arris | 20 (527) | 17 (455) | 4 (94) | 1 (25) | 7 (172) | 2 (56)<br>*4*<br>*(176)* | 10 (276)<br>*25*<br>*(1,145)* | 8 (210) | 39 (1,022) |
| OP | 21 (449) | 15 (345) | 5 (112) | — | 8 (169) | 2 (48)<br>*4*<br>*(179)* | 8 (187)<br>*20*<br>*(800)* | 13 (279) | 36 (808) |
| o | 17 (681) | 21 (860) | 7 (299) | — | 8 (333) | 1 (35)<br>*4*<br>*(152)* | 5 (212)<br>*18*<br>*(754)* | 11 (439) | 36 (1,451) |
| allup | 20 (1,000) | 14 (688) | 4 (200) | — (3) | 5 (220) | 3 (156)<br>*5*<br>*(304)* | 19 (941)<br>*26*<br>*(1,680)* | 7 (332) | 33 (1,620) |
| o | 25 (546) | 19 (424) | 4 (98) | — | 8 (183) | 1 (30)<br>*7*<br>*(173)* | 5 (117)<br>*8*<br>*(185)* | 19 (428) | 26 (567) |
| arplan | 18 (1,233) | 22 (1,504) | 3 (185) | 1 (36) | 7 (486) | 3 (201)<br>*3*<br>*(148)* | 14 (983)<br>*38*<br>*(1,834)* | 5 (310) | 34 (2,339) |
| ) | 18 (1,288) | 16 (1,157) | 6 (421) | — (12) | 2 (140) | 3 (174)<br>*4*<br>*(341)* | 18 (1,263)<br>*24*<br>*(1,931)* | 6 (430) | 33 (2,303) |

Only first leading article where more than one.
Includes regional reports.
These figures are also *included* in the adjoining columns referring to the parties.
Column inches for 1966 may not always be comparable due to changes in column widths.
Includes all leading articles on the election even where more than one per day.
*N.B.* The *Sun* was not tabloid in 1966.

frustrating, at least it lacked a number of factors which in 1966 had complicated papers' traditional functions as channels of communication and fighters in the party battle. This time the strike was the main complication, and it might have damaged the press much more seriously than it did. As *The Times* put it, there were real reasons to fear that London could be entering the stage, which New York went through in the 1960s, 'of a series of strikes leading to a steep reduction in the number of papers. And to a corresponding reduction of personal and political choice for the public.' Although at first glance in 1970 the view across the marmalade remained the same — a choice of eight major national dailies — the precariousness of the industry had increased since 1966. Then the Economist Intelligence Unit had forecast the possible closure of three national dailies within five years. There was talk during the 1970 strike that, if it was prolonged, three papers might indeed close down.

The names in fact remained the same, but much else had changed since 1966. The redistribution of ITV licences and developments in book publishing increased the extent to which British newspapers were part of an integrated multi-media communications industry. For example, *The Times*, which in 1966 was the sole daily newspaper controlled by Lord Astor of Hever, found that it lacked the financial resources to stay competitive; in 1967 it passed into the ownership of Lord Thomson, who personified the multi-media organisation, having interests in Britain alone that ranged from provincial and local newspapers and Scottish Television to the London telephone directories. The injection of £5 million of capital since 1967 led to a complete restyling of *The Times* — more staff, more features, more interpretative and 'depth' journalism and a separate daily *Business News* section. Circulation in 1970 was up by some 60%, but without bringing a profitable return on investment.

In 1970 the *Daily Mirror*, with the rest of the mammoth IPC publishing group (including the *Sunday Mirror* and the *People*), was taken over by its largest shareholder, the Reed paper and packaging group. The effect was probably less noticeable than the ousting of Cecil King from the IPC chairmanship by his colleagues in 1968. King had increasingly emerged as more of a platform figure than other post-war newspaper controllers and had exercised a distinctive personal influence over the politics of the group's papers.

The most 'visible' change, apart from *The Times*, was in the *Sun*. IPC failed to establish it as a 'serious' Labour popular daily in the tradition of its pre-1964 predecessor, the *Daily Herald*. In 1969 it was sold to the Australian newspaper proprietor Rupert Murdoch who printed it on the presses of the *News of the World*, the Sunday paper he had taken over in 1968 from the Carr family. Murdoch made no attempt to hold on to the 'politically aware' readers surviving from the old *Herald* (a 'poaching' advertisement was accepted quite readily from the *Guardian* in the first week). It became a tabloid, fashioned so like the *Mirror* in layout and style that even the *Mirror*'s old slogan 'Forward with the People' (dropped in 1959) was resurrected for the masthead. The imitation paid off and circulation grew rapidly.[1]

Among the press as a whole the trend of circulation growth continued in favour of the 'heavy' papers — *The Times*, *Guardian*, *Daily Telegraph* and *Financial Times*, and the Sunday equivalents. The popular papers themselves showed signs of becoming more 'serious' (e.g. the *Mirror* overseas feature Mirrorscope); and they exploited the seam of financial advertising by developing business news. In 1966 the *Daily Worker* changed its name to the *Morning Star*.

The changes of readership, however, were essentially of degree. Each newspaper's treatment of the election was governed as be- ore by a combination of 'internal' and 'external' factors. Internally, the main factors were the pattern of a paper's readership and its corresponding news values; the strength of its party commitment, and the level of its resources. With or without Cecil King there would be pictures of 'Election Birds' in the *Mirror* ('Pretty girls with armloads of political literature will be bustling down suburban streets. There will be more Election Birds like Brenda in the *Daily Mirror*. Don't miss them . . .').

The 'external' factors largely account for the lack of complications in press coverage. Chief among them was the behaviour of the opinion polls. In 1966 they showed a relentless Labour lead in double figures. This time they were agreeably confused. They 'added a dash of spice and suspense to this election', the *Mail* wrote on election day; 'they are keeping us guessing up to the very last moment'.

By 1970, furthermore, the press seemed to have come to terms

[1] In its approach to cheesecake the *Sun* literally outstripped the *Mirror*.

satisfactorily with the development of election television. The effects of TV on the style of campaign politics were now familiar — the angling of party leaders' speeches and press conferences towards TV coverage, for instance. Familiarity did not imply approval, of course. 'In place of argument we get physical snippets,' *The Times* grumbled in a leader about the trivialising effect of TV (June 5). 'Inside a few years,' it continued next day, 'British elections have passed from being debates to being spectacles.' Debate was now 'an adjunct to television whose intellectual content has mainly been negligible'. None the less, the dominance of TV was now a well-established fact. Moreover, in this election TV was not itself an issue except for a brief moment near the end, when it emerged that Mr. Wilson had forbidden his Foreign Secretary to appear on *Panorama*, forcing the programme on to the issue of defence. There was nothing like the 'TV confrontation' argument of 1966 to make a good newspaper story, though the *Sketch* tried to stir one up on June 9, arguing that 'confrontations' would be preferable to the 'phoney fight' of the daily press conferences. As Table I shows, the proportion of newspaper space given to election TV matters was therefore less than in 1966. TV was perhaps accepted more as a complementary than a rival medium by 1970.[1]

The other 'external' factor which in this election caused the

[1] Apart from occasional articles in, e.g. the *Sunday Times* and the *Economist*, the press refrained from self-analysis in the election. But in general the reader who wishes to study the political role of mass media in Britain will find an increasing amount of material published. Much of it is ephemeral and appears in the weeklies, but the following books published since 1966 may be noted:

Richard Boston (ed.), *The Press We Deserve* (Routledge & Kegan Paul, 1970).
Economist Intelligence Unit, *The National Newspaper Industry* (1966).
Cecil King, *The Future of the Press*, (MacGibbon and Kee, 1967).
D. McQuail, *Towards a Sociology of Mass Communications* (Collier-Macmillan, 1969).
Eric Moonman (ed.), *The Press: A Case for Commitment* (Fabian Tract 391, 1969).
Colin Seymour-Ure, *The Press, Politics and the Public* (Methuen, 1968).
Jeremy Tunstall, *The Westminster Lobby Correspondents* (Routledge & Kegan Paul, 1970).
Jeremy Tunstall (ed.), *Media Sociology* (Constable, 1970).
Francis Williams, *The Right to Know* (Longmans, 1970).
Rex Winsbury, *Government and the Press* (Fabian Tract 379, 1968).
*Sociology of Mass Communicators* (Sociological Review Monograph, No. 13, 1969).
Jay G. Blumler and Denis McQuail, *Television in Politics: Its Uses and Influence* (Faber, 1968).
Jay G. Blumler and John Madge, *Citizenship and Television* (PEP, 1967).
John Whale, *The Half-Shut Eye* (Macmillan, 1969).

press no difficulties was the balance of policy in the parties. No great issue stifled the willing partisanship of papers the way Labour coolness and Conservative warmth over the Common Market had embarrassed respectively the *Mirror* and the *Express* in 1966. 'There is no use complaining that neither party has all the answers,' said the *Mail* on polling day. Indeed, to judge by the *Mail*, Mr. Heath had them all.

The election was straightforward for one last reason. Like TV, the press itself never became a subject of controversy. During the later years of the Wilson government, relations with the press had often been strained, in marked contrast to the initial honeymoon period with its bouquets about his skill in public relations. Eventually he is said to have asserted that no Prime Minister since Lloyd George had suffered such virulent and distorted treatment. Even immediately after announcing the election date on May 18 he remarked in a BBC interview, in retort to a question about the Labour party's 'Yesterday's Men' advertisements, on the dirt flung at him by the 'Tory press'. But in the campaign there was no charge of misreporting like the 1964 argument about George Brown's alleged 3% mortgage promise. Mrs. Castle made a hustings comment about the Labour government being good democrats and working to stop the newspaper strike so that the press could start attacking them again. But only Mr. Callaghan appeared to challenge the press seriously, complaining in a speech at Tamworth on June 7 that 'It is an astonishing phenomenon that the newspapers can find nothing good to say about Mr. Wilson.' *The Times*, *Guardian* and *Telegraph* reported this briefly on the front page ('Heaven and Mr. Wilson know that none of us has done him half the damage Mr. Callaghan did over trade union reforms,' *The Times* commented). Otherwise the press featured as an issue only through the SOGAT strike being quoted, by the *Guardian* for example, as an illustration of the problems of industrial relations.

In this context, how did the national press approach its task as a channel of communication?[1] The most striking general feature was

[1] As before, this chapter cannot make an attempt to deal with Britain's seventeen regional morning papers and more than seventy evening dailies. Although the situation in Scotland was very different (see p. 46), in England and Wales only about 7% of the total morning circulation was provided by the 12 provincial papers (and over half of their readers saw a Fleet St. paper as well). A general impression is that the best of them, such as the *Birmingham Post* and *Yorkshire Post*, provided a thorough coverage of local issues and candidates, plus reports of the main events and speeches further afield. The party leaders con-

[*Continued on page 240*

TABLE 2

*Subjects of Lead Stories during the Election, May 27–June 18, 1970*

| Date | *The Times* | *Guardian* | *Daily Telegraph* | *Daily Express* | *Daily Mail* | *Daily Sketch* | *Daily Mirror* | *Sun* |
|---|---|---|---|---|---|---|---|---|
| May 27 | Con. manifesto | Bobby Moore | Con. manifesto | Bobby Moore | Bobby Moore | Bobby Moore | Bobby Moore | Bobby Moore |
| 28 | Lab. manifesto | Doctors pay | Bobby Moore | Bobby Moore | Bobby Moore | Bobby Moore | World Cup car rally | Bobby Moore |
| 29 | Jenkins attacks Heath | Lab. action on prices | Election sweetening by Lab. | Bobby Moore | NOP poll | Bobby Moore | Bobby Moore | Bobby Moore |
| 30 | Heath speech | Leaders' speeches | Leaders' speeches | Heath speech | Reader Harris quits | Price rises | Wilson speech | Murdered girl |
| June 1 | Opinion polls | Opinion polls | Gallup poll | World Cup | World Cup | Opinion polls | Climbing accident | Wilson on homes |
| 2 | Marplan poll | Opinion polls | Wilson hit by egg | Prices, Heath speech | Heath taunts Brown | Leading article | Child safety | Wilson hit by egg |
| 3 | Opinion polls | Ulster | Wilson hit by egg | Harris poll | Election incidents | World Cup | World Cup | Election incidents |
| 4 | Freeze threat | Benn speech | Benn speech | Freeze threat | NOP poll | Benn speech | Powell and skinheads | Benn speech |
| 5 | Benn speech | Doctors pay | Heath speech: freeze threat | Heath reply to Benn | Heath speech: freeze threat | Doctors pay | Leading article | US Hi-jack |
| 6 | Doctors pay | Fleet St. strike | Fleet St. strike | Fleet St. strike | Doctors pay | Shooting incident | Shooting incident | Shooting incident |
| 8 | Tory battle plan | Doctors pay | Maudling speech on economy | Tory battle plan | Leading article | World Cup | World Cup | World Cup |

I

| | | | | | | | | |
|---|---|---|---|---|---|---|---|---|
| 9 | Fleet St. strike | Cons. attack on economy | Fleet St. strike | Fleet St. strike | Fleet St. strike | Fleet St. strike | Missing children | Missing children |
| 15 | Tories split | Tories split | Gallup poll | Opinion polls | Ted hits at Enoch | World Cup | Leading article | World Cup |
| 16 | Trade figures | Trade figures | Trade figures | Prices row | Prices: Treasury reports | Leading article | Trade figures | Callaghan attack on firms |
| 17 | Marplan poll | Wilson attacks Heath | Powell meeting | Opinion polls | Heath devaluation warning | Heath devaluation warning | Leading article | Opinion polls |
| 18 | Opinion polls | Opinion polls | Housewives' vote is Tory hope | Harris poll | NOP poll | Heath speech | Leading article | Missing children |

## *Sunday Newspapers:*

| Date | *Sunday Times* | *Observer* | *Sunday Telegraph* | *Sunday Express* | *News of the World* | *People* | *Sunday Mirror* |
|---|---|---|---|---|---|---|---|
| May 31 | Opinion poll | Opinion poll | Opinion poll | Wyatt attacks Labour | World Cup | Enoch Powell | Enoch Powell |
| June 7 | Opinion poll | Doctors pay | Heath's council of war | Economy in peril | New police equipment | Egg thrown at Wilson | Wilson in danger |
| 14 | Opinion poll | Heath speech | Opinion polls | Opinion polls | Enoch Powell | Enoch Powell | Enoch Powell |

the dominance of the opinion polls. Out of 93 lead stories related to the election in the eight major dailies during the three weeks before polling day in 1966, 10 (9%) were about polls.[1] This time there were 19 out of 77 (25%), covering a smaller number of days because of the strike.[2] If the *Financial Times* and the Sunday papers are included the figures rise to 30 out of 96 (30%). That is simply a crude measure. Even when polls were not the lead story they were often reported prominently, and papers led with their competitors' polls as readily as with their own. If in 1966 polls were vipers in the bosom of the press, treated somewhat as computerised rivals in the game of prediction, now they were treated as subjects of scrutiny and comparison.[3]

Some papers without their own poll made up for it by consolidating the results of the others. The *Observer*'s weekly 'Poll Analysis' produced a weighted average of polls of the previous week — usually as many as six. The *Sunday Times* supplemented its own Marplan poll with a similar 'Poll of Polls'. Most significantly the tabloid *Sun* had a large 'Top of the Polls' chart. 'At key points of the campaign,' it explained, 'the Sun will publish the latest average of the current results from the five leading pollsters.' This it did on June 2, 4 and 9. That evidently was the sum of the campaign's key points: the chart did not reappear. Instead, on June 17 there was an article emphasising the polls' confusion ('UP THE POLL').

The other tabloids did not play the poll game so seriously. The *Sketch* led with a poll story early in the campaign: 'NOW IT'S NECK AND NECK IN POLLS' (the horse-racing metaphor was an obvious favourite). It showed almost total neglect then until June 17, when a short page one story asked: 'WELL, WHO IS WINNING?' The *Mirror*'s attitude was a mixture of condescension and hostility: 'The blinking British, the most politically sophisticated electorate in the whole wide world . . . have not yet reached the stage of

---

tributed articles to several of them (e.g. *Yorkshire Post*, *Western Mail*), and the *Birmingham Post* published Marplan polls of four key local constituencies. The papers appeared to make no effort to stand in for the national dailies during the strike, partly for technical reasons of printing capacity and distribution facilities. In their loyalties the provincial papers continue preponderantly Conservative.

[1] *British General Election of 1966*, pp. 152–3.

[2] In a daily Radio 4 programme during the strike on 'what the papers would have said' editors indicated that polls would also have been headline news on some of those days.

[3] On the press and the polls, see pp. 171 ff.

mental stagnation, when Andy Capp, or Maudie Littlehampton, or Giles's Grandma can reasonably say: "Of course, I'm not going to vote on June 18th. I have already told Dr. Gallup that I don't know."' (June 1). 'Opinion polls are not, and must never become, the beginning and end of political campaigning, or the beginning or end of democracy,' the same article stated, in phrases the paper picked up again later to open its lead story on election day. This attitude did not prevent it keeping track — very briefly — of the way the polls were going; and the main story on its election page on polling day was headlined: 'OPINION POLLS TURN OUT TO BE THE COMEDY OF THE ELECTION.'

Interest in the polls blurred the distinction between 'quality' and 'popular' papers. The same was true of one or two other aspects of election coverage. The press was very loyal, for instance, to the party manifestos — though they competed on the whole unsuccessfully with the arrest of England's World Cup captain Bobby Moore in Latin America for the headlines (see Table 2). The *Guardian*, *Telegraph* and *The Times* printed them in full, the *Mail* and *Express* in some detail; and even the tabloids gave very full summaries. Every paper gave them leader column comment. Most papers continued to take the usefulness of the manifestos completely for granted, presumably on the same grounds as the *Guardian* — 'they would not be worth the paper they are printed on except for what they tell us about the way political parties wish themselves to be seen'. But assumptions varied about their purpose. The *Telegraph* thought they were 'intended to instruct rather than to inspire': *The Times* thought just the opposite (they were 'bound to be pieces of propaganda and should be read as such'). The *Guardian* implied that manifesto-writing was becoming more difficult for an opposition party: *The Times* thought it was more difficult for a government ('Every line of its manifesto is subject to the mute criticism of its own past policies').

Newspapers of all kinds agreed on the duty of politicians to campaign on issues. Yes, personalities as well as principles were important, the *Mirror* thought. But 'for the love of Mike, give us the facts and cut out the eyewash'. Mr. Wilson's strategy of a quiet election, on grounds of the people not wanting change, was 'strictly ordure'. While the *Mirror* was not 'cynical about democracy' ('The British way of life is the envy of the world'), this was a worry linked to the question of issues by the *Guardian*. 'A campaign devoid of policy content,' a leader reflected after the election announcement, 'can easily create an immediate reaction among some voters; it can also damage democracy'. There had been a 'marked falling away' in the esteem of politicians, was how the *Express* put it: 'There has been too much double talk in politics.' The voters 'will look behind the promises and read between the lines', wrote the *Sketch*, and 'That's what the *Sketch* will be doing too.' When Mr. Wilson declined to answer open questions posed by the *Sketch* (on grounds of the wording) the paper commented: 'We know he wants to make it a "no issue" election . . . but we're one paper that's NOT going to play his game.' The absence of policy discussion was a continual theme of *The Times*: the main responsibility, its leader on polling day said, lay with a Prime Minister who 'planned an election which would be fought not on issues, but on pictures'. 'Both Mr. Heath and Mr. Wilson have so far proved rather better at hurling questions at each other than at answering them,' the *Telegraph* remarked on June 3.

In the absence of policy debate the press dutifully recorded the rituals of the campaign. The leaders' big set speeches were diligently reported. George Brown's hustings tour was mapped with a detail that could be justified, as the *Economist* pointed out, only in terms of sentiment (and nostalgia for a vanishing form of electioneering, perhaps). The tally of eggs thrown at Mr. Wilson was carefully notched. At first these made headlines, probably due to the initial fears of a violent campaign (the rowdiness that Mr. Amery and Mr. Brown met at Sussex and Essex Universities may have attracted particular attention for the same reason). As anxiety receded and Mr. Wilson whisked the eggs to his own advantage ('We have all the arguments: they have all the eggs') they became the *leitmotif* of the election (June 16, *Daily Telegraph*: '14th EGG, THEN A SHOWER'). Mr. Wilson's walkabouts were often contrasted early on with the 'cold' performance of Mr. Heath. Mr. Heath's conversion to the idea a few days before the newspaper strike was viewed much as ducks watch a baby take to water. By the time the papers reappeared they thought he had learnt to swim — though probably too late.

The press conferences were largely treated as an empty ritual: reports were often brief, reluctant, facetious or frustrated. Either the leaders seemed to demonstrate the basic sameness of their policies ('TWEEDLEDUM AND TWEEDLEDEE OVER POLICIES FOR IN-

DUSTRY' — *Guardian,* June 3); or else they bickered and flung challenges at each other that might have gone down all right in the market-place but scarcely in Smith Square. Hence the press gave major prominence to the press conferences only when the issues they themselves were interested in came (or were drawn) to the fore — for example doctors' pay (briefly) and a wages freeze. Only at the end of the campaign, when interest in Mr. Powell was most intense and Mr. Heath mentioned devaluation in a statement issued at the end of one conference that he elaborated next day, did the occasion provide an important focus of election news. As Table 3 shows, the proportion of election coverage provided by conference stories was minute.

In addition to these activities, how far papers themselves discussed issues, as well as criticising the parties for not doing so, depended a good deal on their readership. The popular papers tended to refer to issues in leader column discussion while the 'heavies' ran special features. (Table 1 shows how much more space leading articles took up proportionately in the popular papers.) The two extremes were the *Mirror,* which hooked the issues on to rival personalities (Jenkins *v.* Macleod; Callaghan *v.* Hogg, etc.) in a series headed 'The Men, the Evidence, the *Mirror* Verdict'; and the *Telegraph,* with a regular series of feature-page

TABLE 3

*Coverage of Headquarters press conferences as % of total election coverage (column-inches in brackets).*

| | Con. | Lab. | Lib. |
|---|---|---|---|
| *Daily Mirror* | 1·2 (38) | 2·2 (71) | 0·3 (8) |
| *Daily Express* | 0·6 (15) | 0·9 (25) | 0·2 (6) |
| *Daily Mail* | 0·7 (15) | 1·3 (28) | 0·4 (9) |
| *Sun* | 0·2 (7) | 0·2 (10) | 0·4 (16) |
| *Daily Telegraph* | 1·7 (85) | 1·4 (69) | 0·8 (41) |
| *Daily Sketch* | 0·4 (10) | 0·3 (7) | 0·5 (11) |
| *The Times* | 1·2 (79) | 1·6 (108) | 0·2 (15) |
| *Guardian* | 0·9 (65) | 0·5 (36) | 0·3 (22) |

articles on the economy, education, welfare, etc. In general the style of popular coverage tended to be characteristically more 'personalised' than the 'heavies', and hence to have the effect, possibly, of making the campaign appear more 'presidential'. Except for the *Mail* the popular papers gave twice as much space as the qualities to George Brown's tour, for example. Where a 'serious' paper like the *Guardian* had a series *about* 'Young voters', the populars had pictures *of* young voters (the Election Birds) and solicited letters *from* them ('The *Mirror* wants to hear from you. Now!' — with five pounds for the best letter published.). The *Sun*, with an eye on a 1980 election, even published the views of nine-year-olds. The *Mirror*, as in 1966, published a centre-page interview with Mrs. Wilson (if the Tory High Command envies 'anything at all in the opposite camp it is the Labour leader his wife'). The *Sun* asked: 'Would Ted really get more votes if he had a wife?' and invited readers' views. Fewer papers printed articles by the party leaders than in 1966, but all the populars had 'profiles' and interviews of them, or 'answers to questions'. (This was a major source of Liberal coverage, along with its manifesto.)

The *Mirror*'s 'personalisation' of the campaign was partly also the result of an editorial decision. Its slogan for 1970 was 'Well . . . man for man, who would you put YOUR money on?'. This election, the *Mirror* believed, was 'unique in modern times' in being 'more about men and personalities than it is about political, national or international issues. Man for man — that is what we have to decide,' and the *Mirror* posed the choice (and implied its answers) in the series of vignettes referred to above: Callaghan was the 'calm man in command' at the Home Office, Hogg the 'impetuous understudy', and the like.

The *Sun* made no such decision about the election's content. Just as it copied heavier papers in treating the polls in depth, so it made a serious attempt to discuss issues independently of the campaign speeches. 'We will add a new dimension to press coverage of General Elections,' the *Sun* announced on May 19. This (or was it 'Top of the Polls'?) was presumably it. From June 1 until the strike the *Sun* analysed the rival policies on poverty, education, full employment, law and order, pollution, etc., and gave its own view. The result was that a higher proportion of its coverage went to policy features than of almost any other paper's — and without cutting out other campaign coverage. In terms of column inches the *Sun* printed one third as much again as the *Mirror* about the election, and not far off twice as much as the *Sketch*.

Constituency reports were, as usual, the quality papers' herbaceous border. The end of the strike, like the end of a drought, brought a lot of them out together. The tendency was to combine detailed study of marginal seats with broader regional surveys, so that national coverage would not be sacrificed wholly to the question of which party would have a majority in the next parliament. In addition *The Times* had background articles about the electorate from Professor Richard Rose, commentaries on the campaign — from Wilson's 'style' to the political broadcasts — by its regular specialists; and a good deal of local colour in Patrick Brogan's 'Rural Drive' (through rather than always *in* the countryside), Leonard Beaton's 'Election Notebook' and others of its specialists following the party leaders. A real innovation was the 'Minority View' column. Guessing the next contributor was like a *New Statesman* competition: Lord Redcliffe-Maud, Des Wilson, Arnold Wesker, Lord Harlech, Cecil King, Margaret Drabble, David Triesman, etc. The *Telegraph*'s coverage was much less colourful and imaginative ('Election Sketchbook. By Onlooker'). The *Guardian*, on the other hand, contained the same variety of description and analysis as *The Times*. Where Lord Kennet and Norman St. John Stevas wrote for their parties in *The Times*, Christopher Price and Lord Balniel wrote in the *Guardian*. The *Guardian* tackled the issues the more systematically — covering, as it said, what the electorate meant by an issue (something that might change minds) as well as what the politicians meant (something they felt ought to). The *Guardian* also made a speciality out of long interviews — mixing policies and personalities in lively portraits of (among others) Callaghan, Macleod, Heath and Thorpe ('Faith, Hope and Jeremy'). The quality papers all seemed to provide a greater breadth of coverage than ever, with elaborate pull-out charts for election night of a kind which most readers would have greeted with fumbling incredulity, one suspects, twenty years ago.

In covering the campaign, how far and in what way were the press partisan? The simplest indicator is the leading article. Judged by this, the Conservative party found several supporters early on, while Labour's only gradually declared themselves. With a few exceptions papers seemed unhappy to commit themselves to one or other party in 1970 without reservation; and to the extent that men not measures was a theme, a new candour about party personalities appeared.

Those rooting for the Tories from the start were the *Mail*,

*Sketch*, *Telegraph* and *Express* — reaching a total readership of perhaps twenty million. In a leader headed 'THE GREAT BETRAYAL' the *Mail* stated baldly as early as May 19: '... the truth is that under Labour the British people have suffered the worst Government in this century.' Labour's broken promises had 'badly damaged the public's faith in our political system. For that betrayal we can never forgive Mr. Wilson.' From then on it had never a good word for Labour — except for one thing in its manifesto, 'The phoney Prospectus' — the promise of measures to reduce aircraft noise. The *Sketch* started to tune its conservatism to election pitch by strong criticism of the Labour government's handling of the South African cricket tour controversy (May 20–22). After the party manifestos appeared, its support of the Conservatives was unwavering. Their manifesto was a well-thought out strategy for rescuing Britain from Labour's legacy of raging inflation, high unemployment and economic stagnation (May 27). Labour's, by contrast, was 'a mask to hide six years of Socialist failure' (May 28). The *Telegraph*, similarly, thought the Tory manifesto threw out an impressive challenge and set the party theme 'with compelling simplicity' (though weak on law and order, education and the Health Service); while Labour's was 'a terribly unexciting document and no doubt means to be so'. Its concern later was with the apparent failure of the Tory message to get across rather than with any flaws in it. To the *Express*, in this election as before, the Common Market was the most momentous issue of all. On May 18 it said that unless the parties promised a referendum before entry, the election would simply be a choice between two evils — 'Some choice! Some election!' Yet instead of the issue being a hard brake on its support for the Conservatives, the paper was able to find a happy refuge in their manifesto. Especially welcome is their fresh approach to the Common Market, a leading article noted: 'for behold a pledge to report regularly through Parliament to the Country on any negotiations for entry.' The *Express* settled for that, though a referendum remained the ideal. Its support for the Conservatives mounted to a characteristic climax on June 17 ('MAKE BRITAIN PROUD AND FREE'): 'On practically all counts the Tories have it. They have the better record. The stronger management. The sterner resolve. The clearer purpose. And the greater faith in Britain's role tomorrow.'

In comparison with those Tory papers the endorsement of

Labour by the *Mirror*, *Sun* and *Guardian* was passive and slow to emerge. An early clue to the *Mirror* attitude, like the *Sketch*, was its treatment of the cricket tour controversy — pro-Labour in this case. On June 1 it announced its election plans: it would report the campaign 'factually and impartially. Always has. Always will.' Its own views would be stated candidly and forcibly nearer polling day. They became fairly clear once its series 'The Men, The Evidence, The *Mirror* Verdict' started on June 9. On June 17 the paper openly plumped for Wilson and his team. Mr. Heath with all his earnestness and integrity, hadn't the personality to dominate his own party. How could he lead the nation?

The *Sun* followed the same cliffhanging policy. 'The *Sun*'s growing army of readers is entitled to know which side their newspaper is on,' it announced when the election was called. The answer? Why, naturally 'The *Sun* is on YOUR side'. Commentary on the paper's 'issue a day' increasingly showed what this meant: while both parties had drawbacks, Labour was preferable. The time had come and the *Sun* would vote Labour, it concluded on June 17. Mr. Wilson had the better team and was fundamentally more concerned about ordinary people and social justice, though his initial economic policy had provoked a 'near disaster'.

On a more detailed plane of discussion the *Guardian* behaved in the same kind of way. It found much to approve in both manifestos. As the days passed, a preference for Labour could be inferred from such comments as that Tory emphasis on indirect taxes is not what a responsible and compassionate party ought to advocate (June 2). In the shadow of the newspaper strike a provisional summing-up still gave only implicit endorsement of Labour. But when that was over, the paper spoke plainly and argued that 'candidates ought to be considered as much for their individual merits as for their party labels; that where a Liberal stands a fair chance of coming first or second he should be supported; that Mr. Heath's conservatism is, in the main, of a moderate and progressive character; but that Mr. Wilson's government, in spite of all its failings, deserves to be returned again' (June 15).

The other daily eventually to endorse the Conservatives was *The Times*. To say that alone is to ignore the more intriguing aspects of its policy, however. During the election fever of early May it had said: 'The weakness of the Government's position is their economic record', and sure enough on May 19 it concluded that judged by the economic criteria which the Labour party used to gain office in 1964 and to retain it in 1966, the present government had a wholly inadequate claim on the electorate in 1970. Explicit endorsement of Mr. Heath was clearly foreshadowed. But before that came (and after) the paper showed a sometimes flippant, sometimes cynical impatience of party politics and politicians, which, had it not been expressed in language characteristic of the extraordinarily middle-class and middle-aged election that the paper claimed to witness, might have sounded like real alienation. The cutting edge was sharp from the start: 'The appetite of the British electorate for innovation, radicalism and disturbance is slow to rouse and easy to satisfy. . . . It is hard for the Conservative Party to challenge a Government that appears to answer so well to the conservative instincts of the voters' (May 18). The manifestos were observed with amusement as necessary and harmless rituals. 'When the Labour party comes to a difficulty, it does not do anything so undignified as dodge, it rises gracefully above it'; an example being the section about the economy, where in fact 'Labour have been the stop–stop artists of the go–go years.' Another reason for detachment was parochialism: 'though Mr. Heath is trying to raise the issues, it cannot be pretended that the tone of debate in this election — or the response to it that is reported on our doorsteps — suggests that we are experiencing anything but our most complacent hour' (June 6). On June 8 a leader regretted that 'defence is taboo'. On polling day itself the double column leader, DEAD TO THE WORLD, listed foreign policy issues that had not been discussed: 'What we do not think our business would stock a library, and what we do think our business would not fill a paperback.'

A further cause of detachment was the 'depressing tone' of the campaign, produced (as on June 5) by Wilson's claim that Labour's record was so good that it needed no discussion, by the trivialisation of TV and by Mr. Benn's outburst against Mr. Powell. 'Furthermore, whatever the outcome, the one thing that is certain is that either party will form a Cabinet almost exclusively influenced by the values of 50-year-old Oxford men, advised by Senior Civil Servants who were up at the same time' (June 6). Lastly, the paper announced on June 2 that because the most chilling aspect of modern elections is their impersonal quality, it would write regularly about politicians who would contribute to the quality of parliament regardless of party. Michael Foot came first, followed by a group under the heading 'Intellect in politics'; then 'Does Labour care?' (Mrs. Shirley Williams); and culminating in an invocation of 'the Asquith ideal', which called strenuously for more Liberal M.P.s and in particular for Mrs. Laura Grimond.

Almost every day, then, *The Times* pondered the electoral process in one or another of these ways that detached it largely from the party symbols and machinery with which the battle was fought. Basically, however, it remained firmly in the game; and though its reasoning was economic, its endorsement of the Conservatives was in general terms: 'Mr. Heath . . . offers the prospect of a well managed, moderate liberal democracy with a bias towards freedom.'

Partisanship of course may also colour a paper's news values — both in what it reports and how it does so. The *Morning Star* naturally gave special attention to the Communist party campaign, for instance. Quantitatively, as Table 1 shows, biases in the leader columns were to some extent reflected in the space devoted to the parties, most obviously in the *Mirror*, *Telegraph*, *Mail* and *Sketch*. Qualitatively, the papers that declared themselves editorially early on were rooting for the Tories in their news coverage too. The *Telegraph* provided a wealth of small examples, often in the form of tendentious headlines. 'ELECTION SWEETENERS BY WILSON: EVEN ZOO MONKEYS NOT OVERLOOKED' was the lead on May 29. The story began: 'A series of Government announcements yesterday added up to vote-catching "bribes" on an even more lavish scale than the Conservatives had expected from Mr. Wilson. "Even the monkeys in the zoo have not been overlooked" was one sardonic comment. . . .' On May 27 the Conservative manifesto led the paper, with a glowing picture of Mr. Heath, and the Bobby Moore story took second place. Next day the Bobby Moore story led the paper, with an anti-Labour cartoon next to it and the Labour manifesto in second place. The *Telegraph* often published 'warm' pictures of Mr. Heath on the front page, presumably to counter his 'cold' image.

The *Mail* also provided plenty of excellent examples. 'THREAT TO OUR ROADS', the splash headline over a story on May 26 about the 'disastrous effects' of a £120 million cut in maintenance spending ordered by the government in 1968, turned out to originate in a dossier compiled by Michael Heseltine, Tory shadow Minister of Transport, from reports of thirty county councils. The *Express* did the same sort of thing. It presented its polls in the brightest possible light for the Tories; and it produced on June 2 one of the best scare headlines of the campaign: 'THE 3S. LOAF.' The story began: 'Double price and half value — that was Mr. Edward Heath's prediction last night if Labour gets back in the General Election.' On a similar theme the *Sketch* on May 30 headlined 'ANOTHER SHOPPING SHOCKER', over a story, without sources or details, that 'more than 200 increases' in prices had been announced by manufacturers. 'This boosts the number of increases since January to well over 4,000.' The *Mirror* on the same day not surprisingly took the opposite view: 'WILSON TAUNTS TORIES OVER PRICES.'

The *Mail*'s handling of its polls too was somewhat tendentious. The small initial Labour leads were reported fairly flatly as the headline story, but the NOP 23% lead for Labour in Scotland was given little prominence on page 2. On polling day, with the lead cut to 4·1%, the headline was a blunt 'COME ON TED!'.

Two subjects deserve detailed analysis here because they absorbed the press more heavily in the campaign than any other. They are the economy and Enoch Powell. Treatment of the economy reflected party preferences fairly predictably, both in the news and in the leader columns. There was no dispute, however, that this was the central issue; and most papers had said so by the end of May. Coverage fell into three phases. Between May 27 and June 2 the emphasis was on rising prices. *The Times*, *Telegraph*, *Express* and *Sun* highlighted the section on inflation in the Tory manifesto on May 27 ('TORY MANIFESTO — "WE'LL SLASH PRICES"' — *Sun*); and on May 29 a speech by Mr. Jenkins accusing Mr. Heath of 'dishonesty' over prices got prominent treatment in the heavy papers and the *Mirror* ('LABOUR STEPS INTO TORY WAR ON PRICES' — *Guardian*). The next few days saw a variety of stories about prices, including the *Sketch*'s 'ANOTHER SHOPPING SHOCKER' and the *Express* 'THE 3S. LOAF' scare. The *Mail* on June 1 reported 'GIANT BUS FARE RISES SOON' (which referred in fact to desired rises in some companies, as reported by 'Tory leaders'). The *Guardian* noted 'LEADERS REACH FOR FLOATING VOTERS' POCKET'; and the *Telegraph* had a centre-page feature about prices.

The second phase — an argument about the possibility of a

pay freeze — was begun by *The Times* on June 3, with a report of Lord Cromer's television comments raising doubts about the economy's strength. Most papers took up the theme next day, on the basis of a comment by Mr. Callaghan that the government would have to give attention to wage increases after the election. The *Mail* and *Express* were most sensational ('CALLAGHAN LETS IT OUT: NEW PAY FREEZE THREAT' — *Express*). The *Telegraph* ('HEATH TAUNTS JENKINS') was still concerned with prices, and Mr. Benn's attack on Mr. Powell stole the main headlines in many papers. On June 5 charge and counter-charge flew, with Mr. Heath's claim and Mr. Wilson's denial variously emphasised. Mr. Heath then turned his gaze to the prospect of a national 'crash' after the pay freeze, and the *Guardian*, *Telegraph*, *Mirror* and *Mail* concentrated attention on that.

In the third phase, from June 8 to polling day, the issue broadened out into a discussion of the general state of the economy, turning on the balance of payments and whether there was, or was not, a crisis which might, as Heath hinted in a statement on June 16, lead to a new devaluation. In this final period the effect of party preferences became clearer. On June 7 the *Sunday Express* hooked its lead story ('ELECTION BOMBSHELL — ECONOMY IN PERIL') on the remark allegedly dropped to doctors' representatives by Mr. Crossman (see pp. 154-5). On June 8 all the Conservative papers headlined the Tory charge that Labour was 'hiding the truth' about the economy, while the three Labour papers stressed Labour rebuttals ('CRISIS TALK IS MOONSHINE, SAYS JENKINS' — *Guardian*). June 9 showed the same tendency. On one or other day every Tory paper carried the charge into the leader columns. The *Mirror* said nothing, but the *Sun* and *Guardian* both pointed out that each party had made mistakes in economic management in the past, and that it was not at all clear that either had the answers now. The *Guardian* thought the Tories had marred their generally sober campaign by 'seeming ready to whip up the atmosphere of an immediate economic crisis'.

After the newspaper strike the economy issue, submerged on June 15 almost entirely by news and comment on Mr. Powell, bubbled to the surface on June 16 with the news of unfavourable May Trade figures: 'TRADE GAP PUTS KISS OF LIFE INTO TORY CAMPAIGN' was the *Guardian* headline, and the Tory papers exploited the figures to the full ('£31 m. TRADE BLOW TO LABOUR' —

*Telegraph*). The *Sun* in contrast stressed Mr. Callaghan's accusation that big food chains were deliberately forcing up prices to make things difficult for Labour. Mr. Heath issued his 'devaluation' statement the same day. This kept the issue afloat and was reported in party terms ('DEVALUE WITH LABOUR' — *Mail*; 'THE POUND: HEATH'S LAST FLING' — *Sun*). On election day itself the economy took second place to opinion polls, except in the *Telegraph* and *Sketch* which stressed Tory hopes of getting the 'housewife vote' because of price rise fears. Other Tory papers had less prominent stories on this theme. They were denied a last minute sensational story by the absence of any significant rise in the cost of living index for the previous month: only the *Guardian* reported it.

One is left with the impression, therefore, that while all the papers stressed the economy issue, the Tory press exploited it most fully and sensationally. Labour papers were more moderate and defensive and less prepared (as was *The Times*) to believe that either party had the answers.

Mr. Powell first attracted attention with his boatrocking election address issued on May 30. It made headlines in the *Sunday Mirror* and the *People* and was prominent in all the other Sundays except the *Sunday Telegraph* and the *Sunday Express*. The *Sunday Express* lead story, indeed, was an excellent example of the opposite news values: 'WOODROW WYATT ROCKS WILSON'S BOAT.' On Monday *The Times*, *Telegraph*, *Guardian* and *Sketch* all commented on Mr. Powell's disagreements with the party over immigration and the EEC. Three days later (June 4) he hit the headlines properly because of Mr. Benn's strongly worded attack on him. The repercussions barely died down by the time of the newspaper strike, during which he made two dramatic speeches covered fully by radio and TV. (Comments by journalists on radio confirmed that they would also have been headline news in the press.) When papers reappeared on Sunday, June 14, these, and Mr. Powell's role in the campaign generally, were the subject of universal analysis and comment. *The Times*, for example, devoted almost its entire feature page to him ('THE SPECTRE THAT HAUNTS HEATH'), as well as its lead story.

As Chapter VII pointed out, neither party welcomed the attention given to Mr. Powell. (Table 1 shows that it was far more than was given to the entire Liberal party.) But they cannot have been surprised. He intruded an element into the election which fitted the capacities and traditional preconceptions of the press about elections much more closely than the stuff of party politics in 1970. His subject did not chill with the numb arithmetic of complex economics: it touched strong human feelings. His personality and style were dramatic. Newspapers deal in conflict, and Mr. Powell embodied it at every level.

Yet the tone of Powell's coverage was nearly always 'cool'. One exception was the lunchtime edition of the London *Evening Standard* on June 4. The front page was almost filled with a story by George Gale from Smethwick, headed 'I WITNESS ENOCH'S MAGIC.' It began: 'A moment of undoubted dignity has occurred in this election. It may prove, too, to be a moment of historical significance.' His subsequent report of Mr. Powell's reply to Mr. Benn's charges included other passages of some warmth: 'Here was a man speaking as if filled with a declamatory authority, as if filled with a divine spirit, as if convinced himself that he was only to utter and his words would be taken to be the truth and the gospel.'

The treatment of individual papers reflected loosely their party leanings. No one at all had much to say in Mr. Powell's support, but the Conservative papers naturally handled him in a way which might minimise the possible danger to his party. The *Mail* and *Express*, for instance, were the only two papers not to put Mr. Benn's attack on the front page. The *Mail* did not even spotlight Mr. Heath's retort next day, though the *Express* and other Tory papers made great play of it ('REPUDIATE! HEATH SLAMS "SMEAR"' — *Express*). The *Mail* had no leader comment either, but the *Express* assumed Mr. Benn's speech was a tactic to divide the Tories and 'brand the entire party as Nazis', with the aim of diverting attention from 'the inevitable post-election wage freeze'.

Apart from these examples, 'playing Powell down' meant softening the issue in the leader columns rather than burying it inside the paper. The general Tory approach was to emphasise Mr. Powell's good points and blame Labour if possible for any consequences that might follow from his bad ones. Thus the *Telegraph* thought Mr. Powell's election address was helpful because many Conservative voters would be reluctant to support a Tory party in which such views were never expressed. The paper itself disagreed with him, but even its condemnation of his use of 'the age-old concept of the single universal conspiracy' was on grounds that it invited neglect of the element of truth in what he said. The *Sketch* made clear its disagreement with Mr. Powell right from the start (June 1). It strongly attacked Mr. Benn ('Dial Wedgwood Benn for computerised hate') and ingeniously turned the arguments against the whole Labour government on June 15. Powellism, the *Sketch* explained, was the exploitation of issues for emotional content, with the future placed in the hands of a political Messiah. But 'a Powell takeover would not come through the normal democratic process' — only in a moment of 'national panic'. This might follow an economic collapse: and Mr. Wilson could indeed reduce the country to a state where Powellism was clutched at. The *Express*, after its anti-Benn leader, commented again only to approve, of course, Mr. Powell's views against the Common Market. The *Mail* dismissed Mr. Powell's later speeches as 'a happening': the economy was the real issue. Like its stablemate the *Sketch*, it emphasised that Wilson's double-talk and broken promises were the true threat to the peace of Britain, not 'the excesses of Mr. Enoch Powell' (June 17).

*The Times*, in its 'detached' mood, behaved unlike the other Conservative supporters. Its rebuke of Mr. Benn ('an exceptionally silly man, though able and pleasant enough') concentrated on the fact that 'he has made race an issue in the election, which Mr. Powell's election address had failed to do' (June 5). The 'conspiracy' speeches provoked a new tone of regretful dismissal. The leader on June 15 ('How Fall'n, how changed') thought it 'ludicrous' to suppose Mr. Powell could now lead any British party: 'he has destroyed himself and that is tragic.'

The Labour papers did not beat the Tories with Mr. Powell as much as they might have done. (The *Guardian*, for example, harped just as much as *The Times* on the obvious 'Tory split' note.) The *Sun* condemned Powell most strongly of the three. It reported Mr. Benn's speech fully but without any critical comment, and on June 15 it published a large, front page picture of Mr. Powell, with the heading THIS MAN IS DANGEROUS. 'Let the Tory party *totally* repudiate him now', it urged: he was 'the enemy within'. Next day it spotlighted the names of thirteen candidates who had invited Mr. Powell to speak in their constituencies. Similarly the *News of the World*, Mr. Murdoch's other paper, advised readers the previous day that 'If your Tory candidate is even remotely sympathetic to Enoch Powell you should either vote Labour or Liberal'. Its headline was: 'HAS ENOCH GONE MAD?'. The *Mirror* was more moderate. It had a guilt-by-association headline to its Benn speech story — 'WE GUARD ENOCH, SAY SKINHEADS' — but its comment next day blamed both men: Mr. Powell was 'a national problem', but Mr. Benn's speech was 'inexcusable' and he had 'out-Powelled Powell'. On June 15 it noted that Mr. Powell was an intense embarrassment to Mr. Heath, but that immigration was not a party issue; and contented itself finally with saying such a man could not survive in the Labour party. The *Guardian*, much like the *Sun*, criticised Mr. Heath for not 'moving against' Mr. Powell (June 15). But the paper was alone in finding a good word to say for Mr. Benn. To be sure, he had used Mr. Powell's own worst vice — 'scapegoating': but 'it was Mr. Powell who chose to make immigration the central issue in his election address. Someone therefore had to answer him, and in equally strong terms.'

In the light of party strategy, as the *Express*, *Mail* and *Telegraph* pointed out, the attention given to Mr. Powell threatened to distract voters from the Conservative onslaught on the economy issue. Interpretation of Mr. Powell's activities as a bid for the Tory leadership after a probable election defeat made the extensive coverage of *The Times* and the *Guardian* (particularly the former) more alarming to the Tories than the open attack of the Labour papers. For example *The Times* lead story on June 15 ('CONSERVATIVE ANGER WITH POWELL OVER RIFT ON IMMIGRANTS') reported the 'extreme anger' of the Tories over what they saw as an 'open fight' for the leadership; and next day a page one story about Mr. Heath's press briefing said: 'As speculation began about his future as party leader if the Conservatives lose heavily in Thursday's general election, Mr. Heath firmly shut off all answers about Mr. Enoch Powell and his opinions on immigration.'

Although the Sunday papers have been mentioned intermittently they deserve notice separately. Their attitudes to the election varied considerably. The *Sunday Mirror* (circulation 5,008,000), firmly in the Labour camp, probably devoted less attention to the campaign than any other daily or Sunday. It took a strong line on Powell: its lead story was about him on two of the three Sundays in the campaign proper — May 31 and June 14.

At the other extreme was the *Sunday Times* (1,473,000). The previous October it had set up a special group to plan its coverage ('Insight and Spectrum will combine forces to provide narrative and analysis week by week', etc.). It had its own polls, profiles of the leaders, analysis of the issues and the Labour record, articles giving the background to the manifestos and the leaders' campaigns, special features on topics like the immigrant voters and the Tory hopefuls. These 'Tory hopefuls' were 62 candidates in Labour's most marginal seats, and the feature was based on questioning of every one of them — a typical example of the kind of thoroughness which the paper's resources permitted. A leading article on June 14 endorsed the Conservatives but, as in many of the dailies, a handful of individual candidates regardless of party were picked out for approval.

Of the other mass circulation Sundays the chief feature of the *News of the World* (6,318,000) was its weekly 'Hot Line', in which various leaders of each party answered readers' queries on vital issues. In 1966 it had not endorsed a party. Now, under the new Murdoch regime, it was strongly Labour and anti-Powell. The *Mirror*'s stablemate, the *People* (5,329,000), pro-Labour from the start, made more of an effort than either of those two. It reported the leaders' speeches in some detail and had long articles on Mr. Powell and Mr. Paisley campaigning; and its reporting team set the inflation issue in the context of other countries' performance. Mr. Callaghan contributed an article; and for the Conservatives, Sir Peter Rawlinson wrote on law and order.

The coverage of the *Sunday Express* (4,277,000) was entirely geared towards the achievement of a Tory victory. Already on May 24 its lead story, which warned 'NEW PAY FREEZE AFTER POLL', set the tone for succeeding weeks. Its feature articles were straightforward anti-Labour onslaughts by Mr. Maudling, Mr. Ian Gilmour, Sir Alec Douglas-Home and Mr. Hogg. On May 31 it featured a double page biography by George Hutchinson of Mr. Heath's early life and passage to Westminster; and it continually emphasised that polls (including its own) *can* sometimes go wrong. Mr. Powell was played down.

The *Observer* and *Sunday Telegraph* followed the *Sunday Times*. The *Sunday Telegraph* (768,000) did less spadework and had a good deal of comment (e.g. Peregrine Worsthorne on the absence of statesmanship). There were lengthy reports of speeches, a campaign diary, articles on young voters, distinctive candidates and so on. For psephological matters it called on Hugh Berrington of Newcastle University. Its leader columns were staunchly Conservative and impatient with Mr. Powell's equivocal support of the party.

The *Observer* (857,000) mounted a slighter operation than the other two, but of the same kind. It kept pace with party tactics and the leaders' campaigns, and it made much of Enoch Powell. But there were fewer research-based articles than in the *Sunday Times* and more by people like the editor of *Peace News* on why he would not be voting. Editorially the paper declared on May 24 that it would not endorse a party unless one issue became overriding. None did.

What, finally, was the effect of press coverage of the 1970 election? In a general sense newspapers, as usual, helped to 'integrate' the campaign, by providing a national 'focus' and preparing people to go to vote. How many votes they influenced cannot be judged here (research published since 1966 supports the view that changes produced by media occur between, more than at, election times). But a judgement can be made of effects in relation to party strategies. If we think of the parties having broad campaign plans, how far did the behaviour of the press reinforce or counteract them? The trend of the polls, the confidence of Mr. Wilson and the unease of Mr. Heath all left an overwhelming impression in the press of a Tory defeat well before polling day. As early as June 7 the *Observer* lead story was asserting 'TORIES NEED A MIRACLE NOW'. A week later all the Sundays had written the Tories off. The *Sunday Times* was looking ahead ('the toughest fight is Powell and the leadership') and even the *Sunday Telegraph*, while not actually conceding defeat, made remarks like 'There must at least be a powerful Conservative Opposition'.[1]

Yet paradoxically most aspects of the campaign image presented by the press favoured the Conservatives. Only three perhaps helped Labour. If Labour wanted a 'quiet' campaign, then the newspaper strike was a help: it dampened the Tory economic case — though it also concealed their embarrassment at Enoch Powell. If Labour wanted a 'presidential' campaign, then the

[1] For similar quotations from the dailies, see pp. 165-6

tendency of popular papers to personalise issues was a help — in particular the *Mirror*'s argument that this was a 'men not measures' election. Thirdly the eruption of Enoch Powell was a help: more because it diverted the press for a while from the economic issue again than because Mr. Powell himself lost the Tories votes (which the press did not seem sure about anyway in advance).

On the other hand the very idea of a 'quiet' campaign must have put Labour at a general disadvantage. Newspapers do not want 'quiet' campaigns: the attention to 'unquiet' people like George Brown and Quintin Hogg — let alone Enoch Powell — was evidence in 1970. Also newspapers, so long as they value feature or leader columns, are interested in ideas. From the very start the press did not want a 'no issue' election and did its best to prevent one happening. This intangible advantage to the Conservatives was given real weight by the fortunate fact that the entire press believed, like them, that the economy was the issue to fight on. Furthermore, not only was newspaper opinion preponderantly Conservative, but the Tory papers joined in much earlier than the others and fought their party's battle with greater vim — more so, perhaps, in their choice of news values than in the leader columns.

The effect of the opinion polls is difficult to judge. Their increasing Labour leads must have suited Labour strategy as well as provoking 'Heath succession' stories. Yet the overwhelming race-track approach presumably helped to keep public interest alive and favour the Conservative message in the last few days. The surprise Tory victory may in fact owe little to the newspapers' strategy. But the obsession with polls made one thing clear. 'HEATH HEADS FOR SHOCK VICTORY' was the *Guardian* headline on June 19. The press could take much credit for the shock if not the victory.

CHAPTER XI

# CONSTITUENCY PREPARATIONS 1966–1970

'It was the pirate radio . . .', 'our 100% canvass . . .', 'the rise in council house rents . . .', 'the candidate's flair for publicity . . .', 'the new housing estate . . .'. These were some of the reasons given to us after the election to explain particularly good or particularly bad constituency results. As previous Nuffield studies would suggest, we are inclined to treat such assertions with reserve. The assurance with which exceptional performances are accounted for after the event contrasts with the inability of even the most experienced, well-informed party organisers to predict them beforehand. In any case, the vast majority of individual results conformed to the national pattern. In 1970, the swing from Labour to Conservative was within 1·5% of the national average in 335 out of the total 630 constituencies, and only in 28 did it deviate by more than 4%.

Even when unusual local results did occur, the attempts to account for them in terms of purely local considerations tended to be unsatisfactory. At Rugby, for example, there was a swing to Labour in the 1970 election of 2·7% as against the average movement of 4·8% to the Conservatives, although there were few special factors to distinguish the constituency from its neighbours. According to *Tribune*, the Conservatives fared badly because the sitting Labour M.P., Bill Price, 'fought a four year campaign, writing 30,000 letters, conducting 200 Saturday morning surgeries and fulfilling over 1,000 engagements in the constituency.'[1] Some Conservative sources, on the other hand, blamed Mr. Powell's speech in the area for alienating Conservative-inclined liberal opinion. The *Tribune* analysis failed to show why the candidate's activities apparently paid such handsome dividends while similar efforts in other constituencies were unproductive; and the Conservative explanation merely posed the question why Mr. Powell's speeches had not caused anti-Conservative swings elsewhere in the West Midlands. It is tempting to conclude that, by and large, elections are won and lost nationally: the few local deviations which

[1] *Tribune*, June 26, 1970.

do occur are usually due to chance or to population movements rather than to exceptional constituency organisation or any other clearly local stimulus.

Nevertheless, it would be wrong for several reasons to limit an election study exclusively to the national scene. First of all, there remain significant, albeit small, variations between the results in different types of constituency: between different regions and between cities, suburbs, rural areas and so forth. Some of these are examined in Appendices II and III.

Secondly, although local organisations and individual candidates rarely make an immediate impact, they are probably more important over a longer period. Philip Williams has examined the performance of 'familiar' M.P.s in marginal seats (i.e. those of at least eight years' standing). He argues that in the elections of 1964 and 1966 'familiar' Conservative M.P.s had a better swing by about 1½% to 2% than their colleagues, while 'familiar' Labour men had a better swing than their colleagues by 3 to 3½%.[1] Unfortunately, there is no equally simple test of the long-term impact of a good local organisation, but the Williams study does suggest that — like that of a good candidate — it may be greater in the long term than in the short. Such cumulative influences may explain some of the larger variations in swing between 1955 and 1970 which are given in Appendix I.

Thirdly, even if the candidate or the local organisation is 'worth no more than 1% of the vote' between one election and the next, this can sometimes be decisive. The party battle has been so close that a swing of 4% between Labour and Conservative would have been sufficient to alter the national verdict in every election since the war. In 1950, 1951, 1964 and 1970, a switch by less than 1% of the voters would have robbed the winning party of its majority.

Fourthly, the local parties fulfil the vital function of selecting the candidates. Although this has almost no effect on the election result, it influences the composition of the new parliament and determines the personnel from which future governments will be chosen.

Fifthly, even if local party activity does not influence many votes,

[1] In 'Two notes on the British electoral system', *Parliamentary Affairs*, Winter 1966–67, Philip Williams compares swings between 1950 and 1964; 1951 and 1964; 1950 and 1966; and 1951 and 1966 and maintains that the differences in performances between 'familiar' M.P.s and others cannot be accounted for except in terms of personal followings.

politicians think it does. What is going on in the constituencies affects, through individual M.P.s, the whole climate of politics at Westminster.

Therefore it is necessary to consider the functioning and malfunctioning of local party organisation. Although many local parties only come to life during the campaign, the general success of electioneering efforts must depend on how well the machine has been maintained in the period preceding the election. This chapter is devoted to local party organisation from 1966 to 1970 while the 1970 campaign itself is discussed in Chapter XIII.

We have used several kinds of sources. As in previous Nuffield studies, we spoke with almost every Conservative area agent and Labour regional organiser. We carried out over 100 interviews with local party agents in the pre-election period. During the four weeks before the poll we made contact with area agents, constituency agents and candidates.[1] 95 Labour, 112 Conservative and 30 others (Liberals, Plaid Cymru, Scottish National Party and Democratic Party).[2] We attempted in our questions to cover the years from 1966 as well as the campaign.

[1] While we ourselves saw nearly 100 agents, we should underline our enormous debt to those who helped us in this work, with interviews of very high quality; their names are to be found on p. xv.

[2] The distribution of interviews (using the Conservative area boundaries) by area and by type of constituency was:

| | Constituencies in group | Labour visits | Conservative visits |
|---|---|---|---|
| Greater London | 103 | 7 | 9 |
| Northern | 34 | 2 | 2 |
| North-West | 79 | 14 | 9 |
| Yorkshire | 54 | 10 | 13 |
| East Midlands | 42 | 11 | 7 |
| West Midlands | 60 | 10 | 12 |
| East of England | 40 | 8 | 9 |
| South Eastern | 34 | 3 | 5 |
| Wessex | 37 | 7 | 13 |
| Western | 28 | 9 | 13 |
| Wales and Monmouthshire | 36 | 7 | 8 |
| Scotland | 71 | 7 | 12 |
| Total | 618 | 95 | 112 |
| Safe Labour | 243 | 24 | 20 |
| Marginal Labour | 111 | 40 | 44 |
| Marginal Conservative | 81 | 14 | 19 |
| Safe Conservative and other | 183 | 4 | 10 |

Safe Labour includes the Speaker's seat. Throughout this chapter we have arbitrarily classified as marginal all seats with 1966 majorities of less than 10%. Northern Ireland is excluded throughout. The regional totals differ from the safe and marginal ones because we have included interviews in city and area headquarters.

We also received several dozen constituency magazines and annual reports and some hundreds of balance sheets. After the election we obtained private accounts of the campaign from 109 candidates, and from 40 agents mainly in marginal constituencies.

The material for Chapter XII (The Emergence of Candidates) is different. We have used the biographies of candidates produced by the press departments at the party headquarters; we have examined the files on the individual candidates in a major press archive and we have supplemented this information with a number of interviews.

Despite the quantity of information we have gathered, we are all too aware of its limitations. The constituencies in which we carried out our interviews are not a deliberately random sample. We concentrated on marginals, and we had to a certain extent to tailor our choice to the dictates of geography and convenience. Thus we visited a disproportionate number of constituency organisations with full-time agents simply because the others tended to have no telephone or permanent premises (this incidentally, accounts for the larger number of interviews with Conservatives). Furthermore, some of the information we received was suspect. For example, few local parties keep tallies of their membership and estimates are sometimes over-optimistic. In two cases, which were certainly not typical, agents told us that their membership was 2,300 and 5,000, whereas the annual reports which they gave us showed totals of 900 and 2,700 members. Though we have made allowances for inaccuracies of this sort, much of the factual information must be treated with reserve. We have therefore attempted to draw only the simplest general conclusions about constituency organisation, categorising our findings under a number of sub-headings. After a brief summary of the 1969 Representation of the People Act, we describe in the first part of the chapter the Labour party and in the second the Conservatives.[1]

[1] In this chapter we focus on the Conservative and Labour organisations. For some reference to Plaid Cymru see p. 111 and to the Scottish National Party see pp. 446–62. The Liberals are discussed on pp. 113–17; there are difficulties in assessing their very varied levels of activity. Early in 1970 they had full-time agents in only 18 seats, although in half-a-dozen others there was a full-time secretary or someone paid to manage a 'tote' scheme. The constituencies with full-time agents were:

| | | | |
|---|---|---|---|
| Bodmin* | North Dorset | Cardigan | West Aberdeenshire* |
| North Cornwall* | Tiverton | Chorley | Caithness & Sutherland |
| North Devon* | Torrington | Scarborough & Whitby | Inverness* |
| Colne Valley* | Chippenham | Wavertree | Roxburgh, Selkirk* & Peebles |
| Ladywood* | Eastbourne | | |

* Sitting Liberal Member

[*continued*

The Representation of the People Bill was enacted in 1969 with relatively little controversy, although on a free vote Conservatives recorded themselves against lowering the voting age and parliamentary pressure led to a drastic revision of the proposals for putting party labels on the ballot paper. There was also vigorous objection to non-residents being debarred from election to local councils.

The Act made four significant alterations in the law.[1]

1. *Voting age.* Everyone was to be entitled to vote from the day of his 18th birthday. This provision lowered the age of voting by more than 3½ years since under the previous arrangements, with the cumbrous Y-voter provisions, it was impossible to vote until four months after coming of age and the average delay was 7 months. However, the first register under the new system (which was compiled on October 10, 1969, and came into force on February 16, 1970), failed to record the names of a very large minority of 18 to 21-year-olds. Sample surveys suggested that only 70% were on the register. It was possible to check more exactly as far as the youngest voters were concerned since under the new system their date of birth was recorded on the register if they reached 18-between February 16, 1970, and February 15, 1971. There were only 464,000 of them registered although Census data suggest that there should have been about 800,000.[2]

---

In the seats they held their organisation usually compared favourably with almost any in the country. For example, they claimed 7,000 members in North Cornwall, 5,000 in North Devon, 5,000 in Orpington, 3,000 in Bodmin and 2,000 in Inverness. A number of other seats had substantial memberships, particularly in Wales, but there were many seats where although the Liberals had come second as recently as 1960 or 1964, their organisation had run down almost to nothing. In isolated constituencies there was a sharp growth in activity centring around an individual or a group, but the general picture was one of decline. The areas which gave most encouragement to the party were in a few big cities where from bridgeheads established on the local council there had been a substantial upsurge in activity. In Birmingham, everything centred around Wallace Lawler in Ladywood, and in Liverpool around Cyril Carr in Wavertree; in Leeds Michael Meadowcroft had tried to lead a less spectacular advance on a broader front. The story of local Liberal activities is chronicled in some detail in the *Liberal News*.

[1] There were other minor provisions, mainly of a technical nature. Changes relating to television are referred to on p. 201. The substantial repeal of the 1883 bans on incurring expenses on account 'of bands of music, torches, flags or banners' had no obvious effect in making the 1970 election more colourful or more musical.

[2] The number entitled to vote on June 18 was 273,000 out of this 464,000. i.e. 41%. Since only 35% of the births between February 16, 1952, and February 15, 1953, had occurred by mid-June, this would imply that, when the 1970 register was compiled on October 10, 1969, householders found it appreciably easier to envisage 17-year-olds becoming eligible to vote within the next eighteen months than 16-year-olds.

2. *Election expenses.* The old limit, laid down in 1948, of £450 plus 2*d* per elector in county seats and 1½*d* per elector in boroughs was increased by a flat £300.

3. *Names on ballot papers.* The Home Secretary originally proposed an elaborate scheme for the registration of party labels but anxiety about the litigation that this could provoke together with other objections led to a provision by which any candidate could add a slogan of up to six words after his name. Most candidates used their party label in a simple form. For Labour the recommended words were 'The Labour party candidate'. Most Conservatives just used 'Conservative' though at least one, Mr. Body in Holland-with-Boston, wrote 'Anti-Common Market Conservative' and Mr. Edward Heath, to distinguish himself from an independent challenger who had changed his name to Edward Heath, used the phrase 'leader of the Conservative party'.

4. *Hours of voting.* For all parliamentary elections, polling stations were to open for an extra hour, i.e. from 7 a.m. to 10 p.m. This provision, not endorsed by the Speaker's Conference, was apparently intended to help Labour supporters who traditionally have voted later in the day (the median Conservative vote has usually been cast about 5 p.m. the median Labour vote about 6 p.m.).[1] Among party workers on both sides, unhappiness was expressed about this prolongation of what was already a very long day's electioneering. In fact post-election surveys suggested that only about 4% of voters cast their ballots during the extra hour.

### *Constituency Labour Parties*[2]

*Membership.* In both the Labour and Conservative parties alike, 'membership' often involves a very casual affiliation. Subscriptions are so inefficiently collected that agents and party secretaries rarely have a clear idea of numbers. The figures in the Annual Reports of the National Executive Committee thus give a very misleading impression.[3] According to the 1970 Report, there were precisely

[1] See *The British General Election of 1966*, p. 201.

[2] For a discussion of the role of Transport House, see Chapter II.

[3] Writers on British parties have often over-estimated the information on membership available to the party headquarters. For example, R. T. McKenzie, in *British Political Parties* (2nd edition, p. 4 n.) suggests that 'British parties have fairly accurate rolls of paid-up members' while others, including earlier Nuffield studies, have quoted without qualification the gross figures published by the parties.

680,656 individual party members during the previous year. This not only assumes that constituency Labour parties (CLPs) gave accurate figures but also that all those which affiliated on the basis of the constitutional minimum of 1,000 actually had that many members. In fact, the privately circulated list of individual CLP affiliations shows that only 111 claimed over 1,000 members, the rest presumably having less than 1,000. Even this is almost certainly an over-estimate. We independently obtained membership figures from about a quarter of the local parties listed with over 1,000 members. Half the figures we were given were significantly lower than the official ones and a quarter were under 1,000. It seems, therefore, that only about 80 CLPs had as many as 1,000 nominal members in 1969–70.

In many CLPs, including a large proportion of those in Labour's political strongholds, there were only a few dozen members. To cite a bad but not altogether exceptional case, the fifteen Glasgow CLPs had only 1,786 members combined and some of the Labour-held seats had less than 50 members.[1] Constituency committees still tended to rely on old faithfuls who were recruited in pre-war times and often not replaced when they became too old to continue.[2]

It seems most reasonable to estimate the total membership of the 111 constituencies claiming over 1,000 members at 130,000 (an average of 1,170) and the average membership of the others at 350 to 500. This yields an approximate total membership in 1969–70 in England, Wales and Scotland, of between 310,000 and 385,000.[3]

Despite their inaccuracy, the official figures give a good indi-

[1] This was the figure quoted in a special report to the NEC in early 1969 into the affairs of the party in Glasgow by Reg Underhill, the Assistant National Agent. For interesting if slightly exaggerated stories see *Sunday Times*, March 23, 1969, and *Scotsman*, March 27, 1969.

[2] See Paul Foot's sketches of the CLPs in Salford, Barkston Ash and Harlow, the *Sunday Times*, September 29, 1968.

[3] Although we received membership figures from 67 CLPs, the over-representation of marginal constituencies and those with full-time agents makes it dangerous to extrapolate from them an estimate of total membership. The estimate above is, therefore, made on the following basis:

(*a*) The constituencies affiliating in 1969 with over 1,000 members claimed a total membership of 175,218. Our interviews in a quarter of these constituencies suggest that the actual figures were probably only 75% of the number claimed in their returns to Transport House, i.e. about 130,000.

(*b*) By affiliating at the constitutional minimum the other constituencies all acknowledged memberships below 1,000 and it is unlikely that more than a very few had more than 800. A large proportion clearly had 250 or less. We have therefore assumed an average membership in these constituencies of 350–500.

cation of the relative strength of membership in different types of constituency:

TABLE I

*CLPs claiming over 1,000 members in 1968–9, by type of constituency*

| | Over 1,000 members | Under 1,000 members | % over 1,000 members |
|---|---|---|---|
| Safe Labour . . | 57 | 186 | 23 |
| Marginal Labour . . | 44 | 37 | 54 |
| Marginal Conservative . | 25 | 86 | 23 |
| Safe Conservative and other . . . | 12 | 171 | 7 |
| Total . . . | 138 | 480 | 22 |

Table I shows that the comparatively strong organisations were less concentrated in Labour's best political areas than might have been expected. Most of the marginal Labour seats (the best category) had been Conservative-held before the elections of 1964 and 1966. It is also surprising, perhaps, to find large Labour parties in such safe Conservative constituencies as Barnet, Harrow West, Esher, Reigate, Richmond and Surbiton. The probable explanation is that the Labour party draws a large proportion of its active following from particular sections of the urban middle class (teachers, for instance) which are concentrated in these areas. The weakness of CLPs in safe Labour constituencies, and their consequent uselessness as sources of funds and helpers for marginal seats contrasts sharply with the situation in the Conservative party.

Labour membership appears to have been in decline since the 1950s. This became more pronounced in 1967 and 1968 as the fortunes of the government worsened and measures such as prescription charges were introduced, infuriating many of the activists. The official minimum subscription had been raised from 6*s*. to 12*s*. a year in 1965, but this increase was not responsible for the fall in membership as the full subscription was often not imposed. In some areas, party collectors still called on members each month for 6*d*. or 1*s*. This method had been suitable in a poorer age and it still fostered the sense of a party community, but it often meant that the keenest collectors, generally old timers, covered only a small beat and memberships lapsed simply because no one called for the subscription.

The situation was serious even before the crisis over the Industrial Relations Bill. Indeed, most agents to whom we spoke considered that the bill had been a comparatively unimportant factor in the drop after 1966. They generally emphasised the effects of the government's economic difficulties on local morale: many spoke of the long period when there was great reluctance to go from door to door, simply because collectors were so likely to encounter abuse. Senior party officials, on the other hand, maintained that the quarrel over the 'penal clauses' had badly weakened the organisations in the constituencies.

As the election approached, Transport House experimented in a few selected areas with more modern ideas for collecting subscriptions — through the Giro for example[1] — but little progress had been made by June 1970. Transport House could do no more than encourage the dispirited workers to go on to the doorsteps again. It was only when there was an improvement in the economic situation and in Labour's position in the polls over the winter of 1969–70 that party supporters became less reluctant to canvass for members. By this stage it was a case of too little and too late.

TABLE 2

*Number of CLPs claiming over 1,000 members, 1966–70*

| | –1,000 | 1,001–1,999 | 2,000–2,999 | over 3,000 | Total over 1,000 | Total members in CLPs over 1,000 |
|---|---|---|---|---|---|---|
| 1966 | 393 | 162 | 50 | 13 | 225 | 380,920 |
| 1967 | 433 | 143 | 34 | 8 | 195 | 295,366 |
| 1968 | 470 | 115 | 15 | 8 | 138 | 213,339 |
| 1969 | 507 | 90 | 13 | 8 | 111 | 175,218 |

(Sources: NEC *Annual Reports* and annual *Lists of Affiliated Organisations, Membership, Affiliation Fees and By-election Premiums*.)

*Agents.* The falling number of full-time constituency agents was a major concern of *Socialist Commentary*'s review of Labour organisation in October 1965. In the same month, R. L. Leonard published the results of a survey.[2] This showed that 87% of Labour agents were earning under £1,000 a year and worked long hours in

[1] This had been one of the interim recommendations of the Simpson Committee in September, 1967.

[2] R. L. Leonard, 'Who are Labour's agents?' *New Society*, July 15, 1965.

TABLE 3

*Membership in selected CLPs, 1966–70*

| | 1966–67 | 1967–68 | 1968–69 | 1969–70 |
|---|---|---|---|---|
| Woolwich East . | 5,761 | 5,226 | 4,816 | 4,150 } 6,350* combined |
| Woolwich West . | 4,724 | 4,086 | 3,353 | 3,419 } |
| Lewisham South . | 4,909 | 4,590 | 3,951 | 3,198 |
| Buckingham* . | 1,366 | 1,380 | 1,239 | 957 |
| York . . | 1,901 | 1,744 | 1,134 | 915 |
| Faversham . | 4,648 | 3,872 | 3,005* | 2,588* |

(Sources: Asterisked figures are from constituency annual reports, others from NEC annual reports.)

bad conditions, usually without secretarial assistance. These hardships were causing a drift away from party work. In 1951 there had been 296 full-time agents, but by 1966 there were only 204. Mr. Leonard warned that unless the party took 'urgent steps to improve the conditions of the agency service it is highly doubtful whether it will find adequate replacements for such stalwarts when they eventually retire'. The Plan for an Efficient Party campaign proposed a national agency service under which full-time organisers would receive a guaranteed salary from Transport House. The scheme would provide job security and acceptable salary rates thereby stimulating recruitment. The disadvantages were the cost to Transport House, the disincentive to local parties to raise their own money and the central control which national employment might involve.

A National Agency Scheme was recommended in the interim report of the Simpson Committee and in January 1968, the NEC agreed to provide finance for a partial scheme. £50,000 per annum was to be allotted for three years from the General Election Fund, sufficient to guarantee at least thirty appointments. The interregnum between Len Williams' and Harry Nicholas' general secretaryships delayed the implementation of the scheme until July 1969. With the help of local contributions (often substantial), it was then possible to assign 43 national agency positions,[1] but

[1] These National Agency Scheme appointments were made (* denoting that more than one constituency was covered):

Bedford
Berwick & East Lothian
Billericay
*Bolton
*Bradford
Brighouse & Spenborough
Brighton, Kemptown
Cambridge
Carlisle
*Cardiff

three of these remained unfilled at the time of the general election.[1] The salary scale introduced in 1969 for National Agency Scheme appointments started at £1,000 per annum with three annual increments to a maximum of £1,250. In addition there was a car

TABLE 4

*Number of Labour full-time city party secretaries, agents, organisers and assistants*

| | | | |
|---|---|---|---|
| 1951 | 296 | 1966 | 204 |
| 1955 | 227 | 1967 | 199 |
| 1959 | 243 | 1968 | 177 |
| 1964 | 200 | 1969 | 146 |
| | | (May) 1970 | 141 |

allowance and £50 a year for maintenance. City agents received marginally higher rates.[2]

During 1966–69, while the problems of the agency service were being investigated, they became even more critical. By 1969, there were only 146 agents for the 618 constituencies in England, Wales

Colne Valley
Conway
Darlington
Dover
*Edinburgh
Eton & Slough
*Falmouth & Camborne (with Truro)
Gravesend
Holborn & St. Pancras South
*Hornsey (with Wood Green)
King's Lynn
Keighley
*Leicester
Meriden
Monmouth
Nelson & Colne
Newark
Norwood
*Nottingham South
(with Nottingham West)
Oxford
Peterborough
*Plymouth
Putney
Reading
Rugby
Rushcliffe
Stretford
(Truro — see Falmouth & Camborne)
Wandsworth Central
(Wood Green — see Hornsey)
Wrekin
York

Three appointments were 'held over'; *Bristol North East (with Bristol North West), *Oldbury & Halesowen (with Smethwick), and Cardigan.

[1] The National Union of Labour Organisers favoured an alternative plan. The 1933 Hastings agreement governing the limits of trade union contributions for sponsored candidates was to be revised so that unions would be persuaded to increase their contributions. This idea was rejected by the Simpson Committee on the ground that it might lead to a large drop in the number of sponsored candidates. However, the 1969 Annual Conference approved an increase from 50% to 60% in the proportion of an agent's salary that a sponsoring union could contribute in borough constituencies and from 55% to 65% in county constituencies.

[2] At the same time, Transport House tried to impose improved rates for locally employed agents. Normal salaries were to start at £875 per annum with four annual increments to a maximum of £1,155.

and Scotland. Furthermore, the increased cost of living and the dismal position of the party hindered recruitment. The 12-month certificate course in 1967 attracted only 7 trainees; no course was offered in 1968; and the shortened 9-month course in 1969 had only 8 members. Of these some left organisation work after a year or two.

The National Agency Scheme failed to improve the low morale among agents. A report of the National Union of Labour Organisers complained in August 1969:

> 'If one takes the four years from 1958 to 1961 inclusive, over 80 new agents were appointed. Less than 20 are still employed by the party and several of these are on the regional staff. . . . Probably the biggest simple need of Labour's organising service can be summed up in one word: recognition. . . . A party which advocates industrial democracy really ought to set a better example in its relations with its own employees.'[1]

As Table 5 shows, the shortage of full-time agents varied considerably from region to region. The problem was particularly serious in Scotland and Wales, while East Anglia remained an exceptionally strong area.[2]

TABLE 5

*Number of full-time City Party Secretaries, agents and organisers on eve of 1970 election, by region*

| | No. of full-time agents | No. of constituencies in region | Col. 1 as % of Col. 2 |
|---|---|---|---|
| Greater London | 25 | 100 | 25 |
| Northern | 12 | 38 | 32 |
| North-west | 13 | 79 | 17 |
| Yorkshire | 9 | 51 | 18 |
| East Midlands | 11 | 40 | 28 |
| West Midlands | 8 | 54 | 15 |
| Eastern | 22 | 42 | 52 |
| Western | 14 | 43 | 33 |
| South Eastern | 17 | 64 | 38 |
| Wales and Monmouthshire | 3 | 36 | 8 |
| Scotland | 7 | 71 | 10 |
| All constituencies | 141 | 618 | 23 |

[1] See also J. Minogue, 'Agents want Security', *Guardian*, January 20, 1969.

[2] There is an extremely informative interview with a Labour organiser in Suffolk in Ronald Blythe's *Akenfield, Portrait of an English Village* (Allen Lane, 1969). East Anglia is the only rural part of England where the Labour party had managed to establish a foothold.

TABLE 6

*Number of full-time Labour constituency agents, organisers and assistants on the eve of the 1970 election, by type of constituency*

| | No. of agents | No. of constituencies | Col. 1 as % of Col. 2 |
|---|---|---|---|
| Safe Labour . . . . | 64 | 243 | 26 |
| Marginal Labour . . . | 38 | 81 | 47 |
| Marginal Conservative . . | 27 | 111 | 24 |
| Safe Conservative (and other) . | 5 | 183 | 3 |
| All constituencies . . . | 134 | 618 | 22 |

Ideally it would have been best to direct agents to the marginal constituencies, especially the Labour-held marginals which had to be retained if Labour was to win the election. The National Agency Scheme gave Transport House considerable scope to do this, but it was often impossible to persuade agents to move or to find the funds to set up an agency appointment in a weakly-organised Labour-held marginal seat. As Table 6 shows, the party had achieved some concentration of agents in marginal Labour seats.

*Finance.* As the National Union of Labour Organisers argued in its 1969 report, Labour's constituency finances had been caught in a 'vicious circle':

> 'Since the success of fund-raising ventures depends very largely on the availability of trained organisers in the constituencies, Labour is unlikely to raise the money without the organisers, and yet cannot employ the organisers without first raising the money.'

An examination of two dozen balance sheets for 1969 shows that CLPs employing full-time agents had an average income and expenditure of about £2,500 a year and those without agents about £800 a year. This latter figure is almost certainly too high; as only the more efficient CLPs circulate accounts and send them to the Regional Office, a reasonable estimate would suggest that all CLPs taken together had a combined income and expenditure in the order of £750,000 a year.[1] A similar enquiry by R. L. Leonard in

[1] This figure is arrived at thus:

| | | |
|---|---|---|
| Constituencies with full-time agents | 140 × £2,500 | = £400,000 |
| Constituencies without full-time agents | 480 × £700 | = £336,000 |
| | | £736,000 |

This leaves an average for all CLPs of about £1,200 per year.

K

1962–63 showed an average income for all CLPs of £2,000 a year. This would imply that, taking inflation into account, their incomes in 1969 were less than they had been six years before.[1]

Gambling schemes were by far the largest source of income in most CLPs, the most popular being football totes. Other variations were Grand National draws, Christmas raffles, pontoon and so forth. These generally accounted for well over 50% of CLP income. Some constituencies received grants from a trade union or from Transport House. Income from subscriptions and trade union affiliations was normally below 10% and rarely exceeded 15%. The richest and most successful local parties, such as Norwich or Faversham, generally relied on tote schemes. These were run by door to door collectors who often received a share of the proceeds and who sometimes collected party subscriptions at the same time. In constituencies with full-time agents, two-thirds of the expenditure was generally devoted to their salaries and expenses, and most of the rest to office expenses. In other CLPs office expenses were the main item. The common local argument that employing an agent only meant that he spent his time organising gambling activities in order to meet his salary contained a considerable element of truth.

The financial weakness of the local parties imposed a heavy burden on Transport House. It meant that so far from receiving payments from them (or, at any rate, from the richer CLPs) it had to devote money to the National Agency Scheme and to local grants. This reduced the amount available for advertising and other national needs such as increasing the staff at the headquarters.

There were numerous attempts to improve constituency fund-raising. In August 1965 a 'Golden Prize Clubs Scheme' was started to promote lotteries. Their profits amounted to a meagre £3,555 in 1966–67 and failed to improve in subsequent years. Mr. Robert Maxwell's 'National Fund Raising Foundation' met with no greater success. Early in 1969 a committee was formed under Mr. Callaghan's chairmanship to consider long-term problems of constituency finance. Its members included two of the wealthiest Labour M.P.s, Jack Diamond and Harold Lever, and also Robert Maxwell. It had made little impact by the time of the general election.[2] There was a brief attempt to tap middle income sub-

[1] See R. L. Leonard, *Elections in Britain* (Van Nostrand, 1968), pp. 60–1.
[2] For other fund-raising plans see p. 54.

scriptions, in a 'Fighting Fivers' campaign. Advertisements appeared early in 1969 in the *New Statesman* and other journals, inviting contributions of £5. The idea was modelled on the 'dollars for Democrats' drives in the United States. The response was disappointing, the receipts hardly covered the cost of the advertisements. There were also tentative plans for a major fund-raising campaign on the lines of the Salvation Army Appeal which was said to have topped £1¼ million with an administrative expenditure of about £80,000. After the failure of the early advertisements, the idea was dropped.[1] The poor response to virtually every fund-raising scheme and the lack of any prospect of improvements led in October 1970 to the resignation of Oliver Stutchbury who had acted since 1966 as the party's financial adviser. Commenting that 'financially and organisationally the party is in a critically unhappy position', Mr. Stutchbury wrote to the General Secretary:

> 'My job as the party's fund raising adviser cannot be performed effectively in the present state of the party's organisation in the country. I have resisted the impulse to resign before on the assurance that a high level inquiry was to be instituted at the 1970 conference. No inquiry has been forthcoming, and I can see no point whatever in my carrying on.'[2]

*Local elections.* Besides functioning in parliamentary elections, most constituency parties also organise campaigns for local government elections. It is only in a small proportion of rural constituencies that these are still run on non-party lines. Although the annual municipal and the triennial county council campaigns can be useful in keeping parties in trim for the general election, they can also have the opposite effect. In some areas they are regarded as so important that they consume funds and energies that would, from the viewpoint of the national party, be better conserved.[3] In the middle 1960s many ward parties were dominated by secretaries who were local councillors and who had no wish to complicate life by attracting new recruits on to their ward com-

[1] Another scheme, also called 'Fighting Fivers', was organised before the election campaign with greater success. Instead of advertising, the names of potential donors were suggested by constituency agents.

[2] *Guardian*, October 3, 1970.

[3] In the words of a city agent, 'Being elected to the Council seems to go to [the ward leader's] head and they think [Council] group meetings are more important than party work — even during a campaign.'

mittees.[1] Some senior Labour ministers thus regarded the heavy local election losses in 1967, 1968 and 1969 as a blessing in disguise. As one of them commented to us 'they do nothing for the party outside their own elections. Their motto might as well be "Councillors of the world unite. You have nothing to lose but your chains". . .'. It was hoped that as the other defeated councillors gave way to more energetic replacements, organisation would improve.

Indeed, there were probably some compensations for the massacres inflicted on the Labour party in local elections. In some areas the Conservatives were quite inexperienced in controlling local councils and soon found themselves in trouble. 'Our main local advantage,' said one Labour agent, 'is that the City Council is Conservative and has made a hash of things.' A few CLPs reported that defeated councillors increased their work on the doorstep in their efforts to secure re-election. And there was widespread agreement that the Labour recovery in the 1970 local elections did wonders for morale.

On balance, however, CLPs were severely damaged by their poor performances in local government elections which greatly discouraged party workers and inhibited recruitment. After the general election we received this typical account from a voluntary agent in a Labour-held marginal. It shows the close connection between parliamentary and local election performances.

> 'Since the 1966 parliamentary election, the organisation inside [our] Labour party had fallen to a very low level. Most ward groups had ceased to exist. This reached a lowest level about two years ago, when we lost every council seat we were defending except [one]. Most ward groups gave up the fight before it started. . . . In 1969, we again lost all our council seats excepting [one], but on this occasion by very much smaller majorities than 1968. . . . This year [1970], we held all our seats except one and these by good majorities. Compared with 1968, we went into the parliamentary election with improved organisation in four wards, four new ward groups, enthusiastic but generally inexperienced, scratch organisations in four wards and no organisation at all in two wards. Under these circumstances, it was largely a matter of our doing the best we could.'

A Labour activist in Bradford reported:

[1] The high percentage of Councillors among CLP ward secretaries emerges, for example, from J. M. Bochel's 'Activists in the Conservative and Labour Parties — A Study of Ward Secretaries in Manchester', M.A. Thesis, University of Manchester, 1965.

'In 1968, there was a redistribution of wards and therefore all the seats in the city were due for election in 1968. . . . 57 went to the Conservatives and only 2 to Labour. There has been some comeback. There were 4 gains in 1969 and almost half the seats being contested were won in 1970. . . . But it does mean that the Council is predominantly Conservative and this has had a very bad effect on morale. Some old party workers drifted off and others stayed where they were but were shattered. There were all sorts of jokes such as "now the Labour group on the City council will meet in a telephone kiosk". The scars of 1968 are still not entirely healed. People did stay in the party, however, though they were afraid to go out and canvass on the doorstep.'

A Yorkshire agent put it more simply: 'the more councillors, the stronger the local party'.

*City and borough Labour parties.* The harmful effects of over-concentration on municipal elections were most apparent in the cities and large towns. Here, Labour politics had been long dominated by city-wide committees whose reliance on trade union funds made it unnecessary to press for contributions or for members from the several CLPs in their area. This top-heavy form of organisation often prevented the development of efficient machinery at ward and constituency level. Transport House had made numerous attempts over the years to break the power of the City and Borough Committees and to build up constituency parties, but it had to tread warily: it was much easier to destroy an existing, albeit ineffective, organisation than to build others in its place. As a regional organiser told us:

'I'm all for altering the structure of borough parties. At the moment, there are ward meetings, constituency meetings and borough meetings — in other words, too many levels and too many meetings. There ought to be a change. I wouldn't mind if the borough party became a mere local government committee. The trouble is that at present you can't get the affiliated trade unions to appoint delegates to both borough *and* constituency Labour parties. For example, at a recent selection [in a CLP within a city], there were only two union representatives.'

The situation in London provides a special example of the organisational problems with which the staff at headquarters had to contend. When the Greater London Council was created in 1964, the area covered by the London County Council was greatly extended, and the borough boundaries transformed. The Conservative Central Office accordingly established a 'Greater London

Area'. But the London Labour Party, which covered the areas of Inner London in the old London County Council, vigorously resisted surrendering its identity (and its sources of income) to a larger unit. Accordingly, London affairs — and particularly the running of GLC elections — were entrusted to an unwieldy Co-ordinating Committee drawing its members from the London Labour Party and the other Home Counties areas containing constituencies within the GLC. The arrangement was examined by the Simpson Committee which recommended in its interim report the formation of a Regional Council for Greater London to replace the existing structure. The proposal was the first to be considered by the NEC, which gave its approval at its November 1967 meeting. Consultations with existing Regional Councils followed and a consultative conference took place on January 27, 1968. Detailed proposals were then reconsidered by the NEC. A conference to establish the Greater London Regional Council was finally held on March 31, 1968. Even at this stage there was controversy, the necessary resolution being accepted by 799 votes to 240. After this it was still necessary to complete the administrative arrangements and it was only on January 8, 1969, that the new body finally came into being. By this time, two GLC elections and two borough elections had been fought under the new boundaries, and the GLC together with 27 of the 32 boroughs was firmly in Conservative hands.

In other cities there were even more serious problems. Labour lost control of Birmingham City Council in 1966, Bradford, Bristol, Cardiff, Coventry, Leeds, Leicester, Liverpool, Manchester, Newcastle and Nottingham in 1967 and Glasgow and Sheffield in 1968. Sheffield was recaptured in 1969 but, although there were considerable Labour gains in 1970, no other city was won back and Stoke-on-Trent was lost. Hull was the only borough with three or more M.P.s that stayed continuously in Labour hands.

Party membership was very low, even by Labour standards, and there was an extreme shortage of agents. In 1969, only seven CLPs out of 98 in large provincial cities claimed over 1,000 members;[1] and Transport House had great difficulty in ensuring that each city had at least one full-time organiser. Shortly before the election

[1] Even these figures are almost certainly exaggerated. Our own interviews suggest that Manchester, Wythenshawe was possibly the only CLP in a city outside London with a membership of over 1,000.

National Agency Scheme appointments provided agents in Leicester, Nottingham, Bradford and Edinburgh. No city had three agents and only Birmingham, Bristol, Manchester and Sheffield had two. Only one agent in any city was given specific responsibility for a marginal seat (under National Agency Scheme an agent was appointed to Nottingham South — but he also had to look after Nottingham West). In Liverpool there was no agent at all at the opening of the election. Transport House had long objected that the link between the Liverpool Labour Party and the Trades Council permitted the infiltration of Marxist elements. In 1969 the Trades and Labour Council was finally forced to separate into two bodies and in January 1970 Simon Fraser, previously secretary of the joint organisation and the only full-time agent in the city, became Secretary of the Trades Council. In his final report as Labour party secretary, he noted that 'The state of party organisation at constituency and ward level is at its worst for many years, if not the worst ever'. There was also no Labour agent in Leeds. Here the main problem was the usual one — namely that the organisation was dominated by the Labour group on the City Council. Transport House therefore refused to provide the funds to employ an organiser unless he worked directly under the regional organiser, and only if he did not act as the secretary of the Labour Group on the City Council. The long term aim of Transport House was to improve the CLPs and to reduce the importance of the city parties. Very little progress had been made by 1970.

*Young voters.* Transport House produced attractive birthday cards for those who, under the Representation of the People Act, became entitled to vote on their eighteenth birthday. These, or other locally produced leaflets, were sent by many constituency parties to new voters, usually signed by the M.P. or candidate. A few CLPs also organised special youth forums or dances. The response was generally disappointing. Both major parties found that young people lacked interest in politics. The experience of both Conservative and Labour organisations was summed up by the agent who complained, 'We can't get at the young voters — they never come to the door to ask or answer questions.'

The Young Socialists, never a very successful organisation, had a difficult time. The number of YS branches declined from 571 in 1966 to 348 in 1969. The Simpson Committee's recommendations for their revitalisation had not been in operation for long enough before the election to show any results. According to Transport House there were between 6,000 and 10,000 Young Socialists in 1970.[1]

*Political activity.* The decline in constituency activity had a side effect which members of the Labour government must have welcomed. It meant that there was less political debate and relatively little local pressure against its policies. Motions came to the party conference as before, but they tended to lack weight as the delegates that spoke on their behalf represented a comparatively small, inactive following. A few CLPs continued to be concerned with such issues as Rhodesia, Vietnam and South Africa. There was even the occasional remnant of the Campaign for Nuclear Disarmament. But the main internal opposition to the government came from sections of the PLP and the trade unions. It is significant that the constituencies appear to have been relatively uninvolved in the upheaval over the Industrial Relations Bill. As a Labour official, only half in jest, commented: 'At least that is one good argument for having weak local parties — they don't make trouble.'[2]

### *Conservative Constituency Associations*[3]

*Membership.* The last official Conservative membership statistics were announced at the end of a national membership campaign in 1953 when an all-time record total of 2,805,832 was claimed for England and Wales. Although this may have been a relatively accurate figure, it represented a temporary peak after a special campaign. A detailed private study carried out during the following

[1] P. Abrams and A. Little, 'The Young Activist in British Politics', *British Journal of Sociology*, December 1965, give a figure of 25,000. Though this is possibly an over-estimate, it gives some impression of the decline during the late 1960s. Abrams and Little reckon that the rate of decline of the YS in the decade preceding 1965 had been 5% per annum.

[2] In Autumn 1969, the Labour party launched a programme similar to the Contact Programme of the Conservative Political Centre (see pp. 99–100 and pp. 286–8). It was called 'Participation '69'. Mr. Nicholas said in introducing it:

> 'The Labour party is not, and never has been a party of leaders and led, top dogs and underdogs. . . . Any member of the party has the right to say what he thinks, the right to try and persuade others to his point of view.'

The first discussion topic, the only one before the election, was 'Women and Social Security'. 198 questionnaires were returned by the deadline. The total number of people taking part in the discussions was 2,343. In all, including late replies, 250 questionnaires were returned — a figure that did not compare badly with those obtained by the CPC.

[3] For a discussion of the role of Conservative Central Office see Chapter IV.

year indicated that there were about $2\frac{1}{4}$ million members. Before the 1970 election, it was widely acknowledged in the Conservative party that the age of mass membership had passed. Indeed, 1966–70 was the first time since the war when there was no concerted membership drive during a full length parliament. It is therefore somewhat surprising to find that membership (including Scotland) remained as high as $1\frac{1}{2}$ to $1\frac{1}{4}$ million in 1969–70. This estimate is based on the figures received from 99 Conservative Associations.

TABLE 7

*Conservative membership 1969–70, by type of constituency*

| | Number of constituencies | Number of constituencies in sample | Average membership |
|---|---|---|---|
| Safe Labour | 183 | 15 | 1,300 |
| Marginal Labour | 81 | 42 | 3,050 |
| Marginal Conservative | 111 | 28 | 4,800 |
| Safe Conservative and other | 143 | 14 | 4,600 |
| All constituencies (G.B.) | 618 | 99 | 2,700* |

*The actual figures we received from constituencies indicate higher totals. We have subtracted 10% to allow for their probable over-estimates and for the fact that our sample is biased towards better-organised constituencies.

Table 7 shows that Conservative membership, unlike Labour's, was largest in the constituencies where their party was politically more popular. Throughout the country, there were probably four to five times as many Conservatives as Labour members. Conservative associations in safe Conservative constituencies had about ten times as many members as CLPs in safe Labour constituencies. In the Labour-held marginals, many of which the Conservatives had to recapture if they were to win the election, their numerical advantage was only about 3 to 1.

As we do not have any detailed figures for 1966 and 1967, we cannot give a reliable estimate of the changes in Conservative membership between 1966 and 1969. Our subjective impression based on several constituencies whose membership we traced over the period is that there was a slight increase. But constituency parties were generally well pleased if they obtained sufficient recruits to replace natural wastage. There were few claims of large increases of the sort that were frequently made in the late

1940s and early 1950s. Subscriptions varied from constituency to constituency, with a usual 2*s*. 6*d*. minimum. The difference between Labour and Conservative membership perhaps owed a little to the fact that the Labour subscription was much higher (12*s*.). But too much should not be made of this as the official minimum was rarely insisted on in either party, and a much more important cause of low membership was the failure to collect at all. It is conceivable that Labour to some extent made up for its lack of numbers by having a greater proportion of activists. But the available evidence does not suggest that this was so.

*Agents*. In 1963, Selwyn Lloyd's one man enquiry into the party organisation reported that the agent's job often meant 'working long hours in a rather old-fashioned office . . . out most evenings, usually fully engaged on a Saturday'. Agents were resigning, according to the report, because of the poor financial prospects offered and suitable people were deterred from entering the profession for the same reason. In May 1965, a committee under Lord Chelmer made recommendations to improve the pay and working conditions of agents. Constituency parties were encouraged to regard them as their 'managing directors'. In September 1965 a much improved salary scale was recommended by Sir Michael Fraser. Over the next months, the party managers, area agents and constituency leaders spent considerable time in persuading the constituency associations to accept the extra financial burden. They were unexpectedly successful. From 1966 to 1969 virtually all the advertised vacancies carried salaries up to the scale recommended in 1965. In 1966 about 20% were 'above scale'. This went up to about 35% in 1967, over 40% in 1968 and over 50% in 1969. A higher salary scale was recommended in September 1969.[1] Under its terms Conservative agents would receive almost double the salaries of their Labour counterparts, even after the rises proposed a few months earlier by Transport House.

Higher pay did not, however, remove the severe problems of recruitment facing the Conservative agency service. Until 1969, more left the profession than came into training. There were the usual retirements, deaths and resignations through ill health (16 in 1966, 14 in 1967, 18 in 1968 and 7 in 1969); there were also an

[1] See pp. 97,103.

exceptional number of promotions to Central Office positions, together with a steady loss of agents who did not fit happily into their constituencies or who took better paid jobs outside the party.

TABLE 8

*Conservative city and constituency agents 1966–69*

| | No. coming with training | No. passing final agents' examination | No. leaving the profession | Total no. of full-time agents |
|---|---|---|---|---|
| 1966 | | 35 | 48 | 421 |
| 1967 | 28 | 32 | 40 | 402 |
| 1968 | 16 | 21 | 44 | 409 |
| 1969 | 43 | 20 | 28 | 399 |

A 'cadet agents' scheme was introduced in October 1965 to attract school leavers, the cost being borne by Central Office. Recruitment of cadets was discontinued for reasons of economy between November 1967 and June 1969. Several cadets had qualified by the 1970 election and others took charge of constituencies without full-time agents during the campaign.

TABLE 9

*Number of full-time Conservative city and constituency agents in Spring 1970 by area*

| | No. of full-time agents | No. of constituencies in area | Col. 1 as % of Col. 2 |
|---|---|---|---|
| Greater London . . . . | 58 | 103 | 56 |
| Northern . . . . | 16 | 34 | 47 |
| North-west . . . . | 38 | 79 | 48 |
| Yorkshire . . . . | 33 | 54 | 60 |
| East Midlands . . . . | 26 | 42 | 61 |
| West Midlands . . . . | 41 | 60 | 68 |
| East of England . . . . | 38 | 40 | 95 |
| South-eastern . . . . | 31 | 34 | 91 |
| Wessex . . . . | 34 | 37 | 92 |
| Western . . . . | 24 | 28 | 86 |
| Wales and Monmouthshire . | 18 | 36 | 50 |
| Scotland . . . . | 29 | 71 | 41 |
| Total . . . . | 386 | 618 | 62 |

In Spring 1970 there were 386 full-time agents. Their distribution by area is shown in Table 9. Virtually all associations in marginal and safe Conservative constituencies had a full-time professional; so did a minority of those in safe Labour constituencies. There was a relative shortage of agents in some cities and in Scotland.

*Finance.* In 1966–67 the total income of constituency associations in Great Britain was about £1¾ million a year. This estimate is based on accounts collected from over 400 constituencies. The differences between average incomes in different types of constituency is shown in Table 10. In four-fifths of safe Labour seats, Conservative constituency associations had incomes below £2,000 a year. In four-fifths of safe Conservative seats it was over £4,000 a year.

TABLE 10

*Average annual income of Conservative constituency associations, 1966–67 analysed by type of constituency (England and Wales)*

| | £ |
|---|---|
| Safe Labour | 1,550 |
| Marginal Labour | 3,750 |
| Marginal Conservative | 4,350 |
| Safe Conservative | 4,900 |
| All constituencies | 2,900 |

There were three major sources of income: about a fifth came from subscriptions and donations to the constituency associations (from individual subscribers and local businessmen), a half in payments from the ward branches of the associations (this was mostly raised through small-scale social events and a small proportion from membership subscriptions) and a quarter from social events organised at constituency level. The Conservatives' local income, like Labour's, thus relied little on membership subscriptions or on donations — the proportion coming from local business to the Conservatives was comparable to that from trade unions and Co-operative Societies to CLPs. The main difference was that there were more social events and less gambling in local Conservative associations. In both parties small-time activities provided the bulk of income, and the Conservatives' financial advantage appeared to be a direct function of their larger membership.

As in the Labour party, the largest expenditures of associations employing agents were the salaries of the agents and their secretaries, and the cost of running the constituency offices. These generally accounted for about three-quarters of their resources.[1] One of the major remaining items was the Central Office 'quota'. The 'quota' scheme, a system of voluntary taxation, was introduced in the late 1940s. Assessments were determined by a complex formula based on the size and proportion of the Conservative vote in a given constituency. If Central Office received a direct contribution from an individual or a company within a constituency a part was credited to this quota on the theory that a proportion would have otherwise been contributed to the local association. The quota payments published since 1967 in the Annual Conference handbooks show that these amounted to £227,119 in 1967–68, £292,333 in 1968–69 and £292,489 in 1969–70. During the fifteen months of the Carrington Appeal (part of 1967–68 and 1968–69) £920,723 was received from the constituencies by Central Office. As these figures include the notional 'credits' to local associations on direct contributions from individuals and companies, the amounts actually given by local associations were about 15% less. Even so, they show that Central Office received about £1·2 million from them between 1966–70. Most of this came from associations in safe Conservative seats.

The large constituency response to the Carrington Appeal and their willingness to pay much higher salaries to their agents, indicates that their incomes were more than keeping pace with the increased cost of living. An examination of about three dozen local annual reports for 1969–70 suggests that incomes rose 40% to 50% between 1966 and 1969. Total constituency income in 1969–70 was therefore probably about £2½ million, over three times as large as Labour's.

*Local elections.* The Conservative victories in local elections undoubtedly provided a great fillip to morale. By giving the constituency associations some continuing feeling of belonging to a governing party they possibly prevented the despair and the internal divisions on national policy that might otherwise have developed. In narrowly organisational terms, the local government

[1] For an example of a constituency party budget together with a discussion of constituency finance, see R. L. Leonard, *Elections in Britain* (van Nostrand, 1968) p. 61.

successes had mixed effects. In some strongly Labour wards, which were captured by the Conservatives for the first time within memory, the local Conservative committees gained much encouragement. But too often it was the most active members who had themselves stood as candidates and had little time for association activities. While most agents thought that local elections had aided their organisation 'by giving people practice and by giving them a feeling of success', a minority also pointed out their disadvantages. Some typical remarks were:

> 'There is always a conflict between association work and council activities. . . . A meeting at the constituency office takes second place to a meeting in the Town Hall.'
>
> 'Local government successes have made people placid.'
>
> 'The problem has been the sudden diversion of keen party workers to council work after they have won.'

*City associations.* As in the Labour party, Conservative local organisation was at its weakest in the cities, and for similar reasons. The dominance of city associations and the concentration of funds and efforts on municipal elections had hindered the development of effective constituency and ward committees. Whereas some Labour city parties relied on trade union money, Conservative city associations were supported by local businessmen. These contributions had permitted some city associations to move into expensive central headquarters, as well as to accumulate considerable reserves. They had also encouraged the constituency associations within their boundaries to get out of the habit of raising money for themselves. As costs rose and business contributions fell off in the late 1950s and early 1960s the city associations began to find themselves in financial difficulties and they lacked the members to organise fund-raising social events. By the summer of 1966, most of them were running serious deficits. They had also obtained particularly poor results in the 1964 and 1966 general elections, which had reduced the number of Conservative seats in the major cities outside London from 32 out of 98, to a mere 13.

Central Office, which had long regarded the city machines as 'legacies from the days when the Chamberlains in Birmingham and the formidable Alderman Salvidge in Liverpool were the pacemakers of political organisations', tried after the 1966 election to draw them into its control, presumably hoping to break their power and to encourage the growth of constituency activities in the cities.

A committee was set up by the party chairman at the end of 1966 under the chairmanship of Lord Brooke of Cumnor. It made its report in the summer of 1967, disclosing 'in some cases fairly entrenched inefficiency, in others a record of persistent sourness and friction'. It recommended that 'the area is to be the overall authority, with the city machine an important but integral component'. The cities were to be brought 'within the orbit of the party's Central Board of Finance'.[1] Chief Agents of City associations were to be offered positions as Deputy Central Office Agents and paid by the central party organisation. Only two cities, Bristol and Liverpool, both of them in severe financial straits, accepted these recommendations. All the rest preferred to retain their independence and most of them resisted the Central Office arguments that they should leave the collection of business subscriptions to the Central Board of Finance and concentrate on smaller scale (but organisationally more productive) methods of fund raising.

By 1970, Conservative organisation in most cities had hardly improved. Although it could be argued that a majority of the constituencies within them were safely Labour and would probably be poorly run if they were in smaller towns, it was clear that even in the remaining Conservative-held constituencies and in those that were winnable from Labour the associations had fewer members and were less active than their equivalents elsewhere. In some cities, associations in Conservative-held constituencies were asked to raise their levels of income to £1,000 — by their standards a large amount though it was about a fifth of the sum considered normal elsewhere. City memberships were about a half or a third of the national average. There was also a shortage of constituency agents. In 1970, the Chief Agent in Manchester had only a deputy and two qualified agents for his nine constituencies,[2] and in Liverpool, also with nine constituencies, the Chief Agent had only four trainees.

The decline was perhaps most dramatic in Birmingham. In *The British General Election of 1950* (pp. 25–6), H. G. Nicholas, quoting from the 1949 Birmingham Unionist Association Yearbook, described the Conservative machine at its best:

'"The senior official of the organisation is the Chief Agent. Admin-

[1] Quotations are from Ian Trethowan, 'Brooke's answer to Tory provincial decay', *The Times*, June 29, 1967.
[2] There was also a women's organiser and seven young trainees.

istrative and financial matters are dealt with by the Secretary. The very extensive Women's Organisation is under the supervision of a Women's Organiser, while the Young Unionist movement also has its own organiser. There is a Publicity Officer . . . a Political Officer . . . Organisation Officer." Each of the 13 Birmingham divisions has its own full-time certificated agent with secretarial assistance. Similarly all but one or two of the 38 wards has its organiser, generally certificated; they work under the divisional agents. At a similar level there are 30 or more full-time "missioners" or paid canvassers and subscription collectors.'

By 1970 there were just the Chief Agent, the Assistant Chief agent and five constituency agents. But even this much reduced force was four times as large as Labour's total of two agents within the city.

*Young voters.* At the October 1966 Conservative Conference Mr. du Cann launched 'Action '67' a major Young Conservatives' recruiting drive.

'Action '67 is designed to enable the YCs to broaden their support and to widen their activities. It is a three-phase programme. Phase 1 . . . recruitment of leaders will culminate in a special national YC Rally . . . which Mr. Heath will address. . . . The second of the operations will involve a new approach to YC activities, for example . . . involvement in local community. Phase 3 is a drive for political action, recruitment and development in the branches, and more political activity. . . . I challenge the YCs before the next general election to meet and beat the membership target I have set them of a quarter of a million.'[1]

Although the campaign achieved a small, temporary increase in paper membership, this disappeared within a few months. In 1968, the Young Conservatives participated, under Peter Walker's leadership, in a campaign against Barbara Castle's Transport Bill. In 1969, they were charged with making contact with the 18- to 21-year-olds who had been given the vote by the Representation of the People Act. But few YC branches were strong enough to carry out this work effectively. In most constituencies, special efforts to attract the young voters were limited (as on the Labour side) to sending 'birthday cards'.

*Political activities.* Leading party figures frequently declared their keenness to involve the rank and file members in the making of policy. Mr. du Cann claimed that the political contact pro-

[1] *Conservative Conference Report, 1966*, p. 11.

TABLE 11

*Young Conservatives membership, 1949–68*[1]

| | | | |
|---|---|---|---|
| 1949 | 157,000 | 1966 | 54,000 |
| | | 1967 (mid-year) | 54,000 |
| 1959 | 80,000 | | |
| | | 1967 (end of Action '67) | 62,000 |
| 1964 | 59,000 | 1968 | 50,000 |

gramme of the Conservative Political Centre was 'unprecedented in the work of any British political party to date'. In fact, it was very similar to previous CPC programmes and, as Table 12 suggests, it scarcely made a great impact.[2] This can be gauged from the number of reports received from constituency groups on the monthly discussion topics. The highest total of reports received was 499. This was in February 1967 when the topic was 'Education and the Citizen' and a total of 5,391 people participated.

The formal channels provided by the CPC and by the various party conferences (area conferences, Central Council meetings, YC, women's, local government and trade unionists' conferences and the annual party conferences) were not perhaps as important as the

TABLE 12

*Quarterly average number of groups and people participating in the Conservative Political Centre contact programme, 1966–70*

| | No. of groups sending reports | No. of persons partici-pating | | No. of groups sending reports | No. of persons partici-pating |
|---|---|---|---|---|---|
| 1966 | | | 1968 | | |
| | | | 1st | 405 | 4,060 |
| 2nd | 193 | 2,003 | 2nd | 313 | 3,152 |
| 3rd | 297 | 2,927 | 3rd | 371 | 4,013 |
| 4th | 319 | 3,244 | 4th | 351 | 3,572 |
| 1967 | | | 1969 | | |
| 1st | 427 | 4,517 | 1st | 409 | 4,237 |
| 2nd | 381 | 4,091 | 2nd | 437 | 4,321 |
| 3rd | 317 | 5,370 | 3rd | 314 | 2,936 |
| 4th | 398 | 4,022 | 4th | 393 | 3,942 |
| | | | 1970 | | |
| | | | 1st | 412 | 4,345 |

[1] These estimates, which are based on a Central Office report, are lower than those of P. Abrams and A. Little in 'The Young Activist in British politics', *British Journal of Sociology*, December 1965, who give a figure of 120,000.

[2] See pp. 99–100, 102.

informal ones: letters to party leaders, calls to Central Office or merely grumbles in the constituencies reported via M.P.s' local committee members or agents. It was only during 1968, over the immigration issue, that strong constituency views were expressed. In general, constituency associations continued to concentrate on organisational and social rather than on political activities.

*The 'critical seats' exercise.* Given the uniformity of the swing between one constituency and another, it follows that elections in Britain are won and lost in a few dozen marginals. It was therefore decided at Central Office, soon after the 1966 election, to concentrate even more intensively than before on the seats which it would need to recapture if it was to regain power with a workable majority. These 'critical seats' were basically Labour- or Liberal-held marginals which would be gained with a swing of 5% or less.[1] With the advice of area agents a few seats, where a bigger swing was needed, were included (they were all in Yorkshire — Bradford North, Huddersfield West and Halifax — or in Scotland — Dundee East, Glasgow Kelvingrove and Dundee West); some others which would be recaptured with a lower swing, were excluded (Monmouth, Belper, Falmouth and Camborne, Lichfield and Tamworth, Bury and Radcliffe, Stockport North, Middlesbrough West, Plymouth Sutton, Darlington, South-east Derbyshire, Chorley, Norwich South, Perry Barr and Smethwick). Conservative-held seats were rigorously excluded on the grounds that it was necessary to limit attention and resources to those which had still to be won. When seats were won at by-elections they were removed from the 'critical' list (except for Wellingborough won in December 1970). Before the election it thus included 68 constituencies. The seats which had been won at by-elections were added to the list for the campaign period, but by this time the main exercise had been completed.

'Critical' seats were given help of several kinds. Additional allowances ('marginal weighting')[2] were usually given to agents

[1] Transport House also made efforts to direct its limited resources to marginal seats. The appointments under the national agency scheme were generally to marginal seats and they most frequently received visits from the National Agent and his staff. But there was no attempt to introduce a rigorous definition of marginality. Seats with a Labour majority of 5,000 or a Conservative majority of 3,000 were usually regarded as marginal. This meant that in London alone 23 Labour-held and 8 Conservative-held constituencies were so designated, but they do not appear to have been given much extra assistance.

[2] 'Marginal weighting' allowances, normally about £200 a year, were also given to agents in marginal seats not included in the critical list.

who accepted posts in critical seats. By the 1970 campaign all but three of the English criticals had certificated election agents and all but three of those in Scotland. Nevertheless there were numbers of agency problems. Brighton, Kemptown, was an example of a constituency association which had difficulty in retaining its agents, the last one coming three months before the poll. In Orpington, a controversy involving the candidate, the association's officer and the agent resulted in a gap of several months with no agent. In Halifax the agent left shortly before the election to take up a post outside the party. In other cases, agents withdrew through illness or moved to other posts within the party, and there were some instances where they remained in their posts although they were considered inefficient as the association officers did not want to cause friction by attempting to remove them. Altogether, there were twenty to thirty critical seats in which there was to a greater or lesser extent some difficulty connected with the agent, or which were for a considerable time without an agent.

Front bench speakers were systematically given speaking engagements in the criticals, both before and during the election. The party chairman paid them regular visits and had lengthy consultations with their agents, candidates and associations chairmen. There was a special briefing for agents from the chosen seats in November 1968. In 1969 those within easy reach came individually to Central Office with their candidates and local chairman to discuss the private opinion polls (of about 250 respondents each) which were to be carried out in each constituency over the summer. Those further off received a visitation from Central Office. The polls included questions about the importance of different issues, the names of the M.P. and the Conservative candidate, readership of local newspapers, past voting and voting intention.

In September 1969, the pre-election campaign started in all the English and Welsh criticals. Poster sites were hired by Central Office for an indefinite period until the general election. One of the posters showed a husband, wife and two children, with the caption 'this family pays too much tax'; another showed a car licence '1964 . . . £15, 1969 . . . £25 — Britain was better off with the Conservatives'; a third showed a man with a pound being burnt away in his hand. The number of poster sites varied from constituency to constituency, one of the main factors being simply the availability of sites. Political parties were not permitted to advertise on railway sites. In some areas there was a shortage of suitably prominent places and it was necessary in some cases to wait several months after September 1969 until they became available. The monthly cost of hiring sites varied considerably: the 6 sites in Buckingham, to give an extreme case, cost only £23, while the 18 Hornchurch sites cost £148. In most cases site rentals amounted to £60–£90 a month. The overall cost was about £5,000 a month. Weekly advertisements in the form of leading articles were inserted in local newspapers, the choice of which had been largely determined by the private surveys.[1] In addition, with some initial technical difficulties, an 'opinion formers' exercise was launched. It was copied from some of the direct mailing techniques that Central Office officials had been shown during visits to political campaign organisations in the United States. On the theory that voters were influenced by informal conversations, especially with persons who commanded their respect, parties in America had regularly drawn up lists of the names and addresses of these 'opinion formers' and then sent them party literature and special letters. If simple details about each of them were computerised, it became possible to write to, say, all the doctors or all the barbers on the list. Agents in critical seats were asked to submit the names of about 250 suitable people to Central Office, together with the necessary occupational outlines.[2] Many found difficulties in making the choice and either asked members of their committees to help them (which tended to mean that those who were already in contact with the Conservative party tended to be included on the lists) or submitted a smaller number of names. At the Central Office end, there were delays in processing the information and only about a half-dozen sets of letters or items of party literature had been sent by the time of the election.

Agents and constituency chairmen undoubtedly enjoyed the status they gained by involvement in the critical seats exercise and also, perhaps, its aura of secrecy. Nevertheless, those whom we interviewed generally thought little of its technical aspects. Most of them disliked the 'opinion formers' exercise and almost none

[1] See pp. 192, 197.

[2] They were advised to concentrate on editors, journalists, doctors, dentists, hospital staff, head and senior teachers, bank managers, ladies hairdressers, barbers, clergy, selected shopkeepers, shop stewards, selected milk roundsmen and postmen and selected members of professional associations, club and trade associations.

admitted that the private poll in their constituency had told them anything they did not already know. This was, perhaps, just a reflection of professional pride and it is probable that they and their candidates were influenced in their emphasis on specific issues in election addresses and speeches more than they realised. Indeed, one of the main aims of the critical seats exercise was to avoid helping constituencies in conventional ways — by financial grants and the provision of paid canvassers: it was thought that this would result in sluggishness on the part of local organisations. It was for this reason that help was given in forms that were outside the run of normal association activities.[1]

### *Summary*

By every measure the Conservative organisation at the outset of the 1970 campaign was superior to Labour's. In itself, this was no different from previous elections. But in 1970 the gap was even wider. Whereas the Conservatives had perhaps three times Labour's membership in 1966, the ratio had increased to four or five to one. In 1966 Conservatives had double the number of agents, and now they had well over two and a half times as many. Their advantage in the marginal seats was also greater. In 1966 the total income of Conservative associations was 2–2½ times that of CLPs, while in 1970 it was 3½ times as much. The difference between local contributions to Central Office funds and to those of Transport House had also grown greatly. There were about 8 times as many Young Conservatives as Young Socialists.

Yet the increased Conservative advantage was not the result of marked improvements on their own side. The sole advance about which Central Office could feel unequivocally pleased was the increased fund-raising capacity of Conservative constituency associations. The major explanation for any change in the balance of local party strength lay primarily in the decline on the Labour side.

[1] It was emphasised by both the London and Edinburgh Central Offices that the Scottish critical seats exercise was an 'autonomous operation'. Scottish criticals received much less help than those in England and Wales. They generally received poster sites (except in the far flung Highland seats where these did not exist). But they received little other assistance in the form of 'mutual aid' or of finance. One critical seat reported that it paid for all its own newspaper advertising, another that Central Office paid half, and a third that although Central Office was intending to finance local newspaper advertisements only one had appeared by May 1970. The opinion formers exercise was not systematically carried out.

CHAPTER XII

# THE EMERGENCE OF CANDIDATES

DURING the 1966–70 parliament, the established procedures of candidate selection once again worked straightforwardly in the majority of cases. The usual pattern in both major parties was for a short list of two to five names to emerge from lengthy winnowing by a small sub-committee of the local constituency party. A body generally between 20 and 60 (the Executive Council of the Conservative constituency association or the General Management Committee of the constituency Labour party) then balloted after each aspirant had made a brief speech and answered questions. Their choice was then ratified at a general meeting. On only one occasion was the decision of the Executive Council (General Management Committee) reversed at this late stage. This occurred at Nelson and Colne where the former Conservative candidate, David Waddington, put his name forward at the last moment to fight the by-election and was preferred at a general meeting to David Penfold, whose name had been forwarded by the Executive Council. The Conservatives at times varied the procedure at the short-list stage, usually against Central Office advice; in the extreme case there was a well-publicised if misnamed 'primary' at Reigate, where 500 members of the Conservative Association assembled to hear the two finalists *and* their wives each make a political speech before television cameras.[1] Normally, the Conservatives took cognisance only of the social graces of applicants' wives, while local Labour parties ignored wives altogether.

Constituencies chose much the same sort of person as over the last decade, sometimes a local favourite, sometimes one of a circuit of ex-M.P.s and other meritorious candidates discreetly encouraged by officials of the central party, and sometimes a complete outsider. As always, there was constant politicking and discussion behind the scenes, but few controversies or scandals broke into the press.

There were, however, two distinctive features of selections during this period. First of all, most of the selections for winnable

[1] The television cameras were also allowed to cover the vigorous selection contest for a Conservative candidate to run against Mr. George Brown in Belper.

seats took place on the Conservative side. The 61 Labour gains in 1964 and the 49 in 1966 brought in two large groups of young M.P.s. As the Conservative ranks in parliament were unlikely to be further decimated, Labour hopefuls were restricted to the search for places vacated by retiring members. Their Conservative counterparts had the additional prospect of contesting the marginal constituencies which had recently been lost.[1] Secondly, the political interest of candidate selection also shifted to the Conservatives. In both parties, the choice of local standard-bearer has almost always been decided on astonishingly non-ideological grounds.[2] In the great majority of cases, an aspirant's personality matters more than his position within the political spectrum. Where intra-party factionalism has influenced selections, however, it has more often been within the Labour party. Between 1966 and 1970, however, ideological rumblings tended to come from the Conservative ranks. In the late 1960s there were repeated allegations that Powellites or the Monday Club were attempting to plant amenable candidates and to blacklist others. 55 candidates were members of the Monday Club — and 30 were in the end elected, 10 of them for the first time. But few of them seemed to have owed their selection to concerted action. Paul Williams, the Chairman of the Monday Club from 1964 to 1969, had several rebuffs before he abandoned the search for a seat, while Mr. Harold Soref, chairman of the Club's Africa Group, apparently owed his selection at Ormskirk to his impressive knowledge of local agriculture. Two other selections frequently cited, Sir Brandon Rhys Williams at South Kensington and Mr. Robert Boscawen at Wells, could also be explained without attributing overmuch influence to the Monday Club activists. Nevertheless, the informal list of about 50 candidates maintained at the Monday Club headquarters and the collaboration with local groups of the Club presented a potential danger, which was never realised but which the Conservative leadership could not afford to ignore. On the opposite wing, a

[1] In the five general elections and all the by-elections held on the 1955 boundaries only 160 seats ever changed hands; the remaining 470 invariably stayed with the same party. Since many of those 160 seats were now safely in one camp or the other, it is clear that in much more than three constituencies out of four, it was a party selection conference and not the electorate that irrevocably decided who was to be the M.P.

[2] For two views on Conservative candidate selection see Anthony King, 'The Changing Tories', *New Society*, May 2, 1968, and Andrew Alexander, 'Where are the bright young Tories?', *Sunday Telegraph*, January 26, 1969. More generally, see Michael Rush, *The Selection of Parliamentary Candidates* (Nelson, 1969).

scarcely less keen intelligence network probably operated within the Bow Group. In a few cases, candidates identified with the 'left' of the party encountered organised and awkward questioning at their selection conferences.[1] The heckling of Sir Anthony Meyer at Esher may not only have prevented his selection but may also have given him a tag which handicapped him in other suburban seats, though it was no barrier to his eventual choice in West Flint. During the election, there was an effort to prove that the likely additions to the Conservative benches were to the right of the party — Lord Byers reported on June 16 that a spot check in 82 seats suggested that 24 Tory candidates were in some sense Powellite and the *Sunday Times* after a telephone survey of the 90 successful Conservative M.P.s who did not sit in the 1966 parliament found that 33 expressed sympathy with Enoch Powell's views on immigration.

But, by and large, the rows over candidate selection were not ideologically motivated. The most common source of public complaint was that the selection committee had not chosen a local man.[2] The most vehement and protracted dispute was perhaps in Caithness and Sutherland where the choice fell on John Young who in 1964 had stood against the official candidate. The scars left by that episode — and by the geographic split between the east and west of the constituency — led to several challenges to Mr. Young's selection before it was finally endorsed by a vote of 313 to 64. On the Labour side there was a scandal — and an NEC enquiry — after the *Sunday Times* had alleged fraud in the choice of nominee for the 1969 by-election in North Islington; it emerged that one of the union delegates to the selection conference had been impersonated by another member of the local Labour party.[3]

[1] As an influential Monday Club figure put it, 'Where there is a left-wing Tory M.P. it stirs our people to try to counter his left-wing influence', and he went on to name places where action had been initiated.

[2] For example, in Bedford, Brighouse and Spenborough, Handsworth and Warwick and Leamington, plans to run a local man against the outsider chosen by the Conservative Association were reported. All came to nothing.

[3] The unexpected announcement of the election inevitably caught one or two constituency parties at an awkward moment trying to replace a candidate. In other instances M.P.s and candidates made last minute decisions not to stand and the whole selection process had to be rushed through in a mere ten days or so. In one case, Jonathan Aitken who had been chosen two years earlier, in a rather disputatious selection, to succeed Mr. Turton, the Father of the House, in the safe seat of Thirsk and Malton, withdrew because he was before the courts over the publication of a military document; Mr. Turton stepped into the breach. Another veteran member, Sir Barnett Janner, the Labour M.P. for North-west Leicester withdrew on May 22 on the grounds of ill-health (in fact he accepted a peerage in the Dissolution Honours on May 30); after due pro-

As always, sitting M.P.s were virtually certain of re-endorsement by their parties. Where they decided not to stand again, it was not always possible to say with certainty how far their retirement was voluntary. The reasons of health or business that were cited may occasionally have concealed some row or pressure. But it is clear that this would apply to only a handful of the 78 M.P.s (40 Labour, 27 Conservative and 2 Liberal) who stood down in 1970. Only 16 of the 78 were under 60 and only 8 under 50. Enquiry into these 16 cases suggests that in only five or six was there any question of local pressure: in three instances the problem seems to have been personal, involving drink or divorce and the matter was dealt with entirely without publicity. There were two special situations in Northern Ireland (see p. 330) and in two London seats the trouble became very public.

In Clapham, Mrs. Margaret McKay had a prolonged battle with members of her constituency Labour party over her pro-Arab activities. Finally in May 1970 the National Executive gave the Clapham party permission to consider whether to re-select her but before any meeting was held, Mrs. McKay abandoned the struggle.

Mr. Reader Harris, the Conservative member for Heston and Isleworth since 1950 may have had his political career terminated by his long involvement with the courts following the collapse of the Rolls Razor Company. On the very eve of the election he was at last acquitted of all charges. But a successor had by this time been recommended and was ratified at a general meeting of the Constituency Association on May 29. The vote of 242 to 176 was against the opposition of the retiring member who supported a second candidate.

Among the other younger members who did not stand again, one, Trevor Park, the 43-year-old Labour M.P. for the marginal South-east Derbyshire constituency, announced in September 1968, that he was returning to educational work (although in May 1970 he did seek — unsuccessfully — the supposedly safer nomination in his home town of Rossendale).

In 1968, John Smith, the wealthy Conservative member for the Cities of London and Westminster, announced his withdrawal from politics in protest against the inadequate working conditions and facilities available to M.P.s.

---

cedures had been followed, his son, Mr. Greville Janner, was selected in a close vote. Some indignation was expressed over Sir Barnett's timing and there were local Labour supporters who in protest did their campaign work in neighbouring seats.

Among older members, retirement seems in at least one Conservative case to have been accelerated by constituency hints. On the Labour side there were instances of discreet encouragement to move on being given by the Whips. It had been feared that higher salaries might make it harder for members to sense when the right moment to make way for a younger man had arrived. But in fact there were fewer septuagenarian candidates than ever before — only seven, two Conservatives and five Labour, compared to 19 in 1966 and 23 in 1964 — and 30 in 1955. The oldest of them, the 83-year-old S. O. Davies of Merthyr, was standing as an Independent after being repudiated by his local party explicitly on the grounds of age.

Some M.P.s who did stand again had, of course, heard mutterings against them in their constituencies. On the Labour side, the NEC did not authorise any re-selection meetings except in the cases of Mrs. McKay and Mr. S. O. Davies. But Mr. Paget had brushed with his local party in Northampton when he resigned the whip for a brief time at the end of 1966.

On the Conservative side, there were 'right-wing' challenges to a few M.P.s.[1] The most publicised was a sustained attempt to oust Nigel Fisher from Surbiton because of his liberal views on racial matters. But Mr. Fisher retained the support of the bulk of the active members of his Association; in the end an Independent did stand against him but got only 5% of the vote. On a smaller scale Terence Higgins in Worthing suffered somewhat similar attacks; so did Sir Edward Boyle in Handsworth. While none of these challenges came close to success, they imposed a heavy burden of uncertainty on the members concerned and there is evidence that these attacks made others wary of identifying themselves with liberal causes unpopular with constituency activists.

Mr. James Dance, a 63-year-old farmer, businessman and Etonian, was threatened at Bromsgrove ostensibly because he was not the right sort of person to represent an industrial constituency, though the trouble seems to have been a more personal one between him and a constituency officer: in the end he was given a vote of confidence by 68 to 37; shortly thereafter he announced that he would only serve for one more normal length parliament.

While M.P.s were almost sure of re-nomination, defeated

[1] There were also a few Ulster Unionists who had their special trouble (see p. 330).

members, let alone defeated non-members, could not be certain that their constituencies would not look elsewhere. The newspapers did record some cases where the decision to seek a new candidate was a blow to the former member.[1] One voluntary change of seat was by a sitting M.P., Mr. Atkins, who, assuming that redistribution would give his marginal seat of Merton and Morden to Labour, offered himself for the more secure berth of nearby Spelthorne.

In fact, out of the 48 Conservative M.P.s defeated in 1966, 6 got back in subsequent by-elections and a further 15 in 1970. Six of these 21 were returned for their old seat but 15 found safer constituencies. A further six M.P.s who had been defeated in 1964 managed to get back. Only seven Conservative ex-M.P.s who secured nominations failed in their efforts to return, six of them in seats in which they had persisted manfully ever since 1964.[2] In the circle of a dozen or so Conservatives whose names tended to be mentioned every time a safe seat was looking for a candidate, ex-M.P.s loomed large. Some of the most seemingly attractive — for example, Geoffrey Howe, Peter Thomas and Sir Anthony Meyer — were turned down by half-a-dozen constituencies before they finally found a safe seat. The frequent short-listing and the frequent failure of these favoured candidates illustrates both the initial influence and the ultimate lack of power of the party hierarchy when it comes to candidate selection. Some promising Central Office and Research Department aspirants had a long and sometimes unsuccessful search for a decent seat. But it would be hard to sustain the complaint that political experience was at a discount with Conservative selection conferences.[3]

One of the first Conservative actions after their 1966 disaster had been to clear the candidates panel. All the aspirants on the Central Office list were told that they would have to reapply.[4] A year later there were 400 on the list instead of the previous 600. Those who were eliminated were mainly the elderly and it is indeed arguable that no one who had any serious chance of selection was in fact affected by the purge. Certainly nothing in the selections made

[1] e.g. A. Courtney (Harrow East), G. Lagden (Hornchurch) W. Yates (Wrekin) and A. R. Wise (Rugby).

[2] Only three non-Conservative ex-M.P.s stood. P. Duffy (Labour) was successful. G. Mackie (Liberal) and R. McIntyre (SNP) were not.

[3] Of the 27 Conservatives chosen as replacements for sitting members 11 were ex-M.P.s, 11 had fought unsuccessfully before and 5 were novices. Of the 74 Conservatives who gained seats 7 were ex-M.P.s, 39 had fought unsuccessfully before and 27 were novices.

[4] See pp. 99, 102, 103.

over the next three years suggests a major change in policy either at the centre or in the constituencies. The balance of candidatures in terms of age, education and occupation was much the same, although two out of three groups that had long-standing cause for complaint made some advance. The 15 women and the 9 Jews[1] elected to the Conservative benches represented record totals but there were no additions to the two M.P.s from the trade union wing of the party — Mr. Mawby (elected 1955) and Sir Edward Brown (1964).

On the Labour side, there were some changes in trade union representation. For the first time in the history of the party the miners who at their peak in 1945 had sponsored and elected 39 candidates, did not head the list of sponsoring unions, although among M.P.s miners still provided the most numerous group. Only one of the five miners who retired from parliament was replaced by a miner.

The left-wing leadership of the TGWU and the AEF does not seem to have had any marked effect on their choice of candidates, although the withdrawal of TGWU sponsorship from Mr. George Brown did excite some comment. The fall of twenty in the number of union-sponsored M.P.s was of course mainly due to the loss of seats in the election. If all the seats held at the dissolution had been retained, union sponsored M.P.s would have numbered 126, only 6 less than 1966. But that would understate the continuing decline in the number of working men on the Labour benches, as our exhaustive examination of the background of candidates shows.[2]

Statistics about candidates should always be treated with reserve. The biographical handouts on which they are based are sometimes inaccurate or disingenuous. Moreover it is often impossible to

[1] Data about the religious affiliation of M.P.s is hard to come by. For example about 40 Labour M.P.s admit to being humanist, agnostic or atheist — but *no* Conservatives *seem willing* to advertise their unbelief. Among other denominations the figures for Jews (9 Conservatives, 31 Labour) are probably fairly reliable. So are those for Catholics, of whom there were 37 members elected in 1970 (13 Conservative and 22 Labour as well as Mr. McManus and Miss Devlin from Ulster), the highest figure since the partition of Ireland. Mr. Selwyn Lloyd appears to be the only Conservative Methodist and the remaining active nonconformist members (Methodists and Baptists) form a nebulous group of ecumenical Christian Socialists, about 30 in number. It is clear that the overwhelming bulk of Conservatives and the majority of Labour members are either nominal or practising Anglicans but, except for a few active laymen, it is hard to identify explicitly those who belong to this dominant category. (We are indebted to Mr. John Seagrave for most of this information.)

[2] For the earlier history of sponsored candidates see Martin Harrison, *Trade Unions and the Labour Party* (Longmans, 1960).

*Sponsored candidates*

| 1970 Affiliation to Labour party '000s | | 1966 | | 1970 | |
|---|---|---|---|---|---|
| | | Total | Elected | Total | Elected |
| 1,000 | Transport and General Workers Union | 27 | 27 | 23 | 19 |
| 855 | Amalgamated Union of Engineers and Foundrymen | 17 | 17 | 21 | 16 |
| 305 | National Union of Mineworkers | 28 | 27 | 21 | 20 |
| 650 | National Union of General and Municipal Workers | 10 | 10 | 12 | 12 |
| 281 | Union of Shop Distributive and Allied Workers | 8 | 8 | 7 | 7 |
| 175 | National Union of Railwaymen | 8 | 7 | 6 | 5 |
| 150 | National Union of Public Employees | 5 | 5 | 6 | 6 |
| 58 | Transport Salaried Staffs Association | 5 | 5 | 4 | 4 |
| 65 | Association of Scientific, Technical and Managerial Staffs | 2 | 2 | 4 | 3 |
| 33 | Draughtsmen's and Allied Technicians Association | 2 | 2 | 4 | 4 |
| 69 | Clerical and Administrative Workers Union | 4 | 4 | 3 | 3 |
| 56 | Post Office Engineering Union | 1 | — | 3 | 1 |
| 183 | Union of Post Office Workers | 4 | 4 | 3 | 1 |
| 350 | Electrical, Electronic & Plumbing Trades Union | 2 | 1 | 3 | 3 |
| 87 | British Iron & Steel and Kindred Trades Association | 1 | 1 | 2 | 2 |
| 85 | National Union of Agricultural Workers | 1 | 1 | 2 | — |
| 15 | Musicians Union | 1 | 1 | 2 | 1 |
| | 11 Other Unions (none more than 1 candidate in 1970) | 12 | 10 | 11 | 7 |
| | | 138 | 132 | 137 | 112 |
| | Co-operative party | 24 | 18 | 27 | 17 |
| | All sponsored candidates | 162 | 150 | 164 | 129 |

determine which of several trades constitutes a man's 'first or formative' occupation. The categories into which they have to be sorted are necessarily arbitrary. The word 'farmer' may cover both a titled landowner and a struggling smallholder. In borderline cases the distinction between 'secondary' and 'public' on which some schools are placed has little significance. We have tried to apply the same criteria as in previous Nuffield studies — but we have learnt to be suspicious of building too heavy a superstructure of conclusions upon such necessarily shaky foundations.

But on age, at least, there is little ambiguity and the age balance of the new House was very much as in the old. Miss Devlin, elected in 1969 just before her 22nd birthday, was still easily the youngest M.P. Next came Mr. Reed the 25-year-old Labour member for Sedgefield. It seems to have been the first parliament ever in which no Conservative under 30 was returned.

Only five members of the 1970 parliament had served continuously since before the war and only seven others had experience of

*Age of candidates*

| Age on Jan. 1, 1971 | Conservative | | Labour | | Liberal | |
|---|---|---|---|---|---|---|
| | Elected | Defeated | Elected | Defeated | Elected | Defeated |
| 21–29 . . . | 0 | 39 | 5 | 69 | 0 | 67 |
| 30–39 . . . | 56 | 125 | 47 | 116 | 3 | 111 |
| 40–49 . . . | 119 | 91 | 89 | 113 | 2 | 106 |
| 50–59 . . . | 111 | 34 | 79 | 30 | 1 | 37 |
| 60–69 . . . | 42 | 8 | 61 | 9 | 0 | 5 |
| 70–79 . . . | 2 | 0 | 5 | 0 | 0 | 0 |
| | 360 | 297 | 287 | 337 | 6 | 326 |
| Median age . . | 49 | 38 | 50 | 38 | 39 | 38 |
| Median age of candidates in 1966 . | (48) | (38) | (50) | (34) | (39) | (37) |

*M.P.s parliamentary experience*

| | Con. | Lab. | Other | Total |
|---|---|---|---|---|
| First elected before 1945 election . . | 11 | 4 | 1 | 16 |
| First elected 1945–59 . . . . | 155 | 112 | 3 | 270 |
| First elected 1960–March 1970 . . | 81 | 107 | 6 | 194 |
| First elected 1970 general election . | 83 | 64 | 3 | 150 |
| | 330 | 287 | 13 | 630 |

the pre-war parliament, although four more entered the Commons at war-time by-elections; three pre-war M.P.s were defeated.[1] The number of new members, 150, was the largest since 1945.

For the first time since 1955 the number of women candidates increased — to 98 — but both the Conservative and Labour parties still fielded fewer women than at any election in the 1950s. The 26 elected equalled the 1966 figure. The Conservatives with 15

[1] *Conservative veterans*

R. Turton 67, (1929–)
Sir C. Taylor 60, (1935–)
Sir A. Douglas-Home 68, (1931–45, 1950–1, 1963–)
G. Lloyd 63, (1931–45, 1950–)
Dame I. Ward 75, (1931–45, 1950–)
Sir R. Cary 67, (1935–45, 1951–)
Sir R. Grant-Ferris 63, (1937–45, 1955–)
Q. Hogg 62, (1938–50, 1963–70)
S. Digby 60, (1941–)
Sir F. Maclean 59, (1941–)
R. Bell 56, (1945, 1950–)

*Labour veterans*

G. R. Strauss 69, (1929–31, 1934–)
L. Mallalieu 65, (1931–35 *as Lib.* 1948–)
S. O. Davies 83, (1934– *now Ind.*)
J. Parker 62, (1935–)
T. Driberg 65, (1942–45 *as Ind.* 1945–55, 1959–)

*Defeated Labour veterans*

Miss J. Lee 66, (1929–31, 1945–70)
Sir D. Foot 65, (1931–45 *as Lib.* 1957–70)
Malcolm Macmillan 57, (1935–70)

Together with those in this list three Labour members elected in 1945 complete the roll of septuagenarians: Mr. Rankin 80, Mr. Scholefield Allen 72, and Mr. Weitzman 72.

| | Conservative | | Labour | | Liberal | |
|---|---|---|---|---|---|---|
| | Elected | Defeated | Elected | Defeated | Elected | Defeated |
| Elementary only | 1 | 2 | 55 | 14 | — | 3 |
| Elementary + | 1 | 0 | 4 | 1 | — | 1 |
| Secondary only | 33 | 58 | 45 | 59 | — | 66 |
| Secondary + | 5 | 30 | 29 | 53 | — | 46 |
| Secondary and University | 43 | 65 | 94 | 133 | 3 | 95 |
| Public School only | 80 | 56 | 7 | 13 | — | 27 |
| Public School and University | 167 | 87 | 53 | 64 | 3 | 88 |
| Total | 330 | 298 | 287 | 337 | 6 | 326 |
| Oxford | 99 | 32 | 49 | 35 | 2 | 42 |
| Cambridge | 71 | 38 | 23 | 24 | 1 | 36 |
| Other Universities | 38 | 79 | 82 | 139 | 3 | 110 |
| All Universities | 208 | 149 | 154 | 198 | 6 | 188 |
| Eton | 59 | 10 | 2 | 0 | 2 | 2 |
| Harrow | 14 | 4 | — | 2 | — | 3 |
| Winchester | 9 | 1 | 2 | 1 | — | 2 |
| Other | 161 | 120 | 46 | 57 | 1 | 108 |
| All | 243 | 135 | 50 | 60 | 3 | 115 |

had more women members than ever before but Labour with 10 had its smallest female contingent since the war.

The educational pattern among candidates conforms closely to 1966. Among Conservative candidates the total number of Etonians fell by 15, although 4 more were successful. Appreciably fewer of the defeated Conservatives were either public school or university educated, although among the elected M.P.s the proportions were much the same as before. On the Labour side the long-term increase in the proportion of public school and Oxbridge candidates was checked if not reversed. Compared to 1966 the number with public school backgrounds (110 as against 111) and Oxbridge education (131 as against 140) was slightly down. However, the number of graduates (352 as against 330) was higher.[1]

[1] Data about minor party candidates is particularly hard to obtain but the broad picture is clear.

| | SNP | PC | Comm. |
|---|---|---|---|
| Professional | 36 | 23 | 9 |
| Business | 23 | 7 | — |
| Miscellaneous | 3 | 4 | 9 |
| Worker | 3 | 2 | 40 |
| Total | 65 | 36 | 58 |
| Elementary | — | 1 | 20 |
| Secondary | 55 | 30 | 38 |
| Public | 10 | 5 | — |
| University | 33 | 29 | 6 |
| Median age | 39 | 36 | 39 |

The trend towards white collar Labour candidates continued (even among those sponsored by the unions). Only 108 workers stood compared to 132 in 1966; professional people, 320, provided more than half the Labour slate of candidates. Of the 54 new

*Occupation of candidates 1970*

| | Conservative | | Labour | | Liberal | |
|---|---|---|---|---|---|---|
| | Elected | Defeated | Elected | Defeated | Elected | Defeated |
| Professions | | | | | | |
| Barrister | 60 | 21 | 34 | 18 | 3 | 10 |
| Solicitor | 14 | 29 | 13 | 14 | 1 | 19 |
| Doctor/Dentist | 6 | 9 | 7 | 3 | — | 7 |
| Architect/Surveyor | 3 | 5 | 2 | 1 | — | 6 |
| Civil Engineer | 1 | 2 | 2 | 3 | — | 7 |
| Chartered Secretary/ Accountant | 6 | 19 | 6 | 3 | — | 9 |
| Civil Servant/Local Government | 12 | 1 | 3 | 4 | — | 8 |
| Armed Services | 24 | 3 | — | 1 | — | 5 |
| Teaching | | | | | | |
| University | 1 | 6 | 13 | 26 | — | 11 |
| Adult | 2 | 10 | 10 | 44 | — | 23 |
| School | 6 | 23 | 33 | 45 | 1 | 35 |
| Other Consultants | 14 | 11 | 9 | 12 | — | 15 |
| Scientific Research | — | 5 | 5 | 8 | — | — |
| Total | 149 | 144 | 137 | 183 | 5 | 155 |
| Business | | | | | | |
| Company Director | 80 | 64 | 4 | 14 | — | 24 |
| Company Executive | 14 | 28 | 10 | 17 | — | 39 |
| Commerce/Insurance | 3 | 10 | 5 | 7 | — | 29 |
| Management/Clerical | 1 | 6 | 7 | 8 | — | 4 |
| Small Business | 3 | 4 | 2 | 2 | — | 7 |
| Total | 101 | 112 | 28 | 48 | — | 103 |
| Misc. White Collar | 1 | — | 3 | 7 | — | 11 |
| Private Means | 4 | 1 | — | — | — | — |
| Politicians/Pol. Org. | 10 | 7 | 11 | 16 | — | — |
| Publisher/Journalist | 30 | 10 | 27 | 20 | 1 | 24 |
| Farmer | 31 | 13 | 1 | 2 | — | 9 |
| Housewife | 1 | — | 1 | 6 | — | 10 |
| Student | — | 1 | — | 4 | — | 5 |
| Local admin. | 1 | 6 | 3 | 19 | — | 2 |
| Total | 78 | 38 | 46 | 74 | 1 | 11 |
| Clerk | — | — | 4 | — | — | 1 |
| Miner | — | — | 22 | 1 | — | — |
| Skilled Worker | 2 | 3 | 33 | 24 | — | 5 |
| Semi/Unskilled | — | 1 | 17 | 7 | — | 1 |
| Total | 2 | 4 | 76 | 32 | — | 7 |
| Grand Total | 330 | 298 | 287 | 337 | 6 | 337 |

Labour M.P.s in the 1970 parliament, 32 were professional people, 11 had a business background and one was a housewife; among the 10 who could be classified as workers two were railway clerks who had graduated to administrative jobs and two were draughtsmen. Only two miners, one building worker and a seaman came from indisputably manual occupations.

If the background of the members of the 1970 parliament compared with those returned in 1951 — the last narrow Conservative majority — the contrasts are probably less than most people would imagine. While the proportion of the Parliamentary Labour Party who were graduates has increased from 41% to 53% and the

*Background of M.P.s 1951 and 1970*

| | Conservative | | Labour | |
|---|---|---|---|---|
| | 1951 | 1970 | 1951 | 1970 |
| | % | % | % | % |
| Professional | 41 | 45 | 35 | 40 |
| Business | 37 | 30 | 9 | 10 |
| Miscellaneous White Collar | 22 | 24 | 19 | 16 |
| Workers | — | 1 | 37 | 26 |
| | 100 | 100 | 100 | 100 |
| Elementary | 1 | 1 | 26 | 21 |
| Secondary | 24 | 25 | 54 | 62 |
| Public School | 75 | 74 | 20 | 17 |
| (Eton) | (24) | (18) | (1) | (1) |
| Oxford and Cambridge | 52 | 52 | 19 | 24 |
| Other universities | 10 | 12 | 22 | 29 |

proportion of Etonians on the Conservative benches dropped from 24% to 18%, working men were almost as invisible on the Conservative benches as twenty years ago. On the Labour side they have declined from 37% to 26% of the total, their place being taken by professional people.

The changing impact of class upon the British political scene is also evident in the pattern of candidatures for safe marginal and hopeless seats in the two parties.

On the Conservative side, the public school men, and above all the Etonians, were concentrated in Conservative safe seats; the few Conservatives with working-class occupations almost all stood in hopeless seats. On the Labour side (which for the first time fielded more graduates than the Conservatives) candidates were more evenly distributed in safe or hopeless seats in terms of age and occupation except for the remaining concentration of working men (largely union-sponsored) in safe Labour seats.

There are dangers in being too quantitative in the analysis of members of parliament; there is a temptation to be too much influenced by characteristics which readily lend themselves to

*Background of 1970 Conservative candidates in different types of seat*

| | All Conservative candidates % | In seats held by Conservatives in 1966 with majorities | | In seats held by Labour in 1966 with majorities | |
|---|---|---|---|---|---|
| | | (Safe) Over 10% % | (Marginal) Under 10% % | (Marginal) Under 10% % | (Safe) Over 10% % |
| Eton | 12 | 22 | 23 | 7 | 4 |
| All public school | 62 | 84 | 73 | 58 | 48 |
| University | 57 | 68 | 66 | 51 | 51 |
| Professional | 45 | 48 | 45 | 38 | 45 |
| Business | 34 | 28 | 27 | 37 | 39 |
| Miscellaneous | 18 | 23 | 27 | 25 | 11 |
| Worker | 3 | 1 | 2 | — | 5 |
| Women | 4 | 4 | 3 | 7 | 4 |
| Under 40 | 35 | 10 | 9 | 42 | 54 |

*Background of 1970 Labour candidates in different types of seat*

| | All Labour candidates % | In seats held by Conservatives in 1966 with majorities | | In seats held by Labour in 1966 with majorities | |
|---|---|---|---|---|---|
| | | (Safe) Over 10% % | (Marginal) Under 10% % | (Marginal) Under 10% % | (Safe) Over 10% % |
| Public school | 23 | 24 | 24 | 26 | 20 |
| University | 58 | 60 | 58 | 69 | 54 |
| Professional | 43 | 41 | 39 | 47 | 43 |
| Business | 12 | 12 | 17 | 16 | 9 |
| Miscellaneous | 19 | 24 | 18 | 20 | 17 |
| Worker | 26 | 23 | 25 | 17 | 30 |
| Women | 5 | 9 | 3 | 2 | 4 |
| Under 40 | 37 | 68 | 62 | 27 | 16 |
| Union sponsored | 23 | 6 | 10 | 17 | 46 |

measurement. Intelligence, humanity and emotional stability are much less easily discoverable than education, age and occupation. Until new types of research are attempted, the question of how far a party's slate of M.P.s or candidates is representative in socio-economic terms (important though this may be) can be overstated. The time has come to focus more on the psychology of politicians and the role which they see themselves as playing.[1]

[1] See Denis Kavanagh, *Constituency Electioneering in Britain* (Longman, 1970).

CHAPTER XIII

# CONSTITUENCY CAMPAIGNING

In 1970 there were 1837 candidates. Their varied campaigns do not lend themselves to a simple summary. In this chapter we try to gather factual information from newspapers, post-election surveys, interviews and questionnaires (see pp. xii–xiii) about electioneering methods, the impact of the national leaders and issues at the constituency level.[1] We do not have an answer to the question of whether local Conservative organisation was decisive in the 1970 election, but we present some of the evidence on which it would have to be based. For the sake of convenience the material is presented under several subheadings.



[1] We have not included sketches of individual constituency campaigns of the sort featured in previous books in the Nuffield series. There were two reasons for this. First, the methods and the atmosphere of local electioneering change little between one election and the next: readers who wish to gain a general impression of grass roots campaigning can do so from previous Nuffield studies or from such books as *Political Parties in Action: the Battle of Barons Court* by R. T. Holt and J. E. Turner (Collier-Macmillan, 1968). Secondly, large numbers of individual constituency reports, particularly on marginals, appear in the press during the campaign and many of them give a good impression of the local contests and the activities of the candidates. We found it useful to adopt two rules-of-thumb in following these during the 1970 election: (i) as individual reports were usually brief, we aimed to compare several different ones on a given constituency or region; (ii) we tried, where possible, to refer to accounts in local or regional newspapers as they were generally more detailed than those in the

*Launching the Campaign*

Although there had been intermittent speculation throughout the spring, it was only at the beginning of May that many constituency officials began to treat the prospect of a June election as more than an outside possibility. Most local parties had intended to use the summer to put their organisations into fighting trim, to recruit members and ward helpers, to organise canvassing and to collect postal votes. Candidates had prepared to spend the next months nursing their constituencies, with an early holiday as a prelude to the hard labour of an autumn campaign. Even though the opinion polls and the local elections encouraged Labour and puzzled the Conservatives, few candidates reported during or after the election that they or their supporters had sensed the fast slide to Labour that was being indicated.

The Prime Minister's announcement on May 18, 1970, took Labour more off guard than the Conservatives. Of the Labour agents to whom we spoke during the campaign only one in six claimed to have anticipated a dissolution before the summer and the great majority admitted that they were unprepared. Two-thirds of the Conservatives also said that they expected October but most stated they were ready for June. The task of addressing envelopes for election addresses had been started in only a third of local Labour parties and less than a fifth claimed to have completed a large proportion of them. Even this is probably too generous an estimate as it is based like most of the observations in this chapter, on information taken disproportionately from marginal seats and those with full-time agents, which were better organised than the rest.[1] Almost two-thirds of the Conservatives claimed that their parties had set about addressing envelopes before May 18 and over a third said that the job had been largely completed by then.

In most parts of the country Labour had still to recruit amateur agents and there were even candidates to be chosen. Regional organisers were therefore involved in a disproportionate amount

---

nationals. The *Scotsman*, *Irish Times*, *Birmingham Post*, *Halifax Evening Courier*, *Middlesex County Times and Gazette*, and *Tribune* were among those which gave particularly helpful or evocative reports.

[1] See p. 262. The over-estimates are likely to be greater on the Labour side. Our approximate figures therefore probably underplay the gap between the two parties.

of work in setting up the constituency campaigns. Assistant regional organisers had to spend a great deal of time, especially in the first two weeks of the campaign, giving elementary advice to volunteer agents. They helped them to obtain temporary telephones or premises, to fill in nomination forms, to design election addresses, to understand the technicalities of the law and much more. All agents received daily sheets from the National Agent offering legal and organisational guidance, but the less experienced still required direct help from the regional office. As one regional organiser said during the campaign:

> 'We can honestly say that we were caught unprepared. We were without (several) candidates on May 18. . . . Besides, there has been a problem with agents. In one constituency the agent who had agreed to do the job [on the assumption that the election would be in October] is on an Electricity Board course at the moment and cannot be spared. Another agent is on the Continent. There are no agents in [two marginals]. . . . The initial chaos was intensified by Whit Week. . . . There were also difficulties in the ordering of supplies.'

The following summary from a log book of an assistant regional organiser's activities also give an impression of the difficulties:

2.00 p.m. *Visit to safe Labour seat*: Organisation very poor. Candidate only just selected. This means that ARO has to place orders for printing introductory leaflet.

2.45 p.m. *Visit to Labour-held marginal*: Dispute with newly arrived amateur agent who has altered the venue of an appearance by a cabinet minister the next day without making a new itinerary available to the press. Numerous other small matters.

5.30 p.m. *Visit to another Labour-held marginal.* Here the election agent has only agreed to do the job after much persuasion and on the understanding that the ARO will make regular visits. [He had already spent five days in this constituency the previous week.] ARO tries to obtain accommodation for visiting supporting speaker.

7.30 p.m. *Visit to a third Labour-held marginal*: Attends a public meeting. Calls out amateur agent to persuade him to hire a shorthand typist though they had not provided for one in the budget.

10.00 a.m. *Return to first Labour-held marginal*: Press conference for local candidates and visiting cabinet member. ARO dissuades election agent from sending election envelopes to ward parties for 'filling' without checking against the electoral register that they have been properly addressed. He emphasises that spot checking is not sufficient. ARO reorganises plans for filling and checking the envelopes so that it is done at two centres, and thereby can be more easily controlled.

The Conservative area offices had many fewer of these problems as there were relatively few constituencies without professional agents. While only 128 constituency Labour parties (CLPs) had the services of full-time organisers as election agents,[1] 439 of Conservative associations were manned by certificated agents,[2] 36 others by certificated organisers. Only 141 constituencies were in the charge of 'unqualified' agents. (Most of these were in Scotland and Lancashire.) Conservative area officials (like their Labour opposite numbers) spent much of their time arranging itineraries for visiting front bench speakers and accompanying them to meetings. But they were able to give more time than their counterparts to other functions; such as arranging to transfer helpers from safe to marginal constituencies ('mutual aid'), passing 'intelligence' reports from the constituencies to the Central Office, answering queries from candidates on aspects of policy (or passing them for reply by the Questions of Policy Committee at the Conservative Research Department),[3] and making tours of constituency offices. In the absence of major local crises, their main job was, as one of them put it, 'going round with the oil can.'

Constituency agents and candidates spent the first few days arranging the adoption meeting, booking halls, fixing the schedule of the candidates' activities during the following weeks, placing

[1] National Executive Committee *Annual Report* 1970, p. 9. 'In addition three of these full-time Labour organisers were assisted by full time assistant organisers. Thirteen City and Borough Secretaries supervised the work of election agents within their area. In addition, two members of the organising staff acted as election agents in Cardigan and South Bedfordshire respectively and a retired Regional Organiser acted as the election agent at Windsor. Also employed as election agents were 18 former full-time organisers. Eight trainee agents gave full-time assistance in selected marginal constituencies. . . . Mr. M. Macmillan acted as his own election agent in the Western Isles. In the remaining 458 constituencies, the election agency was undertaken by voluntary workers, many of whom had acted as election agents at previous general elections.'

[2] There were 405 certificated agents, some of whom acted as election agents for more than one constituency.

[3] See p. 142.

orders with printers, planning their campaign budget, organising a 'fighting fund' and finalising arrangements with key party workers. There was considerable dislocation in a number of local parties (particularly on the Conservative side) because committee members were already on holiday or were about to set off. Constituency offices were bombarded by calls from electors who intended to be on holiday on June 18, asking for postal votes. They had to be informed that they were not entitled to them unless their trips were on business or for medical care.

The long Whit weekend, which started five days after the Prime Minister's announcement, gave candidates and agents an opportunity to draft their election addresses. Many were then amended in the light of the party manifesto, which in all the main parties appeared the following week.[1] Although the brunt of planning and setting the campaign in motion fell in almost all cases on the agent and the candidate (and in many Labour and Liberal parties on the candidate alone), they sometimes had the assistance of full-time helpers and occasionally of a formally constituted campaign committee. On both Conservative and Labour sides about half said they had some form of campaign committee with 'departmental directors'. These committees were usually very informal and only in a few places had they been constituted by May.

In 1970, campaigns followed their usual forms. Almost all agents share a broadly similar ideal of what an election campaign should do. They see their job as supervising coherent routine. There is the business of making basic arrangements for meetings and, until two weeks before the poll, of collecting postal votes. There is the task of organising the addressing and filling of envelopes for every household in the constituency, usually for the Post Office's free delivery of the election address. And there is the main exercise of 'achieving a 100% canvass', making door to door contact with every elector in order to create a marked-up register showing who intends to support the party; on this basis, arrangements are then

[1] During the preparatory stages of the campaign the controversy over the South African cricket tour was reaching its climax (see pp. 139–141). But agents on both sides were almost unanimous in their opinion that it had no impact in the constituencies. Predictably, it was a Conservative agent in Yorkshire who expressed the strongest feelings:

> 'We are quite frankly disgusted with the government's attitude, cricket is a religion in Yorkshire. It will not feature in the election address, however. . . . To generate ill feeling in an election on an issue such as this is not playing cricket.'

made to drive electors to the polling station who might otherwise find difficulty in getting there; as polling day proceeds, tellers send the official poll card number of those who have voted to local committee rooms and party workers are sent out to 'knock-up' supporters whose names have not yet been checked off.[1]

The candidate does not loom large in most of this pattern. He has to speak at meetings and to visit committee rooms to keep up the morale of workers but, for most of the time, his role is to go out to meet the people with a loudspeaker car or going from house to house, leaving the agent to get on with administration.

Reality is much more complicated and messy and, as the pages that follow will show, the ideal is seldom achieved.

*Literature*

'You may notice one word missing. The word "Conservative"', a local party leader remarked, showing his M.P.'s election address. When it was unfolded, there emerged a photograph 11 inches by 8 and, in letters over an inch high, the words 'ENOCH POWELL'. The vast majority of candidates were much less flamboyant. Most produced the usual three-folded pamphlets containing a photograph, points of policy, a statement in letter form, a family picture, biographical details and stress on the date 'June 18th', committee room telephone number and so on. Compared to previous years there was a slight increase in the use of a newspaper format, profusely illustrated with scenes of the M.P.s constituency activities; a growing informality in family poses; and an increase (especially on the Labour side) in photographs of 'ordinary people', often with their testimonials to the candidate's work, or their general well-being under the government.

[1] According to the *Parliamentary Election Manual* issued by Conservative Central Office. 'The ideal organisation of the central [constituency] committee room is to have seven departments:

(i) General Office
(ii) Clerical
(iii) Canvassing
(iv) Absent Votes and Removals
(v) Meetings
(vi) Publicity
(vii) Transport

As this is not always practicable, it may be necessary to combine departmental work and the following arrangement is suggested:

(i) General Office and Clerical
(ii) Canvassing, Absent Voters and Removals
(iii) Meetings, Publicity and Transport

The Labour party manual *Party Organisation* gives similar advice, adding, 'such appointments should be made some time before an election is expected'.

Although national party leaders were mentioned relatively little,[1] addresses concentrated, as in previous elections, on national policies. Local issues were most frequently emphasised in Liberal addresses and in Scottish and Welsh constituencies.

According to the post-election survey by Gallup 53% of the electorate said they had read at least one election address, the highest percentage since 1959. Using a slightly wider question ('Have you received any literature from any of the political parties in the last few weeks?') ORC obtained the impressive figure of 83%, higher even than the 65% who recalled seeing a party political broadcast on television.[2] Of the agents in marginal seats who answered our questionnaire three-quarters reported that they had sent a separate copy of the election address to each elector; the others had sent copies to each household. The majority had also produced an introductory leaflet and a large minority had produced a 'final message' for delivery in the last week. These supporting items were generally ordered in quantities of 10,000 to 20,000 for selective distribution. In most places with immigrant populations, there were special leaflets in what were thought to be the appropriate languages.

According to the answers to our questionnaire 90% of local parties ordered some literature produced by the party headquarters. Transport House produced a total 6,922,000 pieces of literature during the campaign (compared with 6,880,000 in 1966). This total included 150,000 copies of the manifesto and 500,000 copies of the abbreviated version *Points from Labour's Plan.* A stock of these remained at Transport House until they were sold at reduced prices in the last week of the campaign. Sales of literature by Conservative Central Office to constituency organisations totalled 6,449,671, including 97,020 copies of the manifesto and 737,042 of the abbreviated version. Table 1 shows the decline since 1951 in the quantity of centrally produced literature and posters. During the 1970 election, local Labour and Conservative parties probably produced about 1½ pieces of literature for each elector — i.e. about 60 million in all, or ten times the quantity of centrally

[1] See pp. 437–42.

[2] The post-election surveys on participation in campaign activities must be treated with caution, as the very large variations in their findings indicate. A summary of the results of the ORC survey appeared in John Whale the *Sunday Times*, June 28, 1970, while those of Gallup and NOP were in their monthly bulletins for July and August. NOP found 79% who claimed to have watched a party political broadcast.

TABLE 1

*The fall in the quantity of literature and posters produced by Conservative Central Office for constituencies, 1951–70*

| | 1951 | 1955 | 1959 | 1964 | 1966 | 1970 |
|---|---|---|---|---|---|---|
| Leaflets | 13,134,187 | 10,607,679 | 6,695,340 | 5,285,556 | 5,266,002 | 5,615,609 |
| Manifesto (full) | 215,810 | 57,690 | 224,734 | 65,579 | 94,770 | 97,020 |
| Manifesto (popular) | 3,175,450 | 1,698,786 | 1,554,682 | 938,396 | 1,167,771 | 737,042 |
| Broadsheet | 2,418,850 | 1,531,000 | 676,460 | 783,100 | Not issued | Not issued |
| | 18,944,297 | 13,895,155 | 9,151,216 | 7,072,631 | 6,528,543 | 6,449,671 |
| Posters | 197,970 | 128,871 | 193,546 | 145,383 | 138,090 | 31,583 |

produced material (and probably much more, as, in our experience, bundles of national leaflets frequently remained undistributed in local party offices). Even in 1951, when the number of centrally produced items was three times larger (and four times greater as a proportion of the electorate), it was still relatively small in comparison with the amount of local material.

*Poster Sites*

The Conservatives displayed 3,490 16-sheet posters on hoardings throughout Great Britain during the campaign,[1] 1,331 of them ordered by Central Office in connection with the 'critical seats' exercise.[2] Agents in critical seats had a choice of four Central Office designs, all of them carrying the slogan 'For a better tomorrow vote Conservative'. The least popular was a photograph of a mother and child, which accounted for only 4% of those shown. The most popular poster (39% of the total) was the wastepaper basket of Labour's broken promises and next (34%) came the ever-diminishing value of the pound ('The £ in your pocket is now worth . . . 15/7').[3] A mere 6% showed Mr. Heath; 17% were locally produced designs.[4] Posters were ordered for a two-week period during the campaign. Sheffield Heeley and Yarmouth had the largest number of sites (32 each) while there were only two in Bristol North-west. There were fifteen or more sites in a majority of 'criticals'. The total cost varied between £99 10*s*. for 22 sites in

[1] For the purposes of this count, 48-sheet hoardings have been counted as 3 16-sheet hoardings.

[2] 864 in English and Welsh 'criticals', 92 in Scottish 'criticals' and 125 48-sheet hoardings on major road intersections and other 'nodal' sites near 'criticals'.

[3] See photographs facing p. 111.

[4] These percentages exclude Scottish 'critical' seats.

Cheadle to £15 15*s*. for 6 sites in Southampton Test and £8 15*s*. for 2 sites in Bristol North-west. There were 2,159 16-sheet sites in non-critical constituencies and a total of 22,000 double crown sites (in all constituencies).

The Labour party produced three posters. Two bore a picture of Harold Wilson and the campaign phrase *Now Britain's Strong . . .*; and one of these had the additional words *Vote Labour* and space for individual candidate's names; the third carried a photograph of Harold and Mary Wilson with a group of children and the words *Their health, their education, their opportunity — when it comes down to it aren't you voting for your children's future as well?*[1] 2,750 16-sheet copies, 10,000 double crown and 15,000 folio, of these were printed but it is unclear how many were displayed. The 48-sheet sites that had been booked for the national 'Yesterday's Men' campaign were offered to the constituencies and 160 (out of 180) of those outside London and 33 (out of 98) of those in Greater London were actually used.

*Window Bills*

No one travelling through Orpington could have failed to be impressed by 'Lubbock' in bright orange or 'Stanbrook' in deep blue displayed in profusion on stakes in front gardens, on trees, garage doors and windows; in Birmingham Ladywood there was a huge set of placards along one floor of a block of council flats reading 'Back Lawler's rents and rates — down fight'; in Solihull the neat Conservative flyposting high on the lamp-posts dominated the main road into Birmingham. But in many parts of the country — it was possible to drive for miles with hardly a sign that an election was in progress — only the odd cluster of posters bore testimony to a party worker's persistent requests to his neighbours. Occasionally in country areas there were posters every one or two hundred yards near the roadside on a sympathetic farmer's land. The reverse side of the candidate's election address was often designed for use as a window-bill. Mainly in the North, there were Conservative or Labour Clubs which provided prominent sites for hoardings. The biggest was perhaps the illuminated board, 20 feet by 50 feet above the Witham Labour Club (in the Maldon constituency) advertising the candidature of Steven Haseler.

According to the Gallup post-election survey, 10% of the

[1] National Executive Committee, *Annual Report* 1970.

electorate claimed to have displayed a window bill. (As there are about 25,000 households in the average constituency, this would mean some 2,500 window bills per constituency, or more if account is taken of households with several bills). In reply to our questionnaire, almost half the agents in critical seats (and a majority of those on the Labour side) estimated their supporters had displayed less than 2,000 window posters; the other half gave higher estimates. We strongly suspect that these, like the Gallup findings, were somewhat exaggerated.

### *Meetings*

Although the coming of television has made it much more difficult to attract a large audience to hear a political speech, election meetings have remained an essential feature of most constituency campaigns and in some parts of the country they have continued to flourish. The evidence of post-election surveys is ambiguous, but two general points emerge — first, there had been some decline in attendance since the 1950s and, second, Conservatives have continued to attract larger audiences.

TABLE 2

*Attendance at political meetings 1959–70*

| | 1959 | 1964 | 1966 | 1970 |
|---|---|---|---|---|
| *Gallup* | | | | |
| Indoor meetings . | 15% | 8% | 7% | 5% |
| Outdoor meetings . | 5% | 8% | 3% | 6% |
| *NOP* . . . | — | — | 4% | 4% |
| *ORC* . . . | — | — | — | 8%* |

* The wording of the NOP and ORC questions is similar: 'Have you been to any meeting organised by any of the political parties in the last four weeks?' Gallup includes separate questions on indoor and outdoor meetings.

TABLE 3

*Attendance at political meetings, 1970 (ORC)*

| | All electors % | Conservative voters % | Labour voters % | Liberal voters % |
|---|---|---|---|---|
| Conservative meetings | 4 | 8 | 2 | 9 |
| Labour meetings . | 3 | 1 | 6 | 7 |
| Liberal meetings . | — | — | — | 5 |
| None . . . | 93 | 91 | 92 | 79 |

The number of meetings varied greatly from constituency to constituency. In rural areas candidates frequently arranged a long series of village meetings. Jeremy Thorpe had as many as five a day, while the Liberal candidate in North Cornwall, John Pardoe, arranged six indoor and about 280 outdoor meetings. There were about four Labour meetings each day in King's Lynn, and the Conservatives said they were having six a day in Falmouth and Camborne. In urban constituencies there were generally very few meetings. There were more meetings in marginal seats, probably because they had more front bench visitors, and more were held by the Conservatives. According to our interviews during the campaign a clear majority of CLPs had fixed less than half-a-dozen meetings, while two-thirds of Conservative associations were having more. Conservatives reported much higher attendances at their adoption meetings than in 1966; the average in Conservative-held seats was 230 and in Labour-held marginals 180. Labour adoption meetings were often scratch affairs limited to the General Management Committee and their friends. The attendance at Labour adoption meetings in Conservative-held seats averaged 40, in Labour-held marginals 130, and in safe Labour constituencies 75.

On the theory that the visit of prominent speakers helped the local candidates to obtain audiences and publicity, the party headquarters directed front benchers to speaking engagements in marginal constituencies. In fact, there were only a handful of speakers on either side who drew large crowds. A Conservative area agent told us:

> 'We are running short of ex-ministers and crowd-drawing names. After all, who is there after Heath, Home, Maudling, Hogg and, God help us, Powell?'

And a Labour regional organiser observed:

> 'Callaghan will fill the town hall. Also Jenkins. Benn's meetings get 3–400. Crossman . . . is more of an intellectual than a platform speaker. Stewart . . . does not get high audiences.'

Another regional organiser said:

> 'Who draws the largest audiences? Harold (Wilson), of course, then George (Brown), without a doubt. And Barbara (Castle). Anybody else? I wouldn't have said so. You can work hard and fail to get a big audience for Crosland, Stewart and the others.'

According to attendance figures supplied by agents after the election, only Mr. Wilson, Mr. Brown and Mr. Callaghan regularly attracted audiences of 500 or more, while Mr. Jenkins, Mrs. Castle and Mr. Healey usually drew 200–300. Mr. Crosland, Mr. Peart, Lord Shackleton, Sir Elwyn Jones, Mr. Denis Howell were among those whose audiences were 100 or less. Mr. Heath and Mr. Powell were the most popular Conservative speakers followed by Mr. Hogg and Sir Alec Douglas-Home, all of whom regularly had audiences of 500 or more. Mr. Maudling and Mr. Macleod had audiences of about 400 while others, including Mr. Barber, Sir Keith Joseph and Mrs. Thatcher addressed gatherings of 200. Others who spoke to meetings of 100 or less, according to admittedly, isolated reports, were Mr. Patrick Jenkin, Sir Peter Rawlinson, Lord Balniel, Lord Carrington, Mr. Chataway, Mr. Pym, Mr. Richard Wood, Mr. Selwyn Lloyd, Mr. Maurice Macmillan, Mr. Terence Higgins, Earl Jellicoe, Mr. Peter Walker and Mr. Robert Carr.

The average attendances at ordinary meetings (excluding adoption meetings) as reported to us by agents during the course of the campaign was 50 for the Conservatives and 40 for Labour. According to our post-election questionnaire, the average attendance in Labour-held marginals throughout the campaign (including adoption and eve of poll meetings) was 100 for both Conservatives and Labour. About 60% of local parties had eve of poll meetings, half of them with attendances of over 150.

In all the reports we received the absence of references to heckling was notable. The stories of eggs being thrown and abuse being shouted were mainly confined to a few days in the travels of Mr. Wilson and Mr. Heath, as well as of Mr. Brown and Mr. Powell. Students at Brighton did shout down Mr. Julian Amery and there were other isolated incidents. But the number of cases that came before the courts was negligible and, by past standards, the election was a very orderly affair.

### *Canvassing*

Local leaders can usually find helpers to address envelopes, to run committee rooms, to act as tellers on election day or as drivers. It is much more difficult to induce them to canvass or to persuade electors to put up posters: the work is more lonely and there is always the fear (seldom justified) of a rude response at the doorstep. The canvass is generally concentrated in a party's best political areas. This is partly because the organisation is usually stronger in these areas; and also because it is most efficient to work where it is easiest to locate party supporters — for this is the principal object of the exercise. However, it does have the effect of distorting the results if they are used to indicate how the constituency is likely to behave. As canvassers are more concerned to find out who their supporters are, they seldom bother, in constituencies where there are more than two candidates, to ask which party an opponent supports. This too makes it difficult to use the canvass as a means of predicting the result. A third difficulty of using the canvass for this purpose is the large number of 'doubtfuls' and the tendency of party workers to put an over-optimistic construction on ambiguous replies at the doorstep. Fourthly, canvassers rarely ask husbands and wives separately for their voting intentions. Thus, although the canvass is, as Holt and Turner have shown,[1] a very effective means of identifying a large proportion of those who will vote for one's party, it is a very dubious form of 'opinion poll'.

As the 1970 election followed so closely on the county and municipal elections, many parties based their canvassing on the registers partially marked up during the earlier campaign. Some relied on more ancient records. The hot weather and the long summer days encouraged canvassers, but also made their job harder

TABLE 4

*Percentage of electorate canvassed (ORC)*

| | All electors | Conservatives % | Labour % | Liberal % |
|---|---|---|---|---|
| By Conservatives . | 28 | 37 | 25 | 28 |
| By Labour . . | 18 | 14 | 27 | 10 |
| By Liberals . . | 6 | 5 | 4 | 36 |

by taking people out of their homes. An exceptionally high proportion of 'outs' was reported in many places. According to the Gallup post election survey 1% of the electorate claimed to have done some canvassing (as against 2% in 1966). NOP reported that 29% of the electorate said they had been canvassed (31% in 1966)

[1] See R. T. Holt and J. E. Turner, *Political Parties in Action* (Collier-Macmillan, 1968), pp. 163–81.

while ORC found a figure of 40%. The NOP and ORC surveys both suggested the Conservatives had reached at least one and a half times as many electors as Labour.

CLPs sent weekly reports to the regional offices. Conservative associations in critical seats submitted canvass returns on June 10 and June 17. Central Office's analysis of the figures apparently showed that the Conservatives were ahead in many constituencies even if the 'againsts' of all parties and all 'doubtfuls' were added together. In view of their inherent unreliability, however, these canvass returns were regarded with reserve and were not made public although they were indirectly referred to as evidence against the opinion polls.

After the election we received canvass returns from thirty-six agents, almost all in marginal seats. The Conservatives claimed on average to have canvassed 75% of the electorate and Labour 66%. The Labour agents had all separated their opponents into 'Conservative' and 'Liberal' but two-thirds of the Conservatives lumped all 'againsts' together. The average percentage of doubtfuls was found by Conservatives to be 25% and by Labour, 13% (the full range was from 5% to 40%). If 'doubtfuls' were added to 'againsts' then almost all Labour canvassing over-estimated the party's vote; on the Conservative side half the canvasses underestimated their party's support and half over-estimated it. The range of error was between an over-estimate of 46% and an underestimate of 13%. The average Labour error was 15%, and the average Conservative error 10%.

*Mutual Aid*

However logical it may seem to party headquarters to transfer activists from safe or hopeless seats to marginals where their efforts may really make a difference, the exercise is fraught with practical difficulties. It can take patient staff-work to overcome the natural reluctance of party workers to leave their home territory. After an evening journey little time may be left for serious activity. The local party workers may find themselves wasting time guiding their visitors about and briefing them and the visitors may feel unwelcome.[1]

[1] Students, however, offered a frequent source of outside aid. Although examinations and the ending of the academic year limited their activity, they were much in evidence in some constituencies, particularly through an energetic, newly recruited organisation, Students for a Labour Victory.

In the Labour party 'mutual aid' arrangements tended to be *ad hoc* and, by general agreement, were poorer than in 1966. The Conservatives had long planned to provide aid to 'critical' seats and a considerable number of constituency associations had agreed to give a specific allocation of 'man-hours' of work or to take responsibility for particular wards or polling districts in a nearby 'critical'. Besides these formal offers, usually arranged through the area office, constituencies sometimes made informal exchanges. The early election and the jitteriness of some Conservative-held constituencies in face of Labour's lead in the polls during the campaign prevented the plans from operating as smoothly as they might otherwise have done. But they were much better than in 1966, and better than Labour's.

According to our interviews during the campaign, at least two-thirds of Conservative associations in Labour-held marginals received 'mutual aid'. In over three-quarters of these constituencies this had been organised through the area office before the campaign; in 10% of them it had been fixed directly with the constituency that was providing the help; and in the remaining 10%, the arrangements were made during the campaign. Slightly over half the CLPs in Labour-held marginals received outside help, arranged in half these constituencies by the regional office before the campaign.

This tallies with the findings of our post-election questionnaire. About two-thirds of the Conservative associations in Labour-held marginals received some outside aid, and in half these cases whole wards or polling districts were assigned to the outside helpers. In two-fifths of these constituencies, the proportion of canvassing by the outsiders was less than 10%, in a quarter of them it was between 10% and 39% and in the remainder of the seats receiving outside aid, it amounted to between 40% and 50% of the total canvassed. On the Labour side, about half the CLPs in Labour-held marginals received some outside help, but it never amounted to more than 40% of the total canvassed and in three-quarters of them it constituted less than 10%.

## *Participation*

According to the Gallup post-election survey, 2% of the electorate did some work for one of the candidates (in addition to the 1% who had taken part in canvassing). According to ORC 5% of Conservatives, 3% of Labour and 3% of Liberals participated actively in the campaign. In answer to our questionnaire, three-quarters of Labour agents in marginal seats said they had fewer than 500 helpers and none claimed over 1,000. Almost half the Conservative agents said they had had more than 1,000 helpers, but only one claimed more than 1,500. Almost all the Conservatives said their organisation was better than in 1966, while Labour agents were equally divided between those who said it was better, worse and the same.

*Polling Day*

Some professional agents expressed doubts about the polling day exercise as operated by most local parties. The object was, of course, to keep a running check throughout the day on the names of supporters who had not yet voted.[1] Unfortunately it often happened that so much manpower was devoted to telling, manning committee rooms and keeping the paper work in order (quite apart from making tea and ordinary sociability), that the actual business of fetching electors to the poll was neglected. There were some superbly efficient local operations but many agents had cause to sigh at the inevitable limitations of untrained volunteer helpers.

In 'knocking up', transport was all important; 40% of Conservative and 60% of Labour agents reported that they had less than 150 cars at their disposal during polling day; 20% of the Conservatives and 10% of Labour had over 350. Labour agents claimed an average of 300 helpers on election day and the Conservatives 600.

The Gallup post-election survey produced the following information about time of voting:

[1] For this purpose the canvassers' marked-up registers are sometimes pinned up on boards in the local committee room and crossed off as tellers' slips arrived from the polling station. 'Knockers-up' are then given slips of paper with the names of the outstanding supporters and told to get them to the poll. A more effective method (the NCR system, or the Reading system as it is called in the Labour party) is to prepare the names of all party supporters in a street on pads with four duplicate copies. Their names are crossed off as the tellers slips come in and 'knockers-up' merely tear off the top sheets, leaving the remaining copies ready for use later after further tellers' reports have come in. According to our questionnaire, constituencies were evenly divided between the NCR/Reading system and more traditional methods of marking off names.

*Time of Voting*

| | 1970 | 1966 |
|---|---|---|
| Before 12 noon . | 27% | 23% |
| 12–4.59 p.m. . | 23% | 26% |
| 5–6.59 p.m. . | 16% | 18% |
| 7–7.59 p.m. . | 18% | 19% |
| 8–8.59 p.m. . | 12% | 14% |
| 9–10 p.m. . | 4% | — |

*Candidates' Activities*

Most candidates are extroverts who get pleasure out of the hard slog of campaigning and incessantly meeting people. But often they are troubled by the sense that by polling day they will still remain unknown to the great bulk of their electors. Some seek publicity in striking ways: one Conservative defending a perilous by-election majority in Swindon went around in a horse and cart; another similarly placed in Meriden used a high powered motor-cycle; in safer Hereford the candidate travelled by helicopter; Mr. Faulds defended Smethwick for Labour with a Union Jack draped around his Land-Rover; the colourful Miss Lestor went round Eton and Slough by bicycle. But a Lancashire candidate lamented:

> 'Avenues for personal electioneering are closing. 20 years ago all the factories and mills invited the candidates into the canteens to address the workers. Since then the factories and mills have been taken over by national firms who are very timid and send out directives from London that no candidate is to be allowed into the canteen.'

Douglas Houghton sought to get round this sort of problem and to multiply his presence in Sowerby by sending out teams with recorded loudspeaker programmes of speech and music and a tape recorder for constituents to dictate questions or comments to him.

Candidates tended to start the mornings by dealing with the press and with correspondence and then to go out knocking on doors or using a loudspeaker van until the evening meetings. In towns there were daytime visits to factory gates while in the country it was necessary to have village meetings at all hours if the whole constituency was to be covered.

A small proportion (mainly Conservatives) had volunteer personal assistants to drive them around, keeping them on time and helping with telephoning about arrangements and doing research for speeches. Wives sometimes performed this chore together with their many other roles; and occasionally it was undertaken by the candidates' children or friends. But we had the impression that while some campaigns were family affairs, few candidates made heavy demands on personal friends; when they did, it often added greatly to their effectiveness.

The replies offered by candidates to our question 'did you enjoy the campaign?' offer an oddly mixed but very human picture of what it felt like to be in the thick of things. The range was from 'I never do' and 'Don't make me laugh' to 'Enormously', 'Loved every minute of it' and 'Yes, except for the result'. A majority fell into the cheerful category, often with a stress on how the weather had helped.

> 'Yes. In summer sunshine and a beautiful countryside, it was marvellous.'
>
> 'Better than most. Shirtsleeve order makes a pleasant change.'
>
> 'Fortunately I made the acquaintance of my opponent and became quite friendly with him so the campaign could be reasonably relaxed.'
>
> 'Campaigning is always lonely. You are cut off from friends, congenial relaxation and good food. But I enjoy electioneering.'
>
> 'It was too strenuous to be pleasurable. . . . I personally prefer more constructive work than campaigning.'
>
> 'On and off. My opponent used the race issue — I hated it and couldn't bring myself to shake hands with him.'
>
> 'I liked speaking at meetings but otherwise it was drudgery from beginning to end.'
>
> 'I enjoyed it but was glad when it was over. Repetition of speeches becomes tedious.'

Perhaps the most eloquent comment came from a disillusioned Liberal:

> 'The joy wore off with time. I'm much more philosophical about standing now. The work is hard and nobody is grateful. You may lose £50 through it although you know you won't win, but to the average voter you are out to line your own pocket. Perhaps the saddest feeling of all is the candidate's reaction to the voters, not vice-versa. They appear stupider than he expects. Most of them are uninterested and many would vote for a clown with the right party label. Too many seem to think that politics is too complicated for them.'

*National Leaders*

During the election we found few Conservative agents or candidates who spoke with eagerness about Mr. Heath or suggested that they were putting his qualities in the forefront of the campaign. It was only a small minority who were actively disloyal, like the one who said, 'Heath's image is bloody awful — he should have been told to get married — he's got the personality of a blanc-mange.' But many covered their embarrassment by stressing that they focused on the local candidate not the party leader; quite a few referred to the popularity of Enoch Powell; and a number commented regretfully that while Ted Heath was popular with many party workers he was not getting across to the mass of voters. But less than one in five mentioned him with enthusiasm or suggested that he was in any way a campaign asset. Candidates writing to us after the election reported that it was only in the last few days that Mr. Heath began to make an impact, but even the relief of victory did not induce many to use very strong terms about his contribution, except for his final television appearance. 'At the end he began to get over better.' 'His last TV dispelled our people's reservations.' 'His standing among party workers rose during the campaign but on the whole he made an unfavourable impression on the voters.'

Mr. Wilson won much praise from his followers, but even this was double-edged. 'He's our greatest asset, the clever little so-and-so,' said one candidate. The Yorkshire comment, 'He's a little God locally', could be balanced by one or two others who said pointedly that they focused on the candidate or the party, not the leader. One extreme plaint was, 'I haven't been flogging my guts out for the last thirty years on behalf of Harold Wilson; I've been doing it for the party.' However, while one or two expressed unease about Mr. Wilson's 'trivialising' campaign, there was very little disparagement of his public appeal and a great majority emphasised that the Wilson–Heath contrast worked powerfully in Labour's favour. Even the post-election comment of Labour candidates, some of them unexpectedly defeated, was on the whole laudatory and only a handful complained that Mr. Wilson had been too smug or had fought too personalised a campaign. However, all the reports showed that while few Labour people felt strongly about Edward Heath, even when they despised him, many Conservatives had a driving hatred of Harold Wilson, even when they admired his cleverness. Yet as far as the mass electorate if not the activists were concerned, there was some evidence to support the verdict of one very senior figure indeed: 'The people wanted Wilson but not Labour, the Conservatives but not Heath.'

*Pressure Groups*

Many organisations and pressure groups were active during the campaign sending questionnaires and propaganda to candidates. The Anti-Common Market League was a well-publicised example, but the most noticeable groups were undoubtedly Aims of Industry and the 'Free Radio'.

Aims of Industry launched a nationwide advertising effort on March 26, 1970, advocating the case for free enterprise. At a cost of about £25,000, 3,800 sixteen-sheet posters, showing four harassed citizens fed up with state interference, were displayed nationwide for about three months. In May and June there were 136 insertions of large advertisements in national and local newspapers. The total bill for the whole Aims of Industry campaign was £134,000.

There were suggestions that the campaign in a number of East Coast constituencies had been significantly affected by the activities of pirate radio operators, seeking revenge on the Labour government which had outlawed them in 1967 and jammed them since. 'Jamming the pirates took the edge off our advantage with young people,' said one East Anglian Labour agent. The coastal area from Dover to King's Lynn contained a disproportionate number of marginal seats. A station calling itself Radio Nord See International, anchored a few miles off the Essex coast, put out increasingly vehement pro-Conservative slogans and gave telephone numbers which sympathisers could contact to obtain literature and to find ways of helping the Conservative cause. Some of these were the numbers of Conservative committee rooms. It was alleged that one million pirate radio leaflets were distributed from 62 local centres. There was also flyposting — one poster showed Harold Wilson dressed as Chairman Mao. In the last week Radio Nord See used the name of Radio Caroline, the best known of the old pirate radio stations. The stridency of the propaganda and its blatant illegality were commented on in the press. However, there were Conservative candidates who said they were glad to accept allies wherever they came from; and it was suggested that Mr. Ronan O'Rahilly, the sponsor of Radio Caroline, had received warm messages from senior people in the Conservative party.[1]

[1] See 'Cons-piracy', *Private Eye*, July 17, 1970, for a circumstantial if unconfirmed account of these matters. See also *Sunday Mirror*, June 14, 1970, and *Daily Telegraph*, June 22, 1970.

*Trade Unions and Co-operative Societies*

Trade unions may, however, be regarded as the most important of all the pressure groups bearing on voters, though their influence can be over-estimated.[1] During a campaign their main help to Labour is informal. It consists in providing an atmosphere favourable to the propagation of Labour ideals and working class identification. Apart from sponsoring some Labour candidates,[2] trade unions give little direct organisational support to CLPs. In May 1970, over 100 full-time trade union and Co-operative Society organisers were members of the National Union of Labour Organisers, many of them former constituency agents. Yet there appears to have been a reluctance on the part of their unions to let them serve as election agents during the campaign, and an equal hesitation on the part of CLPs to accept them. In the words of a senior Labour party official:

> 'It is policy not to use trade union organisers for this purpose. If a sudden trade union dispute arose, the trade union organiser would have to leave. We were thinking of having a trade union organiser as election agent in [a particular constituency]. But there would have been a problem of dual loyalties. There was also a reluctance in the local party to accept an outsider imposed on them.'

In a very few constituencies CLPs did have trade union organisers as election agents. For example, USDAW drafted a full time official to be agent in Bradford South. But we encountered only a single CLP, North Norfolk, which relied heavily on trade union help. Here six organisers of the National Union of Agricultural Workers devoted themselves full time from June 1st: '. . . (they) all have cars and are real pros . . . (they) are doing the bulk of the campaign work . . . You really (cannot) get voluntary canvassers very easily.'

A Bristol candidate told us that the unions were 'like having a whole other organization to help you', while the agent at Bolton was grateful for the help of about 20 mineworkers a day from Wigan. But these were exceptional cases. More typical were these comments. From a CLP with a Co-op sponsored candidate:

> ('Would you estimate that 10% of the work is done by helpers from the Co-op?') 'No. It is less than that. They are mainly old ladies who help with the addressing.'

[1] See *Political Change in Britain*, Chapter 7. [2] See pp. 298–9.

or from a Northern agent:

> 'A few trade unions have offered some help but they are not very punctual or reliable. They aren't very willing to help with the foot-slogging.'

It appears that the lack of union involvement is normal in general elections and did not result in 1970 from annoyance over the Industrial Relations Bill.

*Liberals*

Even more than those of other parties, Liberal campaigns were usually 'do-it-yourself' local affairs. There were constituencies such as North Cornwall, North Devon and Orpington where the organisation was on a spectacularly energetic scale. £2,500 was raised at Mr. Pardoe's Launceston adoption meeting which 800 people attended. But for the most part activities were relatively modest. Only a small minority of candidates had the support to attempt comprehensive canvassing or large indoor meetings. There was very little in the way of mutual aid, though, for example, help did come to Wavertree from the rest of Merseyside. The Federation Secretaries had neither the resources nor the manpower to help the constituencies. The party lacked well-known speakers to go on tour and their M.P.s were all busy fighting their own constituencies.[1]

As the results were to show, Liberal performance varied widely. A few candidates with a flair for publicity and an energetic organisation made a marked impact and often a cadre of a few dozen enthusiasts put on a very presentable campaign. But in our interviews with the other parties, we were most struck by the almost total absence of awareness or anxiety about the Liberal efforts.

*Issues*

Four national issues were most often raised on the doorstep. Almost every candidate mentioned high prices. The Common Market came next followed by taxes and immigration (or Powell-ism). Far behind came housing, and abuse of the social services. No other issues were mentioned by more than a handful of the hundred or so candidates who wrote to us after the election — but

[1] One enterprising headquarters activity on behalf of the more promising Liberal areas was the placing of big advertisements in provincial papers, mainly those covering Wales and the West Country during the ten days after the election was announced. The cost of this operation was £4,000.

many of them, particularly on the Labour side, commented that the election had been almost without issues. One M.P. was typical:

> 'A few mentioned high prices but really almost every point raised when I was canvassing was a personal matter.'

Surprisingly few candidates or agents laid much stress on local issues, and such 'local' issues as were mentioned were often national in essence — unemployment, immigration, housing, council rents, education or transport — which bore especially on the constituency. Anxiety over the third London airport was mentioned in constituencies around all the possible sites and aircraft noise was referred to by several candidates in seats near Heathrow or Gatwick. The Selective Employment Tax came up in seaside resorts, docks nationalisation in Bristol and East London and railway closures in several country districts. Particular aspects of local redevelopment plans, such as the line of a new road or the London Motorway Box, were thought to matter in a number of constituencies; the location of the Chorley/Preston new town seemed important in North-east Lancashire, while the exclusion of Edinburgh from the Scottish development area was said to have caused a few Labour abstentions in the city. Worries over jobs and locally high unemployment rates were touched on quite frequently and the closure of specific local factories seemed to have caused candidates a good deal of trouble. Regional and nationalist problems were always mentioned in the outlying parts of Wales and Scotland. Only one or two mentioned an authentically parochial concern — the closure of a swimming bath, the strike at the steelworks or the scandal on the town council. But when an M.P., representing what most would have regarded as a blighted, problem-ridden London constituency, answered 'Of course not' to our question whether any local issues had mattered, he was being neither perverse nor untypical. About half those we approached on this subject replied negatively, and those who did suggest local issues that might have swayed votes seldom put much emphasis upon them.

### *Immigration*

Despite the deterioration in race relations since 1966, and Mr. Powell's powerful speeches on immigration during the campaign, the 1970 election was not marked by the bitterness, the racial slogans or the obscenities that were apparent in a few constituencies in 1964.[1] This was very largely the result of a determination by party organisers and candidates on all sides that they should not be repeated. In Eton and Slough (one of the few constituencies where immigration was discussed somewhat more bitterly than elsewhere) Miss Joan Lestor, the sitting Labour M.P., was described as 'the first candidate ever heard to tell a supporter that he could stuff his vote — in this case a racialist Labourite in the Aspro factory'.[2] In Bradford, a city with a high immigrant population and a background of troubles, careful plans were made by both parties to play down the immigration issue. According to a leading member of the city Labour party:

> 'The Conservative Chief Agent, David Smith, got the four Conservative candidates to go into the (immigration) question some time ago, and they came out with a relatively moderate line. He wished quite deliberately — it seems — to get immigration out of the way as an issue.'

And a senior Bradford Conservative told us:

> 'As far as the Labour and Conservative parties are concerned, we are determined not to make it an issue. Quite frankly, Powell isn't helping us. The way I reckon it is this: those who support Powell are likely to vote Conservative anyway. So it is best to go after the immigrant vote.'

The same attitude of enlightened self-interest was apparent at the headquarters of the Birmingham Conservative Association. Working lunches with candidates had been organised at which the official Conservative line on immigration was discussed. It was recognised that the immigrant vote was itself important and that this risked being lost through 'Powellite' policies. Indeed, it was officially claimed that Mr. Powell had not been invited to speak in Birmingham during the campaign and that when he came it was only at his own request. The Conservative candidate for nearby Smethwick, Mr. Rathbone, whose views on immigration were suspect, was treated with reserve by party officials.

The towns where the immigration issue was debated most forcefully were Wolverhampton and Huddersfield. In both places National Front candidates had performed well in the 1970 municipal elections, taking 32% of the vote in a straight fight with a Conservative in the St. Peter's ward of Wolverhampton and gaining about 10% of the total vote in Huddersfield, where National

[1] See *The British General Election of 1964*, pp. 360–8.

[2] Corinna Adam, 'Fit for humans?', *New Statesman*, June 19, 1970.

Front candidates stood in 13 out of 15 wards.[1] During the campaign, the Conservative candidate, Geoffrey Wright, in Wolverhampton, North-east, virtually wrote off the immigrant vote, and attempted to attract the working class vote by emphasising his Powellite sympathies. He was hindered by having the same name as the National Front candidate who obtained 5% of the vote. Had there been no National Front candidate, the Conservatives might almost have won the seat. The National Front did not put up a candidate against the Conservative candidate in Huddersfield, East, who favoured a highly restrictive policy on immigration, directing their efforts against the moderate Conservative in Huddersfield, West. There was almost an incident when Communists and members of a Black Power group set up their stalls in one of the parks in the town where a meeting in support of Mr. Powell had been planned. When the Powellite speakers arrived, the police did not allow them to speak on the ground that public order was threatened. It did not appear, however, that this meeting had been called by the National Front. Although their candidate obtained only 1,427 votes (4%), this was sufficient to rob the Conservatives of victory.

Although immigration was widely seen as the main issue in Wolverhampton and Huddersfield, observers noted the relative inactivity of extreme right organisations. As an expert in the field wrote to us after the election:

> 'The National Front made hardly any noticeable impact in Wolverhampton, and it was remarkable, even in an election when it was generally agreed that interest was low nearly everywhere in the country, that there were very few election posters on view in either constituency.'

*Northern Ireland*

The reactions to the O'Neill era and to the upheavals which followed it made 1970 the most important general election in Northern Ireland since the war. The Unionist camp was split and there were challenges in two seats in the name of the Rev. Ian Paisley's Protestant Unionism, and in three other contests where the official candidate was faced by representatives of moderate or extreme Unionism — or both. On the other side, the Nationalist and Republican labels had disappeared; those who used to vote for

[1] There has been regular information about race and politics at the local level in *Race Today*, published monthly by the Institute of Race Relations.

'the green' were now faced with 'Unity' or National Democratic standard-bearers. There had been complex politicking over these candidatures. Two sitting Unionist M.P.s disappeared. Mr. George Currie in North Down was denied re-nomination, while Sir Knox Cunningham in South Antrim resigned at the last moment. Mr. Stratton Mills almost failed to secure re-nomination in Belfast North because of his liberal views. Moves to replace Lord Hamilton, the Unionist M.P. for Fermanagh, by a more right-wing candidate were abandoned under the threat that a moderate Unionist would then intervene to split the vote. The suggestion that there had been a deal to save the Ulster Prime Minister's brother, Robin Chichester-Clark, from Paisleyite opposition in Londonderry provoked one of the few flurries of the campaign. In some constituencies, Labour and Liberal candidates were not prepared to give way to 'Unity' tickets — in Londonderry a very radical 'Derry Labour' candidate stood in protest against 'Unity' support for the veteran Nationalist, Mr. McAteer, while Miss Devlin's socialist or revolutionary views provoked two other Catholics to stand against her in Mid-Ulster — very ineffectively.

The campaign was conducted with unprecedented thoroughness. In contrast to previous elections, almost no result was taken for granted and organisation was tuned to a new pitch. A record number of postal votes were secured and turnout increased everywhere. There was special interest in young voters, for votes at 18 could make a great difference to a country where the higher Catholic birthrate has long been offset by higher Catholic emigration among people in their early twenties. The Northern Ireland contest was not characterised by great arguments over policy, though Mr. Wilson's June 13 onslaught on the Ulster Unionists may have damaged the Labour party in three Belfast seats where any hopes it had were centred. There were few meetings and, in the presence of the Army, the traditional and provocative parades were less evident in Belfast and Londonderry. Granted the history of the previous year, there was a marked absence of violence.

> 'The only incidents to break the uneasy calm in the last fortnight were a mild fracas in Dungiven during an Orange parade there, and a tense confrontation between rival factions at a meeting of the Unity candidate for Fermanagh and South Tyrone, Mr. Frank McManus, in Dungannon.'[1]

[1] *Economist*, June 20, 1970.

Nevertheless, the campaigns had a uniquely Northern Irish style, very much outside the national pattern in Great Britain. Despite the new labels, the battle was on traditional sectarian lines, as the votes were to demonstrate.

*Postal Votes*

One of the most variable features within the remarkable regularities of election statistics was provided by the postal vote. 731,116 electors had their names on the absent voters register and 625,355 of these (85·5%, 0·5% less than in 1966) recorded valid votes — an average of 973 per constituency. More people were eligible for postal votes than in 1966 because the register was three months older (so that more people had moved house) and because the 1969 Act had relaxed the law to allow postal voting by people moving within multi-member boroughs. But the proportion of votes cast by post only rose from 1·9% to 2·1%; in 1964 the figure was 2·5% and in 1951, the record year since the postal vote began in 1949, 2·6%.

In individual seats the figure ranged from 6,499 valid postal votes (10·1%) in Fermanagh and South Tyrone and 6,023 (8·5%) in Mid-Ulster down to 142 (0·6%) in West Ham South, and 78 (0·5%) in Glasgow, Gorbals. In Britain two marginals, Dover (3,319) and Buckingham (2,987), led the 19 seats in which over 2,000 postal votes were cast. All but two of these 19 seats were rural and only 11 of them were really marginal. There seems nothing special about Dover or Buckingham except that they were well organised county constituencies facing close contests. In other similar marginal seats the postal vote was less than half this size. Indeed the special efforts made in marginal seats had an only moderate effect. In the 50 most marginal Labour seats (48 of them were on the Conservative 'critical' list and 29 had full-time Labour agents) the average postal vote recorded was 1,451, only 50% above the national average of 973. What is striking is that in so many marginal seats the postal vote was so low, with Perry Barr (399) and Leicester South-west (541) providing the extreme cases. Had the election been held in October, these figures must have been considerably higher.

Eligibility for the postal or proxy votes varied widely between localities. If a constituency housed a large number of seamen, or of elderly people, or indeed it if contained a substantial hospital or service population or if it had had a large amount of slum clearance, the potential postal vote was greatly increased. But there is no doubt that the main cause of variation in postal electorate lay in the energy and enterprise of local party officials. Both sides claimed to have put great effort into getting electors on to the postal register. Many appointed voluntary postal voting officers for the constituency and even down to ward and polling district. A few, mostly Conservatives, had someone working full-time on the matter for some weeks but the majority, particularly on the Labour side, admitted that the election had come too soon for them to complete their preparations — all applications for postal votes had to be in by June 4. As the essential to success was locating those who were eligible, the garnering of postal votes often depended on sympathetic friends in the right places; doctors, and the matrons of hospitals and nursing homes could help greatly in putting party workers in touch with those eligible by reason of chronic sickness, while council officials could supply lists of people who had moved to new housing. There were stories of intending holiday-makers claiming postal registration on the ground that they would be away on 'export drive' business. The evidence that came our way suggests that such abuses, though widespread, were not on any serious scale; we were on the whole struck by how often the two sides agreed in thinking the postal vote divided between Conservative and Labour in a ratio ranging from 75–25 down to 60–40.

There were 32 seats where the number of postal votes included in the count exceeded the Conservative majority. Although the Conservatives probably won more than half the postal votes in all these constituencies, in relatively few of them was their advantage sufficient to have made the difference between victory and defeat. If the postal vote everywhere divided 3 to 1 in the Conservatives' favour they would owe 17 seats to it, but if the ratio was only 2 to 1 this would drop to only 6 seats. We have made what local enquiries we could in these 17 seats and, though we are dependent on the rough and sometimes conflicting calculations of those present at the count, we would guess that the postal vote was decisive in the six seats listed on the next page.

There is some conflict of evidence about Dover (3,319 postal votes; 1,649 Conservative majority) and the Wrekin (1,270; 518). The balance of local opinion seems narrowly against the postal vote having been decisive in Bolton East (1,374; 471) or Middlesbrough

West (993; 388). In our enquiries on this question we found several Conservative agents who claimed that, although 80% or more of postal electors had been put on the register through their offices, they had received no more than 66% of the postal votes counted.

| | Valid postal votes | Conservative majority |
|---|---|---|
| Ipswich . . . . . . . | 1,673 | 13 |
| King's Lynn . . . . . . | 1,985 | 33 |
| Brighouse and Spenborough . . . | 1,924 | 54 |
| Yardley . . . . . . . | 738 | 120 |
| Leicester, South-west . . . . | 541 | 106 |
| Keighley . . . . . . . | 1,954 | 616 |

If the Conservatives did owe at most eight and possibly only six seats to the postal vote, it sets in a new perspective the remarkable claim by Mr. Macleod at the Smith Square press conference on June 16 that the Conservatives would get 30 seats simply through their superior organisation of the postal vote.

*Expenses*

The total expenses reported by candidates amounted to £1,392,796 or £761 per candidate (compared to £1,070,746 and £667 in 1966).[1] Since the electorate was almost 10% greater this only represents an increase in total expenditure from 8*d* per

| | Average £ per candidate | | | | | % of permitted maximum | | | | |
|---|---|---|---|---|---|---|---|---|---|---|
| | Con. | Lab. | Lib. | Other | All | Con. | Lab. | Lib. | Other | All |
| England . . | 974 | 828 | 513 | 276 | 780 | 80 | 68 | 41 | 24 | 64 |
| Wales . . | 794 | 869 | 585 | 527 | 694 | 68 | 74 | 49 | 45 | 59 |
| Scotland . . | 854 | 854 | 627 | 516 | 713 | 75 | 76 | 40 | 44 | 60 |
| Northern Ireland | 854 | 329 | 211 | 550 | 586 | 62 | 24 | 13 | 37 | 40 |
| Total 1970 . | 949 | 828 | 525 | 424 | 761 | 79 | 68 | 41 | 36 | 63 |
| 1966 . . | 766 | 726 | 501 | 338 | 667 | 89 | 84 | 56 | 41 | 77 |

The average expenditure of the 58 Communists was £269 (1966, £354), of the 36 Plaid Cymru candidates £597 (1966, £379) and of the 65 Scottish Nationalists £644 (1966, £414).

elector to 9*d*. The flat rate increase of £300 in the legal maximum expenditure permitted to any candidate was little used. Many of the agents we met said that increased printing costs were fully swallowing the increased allowance: it was therefore surprising to discover how little they raised their actual expenditure, and to find

[1] All these figures exclude the personal expenses incurred by the candidates which, subject to certain conditions, do not count against the legal maximum. In past elections they have amounted to about 7% of the other expenses returned; in 1970 they amounted to 5%.

that the share of printing in the total outlay only rose from 71% in 1966 to 75% in 1970. Most Conservatives were not short of funds (some made a profit on their election appeal) but they spent on average only 79% of the permitted maximum (as against 89% in 1966 and 92% in 1964). Financial stringencies may possibly have had more to do with Labour's spending only 68% (as against 84% in 1966 and 87% in 1964), and even more with Liberals spending only 41% (as against 56% in 1966 and 66% in 1964).

It is true that the parties spent near to the hilt in marginal seats. In the 50 most marginal Labour-held seats the Conservatives spent 91% of the maximum and Labour 88%. The Liberals in their 25 best seats spent 90%. But it would be hard to show any correlation between expenditure and success. Once again the Conservatives retained Heston and Isleworth, hardly a safe seat, on £488, only 45% of the legal maximum. Labour held Dagenham on £229 (24%), the lowest expenditure by any Labour candidate outside Northern Ireland.

*Late swing*

> 'In our view we "peaked" a week before Polling Day and there are many election agents and candidates who hold the view that had Polling Day been held on June 11 the result would have been in our favour.'

So wrote the National Agent of the Labour party in a report to NEC immediately after the election.

In the days before the poll very few of the agents or candidates to whom we spoke expressed this feeling. Most of the Conservatives remained defiantly puzzled by the opinion polls throughout, and almost everyone in the Labour party was calmly confident. The concern expressed by a Labour regional organiser at the end of the first week in June was exceptional:

> 'Things are going too easily. I'm worried about turnout. You can't *feel* anything. I wish I could see a real response.'

With the wisdom of hindsight just about half the candidates — both Conservative and Labour — whom we questioned claimed to have had some inkling of a last-minute swing against Labour. The other half were equally divided between those who shrugged their shoulders ruefully at their own lack of perception and those who denied that any such swing had taken place. Very little hard evidence was adduced though some Conservatives referred to the unexpected number of 'doubtfuls' coming down on their side in the last few days' canvassing. In so far as candidates had an explanation, they mostly put it down to the impact of the trade figures and the devaluation scare. But one or two others followed the Labour M.P. who blamed

> 'the damned germ in Gordon Banks' tummy [the England goalkeeper could not play in the June 14 World Cup match] that punctured the mood of euphoria'.

Agents were more sceptical than candidates about late swing. Almost a third of them claimed to have detected it, including all of the few who specifically mentioned doing extensive re-canvassing during the last week. The majority of the Conservatives denied that there had been any late movement of opinion on the ground that they had been winning all along. On the Labour side, too, defeat clearly came as a shock to most agents. According to an election day report from a Labour regional office:

> 'The regional organiser phoned all the constituencies within the region, sometimes more than once, and the air of optimism was widespread. All agents thought there would be a high poll. Nearly all commented on the wonderful weather. In short everyone appeared to be very happy with the situation. The optimistic picture was confirmed when [an official] of Transport House rang up to ask how things were going. . . . The regional organiser told him that high turnouts were reported, that there were no complaints and that everything seemed fine. [The Transport House official] said that these impressions were identical to those of 4 or 5 regions he had telephoned.'

### *Organisation and the result*

If we look at the 20 narrowest Conservative victories, those seats which made the difference between a majority of 30 and a minority of 10, we can see how far there is *prima facie* evidence for the election having been won by organisation. The Conservatives were treating 8 of the 20 as 'critical' seats. The Labour party was applying the National Agency Scheme in 4 of them, while 7 were among the 138 seats claiming over 1,000 Labour members. In 6 of them the postal vote alone certainly decided the issue for the Conservatives, and possibly in 8 of them. In almost all the others (which would all have been retained by Labour with a 1·0% smaller swing to the Conservatives) their superior organisation of the postal vote

M

gave a distinct advantage to the Conservatives. The question is whether this, combined with the Conservative advantages in canvassing and publicity, was responsible for the vital last 1·0% of swing.

But we have no real means of telling, except perhaps with the postal vote, how much should be allowed to such forces on polling day. If Labour workers had been less lulled by the polls, their extra efforts on June 18 might have saved Ipswich (majority 13), King's Lynn (33), Brighouse and Spenborough (54) and perhaps even Leicester South-west (106) and Yardley (120). It is hard to see how they could have switched the result in the next seat on the list, Middlesbrough West (338). As the next chapter and Appendix II show, there is no evidence in the voting figures that the Conservatives fared better where they put in special efforts, yet the margin of victory was so small that we cannot exclude the possibility that in 1970 organisation did tilt the balance.

CHAPTER XIV

# THE OUTCOME

POLLING day was fine everywhere and voting passed off without any serious incident. The ORC forecast of a 1% Conservative lead which appeared in the evening papers did not seriously disturb the betting odds and when the polling stations closed at 10 p.m. a Labour victory was expected by virtually everyone on the government side and by most leading Conservatives.[1] At 10.30 p.m. it became known that a survey of voters emerging from the booths in the arch-typical constituency of Gravesend[2] indicated a 4·4% swing to the Conservatives and at 11 p.m. the first result at Guildford showed a 6% swing; the next few results all showed a similar movement and when the two Wolverhampton constituencies each showed a 9% swing, it was plain, although no seats had yet changed hands, that the Conservatives would win the election.[3]

As the night wore on, the television cameras in Smith Square and around the country showed the parties reacting to the unexpected. Interviewed in the small hours Mr. Wilson refused to concede and Mr. Heath refrained from claiming victory — though the story was in both their faces, and in the huge police escort that accompanied Mr. Heath on his 2 a.m. drive from Bexley to a triumphant reception in Smith Square. Because of the longer polling hours, only 430 constituencies were counted on the night (as against 462 in 1966) but at dawn Labour had a net loss of 42 seats. It was not until 2.15 in the afternoon that the 316th Conservative victory was announced although Mr. Wilson (who had driven down the M1 in the early hours of the morning) had admitted defeat in a graceful television interview from 10 Downing Street at midday.[4] As the Conservative majority became absolute,

[1] Some twenty million people stayed up for the results, 75% watching BBC and 20% ITV, while 5% were content with radio. (BBC Audience Research.)

[2] See p. 417.

[3] In fact the first six results all showed a swing that proved to be well above the final average figure. The mean swing at 11.40 p.m. was 6·2% and pointed towards a Conservative majority of 70 or more. It was not till after midnight that the forecasts of the BBC, ITN and the Press Association came down to near the final outcome.

[4] For viewers the sight that must have driven home most abruptly what had happened was the shot soon after lunchtime of a removal van drawn up outside 11 Downing St. and being filled with Mr. Jenkins' crates.

the television cameras were focused on the Queen driving down the course at Royal Ascot, but she later returned to Buckingham Palace to accept Mr. Wilson's resignation at 6.30 p.m. and at 6.50 p.m. she asked Mr. Heath to form a government.

The Conservatives made a net gain of 66 seats and in all 88 constituencies changed hands — records by any post-war standards[1] (although in 10 of the 11 general elections from 1906 to 1945 over 100 constituencies switched sides). The Conservatives won 330 seats, a clear majority of 30 over all parties and ample enough to govern with and probably just adequate to withstand the worst that by-elections could do during a five-year parliament.

One of the most striking features of the results was their nationwide uniformity. As the table on pp. 356–7 shows, every region of the country showed a swing to the Conservatives within 2% of the national average for Britain (4·8%). The movement was lowest in Merseyside, Rural Wales, Humberside, Tyneside and most of Scotland; it was largest in the Black Country and Leicester. But the really big deviations from the norm that had been forecast, on the one side for Scotland and on the other for the West Midlands, did not occur.[2]

There were, however, some constituencies that had startling results. The biggest swing, 11%, toppled Jennie Lee from her safe seat at Cannock and two Labour seats in Bolton went to the Conservatives on 9% and 8% swings. Mr. Diamond at Gloucester was the only cabinet minister to go down to defeat but George Brown at Belper and Sir Dingle Foot at Ipswich were also among the casualties. In all 11 members of the government lost their seats, including both Dr. and Mrs. Dunwoody, the first married couple to hold office simultaneously. The Conservatives surrendered six of their twelve by-election gains and in Northern Ireland they lost North Antrim to Mr. Paisley's Protestant Unionism and Fermanagh and South Tyrone to the Catholic 'Unity' nominee;

[1] In post-war parliaments up to 1966 no government ever lost more than 5 seats net in by-elections. But between 1966 and 1970 Labour lost 15 seats at by-elections and one by floor-crossing, and its clear majority slumped from 96 to 64; however, if the majority had been narrower some of the by-elections caused by government appointments would doubtless have been avoided.

[2] Over the longer run the picture is less uniform. 1970 confirmed the continuing change of political balance between the cities and the rest of the country. Of the 20 seats that Labour held on to in 1970 though they had never won them in the 1950s, 15 were in London or other big cities. Of the 18 seats that the Conservatives won for the first time since 1945, none was in London and one (Leicester, South-west) was in a big city.

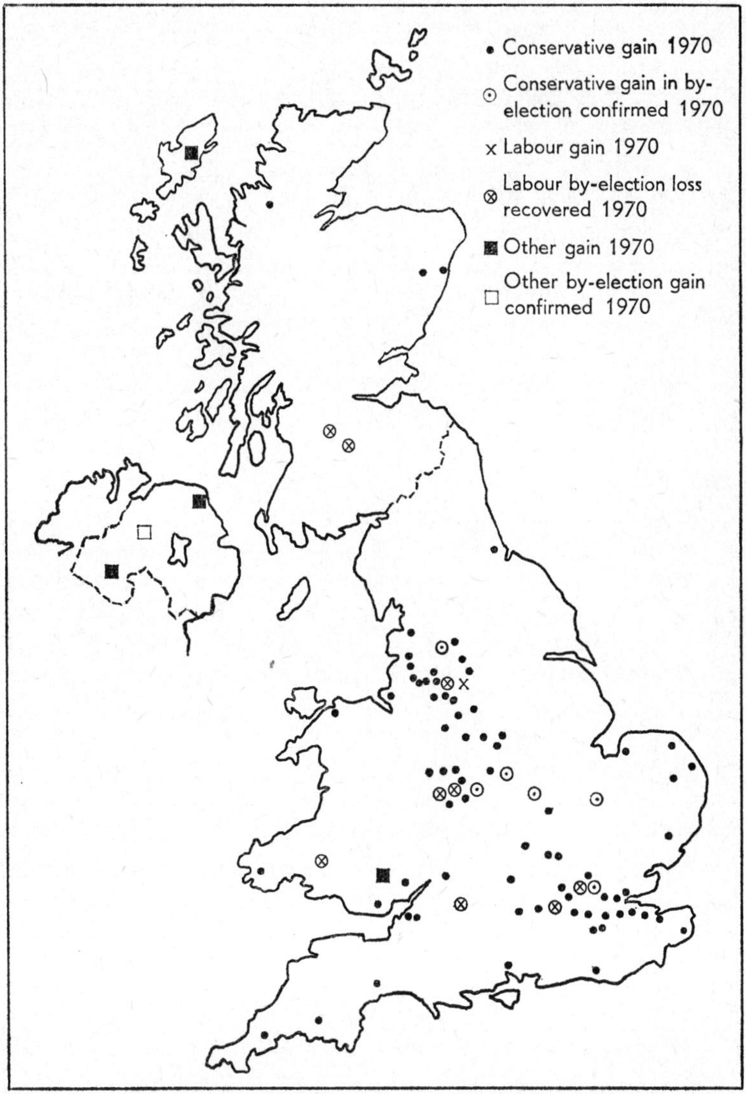


Seats Changing Hands 1966–70

they also failed to win back Mid-Ulster from Miss Devlin. The Liberals lost seven of their thirteen M.P.s and, for the first time, had not a single seat outside the West Country, Wales and Scotland. Jeremy Thorpe's margin of only 366 votes in North Devon justified his concentration on his own constituency during the campaign. Of the other Liberals only Jo Grimond in Orkney and Shetland and Emlyn Hooson in Montgomery had comfortable majorities.

The Liberal vote was down almost everywhere — the average fell from 16·1% in 1966 to 13·5%. But their débâcle was not quite as complete as some have suggested. Their vote per candidate was as high as in 1951 or 1955 and they were fighting on three times as broad a front; moreover their six members in 1970 all won in three-cornered fights, whereas in 1951 and 1955, five of their six members were elected without Conservative opposition. But their importance was less because both the big parties assumed that the presence or absence of Liberal candidates would make little net difference to the outcome — and an analysis of the vote confirms that this assumption was largely vindicated.

On the whole, the nationalists in Wales and Scotland had a very disappointing time. For Plaid Cymru Gwynfor Evans lost Carmarthen and though the party achieved comfortable second places in Merioneth, Caernarvon, Rhondda East, Aberdare and Caerphilly 25 of its 36 candidates lost their deposits. For the Scottish National party Mrs. Ewing lost Hamilton and the party fared very poorly throughout industrial Scotland getting no second places except in Hamilton and West Lothian. It polled strongly only in the North-east and the Highlands, where it cut heavily into the Liberal vote, coming second in seven seats and actually winning that very exceptional constituency, the Western Isles, from Labour.[1]

Fringe parties and independents did very badly. The 58 Communists averaged 1·2% of the vote (their lowest ever) and none rose above 5·8%. The ten National Front candidates averaged 3·6%. Apart from Nationalists and Paisleyites, the only ones outside the three large parties who saved their deposits were the Speaker and one of his opponents, Mr. Donnelly in Pembroke, and the 83-year-old S. O. Davies whose easy victory in Merthyr

[1] In seats where comparisons with 1966 could be made the Plaid Cymru vote was up by 7·5%. In Scotland the SNP made no net improvement in seats they had fought in 1966. Both nationalist parties made their most solid advance in the remoter rural areas. See pp. 401–4.

made him the first M.P. since 1945 to be re-elected after being denied his party's label.

The impact of Mr. Powell himself or of a Powellite appeal by individual candidates is hard to assess. Conservatives were inclined to blame a backlash against Mr. Powell by Irish, as well as by coloured and Liberal voters, for their failure to make some expected gains, for example in Brentford and Chiswick, Ealing North and Eton and Slough. Certainly there is evidence that the turnout of coloured voters was much higher than in previous contests.[1] In the West Midlands the very high swings in Wolverhampton and some nearby constituencies could be taken as proof that Mr. Powell pulled in votes for the Conservatives in his home territory, except that other seats — for example Smethwick, the Wrekin, All Saints, and Selly Oak — showed lower than average swings. The median swing in the 30 seats identified by Deakin and Bourne as having candidates who had spoken in favour of Mr. Powell's views on immigration was 5·0%, only 0·2% more than the national average; since they tended to concentrate in areas which gave all Conservatives a slightly above average swing, no significance can be attached to the difference.

However, if Powellites did not fare especially well, coloured candidates did fare especially badly. The lowest two Liberal votes in the country went to two of their three Asian candidates while Dr. Pitt, a respected West Indian doctor, and a GLC councillor, suffered a 10·8% swing against him when he tried in vain to hold Clapham for Labour. Neither he nor his opponents had raised the question of his colour in the campaign but, despite the rows over the returning Labour M.P., Mrs. McKay (see p. 295), it must have played a major part in producing a swing vastly greater than any other in the London area.

Only 72% of the electorate registered their votes — the smallest turnout for 35 years (only 1918, 1922, 1923 and 1935 offer a lower record of participation). The vote dropped by almost 20% in the Potteries, where there was a Wakes Week, but holidays everywhere seem to have taken their toll. In fact, if allowance is made for the

[1] See Nicholas Deakin and Jenny Bourne, 'Powell, the Minorities and the 1970 Election', *Political Quarterly*, Oct.–Dec. 1970, pp. 399–415, for a full gathering of the limited evidence there is on the complex problem of the net effect of the immigration issue. For some interesting if more tendentious evidence see *Powell and the Election*, ed. John Wood. See also Appendix II, pp. 406–8.

fact that the register was three months older than in 1966 and that 3% or 4% more people must be on holiday in June than in March, it may well be that the apparent fall in turnout of 3·8% did not really reflect any reduction in interest compared to 1966. But by the standards of 1950 and 1951 when the turnout was 10% to 12% higher there has been a real decline.

There was one special and perhaps startling feature in the uniformity of the results. Marginal seats behaved just like other seats. The swing was no greater and no less. It is not of course possible to say how far the activities of the parties were mutually cancelling but the results do not show any obvious return to the Conservatives for all their efforts on the critical seats. The mean swing in the 68 'criticals' they singled out for special treatment was 4·1% as against the nationwide figure of 4·7% If we consider the constituencies that in 1966 ranked from 61st to 90th in marginality the swing in the 14 seats that were in the 'critical' list was 4·2%; the swing in the 16 seats that were not was 5·8%.[1] Labour failed in 16 of the 75 seats that would go Conservative on a 4·8% swing from 1966 and succeeded in 14 (to set against the loss of 15 seats that needed a swing of more than 4·8%).

Despite the magnitude of the swing and the new volatility of the electorate shown in the previous years, the parties drew their support from the various sections of the community in broadly the

*NOP Profile of the Electorate, 1970* (%)

| | All | Men | Women | 18–24 | 25–34 | 35–44 | 45–54 | 55–64 | 65+ |
|---|---|---|---|---|---|---|---|---|---|
| Con. | 46·2 | 42·2 | 49·9 | 42·3 | 41·0 | 46·1 | 43·3 | 47·5 | 56·2 |
| Lab. | 43·8 | 47·3 | 40·6 | 47·2 | 45·8 | 40·6 | 49·1 | 43·7 | 37·1 |
| Lib. | 7·6 | 7·3 | 7·8 | 8·4 | 8·4 | 11·3 | 5·2 | 7·6 | 5·1 |
| Other | 2·4 | 3·2 | 1·7 | 2·1 | 4·8 | 2·0 | 2·4 | 1·2 | 1·6 |
| Swing from 1966 | 4·9 | 4·8 | 5·0 | (0·0) | 6·4 | 9·4 | −0·3 | 1·4 | 6·5 |

| | All | AB | C1 | C2 | DE |
|---|---|---|---|---|---|
| Con. | 46·2 | 79·1 | 59·2 | 34·6 | 33·2 |
| Lab. | 43·8 | 10·4 | 30·5 | 55·4 | 57·3 |
| Lib. | 7·6 | 9·5 | 8·8 | 7·0 | 6·4 |
| Other | 2·4 | 1·0 | 1·5 | 3·0 | 3·1 |
| Swing from 1966 | 4·9 | 6·0 | −0·1 | 2·7 | 7·4 |

[1] Of these 14 critical seats the Conservatives won only 4; of the 16 not on the critical list the Conservatives won 10. The relatively low swing in critical seats may be explained in part by the personal vote which seems to accrue to MPs at the end of their first term in parliament. See p. 404.

same proportions as before. There is no evidence of an especial turnover among target voters any more than in critical seats. An adjusted breakdown of NOP final figures gives a profile of the electorate; the size of sample must limit overmuch reliance on any single figure (there are only about 300 voters in any one age group) and, indeed, if the figures for 1966 are compared with the NOP surveys of May and early June, many of the apparent swings would be still more uniform. The main moral of the table is that the pattern of party support has not been transformed: the old were more Conservative than the young, although the contrasts between age groups were less than many have supposed. Women were more Conservative than men, but by the same amount as in 1966; the middle class were still overwhelmingly Conservative and the working class comfortably Labour.

The amount of wobbling by the electorate may have been without precedent but no startling changes of alignment seem to have underlain their final distribution of support.

The press reaction to the outcome was, above all, one of apologetic plaudits for Mr. Heath, whose qualities the leader-writers suddenly saw in a new light. Their praise for him was mingled with a good deal of self-reproach at being deceived by the polls. As the *Guardian* summed it up:

> 'Mr. Heath's victory is his own. It is a triumph over the opinion polls, over a sceptical press and doubting colleagues, and over Mr. Wilson. It is a personal success achieved by perseverance and determination when the tide seemed against him.'

The popular papers echoed the same theme

> 'Welcome to Mr. Edward Heath. . . . Let there be no mistake, the Tory victory was attained by the Prime Minister's own guts and leadership.' (*Daily Express*)

> 'Well done, Ted Heath. The British love to see an outsider come surging up to pass the favourite. . . . They made it a Heathwave election.' (*Sun*)

> 'The *Mirror* described Harold Wilson and Ted Heath as the Sorcerer and the Sorcerer's Apprentice. . . . On polling day the Nation chose the Sorcerer's Apprentice. . . . Mr. Heath won a man-sized victory. Now he takes on a man-sized job.' (*Daily Mirror*)

> 'This is an exhilarating moment. Britain is alive again. The people have chosen a new Government and a new direction.
>
> Ted Heath's victory is the most thrilling political comeback in memory.

The pundits said his plain speaking would never win. They said that honesty was not enough. They said he needed a gimmick or a wife.

Where are those pundits now? Their reputations are buried under the tattered waste paper of the opinion polls.' (*Daily Mail*)

The *Economist* concluded:

'Only one man has really won this election and that man is Mr. Heath. . . . He did not lose his nerve in the campaign, even when all seemed lost. . . . All parties are alliances, and in the end it was Mr. Heath who held his unruly, strained and unconfident Conservative alliance together. No one did it for him. . . . [In 1967–9] it was neither the Conservative party nor Mr. Heath who was primarily responsible for anything; it was Mr. Wilson and the Labour party who were throwing their victory in 1966 down the drain. So when . . . Mr. Wilson and Mr. Jenkins allowed the wages boom to get under way, the Tory lead in the polls melted in the sun. Mr. Heath was going to be the Tories' scapegoat for that. . . . He is now entirely and for the first time his own man.'

The *Daily Telegraph* was less rapturous

'So the apparently impossible has happened. . . . In the event the electors preferred, in this most "Presidential" of campaigns, Mr. Heath's restless energy, his urge for change, his warnings of dangers ahead to Mr. Wilson's low-keyed complacency. . . . Now the qualities, or as many said the deficiencies, which were held so much against Mr. Heath in his Opposition days — his transparent honesty and courage, his unswerving dedication to politics as the supreme end, his frequent brusqueness and surprising lack of charisma — will be tried in a quite different office. . . .'

*The Times* underlined what the upset did for Mr. Heath:

'Achieving so big a victory against the odds puts Mr. Heath in a position of great stength. He has no personal obligations to anybody. He has relatively few commitments of policy and those are of his own choosing. . . . He will be a considerably more powerful Prime Minister . . . because he made his victory in such difficult circumstances. . . . Undoubtedly Mr. Wilson made a technical mistake. He fought a non-controversial campaign as the man in possession. . . . The result considered simply as a response to the election campaigns of the two parties is a healthy sign for democracy.'

Other papers echoed this verdict

'It would have been deeply depressing if Mr. Wilson had managed to retain power by blandly ignoring the issues and relying on the electors to sit back, enjoy the sunshine and vote for the party which the opinion pollsters tipped to win.' (*Financial Times*)

'Mr. Wilson fought the campaign on a fundamentally complacent ticket, hoping that his skill with the media and his basic political *savoir-faire* would carry a decidedly bad record past the voters when they were not looking.' (*Evening Standard*)

'A great effort has been made by [Mr. Wilson's] government . . . and it has put Britain on the road to recovery. Now the Conservatives will reap the harvest. . . . Mr. Wilson himself, however, is not blameless. His election campaign was too smug by half. . . . Would Labour, if re-elected, have been more adventurous? . . . We shall never know. . . . But the idealism and the crusading spirit which Labour somehow lost after 1964 will have to be recreated — and convincingly — if the Conservatives are not to have another 13-year term.' (*Guardian*)

The wryest note was left to the *Morning Star*.

'Jubilation among City of London speculators yesterday, and gloom among many working class people, sums up the meaning of the Tory victory at the General Election. . . . If a tombstone is to be erected to Mr. Wilson's Government, there should be inscribed on it the words: "Slain by their own hands".'

The press, like the politicians, was startled by the election result. Yet in the days that followed it did little to explain what had happened: the challenge of writing about the new government quickly and naturally swamped the question of how it had got there. In the continued sunshine, with the holidays approaching, the public settled down without much sign of curiosity, to await the slow discovery of whether their decision on June 18 would really make much difference to their lives.

* * *

'Don't forget to mention that we won.' Mr. Heath had every right to tease the various chroniclers of the election.[1] The Conservative victory was plucked from the jaws of defeat and the man who, almost alone, had maintained his confidence while the world had written him off could feel, like President Truman in 1948, an overwhelming sense of self-vindication.

But, despite all the drama of the result, it may be as pertinent to stress that Labour lost the election as that the Conservatives won it. The swing from government to opposition — 4·7% — was indeed the largest in a post-war election. But the government

[1] In a speech to the Conservative Agents' Dinner at Blackpool on October 6, 1970, he referred to that lively book, *The Making of the Prime Minister 1970*, by Andrew Alexander and Alan Watkins (who had had to send it to the printers five days after polling): 'They omitted to say that we won.'

recovery from a 20% deficit in the polls a year before was also without precedent; so was the defeat of a party that at the dissolution had been ahead in all the opinion polls. The outcome can be seen as the reluctant decision of just enough electors that the Conservatives were, marginally, the lesser of two evils. If this is a negative verdict there is much evidence to support it.

The unprecedented volatility of public opinion throughout the 1966 parliament as well as during the campaign argues a lack of conviction or enthusiasm among a substantial proportion of voters. Of those who abandoned Labour in the bad days of 1967 and 1968, many moved only to 'don't know' or to a minor party; among those who did switch to a Conservative voting intention a large proportion switched back again. Moreover, as the private polls showed, many of those who said they would vote Conservative retained their sense of identification with Labour.[1] The lack of enthusiasm was demonstrated in the lowest turnout since 1935 and in the relatively small proportion of people who 'cared very much' which party won (29% according to NOP). This was evident in the poll ratings of the leaders which over the previous two years had been jointly the lowest since such measures were started.[2] And it was shown in

[1] The Conservative panel survey (see pp. 191–2) found these figures:

| | | October 1967 +March 1968 | September 1968 | September 1969 |
|---|---|---|---|---|
| | | % | % | % |
| 'Generally speaking would you describe yourself as Conservative, Labour, Liberal or what?' | Con. | 40 | 38 | 40 |
| | Lab. | 43 | 44 | 42 |
| | Con. lead | −3 | −6 | −2 |
| 'If there were a general election tomorrow how would you vote?' | Con. | 44 | 41 | 45 |
| | Lab. | 32 | 33 | 32 |
| | | +12 | +8 | +13 |

This sort of discrepancy between party identification and voting intention, though long familiar enough in the United States, is a new phenomenon in Britain. There was almost no trace of it in the panel surveys between 1963 and 1966 reported in *Political Change in Britain*.

[2] In, for example, January 1968, the sum of the proportions thinking each party leader handled his job well was, according to Gallup, 65 (Mr. Wilson 33%, Mr. Heath 32%). An index constructed on this basis for the joint popularity of the Prime Minister and the Leader of the Opposition yields the following picture

| | | | |
|---|---|---|---|
| 1960 | 114 | 1965 | 98 |
| 1961 | 103 | 1966 | 94 |
| 1962 | 97 | 1967 | 78 |
| 1963 | 98 | 1968 | 62 |
| 1964 | 105 | 1969 | 67 |

their speeches. 75% of Mr. Wilson's press handouts and 70% of Mr. Heath's consisted of attacks on the other side. Only a twentieth of Mr. Wilson's handouts and a tenth of Mr. Heath's concerned their plans for the future.[1]

Moreover, if there was a critical swing back to the Conservatives in the last four days (and the evidence for this is set out in Chapter VIII), it could only have occurred when a significant proportion of the electorate was in a hesitant and unconvinced mood. If one month's trade figures could create a scare jumbo-sized enough to frighten a million voters away from Labour (even with the aid of a Conservative advantage in last television exchanges and, more obviously, of a powerful speech from Mr. Powell), they were certainly in a fickle and sceptical mood.[2]

However, our argument here does not depend upon accepting that there was a late swing. Even if we were to agree with those who say that the Conservatives were winning all along, we would still have to explain how the voters swung by 5% between the county elections in April and the borough elections in May and how they developed an unprecedented capriciousness in deceiving the poll-sters all through May and early June.

Whether or not there was a late swing to the Conservatives is an interesting sub-argument in any discussion of the 1970 election. But the verdict upon it is much less important than the situation which it highlights: the generally unenthusiastic attitude to the parties shown by the British public as it suffered the economic uncertainties and the post-imperial malaise of the late 1960s. Although the 1970 election gave power to the Conservatives with a workable majority, it was scarcely a resounding victory. The party won only 14 seats more than the minimum needed to form a government — and there were 14 constituencies where less than 750 votes separated their candidates from defeat. Success at this level is almost like scraping through to a football title on goal

[1] See pp. 442–5.

[2] It is ironic that the monthly figures which the public learnt to focus upon were themselves suspect. In 1969 (see *Board of Trade Journal*, September 10, 1969) it was revealed that the export figures had for some years been under-stated by about £12 million per month. The corrective steps that were then taken seem to have been inadequate. On November 16, 1970, it was announced that the monthly export figures still fell 2% short of the actual total, i.e. something like £15 million a month. On this basis the famous £31 million deficit an-nounced on June 15, three days before the poll, may well have been only £16 million or even allowing for the £18·5 million spent on Jumbo-jets, a surplus of £2 million.

average: the title is there and all the rewards that go with it — but it is gained so fortuitously that what demands explanation is why the two teams were so equal. In the days before June 18 responsible people at the top of the Conservative party, facing the probability of defeat, had had consultations on how to manage a smooth transfer to a new leader. The fact that these plans never had to be given effect does not mean that there was no justification for making them. They came very near to being needed. When an election result is narrow, there is always the danger of over-explanation. That otherwise admirable book *The Making of the President 1960* offers a warning: Theodore White presents the reasons for President Kennedy's victory so compellingly that it is hard to understand how the Republicans came within a hairsbreadth of winning.

When an election has a narrow result, it is particularly easy to focus too much attention on the central figures and the last days of the campaign. But the outcome is of course decided cumulatively at different times and at different levels. In the structure of this book we have distinguished between the pre-campaign and campaign periods and between the national and the local battles. But the separation should not be too complete. It is true that the Conservatives entered the election behind and ended ahead, thus providing the first occasion for a long time in which the outcome was probably decided by the campaign; it is also true that the Conservatives' organisational superiority may well account for at least those last 15 victories that saved them from defeat. But the campaign was decisive only because the battles of the previous four years had left so evenly balanced a legacy and local organisation was important only because the national struggle was such a close-run thing.

What thus emerges as the key to the story is the impact on the electorate of Labour's poor record, coupled perhaps with the lack of impact of the Conservative response. In the end Labour's record proved a marginally greater handicap than the muffled alternatives presented by the Conservatives. Dr. Wilson, for all his reassuring skills, had not quite succeeded in healing the scar tissue over the wounds of 1966 to 1969; but there was little enthusiasm about the last-minute switch to a new physician. Yet to say even that may be to present the election too much in personal terms. Admittedly, the coverage of the campaign did concentrate more exclusively on the two party leaders than in any previous contest, and there is no doubt that to an exceptional degree Mr. Wilson and Mr. Heath took personal charge of their parties' efforts. Their ascendancy was all the more remarkable in view of how low they personally had stood in the polls. Yet we would not accept the easy clichés about the 'presidentialisation' of British elections. In the poll data and in the observations made to us in the constituencies we find little evidence that the conduct or personalities of the two leaders were of exceptional importance in shaping votes. Nor, despite all the attention paid to that unattractive work *The Selling of the President*,[1] and despite the innovations in personality presentation — Mr. Wilson's walkabouts and the commercial that introduced Mr. Heath's final television appeal —, do we feel that a fundamental change had come over British electioneering.

Although in these pages we have focused on the specific events and forces that seemed relevant to specific decision on June 18, we do also see the election and what led up to it as part of a wider problem about the evolution of British government and politics. When, rightly or wrongly, the parties are less and less seen as disagreeing over fundamentals, it may be natural for voting loyalties and support for party leaders to decline in intensity. These tendencies have been discussed in previous Nuffield election studies. What the 1970 election did was to highlight trends which had been gathering strength over the years. The mounting importance of economic conditions was especially evident. C. A. E. Goodhart and R. J. Bhansali have demonstrated a remarkable correlation between changes in the economy and swings in the Gallup poll over the 1950s and early 1960s. This seems to have continued in the late 1960s.[2] H. A. Turner and D. A. S. Jackson have argued persuasively that in pre-election periods since the war there have consistently been sharp increases in the levels of wage increase: in pre-election periods hourly earnings have increased by 7·4% compared with an average of only 5·8% in other years.[3] With-

[1] Joe McGinniss, *The Selling of The President* (André Deutsch, 1970).

[2] See C. A. E. Goodhart and R. J. Bhansali, 'Political Economy', (*Political Studies*, March 1970). A note of caution is necessary. The earlier finding that movements in the polls corresponded most closely to changes in unemployment was contradicted in the late 1960s. The Labour recovery took place amid high unemployment. However, other economic indicators, possibly more relevant to the conditions of the late 1960s (such as real disposable income), continue to reveal a close correlation. See S. Brittan, *Steering the Economy* (Penguin, 1971), p. 409 and also his article 'The Political Parties, the Classes and the Economy', *Financial Times*, May 14, 1970.

[3] In 'Wage Inflation and the Election Cycle', *The Times*, March 24, 1970.

out adopting either the econometric determinism inherent in some of this sort of argument, or a totally cynical view of the 'stop–go' management of affairs by the politicians, one can still see the British elector as regularly swayed by attempts to time the increases in his real disposable income. The more volatile his voting support, the greater the reward for the government which can boost incomes and then hold an election before prices show the inevitable spiral. In 1970 the managers of the economy created a brief moment of opportunity like a 'window in space' for a moonshot, when a sense of growing well-being had not been overtaken by shopping-basket anxieties. It is arguable that that 'window' was still open on June 11 but closed by June 18.

Style matters as well as substance on economic and social policy. There is strong evidence, some of it set out in our early chapters, that the leaderships of both parties were very aware of the limits to what would be acceptable to the 'middle mass' of the electorate. This led them to eschew policies which might alienate moderate opinion; they could not, despite all the talk of harsh choices and facing up to unpopularity, take stands that seriously jeopardised short-term well-being for the sake of long-term gain. Quite apart from his stand on immigration, Mr. Powell stood out as the one articulate politician to attempt a breakaway from the sane colourlessness that had characterised the consensus politics of the sixties.

In some degree the two party dog-fight, confined to its relatively narrow areas of conflict by the exigencies of electoral strategy, frustrates clear discussion of central issues.[1] Such major questions as entry into the Common Market, or devaluation, do not fit neatly into the conventional divisions of right and left. They involve problems which, for the most part, can be discussed without deep ideological cleavages. The reason why this was not done more successfully seems to lie as much with the quality of the politicians involved as with the nature of consensus politics itself. For example, Mr. Heath and his colleagues could surely have made more headway before the election in interesting voters in the technical alternatives that they ought to offer. If other Labour ministers had given their minds to it, Mr. Crossman and Mr. Wedgwood Benn would not have stood out so sharply in their efforts to involve people in new ideas about the social services and industry.

[1] Similar views are put forward in Samuel Brittan's stimulating book *Left or Right: the bogus dilemma* (Secker and Warburg, 1968).

But the outsider should hesitate to preach at the politicians, who are after all circumscribed by what their audience will accept. The electorate did seem to see politics increasingly in material, bread-and-butter terms; since their votes so patently reacted to short-term economic benefits, they tempted politicians to focus so heavily upon them. Indeed, though it may have been misguided to place such overwhelming emphasis on getting the balance of payments right, it was perhaps a triumph of political education that the Labour government made such an abstract concept so electorally important. But if it was an abstraction it was still a specifically economic one, not a political or a moral one. In the end the election never seemed to rise above the level the politicians and the public had set each other. But this may have been not only because of scepticism about the politicians' ability to deliver, but also because of creeping doubts about the country's ability to live by bread alone, that the affair proved to such an extent to be 'an unpopularity contest'.

APPENDIX I

# STATISTICS

## The National Results, 1945–70

| | Electorate and turnout | Votes cast | Conservative | Labour | Liberal | Nationalist † | Communist | Others |
|---|---|---|---|---|---|---|---|---|
| 1945 * | 73·3%<br>32,836,419 | 100%<br>24,082,612 | 39·8%<br>9,577,667 | 48·3%<br>11,632,891 | 9·1%<br>2,197,191 | 0·6%<br>138,415 | 0·4%<br>102,760 | 1·8%<br>433,688 |
| 1950 | 84·0%<br>34,269,770 | 100%<br>28,772,671 | 43·5%<br>12,502,567 | 46·1%<br>13,266,592 | 9·1%<br>2,621,548 | 0·6%<br>173,161 | 0·3%<br>91,746 | 0·4%<br>117,057 |
| 1951 | 82·5%<br>34,645,573 | 100%<br>28,595,668 | 48·0%<br>13,717,538 | 48·8%<br>13,948,605 | 2·5%<br>730,556 | 0·5%<br>145,521 | 0·1%<br>21,640 | 0·1%<br>31,808 |
| 1955 | 76·8%<br>34,858,263 | 100%<br>26,760,493 | 49·7%<br>13,311,936 | 46·4%<br>12,404,970 | 2·7%<br>722,405 | 0·9%<br>225,591 | 0·1%<br>33,144 | 0·2%<br>62,447 |
| 1959 | 78·7%<br>35,397,080 | 100%<br>27,859,241 | 49·4%<br>13,749,830 | 43·8%<br>12,215,538 | 5·9%<br>1,638,571 | 0·6%<br>182,788 | 0·1%<br>30,897 | 0·2%<br>61,619 |
| 1964 | 77·1%<br>35,892,572 | 100%<br>27,655,374 | 43·4%<br>12,001,396 | 44·1%<br>12,205,814 | 11·2%<br>3,092,878 | 0·9%<br>249,866 | 0·2%<br>45,932 | 0·2%<br>53,116 |
| 1966 | 75·8%<br>35,964,684 | 100%<br>27,263,606 | 41·9%<br>11,418,433 | 47·9%<br>13,064,951 | 8·5%<br>2,327,533 | 1·2%<br>315,431 | 0·2%<br>62,112 | 0·3%<br>75,146 |
| 1970 | 72·0%<br>39,342,013 | 100%<br>28,344,798 | 46·4%<br>13,145,123 | 43·0%<br>12,178,295 | 7·5%<br>2,117,033 | 2·4%<br>672,356 | 0·1%<br>37,970 | 0·7%<br>196,019 |

* University seats are excluded: other 1945 figures are adjusted to eliminate the distortions introduced by double voting in the 15 two-member seats then existing.

† Including all types of Irish Nationalist.

## The House of Commons, 1945–1970

| | 1945 | 1950 | 1951 | 1955 | 1959 | 1964 | 1966 | 1970 |
|---|---|---|---|---|---|---|---|---|
| Conservative | 213 | 298 | 321 | 345 | 365 | 304 | 253 | 330 |
| Labour . | 393 | 315 | 295 | 277 | 258 | 317 | 363 | 287 |
| Liberal . | 12 | 9 | 6 | 6 | 6 | 9 | 12 | 6 |
| Others . | 22 | 3 | 3 | 2 | 1 | 0 | 2 | 7 |
| Total . | 640 | 625 | 625 | 630 | 630 | 630 | 630 | 630 |

# REGIONAL RESULTS

The tables on the following pages are based on the Standard Regions and the Conurbations, as currently defined by the General Register Office.

*South-East* includes Hants., Berks., Oxon., Beds., Herts., Essex, Surrey, Sussex, Kent and Greater London.
*South-West* includes Dorset, Devon, Cornwall, Somerset, Glos. and Wilts.
*East Anglia* includes Norfolk, Suffolk, Cambs., Ely, Hunts. and the Peterborough constituency.
*East Midlands* includes Lincs. (less Lindsey), Notts., Leics., Northants. (less the Peterborough constituency) and Derbys. (less the High Peak constituency).
*West Midlands* includes Hereford, Worcs., Warwicks., Staffs. and Salop.
*Yorkshire* includes the East and West Ridings, the York constituency and Lindsey.
*North-West* includes Cheshire, Lancs. and the High Peak constituency.
*North* includes the North Riding, Durham, Northumberland, Westmorland and Cumberland.

The sub-regions are largely self-explanatory. When a city or conurbation crosses the boundary of a constituency, the constituency is included if more than half its population lies within the area concerned, e.g. London includes East Surrey and Carshalton but not Epping or Chigwell. Teesside includes Cleveland. The West Midlands conurbation includes Brierley Hill but not Cannock. The Clydeside conurbation includes Hamilton but not West Dunbartonshire.

*Industrial Wales* includes Glamorgan, Monmouthshire and the Llanelli constituency.
*Industrial Scotland* includes all of Ayrshire, Bute, Renfrewshire, Dunbartonshire, Lanarkshire, Stirlingshire, Clackmannan, Midlothian, West Lothian and Fife (except for the East Fife constituency).

The small figures above the percentages indicate the number of seats in which candidates fought, except where they fought all seats. The Conservatives fought every seat except Southampton (Itchen) and Greenock. Labour fought every seat except Southampton (Itchen) and 5 of the 12 seats in Northern Ireland.

| | Seats<br>Con. | <br>Lab. | <br>Other | %<br>voting | Change in %<br>voting<br>1966–70 | Con.<br>% | Lab.<br>% | Lib.<br>% | Other<br>% | Swing<br>1966–<br>70 | Swing<br>1955–<br>70 |
|---|---|---|---|---|---|---|---|---|---|---|---|
| ENGLAND | 292 | 216 | 3 | 71·3 | −4·6 | 510<br>48·4 | 510<br>43·3 | 282<br>13·6 | 88<br>3·5 | 5·1 | 0·8 |
| WALES | 7 | 27 | 2 | 77·4 | −1·6 | 27·7 | 51·6 | 19<br>12·7 | 13·9 | 4·5 | 1·9 |
| SCOTLAND | 23 | 44 | 4 | 74·0 | −1·9 | 70<br>38·5 | 44·5 | 27<br>14·6 | 68<br>12·2 | 2·9 | −5·0 |
| GREAT BRITAIN | 322 | 287 | 9 | 71·9 | −4·2 | 616<br>46·3 | 617<br>43·9 | 328<br>13·7 | 192<br>8·5 | 4·8 | 0·3 |
| NORTHERN IRELAND | 8 | — | 4 | 76·6 | +10·6 | 54·2 | 7<br>21·9 | 4<br>3·9 | 10<br>35·5 | — | — |
| UNITED KINGDOM | 330 | 287 | 13 | 72·0 | −3·8 | 628<br>46·5 | 624<br>43·5 | 332<br>13·5 | 202<br>10·8 | 4·7 | 0·1 |
| SOUTH-EAST REGION | 127 | 60 | 1 | 69·4 | −5·9 | 187<br>51·0 | 187<br>38·8 | 128<br>13·0 | 42<br>4·9 | 5·2 | 1·1 |
| Inner London | 9 | 33 | — | 58·4 | −6·5 | 42·4 | 53·2 | 17<br>7·9 | 15<br>3·0 | 4·5 | −1·3 |
| Outer London | 39 | 22 | — | 68·1 | −8·1 | 49·1 | 41·4 | 42<br>12·5 | 15<br>2·0 | 4·3 | −0·3 |
| Rest of Region | 79 | 5 | 1 | 73·4 | −5·0 | 84<br>54·1 | 84<br>34·0 | 69<br>13·8 | 12<br>9·0 | 5·1 | 0·5 |
| SOUTH-WEST REGION | 35 | 6 | 2 | 76·2 | −3·8 | 51·1 | 34·3 | 35<br>17·8 | 5<br>1·1 | 5·0 | 2·2 |
| Devon and Cornwall | 12 | 1 | 2 | 77·2 | −3·6 | 51·3 | 27·9 | 13<br>24·0 | 2<br>1·2 | 4·5 | 1·6 |
| Rest of Region | 23 | 5 | — | 75·7 | −3·8 | 51·1 | 37·5 | 22<br>14·4 | 3<br>1·1 | 5·3 | 2·9 |
| EAST ANGLIA REGION | 17 | 1 | — | 76·4 | −3·7 | 53·0 | 40·9 | 10<br>9·8 | 2<br>3·2 | 5·5 | 3·6 |
| EAST MIDLANDS REGION | 16 | 19 | — | 73·9 | −3·6 | 47·4 | 48·5 | 12<br>9·6 | 6<br>3·7 | 5·9 | 2·8 |
| WEST MIDLANDS REGION | 30 | 24 | — | 69·7 | −5·1 | 50·5 | 45·0 | 20<br>12·3 | 12<br>1·8 | 5·8 | 2·9 |
| Conurbation | 12 | 15 | — | 67·9 | −3·9 | 50·7 | 46·1 | 8<br>10·8 | 8<br>2·0 | 6·1 | 4·0 |
| Rest of Region | 18 | 9 | — | 71·2 | −6·4 | 50·4 | 44·0 | 12<br>13·0 | 4<br>1·4 | 5·6 | 1·7 |
| YORKSHIRE REGION | 19 | 36 | — | 71·6 | −4·0 | 40·3 | 52·0 | 28<br>13·3 | 10<br>1·9 | 4·6 | −0·5 |
| Conurbation | 7 | 16 | — | 73·0 | −3·5 | 41·6 | 48·9 | 16<br>13·3 | 5<br>1·7 | 4·8 | 0·2 |
| Rest of Region | 12 | 20 | — | 70·5 | −4·4 | 40·7 | 52·3 | 16<br>13·6 | 5<br>2·1 | 4·4 | −1·2 |
| NORTH-WEST REGION | 38 | 41 | — | 71·7 | −2·8 | 46·6 | 45·7 | 35<br>15·0 | 10<br>3·0 | 5·0 | −2·3 |
| S.E. Lancashire Conurbation | 11 | 18 | — | 71·3 | −2·7 | 45·6 | 45·2 | 13<br>18·1 | 3<br>1·9 | 5·7 | −1·5 |
| Merseyside Conurbation | 6 | 9 | — | 67·7 | −1·9 | 46·2 | 47·7 | 4<br>15·2 | 3<br>3·6 | 3·0 | −6·4 |
| Rest of Region | 21 | 14 | — | 73·5 | −3·5 | 47·6 | 45·4 | 18<br>12·8 | 4<br>3·2 | 5·3 | −1·4 |
| NORTHERN REGION | 10 | 29 | — | 72·3 | −3·4 | 41·2 | 54·8 | 10<br>15·9 | 1<br>0·9 | 3·9 | −2·1 |
| Tyneside Conurbation | 2 | 8 | — | 71·2 | −3·6 | 40·7 | 57·7 | 2<br>8·4 | — | 3·8 | −3·7 |
| Rest of Region | 8 | 21 | — | 72·6 | −3·4 | 41·4 | 53·8 | 8<br>17·7 | 1<br>0·9 | 3·9 | −1·6 |

| | Seats Con. | Seats Lab. | Seats Other | % voting | Change in % voting 1966–70 | Con. % | Lab. % | Lib. % | Other % | Swing 1966–70 | Swing 1955–70 |
|---|---|---|---|---|---|---|---|---|---|---|---|
| WALES | 7 | 27 | 2 | 77·4 | −1·6 | 27·7 | 51·6 | [19] 12·7 | 13·9 | 4·5 | 1·9 |
| Industrial Wales | 4 | 19 | 1 | 76·1 | −2·0 | 26·4 | 57·4 | [7] 7·8 | 13·7 | 4·8 | 1·3 |
| Rural Wales | 3 | 8 | 1 | 80·3 | −0·8 | 30·5 | 39·1 | 16·2 | 14·3 | 3·5 | 3·1 |
| SCOTLAND | 23 | 44 | 4 | 74·0 | −1·9 | [70] 38·5 | 44·5 | [27] 14·6 | [68] 12·2 | 2·9 | −5·0 |
| Clydeside Conurbation | 3 | 21 | — | 71·3 | −2·9 | 35·4 | 52·0 | [3] 7·6 | [23] 11·2 | 3·0 | −6·6 |
| Rest of Industrial Belt | 6 | 18 | — | 76·0 | −2·3 | 37·5 | 49·0 | [9] 11·4 | [23] 11·3 | 2·7 | −5·0 |
| Highlands | 2 | 1 | 3 | 72·4 | +1·6 | 31·7 | 27·6 | [4] 34·9 | [5] 19·0 | 3·4 | −7·5 |
| Rest of Scotland | 12 | 4 | 1 | 75·0 | −0·9 | 45·6 | 31·3 | [11] 15·3 | 13·8 | 2·5 | −2·5 |
| GREATER LONDON | 48 | 55 | — | 64·5 | −7·3 | 46·9 | 45·3 | [59] 11·4 | [30] 2·4 | 4·5 | −0·2 |
| GLASGOW | 2 | 13 | — | 66·8 | −4·3 | 35·5 | 54·9 | — | [14] 10·0 | 2·9 | −8·5 |
| BIRMINGHAM | 6 | 7 | — | 65·2 | −3·8 | 48·0 | 48·9 | [4] 11·8 | [5] 2·0 | 5·6 | −0·2 |
| LIVERPOOL | 2 | 7 | — | 63·1 | −1·4 | 44·2 | 51·4 | [1] 28·4 | [1] 4·2 | 2·9 | −6·5 |
| MANCHESTER | 2 | 7 | — | 66·2 | −1·6 | 43·6 | 53·5 | [2] 9·1 | [2] 2·2 | 4·5 | −5·7 |
| EDINBURGH | 4 | 3 | — | 73·7 | −3·1 | 45·4 | 41·3 | [6] 8·1 | [6] 7·2 | 2·8 | −4·4 |
| BRISTOL | 3 | 3 | — | 70·6 | −4·3 | 46·7 | 48·7 | [3] 10·1 | [1] 0·4 | 3·9 | 0·6 |
| LEEDS | 2 | 4 | — | 66·0 | −4·1 | 42·7 | 50·0 | [4] 11·0 | [2] 1·0 | 3·3 | −1·5 |
| SHEFFIELD | 2 | 4 | — | 66·0 | −5·0 | 39·1 | 57·0 | [2] 7·2 | [3] 1·8 | 5·6 | −2·4 |
| BRADFORD | 1 | 3 | — | 71·7 | −2·6 | 44·1 | 51·6 | [2] 8·8 | — | 4·3 | −0·9 |
| LEICESTER | 2 | 2 | — | 71·3 | −2·7 | 49·6 | 44·5 | [2] 7·2 | [3] 3·3 | 6·8 | 3·1 |
| NOTTINGHAM | 1 | 3 | — | 68·0 | −6·0 | 45·9 | 51·4 | [1] 7·7 | [1] 1·5 | 4·4 | −2·2 |
| NEWCASTLE | 1 | 3 | — | 69·7 | −5·1 | 41·7 | 57·2 | [1] 7·4 | — | 3·1 | −5·1 |
| TEESSIDE | 1 | 3 | — | 70·9 | −6·5 | 43·7 | 56·1 | — | [1] 0·9 | 5·5 | −4·2 |
| BELFAST | 3 | — | 1 | 77·2 | +9·1 | 54·8 | [3] 34·0 | — | [2] 36·0 | 3·1 | −8·1 |
| CARDIFF | 1 | 2 | — | 73·5 | −4·2 | 41·6 | 48·3 | [2] 4·8 | 7·0 | 4·1 | −3·7 |
| COVENTRY | — | 3 | — | 73·0 | −5·7 | 43·5 | 56·0 | — | [1] 1·4 | 3·8 | −2·5 |
| KINGSTON UPON HULL | — | 3 | — | 67·8 | −6·5 | 34·6 | 64·0 | — | [1] 3·9 | 0·8 | −8·8 |
| PORTSMOUTH | 2 | 1 | — | 70·5 | −3·2 | 55·1 | 37·8 | [1] 12·7 | [1] 1·7 | 3·5 | −3·2 |
| STOKE ON TRENT | — | 3 | — | 51·2 | −19·4 | 36·7 | 62·9 | — | [1] 1·1 | 4·7 | 1·6 |

# CONSTITUENCY RESULTS

On the right-hand side these tables present the election results in virtually the same form used in previous Nuffield studies.

The swing (the average of the Conservative % gain and the Labour % loss) is given only where the two main parties shared the top two places in the poll, both in 1966 and 1970. Where there was a straight fight in both years, the swing is printed in italic type.

The Liberal 1966–70 column shows the increase or decrease in the Liberal % of the total vote. The 1966 Liberal vote is given in brackets where Liberals withdrew in 1970. A * denotes Liberal intervention in 1970.

In the other column a C denotes that the candidate was a Communist. An N denotes that the candidate was a Nationalist (Plaid Cymru or Scottish National Party).

A † indicates that the seat was won in 1970 by a different party from 1966. A ‡ indicates that the seat changed hands in a by-election during the 1966–70 Parliament.

On the left-hand side of these tables there are listed, for the 618 constituencies in Great Britain (but not the 12 in Northern Ireland), some of the most significant characteristics revealed by the 10% sample Census of 1966. In 1969, for the first time ever, the Registrars-General for England and Wales, and Scotland, published findings arranged on a constituency basis. (See *1966 Census: General and Parliamentary Tables*, H.M.S.O., Nov. 1969). The figures in the tables that followed were derived by Clive Payne and Ivor Crewe from the computer tape on which the H.M.S.O. publication was based.

% non-manual: The proportion of employed and retired males in the Registrar-General's Occupational Categories 1, 2, 3, 4, 5, 6 and 13.
% professional and managerial: The proportion of employed and retired males in the Registrar-General's Occupational Categories 1, 2, 3, 4 and 13.
% owner-occupiers: The proportion of households owned or being bought by the occupier.
% council tenants: The proportion of households under council ownership.
% with full plumbing: The proportion of households with hot water, bathroom and exclusive use of an indoor W.C.
% with cars: The proportion of households with at least one car.
% born in New Commonwealth: The proportion of the population born in Commonwealth countries other than Canada, Australia and New Zealand. (This is, of course, not the same as '% non-White' since it includes many children of British soldiers and civilians serving in India and elsewhere, as well as Cypriots, Maltese and others, and since it does not include non-White residents born in the United Kingdom or in countries outside the Commonwealth.)
% young voters: The proportion of the population who in April 1966 were between 15 and 19 and who in 1970 would have been between 19 and 23.
% retired: The proportion of the male population over 15 who were recorded as retired in the 1966 Census.

At the end of the Constituency Tables there is a list of constituencies exceptionally marked out by one special characteristic.

% engaged in agriculture: The proportion of the economically active population recorded in the Registrar-General's Occupational Category I – 'agriculture, forestry, fishing'.
% engaged in mining: The proportion of the economically active population recorded in the Registrar-General's Occupational Category II – mining and quarrying. (Although the great majority are coal-mining constituencies,

Truro enters this list primarily because of china-clay quarrying and there is much ironstone working in Penistone and Wrexham.)

% in H.M. Services: The proportion of employed and retired males in the Registrar-General's Occupational Categories XVI and XVII.

% born in Ireland: The proportion of the population born anywhere in Ireland, North or South.

*Distribution of Census Characteristics by Constituency*

(This table is designed to show the approximate rank ordering of all constituencies in the following tables as well as the range between the highest and lowest figures recorded for any characteristic.)

| Ranking order in Decile | Rank order in number | % Non-manual | % Professional & managerial | % Owner-Occupiers | % Council Tenants | % With full plumbing | % With cars | % Born in New Commonwealth | % Young voters | % Retired |
|---|---|---|---|---|---|---|---|---|---|---|
| 0% | 1 | 12·0 | 2·5 | 1·6 | 1·6 | 17·4 | 7·6 | 0·0 | 6·3 | 4·7 |
| 10% | 62 | 19·9 | 7·2 | 20·4 | 12·0 | 50·9 | 27·7 | 0·2 | 8·6 | 7·6 |
| 20% | 124 | 23·7 | 9·2 | 31·4 | 16·3 | 62·7 | 33·7 | 0·3 | 9·2 | 8·4 |
| 30% | 185 | 26·2 | 11·2 | 36·5 | 18·8 | 68·3 | 36·1 | 0·4 | 9·6 | 9·1 |
| 40% | 247 | 28·4 | 12·5 | 42·6 | 22·0 | 72·0 | 39·4 | 0·6 | 9·8 | 9·7 |
| 50% | 309 | 30·7 | 14·7 | 46·9 | 24·6 | 75·4 | 43·7 | 0·8 | 10·1 | 10·1 |
| 60% | 371 | 33·9 | 16·5 | 50·1 | 27·2 | 79·0 | 47·4 | 1·1 | 10·4 | 10·8 |
| 70% | 433 | 36·9 | 18·2 | 53·6 | 30·9 | 81·7 | 51·8 | 1·5 | 10·7 | 11·6 |
| 80% | 494 | 40·8 | 20·3 | 57·1 | 36·7 | 84·8 | 55·8 | 2·2 | 11·1 | 12·6 |
| 90% | 556 | 47·5 | 24·4 | 61·9 | 49·8 | 88·8 | 59·8 | 4·7 | 11·6 | 14·7 |
| 100% | 618 | 74·1 | 41·5 | 79·0 | 87·0 | 97·0 | 73·6 | 15·8 | 15·9 | 29·8 |
| Mean | — | 32·6 | 15·3 | 44·0 | 27·7 | 73·1 | 43·6 | 1·7 | 10·2 | 10·8 |

## *Inner London Boroughs*

| % Non-manual | % Professional & managerial | % Owner-Occupiers | % Council Tenants | % With full plumbing | % With cars | % Born in New Commonwealth | % Young voters | % Retired | Constituency | % Voting 1970 | Change in % voting 1966–70 | Con. % | Lab. % | Lib. % | Other % | Lib. + or − % | Swing 1966–70 | Swing 1955–70 |
|---|---|---|---|---|---|---|---|---|---|---|---|---|---|---|---|---|---|---|
| 40·7 | 14·3 | 11·3 | 14·3 | 49·9 | 28·9 | 6·4 | 8·4 | 7·7 | Barons Court | 67·3 | −7·9 | 44·1 | 48·0 | 7·9 | — | +0·7 | 3·3 | −1·8 |
| 28·1 | 8·6 | 8·8 | 36·3 | 47·6 | 29·1 | 3·3 | 10·6 | 6·5 | Battersea, North | 58·9 | −4·3 | 27·8 | 65·5 | 5·7 | 1·0 C | * | 4·8 | 2·9 |
| 35·6 | 11·4 | 27·9 | 8·8 | 48·5 | 32·4 | 11·6 | 8·2 | 7·8 | South | 63·6 | −9·3 | 41·8 | 49·5 | 5·4 | 3·3 | −3·5 | 3·5 | −4·9 |
| 22·0 | 6·6 | 1·7 | 64·4 | 57·6 | 27·1 | 1·2 | 10·2 | 7·6 | Bermondsey | 52·9 | −8·0 | 23·1 | 76·9 | — | — | — | *3·7* | 3·8 |
| 21·9 | 6·7 | 3·9 | 52·6 | 50·9 | 24·9 | 3·7 | 9·7 | 9·4 | Bethnal Green | 50·4 | −7·3 | 23·2 | 64·3 | 12·6 | — | −0·7 | 5·8 | 5·8 |
| 39·0 | 15·1 | 28·3 | 25·7 | 59·9 | 37·7 | 6·1 | 10·3 | 8·2 | Camberwell, Dulwich | 64·4 | −9·3 | 45·1 | 47·2 | 7·7 | — | −1·7 | 5·6 | −2·8 |
| 20·7 | 5·2 | 9·2 | 40·7 | 44·4 | 27·7 | 7·9 | 10·5 | 7·0 | Peckham | 49·9 | −5·8 | 32·5 | 67·5 | — | — | — | *4·5* | *0·2* |
| 68·7 | 38·6 | 15·8 | 10·0 | 80·5 | 38·3 | 4·7 | 8·7 | 8·2 | Chelsea | 54·9 | −8·2 | 65·4 | 23·7 | 8·8 | 2·1 | −3·2 | 5·0 | −2·5 |
| 59·2 | 32·1 | 7·2 | 21·8 | 69·8 | 29·9 | 3·0 | 7·2 | 7·3 | Cities of London & Westminster | 54·6 | −5·4 | 59·4 | 31·3 | 8·4 | 0·9 | −1·8 | 4·3 | −6·2 |
| 24·4 | 7·2 | 17·7 | 28·8 | 38·5 | 31·7 | 8·6 | 9·2 | 9·0 | Deptford | 54·7 | −5·3 | 31·6 | 63·0 | — | 5·5 | — | 4·5 | 0·0 |
| 37·9 | 11·2 | 22·6 | 11·3 | 45·0 | 30·3 | 6·0 | 8·4 | 7·8 | Fulham | 68·8 | −7·6 | 43·2 | 55·0 | — | 1·4<br>0·4 | — | 4·2 | −0·9 |
| 34·0 | 13·3 | 23·9 | 38·2 | 68·7 | 39·6 | 2·2 | 10·5 | 10·0 | Greenwich | 65·8 | −1·9 | 35·4 | 55·8 | 8·9 | — | * | 4·7 | −1·4 |
| 22·4 | 7·2 | 12·9 | 30·1 | 40·4 | 26·4 | 8·8 | 9·3 | 8·0 | Hackney, Central | 50·8 | −6·8 | 34·6 | 64·4 | — | 0·9 | [14·1] | 5·9 | −1·4 |
| 27·9 | 7·3 | 13·9 | 25·9 | 51·6 | 24·4 | 9·8 | 9·1 | 7·5 | Hammersmith, North | 62·3 | −1·6 | 37·3 | 62·7 | — | — | — | *6·1* | *−1·5* |
| 60·6 | 29·9 | 16·6 | 9·5 | 62·8 | 34·0 | 7·5 | 8·0 | 6·5 | Hampstead † | 63·4 | −9·0 | 46·6 | 45·6 | 7·8 | — | −2·8 | 2·8 | −11·5 |

| | | | | | | | | | | | | | | | | | | |
|---|---|---|---|---|---|---|---|---|---|---|---|---|---|---|---|---|---|---|
| 41·5 | 17·8 | 2·1 | 35·3 | 65·6 | 21·3 | 5·5 | 8·1 | 7·4 | Holborn & St. Pancras South . . | 54·1 | −11·5 | 44·9 | 55·2 | — | — | — | *4·4* | −3·8 |
| 29·7 | 9·6 | 15·6 | 20·0 | 38·9 | 26·6 | 11·0 | 8·6 | 7·0 | Islington, East . . | 51·8 | −5·2 | 38·3 | 61·8 | — | — | [8·8] | 2·8 | *−1·4* |
| 29·1 | 9·5 | 19·1 | 13·9 | 34·5 | 24·6 | 15·8 | 8·6 | 7·8 | North . . | 49·0 | −5·2 | 35·6 | 58·9 | — | 5·6<br>5·5 | [9·9] | 2·7 | −1·3 |
| 24·5 | 7·7 | 10·8 | 18·9 | 32·9 | 22·4 | 12·9 | 8·5 | 6·6 | South-west . | 48·9 | −2·1 | 31·2 | 60·9 | — | 2·4 C | — | 5·8 | 3·3 |
| 38·3 | 13·8 | 9·9 | 13·5 | 50·2 | 22·7 | 9·8 | 8·1 | 5·3 | Kensington, North . | 57·5 | −4·6 | 39·2 | 52·8 | 8·0 | — | −0·5 | 2·2 | −2·9 |
| 74·1 | 41·5 | 14·4 | 1·6 | 71·0 | 34·7 | 9·5 | 8·9 | 4·7 | South . . | 49·9 | −8·2 | 75·7 | 24·3 | — | — | [15·0] | 3·1 | *−6·8* |
| 30·6 | 8·2 | 12·0 | 29·3 | 48·6 | 26·0 | 11·5 | 9·0 | 7·7 | Lambeth, Brixton . | 52·6 | −4·4 | 42·7 | 57·3 | — | — | — | *4·0* | *−0·3* |
| 39·5 | 12·8 | 25·8 | 20·0 | 57·4 | 33·5 | 10·8 | 9·4 | 9·1 | Norwood . . | 65·7 | −6·1 | 45·6 | 47·4 | 7·0 | — | −1·4 | 2·0 | −6·5 |
| 26·3 | 7·5 | 4·2 | 49·7 | 60·6 | 25·7 | 4·3 | 10·1 | 7·7 | Vauxhall . . | 54·5 | −4·1 | 36·4 | 63·6 | — | — | — | *3·0* | 1·1 |
| 43·0 | 15·1 | 37·6 | 19·9 | 71·0 | 39·4 | 5·4 | 9·1 | 10·3 | Lewisham, North . | 68·6 | −8·8 | 48·6 | 51·5 | — | — | — | *1·6* | *−5·4* |
| 36·2 | 11·6 | 32·5 | 47·6 | 81·1 | 39·0 | 2·1 | 11·2 | 11·4 | South . . | 65·9 | −9·3 | 40·6 | 57·0 | — | 2·4 | [12·9] | 5·1 | −0·8 |
| 43·7 | 15·9 | 38·9 | 18·7 | 71·7 | 40·9 | 4·8 | 9·4 | 9·3 | West † . . | 68·2 | −7·5 | 51·0 | 49·0 | — | — | — | *3·5* | *−4·0* |
| 34·7 | 12·6 | 6·1 | 27·1 | 44·7 | 24·1 | 13·1 | 7·5 | 6·6 | Paddington, North . | 62·6 | −3·7 | 40·4 | 54·8 | 4·8 | — | −4·5 | 5·9 | −3·8 |
| 56·6 | 27·9 | 7·8 | 15·3 | 61·6 | 24·1 | 10·0 | 6·8 | 6·3 | South . . | 57·5 | −4·9 | 53·2 | 40·0 | 6·9 | — | −3·3 | 3·2 | −5·2 |
| 19·3 | 6·2 | 5·1 | 54·6 | 55·9 | 27·4 | 4·1 | 11·1 | 6·9 | Poplar . . . | 48·8 | −8·9 | 19·6 | 80·4 | — | — | — | *4·1* | 1·2 |
| 68·1 | 41·5 | 8·2 | 9·7 | 74·1 | 31·7 | 5·0 | 7·6 | 7·2 | St. Marylebone . | 59·6 | −5·4 | 62·1 | 29·3 | 8·6 | — | −2·0 | 3·3 | *−4·3* |
| 34·3 | 11·2 | 14·0 | 25·4 | 45·2 | 26·5 | 8·5 | 8·5 | 9·0 | St. Pancras, North . | 55·5 | −7·9 | 38·3 | 59·3 | — | 2·4 C | — | 5·6 | −2·4 |
| 23·1 | 6·1 | 2·0 | 54·6 | 59·5 | 22·3 | 2·6 | 10·5 | 9·0 | Shoreditch & Finsbury | 48·7 | −4·8 | 33·1 | 66·9 | — | — | — | 6·5 | 6·6 |
| 22·7 | 5·5 | 1·6 | 41·5 | 44·7 | 24·9 | 3·0 | 10·1 | 7·1 | Southwark . . | 48·2 | −5·8 | 28·2 | 67·3 | — | 4·5 C | — | 6·3 | 1·9 |
| 20·3 | 6·1 | 2·7 | 45·5 | 48·3 | 22·4 | 8·3 | 10·9 | 7·0 | Stepney . . . | 44·9 | −5·8 | 19·4 | 74·8 | — | 5·8 C | — | 2·0 | 1·2 |
| 29·6 | 10·0 | 15·6 | 29·5 | 48·9 | 26·2 | 14·4 | 9·8 | 8·2 | Stoke Newington & Hackney, North | 50·1 | −5·7 | 34·7 | 62·8 | — | 2·4 C | — | 5·4 | −2·7 |
| 36·9 | 11·6 | 28·2 | 15·0 | 52·2 | 32·7 | 8·5 | 7·7 | 10·2 | Wandsworth, Central | 62·6 | −11·6 | 46·0 | 54·0 | — | — | [8·2] | 2·9 | *−5·1* |
| 37·5 | 12·2 | 21·2 | 24·1 | 60·4 | 31·6 | 9·5 | 9·6 | 7·7 | Clapham † . | 62·9 | −10·1 | 49·8 | 40·4 | 8·9 | 0·7<br>0·2 | +1·1 | 10·2 | 4·9 |
| 45·9 | 18·4 | 23·9 | 34·6 | 73·5 | 40·9 | 2·9 | 11·1 | 8·1 | Putney . . | 68·9 | −10·0 | 45·0 | 47·6 | 7·4 | — | −2·5 | 1·8 | −8·4 |
| 51·6 | 19·9 | 35·2 | 16·7 | 70·3 | 40·3 | 5·7 | 8·8 | 9·2 | Streatham . | 66·8 | −3·6 | 54·2 | 38·3 | 7·6 | — | * | 3·3 | −7·6 |
| 30·0 | 8·7 | 37·7 | 33·5 | 60·1 | 37·1 | 3·2 | 10·7 | 10·4 | Woolwich, East . | 60·7 | −6·3 | 34·6 | 65·4 | — | — | — | *6·2* | *−1·1* |
| 47·8 | 18·5 | 46·5 | 35·4 | 84·5 | 48·3 | 1·7 | 12·2 | 10·2 | West . . . | 72·1 | −9·3 | 49·3 | 50·8 | — | — | — | 4·0 | *−2·8* |

*English Boroughs*

| % Non-manual | % Professional & managerial | % Owner-Occupiers | % Council Tenants | % With full plumbing | % With cars | % Born in New Commonwealth | % Young voters | % Retired | Constituency | % Voting 1970 | Change in % voting 1966–70 | Con. % | Lab. % | Lib. % | Other % | Lib. + or − % | Swing 1966–70 | Swing 1955–70 |
|---|---|---|---|---|---|---|---|---|---|---|---|---|---|---|---|---|---|---|
| 24·8 | 11·4 | 69·1 | 12·2 | 58·5 | 33·4 | 0·3 | 9·5 | 12·4 | Accrington | 80·3 | −2·8 | 49·3 | 50·7 | — | — | [10·9] | 7·8 | *0·8* |
| 35·8 | 13·3 | 32·5 | 13·4 | 61·3 | 36·1 | 5·1 | 9·4 | 9·0 | Acton ‡ | 66·6 | −7·3 | 45·7 | 48·0 | 5·4 | 0·9 C | * | 6·6 | −0·5 |
| 49·6 | 25·7 | 62·0 | 16·3 | 86·1 | 51·2 | 0·5 | 8·2 | 8·7 | Altrincham & Sale | 74·1 | −3·8 | 53·2 | 31·8 | 15·0 | — | −2·2 | 4·1 | −8·0 |
| 26·5 | 10·2 | 49·7 | 25·3 | 63·6 | 31·5 | 1·5 | 9·9 | 11·7 | Ashton under Lyne | 71·4 | −2·3 | 45·5 | 54·5 | — | — | — | *4·2* | *−2·6* |
| 27·2 | 9·1 | 23·2 | 66·6 | 72·0 | 38·6 | 1·3 | 11·1 | 10·3 | Barking | 61·7 | −10·3 | 30·6 | 69·4 | — | — | [12·0] | 2·8 | −0·2 |
| 19·6 | 8·2 | 35·9 | 40·7 | 69·6 | 34·2 | 0·1 | 10·5 | 12·7 | Barnsley | 71·3 | −2·1 | 20·0 | 64·8 | 15·2 | — | * | 3·3 | 0·4 |
| 26·5 | 9·5 | 66·1 | 17·5 | 70·7 | 39·1 | 0·4 | 10·6 | 13·3 | Barrow-in-Furness | 73·8 | −3·0 | 43·9 | 56·1 | — | — | — | *4·2* | *−2·9* |
| 41·3 | 16·9 | 48·3 | 22·2 | 83·4 | 42·9 | 1·5 | 10·2 | 12·0 | Bath | 77·1 | −3·4 | 49·0 | 36·1 | 13·1 | 1·8 | −2·7 | 5·5 | −0·8 |
| 24·7 | 11·2 | 41·6 | 25·7 | 69·8 | 34·0 | 1·8 | 10·2 | 9·5 | Batley & Morley | 72·7 | −2·6 | 34·5 | 50·4 | 15·1 | — | +0·3 | 5·6 | 2·2 |
| 36·5 | 16·7 | 49·2 | 24·9 | 83·9 | 45·1 | 0·3 | 11·0 | 10·1 | Bebington † | 75·4 | −4·3 | 50·6 | 49·4 | — | — | — | *2·6* | *−8·1* |
| 59·1 | 30·2 | 59·7 | 7·9 | 82·8 | 55·6 | 2·1 | 9·5 | 11·3 | Beckenham | 68·7 | −9·0 | 57·8 | 24·5 | 17·7 | — | −4·0 | 4·3 | −2·3 |
| 49·5 | 20·3 | 75·6 | 12·1 | 92·1 | 57·8 | 1·2 | 9·1 | 9·7 | Bexley | 76·3 | −9·6 | 53·0 | 37·2 | 6·3 | 1·8<br>1·5 | −1·7 | 5·8 | 3·6 |
| 23·2 | 10·9 | 39·4 | 48·3 | 82·3 | 47·0 | 2·0 | 9·6 | 6·7 | Bilston | 69·4 | −3·8 | 49·1 | 50·9 | — | — | — | *6·0* | *6·7* |
| 27·0 | 12·6 | 34·9 | 22·9 | 68·0 | 31·3 | 0·6 | 11·4 | 10·1 | Birkenhead | 71·1 | −1·8 | 36·6 | 50·7 | 11·9 | 0·9 C | * | 3·8 | −3·6 |
| 14·9 | 4·6 | 28·8 | 31·8 | 29·5 | 25·9 | 13·8 | 9·8 | 7·2 | Birmingham, All Saints | 60·8 | −4·3 | 35·2 | 54·6 | 10·3 | — | * | −1·2 | −7·9 |
| 18·2 | 6·6 | 27·5 | 49·0 | 47·6 | 33·0 | 5·2 | 10·8 | 8·5 | Aston | 58·9 | −5·4 | 42·4 | 55·1 | — | 2·5 | — | 4·5 | 3·3 |
| 40·1 | 19·5 | 37·7 | 28·1 | 76·6 | 44·9 | 4·8 | 9·8 | 9·2 | Edgbaston | 63·7 | −4·2 | 63·2 | 34·8 | — | 1·9 | [13·8] | 3·5 | −3·5 |
| 37·3 | 15·7 | 48·8 | 39·4 | 75·1 | 50·0 | 0·7 | 10·3 | 9·0 | Hall Green | 67·9 | −5·8 | 60·4 | 39·6 | — | — | [12·9] | 6·6 | *−1·2* |
| 25·9 | 11·2 | 46·7 | 20·4 | 53·5 | 34·6 | 12·1 | 10·3 | 7·9 | Handsworth | 65·3 | +2·1 | 53·0 | 47·0 | — | — | — | 1·0 | −9·7 |
| 14·5 | 3·7 | 2·2 | 87·0 | 43·0 | 21·3 | 2·2 | 13·3 | 5·3 | Ladywood ‡ | 62·3 | +2·7 | 21·6 | 43·4 | 35·0 | — | +11·3 | — | — |
| 27·9 | 11·9 | 34·3 | 50·0 | 89·1 | 49·9 | 0·6 | 12·6 | 6·7 | Northfield | 68·5 | −6·6 | 48·6 | 50·5 | — | 0·9 C | — | 8·6 | 1·9 |
| 25·7 | 10·2 | 57·1 | 33·3 | 80·5 | 47·6 | 0·4 | 10·6 | 7·5 | Perry Barr | 70·7 | −5·5 | 51·8 | 48·2 | — | — | — | *6·8* | 4·1 |
| 27·7 | 12·8 | 40·7 | 16·8 | 56·8 | 39·1 | 7·9 | 8·9 | 8·6 | Selly Oak | 64·1 | −2·3 | 52·2 | 47·8 | — | — | [11·8] | 1·1 | *−5·3* |
| 16·3 | 5·2 | 28·9 | 41·1 | 38·0 | 28·0 | 7·0 | 10·6 | 7·2 | Small Heath | 58·0 | −1·6 | 30·7 | 61·1 | 7·8 | 0·5 | * | 5·2 | −4·4 |
| 18·2 | 6·1 | 35·4 | 29·0 | 50·4 | 31·0 | 9·0 | 9·9 | 8·0 | Sparkbrook | 65·0 | −1·8 | 40·8 | 52·7 | 6·5 | — | * | 4·6 | −1·6 |
| 21·7 | 7·1 | 31·6 | 54·5 | 77·9 | 41·6 | 1·3 | 13·6 | 7·5 | Stechford | 64·0 | −6·3 | 39·5 | 56·2 | — | 3·6<br>0·7 C | — | 7·1 | 0·1 |
| 25·5 | 10·3 | 45·1 | 41·7 | 83·2 | 47·7 | 0·7 | 12·4 | 7·9 | Yardley † | 69·8 | −7·8 | 50·1 | 49·9 | — | — | — | *6·5* | *3·6* |
| 24·1 | 10·8 | 60·6 | 20·9 | 49·1 | 32·2 | 2·1 | 10·1 | 11·6 | Blackburn | 75·6 | −3·6 | 46·8 | 53·2 | — | — | — | *5·1* | −2·8 |
| 39·3 | 17·6 | 68·0 | 12·7 | 88·9 | 35·7 | 0·5 | 7·9 | 17·7 | Blackpool, North | 68·5 | −4·4 | 55·3 | 32·4 | 12·3 | — | −6·6 | 4·9 | −9·8 |
| 34·5 | 14·0 | 71·5 | 7·8 | 85·7 | 38·1 | 0·4 | 8·2 | 15·5 | South | 68·4 | −2·1 | 52·8 | 33·0 | 14·2 | — | * | 5·7 | −6·4 |
| 19·8 | 7·6 | 30·1 | 44·1 | 72·7 | 34·7 | 0·2 | 10·4 | 13·1 | Blyth | 71·7 | −2·7 | 25·8 | 74·2 | — | — | — | *4·0* | *−1·1* |
| 26·6 | 10·9 | 55·6 | 28·8 | 65·1 | 33·0 | 1·3 | 11·3 | 11·3 | Bolton, East † | 73·6 | −3·4 | 50·5 | 49·5 | — | — | — | *9·8* | *−3·0* |
| 27·7 | 13·7 | 65·3 | 13·9 | 51·8 | 31·5 | 2·6 | 9·3 | 12·2 | West † | 74·0 | −4·3 | 51·7 | 48·3 | — | — | [11·7] | 8·1 | — |
| 22·1 | 6·5 | 21·3 | 42·6 | 70·5 | 25·8 | 0·6 | 13·1 | 6·9 | Bootle | 65·2 | −3·0 | 36·4 | 63·6 | — | — | — | −0·3 | *−11·7* |
| 46·5 | 23·6 | 58·9 | 7·8 | 87·3 | 51·4 | 1·2 | 8·0 | 22·4 | Bournemouth, East | 70·8 | −3·9 | 62·4 | 21·2 | 16·4 | — | −1·6 | 5·6 | −0·5 |
| 41·4 | 19·1 | 51·8 | 13·9 | 84·2 | 47·8 | 0·7 | 7·6 | 20·4 | West | 69·3 | −4·1 | 56·2 | 27·6 | 16·2 | — | −2·0 | 5·2 | −3·5 |

| | | | | | | | | | | | | | | | | | |
|---|---|---|---|---|---|---|---|---|---|---|---|---|---|---|---|---|---|
| 14·3 | 5·2 | 47·6 | 23·5 | 50·4 | 19·3 | 11·9 | 10·9 | 9·6 | Bradford, East | 64·9 | −0·3 | 31·3 | 66·2 | 2·5 | — | * | 2·1 | −5·8 |
| 29·3 | 11·5 | 56·8 | 25·9 | 77·7 | 34·2 | 3·1 | 11·4 | 9·8 | North | 74·0 | −3·7 | 47·9 | 52·1 | — | — | — | 3·2 | −2·2 |
| 27·8 | 12·6 | 59·0 | 25·0 | 75·1 | 35·0 | 0·7 | 11·0 | 9·2 | South | 72·2 | −3·5 | 41·6 | 45·9 | 12·5 | — | +0·4 | 6·5 | 2·1 |
| 33·1 | 15·2 | 64·0 | 18·3 | 70·3 | 33·7 | 3·8 | 9·3 | 11·0 | West † | 74·0 | −2·6 | 52·0 | 48·1 | — | — | — | 4·0 | −1·9 |
| 42·1 | 17·8 | 31·7 | 17·0 | 61·5 | 37·2 | 4·8 | 8·2 | 8·7 | Brentford & Chiswick | 73·2 | −8·9 | 49·1 | 50·9 | — | — | [6·7] | 0·1 | −3·9 |
| 29·2 | 14·7 | 54·7 | 18·1 | 71·8 | 38·4 | 0·8 | 9·3 | 11·3 | Brighouse & Spenborough † | 80·5 | −3·4 | 46·3 | 46·1 | 7·6 | — | * | 4·9 | 1·8 |
| 31·8 | 12·6 | 40·5 | 27·1 | 75·4 | 34·0 | 1·4 | 10·2 | 14·5 | Brighton, Kemptown † | 75·1 | −4·9 | 49·3 | 42·9 | 7·8 | — | * | 4·0 | −3·2 |
| 44·3 | 20·3 | 46·6 | 11·6 | 74·7 | 36·2 | 1·2 | 8·6 | 16·1 | Pavilion | 66·6 | −3·7 | 61·9 | 35·0 | — | 3·1 | — | 5·3 | −4·6 |
| 22·2 | 7·8 | 59·0 | 17·1 | 50·7 | 33·5 | 5·3 | 8·6 | 13·8 | Bristol, Central | 66·7 | −3·2 | 37·9 | 51·4 | 10·7 | — | * | 4·7 | 3·8 |
| 36·8 | 13·7 | 63·2 | 21·3 | 77·8 | 49·0 | 1·6 | 9·4 | 11·8 | North-east † | 72·1 | −4·9 | 50·5 | 49·5 | — | — | — | 4·7 | 1·4 |
| 36·9 | 17·6 | 38·7 | 53·6 | 91·4 | 52·0 | 0·7 | 14·6 | 9·0 | North-west † | 78·1 | −3·9 | 47·6 | 45·5 | 6·5 | 0·5 C | * | 1·7 | 2·9 |
| 23·8 | 7·2 | 38·7 | 51·7 | 79·3 | 41·8 | 0·4 | 12·0 | 9·4 | South | 65·0 | −4·5 | 38·2 | 61·8 | — | — | — | 5·3 | 2·3 |
| 30·2 | 10·8 | 63·6 | 26·1 | 80·0 | 51·9 | 0·5 | 9·7 | 8·9 | South-east | 72·1 | −4·0 | 44·6 | 55·4 | — | — | — | 6·0 | 4·1 |
| 59·6 | 28·5 | 45·0 | 3·0 | 77·1 | 45·9 | 2·4 | 7·8 | 13·8 | West | 66·3 | −5·8 | 60·2 | 24·5 | 15·3 | — | −4·3 | 1·4 | −7·4 |
| 60·3 | 32·3 | 61·4 | 15·5 | 86·1 | 57·8 | 1·6 | 10·0 | 9·8 | Bromley | 69·4 | −8·3 | 59·4 | 24·8 | 15·9 | — | −5·1 | 4·5 | −0·9 |
| 21·9 | 9·6 | 62·7 | 17·8 | 49·6 | 30·0 | 0·8 | 10·3 | 12·0 | Burnley | 75·8 | −4·1 | 34·9 | 57·0 | 8·1 | — | −3·8 | 5·4 | −5·4 |
| 30·5 | 14·0 | 60·1 | 22·2 | 68·2 | 39·3 | 0·5 | 10·4 | 9·6 | Bury & Radcliffe † | 75·7 | −5·6 | 52·8 | 47·2 | — | — | [8·7] | 7·0 | −0·7 |
| 43·2 | 20·4 | 41·9 | 27·1 | 74·4 | 45·5 | 1·5 | 12·1 | 10·1 | Cambridge † ‡ | 73·0 | −7·0 | 55·3 | 44·7 | — | — | [10·2] | 6·4 | −2·2 |
| 31·3 | 13·1 | 39·0 | 45·1 | 71·7 | 38·3 | 0·4 | 10·6 | 11·2 | Carlisle | 78·6 | −4·9 | 46·8 | 53·2 | — | — | — | 2·9 | −3·7 |
| 41·7 | 17·6 | 51·3 | 24·5 | 78·8 | 50·4 | 1·2 | 10·2 | 11·3 | Cheltenham | 75·5 | −1·7 | 50·2 | 31·3 | 18·5 | — | * | 6·0 | 0·2 |
| 23·2 | 9·4 | 36·4 | 32·8 | 71·9 | 37·3 | 0·3 | 10·2 | 11·4 | Chesterfield | 72·5 | −4·3 | 31·5 | 59·0 | 9·5 | — | −2·7 | 3·9 | −6·1 |
| 22·9 | 9·3 | 52·9 | 29·7 | 77·9 | 47·7 | 1·6 | 10·6 | 7·4 | Coventry, East | 70·6 | −6·8 | 39·3 | 59·3 | — | 1·4 C | [7·0] | 5·4 | −3·8 |
| 24·6 | 10·2 | 63·5 | 17·3 | 72·4 | 49·5 | 5·0 | 11·2 | 7·4 | North | 74·7 | −4·0 | 43·3 | 56·7 | — | — | — | 2·6 | −3·2 |
| 31·1 | 15·1 | 55·7 | 20·5 | 73·8 | 50·3 | 4·1 | 10·9 | 7·2 | South | 74·5 | −5·7 | 48·1 | 51·9 | — | — | — | 3·0 | −0·3 |
| 42·1 | 19·5 | 49·8 | 17·9 | 78·2 | 37·8 | 0·4 | 10·8 | 10·8 | Crosby | 71·4 | −0·7 | 56·7 | 43·3 | — | — | — | 2·7 | −11·3 |
| 45·2 | 16·7 | 53·0 | 9·4 | 73·7 | 43·9 | 5·2 | 9·2 | 9·7 | Croydon, North-east | 69·7 | −6·6 | 49·7 | 40·0 | 10·3 | — | −4·0 | 4·2 | −4·4 |
| 46·5 | 19·0 | 53·9 | 10·8 | 72·8 | 44·7 | 5·4 | 9·3 | 9·5 | North-west | 67·7 | −6·7 | 49·9 | 38·0 | 12·1 | — | −3·7 | 2·6 | −5·5 |
| 44·6 | 20·3 | 42·2 | 29·3 | 79·2 | 51·3 | 2·5 | 11·6 | 8·2 | South † | 71·4 | −4·7 | 49·7 | 42·7 | 7·0 | 0·6 | −3·7 | 3·6 | −3·4 |
| 24·3 | 6·9 | 24·6 | 67·6 | 87·9 | 44·2 | 0·7 | 11·9 | 10·1 | Dagenham | 59·1 | −8·3 | 27·0 | 70·7 | — | 2·2 C | — | 4·3 | 2·0 |
| 28·4 | 11·3 | 57·5 | 19·4 | 68·0 | 37·7 | 0·5 | 9·9 | 12·3 | Darlington | 76·5 | −5·8 | 40·6 | 48·5 | 10·9 | — | +2·7 | 0·7 | −6·6 |
| 23·8 | 8·4 | 40·9 | 30·5 | 62·7 | 36·8 | 0·6 | 11·0 | 9·2 | Derby, North | 64·2 | −6·6 | 45·3 | 54·7 | — | — | — | 7·1 | 1·0 |
| 28·0 | 9·8 | 50·7 | 25·8 | 55·4 | 35·0 | 5·7 | 9·7 | 11·1 | South | 67·3 | −5·3 | 45·6 | 54·4 | — | — | [10·7] | 8·4 | 3·1 |
| 26·1 | 12·1 | 43·4 | 30·1 | 71·7 | 34·0 | 2·1 | 10·7 | 10·3 | Dewsbury | 74·6 | −3·3 | 38·7 | 48·7 | 12·6 | — | −5·1 | 7·4 | 3·3 |
| 29·4 | 12·4 | 43·8 | 34·6 | 76·3 | 37·3 | 1·3 | 11·3 | 12·7 | Doncaster | 74·9 | −6·2 | 43·4 | 50·7 | 5·9 | — | * | 3·1 | −5·4 |
| 26·6 | 13·5 | 41·2 | 43·5 | 79·5 | 47·2 | 2·2 | 10·4 | 8·7 | Dudley ‡ | 71·9 | −1·9 | 49·7 | 50·3 | — | — | — | 8·8 | 9·4 |
| 42·1 | 19·1 | 62·0 | 18·4 | 95·2 | 58·0 | 1·8 | 10·1 | 7·2 | Ealing, North | 72·7 | −9·5 | 49·7 | 50·3 | — | — | [7·9] | 2·3 | −0·6 |
| 51·9 | 23·2 | 45·1 | 6·8 | 71·5 | 42·0 | 5·7 | 7·2 | 9·8 | South | 65·4 | −7·9 | 55·0 | 34·3 | 10·8 | — | −1·9 | 3·6 | −4·0 |
| 26·9 | 7·9 | 42·5 | 12·7 | 44·7 | 34·5 | 5·6 | 9·3 | 8·2 | East Ham, North | 52·6 | −12·1 | 40·1 | 59·9 | — | — | — | 6·0 | −0·8 |
| 29·3 | 8·2 | 43·8 | 25·6 | 50·9 | 37·9 | 2·9 | 9·7 | 9·4 | South | 55·2 | −10·5 | 38·1 | 61·9 | — | — | — | 8·0 | 2·2 |
| 29·5 | 11·1 | 45·1 | 32·1 | 73·9 | 35·8 | 0·3 | 9·8 | 10·9 | Eccles | 72·6 | −1·5 | 42·9 | 55·6 | — | 1·5 C | — | 4·7 | −3·9 |
| 34·5 | 14·4 | 56·5 | 19·3 | 70·4 | 45·1 | 2·5 | 9·0 | 9·6 | Edmonton | 66·5 | −5·6 | 44·0 | 49·1 | 7·0 | — | * | 6·0 | 4·0 |
| 28·5 | 10·3 | 55·9 | 23·0 | 73·9 | 50·7 | 0·9 | 10·1 | 7·7 | Enfield, East | 66·7 | −8·5 | 38·5 | 51·0 | 10·5 | — | −1·8 | 4·8 | 4·6 |
| 58·6 | 30·6 | 69·5 | 14·4 | 89·4 | 62·6 | 0·9 | 10·1 | 9·1 | West | 71·2 | −8·9 | 57·9 | 26·2 | 12·8 | 3·1 | −6·0 | 2·6 | −1·9 |
| 36·4 | 14·2 | 58·1 | 23·5 | 79·1 | 50·9 | 1·8 | 9·8 | 9·5 | Erith & Crayford | 71·4 | −10·3 | 44·1 | 55·9 | — | — | [8·8] | 4·7 | 4·5 |
| 30·2 | 13·7 | 45·4 | 34·7 | 83·7 | 54·2 | 5·2 | 10·5 | 5·6 | Eton & Slough | 77·8 | −7·5 | 43·8 | 49·2 | 7·0 | — | * | 2·1 | 0·4 |
| 38·1 | 16·1 | 52·4 | 27·2 | 82·4 | 47·1 | 0·9 | 11·2 | 13·5 | Exeter † | 81·1 | −2·6 | 45·0 | 42·4 | 12·6 | — | +2·0 | 5·2 | −5·0 |
| 35·6 | 13·8 | 49·1 | 32·2 | 89·7 | 57·0 | 2·4 | 11·4 | 7·1 | Feltham | 68·1 | −9·2 | 38·9 | 52·5 | 8·6 | — | −3·9 | 3·4 | −2·5 |
| 55·3 | 29·7 | 52·2 | 10·9 | 80·2 | 51·2 | 3·6 | 9·5 | 8·8 | Finchley | 65·5 | −9·8 | 53·8 | 30·2 | 16·1 | — | −9·3 | 2·6 | 0·2 |
| 26·0 | 10·0 | 26·2 | 53·2 | 81·8 | 30·6 | 0·2 | 13·2 | 10·9 | Gateshead, East | 70·7 | −5·0 | 35·2 | 64·8 | — | — | — | 4·8 | −8·4 |

*English Boroughs—continued*

| % Non-manual | % Professional & managerial | % Owner-Occupiers | % Council Tenants | % With full plumbing | % With cars | % Born in New Commonwealth | % Young voters | % Retired | Constituency | % Voting 1970 | Change in % voting 1966–70 | Con. % | Lab. % | Lib. % | Other % | Lib. + or − % | Swing 1966–70 | Swing 1955–70 |
|---|---|---|---|---|---|---|---|---|---|---|---|---|---|---|---|---|---|---|
| 18·3 | 6·1 | 19·4 | 24·1 | 42·9 | 21·3 | 0·2 | 10·4 | 11·1 | Gateshead, West | 66·6 | −3·5 | 31·9 | 68·1 | — | — | — | *6·7* | *−2·8* |
| 33·9 | 12·1 | 63·8 | 18·2 | 77·1 | 45·0 | 2·2 | 10·3 | 12·5 | Gillingham | 73·4 | −5·1 | 58·8 | 41·2 | — | — | [8·7] | 5·0 | *3·4* |
| 32·6 | 11·2 | 53·5 | 26·8 | 71·8 | 48·1 | 2·2 | 10·3 | 9·7 | Gloucester † | 76·1 | −1·4 | 46·9 | 44·6 | 8·5 | — | −6·7 | 7·3 | 2·0 |
| 35·2 | 14·5 | 62·2 | 17·8 | 85·6 | 52·3 | 2·1 | 10·6 | 11·7 | Gosport & Fareham | 71·7 | −3·6 | 54·3 | 29·4 | 16·3 | — | +2·3 | 3·7 | −0·2 |
| 27·3 | 13·5 | 54·0 | 20·8 | 62·4 | 37·9 | 0·4 | 11·7 | 9·1 | Grimsby | 68·4 | −5·8 | 38·9 | 52·5 | 8·6 | — | — | 2·1 | −3·0 |
| 27·0 | 13·5 | 55·5 | 23·6 | 71·8 | 34·8 | 1·6 | 10·0 | 10·0 | Halifax | 73·5 | −6·9 | 48·9 | 49·3 | — | 1·7 | [10·7] | 5·4 | −1·6 |
| 48·3 | 23·4 | 65·3 | 6·2 | 87·0 | 49·8 | 2·6 | 8·4 | 9·2 | Harrow, Central | 71·7 | −8·5 | 50·2 | 38·2 | 10·5 | 1·1 | −4·0 | 3·7 | −4·0 |
| 51·3 | 27·2 | 65·1 | 16·0 | 92·9 | 61·5 | 2·1 | 10·7 | 6·7 | East † | 76·0 | −6·8 | 51·0 | 40·5 | 8·3 | 0·2 | −3·8 | 5·7 | 0·8 |
| 63·6 | 33·8 | 74·6 | 8·5 | 95·1 | 61·9 | 1·8 | 9·1 | 9·9 | West | 72·8 | −7·4 | 59·5 | 27·4 | 13·0 | — | −5·0 | 3·9 | −3·9 |
| 22·1 | 9·4 | 44·5 | 36·0 | 66·0 | 30·3 | 0·3 | 11·7 | 10·8 | The Hartlepools | 74·4 | −4·1 | 42·2 | 57·9 | — | — | — | *1·5* | *−6·2* |
| 40·1 | 18·1 | 47·4 | 13·5 | 77·0 | 33·8 | 1·0 | 8·8 | 21·3 | Hastings | 72·8 | −3·6 | 50·6 | 33·7 | 15·7 | — | −9·9 | 5·4 | −3·2 |
| 32·5 | 13·9 | 58·4 | 24·1 | 92·7 | 57·8 | 1·7 | 10·2 | 6·2 | Hayes & Harlington | 67·2 | −5·5 | 41·2 | 57·7 | — | 1·1 C | — | 5·1 | 1·1 |
| 48·6 | 25·9 | 51·8 | 30·2 | 88·4 | 55·8 | 2·3 | 11·4 | 10·3 | Hendon, North | 71·0 | −9·0 | 49·3 | 40·7 | 10·0 | — | +1·2 | 3·6 | −0·4 |
| 59·9 | 34·7 | 51·7 | 12·5 | 83·3 | 50·2 | 5·3 | 9·6 | 8·4 | South | 65·9 | −6·9 | 51·7 | 34·7 | 13·6 | — | −6·5 | 3·1 | −4·5 |
| 44·1 | 19·2 | 64·0 | 10·9 | 79·0 | 51·5 | 3·7 | 8·5 | 11·0 | Heston & Isleworth | 71·5 | −8·4 | 56·0 | 44·0 | — | — | [13·5] | 4·8 | *−1·3* |
| 46·4 | 20·7 | 77·0 | 11·0 | 92·5 | 60·9 | 0·9 | 10·0 | 7·7 | Hornchurch † | 72·8 | −8·3 | 49·7 | 41·7 | 8·6 | — | * | 6·1 | 2·9 |
| 48·6 | 19·4 | 31·6 | 7·8 | 59·1 | 35·2 | 11·9 | 8·7 | 7·8 | Hornsey | 67·4 | −5·3 | 49·1 | 40·5 | 8·6 | 1·4 C 0·4 | −1·9 | 3·7 | −7·5 |
| 46·9 | 24·7 | 43·4 | 11·3 | 85·3 | 38·3 | 1·8 | 7·6 | 17·1 | Hove | 66·7 | −5·4 | 68·7 | 31·3 | — | — | [16·0] | 2·9 | −5·5 |
| 25·1 | 12·0 | 42·6 | 35·0 | 72·6 | 34·7 | 4·1 | 10·9 | 9·3 | Huddersfield, East | 75·5 | −2·4 | 38·0 | 50·2 | 11·1 | 0·8 C | −4·9 | 7·8 | −1·0 |
| 33·6 | 16·5 | 62·7 | 12·7 | 71·0 | 37·4 | 3·5 | 8·6 | 11·8 | West | 77·4 | −4·9 | 40·6 | 41·0 | 14·9 | 3·5 | −8·2 | 5·2 | — |
| 51·5 | 21·2 | 71·5 | 11·9 | 89·2 | 57·5 | 1·4 | 9·3 | 8·5 | Ilford, North | 68·6 | −8·1 | 52·5 | 36·2 | 11·3 | — | −2·3 | 4·9 | −2·0 |
| 47·8 | 18·7 | 58·9 | 11·4 | 69·8 | 44·6 | 2·9 | 9·4 | 10·0 | South † | 68·1 | −8·8 | 46·3 | 43·0 | 8·4 | 1·8 0·5 | −2·2 | 4·5 | −5·1 |
| 31·6 | 12·5 | 52·1 | 28·9 | 67·3 | 45·9 | 1·7 | 10·9 | 11·2 | Ipswich † | 72·7 | −4·8 | 44·1 | 44·0 | 8·2 | 3·7 | −2·0 | 5·7 | 2·9 |
| 26·3 | 11·8 | 25·3 | 50·9 | 75·8 | 31·3 | 0·2 | 10·8 | 10·4 | Jarrow | 74·5 | −2·2 | 36·5 | 63·5 | — | — | — | *4·1* | *−0·2* |
| 27·2 | 14·0 | 62·4 | 18·6 | 73·0 | 38·8 | 0·5 | 9·5 | 11·0 | Keighley † | 80·8 | −2·7 | 50·8 | 49·3 | — | — | — | *5·8* | 4·8 |
| | | | | | | | | | Kingston upon Hull, | | | | | | | | | |
| 22·6 | 7·7 | 22·8 | 45·7 | 68·3 | 29·9 | 0·5 | 14·0 | 8·4 | East | 68·2 | −5·3 | 28·6 | 71·4 | — | — | [12·9] | 0·5 | −9·3 |
| 32·1 | 12·0 | 34·9 | 23·0 | 62·2 | 31·4 | 0·6 | 11·1 | 10·6 | North | 70·1 | −8·9 | 38·9 | 57·2 | — | 3·9 | [7·8] | −0·0 | −9·7 |
| 24·4 | 9·1 | 32·9 | 22·1 | 55·5 | 27·3 | 0·3 | 11·6 | 10·3 | West | 64·8 | −5·6 | 37·7 | 62·3 | — | — | — | *2·5* | *−6·3* |
| 54·2 | 28·0 | 59·7 | 12·9 | 81·7 | 54·6 | 1·9 | 9·8 | 9·5 | Kingston upon Thames | 69·1 | −7·8 | 56·7 | 31·7 | 11·7 | — | −3·5 | 3·7 | −3·4 |
| 27·4 | 10·7 | 36·5 | 46·1 | 85·9 | 31·7 | 0·7 | 11·3 | 9·8 | Leeds, East | 65·9 | −6·9 | 41·9 | 57·1 | — | 1·0 C | — | 3·9 | −2·4 |
| 40·6 | 20·4 | 51·2 | 24·1 | 85·9 | 36·5 | 5·5 | 10·2 | 10·3 | North-east | 65·4 | −2·8 | 57·0 | 43·0 | — | — | — | *0·2* | *−4·5* |
| 48·5 | 23·7 | 49·6 | 27·0 | 85·3 | 43·7 | 1·0 | 11·6 | 10·8 | North-west | 69·8 | −3·3 | 52·1 | 37·1 | 10·8 | — | * | 1·9 | −8·3 |
| 20·4 | 6·8 | 32·8 | 36·0 | 67·1 | 24·4 | 1·1 | 10·3 | 11·1 | South | 66·0 | −2·2 | 28·5 | 59·8 | 11·7 | — | * | 4·2 | −0·5 |
| 18·6 | 6·9 | 17·9 | 30·2 | 48·6 | 19·2 | 4·1 | 9·7 | 10·0 | South-east | 58·4 | −3·1 | 29·7 | 62·7 | 6·5 | 1·1 C | * | 5·4 | −0·3 |
| 23·7 | 8·6 | 40·8 | 31·0 | 70·6 | 29·6 | 0·8 | 9·9 | 9·0 | West | 65·7 | −6·3 | 35·4 | 51·8 | 12·8 | — | +1·1 | 3·9 | −1·5 |

| | | | | | | | | | | | | | | | | | | |
|---|---|---|---|---|---|---|---|---|---|---|---|---|---|---|---|---|---|---|
| 21·4 | 8·4 | 50·0 | 14·2 | 42·9 | 34·6 | 4·2 | 10·1 | 9·7 | Leicester, North-east | 71·0 | −4·4 | 45·9 | 48·8 | — | 5·3 | [11·8] | 8·5 | 5·1 |
| 24·5 | 9·4 | 42·7 | 28·9 | 60·6 | 38·1 | 2·0 | 12·7 | 9·3 | North-west | 70·9 | −2·9 | 41·4 | 48·5 | 7·6 | 2·5 | * | 7·4 | 0·7 |
| 45·2 | 24·9 | 61·9 | 8·2 | 68·6 | 48·2 | 7·2 | 9·9 | 10·7 | South-east | 71·9 | −1·4 | 62·7 | 37·4 | — | — | — | *2·8* | *−1·6* |
| 25·3 | 10·1 | 34·2 | 43·2 | 53·9 | 36·5 | 1·2 | 11·3 | 10·3 | South-west † ‡ | 71·4 | −2·6 | 45·7 | 45·3 | 6·6 | 2·3 | * | 8·8 | 6·0 |
| 21·0 | 8·3 | 50·5 | 32·5 | 71·0 | 32·7 | 0·0 | 10·0 | 12·1 | Leigh | 71·0 | −3·4 | 33·5 | 58·2 | — | 8·3 | — | 6·3 | 0·0 |
| 32·5 | 9·4 | 38·7 | 12·0 | 46·9 | 34·9 | 4·3 | 9·2 | 10·1 | Leyton | 62·1 | −14·1 | 43·4 | 56·6 | — | — | [7·8] | 2·1 | 0·7 |
| 30·2 | 10·4 | 42·8 | 32·8 | 68·8 | 39·9 | 0·6 | 10·6 | 11·2 | Lincoln | 74·5 | −4·2 | 39·0 | 51·0 | — | 10·0 | — | 2·3 | 0·1 |
| 19·5 | 5·5 | 25·8 | 6·6 | 32·6 | 19·6 | 1·0 | 9·9 | 8·2 | Liverpool, Edge Hill | 58·7 | −1·9 | 42·3 | 57·7 | — | — | — | *5·3* | *−6·3* |
| 17·2 | 5·4 | 10·8 | 36·2 | 49·1 | 12·2 | 3·0 | 12·2 | 8·2 | Exchange | 53·5 | +2·7 | 25·2 | 70·6 | — | 4·2 C | — | 1·1 | −12·3 |
| 39·0 | 16·5 | 42·5 | 41·7 | 87·0 | 42·2 | 0·4 | 13·8 | 8·5 | Garston | 65·7 | −2·5 | 57·0 | 43·1 | — | — | — | *2·6* | *−6·6* |
| 20·7 | 5·7 | 27·9 | 9·7 | 42·3 | 23·7 | 0·4 | 10·1 | 9·2 | Kirkdale | 63·7 | −2·0 | 43·5 | 56·5 | — | — | — | *2·8* | *−8·6* |
| 13·1 | 3·7 | 9·1 | 36·9 | 35·2 | 12·1 | 0·4 | 12·4 | 7·7 | Scotland | 50·6 | −1·2 | 25·3 | 74·8 | — | — | — | −0·7 | *−9·8* |
| 28·0 | 9·8 | 25·8 | 9·4 | 48·6 | 22·2 | 1·4 | 10·7 | 10·0 | Toxteth | 62·3 | −3·6 | 45·6 | 54·4 | — | — | — | 2·2 | *−10·6* |
| 26·1 | 7·2 | 29·2 | 34·1 | 65·5 | 27·7 | 0·2 | 11·4 | 11·8 | Walton | 68·0 | −3·2 | 44·0 | 56·0 | — | — | — | 1·3 | *−9·2* |
| 42·5 | 18·4 | 49·4 | 21·6 | 85·8 | 38·8 | 0·4 | 10·7 | 10·1 | Wavertree | 69·2 | −1·7 | 46·6 | 25·0 | 28·4 | — | +11·2 | — | — |
| 26·2 | 8·6 | 17·8 | 74·5 | 81·9 | 32·0 | 0·1 | 14·6 | 9·7 | West Derby | 64·3 | −3·3 | 42·7 | 57·3 | — | — | — | *−0·4* | *−10·6* |
| 26·2 | 11·5 | 53·4 | 16·2 | 68·2 | 42·3 | 3·3 | 10·1 | 8·1 | Luton † | 73·2 | −6·0 | 51·0 | 48·0 | — | 1·0 C | [6·4] | 4·1 | −3·1 |
| 23·6 | 7·5 | 32·8 | 13·9 | 42·8 | 21·5 | 4·5 | 9·7 | 9·0 | Manchester, Ardwick | 59·9 | +0·8 | 43·9 | 56·1 | — | — | — | 8·5 | *−3·7* |
| 32·4 | 12·9 | 45·3 | 27·0 | 71·0 | 32·9 | 0·2 | 10·6 | 8·8 | Blackley | 69·5 | −6·0 | 46·8 | 53·2 | — | — | [10·5] | *4·4* | *−9·2* |
| 18·4 | 4·9 | 25·4 | 20·0 | 38·2 | 16·5 | 2·1 | 10·3 | 7·7 | Cheetham | 55·8 | −1·1 | 35·9 | 64·1 | — | — | — | *6·8* | *−1·9* |
| 16·0 | 4·7 | 12·0 | 30·5 | 36·9 | 12·5 | 1·3 | 10·4 | 8·5 | Exchange | 57·0 | +3·3 | 27·8 | 68·5 | — | 3·7 | — | 3·1 | −9·4 |
| 28·4 | 10·5 | 50·2 | 18·0 | 62·9 | 32·8 | 0·4 | 9·5 | 10·0 | Gorton | 71·9 | −0·7 | 39·7 | 53·5 | 6·8 | — | * | 3·2 | −6·5 |
| 31·5 | 13·7 | 39·5 | 8·5 | 62·1 | 29·1 | 9·6 | 10·1 | 8·8 | Moss Side | 64·4 | −1·0 | 52·9 | 47·1 | — | — | [12·9] | 1·1 | *−11·4* |
| 22·0 | 7·2 | 39·7 | 16·9 | 43·8 | 25·9 | 0·4 | 9·8 | 10·2 | Openshaw | 64·0 | −1·9 | 38·1 | 60·2 | — | 1·7 C | — | 6·1 | −1·3 |
| 39·4 | 14·9 | 36·7 | 32·7 | 80·6 | 36·1 | 1·3 | 10·1 | 11·5 | Withington | 67·8 | −3·3 | 48·6 | 39·6 | 11·7 | — | −4·1 | 3·7 | −9·9 |
| 35·5 | 14·8 | 24·7 | 66·3 | 95·1 | 39·9 | 0·4 | 15·9 | 6·9 | Wythenshawe | 70·2 | −4·6 | 44·8 | 55·3 | — | — | [11·1] | 3·4 | *−8·1* |
| 50·7 | 20·8 | 60·1 | 24·2 | 90·9 | 47·7 | 1·7 | 8·3 | 12·1 | Merton & Morden | 73·0 | −8·3 | 50·8 | 41·4 | 7·8 | — | * | 4·2 | −2·5 |
| 15·0 | 5·3 | 23·5 | 50·0 | 58·4 | 22·7 | 1·2 | 14·0 | 7·6 | Middlesbrough, East | 60·5 | −7·8 | 29·0 | 71·0 | — | — | — | *4·1* | *−8·6* |
| 35·4 | 15·1 | 62·5 | 18·8 | 68·7 | 42·8 | 0·6 | 10·6 | 9·8 | West † | 75·1 | −6·3 | 50·4 | 49·6 | — | — | — | *4·9* | *−8·0* |
| 42·6 | 17·6 | 57·1 | 18·2 | 83·3 | 50·5 | 2·3 | 9·5 | 9·5 | Mitcham | 68·8 | −10·7 | 54·6 | 44·2 | — | 1·3 C | [8·4] | 4·7 | −1·3 |
| 23·1 | 11·5 | 69·0 | 16·8 | 57·5 | 36·1 | 1·6 | 9·8 | 13·7 | Nelson & Colne ‡ † | 78·2 | −2·8 | 51·8 | 48·2 | — | — | — | 8·0 | *4·6* |
| 29·1 | 13·4 | 49·2 | 35·6 | 80·7 | 42·4 | 0·2 | 10·8 | 9·7 | Newcastle under Lyme | 65·5 | −14·5 | 44·3 | 48·9 | 4·3 | 2·6 | * | 9·5 | 4·5 |
| | | | | | | | | | Newcastle upon Tyne, | | | | | | | | | |
| 14·9 | 4·1 | 10·8 | 32·8 | 42·2 | 15·0 | 1·4 | 8·9 | 11·6 | Central | 61·5 | −4·4 | 22·0 | 70·6 | 7·4 | — | * | 3·1 | −7·7 |
| 31·3 | 11·4 | 33·3 | 35·6 | 74·8 | 30·5 | 0·3 | 10·9 | 11·9 | East | 75·6 | −4·9 | 41·7 | 58·4 | — | — | — | *1·4* | *−6·3* |
| 44·6 | 21·2 | 35·7 | 9·5 | 54·1 | 30·3 | 1·8 | 8·2 | 15·2 | North | 67·7 | −7·3 | 56·1 | 43·9 | — | — | [9·5] | 1·7 | *−7·8* |
| 31·7 | 12·5 | 33·8 | 52·3 | 90·7 | 37·0 | 0·3 | 13·1 | 11·8 | West | 70·6 | −5·2 | 41·3 | 58·7 | — | — | — | *3·9* | *−3·1* |
| 27·9 | 11·9 | 55·2 | 24·5 | 70·4 | 39·5 | 1·9 | 10·0 | 11·5 | Northampton | 72·0 | −4·4 | 48·8 | 51·2 | — | — | — | *5·6* | *1·6* |
| 22·2 | 7·2 | 25·2 | 43·9 | 60·9 | 36·8 | 0·3 | 10·1 | 14·3 | Norwich, North | 71·3 | −2·9 | 38·2 | 59·7 | — | 2·1 | — | 4·8 | −0·1 |
| 34·0 | 14·3 | 33·0 | 42·8 | 74·1 | 44·8 | 0·6 | 11·7 | 12·3 | South † | 78·2 | −4·9 | 47·0 | 44·7 | 8·3 | — | * | 5·9 | −1·3 |
| 19·8 | 7·4 | 22·6 | 13·4 | 31·1 | 23·7 | 6·1 | 10·2 | 10·4 | Nottingham, Central | 60·2 | −7·6 | 44·4 | 55·6 | — | — | — | *3·3* | *−6·5* |
| 28·0 | 12·4 | 34·8 | 36·4 | 70·0 | 37·8 | 0·8 | 10·0 | 10·7 | North | 69·4 | −4·7 | 38·0 | 52·8 | 7·7 | 1·5 C | * | 4·4 | −1·1 |
| 32·3 | 14·2 | 34·9 | 27·9 | 67·2 | 41·6 | 2·8 | 10·4 | 8·8 | South † | 70·0 | −5·6 | 53·8 | 46·3 | — | — | — | *4·1* | *−3·1* |
| 31·4 | 12·7 | 27·5 | 58·4 | 84·9 | 43·3 | 0·4 | 12·4 | 9·5 | West | 70·9 | −7·4 | 47·2 | 52·8 | — | — | — | *5·2* | *1·3* |
| 27·7 | 13·7 | 48·4 | 36·2 | 74·6 | 49·7 | 1·7 | 9·7 | 9·7 | Oldbury & Halesowen † | 72·2 | −4·5 | 52·6 | 47·4 | — | — | — | *5·8* | 7·4 |
| 21·7 | 10·1 | 48·4 | 25·3 | 54·1 | 29·6 | 1·5 | 10·2 | 10·9 | Oldham, East | 65·2 | −7·5 | 48·9 | 51·1 | — | — | [14·4] | 6·6 | −1·6 |
| 25·9 | 10·3 | 54·0 | 18·2 | 54·4 | 31·1 | 1·1 | 9·6 | 11·6 | West ‡ | 67·0 | −5·4 | 43·1 | 48·1 | 8·8 | — | * | 8·7 | 1·6 |
| 33·1 | 14·6 | 46·2 | 22·7 | 80·1 | 47·2 | 3·3 | 12·0 | 10·1 | Oxford † | 74·5 | −4·7 | 47·0 | 43·4 | 9·6 | — | −2·1 | 4·1 | −5·6 |
| 23·3 | 7·6 | 32·5 | 30·2 | 63·8 | 32·5 | 1·5 | 11·7 | 11·9 | Plymouth, Devonport | 71·0 | −5·2 | 51·6 | 48·4 | — | — | — | *1·3* | 1·5 |
| 29·7 | 11·6 | 41·2 | 34·5 | 73·0 | 43·9 | 1·0 | 11·0 | 13·2 | Sutton | 72·3 | −6·6 | 49·4 | 50·6 | — | — | — | *3·9* | *−4·0* |

*English Boroughs—continued*

| % Non-manual | % Professional & managerial | % Owner-Occupiers | % Council Tenants | % With full plumbing | % With cars | % Born in New Commonwealth | % Young voters | % Retired | Constituency | % Voting 1970 | Change in % voting 1966–70 | Con. % | Lab. % | Lib. % | Other % | Lib. + or − % | Swing 1966–70 | Swing 1955–70 |
|---|---|---|---|---|---|---|---|---|---|---|---|---|---|---|---|---|---|---|
| 17·7 | 8·1 | 37·1 | 39·3 | 74·8 | 32·7 | 0·2 | 11·1 | 10·7 | Pontefract | 70·6 | −5·0 | 25·2 | 74·8 | — | — | — | *3·5* | *1·4* |
| 35·8 | 18·9 | 61·4 | 16·8 | 89·5 | 57·9 | 0·9 | 8·6 | 15·0 | Poole | 74·2 | −4·8 | 53·1 | 30·1 | 16·8 | — | +1·1 | 6·1 | 1·8 |
| 37·4 | 17·3 | 52·8 | 34·1 | 88·2 | 53·4 | 1·7 | 11·2 | 12·1 | Portsmouth, Langstone | 71·4 | −2·7 | 54·4 | 32·9 | 12·7 | — | −2·1 | 4·9 | −3·5 |
| 36·8 | 12·5 | 53·3 | 8·2 | 64·2 | 35·2 | 2·0 | 8·8 | 15·7 | South | 67·4 | −3·4 | 63·4 | 36·6 | — | — | — | *2·7* | *−3·8* |
| 22·9 | 7·9 | 44·9 | 18·5 | 51·5 | 29·1 | 2·2 | 11·3 | 11·1 | West | 72·3 | −4·2 | 47·7 | 50·6 | — | 1·7 | — | 0·3 | −5·6 |
| 29·0 | 12·4 | 55·5 | 25·3 | 68·0 | 34·6 | 2·7 | 10·3 | 11·0 | Preston, North † | 76·9 | −4·2 | 50·6 | 43·2 | 6·1 | — | * | 6·7 | 0·3 |
| 25·3 | 9·3 | 61·3 | 18·4 | 68·2 | 35·4 | 2·0 | 9·0 | 10·0 | South † | 75·8 | −4·1 | 51·7 | 48·3 | — | — | — | *5·3* | *1·1* |
| 39·4 | 20·5 | 62·8 | 23·4 | 87·9 | 47·4 | 0·2 | 8·9 | 8·5 | Pudsey | 79·2 | −4·1 | 49·2 | 37·1 | 13·7 | — | −2·1 | 3·5 | 0·7 |
| 33·9 | 14·0 | 50·1 | 18·3 | 68·9 | 43·0 | 3·2 | 10·4 | 9·8 | Reading † | 74·1 | −9·9 | 50·3 | 47·9 | — | 1·9 | [6·3] | 5·4 | 1·5 |
| 57·5 | 27·9 | 40·6 | 16·2 | 81·8 | 45·7 | 2·8 | 8·3 | 10·3 | Richmond | 71·7 | −7·7 | 51·3 | 31·7 | 17·0 | — | +1·9 | 2·7 | −3·8 |
| 27·1 | 13·4 | 45·6 | 27·5 | 62·4 | 33·4 | 2·5 | 9·8 | 10·7 | Rochdale | 72·9 | −6·0 | 28·0 | 41·6 | 30·4 | — | +11·1 | — | — |
| 29·9 | 12·1 | 50·3 | 26·5 | 72·8 | 45·3 | 1·8 | 10·5 | 9·5 | Rochester & Chatham † | 71·5 | −6·6 | 54·8 | 45·2 | — | — | — | *6·9* | *7·2* |
| 38·0 | 14·9 | 50·1 | 37·7 | 89·7 | 54·8 | 0·7 | 13·6 | 7·0 | Romford | 66·8 | −8·7 | 47·4 | 52·6 | — | — | — | *4·8* | *−0·1* |
| 25·8 | 14·4 | 54·2 | 24·6 | 64·0 | 33·9 | 0·4 | 9·6 | 12·7 | Rossendale † | 78·2 | −2·2 | 52·4 | 47·6 | — | — | — | *7·8* | *5·7* |
| 21·3 | 9·1 | 36·6 | 39·8 | 64·7 | 37·2 | 0·8 | 10·8 | 9·5 | Rotherham | 62·9 | −5·9 | 33·6 | 66·4 | — | — | — | *3·3* | *−3·1* |
| 18·5 | 8·9 | 36·5 | 42·6 | 71·2 | 42·7 | 1·1 | 10·5 | 8·5 | Rowley Regis & Tipton | 63·5 | −5·8 | 38·3 | 61·7 | — | — | — | *4·1* | 3·6 |
| 57·4 | 30·3 | 69·8 | 12·8 | 96·5 | 64·5 | 1·5 | 10·0 | 7·8 | Ruislip-Northwood | 73·1 | −8·6 | 60·7 | 28·9 | 10·5 | — | −4·7 | 6·9 | 0·7 |
| 17·3 | 6·0 | 36·8 | 30·0 | 62·1 | 29·3 | 0·3 | 11·6 | 13·4 | St. Helens | 64·5 | −4·1 | 34·3 | 65·7 | — | — | — | *5·1* | *−1·4* |
| 21·4 | 8·7 | 24·6 | 23·0 | 43·7 | 21·7 | 1·0 | 12·1 | 8·7 | Salford, East | 62·3 | +1·1 | 33·7 | 55·8 | 10·6 | — | * | 6·1 | −8·8 |
| 24·6 | 7·4 | 32·7 | 24·6 | 47·4 | 24·3 | 0·8 | 10·8 | 9·4 | West | 65·6 | −1·6 | 45·7 | 54·3 | — | — | — | *4·9* | *−3·3* |
| 18·9 | 6·6 | 36·8 | 24·8 | 52·6 | 34·8 | 1·5 | 10·3 | 9·0 | Sheffield, Attercliffe | 63·5 | −4·2 | 28·9 | 69·6 | — | 1·5 | — | 6·9 | *0·6* |
| 17·0 | 6·0 | 21·5 | 61·7 | 75·2 | 27·8 | 1·6 | 8·7 | 13·1 | Brightside | 62·0 | −4·2 | 25·8 | 72·2 | — | 2·0 C | — | 4·1 | −4·5 |
| 52·7 | 30·9 | 60·4 | 3·2 | 65·6 | 48·5 | 1·7 | 10·0 | 11·8 | Hallam | 69·8 | −5·2 | 61·3 | 31·4 | 7·3 | — | −8·9 | 5·5 | −1·2 |
| 36·5 | 18·1 | 47·3 | 22·7 | 64·9 | 42·3 | 1·6 | 9·4 | 9·9 | Heeley † | 73·4 | −5·2 | 47·0 | 45·9 | 7·1 | — | * | 4·6 | −10·3 |
| 23·0 | 9·7 | 32·9 | 25·6 | 49·8 | 32·9 | 0·5 | 8·8 | 10·4 | Hillsborough | 65·0 | −5·2 | 37·9 | 62·1 | — | — | — | *5·8* | *−3·3* |
| 13·9 | 3·8 | 12·5 | 67·9 | 75·4 | 22·7 | 1·5 | 11·3 | 9·6 | Park | 58·5 | −6·4 | 22·7 | 75·3 | — | 2·1 C | — | 5·6 | −3·1 |
| 20·3 | 6·8 | 39·6 | 28·1 | 49·8 | 34·7 | 6·6 | 9·4 | 10·0 | Smethwick | 68·2 | −7·2 | 45·4 | 52·2 | 2·4 | — | * | 1·7 | 4·7 |
| 28·8 | 11·0 | 54·4 | 18·8 | 73·3 | 46·4 | 10·6 | 9·5 | 7·2 | Southall | 64·5 | −6·3 | 42·0 | 53·7 | — | 4·4 | — | 1·3 | 1·3 |
| 29·8 | 11·2 | 43·5 | 29·4 | 75·7 | 44·5 | 2·0 | 11·1 | 8·1 | Southampton, Itchen | 54·1 | +5·1 | — | — | — | 67·2<br>21·9<br>10·9 | — | — | — |
| 35·0 | 16·1 | 41·1 | 30·9 | 75·4 | 45·2 | 1·1 | 10·6 | 11·1 | Test † | 73·3 | −4·8 | 47·5 | 44·1 | 8·4 | — | +0·3 | 4·1 | −1·9 |
| 41·6 | 18·1 | 46·9 | 13·2 | 71·1 | 36·5 | 1·7 | 9·4 | 15·1 | Southend, East | 71·3 | −5·7 | 58·5 | 41·5 | — | — | [10·6] | 7·9 | 0·3 |
| 53·0 | 24·1 | 64·0 | 9·4 | 86·8 | 46·9 | 1·1 | 9·5 | 15·4 | West | 70·8 | −7·6 | 60·1 | 25·5 | 14·5 | — | −7·2 | 5·6 | −4·4 |
| 62·2 | 31·2 | 64·6 | 7·0 | 81·6 | 52·4 | 3·1 | 8·7 | 10·2 | Southgate | 67·7 | −7·5 | 60·7 | 24·8 | 14·4 | — | −7·5 | 3·5 | −3·2 |
| 45·7 | 24·9 | 61·8 | 6·8 | 77·6 | 42·7 | 0·8 | 7·8 | 16·6 | Southport | 70·6 | −2·1 | 50·2 | 19·6 | 30·2 | — | +10·5 | — | — |
| 24·5 | 11·7 | 23·3 | 41·4 | 64·4 | 23·9 | 0·5 | 11·6 | 12·2 | South Shields | 66·8 | −1·9 | 39·8 | 60·2 | — | — | — | *4·5* | *−0·6* |
| 36·4 | 15·8 | 61·0 | 12·7 | 71·5 | 40·4 | 0·5 | 9·7 | 10·1 | Stockport, North † | 74·9 | −4·3 | 46·0 | 43·8 | 10·2 | — | * | 5·3 | −4·3 |
| 29·2 | 12·1 | 52·2 | 24·1 | 70·1 | 36·0 | 0·5 | 10·4 | 9·5 | South | 73·3 | −3·4 | 40·7 | 46·5 | 12·8 | — | * | 3·0 | −8·3 |

| | | | | | | | | | | | | | | | | | |
|---|---|---|---|---|---|---|---|---|---|---|---|---|---|---|---|---|---|
| [illegible] | [illegible] | 47·0 | 37·6 | 77·0 | 36·8 | 0·5 | 10·5 | 10·2 | Stockton on Tees | 73·2 | −4·2 | 44·2 | 54·9 | — | 0·9 C | — | 5·4 | −0·9 |
| 18·2 | 6·6 | 44·2 | 31·1 | 58·5 | 30·0 | 0·9 | 11·2 | 9·9 | Stoke on Trent, Central | 50·0 | −18·3 | 37·4 | 62·6 | — | — | — | 5·5 | 1·3 |
| 17·4 | 7·0 | 50·3 | 32·5 | 66·5 | 35·7 | 0·5 | 11·8 | 10·1 | North | 53·0 | −19·5 | 33·8 | 66·2 | — | — | — | 5·3 | 0·7 |
| 19·9 | 8·6 | 42·7 | 35·4 | 69·3 | 36·4 | 0·5 | 11·4 | 10·3 | South | 50·7 | −20·4 | 38·7 | 60·2 | — | 1·1 C | — | 3·4 | 2·8 |
| 38·6 | 16·0 | 56·8 | 19·8 | 83·1 | 43·1 | 2·3 | 10·4 | 8·7 | Stretford † | 74·9 | −2·2 | 53·8 | 46·2 | — | — | [12·2] | 7·0 | −7·1 |
| 21·8 | 8·7 | 34·2 | 42·4 | 65·9 | 26·9 | 0·3 | 10·7 | 11·8 | Sunderland, North | 69·8 | −4·7 | 39·9 | 60·6 | — | — | — | 0·1 | −7·5 |
| 25·1 | 11·1 | 32·2 | 49·8 | 75·8 | 30·3 | 0·3 | 12·8 | 10·2 | South | 70·2 | −5·3 | 43·6 | 56·4 | — | — | — | 1·0 | −8·3 |
| 52·1 | 24·3 | 60·7 | 9·7 | 87·7 | 57·6 | 2·0 | 9·3 | 8·2 | Surbiton | 70·4 | −6·6 | 51·7 | 31·2 | 12·0 | 5·1 | — | 2·4 | −4·6 |
| 57·1 | 29·0 | 72·6 | 5·8 | 87·4 | 58·2 | 1·5 | 8·1 | 10·0 | Sutton & Cheam | 67·6 | −8·7 | 58·1 | 27·3 | 14·6 | — | −4·1 | 5·0 | −0·6 |
| 51·1 | 28·9 | 63·1 | 21·8 | 87·7 | 62·6 | 1·1 | 9·2 | 8·6 | Sutton Coldfield | 68·9 | −7·4 | 57·4 | 28·3 | 14·3 | — | −8·6 | 0·6 | −5·4 |
| 24·7 | 10·0 | 54·2 | 34·5 | 82·8 | 42·4 | 1·7 | 10·6 | 11·1 | Swindon ‡ | 75·6 | +2·1 | 43·5 | 55·5 | — | 1·0 C | — | 6·3 | −1·1 |
| 44·3 | 24·4 | 64·5 | 12·8 | 87·1 | 46·5 | 0·6 | 7·5 | 22·2 | Torquay | 73·9 | −3·5 | 55·6 | 26·1 | 18·3 | — | −3·7 | 4·3 | −2·7 |
| 29·1 | 9·8 | 36·0 | 8·8 | 42·5 | 31·2 | 11·9 | 8·8 | 9·2 | Tottenham | 55·3 | −4·5 | 38·7 | 61·3 | — | — | — | 4·0 | −1·3 |
| 53·7 | 25·3 | 57·4 | 9·4 | 79·2 | 53·0 | 2·3 | 8·5 | 9·1 | Twickenham | 70·9 | −7·7 | 54·4 | 32·3 | 12·4 | 0·9 | −5·9 | 4·2 | −3·0 |
| 41·5 | 20·9 | 49·4 | 24·5 | 79·7 | 39·6 | 0·8 | 10·3 | 11·4 | Tynemouth | 75·9 | −2·6 | 51·4 | 39·9 | 8·7 | — | * | 2·8 | −3·9 |
| 28·7 | 13·6 | 37·4 | 43·2 | 79·6 | 38·7 | 0·6 | 10·4 | 11·7 | Wakefield | 72·8 | −0·6 | 33·3 | 58·1 | 8·6 | — | * | 3·0 | −2·0 |
| 40·0 | 16·3 | 49·1 | 18·7 | 82·7 | 34·9 | 0·3 | 9·8 | 10·5 | Wallasey | 74·9 | −1·2 | 45·0 | 39·2 | 10·4 | 5·5 | −3·4 | 2·3 | −10·6 |
| 30·6 | 11·3 | 31·2 | 41·3 | 78·6 | 36·2 | 0·4 | 11·2 | 9·6 | Wallsend | 74·4 | −3·1 | 38·7 | 61·3 | — | — | — | 3·9 | −3·5 |
| 19·9 | 8·1 | 26·4 | 57·9 | 82·0 | 42·8 | 0·7 | 11·9 | 8·1 | Walsall, North | 66·9 | −4·0 | 41·7 | 57·1 | — | 1·2 C | — | 7·4 | 4·9 |
| 33·5 | 16·9 | 57·7 | 23·5 | 81·2 | 55·3 | 3·6 | 9·3 | 7·2 | South | 73·0 | −4·3 | 59·5 | 40·5 | — | — | — | 6·1 | 6·8 |
| 37·8 | 16·7 | 49·2 | 19·1 | 66·7 | 40·1 | 2·5 | 9·0 | 10·5 | Walthamstow, East † ‡ | 71·0 | −9·2 | 46·7 | 45·0 | 8·3 | — | −1·5 | 3·6 | −0·7 |
| 25·8 | 8·0 | 29·7 | 20·6 | 55·2 | 35·3 | 2·2 | 10·6 | 9·6 | West ‡ | 65·2 | −5·8 | 34·4 | 54·5 | 11·2 | — | −2·9 | 8·2 | 5·7 |
| 61·3 | 32·5 | 64·2 | 11·8 | 86·4 | 55·8 | 1·4 | 9·2 | 9·2 | Wanstead & Woodford | 67·7 | −9·2 | 61·2 | 26·0 | 12·9 | — | −5·2 | 2·5 | −5·4 |
| 18·5 | 5·7 | 35·0 | 34·6 | 61·9 | 33·1 | 0·3 | 12·1 | 10·0 | Warrington | 65·2 | −3·7 | 35·7 | 64·3 | — | — | [9·1] | 4·9 | −7·2 |
| 36·9 | 16·7 | 54·7 | 20·6 | 77·5 | 50·2 | 1·9 | 9·1 | 9·1 | Watford | 75·5 | −7·4 | 45·5 | 45·7 | 8·8 | — | * | 4·3 | −2·1 |
| 17·9 | 8·2 | 29·5 | 52·4 | 71·8 | 40·6 | 2·5 | 10·9 | 7·0 | Wednesbury | 68·2 | −3·8 | 46·2 | 53·8 | — | — | — | 5·1 | 6·6 |
| 56·4 | 28·5 | 72·7 | 8·4 | 93·0 | 58·7 | 2·4 | 9·5 | 8·7 | Wembley, North | 72·1 | −8·8 | 53·4 | 34·7 | 11·9 | — | −3·5 | 3·6 | −3·2 |
| 45·1 | 19·7 | 70·5 | 5·1 | 85·2 | 50·0 | 8·0 | 8·0 | 8·9 | South | 69·0 | −10·3 | 53·6 | 46·4 | — | — | [12·9] | 1·9 | −4·9 |
| 19·9 | 8·9 | 34·8 | 50·2 | 84·4 | 41·0 | 3·7 | 11·9 | 7·6 | West Bromwich | 62·1 | −6·8 | 44·8 | 55·2 | — | — | — | 2·6 | 6·6 |
| 24·4 | 7·0 | 26·8 | 18·6 | 36·7 | 31·5 | 6·1 | 10·8 | 8·4 | West Ham, North | 50·4 | −11·4 | 25·5 | 63·2 | 11·3 | — | −6·4 | 5·7 | 1·2 |
| 18·2 | 5·6 | 18·9 | 34·1 | 42·0 | 30·3 | 2·0 | 12·2 | 8·4 | South | 48·9 | −13·0 | 22·3 | 77·7 | — | — | [11·3] | 5·1 | 5·4 |
| 22·7 | 10·5 | 41·9 | 32·6 | 64·3 | 30·1 | 0·2 | 11·2 | 12·9 | Wigan | 72·3 | −3·7 | 30·9 | 67·5 | — | 1·6 C | — | 5·6 | −1·6 |
| 36·9 | 15·4 | 31·4 | 8·8 | 57·4 | 33·4 | 10·8 | 7·9 | 7·2 | Willesden, East | 62·4 | −8·7 | 43·7 | 56·3 | — | — | [6·9] | 2·5 | −5·6 |
| 24·4 | 8·2 | 30·6 | 11·4 | 48·8 | 28·6 | 13·3 | 9·3 | 7·8 | West | 59·3 | −4·4 | 31·2 | 67·2 | — | 1·6 C | — | 2·0 | −6·3 |
| 54·8 | 27·6 | 47·9 | 6·4 | 69·6 | 45·4 | 4·3 | 8·9 | 10·0 | Wimbledon | 66·9 | −8·1 | 53·5 | 29·9 | 16·6 | — | −1·5 | 2·4 | −3·8 |
| | | | | | | | | | Wolverhampton, | | | | | | | | | |
| 18·3 | 7·1 | 31·3 | 50·3 | 64·6 | 36·0 | 6·0 | 12·2 | 8·4 | North-east | 66·7 | −2·6 | 44·9 | 50·4 | — | 4·7 | — | 9·1 | 9·4 |
| 34·1 | 17·2 | 49·6 | 24·1 | 74·2 | 44·8 | 8·4 | 9·6 | 9·7 | South-west | 76·0 | +2·5 | 64·3 | 28·8 | 6·0 | 0·5 C<br>0·2<br>0·1 | * | 8·7 | 7·8 |
| 32·7 | 11·3 | 34·3 | 30·4 | 57·5 | 35·6 | 5·9 | 9·3 | 10·6 | Wood Green | 60·9 | −6·4 | 42·9 | 57·1 | — | — | — | 3·7 | −3·2 |
| 33·4 | 14·9 | 49·8 | 26·2 | 74·2 | 50·5 | 0·8 | 10·2 | 9·7 | Worcester | 72·8 | −5·1 | 58·3 | 41·7 | — | — | — | 4·8 | 1·5 |
| 54·4 | 27·7 | 64·5 | 9·4 | 86·0 | 41·5 | 1·4 | 6·3 | 29·8 | Worthing | 70·0 | −5·7 | 65·6 | 17·8 | 16·6 | — | −1·3 | 4·3 | −3·2 |
| 32·0 | 12·1 | 49·4 | 29·4 | 76·0 | 33·1 | 0·6 | 11·1 | 10·5 | York | 76·3 | −6·4 | 48·1 | 51·9 | — | — | — | 3·3 | −2·8 |

## English Counties

| % Non-manual | % Professional & managerial | % Owner-Occupiers | % Council Tenants | % With full plumbing | % With cars | % Born in New Commonwealth | % Young voters | % Retired | Constituency | % Voting 1970 | Change in % voting 1966–70 | Con. % | Lab. % | Lib. % | Other % | Lib. + or − % | Swing 1966–70 | Swing 1955–70 |
|---|---|---|---|---|---|---|---|---|---|---|---|---|---|---|---|---|---|---|
| 36·5 | 16·9 | 55·2 | 19·0 | 82·1 | 51·2 | 4·0 | 9·8 | 8·7 | Bedfordshire, Bedford † | 77·2 | −4·4 | 50·5 | 40·4 | 9·1 | — | −1·2 | 5·5 | −0·5 |
| 31·5 | 15·7 | 45·9 | 25·6 | 74·0 | 61·3 | 0·8 | 9·9 | 9·8 | Mid | 77·4 | −4·9 | 52·5 | 33·7 | 13·8 | — | −0·2 | 6·4 | 4·7 |
| 32·0 | 15·2 | 60·3 | 23·3 | 86·1 | 58·9 | 1·2 | 9·6 | 6·1 | South † | 77·3 | −6·4 | 48·7 | 42·4 | 8·9 | — | −1·4 | 6·1 | 0·4 |
| 37·4 | 19·1 | 48·8 | 23·7 | 86·8 | 63·0 | 1·2 | 10·0 | 7·4 | Berkshire, Abingdon | 77·6 | −4·9 | 54·4 | 34·8 | 10·8 | — | −2·0 | 7·1 | 0·6 |
| 38·7 | 18·6 | 53·2 | 21·2 | 85·0 | 59·4 | 1·4 | 11·4 | 8·9 | Newbury | 72·6 | −6·5 | 48·8 | 29·9 | 21·3 | — | +4·6 | 5·8 | 1·4 |
| 44·8 | 23·9 | 55·5 | 18·9 | 84·4 | 62·2 | 1·3 | 9·8 | 7·4 | Windsor | 70·6 | −5·7 | 58·9 | 29·6 | 11·6 | — | −5·4 | 6·6 | 1·3 |
| 47·2 | 24·0 | 60·5 | 21·4 | 87·2 | 68·9 | 1·6 | 10·0 | 7·2 | Wokingham | 72·2 | −7·0 | 55·0 | 28·8 | 16·2 | — | −1·5 | 6·4 | −1·8 |
| | | | | | | | | | Buckinghamshire, | | | | | | | | | |
| 38·8 | 20·5 | 51·6 | 26·0 | 85·9 | 61·3 | 1·9 | 11·0 | 8·1 | Aylesbury | 75·6 | −4·3 | 53·3 | 35·0 | 11·7 | — | −5·9 | 5·4 | 2·1 |
| 27·8 | 13·8 | 45·4 | 29·7 | 78·0 | 54·6 | 0·8 | 10·6 | 10·5 | Buckingham † | 81·8 | −3·9 | 47·5 | 43·2 | 9·3 | — | −0·1 | 4·3 | 0·9 |
| 50·9 | 32·1 | 56·3 | 23·3 | 91·4 | 70·9 | 1·1 | 10·6 | 7·4 | South | 72·8 | −7·5 | 58·7 | 24·1 | 17·2 | — | −5·9 | 4·5 | −1·8 |
| 35·5 | 20·0 | 57·0 | 22·8 | 84·9 | 62·5 | 2·8 | 10·1 | 8·0 | Wycombe | 74·8 | −5·9 | 55·9 | 32·5 | 11·6 | — | −1·0 | 6·2 | 4·0 |
| 34·0 | 19·7 | 47·2 | 24·0 | 73·7 | 62·3 | 0·9 | 8·7 | 10·6 | Cambridgeshire | 75·5 | −3·6 | 54·6 | 33·8 | 11·6 | — | −2·7 | 5·6 | 6·1 |
| 58·0 | 32·4 | 72·2 | 16·3 | 93·1 | 62·6 | 0·4 | 9·5 | 8·1 | Cheshire, Cheadle † | 79·9 | −2·5 | 46·3 | 9·4 | 44·3 | — | +1·9 | — | — |
| 40·2 | 19·9 | 50·4 | 25·0 | 80·6 | 50·4 | 1·0 | 9·1 | 9·6 | City of Chester | 73·2 | −4·9 | 52·0 | 38·0 | 10·0 | — | −3·8 | 4·1 | −5·5 |
| 25·9 | 9·9 | 55·8 | 26·4 | 71·5 | 41·8 | 0·6 | 10·5 | 11·5 | Crewe | 71·0 | −4·6 | 45·7 | 54·3 | — | — | — | 6·7 | 3·4 |
| 50·3 | 30·9 | 58·5 | 21·4 | 87·3 | 63·7 | 0·7 | 8·9 | 10·1 | Knutsford | 74·8 | −4·4 | 59·8 | 20·9 | 19·3 | — | −5·7 | — | −5·8 |
| 38·7 | 22·1 | 53·6 | 23·7 | 77·4 | 52·0 | 0·4 | 9·0 | 10·8 | Macclesfield | 76·3 | −5·4 | 52·1 | 33·3 | 14·6 | — | +0·3 | 5·4 | −0·6 |
| 28·9 | 15·8 | 51·5 | 24·0 | 74·9 | 55·0 | 0·4 | 10·1 | 11·0 | Nantwich | 77·6 | −1·7 | 46·2 | 34·3 | 19·5 | — | +1·1 | 3·0 | −5·1 |
| 30·9 | 15·0 | 47·9 | 31·0 | 76·5 | 54·6 | 0·2 | 11·3 | 11·5 | Northwich | 78·5 | −3·9 | 51·3 | 39·7 | 9·1 | — | −2·7 | 4·9 | −3·6 |
| 39·1 | 21·9 | 63·0 | 18·8 | 80·8 | 56·1 | 0·3 | 9·4 | 10·6 | Runcorn | 76·9 | −5·2 | 53·5 | 34·3 | 12·2 | — | −2·7 | 3·8 | −4·5 |
| 26·4 | 11·7 | 42·0 | 35·8 | 66·2 | 33·2 | 0·8 | 9·8 | 10·1 | Stalybridge & Hyde | 73·5 | −0·1 | 41·3 | 47·4 | 11·3 | — | * | 3·9 | −2·9 |
| 43·7 | 24·0 | 57·9 | 24·6 | 90·9 | 58·0 | 0·6 | 9·7 | 10·1 | Wirral | 74·2 | −5·5 | 55·1 | 31·7 | 13·2 | — | −5·6 | 4·2 | −5·7 |
| 31·0 | 16·6 | 53·6 | 18·6 | 75·1 | 54·9 | 0·9 | 8·8 | 18·4 | Cornwall, Bodmin † | 80·7 | −3·7 | 48·3 | 12·8 | 38·9 | — | −7·7 | — | — |
| 29·6 | 15·5 | 56·6 | 18·3 | 63·4 | 49·9 | 0·9 | 8·7 | 17·0 | Falmouth & Camborne † | 77·8 | −4·8 | 44·5 | 41·4 | 12·1 | 2·0 | −1·3 | 5·2 | 2·8 |
| 33·8 | 21·4 | 54·9 | 13·3 | 76·3 | 61·1 | 0·9 | 8·9 | 16·6 | North | 85·3 | −2·3 | 47·1 | 4·3 | 48·6 | — | +0·1 | — | — |
| 34·4 | 21·0 | 50·9 | 19·2 | 71·4 | 46·4 | 0·9 | 8·6 | 16·0 | St. Ives | 75·1 | −2·8 | 50·9 | 27·2 | 21·9 | — | −5·8 | 6·7 | 0·7 |
| 34·5 | 20·0 | 54·8 | 18·5 | 71·6 | 57·4 | 0·6 | 8·2 | 17·3 | Truro | 76·6 | −2·7 | 49·3 | 33·0 | 17·7 | — | −4·9 | 6·4 | 2·7 |
| 31·5 | 19·1 | 45·8 | 16·3 | 77·5 | 58·0 | 0·4 | 11·3 | 13·5 | Cumberland, Penrith & the Border | 74·4 | −4·3 | 59·0 | 25·4 | 15·6 | — | −1·3 | 5·6 | −0·5 |
| 23·7 | 11·4 | 35·7 | 39·9 | 77·7 | 42·2 | 0·2 | 12·1 | 11·7 | Whitehaven | 78·3 | −0·5 | 41·7 | 58·3 | — | — | — | *3·7* | *−0·3* |
| 24·9 | 11·7 | 42·1 | 30·3 | 73·1 | 40·3 | 0·2 | 11·1 | 13·6 | Workington | 77·4 | −3·0 | 38·3 | 61·7 | — | — | — | *1·7* | *−2·3* |
| 32·5 | 16·4 | 58·9 | 17·6 | 74·4 | 52·8 | 0·2 | 9·7 | 11·0 | Derbyshire, Belper † | 80·1 | −4·1 | 51·5 | 48·5 | — | — | — | *4·8* | *7·1* |
| 14·0 | 5·8 | 32·8 | 31·2 | 66·9 | 33·7 | 0·1 | 10·4 | 13·5 | Bolsover | 70·8 | −3·9 | 22·5 | 77·5 | — | — | — | *4·1* | *1·4* |
| 30·2 | 16·1 | 51·2 | 17·6 | 71·7 | 44·3 | 0·2 | 10·8 | 11·9 | High Peak † | 80·7 | −3·5 | 43·7 | 40·4 | 15·9 | — | −3·6 | 2·8 | −5·2 |
| 18·1 | 7·7 | 52·1 | 23·0 | 64·4 | 37·8 | 0·1 | 10·4 | 11·8 | Ilkeston | 74·2 | −2·0 | 28·9 | 59·9 | 11·2 | — | * | 4·6 | 3·7 |

| | | | | | | | | | | | | | | | | | | |
|---|---|---|---|---|---|---|---|---|---|---|---|---|---|---|---|---|---|---|
| 24·6 | 11·7 | 39·5 | 37·6 | 80·5 | 45·9 | 0·1 | 10·8 | 10·0 | North-east . . | 69·8 | −4·1 | 39·1 | 60·9 | — | — | — | *6·1* | *5·6* |
| 28·2 | 11·5 | 53·1 | 27·1 | 79·2 | 48·9 | 0·5 | 9·8 | 9·5 | South-east † . | 75·3 | −6·5 | 52·2 | 47·8 | — | — | — | *6·8* | *3·8* |
| 30·7 | 19·4 | 49·2 | 17·5 | 68·7 | 53·1 | 0·2 | 9·8 | 11·6 | West . . . | 76·7 | −6·8 | 61·9 | 38·1 | — | — | [13·2] | 5·7 | *2·3* |
| 40·9 | 25·3 | 58·4 | 16·1 | 85·4 | 55·8 | 1·1 | 8·4 | 22·8 | Devon, Honiton . | 76·7 | −2·0 | 59·5 | 20·0 | 20·5 | — | +1·7 | 5·9 | — |
| 33·9 | 19·7 | 56·9 | 14·1 | 80·1 | 54·7 | 0·9 | 9·1 | 17·2 | North . . | 84·9 | −0·5 | 43·2 | 12·3 | 44·1 | 0·4 | +0·5 | — | — |
| 38·3 | 20·6 | 59·8 | 13·1 | 82·8 | 63·7 | 1·3 | 8·8 | 15·0 | Tavistock . | 75·5 | −6·0 | 57·1 | 19·9 | 23·0 | — | −7·6 | — | — |
| 34·4 | 19·4 | 49·4 | 20·7 | 78·8 | 54·8 | 0·6 | 8·7 | 19·0 | Tiverton . . | 77·0 | −3·7 | 55·2 | 24·2 | 20·6 | — | −3·8 | 4·7 | 1·2 |
| 29·7 | 17·2 | 55·1 | 14·1 | 71·6 | 55·2 | 0·8 | 9·4 | 16·5 | Torrington . . | 80·7 | −5·1 | 54·0 | 17·0 | 29·0 | — | −8·5 | — | — |
| 34·5 | 19·7 | 53·6 | 18·0 | 81·8 | 55·8 | 1·0 | 8·6 | 19·5 | Totnes . . | 76·7 | −2·8 | 54·9 | 28·6 | 16·6 | — | −4·1 | 5·0 | 1·7 |
| 36·6 | 21·1 | 54·4 | 17·7 | 84·0 | 65·8 | 1·4 | 9·3 | 17·3 | Dorset, North . | 78·6 | −2·7 | 57·9 | 17·5 | 24·6 | — | −10·6 | — | — |
| 36·2 | 16·4 | 52·5 | 19·3 | 80·6 | 51·8 | 1·2 | 9·6 | 13·3 | South . . | 79·1 | −1·9 | 52·1 | 39·1 | 8·8 | — | −2·9 | 4·6 | 0·3 |
| 36·6 | 20·8 | 45·3 | 19·9 | 78·2 | 60·2 | 1·1 | 8·7 | 15·1 | West . . . | 76·9 | −4·0 | 54·2 | 27·1 | 18·8 | — | −1·9 | 5·5 | 4·0 |
| | | | | | | | | | Durham, | | | | | | | | | |
| 20·0 | 9·0 | 45·4 | 23·1 | 58·1 | 37·2 | 0·1 | 11·5 | 13·9 | Bishop Auckland | 70·8 | −2·7 | 39·3 | 60·7 | — | — | — | *4·2* | *−3·0* |
| 28·5 | 12·0 | 42·9 | 34·2 | 69·4 | 36·8 | 1·1 | 9·2 | 12·0 | Blaydon . . | 72·3 | −5·1 | 35·1 | 64·9 | — | — | — | *4·3* | *1·6* |
| 24·2 | 9·6 | 35·5 | 45·1 | 70·1 | 34·4 | 0·2 | 10·1 | 13·2 | Chester-le-Street . | 73·7 | −1·2 | 28·4 | 71·6 | — | — | — | *5·4* | *4·7* |
| 18·8 | 7·3 | 34·1 | 35·5 | 58·0 | 31·5 | 0·1 | 11·1 | 14·5 | Consett . . | 70·2 | −3·3 | 29·1 | 70·9 | — | — | — | *2·4* | *−3·8* |
| 27·0 | 11·3 | 33·1 | 46·6 | 74·0 | 36·3 | 0·3 | 10·5 | 12·9 | Durham . . | 73·3 | −1·4 | 33·1 | 66·9 | — | — | — | *3·7* | *−0·8* |
| 13·8 | 5·5 | 26·0 | 50·3 | 73·5 | 29·8 | 0·1 | 10·6 | 13·9 | Easington . . | 69·3 | −1·3 | 20·2 | 79·8 | — | — | — | *1·6* | *−0·7* |
| 19·9 | 7·6 | 25·5 | 55·5 | 74·8 | 31·9 | 0·1 | 10·5 | 13·0 | Houghton-le-Spring | 71·6 | −2·3 | 26·6 | 73·4 | — | — | — | *4·1* | *2·7* |
| 19·5 | 8·4 | 32·5 | 35·8 | 62·4 | 34·9 | 0·1 | 10·1 | 15·3 | North-west . | 72·9 | −0·5 | 30·4 | 69·6 | — | — | — | *4·0* | *−2·2* |
| 27·5 | 11·0 | 31·5 | 45·9 | 79·5 | 44·6 | 0·3 | 10·5 | 9·5 | Sedgefield . . | 72·7 | −3·3 | 39·5 | 60·5 | — | — | — | *4·1* | *−0·8* |
| 24·3 | 15·0 | 43·8 | 27·6 | 65·5 | 53·8 | 0·2 | 10·8 | 11·8 | Isle of Ely . . | 71·9 | −4·0 | 59·9 | 40·1 | — | — | [11·4] | 8·4 | *2·5* |
| 41·0 | 18·6 | 47·4 | 42·3 | 89·2 | 60·6 | 0·9 | 10·6 | 7·5 | Essex, Billericay † . | 74·3 | −9·8 | 52·2 | 47·8 | — | — | [8·8] | 3·1 | *−2·6* |
| 45·6 | 21·9 | 54·7 | 26·5 | 83·1 | 59·4 | 1·0 | 9·9 | 9·6 | Chelmsford . | 75·6 | −6·9 | 55·2 | 35·6 | 8·7 | 0·5 | −5·2 | 5·7 | 4·1 |
| 46·7 | 25·4 | 46·9 | 36·9 | 90·7 | 62·7 | 0·5 | 12·0 | 6·8 | Chigwell . . | 72·7 | −8·6 | 59·5 | 40·5 | — | — | [11·3] | 6·6 | *7·0* |
| 37·4 | 19·1 | 55·0 | 22·1 | 71·6 | 51·8 | 1·3 | 10·1 | 13·1 | Colchester . . | 77·6 | −4·7 | 52·6 | 35·0 | 12·5 | — | +1·8 | 7·9 | 3·3 |
| 41·1 | 21·0 | 41·2 | 48·3 | 91·9 | 59·6 | 0·7 | 10·4 | 6·2 | Epping † . . | 73·3 | −9·2 | 51·5 | 48·5 | — | — | [12·6] | 6·2 | −1·6 |
| 36·2 | 18·4 | 68·8 | 10·9 | 81·3 | 45·2 | 0·5 | 8·1 | 21·6 | Harwich . . | 74·5 | +0·1 | 53·5 | 32·6 | 13·9 | — | −3·6 | 4·2 | −0·7 |
| 31·5 | 15·9 | 48·4 | 26·0 | 76·4 | 53·0 | 0·6 | 9·2 | 11·8 | Maldon . . | 79·9 | −3·5 | 50·6 | 39·8 | 9·7 | — | −0·5 | 4·9 | 4·8 |
| 34·4 | 19·6 | 46·2 | 22·5 | 73·7 | 59·2 | 0·7 | 8·9 | 13·0 | Saffron Walden . | 77·2 | −5·3 | 52·9 | 32·1 | 15·0 | — | +2·3 | 6·6 | 2·0 |
| 42·3 | 18·2 | 79·1 | 8·8 | 86·3 | 55·2 | 0·6 | 8·4 | 12·8 | South-east . | 72·0 | −5·4 | 57·7 | 32·9 | 9·5 | — | −2·3 | 8·1 | 2·7 |
| 27·3 | 9·5 | 39·1 | 44·8 | 82·1 | 51·9 | 1·0 | 13·3 | 7·6 | Thurrock . . | 65·7 | −7·0 | 35·2 | 55·8 | 9·1 | — | −3·5 | 6·7 | 5·9 |
| 35·5 | 20·5 | 46·4 | 22·7 | 84·8 | 62·1 | 0·9 | 9·5 | 10·8 | Gloucestershire, Cirencester & Tewksb'y | 73·8 | −1·1 | 56·0 | 29·9 | 14·0 | — | * | 4·9 | — |
| 37·4 | 17·7 | 61·9 | 22·7 | 82·4 | 66·6 | 0·6 | 9·4 | 7·3 | South . . | 78·6 | −5·7 | 50·9 | 37·9 | 11·2 | — | −0·7 | 5·4 | 4·5 |
| 31·5 | 16·6 | 55·4 | 22·0 | 79·4 | 55·1 | 0·8 | 10·4 | 11·6 | Stroud . . | 80·3 | −4·7 | 51·1 | 36·1 | 12·8 | — | −3·8 | 5·9 | 3·3 |
| 28·4 | 14·3 | 61·1 | 17·7 | 73·7 | 58·0 | 0·4 | 9·9 | 12·0 | West . . . | 77·0 | −1·0 | 43·9 | 46·1 | 10·0 | — | −3·7 | 7·5 | 3·8 |
| 42·5 | 19·4 | 52·8 | 18·1 | 84·4 | 64·0 | 2·4 | 11·2 | 7·3 | Hampshire, Aldershot | 70·9 | −4·5 | 55·8 | 31·6 | 12·6 | — | −6·5 | 3·7 | 0·2 |
| 32·7 | 17·1 | 44·1 | 26·1 | 85·7 | 59·4 | 1·4 | 10·0 | 9·1 | Basingstoke . | 75·0 | −3·5 | 50·9 | 37·2 | 11·9 | — | −2·9 | 3·7 | −0·3 |
| 35·8 | 16·8 | 60·7 | 20·9 | 79·5 | 59·0 | 0·7 | 10·2 | 10·7 | Eastleigh . . | 78·4 | −5·3 | 51·0 | 37·5 | 11·5 | — | +1·0 | 6·1 | 6·1 |
| 38·3 | 22·0 | 63·1 | 13·7 | 84·1 | 63·4 | 1·5 | 9·8 | 19·2 | New Forest . | 71·9 | −2·3 | 60·1 | 22·7 | 17·2 | — | −4·8 | 6·5 | −0·0 |
| 87·6 | 20·9 | 53·7 | 16·3 | 81·9 | 61·5 | 1·8 | 10·7 | 12·9 | Petersfield . | 72·1 | −3·6 | 60·5 | 20·5 | 15·5 | 3·5 | −8·4 | — | 0·2 |
| 38·9 | 19·7 | 44·0 | 25·2 | 83·6 | 59·0 | 1·6 | 11·1 | 11·3 | Winchester . | 74·7 | −3·2 | 55·0 | 25·7 | 19·3 | — | +1·3 | 4·1 | −0·7 |
| | | | | | | | | | Herefordshire, | | | | | | | | | |
| 32·4 | 16·8 | 46·4 | 28·8 | 76·3 | 56·5 | 0·9 | 10·0 | 10·5 | Hereford . . | 73·4 | −3·9 | 53·2 | 34·8 | 12·0 | — | −5·8 | — | — |
| 30·5 | 19·9 | 43·8 | 15·1 | 64·0 | 61·2 | 0·5 | 11·3 | 11·5 | Leominster . | 72·8 | −2·3 | 58·0 | 20·8 | 21·2 | — | −4·9 | 4·0 | — |

*English Counties—continued*

| % Non-manual | % Professional & managerial | % Owner-Occupiers | % Council Tenants | % With full plumbing | % With cars | % Born in New Commonwealth | % Young voters | % Retired | Constituency | % Voting 1970 | Change in % voting 1966–70 | Con. % | Lab. % | Lib. % | Other % | Lib. + or − % | Swing 1966–70 | Swing 1955–70 |
|---|---|---|---|---|---|---|---|---|---|---|---|---|---|---|---|---|---|---|
| 54·1 | 26·9 | 57·8 | 25·6 | 90·8 | 61·2 | 1·0 | 11·1 | 7·3 | Hertfordshire, Barnet | 71·3 | −9·2 | 52·3 | 35·4 | 12·3 | — | −3·9 | 3·3 | −2·3 |
| 39·8 | 21·0 | 55·5 | 24·5 | 84·9 | 60·9 | 0·7 | 10·1 | 7·7 | East . . | 73·5 | −6·6 | 54·7 | 34·3 | 11·0 | — | −4·0 | 6·1 | 3·3 |
| 43·3 | 24·5 | 43·0 | 41·8 | 88·5 | 63·9 | 0·9 | 10·9 | 8·4 | Hemel Hempstead | 78·3 | −6·4 | 52·0 | 36·1 | 11·9 | — | −2·0 | 6·5 | 1·8 |
| 45·8 | 23·8 | 34·1 | 51·1 | 91·3 | 63·2 | 0·9 | 10·8 | 6·9 | Hertford . . | 78·7 | −5·0 | 52·6 | 38·8 | 8·6 | — | * | 6·3 | 0·1 |
| 37·5 | 18·5 | 31·0 | 52·4 | 89·3 | 58·9 | 1·7 | 10·0 | 6·2 | Hitchin . . | 77·5 | −4·8 | 44·2 | 48·5 | 7·3 | — | * | 4·4 | −3·1 |
| 44·9 | 22·6 | 55·9 | 21·5 | 84·4 | 58·8 | 2·3 | 9·5 | 7·7 | St. Albans . | 76·2 | −6·8 | 51·5 | 35·0 | 13·5 | — | +2·9 | 5·2 | 0·7 |
| 44·8 | 25·4 | 53·1 | 30·5 | 91·6 | 65·7 | 0·8 | 12·3 | 6·9 | South-west . | 75·8 | −7·3 | 50·3 | 37·3 | 11·5 | 0·8 | −2·3 | 3·9 | −0·4 |
| 29·9 | 16·5 | 43·1 | 27·5 | 77·9 | 62·4 | 0·9 | 10·4 | 8·1 | Huntingdonshire . | 75·3 | −2·3 | 54·7 | 35·1 | 10·2 | — | −4·0 | 3·5 | 1·4 |
| 32·8 | 17·1 | 50·0 | 25·3 | 79·7 | 54·4 | 1·4 | 10·5 | 13·3 | Kent, Ashford . . | 72·6 | −2·9 | 54·9 | 28·9 | 16·3 | — | −2·7 | 3·5 | 2·5 |
| 41·0 | 20·5 | 57·7 | 17·5 | 83·4 | 46·0 | 1·0 | 9·3 | 18·1 | Canterbury . | 74·6 | −1·5 | 55·4 | 25·3 | 19·3 | — | −2·7 | 4·2 | −1·5 |
| 47·6 | 21·6 | 55·6 | 28·5 | 90·5 | 58·3 | 1·4 | 11·2 | 8·8 | Chislehurst † . | 75·5 | −8·7 | 49·1 | 42·4 | 8·5 | — | −2·9 | 4·2 | −0·6 |
| 36·6 | 16·1 | 55·0 | 26·1 | 79·9 | 56·5 | 1·1 | 9·8 | 8·0 | Dartford † . | 74·1 | −6·7 | 46·0 | 45·0 | 9·0 | — | −3·0 | 6·3 | 4·9 |
| 32·4 | 15·7 | 46·4 | 20·7 | 77·4 | 41·7 | 1·5 | 10·8 | 14·5 | Dover † . . | 80·7 | −3·5 | 51·4 | 48·6 | — | — | [7·2] | 4·3 | *−1·5* |
| 26·6 | 12·5 | 49·5 | 24·6 | 69·7 | 44·2 | 0·8 | 9·2 | 14·3 | Faversham † . | 78·2 | −1·8 | 53·4 | 46·6 | — | — | — | *5·9* | *3·5* |
| 39·6 | 20·1 | 51·8 | 13·1 | 78·6 | 44·8 | 1·4 | 9·3 | 18·0 | Folkestone & Hythe . . | 68·8 | −1·8 | 64·3 | 32·8 | — | 2·9 | — | 6·2 | 0·8 |
| 32·4 | 15·4 | 53·9 | 24·6 | 78·1 | 51·2 | 2·1 | 11·0 | 7·9 | Gravesend † . | 76·0 | −6·1 | 46·9 | 45·0 | 8·2 | — | −0·2 | 4·9 | −2·1 |
| 39·0 | 18·8 | 57·8 | 14·9 | 80·6 | 38·2 | 0·9 | 8·7 | 21·7 | Isle of Thanet . | 72·4 | −3·3 | 51·9 | 33·7 | 11·1 | 3·3 | −1·8 | 5·1 | −3·1 |
| 38·8 | 18·9 | 51·0 | 23·4 | 74·8 | 56·5 | 1·0 | 9·8 | 10·7 | Maidstone . . | 72·2 | −2·1 | 51·4 | 30·3 | 18·3 | — | * | 5·9 | 2·7 |
| 57·4 | 29·9 | 67·0 | 18·9 | 90·5 | 64·2 | 0·9 | 10·4 | 8·7 | Orpington † . | 79·2 | −7·8 | 47·3 | 8·0 | 44·7 | — | −1·9 | — | — |
| 44·4 | 26·6 | 52·8 | 18·1 | 79·9 | 60·3 | 1·1 | 9·5 | 9·4 | Sevenoaks . . | 73·9 | −5·3 | 54·1 | 25·5 | 20·4 | — | +3·2 | 5·2 | 2·5 |
| 45·5 | 22·5 | 49·4 | 20·4 | 77·2 | 53·3 | 1·5 | 9·4 | 11·8 | Tonbridge . . | 72·0 | −5·3 | 53·2 | 29·9 | 17·0 | — | −1·4 | 5·7 | 1·2 |
| 27·8 | 13·2 | 61·8 | 19·9 | 72·2 | 44·5 | 0·4 | 10·2 | 10·9 | Lancashire, Chorley † | 79·0 | −2·1 | 47·3 | 44·3 | 7·9 | 0·6 | * | 6·3 | 2·9 |
| 31·0 | 17·9 | 65·5 | 14·1 | 64·5 | 44·9 | 0·7 | 9·2 | 12·4 | Clitheroe . . | 79·3 | −4·2 | 51·7 | 35·8 | 12·6 | — | −1·3 | 5·0 | 1·5 |
| 35·1 | 17·7 | 76·0 | 10·5 | 60·8 | 44·8 | 0·3 | 9·3 | 11·0 | Darwen . . | 76·7 | −5·9 | 52·4 | 34·6 | 13·1 | — | −6·1 | 7·1 | 0·2 |
| 25·5 | 10·4 | 44·4 | 43·7 | 78·6 | 38·8 | 0·2 | 11·2 | 8·9 | Farnworth . . | 72·3 | −2·5 | 41·5 | 58·5 | — | — | — | *7·7* | *−0·8* |
| 27·2 | 12·4 | 49·9 | 27·1 | 66·3 | 37·5 | 0·3 | 9·7 | 10·4 | Heywood & Royton | 76·1 | −3·4 | 44·1 | 45·7 | 10·2 | — | −3·1 | 4·8 | −4·1 |
| 25·7 | 10·3 | 27·6 | 62·9 | 92·2 | 37·7 | 0·3 | 14·4 | 6·3 | Huyton . . | 67·3 | −2·8 | 33·9 | 63·1 | — | 1·7<br>1·2 C | — | 2·3 | −11·9 |
| 23·7 | 9·9 | 50·3 | 26·4 | 66·9 | 40·5 | 0·1 | 10·0 | 11·0 | Ince . . . | 70·7 | −4·7 | 31·5 | 68·5 | — | — | — | *5·2* | *4·3* |
| 28·9 | 13·0 | 56·5 | 22·8 | 79·0 | 43·8 | 0·4 | 9·7 | 11·8 | Lancaster † . | 80·0 | +0·4 | 49·1 | 44·5 | 6·4 | — | * | 4·9 | −4·2 |
| 39·4 | 17·8 | 53·6 | 32·7 | 84·6 | 43·1 | 0·2 | 10·6 | 8·0 | Middleton & Prestwich † . | 74·7 | −3·3 | 43·8 | 41·9 | 14·3 | — | −3·4 | 4·5 | −10·6 |
| 38·4 | 20·1 | 66·5 | 10·9 | 84·8 | 46·0 | 0·5 | 8·4 | 21·2 | Morecambe & Lonsdale . | 72·6 | −3·9 | 57·0 | 28·9 | 14·1 | — | −4·2 | 3·0 | −7·2 |
| 28·7 | 12·4 | 53·9 | 26·8 | 79·6 | 46·1 | 0·2 | 9·2 | 10·2 | Newton . . | 74·3 | −3·7 | 38·9 | 52·5 | 8·6 | — | * | 6·0 | 1·1 |

| | | | | | | | | | | | | | | | | | | |
|---|---|---|---|---|---|---|---|---|---|---|---|---|---|---|---|---|---|---|
| 35·6 | 18·4 | 71·7 | 13·2 | 87·4 | 49·1 | 0·2 | 9·1 | 17·0 | North Fylde | 68·3 | −5·0 | 68·9 | 31·2 | — | — | [13·4] | 7·6 | −3·4 |
| 47·4 | 25·9 | 68·3 | 14·0 | 86·1 | 62·5 | 0·4 | 9·0 | 8·6 | Ormskirk | 72·5 | −1·4 | 61·4 | 38·6 | — | — | — | 2·6 | −7·0 |
| 47·3 | 25·2 | 68·2 | 11·0 | 88·8 | 56·4 | 0·4 | 9·4 | 13·7 | South Fylde | 72·7 | −1·8 | 63·6 | 21·5 | 14·9 | — | −6·2 | 6·1 | −4·4 |
| 26·3 | 12·7 | 59·0 | 22·1 | 70·3 | 42·9 | 0·3 | 9·6 | 9·7 | Westhoughton | 76·9 | −1·8 | 44·6 | 55·4 | — | — | — | 9·5 | 5·5 |
| 23·9 | 9·7 | 41·2 | 40·3 | 83·5 | 39·4 | 0·2 | 11·5 | 8·7 | Widnes | 68·7 | −4·0 | 42·3 | 57·7 | — | — | — | 3·0 | −5·8 |
| | | | | | | | | | Leicestershire, | | | | | | | | | |
| 22·3 | 11·7 | 58·9 | 21·3 | 68·6 | 50·2 | 0·2 | 10·0 | 9·7 | Bosworth † | 77·3 | −2·5 | 50·9 | 49·1 | — | — | [13·8] | 8·0 | 4·9 |
| 35·8 | 18·2 | 63·4 | 20·0 | 81·2 | 59·4 | 0·3 | 9·4 | 8·3 | Harborough | 77·3 | −4·3 | 56·4 | 32·3 | 11·4 | — | −6·3 | 7·1 | 2·0 |
| 29·3 | 15·3 | 49·5 | 26·0 | 70·8 | 48·5 | 1·3 | 10·3 | 9·7 | Loughborough | 79·1 | −3·2 | 44·3 | 45·4 | 10·3 | — | −2·5 | 6·1 | 4·3 |
| 33·0 | 18·1 | 55·9 | 21·5 | 78·3 | 54·5 | 0·5 | 10·1 | 8·5 | Melton | 76·0 | −4·4 | 56·1 | 30·2 | 13·7 | — | −2·1 | 7·0 | 2·0 |
| 21·6 | 9·7 | 51·5 | 29·4 | 78·4 | 48·9 | 0·7 | 10·9 | 8·8 | Lincolnshire, Brigg | 67·6 | −4·8 | 46·6 | 53·4 | — | — | — | 6·7 | 1·6 |
| 26·5 | 14·3 | 47·4 | 20·2 | 69·3 | 55·0 | 0·7 | 9·7 | 11·0 | Gainsborough | 74·7 | −1·1 | 50·2 | 32·7 | 17·1 | — | +1·8 | 3·9 | 3·0 |
| 31·0 | 14·6 | 45·7 | 23·8 | 73·7 | 55·1 | 0·9 | 11·0 | 9·9 | Grantham | 76·5 | −4·0 | 58·7 | 41·3 | — | — | [8·7] | 6·6 | 6·2 |
| | | | | | | | | | Holland with | | | | | | | | | |
| 26·7 | 15·3 | 46·0 | 29·0 | 67·4 | 56·8 | 0·2 | 9·7 | 10·7 | Boston | 74·9 | −0·1 | 58·1 | 41·9 | — | — | — | 7·8 | −0·4 |
| 29·6 | 17·9 | 48·5 | 16·5 | 75·7 | 54·2 | 0·4 | 8·9 | 16·4 | Horncastle | 74·3 | −1·7 | 55·4 | 25·4 | 19·2 | — | −4·1 | 6·7 | −1·9 |
| 31·4 | 16·5 | 59·5 | 15·7 | 75·3 | 51·8 | 0·5 | 10·7 | 11·6 | Louth | 71·6 | −2·8 | 53·1 | 33·9 | 13·0 | — | −3·8 | 4·8 | 0·8 |
| | | | | | | | | | Rutland & | | | | | | | | | |
| 30·9 | 16·6 | 35·2 | 26·3 | 73·5 | 58·3 | 0·8 | 10·6 | 10·2 | Stamford | 75·4 | −2·2 | 60·1 | 39·9 | — | — | — | 6·7 | 5·8 |
| 47·5 | 23·1 | 62·3 | 16·5 | 90·9 | 67·7 | 0·9 | 10·1 | 6·4 | Middlesex, Spelthorne | 73·3 | −7·6 | 54·2 | 36·3 | 9·5 | — | −4·0 | 6·4 | 0·6 |
| 37·9 | 19·0 | 51·5 | 31·6 | 87·4 | 60·0 | 2·2 | 10·8 | 7·6 | Uxbridge † | 74·9 | −7·7 | 49·4 | 41·7 | 9·0 | — | −1·9 | 4·8 | 4·8 |
| 39·5 | 18·5 | 64·5 | 14·0 | 79·4 | 66·5 | 0·5 | 9·6 | 11·1 | Norfolk, Central | 76·7 | −3·1 | 56·6 | 32·7 | 10·6 | — | * | 7·7 | 4·7 |
| 27·7 | 14·5 | 44·6 | 24·9 | 67·5 | 54·6 | 0·4 | 9·7 | 13·6 | King's Lynn † | 78·2 | −4·7 | 50·1 | 49·9 | — | — | — | 2·3 | −1·6 |
| 29·4 | 16·7 | 43·2 | 20·8 | 64·9 | 53·3 | 0·6 | 9·2 | 17·5 | North † | 80·3 | −2·9 | 55·3 | 44·7 | — | — | — | 6·2 | 6·8 |
| 24·4 | 15·0 | 41·0 | 27·9 | 66·5 | 56·8 | 0·6 | 10·2 | 13·4 | South | 78·0 | −3·4 | 51·9 | 39·4 | 8·7 | — | −2·0 | 6·1 | 4·2 |
| 22·4 | 13·3 | 41·8 | 22·9 | 67·2 | 59·2 | 0·6 | 9·6 | 14·2 | South-west | 80·5 | −3·5 | 57·3 | 42·7 | — | — | — | 6·2 | 7·6 |
| 28·7 | 14·8 | 49·9 | 27·2 | 66·4 | 42·3 | 0·4 | 9·7 | 14·5 | Yarmouth † | 77·3 | −2·6 | 49·6 | 42·8 | 7·6 | — | * | 4·3 | 2·3 |
| | | | | | | | | | Northamptonshire, | | | | | | | | | |
| 24·8 | 12·2 | 39·6 | 44·5 | 80·3 | 49·9 | 0·5 | 10·4 | 9·2 | Kettering | 75·9 | −5·4 | 42·5 | 48·3 | 9·3 | — | −2·5 | 5·6 | 2·3 |
| 27·8 | 13·0 | 48·0 | 26·9 | 72·4 | 51·5 | 1·7 | 10·4 | 10·2 | Peterborough | 78·1 | −3·4 | 54·1 | 45·9 | — | — | [7·9] | 4·1 | 0·8 |
| 33·1 | 17·7 | 50·5 | 29·2 | 81·0 | 60·3 | 0·5 | 9·5 | 10·1 | South | 77·9 | −4·3 | 51·2 | 37·2 | 11·7 | — | * | 4·1 | 1·6 |
| 24·4 | 12·8 | 53·6 | 29·5 | 72·3 | 48·1 | 1·1 | 9·8 | 11·9 | Wellingborough † ‡ | 81·4 | −5·0 | 52·2 | 47·8 | — | — | — | 4·6 | 3·3 |
| | | | | | | | | | Northumberland, | | | | | | | | | |
| | | | | | | | | | Berwick-upon- | | | | | | | | | |
| 27·6 | 15·7 | 30·2 | 29·5 | 83·3 | 46·2 | 0·4 | 9·7 | 14·4 | Tweed | 73·7 | −2·9 | 50·7 | 27·4 | 22·0 | — | +2·6 | 4·3 | 1·3 |
| 35·4 | 20·9 | 40·9 | 29·1 | 83·1 | 52·7 | 0·3 | 10·6 | 11·9 | Hexham | 75·4 | −3·1 | 52·0 | 35·3 | 12·8 | — | −2·1 | 2·8 | −5·7 |
| 19·9 | 8·7 | 33·3 | 31·1 | 69·5 | 39·4 | 0·3 | 10·3 | 13·1 | Morpeth | 76·1 | −0·9 | 26·3 | 60·4 | 13·3 | — | * | 7·3 | 3·5 |
| | | | | | | | | | Nottinghamshire, | | | | | | | | | |
| 17·0 | 7·9 | 44·7 | 29·9 | 65·6 | 38·4 | 0·2 | 10·0 | 12·0 | Ashfield | 70·1 | −3·2 | 31·8 | 68·2 | — | — | — | 5·4 | 3·7 |
| 23·2 | 11·7 | 35·0 | 27·5 | 73·6 | 46·3 | 0·5 | 11·2 | 10·2 | Bassetlaw | 76·4 | +3·2 | 39·2 | 54·9 | 5·9 | — | * | 3·8 | 0·3 |
| 38·8 | 19·3 | 55·1 | 19·6 | 83·1 | 55·7 | 0·5 | 9·2 | 8·6 | Carlton | 74·7 | −7·8 | 59·6 | 40·4 | — | — | [15·2] | 6·4 | 2·5 |
| 21·6 | 10·9 | 43·9 | 26·1 | 72·9 | 42·7 | 0·5 | 10·7 | 10·9 | Mansfield | 68·7 | −6·2 | 32·5 | 66·1 | — | 1·4 C | [12·2] | 4·2 | 1·7 |
| 26·6 | 13·3 | 36·0 | 24·7 | 79·4 | 49·8 | 0·5 | 10·6 | 10·5 | Newark | 75·8 | −5·3 | 48·8 | 51·2 | — | — | — | 5·5 | 1·3 |
| 36·1 | 16·9 | 56·5 | 20·1 | 80·3 | 53·5 | 0·6 | 9·5 | 9·2 | Rushcliffe † | 79·6 | −5·8 | 51·7 | 41·4 | 7·0 | — | −2·1 | 5·5 | 3·3 |
| 31·3 | 15·5 | 47·7 | 24·9 | 80·9 | 61·0 | 1·0 | 10·8 | 9·5 | Oxfordshire, Banbury | 77·4 | −4·6 | 53·4 | 36·6 | 10·0 | — | −2·2 | 4·8 | 4·0 |
| 36·2 | 18·8 | 49·7 | 20·4 | 81·5 | 64·3 | 1·3 | 11·0 | 8·5 | Henley | 74·0 | −1·2 | 53·4 | 30·8 | 14·2 | 1·5 | * | 5·9 | 2·7 |
| 27·4 | 18·2 | 43·0 | 21·5 | 68·1 | 56·1 | 0·3 | 10·0 | 12·1 | Shropshire, Ludlow | 73·3 | −0·6 | 54·8 | 31·7 | 13·5 | — | * | 6·7 | −0·1 |
| 26·9 | 15·0 | 42·4 | 24·4 | 71·4 | 56·9 | 0·7 | 10·9 | 12·3 | Oswestry | 72·1 | −1·2 | 50·7 | 26·9 | 22·3 | — | +6·0 | 5·5 | −2·9 |

## *English Counties—continued*

| % Non-manual | % Professional & managerial | % Owner-Occupiers | % Council Tenants | % With full plumbing | % With cars | % Born in New Commonwealth | % Young voters | % Retired | Constituency | % Voting 1970 | Change in % voting 1966–70 | Con. % | Lab. % | Lib. % | Other % | Lib. + or − % | Swing 1966–70 | Swing 1955–70 |
|---|---|---|---|---|---|---|---|---|---|---|---|---|---|---|---|---|---|---|
| 35·2 | 17·1 | 50·0 | 24·2 | 79·3 | 53·3 | 0·5 | 10·2 | 9·0 | Shropshire, Shrewsbury | 73·1 | −3·4 | 53·9 | 31·9 | 14·2 | – | −3·0 | 7·1 | 0·1 |
| 25·6 | 12·4 | 40·5 | 36·7 | 81·7 | 53·6 | 1·3 | 10·8 | 7·7 | Wrekin † | 78·8 | −2·5 | 50·5 | 49·5 | — | — | — | *1·4* | *−3·1* |
| 30·6 | 16·6 | 51·9 | 25·8 | 83·2 | 54·7 | 0·4 | 10·1 | 14·5 | Somerset, Bridgwater | 77·2 | −3·0 | 52·4 | 35·8 | 11·9 | — | −5·6 | 5·1 | −0·9 |
| 38·6 | 22·0 | 58·1 | 23·8 | 84·8 | 62·0 | 0·6 | 9·7 | 12·7 | North | 79·1 | −6·2 | 58·1 | 41·9 | — | — | [10·9] | 6·2 | *3·9* |
| 37·6 | 18·2 | 47·2 | 28·9 | 81·4 | 56·6 | 1·1 | 10·5 | 12·7 | Taunton | 79·0 | −6·2 | 53·6 | 36·5 | 10·0 | — | −1·6 | 5·2 | 2·2 |
| 30·3 | 17·2 | 47·6 | 24·6 | 76·0 | 58·8 | 0·7 | 10·1 | 12·7 | Wells | 77·4 | −4·1 | 49·6 | 32·3 | 18·1 | — | −3·3 | 5·0 | 2·2 |
| 40·9 | 21·1 | 58·2 | 18·2 | 85·9 | 53·6 | 1·0 | 9·3 | 15·7 | Weston super Mare | 73·7 | −5·4 | 57·9 | 24·8 | 17·3 | — | −1·8 | 4·9 | 3·9 |
| 30·7 | 16·1 | 47·6 | 28·0 | 77·6 | 58·4 | 0·9 | 11·0 | 12·2 | Yeovil | 79·3 | −4·3 | 49·7 | 37·0 | 13·3 | — | −4·3 | 4·4 | 2·1 |
| 34·5 | 20·3 | 52·6 | 32·8 | 85·6 | 59·0 | 0·4 | 9·0 | 7·0 | Staffordshire, Brierley Hill | 73·3 | −5·7 | 60·6 | 39·4 | — | — | — | *9·5* | *11·6* |
| 25·4 | 11·7 | 49·7 | 24·1 | 65·0 | 44·6 | 1·1 | 11·5 | 9·2 | Burton | 75·6 | −3·1 | 54·3 | 45·7 | — | — | — | *4·0* | *1·1* |
| 23·2 | 11·8 | 41·1 | 35·9 | 77·6 | 51·5 | 0·6 | 10·2 | 7·8 | Cannock † | 70·8 | −2·8 | 51·2 | 48·8 | — | — | — | *11·0* | *10·4* |
| 27·1 | 14·6 | 60·7 | 17·5 | 72·7 | 53·7 | 0·2 | 10·2 | 10·0 | Leek † | 67·1 | −11·6 | 46·1 | 43·6 | 10·3 | — | * | 7·4 | 2·2 |
| 31·8 | 17·2 | 46·5 | 30·5 | 82·6 | 58·5 | 0·4 | 9·8 | 8·8 | Lichfield & Tamworth † | 73·6 | −5·2 | 51·6 | 48·4 | — | — | — | *5·6* | *5·6* |
| 39·0 | 20·2 | 49·4 | 25·3 | 82·2 | 57·6 | 1·0 | 10·0 | 8·9 | Stafford & Stone | 73·4 | −6·1 | 54·8 | 37·2 | 8·0 | — | −3·0 | 3·9 | −1·1 |
| 27·9 | 15·2 | 37·1 | 28·8 | 77·6 | 56·4 | 1·2 | 10·5 | 9·8 | Suffolk, Bury St. Edmunds | 77·2 | −1·6 | 61·2 | 38·8 | — | — | — | *6·6* | *6·0* |
| 26·6 | 16·4 | 45·4 | 19·7 | 61·9 | 58·0 | 0·8 | 8·5 | 15·0 | Eye | 78·1 | −3·4 | 52·4 | 35·6 | 12·0 | — | −6·4 | 4·6 | 7·5 |
| 29·6 | 14·9 | 57·4 | 17·0 | 69·7 | 45·4 | 0·4 | 9·9 | 13·1 | Lowestoft | 78·7 | −4·5 | 50·7 | 41·0 | 8·3 | — | −0·3 | 4·5 | 7·0 |
| 32·8 | 17·5 | 52·4 | 17·7 | 77·4 | 56·2 | 0·9 | 9·5 | 14·7 | Sudbury & Woodbridge | 75·9 | −4·4 | 54·6 | 33·4 | 12·0 | — | −0·8 | 4·0 | 2·9 |
| 52·4 | 27·7 | 55·1 | 31·6 | 89·1 | 59·3 | 1·1 | 9·9 | 10·8 | Surrey, Carshalton | 71·2 | −8·1 | 54·0 | 33·4 | 12·7 | — | −4·5 | 4·7 | −0·2 |
| 43·0 | 22·8 | 61·4 | 17·5 | 83·3 | 66·6 | 1·3 | 9·5 | 8·3 | Chertsey | 71·1 | −6·9 | 56·6 | 32·5 | 10·9 | — | −5·9 | 5·2 | 0·9 |
| 50·4 | 29·7 | 58·4 | 16·0 | 83·4 | 66·8 | 1·3 | 9·9 | 10·2 | Dorking | 73·0 | −6·0 | 59·0 | 24·5 | 16·5 | — | −1·3 | 4·6 | 0·1 |
| 67·7 | 37·3 | 74·8 | 10·2 | 92·4 | 67·1 | 1·5 | 9·7 | 9·0 | East | 73·1 | −6·2 | 62·0 | 17·7 | 20·4 | — | −8·6 | — | — |
| 63·6 | 35·6 | 71·4 | 11·1 | 91·9 | 66·2 | 1·6 | 9·2 | 9·4 | Epsom | 72·5 | −6·8 | 61·4 | 22·1 | 16·5 | — | −4·9 | 4·4 | −1·8 |
| 58·9 | 35·9 | 63·5 | 13·5 | 89·5 | 66·6 | 1·3 | 10·1 | 9·1 | Esher | 72·1 | −6·0 | 61·8 | 23·7 | 14·5 | — | −4·7 | 4·1 | −0·4 |
| 45·6 | 26·7 | 55·7 | 19·4 | 84·1 | 59·8 | 1·7 | 10·3 | 12·0 | Farnham | 73·6 | −6·4 | 56·9 | 20·1 | 23·1 | — | −4·9 | — | — |
| 47·5 | 24·8 | 52·9 | 21·4 | 85·1 | 58·6 | 1·5 | 9·9 | 10·7 | Guildford | 72·1 | −6·6 | 55·4 | 26·7 | 18·0 | — | +1·3 | 5·6 | 1·1 |
| 48·4 | 26·4 | 53·0 | 23·9 | 87·2 | 61·4 | 1·3 | 10·8 | 9·6 | Reigate | 73·9 | −6·2 | 53·9 | 29·2 | 16·9 | — | −3·1 | 5·0 | 0·6 |
| 48·8 | 27·8 | 57·5 | 22·0 | 88·8 | 65·8 | 2·3 | 11·0 | 7·7 | Woking | 70·1 | −7·0 | 56·7 | 28·4 | 14·9 | — | −2·9 | 3·9 | −0·3 |
| 49·1 | 24·6 | 56·7 | 13·4 | 82·2 | 40·7 | 1·1 | 6·5 | 25·1 | East Sussex, Eastbourne | 73·7 | −3·5 | 48·8 | 13·7 | 37·6 | — | +7·8 | — | — |
| 47·2 | 28·5 | 59·0 | 14·4 | 87·9 | 62·1 | 1·6 | 9·1 | 13·4 | East Grinstead | 72·5 | −4·3 | 61·2 | 19·2 | 19·7 | — | −4·1 | — | — |
| 48·1 | 25·6 | 63·0 | 15·0 | 89·6 | 53·6 | 1·1 | 8·3 | 16·7 | Lewes | 72·8 | −3·5 | 58·3 | 25·9 | 15·8 | — | −2·4 | 3·6 | −0·6 |
| 45·9 | 28·4 | 58·1 | 11·9 | 82·4 | 50·3 | 1·5 | 8·1 | 26·4 | Rye | 73·9 | −1·8 | 64·2 | 18·0 | 17·8 | — | −3·8 | — | 0·2 |

| | | | | | | | | | | | | | | | | | | |
|---|---|---|---|---|---|---|---|---|---|---|---|---|---|---|---|---|---|---|
| 44·7 | 24·4 | 65·0 | 16·7 | 91·6 | 50·8 | 1·3 | 8·1 | 21·6 | West Sussex, Arundel & Shoreham . | 71·8 | −4·0 | 60·8 | 22·9 | 16·3 | — | +0·1 | 5·4 | −0·9 |
| 41·9 | 23·3 | 54·8 | 16·0 | 86·1 | 54·7 | 1·5 | 8·9 | 18·8 | Chichester . . | 69·9 | −3·3 | 62·6 | 20·7 | 16·8 | — | −1·0 | 5·0 | 0·2 |
| 40·8 | 22·3 | 40·2 | 39·0 | 90·9 | 62·7 | 1·2 | 11·2 | 9·3 | Horsham . . | 74·0 | −5·0 | 53·7 | 35·4 | 11·0 | — | −6·1 | 4·8 | −3·5 |
| | | | | | | | | | Warwickshire, | | | | | | | | | |
| 28·1 | 14·9 | 54·1 | 23·1 | 81·5 | 60·4 | 0·4 | 11·1 | 7·0 | Meriden † ‡ . | 75·6 | −10·1 | 53·1 | 46·9 | — | — | — | *6·8* | *4·4* |
| 20·8 | 8·9 | 55·1 | 26·5 | 74·8 | 48·9 | 0·7 | 11·1 | 7·9 | Nuneaton . | 76·2 | −3·5 | 32·8 | 57·4 | 9·8 | — | −4·7 | −1·1 | −0·9 |
| 37·1 | 18·2 | 62·5 | 18·4 | 81·0 | 56·5 | 2·0 | 10·1 | 9·2 | Rugby . . | 81·5 | −3·4 | 46·6 | 52·9 | — | 0·5 | — | −2·7 | −1·3 |
| 56·1 | 33·1 | 72·8 | 12·0 | 95·6 | 73·6 | 0·4 | 9·1 | 6·5 | Solihull . . | 73·2 | −1·6 | 64·3 | 22·4 | 13·3 | — | * | 5·2 | −1·3 |
| 38·1 | 22·5 | 47·8 | 23·0 | 80·4 | 63·5 | 0·8 | 9·7 | 9·5 | Stratford . . | 74·1 | −4·0 | 58·1 | 23·5 | 18·4 | — | +3·4 | 6·5 | −1·3 |
| 38·9 | 20·9 | 55·3 | 21·5 | 83·3 | 58·4 | 2·5 | 10·1 | 7·4 | Warwick & Leamington . | 72·6 | −6·3 | 63·4 | 36·6 | — | — | [12·3] | 5·6 | *−1·1* |
| 33·2 | 20·0 | 46·9 | 19·7 | 83·0 | 55·6 | 0·4 | 9·8 | 12·6 | Westmorland . . | 71·9 | −3·6 | 55·3 | 20·1 | 24·5 | — | −1·0 | — | — |
| 38·2 | 19·5 | 58·9 | 12·1 | 77·7 | 44·4 | 1·0 | 8·4 | 17·7 | Isle of Wight . . | 72·1 | −3·0 | 52·4 | 22·6 | 22·2 | 2·8 | −0·2 | 5·1 | 2·3 |
| 30·2 | 15·0 | 46·0 | 26·1 | 79·3 | 60·0 | 1·6 | 11·5 | 8·8 | Wiltshire, Chippenham | 77·4 | −6·9 | 49·7 | 22·1 | 28·2 | — | −9·9 | — | — |
| 30·5 | 15·0 | 47·2 | 23·3 | 83·9 | 58·4 | 1·0 | 9·8 | 9·4 | Devizes . . | 76·2 | −4·9 | 51·7 | 37·1 | 11·3 | — | −4·8 | 4·6 | 4·6 |
| 38·0 | 16·8 | 42·8 | 21·3 | 81·3 | 54·5 | 2·0 | 10·5 | 10·2 | Salisbury . . | 71·8 | −5·8 | 60·3 | 39·7 | — | — | — | *5·2* | 0·2 |
| 31·3 | 16·9 | 50·8 | 25·4 | 79·0 | 53·9 | 1·4 | 9·8 | 12·8 | Westbury . | 77·9 | −4·6 | 50·3 | 33·0 | 16·7 | — | −2·0 | 5·8 | 4·7 |
| | | | | | | | | | Worcestershire, | | | | | | | | | |
| 35·3 | 18·6 | 60·0 | 20·5 | 81·2 | 65·1 | 1·0 | 9·2 | 8·3 | Bromsgrove . | 76·5 | −3·4 | 58·5 | 41·5 | — | — | — | *5·4* | 3·3 |
| 30·0 | 15·7 | 50·0 | 25·9 | 74·6 | 58·0 | 0·8 | 10·7 | 9·1 | Kidderminster . | 73·8 | −1·7 | 51·8 | 34·2 | 14·0 | — | * | 5·4 | −0·6 |
| 37·6 | 20·2 | 47·1 | 25·1 | 77·3 | 60·4 | 0·9 | 10·3 | 11·6 | South . . | 72·1 | −3·5 | 60·4 | 25·3 | 14·3 | — | −5·9 | 5·7 | 1·6 |
| | | | | | | | | | Yorks. East Riding | | | | | | | | | |
| 39·2 | 22·4 | 57·6 | 18·2 | 85·5 | 44·7 | 0·3 | 8·7 | 17·3 | Bridlington. . | 69·8 | −1·7 | 58·1 | 26·8 | 15·1 | — | −0·7 | 3·2 | −5·2 |
| 48·2 | 27·8 | 59·5 | 18·5 | 83·7 | 57·5 | 0·6 | 9·9 | 10·1 | Haltemprice . | 74·9 | −1·6 | 53·6 | 28·3 | 18·1 | — | +0·4 | −0·7 | −6·2 |
| 29·8 | 18·4 | 45·1 | 19·4 | 70·8 | 51·3 | 0·4 | 11·0 | 12·6 | Howden . . | 70·9 | −0·9 | 57·0 | 24·7 | 17·9 | 0·4 | −4·6 | 4·3 | −0·0 |
| | | | | | | | | | Yorks. North Riding | | | | | | | | | |
| 24·6 | 11·1 | 50·1 | 27·2 | 72·7 | 40·4 | 0·4 | 11·0 | 10·7 | Cleveland . . | 72·9 | −8·2 | 46·2 | 53·8 | — | — | [11·3] | 5·5 | *−3·6* |
| 35·9 | 21·6 | 48·3 | 17·6 | 83·1 | 60·2 | 1·1 | 11·1 | 9·5 | Richmond . . | 68·4 | −2·9 | 62·8 | 26·2 | 11·0 | — | −7·8 | 2·3 | −5·3 |
| 35·9 | 19·7 | 54·0 | 20·8 | 86·8 | 40·8 | 0·5 | 8·5 | 17·4 | Scarborough & Whitby . | 71·5 | −2·6 | 49·9 | 18·7 | 31·5 | — | −0·4 | — | — |
| 32·7 | 17·2 | 50·6 | 17·2 | 81·9 | 56·4 | 0·6 | 10·0 | 10·8 | Thirsk & Malton | 72·3 | +2·1 | 66·9 | 33·1 | — | — | — | *5·3* | *−2·2* |
| | | | | | | | | | Yorks. West Riding | | | | | | | | | |
| 36·0 | 21·0 | 52·6 | 24·7 | 84·8 | 53·8 | 0·5 | 10·3 | 11·2 | Barkston Ash . | 75·6 | −4·3 | 59·6 | 40·4 | — | — | — | *3·3* | 2·3 |
| 27·4 | 15·4 | 58·0 | 16·5 | 71·3 | 43·1 | 0·1 | 9·8 | 12·0 | Colne Valley † . | 80·8 | −5·4 | 22·0 | 39·9 | 38·1 | — | −10·5 | — | — |
| 14·8 | 6·3 | 30·2 | 39·2 | 60·3 | 29·5 | 0·2 | 11·3 | 12·3 | Dearne Valley . | 71·9 | −1·8 | 15·1 | 75·1 | 9·8 | — | * | 4·0 | −2·0 |
| 19·2 | 8·4 | 31·7 | 28·2 | 77·7 | 39·5 | 0·4 | 11·4 | 10·9 | Don Valley . | 73·2 | −5·2 | 30·5 | 69·4 | — | — | — | *5·4* | *4·2* |
| 18·3 | 8·9 | 33·2 | 37·6 | 72·0 | 37·6 | 0·3 | 11·4 | 10·0 | Goole . . | 69·4 | −3·7 | 39·8 | 60·2 | — | — | — | 4·6 | *2·0* |
| 50·6 | 25·7 | 59·5 | 12·0 | 88·8 | 49·5 | 0·6 | 8·8 | 12·4 | Harrogate . . | 69·9 | −4·5 | 59·8 | 20·1 | 20·2 | — | −2·7 | — | — |
| 12·0 | 5·2 | 24·3 | 37·3 | 69·8 | 30·3 | 0·1 | 12·1 | 13·0 | Hemsworth . | 71·8 | −4·3 | 19·2 | 80·8 | — | — | — | *4·6* | *2·5* |
| 22·7 | 9·7 | 44·5 | 30·9 | 74·2 | 36·8 | 0·1 | 9·8 | 12·3 | Normanton. . | 71·6 | −2·7 | 31·6 | 68·4 | — | — | — | *8·0* | *5·1* |
| 23·7 | 11·7 | 36·5 | 40·3 | 72·6 | 42·4 | 0·2 | 11·1 | 10·3 | Penistone . . | 73·9 | −4·9 | 27·7 | 58·7 | 13·6 | — | −0·6 | 3·9 | −3·2 |
| 41·5 | 25·0 | 53·4 | 20·3 | 83·6 | 55·8 | 0·6 | 9·6 | 10·8 | Ripon . . | 73·7 | −5·2 | 60·7 | 26·2 | 13·1 | — | −8·8 | 4·1 | −1·7 |
| 19·5 | 9·2 | 32·2 | 36·9 | 76·8 | 41·5 | 0·1 | 11·2 | 10·1 | Rother Valley . | 70·6 | −2·8 | 28·2 | 71·8 | — | — | — | *5·0* | *3·8* |
| 38·9 | 20·2 | 63·6 | 23·8 | 85·0 | 44·6 | 0·2 | 9·7 | 10·6 | Shipley . . | 82·4 | −4·2 | 50·4 | 38·9 | 10·8 | — | −0·1 | 3·9 | −0·9 |
| 27·9 | 16·1 | 55·3 | 16·3 | 72·8 | 47·5 | 0·4 | 10·0 | 12·2 | Skipton . . | 78·7 | −3·3 | 51·3 | 29·6 | 19·1 | — | −1·8 | 5·4 | −0·3 |
| 24·1 | 12·5 | 54·5 | 16·2 | 60·3 | 36·2 | 0·5 | 9·9 | 10·6 | Sowerby . . | 75·6 | −2·1 | 42·6 | 43·8 | 13·6 | — | * | 6·3 | 2·5 |

## *Welsh Boroughs*

| % Non-manual | % Professional & managerial | % Owner-Occupiers | % Council Tenants | % With full plumbing | % With cars | % Born in New Commonwealth | % Young voters | % Retired | Constituency | % Voting 1970 | Change in % voting 1966–70 | Con. % | Lab. % | Lib. % | Other % | Lib. + or − % | Swing 1966–70 | Swing 1955–70 |
|---|---|---|---|---|---|---|---|---|---|---|---|---|---|---|---|---|---|---|
| 18·2 | 7·9 | 58·5 | 16·4 | 43·5 | 32·4 | 0·2 | 10·0 | 16·0 | Aberdare . . . | 78·0 | +1·0 | 6·5 | 60·0 | — | 30·0 N<br>3·5 C | — | — | — |
| 46·3 | 20·8 | 59·7 | 15·1 | 73·4 | 48·5 | 0·8 | 11·1 | 10·7 | Cardiff, North † . | 76·6 | −2·4 | 47·0 | 43·2 | 5·8 | 4·1 N | * | 2·6 | −7·4 |
| 32·1 | 13·5 | 45·5 | 28·0 | 66·9 | 43·1 | 1·2 | 11·9 | 10·3 | South-east . | 73·2 | −5·8 | 41·1 | 51·9 | — | 1·9<br>5·1 N | [7·4] | 5·1 | −2·0 |
| 30·2 | 11·0 | 41·7 | 33·8 | 64·8 | 39·0 | 1·2 | 11·2 | 11·5 | West . . . | 71·0 | −4·1 | 36·5 | 49·8 | 3·7 | 10·1 N | * | 4·4 | −1·4 |
| 20·7 | 7·2 | 51·1 | 26·8 | 49·0 | 33·4 | 0·2 | 10·4 | 15·4 | Merthyr Tydfil (†) . | 77·9 | +4·0 | 9·9 | 28·7 | — | 52·0<br>9·6 N | — | — | — |
| 27·6 | 12·3 | 53·8 | 25·1 | 74·4 | 43·9 | 0·9 | 11·2 | 9·5 | Newport . . | 75·7 | −3·1 | 40·7 | 55·7 | — | 3·7 N | — | 2·3 | −3·8 |
| 16·4 | 5·7 | 60·4 | 13·3 | 34·1 | 28·7 | 0·0 | 10·4 | 14·3 | Rhondda, East . | 77·5 | −1·0 | 4·8 | 68·7 | — | 2·3 C<br>24·3 N | — | — | — |
| 18·6 | 6·5 | 71·2 | 7·6 | 34·3 | 28·6 | 0·1 | 9·8 | 18·8 | West . . . | 81·5 | +1·2 | 6·4 | 74·8 | — | 4·8 C<br>14·1 N | — | — | — |
| 21·6 | 7·6 | 48·9 | 33·6 | 65·5 | 38·0 | 0·3 | 10·9 | 11·5 | Swansea, East . . | 70·1 | −3·7 | 19·9 | 68·5 | — | 1·4 C<br>10·2 N | — | 5·6 | −1·9 |
| 39·6 | 19·5 | 53·0 | 27·4 | 78·3 | 47·3 | 0·7 | 10·3 | 12·3 | West . . . | 75·8 | −4·6 | 43·6 | 50·2 | — | 6·2 N | — | 3·1 | −2·1 |

## Welsh Counties

| % Non-manual | % Professional & managerial | % Owner-Occupiers | % Council Tenants | % With full plumbing | % With cars | % Born in New Commonwealth | % Young voters | % Retired | Constituency | % Voting 1970 | Change in % voting 1966–70 | Con. % | Lab. % | Lib. % | Other % | Lib. + or − % | Swing 1966–70 | Swing 1955–70 |
|---|---|---|---|---|---|---|---|---|---|---|---|---|---|---|---|---|---|---|
| 31·4 | 18·9 | 43·0 | 25·9 | 68·6 | 55·4 | 0·6 | 9·7 | 13·9 | Anglesey . . . | 78·2 | +5·0 | 28·5 | 43·2 | 6·2 | 22·1 N | * | 2·5 | — |
| 26·4 | 13·8 | 49·7 | 21·4 | 65·6 | 56·2 | 0·3 | 9·5 | 14·1 | Brecon & Radnor . | 81·9 | +1·4 | 32·2 | 43·4 | 18·9 | 5·4 N | * | 4·9 | 2·7 |
| | | | | | | | | | Caernarvonshire, | | | | | | | | | |
| 30·2 | 15·8 | 51·7 | 19·6 | 62·2 | 53·1 | 0·2 | 8·7 | 15·9 | Caernarvon . | 81·7 | +3·3 | 20·1 | 40·1 | 6·5 | 33·4 N | * | — | — |
| 35·3 | 18·3 | 49·1 | 21·9 | 76·2 | 45·7 | 0·5 | 9·8 | 17·4 | Conway † . . | 82·0 | −1·8 | 42·4 | 40·2 | 6·6 | 10·8 N | * | 1·9 | −5·1 |
| 34·1 | 20·3 | 54·8 | 14·4 | 66·2 | 59·6 | 0·4 | 9·7 | 17·2 | Cardigan . . . | 82·0 | +1·0 | 17·3 | 33·5 | 29·6 | 19·7 N | −5·8 | — | — |
| | | | | | | | | | Carmarthenshire, | | | | | | | | | |
| 25·8 | 12·9 | 55·6 | 16·9 | 62·0 | 58·0 | 0·1 | 9·3 | 14·2 | Carmarthen ‡ . | 83·7 | +1·1 | 10·1 | 38·0 | 21·8 | 30·1 N | −4·3 | — | — |
| 21·0 | 8·9 | 53·4 | 30·4 | 66·4 | 43·4 | 0·1 | 9·3 | 14·9 | Llanelli . . | 77·4 | +1·2 | 11·6 | 62·8 | 7·7 | 1·2 C 16·8 N | * | — | — |
| | | | | | | | | | Denbighshire, | | | | | | | | | |
| 35·0 | 20·7 | 52·7 | 16·9 | 77·5 | 52·4 | 0·3 | 9·4 | 17·6 | Denbigh . . | 78·5 | −2·5 | 44·6 | 26·3 | 18·1 | 11·0 N | −11·1 | — | — |
| 23·7 | 10·0 | 34·7 | 43·9 | 77·8 | 46·2 | 0·1 | 11·6 | 11·9 | Wrexham . . | 75·1 | −2·1 | 28·6 | 56·8 | 9·3 | 5·3 N | −3·1 | 2·9 | −2·3 |
| 20·7 | 10·2 | 50·2 | 29·2 | 76·2 | 50·5 | 0·3 | 11·2 | 9·6 | Flintshire, East . | 81·2 | −5·3 | 38·3 | 46·1 | 11·2 | 4·4 N | −2·1 | 5·0 | −1·3 |
| 34·5 | 17·1 | 59·5 | 18·2 | 80·7 | 49·7 | 0·4 | 9·5 | 17·2 | West . . . | 77·8 | −4·1 | 46·5 | 30·2 | 16·5 | 6·9 N | −0·5 | 4·5 | −3·0 |
| 21·8 | 9·5 | 47·7 | 40·0 | 77·8 | 42·2 | 0·4 | 11·1 | 11·7 | Glamorgan, Aberavon | 74·8 | −3·5 | 22·3 | 67·0 | — | 8·4 N 2·4 C | — | 4·9 | −2·8 |
| 45·5 | 23·6 | 60·3 | 18·5 | 81·0 | 55·9 | 0·5 | 9·8 | 11·9 | Barry . . | 79·2 | −4·4 | 53·8 | 39·2 | — | 7·1 N | — | 6·0 | −0·6 |
| 20·5 | 8·2 | 47·6 | 24·0 | 58·0 | 38·5 | 0·1 | 11·4 | 12·8 | Caerphilly . . | 78·1 | +1·3 | 9·7 | 61·8 | — | 28·5 N | — | — | — |
| 24·0 | 11·2 | 60·7 | 22·8 | 64·0 | 48·3 | 0·1 | 9·1 | 14·6 | Gower . . | 76·9 | −1·0 | 22·6 | 63·4 | — | 14·0 N | — | 6·8 | 3·2 |
| 20·2 | 9·3 | 53·7 | 27·5 | 62·5 | 42·1 | 0·1 | 10·3 | 13·2 | Neath . . | 75·3 | −3·4 | 17·0 | 71·4 | — | 1·5 10·1 N | — | 4·6 | −0·8 |
| 23·2 | 9·6 | 52·7 | 25·1 | 66·4 | 45·4 | 0·3 | 10·1 | 12·5 | Ogmore . . | 75·6 | −2·8 | 21·0 | 67·3 | — | 11·7 N | [14·1] | 5·2 | 2·4 |
| 24·5 | 11·5 | 45·9 | 28·7 | 64·8 | 45·0 | 0·2 | 11·2 | 10·3 | Pontypridd . | 74·4 | −0·3 | 16·9 | 58·5 | 14·2 | 10·4 N | — | 4·1 | 0·3 |
| 29·7 | 17·7 | 51·6 | 16·7 | 68·2 | 52·3 | 0·3 | 9·5 | 15·4 | Merioneth . . | 84·3 | −1·5 | 13·3 | 39·8 | 22·6 | 24·3 N | −12·9 | — | — |
| | | | | | | | | | Monmouthshire, | | | | | | | | | |
| 15·3 | 5·3 | 53·5 | 24·2 | 53·0 | 34·4 | 0·1 | 10·1 | 13·6 | Abertillery . . | 75·0 | +1·7 | 12·4 | 81·4 | — | 6·2 N | — | 3·6 | 0·3 |
| 17·2 | 7·0 | 37·9 | 35·2 | 60·8 | 40·8 | 0·1 | 11·9 | 12·2 | Bedwellty . . | 76·6 | −0·1 | 15·4 | 74·6 | — | 10·0 N | — | 6·7 | 2·9 |
| 15·9 | 5·7 | 54·3 | 30·1 | 61·7 | 34·0 | 0·1 | 11·0 | 12·8 | Ebbw Vale . | 78·3 | −1·0 | 7·1 | 72·4 | 14·5 | 6·0 N | * | — | — |
| 32·6 | 17·6 | 42·8 | 38·0 | 81·1 | 59·0 | 0·4 | 10·3 | 11·1 | Monmouth † | 80·5 | −3·9 | 46·5 | 44·3 | 6·7 | 2·5 N | * | 3·9 | −6·1 |
| 18·9 | 7·0 | 37·5 | 44·4 | 68·6 | 43·8 | 0·1 | 11·2 | 12·1 | Pontypool . . | 71·9 | −3·5 | 22·9 | 70·7 | — | 1·1 C 5·3 N | — | 4·4 | −1·0 |
| 27·1 | 17·0 | 46·1 | 17·9 | 58·3 | 61·3 | 0·1 | 9·0 | 12·0 | Montgomery . . | 82·3 | −0·5 | 29·7 | 20·1 | 38·4 | 11·8 N | −3·1 | — | — |
| 28·0 | 15·5 | 49·0 | 26·0 | 73·5 | 55·4 | 0·6 | 11·7 | 12·1 | Pembroke † . . | 77·9 | −1·9 | 34·7 | 32·5 | 4·6 | 21·5 6·7 N | −6·1 | 7·1 | — |

## *Scottish Burghs*

| % Non-manual | % Professional & managerial | % Owner-Occupiers | % Council Tenants | % With full plumbing | % With cars | % Born in New Commonwealth | % Young voters | % Retired | Constituency | % Voting 1970 | Change in % voting 1966–70 | Con. % | Lab. % | Lib. % | Other % | Lib. + or − % | Swing 1966–70 | Swing 1955–70 |
|---|---|---|---|---|---|---|---|---|---|---|---|---|---|---|---|---|---|---|
| 24·2 | 7·7 | 15·4 | 56·5 | 63·6 | 30·6 | 0·4 | 12·3 | 9·9 | Aberdeen, North . | 69·9 | −2·2 | 22·0 | 62·1 | 6·4 | 1·2 C<br>8·4 N | −3·9 | 3·4 | −3·1 |
| 42·7 | 21·1 | 42·1 | 30·4 | 68·4 | 41·8 | 0·6 | 10·3 | 10·4 | South † . | 77·2 | −4·1 | 45·4 | 43·3 | 6·0 | 5·3 N | −5·5 | 2·8 | −6·7 |
| 23·7 | 8·4 | 13·2 | 74·4 | 84·0 | 27·7 | 0·1 | 11·5 | 8·3 | Coatbridge & Airdrie . | 76·3 | −0·7 | 35·1 | 58·9 | — | 6·0 N | — | 2·3 | −6·0 |
| 28·4 | 11·6 | 20·4 | 44·9 | 63·7 | 32·0 | 0·6 | 11·8 | 9·9 | Dundee, East . | 76·5 | −2·4 | 42·4 | 48·3 | — | 0·4<br>8·9 N | — | 3·3 | 1·3 |
| 25·6 | 10·9 | 17·0 | 51·4 | 68·6 | 30·6 | 0·6 | 11·2 | 8·3 | West . . | 76·7 | −3·2 | 38·2 | 51·5 | — | 1·6 C<br>8·7 N | [7·0] | 1·7 | −4·9 |
| 24·1 | 8·6 | 18·6 | 65·3 | 85·3 | 35·6 | 0·4 | 11·0 | 9·8 | Dunfermline . . | 74·0 | −2·4 | 32·0 | 57·1 | — | 1·2 C<br>9·7 N | — | 3·7 | −1·5 |
| 30·0 | 8·5 | 41·0 | 9·7 | 39·2 | 16·3 | 0·8 | 7·8 | 12·9 | Edinburgh, Central . | 66·0 | −2·8 | 38·6 | 46·2 | 7·2 | 8·0 N | * | 4·8 | −2·3 |
| 31·7 | 12·0 | 34·1 | 53·2 | 89·0 | 29·9 | 0·4 | 11·1 | 10·8 | East . . | 74·5 | −2·9 | 39·0 | 51·9 | — | 1·0 C<br>8·2 N | — | 4·0 | −3·9 |
| 32·3 | 12·9 | 48·6 | 12·8 | 52·7 | 24·0 | 0·6 | 8·1 | 11·5 | Leith . . | 73·2 | −2·9 | 41·0 | 46·3 | 5·7 | 7·0 N | * | 4·7 | 5·9 |
| 42·8 | 19·0 | 55·8 | 4·0 | 62·1 | 26·4 | 1·0 | 8·4 | 9·4 | North . . | 70·1 | −3·7 | 52·9 | 37·1 | 10·1 | — | −0·4 | 2·3 | −3·8 |
| 41·2 | 17·3 | 44·8 | 30·6 | 87·1 | 37·6 | 0·7 | 11·1 | 9·5 | Pentlands . . | 77·0 | −3·5 | 46·1 | 39·4 | 8·6 | 5·9 N | −1·7 | 3·3 | −6·1 |
| 47·0 | 23·3 | 50·4 | 33·4 | 89·7 | 37·9 | 1·4 | 14·4 | 10·2 | South . . | 74·1 | −3·5 | 48·1 | 36·5 | 8·4 | 6·9 N | * | −1·0 | −11·7 |
| 47·0 | 23·8 | 47·3 | 36·7 | 96·8 | 43·6 | 0·7 | 11·3 | 7·7 | West . . | 75·1 | −3·6 | 49·2 | 35·8 | 8·2 | 6·8 N | −4·6 | 2·1 | −10·3 |

| | | | | | | | | | | | | | | | | | | |
|---|---|---|---|---|---|---|---|---|---|---|---|---|---|---|---|---|---|---|
| 12·3 | 2·5 | 16·0 | 16·2 | 17·4 | 7·6 | 0·1 | 8·9 | 9·4 | Glasgow, Bridgeton | 56·3 | −2·5 | 21·6 | 62·9 | — | 6·7<br>8·8 N | — | 3·6 | −9·2 |
| 39·3 | 15·1 | 33·3 | 41·1 | 90·0 | 30·9 | 0·4 | 12·4 | 8·2 | Cathcart | 74·4 | −5·3 | 54·2 | 45·0 | — | 0·8 | — | 3·4 | −18·1 |
| 17·3 | 3·9 | 11·7 | 26·0 | 20·7 | 9·2 | 0·7 | 8·8 | 10·0 | Central | 59·2 | +0·5 | 19·9 | 66·0 | — | 14·1 N | — | 1·8 | −11·3 |
| 37·0 | 13·9 | 18·9 | 64·4 | 97·0 | 32·6 | 0·8 | 12·6 | 9·8 | Craigton | 74·9 | −5·5 | 36·5 | 55·7 | — | 7·9 N | — | 3·0 | −9·9 |
| 14·8 | 2·5 | 15·7 | 17·9 | 25·4 | 8·5 | 1·7 | 8·5 | 8·8 | Gorbals | 59·7 | −2·0 | 20·8 | 69·3 | — | 2·5 C<br>7·4 N | — | 0·8 | −9·8 |
| 16·1 | 4·0 | 25·5 | 15·8 | 31·9 | 11·7 | 0·8 | 9·1 | 9·0 | Govan | 63·2 | −4·3 | 28·2 | 60·1 | — | 1·5 C<br>10·3 N | — | 3·9 | −4·0 |
| 50·2 | 24·7 | 46·6 | 6·5 | 65·1 | 32·0 | 0·5 | 8·0 | 11·8 | Hillhead | 69·5 | −4·1 | 61·3 | 30·5 | — | 8·2 N | — | 2·5 | −2·2 |
| 32·5 | 11·4 | 23·8 | 8·0 | 41·5 | 15·7 | 4·6 | 9·2 | 9·5 | Kelvingrove | 60·1 | −6·2 | 46·3 | 53·7 | — | — | — | *4·2* | *−9·0* |
| 19·0 | 3·8 | 9·8 | 67·8 | 73·7 | 15·9 | 0·1 | 12·4 | 8·5 | Maryhill | 63·8 | −4·7 | 23·0 | 65·6 | — | 11·4 N | — | 2·3 | −8·5 |
| 34·3 | 12·6 | 24·7 | 54·9 | 90·4 | 26·1 | 0·3 | 12·4 | 8·3 | Pollok ‡ | 72·6 | −6·5 | 44·8 | 46·2 | — | 9·1 N | — | 1·7 | −12·0 |
| 22·2 | 5·1 | 9·7 | 77·2 | 89·8 | 19·5 | 0·1 | 14·5 | 7·2 | Provan | 65·4 | −5·4 | 27·9 | 60·8 | — | 1·4 C<br>9·8 N | — | 1·6 | −16·1 |
| 27·8 | 8·0 | 9·2 | 83·5 | 93·1 | 26·6 | 0·1 | 14·4 | 7·7 | Scotstoun | 70·4 | −4·0 | 31·4 | 57·4 | — | 1·9 C<br>9·4 N | — | 1·5 | −13·6 |
| 20·2 | 5·2 | 14·5 | 54·1 | 63·1 | 16·2 | 0·1 | 12·0 | 10·0 | Shettleston | 63·6 | −5·1 | 26·7 | 59·9 | — | 13·4 N | — | 5·1 | −8·7 |
| 19·8 | 3·7 | 12·2 | 51·3 | 58·0 | 15·7 | 0·2 | 10·1 | 10·8 | Springburn | 61·2 | −5·4 | 19·6 | 64·3 | — | 1·8 C<br>14·3 N | — | 2·1 | −12·0 |
| 33·9 | 13·3 | 28·2 | 2·8 | 39·2 | 18·1 | 2·2 | 8·6 | 9·1 | Woodside | 63·8 | −9·3 | 41·5 | 47·4 | — | 2·7<br>8·4 N | — | 1·5 | −9·0 |
| 22·9 | 9·2 | 18·4 | 56·3 | 74·1 | 24·0 | 0·3 | 11·8 | 9·5 | Greenock | 75·9 | +2·2 | — | 53·7 | 44·7 | 1·6 C | +21·5 | — | — |
| 24·4 | 10·0 | 21·2 | 58·8 | 76·6 | 34·0 | 0·4 | 10·9 | 11·7 | Kirkcaldy | 74·5 | −0·9 | 32·2 | 56·0 | — | 11·9 N | — | 4·4 | −2·7 |
| 26·0 | 8·7 | 19·2 | 60·4 | 74·1 | 28·5 | 0·3 | 11·3 | 9·6 | Paisley | 71·5 | −4·8 | 32·4 | 54·1 | 6·2 | 7·3 N | −10·6 | 7·5 | −4·4 |
| 29·1 | 12·5 | 23·8 | 62·0 | 82·7 | 38·0 | 0·5 | 10·5 | 8·6 | Stirling & Falkirk | 73·2 | −4·0 | 34·8 | 50·7 | — | 14·5 N | — | 2·7 | −6·5 |

## *Scottish Counties*

| % Non-manual | % Professional & managerial | % Owner-Occupiers | % Council Tenants | % With full plumbing | % With cars | % Born in New Commonwealth | % Young voters | % Retired | Constituency | % Voting 1970 | Change in % voting 1966–70 | Con. % | Lab. % | Lib. % | Other % | Lib. + or − % | Swing 1966–70 | Swing 1955–70 |
|---|---|---|---|---|---|---|---|---|---|---|---|---|---|---|---|---|---|---|
| 25·9 | 17·2 | 34·3 | 32·2 | 73·3 | 51·4 | 0·3 | 11·3 | 12·2 | Aberdeenshire, East . | 68·8 | +0·6 | 40·9 | 18·0 | 11·3 | 29·8 N | −16·3 | — | — |
| 30·2 | 19·3 | 36·8 | 26·2 | 76·3 | 48·7 | 0·5 | 10·6 | 13·1 | West † . . | 75·8 | −0·5 | 46·6 | 15·6 | 32·5 | 5·3 N | −10·6 | — | — |
| 28·1 | 17·3 | 33·1 | 28·5 | 73·8 | 49·1 | 0·4 | 10·4 | 13·4 | Angus, North & Mearns | 74·7 | −1·6 | 53·1 | 18·4 | 11·6 | 16·9 N | −17·8 | 2·2 | −1·6 |
| 29·7 | 17·7 | 31·0 | 33·8 | 75·4 | 45·2 | 0·4 | 9·7 | 12·6 | South . . | 73·9 | +2·7 | 56·2 | 20·8 | — | 23·1 N | — | — | — |
| 31·3 | 20·0 | 35·3 | 28·8 | 81·0 | 43·4 | 0·4 | 8·4 | 15·0 | Argyll . . . | 74·3 | +2·0 | 44·8 | 25·3 | — | 29·9 N | [26·7] | — | — |
| 36·0 | 17·8 | 39·6 | 46·3 | 88·1 | 40·5 | 0·4 | 10·7 | 10·6 | Ayrshire, Ayr . . | 81·6 | −3·7 | 52·7 | 42·1 | — | 5·2 N | — | 4·7 | −3·8 |
| 33·2 | 17·4 | 38·1 | 42·8 | 83·0 | 34·7 | 0·3 | 9·6 | 16·7 | Bute & North Ayrshire . . | 73·6 | −2·4 | 53·6 | 35·4 | — | 11·0 N | [10·7] | 5·1 | −5·4 |
| 25·8 | 13·0 | 23·0 | 63·5 | 88·7 | 37·7 | 0·2 | 11·0 | 9·4 | Central . . | 80·7 | −1·4 | 41·8 | 52·4 | — | 0·7<br>5·1 N | — | 2·4 | −5·5 |
| 24·4 | 11·5 | 22·4 | 62·4 | 80·6 | 37·1 | 0·2 | 10·5 | 9·3 | Kilmarnock . | 79·2 | +0·2 | 27·8 | 59·3 | 6·0 | 6·9 N | * | 2·8 | −4·9 |
| 19·5 | 11·4 | 18·5 | 65·7 | 93·1 | 38·5 | 0·2 | 11·7 | 10·8 | South . . | 76·9 | +1·8 | 30·2 | 61·8 | — | 8·0 N | — | 1·4 | −4·2 |
| 30·1 | 20·5 | 41·6 | 30·1 | 75·7 | 50·4 | 0·3 | 9·7 | 13·3 | Banff . . . | 68·9 | +3·8 | 38·7 | 17·4 | 21·0 | 22·9 N | −13·4 | — | — |
| 27·8 | 16·0 | 24·8 | 46·1 | 90·1 | 44·6 | 0·3 | 10·6 | 10·8 | Berwick & East Lothian . . | 83·7 | −2·4 | 44·2 | 45·6 | — | 10·2 N | — | 1·3 | −4·0 |
| 28·9 | 14·7 | 31·6 | 33·7 | 80·3 | 53·4 | 0·3 | 10·0 | 10·9 | Caithness & Sutherland | 83·1 | +3·9 | 22·4 | 36·8 | 25·4 | 15·5 N | −13·5 | — | — |
| 28·5 | 15·5 | 31·4 | 41·2 | 86·9 | 45·9 | 0·3 | 11·1 | 11·1 | Dumfries . . . | 76·1 | −4·1 | 53·1 | 33·5 | — | 13·4 N | [5·9] | 5·0 | −1·5 |
| 39·1 | 19·3 | 32·8 | 56·5 | 89·4 | 42·4 | 0·3 | 10·1 | 8·0 | Dunbartonshire, East | 77·6 | −3·0 | 37·0 | 44·7 | 4·8 | 2·3 C<br>11·3 N | * | 4·1 | −2·7 |
| 32·1 | 14·7 | 29·4 | 51·8 | 86·1 | 35·3 | 0·4 | 11·2 | 10·1 | West . . | 77·8 | −4·2 | 37·1 | 50·9 | — | 12·0 N | — | 2·7 | −4·5 |

| | | | | | | | | | | | | | | | | | | |
|---|---|---|---|---|---|---|---|---|---|---|---|---|---|---|---|---|---|---|
| 32·7 | 17·7 | 37·8 | 34·8 | 85·1 | 46·3 | 0·9 | 10·8 | 12·5 | Fife, East | 74·4 | −1·7 | 54·6 | 24·6 | 9·0 | 11·8 N | −0·5 | 1·5 | −5·6 |
| 20·4 | 8·1 | 14·8 | 65·8 | 89·0 | 38·1 | 0·3 | 12·0 | 10·3 | West | 74·2 | −2·6 | 26·2 | 61·1 | — | 1·8 C<br>11·0 N | — | 4·4 | 1·5 |
| 30·2 | 19·8 | 37·7 | 30·3 | 86·7 | 53·3 | 0·4 | 9·8 | 11·2 | Galloway | 72·0 | +5·5 | 50·3 | 20·3 | 8·8 | 20·6 N | * | — | — |
| 34·1 | 17·9 | 35·9 | 35·1 | 79·3 | 47·9 | 0·6 | 9·7 | 11·4 | Inverness | 72·3 | +0·2 | 31·5 | 23·0 | 38·3 | 7·1 N | −1·1 | — | — |
| 27·9 | 10·4 | 23·3 | 65·8 | 87·2 | 33·0 | 0·1 | 11·8 | 7·9 | Lanarkshire, Bothwell | 75·3 | −2·5 | 32·5 | 54·7 | — | 12·8 N | — | 1·2 | −6·9 |
| 25·3 | 11·0 | 21·9 | 67·8 | 83·6 | 32·0 | 0·1 | 10·4 | 9·6 | Hamilton ‡ | 79·8 | +6·5 | 11·4 | 53·0 | — | 0·6<br>35·1 N | — | — | — |
| 31·6 | 14·9 | 19·9 | 67·7 | 91·8 | 47·6 | 0·2 | 10·7 | 9·0 | Lanark | 79·5 | −4·3 | 41·4 | 45·0 | — | 1·9 C<br>11·7 N | — | 4·9 | −3·0 |
| 24·3 | 8·8 | 15·4 | 70·9 | 81·4 | 29·6 | 0·0 | 11·1 | 9·9 | Motherwell | 73·5 | −0·9 | 32·2 | 53·2 | — | 4·7 C<br>9·9 N | — | 2·3 | −6·7 |
| 28·5 | 11·9 | 30·4 | 56·9 | 90·8 | 38·5 | 0·2 | 11·7 | 9·6 | North | 77·7 | −1·0 | 40·0 | 51·8 | — | 8·2 N | — | 5·0 | 1·8 |
| 36·2 | 15·5 | 34·2 | 51·3 | 84·4 | 33·3 | 0·2 | 10·2 | 10·3 | Rutherglen | 79·5 | −4·7 | 43·3 | 52·3 | — | 4·4 | — | 2·8 | −7·4 |
| 25·1 | 12·6 | 18·4 | 61·8 | 94·4 | 41·8 | 0·4 | 11·8 | 8·9 | Midlothian | 75·6 | −1·9 | 31·5 | 53·0 | — | 15·6 N | — | 4·1 | −0·6 |
| 31·0 | 17·8 | 35·6 | 29·4 | 81·7 | 49·2 | 0·9 | 10·0 | 9·9 | Moray & Nairn | 72·2 | +4·1 | 49·4 | 22·8 | — | 27·8 N | [17·8] | — | — |
| 26·2 | 15·5 | 48·9 | 19·0 | 59·3 | 46·8 | 0·2 | 9·8 | 15·9 | Orkney & Zetland | 65·7 | +0·5 | 31·9 | 21·1 | 47·0 | — | −12·1 | — | — |
| 36·1 | 24·1 | 35·5 | 21·7 | 82·5 | 53·1 | 0·7 | 10·4 | 12·5 | Perthshire, Kinross & West | 74·1 | +0·7 | 57·4 | 15·2 | 8·9 | 18·6 N | * | — | — |
| 36·4 | 17·6 | 32·5 | 35·9 | 78·2 | 45·0 | 0·4 | 9·8 | 11·4 | Perth & East | 73·6 | +1·3 | 52·1 | 23·8 | 7·2 | 17·0 N | * | −0·2 | — |
| 52·2 | 29·6 | 58·1 | 33·1 | 92·0 | 50·9 | 0·5 | 9·9 | 9·3 | Renfrewshire, East | 76·2 | −3·7 | 52·1 | 28·7 | 12·6 | 6·7 N | −1·2 | 1·7 | −6·6 |
| 29·8 | 15·1 | 22·7 | 59·5 | 88·8 | 36·5 | 0·4 | 11·1 | 9·2 | West | 79·5 | −2·2 | 43·2 | 48·0 | — | 8·8 N | — | 1·9 | −7·6 |
| 27·3 | 17·1 | 41·9 | 21·3 | 79·8 | 50·8 | 0·6 | 10·2 | 14·2 | Ross & Cromarty † | 71·7 | +0·5 | 33·2 | 26·0 | 29·1 | 11·9 N | −13·0 | — | — |
| 29·3 | 16·7 | 34·4 | 34·0 | 78·6 | 43·9 | 0·4 | 10·7 | 10·3 | Roxburgh, Selkirk & Peebles | 80·7 | −4·1 | 41·1 | 9·6 | 42·3 | 0·2<br>6·8 N | −3·4 | — | — |
| 23·6 | 10·1 | 18·7 | 70·6 | 92·2 | 41·5 | 0·3 | 12·6 | 9·1 | Stirlingshire, Clackmannan & East | 75·6 | −1·9 | 28·2 | 50·7 | 5·6 | 15·5 N | * | 4·1 | −2·6 |
| 26·3 | 14·4 | 19·4 | 66·7 | 93·2 | 41·6 | 0·5 | 11·9 | 8·6 | West | 78·9 | −3·5 | 29·7 | 48·9 | — | 21·4 N | — | 2·0 | −5·0 |
| 22·5 | 8·9 | 15·2 | 68·7 | 86·5 | 33·8 | 0·2 | 11·5 | 9·6 | West Lothian | 76·1 | −3·5 | 18·1 | 52·9 | — | 0·8 C<br>28·2 N | — | — | — |
| 16·1 | 8·5 | 70·5 | 15·7 | 59·0 | 30·6 | 0·0 | 8·5 | 18·0 | Western Isles † | 64·8 | +3·3 | 18·5 | 38·4 | — | 43·1 N | [18·8] | — | — |

## *Northern Ireland*

| Constituency | % voting 1970 | Change in % voting 1966–70 | Ulster Unionist % | N.I. Lab. % | Lib. % | Other Unionist % | Anti-Unionist % | Swing 1966–70 | Swing 1955–70 |
|---|---|---|---|---|---|---|---|---|---|
| Belfast, East . . | 75·7 | +7·5 | 59·5 | 40·5 | — | — | — | 4·8 | *−6·7* |
| North . . . | 78·3 | +12·8 | 48·5 | 31·9 | — | Prot. 18·9<br>Ind. 0·7 | — | 0·8 | −9·3 |
| South . . . | 68·4 | +5·2 | 70·4 | 29·6 | — | — | — | 5·1 | *−10·0* |
| West . . . | 84·6 | +9·8 | 47·2 | — | — | — | R. Lab. 52·8 | — | — |
| Antrim, North † . . | 73·1 | +16·4 | 36·7 | 11·1 | 3·5 | Prot. 41·3 | N. Dem. 7·4 | — | — |
| South . . | 67·9 | +12·0 | 61·2 | 20·5 | 0·9 | Ind. 11·2 | N. Dem. 6·2 | — | — |
| Armagh . . . | 78·5 | +15·2 | 55·3 | 12·9 | — | — | Unity 31·8 | — | — |
| Down, North . . | 66·8 | +17·9 | 68·9 | 17·7 | 1·3 | Ind. U. 7·9<br>Ind. 4·1 | — | — | — |
| South . . . | 74·0 | +9·1 | 54·3 | — | 12·0 | — | Unity 33·7 | — | — |
| Fermanagh & South Tyrone † . . | 92·1 | +6·0 | 48·9 | — | — | — | Unity 51·1 | — | — |
| Londonderry . . | 81·2 | +4·8 | 53·1 | — | — | — | Unity 36·6<br>Derry Lab. 10·3 | — | — |
| Mid-Ulster †‡ . | 91·0 | +7·0 | 45·1 | — | — | — | Ind. Unity 53·1<br>Ind. 1·1<br>N. Soc. 0·3 | — | — |

| Highest Swings | | Highest Turnout | | Biggest Turnout Increase | |
|---|---|---|---|---|---|
| % | | % | | See N. Ireland results. All 12 seats showed increases from 4·8% to 17·9%. Other increases: | |
| 11·0 | Cannock | 92·1 | Fermanagh & S. Tyrone | % | |
| 10·1 | Wandsworth, Clapham | 91·0 | Mid-Ulster | +6·5 | Hamilton |
| 9·8 | Bolton, East | 85·3 | Cornwall, North | +5·5 | Galloway |
| 9·5 | Newcastle under Lyme | 84·9 | Devon, North | +5·1 | Southampton, Itchen |
| 9·5 | Westhoughton | 84·6 | Belfast, West | +5·0 | Anglesey |
| 9·5 | Brierley Hill | 84·3 | Merioneth | +4·0 | Merthyr Tydfil |
| 9·1 | Wolverhampton, North-East | 83·7 | Berwick & E. Lothian | +3·9 | Caithness & Sutherland |
| 8·8 | Leicester, South-West | 83·7 | Carmarthen | | |
| 8·8 | Dudley | 83·1 | Caithness & Sutherland | | |
| 8·7 | Wolverhampton, South-West | 82·4 | Shipley | | |

| Lowest Swings | | Lowest Turnout | | Biggest Turnout Decrease | |
|---|---|---|---|---|---|
| % | | % | | % | |
| −2·7 | Rugby | 44·9 | Stepney | −20·4 | Stoke-on-Trent, South |
| −1·2 | Birmingham, All Saints | 48·2 | Southwark | −19·5 | Stoke-on-Trent, North |
| −1·1 | Nuneaton | 48·7 | Shoreditch & Finsbury | −18·3 | Stoke-on-Trent, Central |
| −1·0 | Edinburgh, South | 48·7 | West Ham, South | −14·5 | Newcastle under Lyme |
| −0·7 | Haltemprice | 48·8 | Poplar | −14·1 | Leyton |
| −0·7 | Liverpool, Scotland | 48·9 | Islington, South-West | −13·0 | West Han, South |
| −0·4 | Liverpool, West Derby | 49·0 | Islington, North | −12·1 | East Ham, North |
| −0·3 | Bootle | 49·9 | Kensington, South | −11·6 | Leek |
| −0·2 | Perth & E. Perthshire | 49·9 | Camberwell, Peckham | −11·6 | Wandsworth, Central |
| −0·0 | Kingston on Hull, North | 50·0 | Stoke-on-Trent, Central | −11·5 | Holborn & St. Pancras, North |

## *50 Most Agricultural Seats*

% of employed engaged in agriculture

| | | | | | |
|---|---|---|---|---|---|
| 30·3 | Montgomery | 21·6 | North Angus & Mearns | 15·8 | Bodmin |
| 30·0 | Orkney & Zetland | 21·5 | Caithness & Sutherland | 15·7 | Gainsborough |
| 29·1 | Galloway | 21·0 | Penrith & the Border | 15·5 | South Angus |
| 27·7 | Holland with Boston | 20·6 | Norfolk, South | 15·4 | St. Ives |
| 27·7 | Aberdeenshire, East | 19·9 | Ross & Cromarty | 15·0 | Dumfries |
| 27·7 | Banff | 19·8 | Norfolk, North | 15·0 | Denbigh |
| 27·0 | Cardigan | 18·7 | Cornwall, North | 14·9 | Moray & Nairn |
| 25·1 | Norfolk, South-West | 18·6 | King's Lynn | 14·1 | Dorset, North |
| 24·3 | Torrington | 18·2 | Argyll | 14·0 | Dorset, West |
| 24·2 | Aberdeenshire, West | 17·9 | Brecon & Radnor | 13·9 | Tiverton |
| 23·8 | Leominster | 17·9 | Ludlow | 13·9 | Richmond, Yorks. |
| 23·7 | Carmarthen | 17·8 | Thirsk & Malton | 13·8 | Saffron Walden |
| 23·4 | Howden | 17·7 | Berwick upon Tweed | 13·6 | Rutland & Stamford |
| 22·8 | Kinross & W. Perthshire | 17·6 | Berwick & E. Lothian | 13·5 | Devon, North |
| 22·8 | Horncastle | 17·2 | Pembroke | 13·4 | Fife, East |
| 22·7 | Isle of Ely | 17·2 | Oswestry | 13·2 | Bridlington |
| 21·7 | Eye | 16·1 | Merioneth | | |

## *50 Most Mining Seats*

% of employed engaged in mining or quarrying

| | | | | | |
|---|---|---|---|---|---|
| 40·7 | Hemsworth | 21·2 | Aberdare | 12·6 | Gower |
| 40·3 | Bolsover | 19·5 | Normanton | 12·4 | Merthyr Tydfil |
| 38·5 | Easington | 19·5 | Durham | 12·1 | Leigh |
| 36·3 | Morpeth | 18·7 | Rhondda, West | 11·6 | Goole |
| 31·5 | Dearne Valley | 18·5 | Ogmore | 11·5 | Truro (China Clay) |
| 29·9 | Abertillery | 18·5 | Durham, North-West | 11·4 | Kirkcaldy Burghs |
| 28·0 | Houghton-le-Spring | 17·3 | Chester-le-Street | 11·1 | Bosworth |
| 27·0 | Ashfield | 17·1 | Fife, West | 10·7 | Nottingham, North |
| 26·3 | Blyth | 17·1 | Rhondda, East | 10·7 | Pontypridd |
| 25·6 | Ayrshire, South | 17·0 | Newark | 10·4 | Cannock |
| 25·1 | Mansfield | 17·0 | Consett | 10·4 | Whitehaven |
| 24·6 | Don Valley | 16·3 | Midlothian | 10·3 | Wrexham |
| 24·1 | Pontefract | 15·5 | Derbyshire, North-East | 9·9 | Lanarkshire, North |
| 23·9 | Caerphilly | 15·5 | Bassetlaw | 9·9 | Chesterfield |
| 23·8 | Barnsley | 14·0 | Ebbw Vale | 9·8 | Llanelli |
| 23·5 | Bedwellty | 14·0 | Ilkeston | 9·6 | Penistone |
| 21·3 | Rother Valley | 13·4 | Wakefield | | |

## 25 Seats With Most Irish Born

% born anywhere in Ireland

| | |
|---|---|
| 14·5 | Willesden, East |
| 10·9 | Hammersmith, North |
| 10·1 | Manchester, Ardwick |
| 10·0 | Willesden, West |
| 9·6 | Kensington, North |
| 9·5 | Islington, North |
| 9·3 | Paddington, North |
| 9·2 | Glasgow, Gorbals |
| 9·0 | Barons Court |
| 8·7 | Birmingham, Sparkbrook |
| 8·6 | St. Pancras, North |
| 8·5 | Paddington, South |
| 8·1 | Manchester, Moss Side |
| 7·9 | Birmingham, Ladywood |
| 7·6 | Birmingham, Small Heath |
| 7·6 | Coventry, South |
| 7·3 | Acton |
| 7·3 | Hampstead |
| 7·1 | Birmingham, Selly Oak |
| 6·9 | Birmingham, Handsworth |
| 6·8 | Holborn & St. Pancras, South |
| 6·7 | Birmingham, All Saints |
| 6·6 | Manchester, Exchange |
| 6·5 | Islington, East |
| 6·5 | Coventry, North |

## 20 Seats With Most Servicemen

% of employed in H.M. Forces

| | |
|---|---|
| 20·0 | Plymouth, Devonport |
| 19·4 | Portsmouth, West |
| 18·7 | Moray & Nairn |
| 17·6 | Richmond, Yorks. |
| 16·7 | Gosport & Fareham |
| 16·0 | Aldershot |
| 15·0 | Huntingdonshire |
| 14·9 | Grantham |
| 14·7 | Salisbury |
| 14·3 | Bury St. Edmunds |
| 13·2 | Petersfield |
| 13·2 | Chippenham |
| 12·3 | Rutland & Stamford |
| 11·5 | Gainsborough |
| 11·5 | Portsmouth, South |
| 10·9 | Henley |
| 10·9 | Devizes |
| 10·7 | Gillingham |
| 10·6 | Tavistock |
| 10·4 | Norfolk, South-West |

# BY-ELECTIONS 1966–70

| Constituency | Date | % voting | Con. % | Lab. % | Lib. % | Other % | Swing '66-By-election | Swing By-election-'70 |
|---|---|---|---|---|---|---|---|---|
| Carmarthen | *1966* | *82·6* | *11·6* | *46·2* | *26·1* | *16·1* N | — | — |
| *Plaid Cymru gain* | 14.7.66 | 74·9 | 7·1 | 33·1 | 20·8 | 39·0 N | — | — |
| *Labour recovery* | *1970* | *83·7* | *10·1* | *38·0* | *21·8* | *30·1* N | — | — |
| Glasgow, Pollok | *1966* | *79·0* | *47·6* | *52·4* | — | — | — | — |
| *Conservative gain* | 9.3.67 | 75·7 | 36·9 | 31·2 | 1·9 | 28·2 N<br>1·8 C | +5·3 | — |
| *Labour recovery* | *1970* | *72·6* | *44·8* | *46·2* | — | *9·1* N | — | −3·6 |
| Nuneaton | *1966* | *79·7* | *31·5* | *54·0* | *14·5* | — | — | — |
| | 93.67 | 66·1 | 32·7 | 42·1 | 17·6 | 6·4<br>1·2 | +6·5 | — |
| | *1970* | *76·2* | *32·8* | *57·4* | *9·8* | — | — | −7·6 |
| Rhondda, West | *1966* | *80·3* | *7·8* | *76·1* | — | *8·7* N<br>*7·4* C | — | — |
| | 9.3.67 | 82·2 | 4·3 | 49·0 | — | 39·9 N<br>6·8 C | — | — |
| | *1970* | *81·5* | *6·4* | *74·8* | — | *14·0* N<br>*18·8* C | — | — |
| Honiton | *1966* | *78·6* | *54·4* | *26·7* | *18·9* | — | — | — |
| | 16.3.67 | 72·6 | 57·0 | 20·4 | 22·6 | — | — | — |
| | *1970* | *76·7* | *59·5* | *20·0* | *20·5* | — | — | — |
| Brierley Hill | *1966* | *79·0* | *51·2* | *48·8* | — | — | — | — |
| | 27.4.67 | 68·0 | 53·8 | 36·2 | 7·8 | 2·2 | +7·6 | — |
| | *1970* | *73·3* | *60·6* | *39·4* | — | — | — | +1·8 |
| Cambridge | *1966* | *80·0* | *43·4* | *45·5* | *10·2* | *0·9* | — | — |
| *Conservative gain* | 21.9.67 | 65·7 | 51·6 | 36·6 | 11·8 | — | +8·6 | — |
| | *1970* | *73·0* | *55·3* | *44·7* | — | — | — | −2·2 |
| Walthamstow, West | *1966* | *71·0* | *24·8* | *61·2* | *14·0* | — | — | — |
| *Conservative gain* | 21.9.67 | 54·0 | 37·0 | 36·7 | 22·9 | 3·0, 0·4 | +18·4 | — |
| *Labour recovery* | *1970* | *65·2* | *34·4* | *54·5* | *11·2* | — | — | −10·2 |
| Hamilton | *1966* | *73·3* | *28·8* | *71·2* | — | — | — | — |
| *SNP gain* | 2.11.67 | 73·7 | 12·5 | 41·5 | — | 46·0 N | — | — |
| *Labour recovery* | *1970* | *79·8* | *11·4* | *53·0* | — | *35·1 N*<br>*0·6* | — | — |
| Leicester, South-West | *1966* | *74·0* | *41·3* | *58·7* | — | — | — | — |
| *Conservative gain* | 2.11.67 | 57·5 | 51·6 | 35·9 | 12·5 | — | +16·6 | — |
| | *1970* | *71·9* | *45·7* | *45·3* | *6·6* | *2·4* | — | −7·7 |
| Manchester, Gorton | *1966* | *72·6* | *39·9* | *60·1* | — | — | — | — |
| | 2.11.67 | 72·4 | 44·5 | 45·9 | 5·9 | 2·7<br>1·0 C | +9·4 | — |
| | *1970* | *71·9* | *39·7* | *53·5* | *6·8* | — | — | −6·2 |
| Derbyshire, West | *1966* | *83·4* | *49·6* | *37·2* | *13·2* | — | — | — |
| | 23.11.67 | 64·5 | 56·7 | 18·3 | 19·8 | 5·2 | — | — |
| | *1970* | *76·7* | *61·9* | *38·1* | — | — | — | — |
| South Kensington | *1966* | *58·1* | *65·1* | *19·8* | *15·1* | — | — | — |
| | 14.3.68 | 40·0 | 75·5 | 8·6 | 12·6 | 3·1<br>0·2 | +10·8 | — |
| | *1970* | *49·9* | *75·7* | *24·3* | — | — | — | −7·8 |
| Acton | *1966* | *74·0* | *42·3* | *57·7* | — | — | — | — |
| *Conservative gain* | 28.3.68 | 59·7 | 48·7 | 33·9 | 11·4 | 6·0 | +15·1 | — |
| *Labour recovery* | *1970* | *66·6* | *45·7* | *48·0* | *5·4* | *0·9* C | — | −8·6 |
| Dudley | *1966* | *73·9* | *40·9* | *59·1* | — | — | — | — |
| *Conservative gain* | 28.3.68 | 63·5 | 58·1 | 34·0 | 7·9 | — | +21·2 | — |
| *Labour recovery* | *1970* | *71·9* | *49·7* | *50·3* | — | — | — | −12·4 |

| Constituency | Date | % voting | Con. % | Lab. % | Lib. % | Other % | Swing '66-By-election | Swing By-election-'70 |
|---|---|---|---|---|---|---|---|---|
| Meriden . . . | *1966* | *85·7* | *46·4* | *53·6* | — | — | — | — |
| *Conservative gain* | 28.3.68 | 66·0 | 64·8 | 35·2 | — | — | *+18·4* | — |
| | *1970* | *75·6* | *53·1* | *46·9* | — | — | — | *−11·7* |
| Warwick & Leamington . | *1966* | *78·9* | *51·6* | *36·1* | *12·3* | — | — | — |
| | 28.3.68 | 58·5 | 68·3 | 16·5 | 15·2 | — | +18·2 | — |
| | *1970* | *72·6* | *63·4* | *36·6* | — | — | — | −12·5 |
| Oldham, West . . | *1966* | *70·9* | *38·8* | *61·2* | — | — | — | — |
| *Conservative gain* | 13.6.68 | 54·7 | 46·5 | 33·6 | 6·7 | 13·2 | +17·7 | — |
| *Labour recovery* | *1970* | *67·0* | *43·1* | *48·1* | *8·8* | — | — | −9·0 |
| Sheffield, Brightside | *1966* | *66·2* | *21·3* | *75·9* | — | *2·8* C | — | — |
| | 13.6.68 | 49·8 | 34·8 | 55·2 | — | 4·1 C<br>3·6<br>2·3 | +17·1 | — |
| | *1970* | *62·0* | *25·8* | *72·2* | — | *2·0* C | — | −13·0 |
| Nelson & Colne . . | *1966* | *80·9* | *37·0* | *49·3* | — | *13·7* | — | — |
| *Conservative gain* | 27.6.68 | 74·2 | 48·9 | 38·4 | 9·0 | 3·7 | +11·4 | — |
| | *1970* | *78·2* | *51·8* | *48·2* | — | — | — | −3·5 |
| Caerphilly . . | *1966* | *76·7* | *14·6* | *74·3* | — | *11·1* N | — | — |
| | 18.7.68 | 75·9 | 10·4 | 45·7 | 3·5 | 40·4 N | — | — |
| | *1970* | *78·1* | *9·7* | *61·8* | — | *28·5* N | — | — |
| Bassetlaw . . . | *1966* | *73·3* | *38·4* | *61·6* | — | — | — | — |
| | 31.10.68 | 68·0 | 47·9 | 49·6 | — | 2·5 | +10·8 | — |
| | *1970* | *76·4* | *39·2* | *54·9* | *5·9* | — | — | −7·0 |
| New Forest . | *1966* | *74·2* | *51·2* | *26·7* | *22·1* | — | — | — |
| | 7.11.68 | 55·9 | 66·3 | 13·8 | 19·9 | — | — | — |
| | *1970* | *71·9* | *60·1* | *22·7* | *17·2* | — | — | — |
| Walthamstow, East . | *1966* | *80·1* | *42·3* | *47·8* | *9·8* | — | — | — |
| *Conservative gain* | 27.3.69 | 51·2 | 63·1 | 36·9 | — | — | +15·9 | — |
| | *1970* | *71·0* | *46·7* | *45·0* | *8·3* | — | — | −12·3 |
| Brighton Pavilion . . | *1966* | *70·3* | *58·1* | *41·9* | — | — | — | — |
| | 27.3.69 | 45·1 | 70·6 | 18·6 | 10·8 | — | +17·9 | — |
| | *1970* | *66·6* | *61·9* | *35·0* | — | *3·1* | — | −12·6 |
| Weston Super Mare | *1966* | *79·1* | *52·1* | *28·8* | *19·1* | — | — | — |
| | 27.3.69 | 60·8 | 65·7 | 14·6 | 19·7 | — | — | — |
| | *1970* | *73·7* | *57·9* | *24·8* | *17·3* | — | — | — |
| Mid Ulster . | *1966* | *83·8* | *52·3* | — | — | *47·7* | — | — |
| *Ind. Unity gain* | 17.4.69 | 91·8 | 46·7 | — | — | 53·3 | | |
| | *1970* | *91·0* | *45·1* | — | — | *53·5*<br>*1·1, 0·3* | — | — |
| | *1966* | *73·2* | *57·2* | *25·1* | *17·7* | — | — | — |
| Chichester | 27.5.69 | 53·4 | 74·2 | 12·2 | 13·6 | — | — | — |
| | *1970* | *69·9* | *62·6* | *20·7* | *16·8* | — | — | — |
| Birmingham, Ladywood . | *1966* | *59·7* | *17·4* | *58·9* | *23·7* | — | — | — |
| *Liberal gain* | 27.6.69 | 51·9 | 16·8 | 25·5 | 54·4 | 3·0<br>0·4 | — | — |
| *Labour recovery* | *1970* | *62·3* | *21·6* | *43·4* | *35·0* | — | — | — |
| Glasgow, Gorbals . | *1966* | *61·7* | *22·8* | *73·0* | — | *4·2* C | — | — |
| | 30.10.69 | 58·5 | 18·6 | 53·4 | — | 25·0 N<br>2·5 C<br>0·5 | — | — |
| | *1970* | *59·7* | *20·8* | *69·3* | — | *7·4* N<br>*2·5* C | — | — |
| Islington, North . . | *1966* | *54·2* | *30·7* | *59·5* | *9·9* | — | — | — |
| | 30.10.69 | 32·8 | 38·9 | 49·2 | 10·2 | 1·7 | +9·3 | — |
| | *1970* | *49·0* | *35·6* | *58·9* | — | *5·6* | — | −6·5 |

| Constituency | Date | % voting | Con. % | Lab. % | Lib. % | Other % | Swing '66-By-election | Swing By-election-'70 |
|---|---|---|---|---|---|---|---|---|
| Newcastle under Lyme . | *1966* | *79·9* | *38·2* | *61·8* | — | — | — | — |
| | 30.10.69 | 72·3 | 43·9 | 46·1 | 6·4 | 3·6 | +10·7 | — |
| | *1970* | *65·5* | *44·3* | *48·9* | *4·3* | *2·6* | — | −1·2 |
| Paddington, North . | *1966* | *66·4* | *32·5* | *58·9* | *8·6* | — | — | — |
| | 30.10.69 | 46·3 | 48·4 | 51·6 | — | — | +11·6 | — |
| | *1970* | *62·6* | *40·4* | *54·8* | *4·8* | — | — | −5·6 |
| Swindon . . . | *1966* | *73·5* | *36·7* | *61·3* | — | *2·0* C | — | — |
| *Conservative gain* | 30.10.69 | 69·8 | 41·7 | 40·6 | 15·3 | 1·3 C<br>1·2 | +12·9 | — |
| *Labour recovery* | *1970* | *75·6* | *43·5* | *55·5* | — | *1·0* C | — | −6·6 |
| Wellingborough . . | *1966* | *86·5* | *47·6* | *52·4* | — | — | — | — |
| *Conservative gain* | 4.12.69 | 69·6 | 54·4 | 39·8 | 5·8 | — | +9·7 | — |
| | *1970* | *81·4* | *52·2* | *47·8* | — | — | — | −5·1 |
| Louth . . . | *1966* | *74·4* | *46·4* | *36·9* | *16·8* | — | — | — |
| | 4.12.69 | 44·7 | 58·0 | 19·9 | 17·8 | 4·3 | +14·3 | — |
| | *1970* | *71·6* | *53·1* | *33·9* | *13·0* | — | — | −9·5 |
| Bridgwater . . . | *1966* | *80·2* | *44·4* | *38·1* | *17·5* | — | — | — |
| | 12.3.70 | 70·3 | 55·5 | 31·9 | 12·6 | — | +8·7 | — |
| | *1970* | *77·6* | *52·4* | *35·8* | *11·9* | — | — | −3·5 |
| Ayrshire, South . . | *1966* | *75·1* | *32·8* | *67·2* | — | — | — | — |
| | 19.3.70 | 76·4 | 25·6 | 54·1 | — | 20·3 N | +3·0 | — |
| | *1970* | *76·9* | *30·2* | *61·8* | — | *8·0* N | — | −1·6 |

APPENDIX II

# AN ANALYSIS OF THE RESULTS

By Michael Steed

If the result of the 1970 election is compared with that in 1966, in terms either of the party shares of the vote or of the turnover in seats, it is the sharp movement from Labour to Conservative (the largest change at any general election since 1945) that strikes the attention. But if the result is expressed in a way which, though unusual in Britain, is quite normal in France, in terms of the party share of the registered electorate, it is the appearance of a shift from Labour to abstention that is most prominent. The first column of Table 1 appears to offer support for the theory, so widely bruited after the result was known, that the Conservatives won through Labour apathy rather than through a positive switch of votes. But such global figures are also misleading in that the Liberals and nationalists fought only some of the seats (and on a different pattern from 1966). All the analysis in this appendix is therefore in terms of four specific measures of change applied to the 615 constituencies in Great Britain where the results in 1966 and 1970 can conveniently be compared.[1]

Table 1

*The overall result in Great Britain*[2]

| | % of registered electorate | | % of total votes cast | | % of two-party vote | |
|---|---|---|---|---|---|---|
| Conservative | 33·2 | +1·7 | 46·1 | +4·6 | 51·3 | +5·3 |
| Labour | 31·5 | −5·6 | 43·8 | −4·9 | 48·7 | −5·3 |
| Liberal | 5·5 | −1·1 | 7·7 | −0·9 | | — |
| SNP and Plaid Cymru | 1·3 | +0·8 | 1·8 | +1·1 | | — |
| Others | 0·4 | — | 0·6 | +0·1 | | — |
| Non-voters | 28·1 | +4·2 | | — | | — |
| 'Swing' to Conservative | | 3·6 | | 4·8 | | 5·3 |

[1] The three non-comparable seats are Greenock (see p. 401), Merthyr Tydfil (see p. 296) and the Speaker's seat, Southampton, Itchen.

[2] All figures in this appendix, unless otherwise stated, refer to Great Britain only. Northern Ireland (see below p. 411) showed, as always in its electoral behaviour, how little it is integrated with the rest of the United Kingdom.

1. The swing to Conservative on the basis of the two-party vote[1] (a mean swing of 4·7%).
2. The change in turnout in terms of the total electorate (a mean drop of 4·3%).
3. The change in the Liberal share of the vote (a mean drop of 3·0% in seats fought both times).[2]
4. The change in the nationalist vote (no single figure can meaningfully be given for this because of the irregular basis for comparison; however, the varying impact of the nationalist presence was, for the first time at a general election, a major factor to be taken into account in any analysis of the results).

The first task of this appendix is to examine the relationship between these four changes. The fundamental and perhaps surprising conclusion is that the first movement is quite unrelated to the other three.

*Liberals, nationalists and turnout.* The one clear causal relationship lies in the impact of Liberal and nationalist candidatures on turnout. Table 2 shows the extent to which turnout was affected by the presence or absence of a Liberal or a nationalist; above all it makes plain the extent to which Plaid Cymru and the Scottish National Party in some constituencies managed to mobilise people who otherwise would not have voted. By contrast some of the drop in turnout in England reflected the declining ability of the Liberal party to hold on to such voters. The largest average fall in turnout occurred in the seats where a Liberal candidate stood in 1966 but not in 1970; but the drop was also higher where Liberals stood both times and lost votes than in straight fights. In the seats where the Liberal loss of votes was highest, the drop in turnout was greatest. In the 28 English seats in which the Liberal loss was more than twice the national average (i.e. over 6%), the decrease in turnout averaged 5·4%. These differences indicate that there

[1] As in the 1964 and 1966 Nuffield studies swing is for the purposes of this analysis defined as the two-party swing. For the difference between this and the more conventional method of averaging the changes in the two parties' shares of the total vote see *The British General Election of 1964*, pp. 337–8. An example of the difference lies in Perth and East Perthshire where the 1970 Conservative vote fell by 269 and Labour's fell by 939; this is expressed as a swing of 0·2% to Labour by the conventional method but as one of 1·7% to Conservative on the two-party basis. To retain comparability with past tables, however, the conventional definition is used for the constituency and regional tables on pp. 360–85 and in Table 10 on p. 414 which shows the relationship of seats and votes.

[2] There were 243 seats fought by all three parties at both elections in which comparison is meaningful.

TABLE 2

*Nationalist and Liberal effect on turnout*

| Liberal candidates 1966 and 1970 | Change in turnout | | | | | | All seats | Mean change in turn-out |
|---|---|---|---|---|---|---|---|---|
| | Increase | Decrease | | | | | | |
| | | up to 1·9% | 2·0–3·9% | 4·0–5·9% | 6·0–7·9% | over 8·0% | | |
| Both elections | 10 | 23 | 68 | 72 | 43 | 27 | 243 | −4·7 |
| Neither election | 14 | 32 | 68 | 73 | 24 | 13 | 224 | −4·0 |
| Liberal intervention 1970 | 12 | 20 | 25 | 17 | 6 | 4 | 84 | −2·8 |
| Liberal withdrawal 1970 | 3 | 1 | 10 | 18 | 13 | 19 | 64 | −6·0 |
| All seats (Great Britain) | 39 | 76 | 171 | 180 | 86 | 63 | 615 | −4·3 |
| Nationalist 1966 vote: | | | | | | | | |
| decrease or increase up to 5% | 3 | 7 | 10 | 10 | 0 | 1 | 31 | −3·0 |
| increase over 5% | 9 | 2 | 0 | 0 | 0 | 0 | 11 | +1·2 |
| Nationalist intervention 1970: | | | | | | | | |
| Nationalist vote under 10% | 4 | 6 | 17 | 9 | 1 | 0 | 37 | −2·7 |
| Nationalist vote over 10% and under 20% | 3 | 4 | 5 | 2 | 0 | 0 | 14 | −1·4 |
| Nationalist vote over 20% | 7 | 0 | 0 | 0 | 0 | 0 | 7 | +4·0 |
| No nationalist candidate | 1 | 0 | 1 | 2 | 1 | 0 | 5 | −3·9 |
| All Scots and Welsh seats | 27 | 19 | 33 | 23 | 2 | 1 | 105 | −1·8 |

was abstention by about one quarter of the 1966 Liberal voters who had no candidate in 1970 and by about one quarter of those who deserted the Liberals in seats fought both times. Similarly, the difference in turnout drop between the seats with Liberal intervention and those with no Liberal in either year (1·3%) is almost exactly one quarter of the average vote for Liberal candidates who intervened.[1]

Similar calculations suggest that with the nationalist parties the relationship is even stronger. In most seats they received about one quarter of their support from people who would otherwise have abstained; however in the score of constituencies in which nationalist candidates did best something like half of their support can be explained in terms of the mobilisation of non-voters.[2] As a

[1] In 1966 it seems that at least one quarter of Liberal voters were, in the absence of a Liberal candidate, abstainers (see *The British General Election of 1966*, p. 275) but in the 1950s, when the level of the Liberal vote was more comparable with that of 1970, the number of would-be Liberals who abstained seems to have been insignificant.

[2] This calculation cannot take into account the possibility that the presence of a nationalist candidate (especially one receiving a good deal of support) increased interest in the election and so brought out increased numbers of apathetic Conservative and Labour voters. To the extent that this seems plausible, the estimates given above may be reduced.

result the overall drop in turnout in Scotland and Wales was much lower than in England. It seems likely that, had it not been for the impact of the nationalists and the increase in Liberal candidatures, the overall drop in Great Britain would have reached 4·8% (which was the average turnout drop in seats in England with no change in Liberal candidature).

*Liberals and nationalists.* It is quite clear that in Scotland and Wales a part of the Liberal vote switched to the nationalists. In many seats, for example East Aberdeenshire or Anglesey, a substantial majority of the nationalist vote in 1970 must have come from people who voted Liberal in 1964 or 1966. While it is not possible to calculate the proportion exactly, at least a third of those who voted nationalist could be regarded as people who would otherwise have voted Liberal. This can be seen most clearly from the few seats in Scotland or Wales, such as Brecon & Radnor or Inverness, in which the Liberals did well.

*Liberals, nationalists and swing.* However, there is no evidence to suggest a relationship between the Liberal/nationalist vote and the swing to the Conservatives. It is quite clear that nationalists, like Liberals, took more from the weaker of the two main parties in seats where one was dominant — Labour suffered more from the SNP in Galloway, the Conservatives more from Plaid Cymru in Aberdare. But in more marginal seats both nationalists and Liberals seem to have drawn support from Conservative and Labour in virtually equal proportions; about the same number of 1966 Liberals seem to have voted Conservative as voted Labour.[1] In the 75 most marginal Labour-held seats (susceptible to a swing of 5%), the swing in the 24 seats with a Liberal candidate in 1966 and 1970 was 4·8% compared to 4·9% in the 10 where the Liberal party withdrew. The swing was 4·3% in the 21 marginal Labour seats with a Liberal candidate in 1970 but not in 1966 which, though lower than the national average, was higher than the swing of 3·9% in the 38 seats with no Liberal in either year. Nor can any evidence of areas where the Liberal 'take' seems to have been unequal be found by comparing neighbouring seats.[2] Indeed

[1] With one quarter of a Liberal candidate's vote coming from abstainers only a markedly unequal drawing of votes from Labour and Conservative would have any significant effect on the swing. Thus in a marginal seat where a Liberal intervened and won 8% of the vote drawn 55:45 from the major parties, he would affect the swing by only 0·3%.

[2] Clear instances of the total lack of any effect on the swing from the behaviour of Liberal candidates occur in three pairs of neighbouring seats which are

there is only one seat (Brentford & Chiswick) where a really plausible case can be made for Liberal withdrawal having affected the result.[1] Perhaps for the first time at any general election since the First World War there does not seem to be any seat where there is a case for saying that Liberal intervention decided the outcome. Because virtually all of the Scottish and all the Welsh seats were fought by the nationalist parties, it is not possible to prove so clearly that they too drew votes equally from Conservative and Labour. However, the complete absence of any relationship between the swing and the size of the votes for nationalists who intervened would suggest that this was so. The swing in Scotland was low but this does not appear to have been due to the SNP vote; in 9 seats where no nationalist stood or where the nationalist vote was within 1% of its 1966 level the mean swing was 3·2%, almost precisely the Scottish average.

It therefore seems quite clear that movement between the three smaller and the two larger parties had no net effect on the fortunes of the larger parties; the national swing between Labour and Conservative primarily reflects the direct movement between them; and secondarily the changes in the electorate; it may also reflect differential abstention.

*Turnout and swing*. The possibility that the swing was due to a disproportionate number of Labour voters staying at home merits careful examination. It fits with the overall changes in party shares of the electorate; it has a psychological plausibility; and it has received some support from survey evidence. Given the clear effect on turnout of Liberal candidatures and nationalist performance, the following table covers only seats in which no nationalist was present and in which Liberals stood either both in 1966 and 1970 or on neither occasion.

From Table 3 it is clear that the variation in the size of the swing from one constituency to another was not caused by differential turnout of Labour supporters. Indeed it would be hard to devise a distribution that showed more unequivocally the lack of any re-

---

politically and socially similar: Merton & Morden (Liberal intervention; swing +4·6%) and Mitcham (withdrawal; +4·7%), Halifax (withdrawal; +6·1%) and Sowerby (intervention; +6·2%) and Oldham, East (withdrawal; +7·9%) and West (intervention; +8·5%).

[1] Three possible, but on the whole unlikely, instances are Liberal withdrawal helping Labour to retain North Ealing; Liberal withdrawal giving Bosworth to the Conservatives; and a sharp drop in Liberal support giving Gloucester to the Conservatives.

lationship between the variations in swing and the drop in turnout.[1] This finding appears to be in conflict with the claim by the pollsters that differential abstention was 'a small but contributory factor in the final result [which] explains part of the discrepancy between the poll predictions and the result'.[2] The conflict is only

TABLE 3

*Swing and turnout*

| Change in turnout | Swing | | | | | | | No. of all seats |
|---|---|---|---|---|---|---|---|---|
| | To Labour | To Conservative | | | | | Mean | |
| | | Up to 1·9% | 2·0–3·9% | 4·0–5·9% | 6·0–7·9% | over 8·0% | | |
| Decrease over 8·0% | 0 | 3 | 9 | 20 | 4 | 3 | +4·7% | 39 |
| −6·0–7·9% | 1 | 2 | 17 | 25 | 19 | 2 | +4·9% | 66 |
| −4·0–5·9% | 0 | 10 | 26 | 59 | 28 | 6 | +5·0% | 129 |
| −2·0–3·9% | 3 | 7 | 18 | 45 | 25 | 13 | +5·1% | 111 |
| Decrease up to 2·0% | 1 | 2 | 11 | 11 | 11 | 4 | +5·1% | 40 |
| Increase | 0 | 2 | 1 | 3 | 1 | 2 | +5·0% | 9 |
| All seats | 5 | 26 | 82 | 163 | 88 | 30 | +5·0% | 394 |

apparent to the extent that this factor is used as an explanation of the 'swing' between the poll predictions and the final outcome. Our analysis here is concerned with the non-appearance of differential abstention as a factor in the swing between 1966 and 1970. Apathy among Labour voters could have contributed to the discrepancy between the poll findings and the result while at the same time not affecting the outcome of the election nor contributing to the swing. This is because the differential turnout as between different types of constituency, rather than as between electors of different party loyalty affected the national total of votes as it had done for at least three elections. Therefore when constituencies make unequal contributions to the national total of votes cast (although of course having equal representation in the

[1] But the above average swing which gave Leek to the Conservatives probably reflected the loss of Labour voters on holiday in the Potteries fringe of the constituency. See p. 138.

[2] See R. Rose (ed.), *The Polls and the 1970 Election* (University of Strathclyde Survey Research Centre Occasional Paper, No. 7), p. 34. The words are those used by NOP but similar claims are made by other pollsters.

House), a party with a disproportionately large number of victories in low turnout seats polls less than its full strength. This has been Labour's fate, at least since 1959.[1] Thus a survey can find more apathy among Labour supporters even when apathy is affecting each party's supporters equally within each constituency. The full turnout of such apathetic voters would not alter the outcome in any seat but it would bring up Labour's share of the national vote and—in 1970 it would have brought Labour's share of the vote closer to the poll findings.

We can find support for this theory if we consider what would have happened if there had been compulsory voting and a turnout of 100% everywhere. For this exercise we assume that party shares of the vote in each constituency remained exactly as in 1970. The overall share of the national vote in the United Kingdom would then compare with the actual result:

| | Actual (turnout 72·0%) | | Simulated (turnout 100·0%) | |
|---|---|---|---|---|
| Conservative | 46·4% | (51·9%) | 46·2% | (51·5%) |
| Labour | 43·0% | (48·1%) | 43·5% | (48·5%) |
| Others | 10·6% | | 10·3% | |

A simulation of the 1970 election with turnout in each constituency exactly as it was in 1950 brings the Conservative lead down to 2·6%.

*Bases of turnout change.* Two of the main movements in the 1970 election essentially represented the return of the pendulum. The swing to the Conservatives and the drop in the Liberal vote reversed the trends of the 1964–66 and 1959–66 periods respectively. But the third main movement evident in 1970—the increase in abstention—was a cumulative trend: it followed the pattern of declining participation that has characterised every election since 1950, with the sole exception of 1959. Of the turnout decrease of 4·3% (4·8% in seats with comparable candidatures), a small part represented the ageing of the register between the end of March and mid-June (probably a little over 1%) while rather more was due to holiday-makers being unable to vote in a June election.[2] However, where nationalists were doing well (see p. 388) or where

[1] See *The British General Election of 1966*, p. 272.
[2] See p. 138.

close by-elections stimulated interest (see p. 408) turnout did not fall; this would underline the real increase in voluntary abstention in most constituencies. Indeed, although the fall was much less than 5% in terms of genuine voluntary abstention, this was only in comparison with the 1966 election which vied with the 1918, 1923 and 1935 elections in holding the record for non-voting. The fall from the 1950 level was 12%.

Apart from the few seats stirred up by recent by-elections or by strong nationalist challenges, the fall in turnout affected virtually every constituency. Here and there a personality increased the interest of electors — Mr. Davies produced a 4·0% increase in Merthyr Tydfil and Mr. Powell, whatever else he achieved, was probably responsible for the 2·5% increase in turnout in his own South-west Wolverhampton. Regionally the fall in turnout was greatest in the South-east, and was especially marked in the suburban ring around London (perhaps because people in these areas tended to take earlier and longer holidays). But, whereas it was in the large cities and mining areas that non-voting had spread most spectacularly since 1955, the movement since 1966 was higher in all urban areas and lower in mining and rural seats.

The elector who opted out could of course have no direct effect on the outcome of the contest. But the increasing potential represented by the 28% of the theoretical electorate who were non-voters (although a half to two-thirds of them could certainly have voted if they had wished) can be shown by an imaginary exercise in which the non-voting total is compared to the vote for the winning party in each constituency. There were 89 constituencies in which the non-voters were more numerous than those who cast ballots for the elected member, as Table 4 shows; in 1959 there were only eight such seats.

TABLE 4

*General election results 1959–70 if non-voters were a party*

| | 1959 | 1964 | 1966 | 1970 |
|---|---|---|---|---|
| Conservative | 363 | 297 | 243 | 314 |
| Labour | 252 | 297 | 340 | 217 |
| Non-voters | 8 | 29 | 34 | 89 |
| Liberal | 6 | 7 | 12 | 5 |
| Others | 1 | 0 | 1 | 5 |

*Divergences in swing.* The 1966–70 swing of 4·7% was even more uniform than usual. As Table 5 shows the differences between types of constituency were less than in 1964 or 1966; the number of exceptional swings caused by third-party effects was cut by the decline of the Liberals; the regional variation was no greater than in 1966 and a good deal less than in 1964. Ignoring swings which were affected by third-party activity and leaving aside certain regions and special cases discussed later, there was no instance of a swing to the Conservatives of more than 10%; and there

TABLE 5

*Voting according to type of constituency*

| No. of seats | Type | Average swing since | | Average change in turnout since | | Average drop in Liberal vote since 1966 |
|---|---|---|---|---|---|---|
| | | 1959 | 1966 | 1955 | 1966 | |
| | | % | % | % | % | % |
| 146 | Large cities . | −5·6 | +3·8 | −8·6 | −5·0 | −1·1 |
| 248 | Other urban . | −2·2 | +5·2 | −6·2 | −5·3 | −2·9 |
| 82 | 25–50% rural . | −0·5 | +5·2 | −3·1 | −3·2 | −3·3 |
| 64 | 50–75% rural . | +0·5 | +5·2 | −0·7 | −2·7 | −3·8 |
| 28 | Over 75% rural | +1·0 | +5·3 | −0·6 | −1·8 | −4·3 |
| 45 | Partly mining . | −1·8 | +3·4 | −4·6 | −2·8 | −2·8 |
| 27 | Mining . . | +0·2 | +3·6 | −6·0 | −2·2 | — |
| 615 | All seats . | −2·3 | +4·7 | −5·5 | −4·3 | −3·0 |

*Definitions:* Rural and mining categories (which overlap) are defined in *The British General Election of 1964* (p. 341). The term 'urban' is used for constituencies falling outside any rural, mining or large city category. Large cities are the former County of London and the 18 provincial cities with more than 200,000 population.

was only one constituency in which a swing to Labour remains inexplicable (Rugby, 2·7%).

The swing of 4·7% represents nationally a net loss of about one-tenth of Labour's 1966 support to the Conservatives. But the proportion of the Labour vote lost was much lower in strongly Labour seats than in those with a weak Labour vote. In 24 seats with Labour votes in 1966 of over 70% and with straight fights in 1966 and 1970, the swing still averaged 4·7%, equivalent to a loss of less than one-sixteenth of the 1966 Labour vote.[1]

[1] For the reasons why the swing rather than the proportional loss should be uniform see *Political Change in Britain*, p. 303 ff.

The one region which, as a whole, differed in its movement to the Conservatives was Scotland. The average swing there was only 3·3% and this figure falls to 2·8% if a dozen seats in the fringes are excluded. Apart from these seats, the low swing extended to every part of Scotland. It was clearly a national Scottish swing to be contrasted with the average swing of 4·9% in England and Wales. In seven seats there was actually a swing to Labour and outside the fringes only seven individual swings to Conservative topped 5%.

This is the fifth successive election in which, regardless of the direction of the national swing, Labour has done better in Scotland. The long-term swing since 1955, when the present constituency boundaries were fixed, was 5·8% to Labour compared with a swing to Labour in England and Wales of only 0·3% over the same period. The Conservatives regained three seats in Scotland in 1970 but, with only 23 out of 71 seats, the number of Scottish Conservative M.P.s is lower than at any time between 1931 and 1966. Twelve of the Conservative seats, including all three 1970 gains, are among the 19 seats to the north of Stirling. Even on the occasion of the biggest nation-wide swing against Labour since 1931, the Conservative party could not gain a single seat in central Scotland.

In North-west England a fairly average regional swing concealed two quite diverse areas. In 18 seats in or around Merseyside the swing was only just half the national average at 2·5%. As with Scotland this represented a cumulative trend to Labour; since 1955 these seats have shown a staggering 8·5% swing to Labour. But in 16 seats in the textile towns of Lancashire, in an area north-east of and including Oldham, Bolton and Darwen the 1966–70 swing to the Conservatives, 7·4%, was three times that on Merseyside. This divergence to the right in 1970 is in sharp contrast with the above average Labour swings the textile towns had shown in 1959, 1964 and 1966. The Conservatives gained 2 seats which had been Labour at each general election since the war, Nelson & Colne and Rossendale; overall, however, the net swing in the area since 1955 has been to Labour.

There were two other pockets on the North-east coast which showed a markedly low swing — Hull (its four seats, including Haltemprice, had an average swing to the Conservatives of 1·4%) and Tyneside–Wearside (where twelve borough seats had an average swing of 3·0%, with Sunderland, 0·6%, producing the lowest swing recorded in any multi-member borough). Both followed pro-Labour trends of previous elections, the swing since 1955 being 5·8% in Hull and 5·2% in Tyneside–Wearside. But otherwise the swing in Yorkshire and the North-east was near the average.

By contrast, there were two areas in the Midlands which swung disproportionately to the Conservatives. In six constituencies partly or wholly in the Black Country boroughs of Dudley and Wolverhampton the swing, 9·0%, was nearly twice the national average, while in a dozen seats in and immediately adjoining Derby and Leicester, it averaged 7·2%. Both these areas were isolated pockets, the swing in neighbouring Black Country boroughs or in Nottinghamshire being close to the national average. In both areas the large swings again followed pro-Conservative trends at previous elections. The swing to Conservative since 1955 was 9·6% in the Dudley–Wolverhampton area and 3·2% in the Derby–Leicester area. As a result among these 18 seats there were four, including those of George Brown and Jennie Lee, which went Conservative for the first time at a general election since the war.

The most noteworthy feature about these exceptional regional and local swings was that six of the seven instances reflected cumulative trends rather than pendulum movements; their divergence from the national average represented a continuance of the divergence shown at previous elections rather than, as in the one exception in Lancashire, a reversal of it. It suggests that in seeking explanations for regional variations in recent elections it is more important to distinguish areas where there has been a longer term secular trend, either to the right or to the left, than to distinguish areas where the swing has been high or low.

A similar question arises when the swing is analysed by type of constituency in Table 5. The difference in swing between large cities, rural areas and mining seats which was so prominent in 1964 and 1966 was again present though in less marked degree. Again the differences were cumulative. While nationally the 1966–70 swing of 4·7% to Conservative represents a recovery of two-thirds of the 1959–66 swing of 7·0% to Labour, in the large cities less than half the ground lost was regained. In distinctly rural areas the Conservatives more than made good their precious losses. Thus the long-term secular trend has been towards Labour in the major cities and towards the Conservatives in the suburban and rural areas.

This divergence between city and country seems to date from 1955; in the first three post-war elections the swing to the Conservatives was lower than average in rural areas while most big cities went more strongly to them. (Glasgow, Liverpool and Newcastle, where the secular trend to Labour goes back nearly twenty-five years, are, however, exceptions.) Some of the apparent regional swings reflect the recent contrast in urban and rural trends — the high East Anglian swing was mainly a rural one and the low North-western swing was essentially urban. The breakdown in Table 6 of the swing since 1955 by standard regions and by types of constituency explores the cross-cutting of regional and social differences.

It is apparent that the movements of opinion over the last few years have been developed along cross-cutting lines with both

TABLE 6

*Long-term swing by region and type of constituency**

| Region | Type of constituency | | | | | All seats |
|---|---|---|---|---|---|---|
| | Over 50% rural | 25–50% rural | Mining | Large cities | Other urban | |
| Scotland | −2·4 | *−1·7* | −4·9 | −9·2 | −6·0 | −5·8 |
| Wales | *+3·8* | *−3·3* | −4·9 | *−3·8* | *−2·7* | −2·9 |
| Northern | *+1·0* | −0·5 | −0·7 | *−6·7* | −5·4 | −2·8 |
| North-west | — | *−0·3* | *−0·9* | −7·9 | −3·3 | −4·0 |
| Yorkshire | *+1·5* | *+1·1* | +0·7 | −3·9 | −0·9 | −1·3 |
| East Midland | *+3·8* | +2·6 | +2·0 | *+0·8* | *+1·9* | +2·0 |
| West Midland | *+3·6* | *−0·1* | *+4·6* | −1·3 | −5·2 | +1·9 |
| East Anglia | +5·2 | *+4·4* | — | — | *−0·2* | +3·6 |
| South-east | +3·7 | +2·9 | — | −1·8 | +0·3 | +0·2 |
| South-west | +5·2 | *+2·4* | — | +2·0 | *−0·2* | +3·2 |
| All seats | +2·6 | +0·9 | −1·2 | −3·7 | −1·0 | −0·9 |

* Table 6 shows the mean 1955–70 swing (plus to Conservative; minus to Labour) for the seats in each group. Two of the rural and both mining categories in Table 5 on p. 394 are combined so as to ensure adequate numbers in each cell. Italics indicate a figure relating to less than 10 seats; a dash that there were less than three seats in this category. Seven seats in Table 5 on p. 394 which had no Conservative candidate in 1955 are excluded from this table.

city–country and North–South cleavages. Within each region the cities have moved relatively more towards Labour than the surrounding areas: within each type of seat the swing has been more to Labour in Scotland, Wales and the three Northern regions of England and more to the Conservatives in the five Midland and Southern English regions. As the net national movement since 1955 has been so small the figures in this table are a close approximation to the secular trends to Labour or Conservative over the last fifteen years which have produced much of the diversity of swing at each of the last four general elections.

The separation of the regions and categories into these two divisions in Table 7 shows how the composition of the 1955 and 1970 parliaments, while very similar overall, differed markedly in detail.

TABLE 7

*1955 parliament by city and region breakdown*

| | North, Wales and Scotland | | | Midlands and South | | | All seats (GB) | | |
|---|---|---|---|---|---|---|---|---|---|
| | Con. | Lab. | Other | Con. | Lab. | Other | Con. | Lab. | Other |
| Large cities . | 30 | 36 | — | 28 | 52 | — | 58 | 88 | — |
| Remainder . | 91 | 117 | 6 | 185 | 72 | 1 | 276 | 189 | 7 |
| All seats . | 121 | 153 | 6 | 213 | 124 | 1 | 334 | 277 | 7 |

*1970 parliament by city and region breakdown*

| | North, Wales and Scotland | | | Midlands and South | | | All seats (GB) | | |
|---|---|---|---|---|---|---|---|---|---|
| | Con. | Lab. | Other | Con. | Lab. | Other | Con. | Lab. | Other |
| Large cities . | 17 | 49 | — | 24 | 56 | — | 41 | 105 | — |
| Remainder . | 80 | 128 | 6 | 201 | 54 | 3 | 281 | 182 | 9 |
| All seats . | 97 | 177 | 6 | 225 | 110 | 3 | 322 | 287 | 9 |

The 1970 parliamentary Conservative party was stronger in more Conservative areas while the 1970 parliamentary Labour party much more dependent on more Labour areas. The Conservative weakness in the North, Wales and Scotland and in the cities is clearly shown in Table 7. In 1970 the Labour party held only two seats (in the two large cities, Plymouth and Portsmouth) among all the 53 seats in the counties along the South coast, com-

Variations in constituency swings 1966-70 (on a two-party basis)

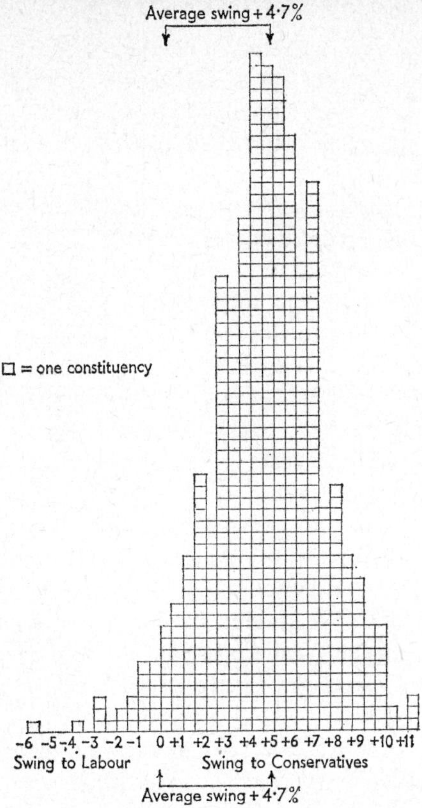


The extreme swings, Hamilton (−11·2%) and Colne Valley (+19·3%) are not marked.

The standard deviation from the mean two-party swing over the four-year period 1966–70 was 2·6%; over the 18 month period 1964–6 it was 2·1% and over the five years 1959–64 it was 3·1%.

Variations in change in Liberal % 1966-70

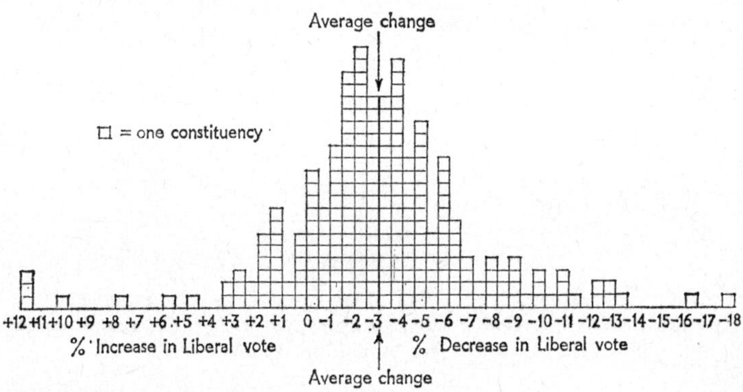

pared with 11 in the 1966 parliament. For the first time since the war no Labour M.P. sat for an English seat which was mainly rural, and the long tradition of representation of the National Union of Agricultural Workers through Labour-held seats in East Anglia was broken.

*Divergences in Liberal performance.* The average drop of 3·0% in the Liberal vote in comparable seats meant that the party lost most of what it had gained in the three elections up to its post-war peak of 1964. The full drop 1964–70 averaged 5·9% and brought the party back roughly to the level of its vote in 1950.[1] The poll of 7·7% of the total votes cast in Great Britain and of 13·7% of the votes cast in the 328 British seats fought suggests that the party would have got about 11% of the total vote if every seat had been fought. The party won 6 seats (1·0% of the total), the same as in 1951, 1955 and 1959. However, two of the 1959 victories and three of the 1955 ones were dependent on Conservative support whereas all six successes in 1970 were won against both major parties.

The drop in Liberal support was largest in Scotland (average 7·6%) and Wales (5·4%) while in the North (1·0%), in the North-west (1·4%) and in the West Midlands (1·5%) regions of England it was much below average. The relatively small drop in the large city seats (see Table 5, p. 394) represented actual gains in some instances, but the average fall in other urban seats conceals big losses of the Orpington period vote in many suburban seats.

As a rule the drop was greater in seats where the 1966 Liberal vote was larger, in contrast to the 1964–66 decline in Liberal support which had been greatest in the weaker Liberal seats. Particularly in view of the large losses in many seats where Liberal candidates were in a position to squeeze a third or fourth party candidate's vote,[2] it seems clear that the loss of Liberal votes in 1970 represented a broad decline in the desire to have Liberal M.P.s. By contrast the 1966 Liberal pattern of losing votes except where the party was locally credible could be seen as a frustration of the desire to have Liberal M.P.s.

[1] 1950 is still regarded by the Liberal party as a disaster year, largely because 319 out of 478 deposits were lost. In 1970 the deposit loss (182 out of 332 including Northern Ireland) was not so great but fewer seats were won; there was an average rise of 0·1% in the Liberal vote in the seats fought both in 1950 and 1970.

[2] But two Liberals survived in face of the trend — in North Cornwall and in Roxburgh, Selkirk & Peebles — by squeezing still further the already minimal Labour vote.

However, despite the general decline in Liberal support, there were some quite extraordinary upsurges in individual seats. In general the variation of Liberal performance was, as the histograms show, far more than the variation of the Labour–Conservative swing: clearly a candidate standing for the Liberals has a far greater opportunity to resist a trend against his party than one standing for the Conservatives or Labour; potential Liberal voters were inclined to vote or not vote Liberal according to local as well as national circumstances.

In the 243 comparable constituencies there were 36 instances of an increase in the Liberal share of the vote,[1] 4 of them of more than 10%—in Birmingham, Ladywood; Liverpool, Wavertree; Rochdale; and Southport. In 9 of these 36, including the 4 large ones, the Liberal candidate was a leading figure on the local borough council. In some cases, notably those of Alderman Wallace Lawler in Birmingham and Councillor Cyril Carr in Liverpool, he had been personally very much responsible for building up Liberal strength on the Council. In another 9 or 10 cases, the increase in parliamentary vote followed successes in municipal elections over the last three years (when the Liberal party was making no net progress in municipal elections elsewhere). It was a bleak election for the Liberals: its parliamentary representation was halved, nationalist candidates took some of its Celtic-fringe bridgeheads and its vote in England fell most in the few seats like Chippenham or Torrington which it might have hoped to win. If there was any comfort for the party, it lay in this evidence that patient work at the municipal level could mobilise support in an entirely new and different type of electorate.

*Divergences in nationalist performance.* Following their by-elections successes during the previous four years both Plaid Cymru and the Scottish National party made an all-out effort to turn the electoral battles in Wales and Scotland into referenda on independence. Plaid Cymru fought all 36 seats in Wales (their previous maximum was 23 in 1964) and the SNP took on 65 of Scotland's 71 constituencies (23 in 1966). But neither came anywhere near the level of their by-election performance; in 7 seats fought in by-

[1] Greenock, which is excluded, was not comparable because the Conservatives did not stand in 1970. The Liberal candidate, a burgh council leader, increased the Liberal vote by 21·5%. The Greenock Liberals had eliminated Conservative representation from the council by 1966, since when no Conservatives had fought in municipal elections.

elections during the 1966 parliament the nationalist vote had averaged almost one-third of the votes cast but in the same seats in June 1970 it was well under a fifth. South Ayrshire, which was fought at a by-election as late as March 1970, showed a fall in the SNP vote from 20·3% to only 8·0%. Overall, Plaid Cymru polled 11·5% of the votes cast in Wales and the SNP 11·4% of those cast in Scotland.[1] Both parties lost two-thirds of their deposits.

It makes little sense to attempt any overall comparison with their previous performance because the changes since 1966 varied so much from constituency to constituency. In Wales the 8 seats with a dramatic rise in the Plaid Cymru vote fell into two groups. The first was the crescent of five rural constituencies from Anglesey to Carmarthen which are overwhelmingly Welsh-speaking and which were up to a decade ago the main bastion of the Liberal party: this group shows the marked relationship between the Plaid Cymru performance and the strength of Celtic culture, as measured by the proportion of Welsh-speakers.

TABLE 8

*Welsh-speakers and Plaid Cymru*

| % able to speak Welsh 1961 Census | No. of seats | Plaid Cymru performance | | |
|---|---|---|---|---|
| | | Deposits saved | Mean % vote | Change on previous vote* |
| Over 70 . . | 6 | 6 | 24·4 | +11·4 |
| 25–60 . . | 8 | 3 | 13·6 | + 7·3 |
| 10–25 . . | 12 | 2 | 10·9 | + 5·0 |
| Under 10 . . | 10 | 0 | 6·0 | − 0·1 |

* Mean change compared with 1966 in 20 seats or, in 7 seats uncontested in 1966, with a previous contest in the last 15 years.

However the second group of three upper valley seats in South Wales (Aberdare, Caerphilly and East Rhondda), where the Plaid Cymru vote rose by 18·5% on average, do not fit the pattern of this table. Apart from this aberrant pocket of strength in South Wales, the Plaid Cymru vote in each constituency in 1970 corresponded closely with the extent to which it had resisted anglicisation. Although in previous elections it was evident that Plaid Cymru had a slightly stronger appeal in Welsh-speaking areas,[2] the

[1] The SNP share of the votes cast in the 65 seats it fought in 1970 was 12·2%.
[2] See *The British General Election of 1964*, p. 355.

growth of Plaid Cymru as a party concentrated in the Celtic heartland of western Wales is a new feature.

The SNP performance in Scotland was even more varied. In the Forth–Tay area which yielded the SNP's best results in 1966[1] some ground was lost; in northern Scottish seats which had previously shown no sign of interest in nationalism electorally there was a major breakthrough for the SNP; in the rest of Scotland the party's low vote was merely maintained.

The SNP breakthrough occurred mainly in the eleven county constituencies from Angus and Argyll northwards which the party fought. Galloway — a socially similar constituency in the south-west corner of Scotland — can conveniently be grouped with them. It is noteworthy that the SNP made no headway in Aberdeen and Dundee, the only large cities in this region. The SNP vote averaged 21·2% in these 12 seats and in 9 they saved their deposits. It is quite clear that most of the new SNP votes here were former Liberals. Yet prior to this election the SNP had made no impact in this rural fringe of Scotland. Only one seat was fought in 1966 (East Aberdeenshire where the 1966 vote of 8·6% jumped to 29·8% in 1970) and only one other had been fought by the SNP since the war; that was Western Isles, and the 5·0% won in 1951 stands in sharp contrast to the 43·1% in 1970, which made this isolated constituency the first ever to return a Scottish Nationalist at a general election.

A very different picture was offered by the 11 seats of the Forth–Tay area where the SNP had shown its strength in 1966 (the average vote was 18·7% and all eleven deposits were saved). In 1970 the average vote declined to 15·9% and three deposits were forfeited. The remaining 42 seats contested include Hamilton, where Mrs. Ewing did well to retain a higher proportion of her vote than any other nationalist fighting to maintain a by-election advance. But among the 42 seats Hamilton was a totally isolated oasis for the SNP; their average in the other 41 was 9·0% and all but five deposits were lost (three were saved in Glasgow where the average vote was 10·0%). In the ten among them which had been fought in 1966 the average vote increased by a mere 0·8%.

Both nationalist parties had in 1967–68 been regarded primarily as a threat to Labour in its industrial strongholds of South Wales and Central Scotland. But in 1970 it turned out that they

[1] See *The British General Election of 1966*, p. 290.

had much more appeal to the traditional values of the rural fringes and they threatened equally both main parties. This is very apparent if the 1970 results are considered in terms of an electoral base for any further advance. The most winnable seat for the nationalists is now Caernarvon, which would fall to the equivalent of a swing of under 5%.[1] Three more (Carmarthen, East Aberdeenshire and Argyll) would go on a similar movement of 10%, and another five (Hamilton, Merioneth, Banffshire, Cardigan and Moray & Nairn) on one of 15%. Eight of these nine seats are in 'fringe' areas and four of the five that are vulnerable to an SNP advance are Conservative-held.

*Personal votes for candidates.* A small but consistent bonus seems to have attached to retiring M.P.s in 1970. Table 9 shows how the swing was a little below average where a Conservative member stood down in 1970 and a little above where a Labour member did so; conversely, in the constituencies where a member newly elected in 1966 had had four years to build up a personal following, the swing was a little above average for Conservatives and a little below for Labour as Table 9 shows. The mean difference between

TABLE 9

| Retiring M.P.s 1966 and 1970 | | No. of seats | Mean swing |
|---|---|---|---|
| None 1966 | Con. 1970 | 19 | 5·3 |
| None 1966 | Lab. 1970 | 21 | 4·3 |
| Con. 1966 | None 1970 | 27 | 4·5 |
| Lab. 1966 | None 1970 | 51 | 5·0 |
| Con. 1966 | Lab. 1970 | 43 | 3·8 |
| Lab. 1966 | Con. 1970 | 12 | 6·8 |

the swing in these situations and the national average amounts to 0·4%. This figure is confirmed by seats where retiring M.P.s in 1966 and 1970 were from opposite parties, though the high swing in the last group in Table 9 reflects by-election effects as well, since all had been won since 1966.[2] There were 5 Labour M.P.s in such seats who should have been defeated on the national swing but whose personal following may have helped their re-election.[3]

[1] The Plaid Cymru vote in Caernarvon was 45·4% of the votes cast for the Plaid Cymru candidate and the winning party; hence Caernarvon would be won by Plaid Cymru on the equivalent of a swing of 4·7%.

[2] See pp. 408–9.

[3] M. Barnes (Brentford & Chiswick), F. Judd (West Portsmouth), J. Mackintosh (Berwick & East Lothian), R. Moyle (North Lewisham), D. Owen (Plymouth Sutton), and W. Price (Rugby).

Some Liberal M.P.s also probably held their seats on personal votes.[1]

*Women candidates.* As in 1964 and 1966, an examination of the constituencies in which either of the two main parties had had a women candidate in only one of the last two elections shows up no clear evidence that the sex of the candidate affected voting. But among Liberal candidates women fared distinctly worse: the drop in the Liberal vote in the dozen constituencies where a woman replaced a 1966 man was much higher than average at 4·9%, while in the dozen where a man replaced a woman the fall was low at 2·1%. This difference of 2·8% is very consistent with similar findings in 1966 (difference 3·5%) and 1964 (difference 3·8%). The fact that it has appeared at three successive elections in different conditions suggests that, to uncertainly Liberal voters, a female candidate is less acceptable than a male.

*The impact of candidates' position on issues.* Two issues on which both party leaderships were agreed but on which a substantial number of candidates dissented from their party's policy came to the fore during the election campaign — British entry into the European Economic Community and Enoch Powell's views on immigration. In both cases there was considerable evidence in the opinion polls to suggest that the dissenting views (opposition to British entry and support for Mr. Powell) had substantial support among the electorate. If, therefore, British electors do sometimes allow their votes to be decided by the candidate's views as opposed to his party's, these two issues provided obvious occasions to do so. The results in 1970 fully support the evidence of previous elections that candidates' views very seldom matter.

Among the Conservative candidates in England who made clear in their election addresses that they opposed British entry into the EEC[2] the swing averaged 5·4%; among those who indicated some degree of support it was 4·6%. However, if the few seats in areas already established as having a specially high or low swing

[1] More generally see P. M. Williams, 'Two Notes on the British Electoral System', *Parliamentary Affairs*, Winter 1966–67, pp. 13–30.

[2] Candidates who opposed British entry are those classified in the table on p. 440 as being opposed either fully or with reservations; those supporting are those classified as supporting it either fully or with reservations. Scotland and Wales are excluded from the analysis of the effects of candidates' views on the EEC because in those regions voters could express their views on the matter through voting nationalist.

are excluded this small difference disappears entirely (the averages becoming 5·0% and 5·1%). Among Labour candidates the average swing for the declared anti-European candidates was 5·4% while pro-European candidates kept the swing slightly lower at 4·6%. This difference persists (the averages becoming 5·0% and 4·3%) if the same type of seats in areas of established high or low swing are excluded; furthermore, if the performance of the pro-European Labour candidates is examined seat by seat in comparison with the constituencies around them, two-thirds of them did better than their neighbours and the average difference between the swing against the pro-European Labour candidates and the swing against their neighbours was 0·5%. If this figure is significant the explanation could be that the Labour candidates favouring entry were people of a sort who attracted a strong personal following. It should be borne in mind that the evidence, such as it is, suggests that the candidates who did better were those who expressed views that were contrary to the majority recorded in the opinion polls. Among Liberal candidates too few opposed entry to allow a significant test of their performance but the fact that the average decline in the vote of the many who expressed pro-European views was, at 2·8%, so close to the national average decline of 3·0%, suggests that the Liberal party's views on Europe did not cost it votes.

Taking declared support for repatriation[1] as the test of support for Mr. Powell, the Powellite Conservative candidates fared exactly as their party did nationally — an average swing of 4·7%. When we look at these Conservative candidates by the type of seat they fought to test whether Powellism attracted votes in constituencies affected by immigration while repelling some more liberal Conservative voters elsewhere, the swing remains persistently the same for Powellite and non-Powellite candidates.[2]

*Immigration.* However, the evidence that Mr. Powell helped the Labour party by mobilising support for it from coloured immigrants is extremely strong. Bradford, Leeds, Leicester and Manchester each contain one constituency which can be identi-

[1] Candidates classified on p. 438 as supporting compulsory or voluntary repatriation of Commonwealth immigrants.

[2] This evidence is supported by Deakin and Bourne who identify rather fewer Powellite Conservative candidates on an impressionistic basis and also find no difference in the performance of these candidates compared to the national swing. See N. Deakin and J. Bourne 'Powell, the Minorities and the 1970 Election', *Political Quarterly*, October–December, 1970 pp. 399–415.

fied as having a greater immigrant population[1] than any of the others;[2] in each city this constituency swung less than the rest. Taking these four cities together, the average swing in the four immigrant constituencies was 1·4% and the decline in turnout only 1·4%; in the nineteen other divisions the swing was 5·1% and the drop in turnout 2·8%. In Birmingham the average swing in the five constituencies where immigrants provided more than 7% of the population was only 1·6% compared with an average swing of 7·0% in the five constituencies where immigrants provided under 2% of the population; the drop in turnout in the two groups of seats was respectively 1·6% and 6·2%. The evidence in Greater London is much less clear.[3] But certainly in the rest of the country it is quite evident that immigrant turnout in 1970 was considerably above that of 1966 and that in the great majority of cases they voted Labour.

If this mobilization brought immigrants out to vote in the same proportion as the rest of the electorate, and if all who voted supported Labour, there would be over a dozen seats in which the immigrant vote ensured a Labour victory. But as most of these constituencies were in Greater London, and as none of those outside London would have gone Conservative on the national swing, the impact, in terms of seats, of the overwhelming immigrant vote for Labour remains problematical. It is, on the other hand, clear that the Conservatives ceased to benefit from local anti-immigrant voting in the three places where they had picked up such votes in 1964: in Smethwick, Eton & Slough and Southall the swing averaged only 1·7%. This suggests that any Conservative gains through local anti-immigrant feeling are likely to be temporary. There is, however, no way of using election statistics to test the theory that Powellism brought votes to the Conservative party nationally, regardless of whether such recruits lived in an area affected by immigration or had a Powellite candidate.

[1] The 1966 Census figure of the proportion of the population in a constituency born in the New Commonwealth is taken as the immigrant population; see p. 358 ff.

[2] Bradford, East; Leeds, North east; Leicester, South-east; and Manchester, Moss Side.

[3] Analysis in Greater London may be frustrated by the facts that almost every constituency in the central area has a large immigrant population and that there are sizeable groups 'born in the New Commonwealth' in London (such as African students or Cypriots) who may not think of themselves or be thought of as coloured immigrants in the same way as West Indian, Pakistani or Indian immigrant workers.

But if it is unlikely that coloured immigration swayed many white voters in 1970, it is absolutely clear that white electors were unwilling to cast a ballot for a coloured candidate. Labour lost Wandsworth Clapham on a swing which was enormous by South London standards almost certainly because their candidate, Dr. Pitt, was black; the large drop in turnout and the increase in the Liberal vote show that the swing was part of a defection of 1966 Labour voters in all directions. Three Liberal candidates of Asian origin also fared extremely poorly. The ones who intervened in East Bradford and Smethwick received barely half the vote achieved by intervening candidates in any other constituency in the country, while in Sheffield Hallam the decline in the Liberal vote since 1966 recorded by the Sikh candidate was three times the national average.

*Irish voters.* The other major immigrant group in Great Britain, the Irish, have traditionally caused little electoral concern and have traditionally voted Labour. In 1970 events in Ulster and Mr. Powell's attacks on their rights to British citizenship were expected to have strengthened their preference for the Labour party. A survey by the *Irish Post*[1] which found the 'Irish vote' splitting 84:16 between Labour and Conservative, cited the Ulster situation as the reason for this; it did not however produce any comparable figures for 1966, although it suggested that the turnout of Irish voters was up. The swing in the seats with most Irish-born voters was lower than the national average but not enough below the average swing in large cities (where the Irish congregate) for any firm conclusion to be drawn. If the *Irish Post* proportions are applied to the Irish-born vote in each constituency as measured by the 1966 census, Labour would definitely owe six seats to the Irish vote — Acton, Barons Court, Brentford & Chiswick, South Coventry, North Ealing, and Watford — and might owe five others to it.[2]

*The sequel to earlier elections.* The 1970 results showed that, as in 1964, the impact of a dramatic by-election can have a long-term effect on the vote in a constituency. In the 10 seats where a by-election during the 1966 parliament had made a previously safe seat seem marginal,[3] turnout increased compared to 1966 by 0·2%

[1] *Irish Post*, July 11, 1970.

[2] Birmingham, Northfield; Camberwell, Dulwich; Lambeth, Norwood; Northampton; and Wandsworth, Putney.

[3] This is defined as seats in which the 1966 plurality had been more than 10% of the votes cast but where the by-election plurality fell below 10%. Newcastle-under-Lyme, where 1970 turnout was affected by the local Wakes Week, is excluded from this analysis.

on average. In the 12 seats which a Conservative won at a by-election during the 1966 parliament, the 1966–70 swing was exceptionally high (on average 6·8%). In other words, the earlier Conservative victory must have helped to secure some support from people who would have stuck by their 1966 Labour allegiance if they had not actually made that by-election switch to the Conservatives. South-west Leicester and Nelson & Colne may only have elected Conservatives in 1970 because they had chanced to have a by-election at the right period in 1967 and 1968. This accidental factor probably trebled the SNP vote in Hamilton and doubled the Plaid Cymruy vote in Caerphilly.

Several other unusual individual results show a return to the normal voting pattern of the constituency following the effect on 1966 voting of an earlier by-election. Clear instances are provided in Nuneaton by the 1970 swing to Labour; in Leyton by the huge drop in the 1970 turnout and in West Lothian by the biggest of all the 1970 drops in nationalist support. A remarkably long-term effect possibly explains the unexpected Conservative gain in Gloucester; at a by-election in 1957 many Conservative voters went Liberal: in 1970, with a swing of 8·4% and a 6·6% drop in the Liberal vote, the constituency reverted to an earlier pattern.

A comparison between the results of the by-elections immediately preceding the general election and the general election itself shows the same movement of opinion back to the government that has been observable in every contest since 1931. In the 10 seats which had had by-elections during the preceding twelve months, the swing back to Labour between the by-election result and the general election averaged 5·1%. In the two which had taken place in 1970, it averaged 1·7%. In view of the small number of seats involved, both figures are remarkably close to the normal swing back.[1]

*Marginal seats.* Both precedent and the attention given to them in 1970 suggested that marginal seats would deviate from the national pattern. In 1964 and 1966, abstention and Liberal voting had been markedly different from the rest of the country: a close contest between the two main parties squeezed potential Liberals and abstainers into voting Conservative or Labour. In 1970 even more attention than previously was focused on the marginal seats

[1] Including 1970, the swing back to the government in seats which had by-elections during the twelve-month period preceding a general election has averaged 3·4% in the elections from 1951 onwards; over the previous six months the average swing back is 2·3%.

by the Conservatives 'critical seats' exercise;[1] throughout the general election campaign it was claimed that as a result the Conservative party's performance in marginal seats would be better than the national swing.

This was not to have been the case. In the 100 seats with the lowest 1966 Labour majority over Conservative, the turnout dropped more than normal (by 5·5% on average) and the Liberal vote dropped less (by 1·7% on average); in other words, although turnout remained higher and Liberal votes lower in marginal seats, the squeeze was working much less in 1970. As for the swing, the average in these marginal seats was 4·4%. This below-average figure was entirely due to the number of marginal seats in which a Labour M.P. was retiring where a Conservative member had done so in 1966 and where, as already shown (see page 404), the Conservatives lost a bonus they had had in 1966 while Labour gained one in 1970. Excluding constituencies in which the 1970 retiring member was from the opposite party to the 1966 retiring member, the swing was exactly the national average at 4·7%. The Conservative party's critical seats exercise reaped no reward that election statistics can measure: among the sixty Labour marginals selected in England and Wales the swing averaged only 4·2% as against an average swing of 4·9% in all other seats in England and Wales.[2]

*Minor parties.* The Communist party nominated 58 candidates — more than in any previous election apart from 1950. But their popular support reached an all-time low, perhaps because of the introduction of party labels on the ballot paper. The average vote was 1·8%, a mean drop of 1·3% in constituencies also fought in 1966. In many constituencies the 1966 Communist vote was cut by two-thirds and in only one seat (Motherwell) was there a significant increase. In two seats where the Communists were traditionally strong, East Rhondda and West Fife, they won only 2·3% and 1·8% of the vote; it seems that the nationalist parties profited most by this decline. The National Front, fighting for the first time, fielded ten candidates and scored an average vote of 3·6%. None got more than 5·6%. In two seats where a British National party candidate had fought in 1966, Deptford and Southall, the Front's vote in 1970 was lower.

There were 64 other candidates standing under a variety of

[1] See pp. 288–9 and p. 342.

[2] Nor was the exercise responsible for the Conservatives' extra victories (see pp. 412–13) above what they would have won on a uniform swing. See p. 342 n.

labels in Great Britain,[1] all but two of whom received the usual low vote. Their support tended to be higher where no Liberal was standing[2] but no identifiable group, such as the anti-EEC or anti-immigrant candidates, were able to poll better than average. The two outstandingly high votes were for M.P.s elected as Labour in 1966 — Mr. Donnelly, who polled 21·5% in Pembroke[3] and Mr. Davies, who was the first rebel to beat an official party nominee since 1945, securing 51·9% of the vote in Merthyr Tydfil.[4] Seven other candidates, several with a base in local government, were the only others to top 5%.[5]

*Northern Ireland.* The troubles in Northern Ireland produced a marked increase of interest in the election and a polarisation along traditional Orange–Green lines. The number of candidates, 33, as well as the variety of party labels was the largest since partition. Turnout went up substantially in each constituency, increasing overall from 66·1% to 76·6%, the highest since 1951. The return of Mid-Ulster and Fermanagh and South Tyrone to their traditional polls of over 90% brought both back to their normal anti-Unionist allegiance while in and around Belfast the non-sectarian Labour and Liberal votes dropped. In four seats the Unionist vote was split between official and independent candidates; in North Antrim Mr. Paisley, standing as Protestant Unionist, defeated the Unionist member.

*Split votes.* Party leaders and political observers had probably realised by 1970 how little the Liberals had affected the fortunes of the major parties; at any rate they showed little concern about 'splitting the vote'. But in Scotland and Wales there was concern both about whether nationalist intervention would lose seats as between the two main parties and about the splitting of a 'Home Rule vote' between Liberal and nationalist candidates. In the event only the latter seems to have had any justification.

The evidence of the total lack of any effect on the swing from

[1] Excluding the Speaker's seat.

[2] The median vote for 34 candidates competing with a Liberal was 0·8%; that of the 30 who had no Liberal against them was 2·2%.

[3] See pp. 112–13.

[4] See p. 296.

[5] These were a local borough councillor in Lincoln (10·0%), another in Leigh (8·3%), a Baptist minister standing as a Protestant in Glasgow Bridgeton (6·7%), a borough councillor who left the Conservative party in opposition to the EEC in Wallasey (5·5%), a 'New Liberal' who fights all elections, parliamentary, GLC and borough in Islington (5·5%), an anti-immigration candidate in North-east Leicester (5·3%) and a self-proclaimed Powellite Conservative in Surbiton (5·1%).

Liberal or nationalist interventions (see pp. 389–90) makes it unlikely that candidates of these parties decided the outcome, as between the two main parties in any seat. But the National Front candidate in West Huddersfield probably prevented the seat from going Conservative, while Mr. Donnelly in Pembroke presumably cost his former party that seat; the trio of moderate candidates in North Antrim (all of whom lost their deposits) were probably jointly responsible for allowing the election of Mr. Paisley instead of the official Unionist.

There are 6 seats which a united 'Home Rule' vote, Liberal and nationalist, would certainly have won — Banff, Carmarthen and Merioneth, where nationalists were second, and Caithness & Sutherland, Cardigan and Ross & Cromarty, where Liberals held the challenging position.[1] In East Aberdeenshire and Caernarvon, with nationalists challenging, the result would have been touch-and-go, but, if we assume some preference among the voters of the weaker major party to see the other major party ousted, these two would almost certainly have gone nationalist in straight fights or with transferable voting. Argyll, too, might possibly have done so. On the same basis second-place Liberals would have been virtually certain to win Birmingham, Ladywood; Cheadle; Colne Valley; Orpington; and Rochdale; they would have been probable victors in West Aberdeenshire and possible victors in Bodmin and Liverpool, Wavertree.

Accepting the probable victories but not the possible ones, the outcome of an election with straight fights between the two leading candidates (or with the alternative voting system)[2] would have been Conservative 325 (instead of 330), Labour 279 (287), Liberal 15 (6), Nationalist 6 (1) and Others 5 (6). As fuel for the controversies which suggestions of a nationalist Liberal pact have always provoked, particularly in Scotland, we can offer this evidence that such a pact could have produced a 'Home Rule' contingent of nine Scottish and five Welsh M.P.s (instead of four and one).

*The relationship between seats and votes.* A combination of chance

[1] The evidence of switching between voting Liberal and Nationalist is sufficiently strong for the assumption of a 'Home Rule' vote to be made but voting for these parties can, of course, represent a common alienation from the two-party system or defence of common cultural values rather than similar support for devolution.

[2] For a discussion of this in earlier elections, see D. Butler, A. Stevens and D. Stokes, 'The strength of the Liberals under different electoral systems', *Parliamentary Affairs*, Winter 1968, pp. 10–15.

factors produced a greater gain in seats for the Conservatives than would have been produced by a uniform swing. There were 67 seats won by Labour in 1966 that would have gone Conservative in 1970 on a uniform 4·7% swing; in the event, 12 of these were saved by Labour but the Conservatives more than made up by taking 20 that required a larger swing. The slight regional variation in swing favoured the Conservatives; the pockets of high swing in the Midlands and Lancashire (discussed on pp. 394–6) contained 7 out of these 20 while the pockets of low swing in Scotland and Northern England contained only 4 vulnerable Labour marginals, 3 of which were saved. But the Conservatives were also favoured by the luck of the draw in winning more seats than Labour on very small pluralities.[1]

However, personal votes, regional swings and other local factors also produced a rather larger than usual number of results which would not have been predicted from a uniform swing. Labour held on to 9 seats[2] which were vulnerable to a swing of 3·7% (1% less than the average) while the Conservatives made thirteen gains[3] on 1966 in seats which required a swing of more than 5·7% (1% more than the average). In 1966 there had been only 8 such seats[4] compared with this total of 22.

Table 10[5] shows how the composition of the House of Commons would be affected by uniform swings from the 1970 result.

This table can be usefully compared with a similar one based on the results of the 1955 general election[6] since the overall distribution of the national votes in the United Kingdom shows no net conventional swing between 1955 and 1970. In 1970 the Conservatives were 13 seats down and Labour 12 seats up compared with 1955; but if the differences between the 1955 and the 1970 tables for the various levels of projected swing are examined, there is an average of 23 seats 'transferred' from Conservative to Labour. This is a measure of the disappearance of the bias against Labour

[1] Eight Conservative seats were won by pluralities of under 1% and fifty-nine by less than 5%; the respective numbers won by Labour were 5 and 38.

[2] Brentford & Chiswick; Berwick & East Lothian; North Ealing; Glasgow, Pollok; Lambeth, Norwood; North Lewisham; West Portsmouth; Rugby; and Wandsworth, Putney.

[3] Birmingham, Yardley; East Bolton; West Bolton; Bosworth; Cannock; Dartford; Gloucester; Leek; South-west Leicester; Ipswich; Nelson & Colne; Pembroke; and Wandsworth, Clapham.

[4] See *The British General Election of 1966*, p. 293.

[5] Table 10, like similar tables in past Nuffield studies, uses the conventional definition of swing, not the 'two-party swing' used elsewhere in this appendix.

[6] See *The British General Election of 1955*, p. 208.

TABLE 10

*Seats and votes 1970**

| To Conservative | | | Swing | To Labour | | |
|---|---|---|---|---|---|---|
| Con. | Lab. | Con. lead over Lab. | | Lab. | Con. | Lab. lead over Con. |
| 331 | 289 | 42 | Actual result | 289 | 331 | −42 |
| 349 | 272 | 77 | 1% | 308 | 312 | −4 |
| 365 | 257 | 108 | 2% | 338 | 282 | 56 |
| 382 | 241 | 141 | 3% | 350 | 268 | 82 |
| 400 | 222 | 178 | 4% | 364 | 254 | 110 |
| 408 | 214 | 194 | 5% | 377 | 242 | 135 |
| 425 | 198 | 227 | 6% | 392 | 227 | 165 |
| 450 | 173 | 277 | 7% | 410 | 209 | 201 |
| 466 | 156 | 310 | 8% | 421 | 198 | 223 |
| 476 | 146 | 330 | 9% | 449 | 170 | 279 |
| 482 | 140 | 342 | 10% | 474 | 144 | 330 |
| 535 | 85 | 450 | 15% | 543 | 71 | 472 |

* Allowance is made in this table for seats that would be gained or lost by other parties as a consequence of uniform swings between the two major parties: hence the total of seats in the table varies slightly. The Speaker's seat is treated as Labour and the two seats won by major party rebels (North Antrim and Merthyr Tydfil) classified as belonging to the major parties.

in the relationship between seats and votes between 1955 and 1970;[1] the actual 1970 result, because of the accidental factors discussed above, produced about 10 more Conservative and 10 fewer Labour seats than the basic relationship would indicate.

*Redistribution.*[2] Table 10 will, however, not be precisely applicable to the next general election because of the redistribution of boundaries authorised by parliament in November 1970. The exact effect of the new boundaries will vary at different levels of swing from the 1970 election result and any specific predictions must be subject to a margin of error. However, as an approximate guide to the future, the following calculations indicate what might have happened had the 1970 general election been fought on the new boundaries.

The major changes are a result of the shift of population from the centres of the conurbations to the surrounding fringes of suburb, new town, commuting centres and countryside. Greater London loses 11 seats in return for which 16 new seats are created in South-east England, 2 in outer fringe boroughs of the GLC and

[1] For discussion of the reasons for the disappearance of the bias see *The British General Election of 1966*, pp. 294–5. The results of the 1970 election do not add any significant evidence.

[2] I am indebted to Peter Pulzer for help in compiling these estimates; it should be possible in time to produce more certain estimates, particularly following the London Borough elections in May 1971 and the 1971 Census.

1 or more in each of the counties of the region. It is from this transfer that the Conservatives will derive most benefit; the 11 disappearing seats were held in 1970 in a proportion of something like 8 Labour to 3 Conservative[1] while the Conservatives would probably have taken some three-quarters of the new seats — a net increase of 13 in the overall Conservative parliamentary majority.

However, the same changes in and around provincial cities look more like cancelling each other out. Nine seats disappearing in large cities are compensated for by 9 new seats on conurbation fringes (not always the same ones); this suggests an estimated net transfer of about 2 seats from Labour to the Conservatives. The three instances outside London and the large cities of seats being abolished and the three new ones being created should produce no net change.

Against this must be offset the seats which boundary changes (mostly caused by adjustment to new local government boundaries) look likely to switch from one side to the other. Thus Mr. Brown would probably not have lost his seat at Belper had the areas which were transferred to Derby County Borough in 1968 been added to the parliamentary seats for Derby, as the parliamentary boundary commissioners recommended. Labour should derive a net benefit through this kind of change since there seem to be approximately four prospective 'gains' from Conservative on this basis as against about one in the opposite direction.

From these estimates it would seem that the net Conservative benefit from redistribution would have been less than was implied in some of the speculation at the time of the controversy in 1969 over Mr. Callaghan's refusal to implement the changes. Our estimates suggest that there would have been eight more Conservative[2] and three fewer Labour M.P.s in June 1970 under the new boundaries, a net increase in the Conservative majority of eleven. It seems reasonable, therefore, to say that on any particular swing level from the 1970 result the Conservative majority would be anywhere between five and fifteen higher than that shown in Table 10 as a result of redistribution.

[1] Seats are identified according to which party looks like the net loser from each set of changes: e.g. in Kensington & Chelsea a safe Conservative seat (South Kensington) is divided between Labour North Kensington and Conservative Chelsea but since the new Kensington seat would certainly be Conservative, this is identified as a Labour loss.

[2] But the Liberals might have taken the new seat at Hazel Grove in Cheshire while Mr. Thorpe would have been in grave danger of losing North Devon on its enlarged boundaries.

APPENDIX III

# ANALYSING THE CENSUS DATA

By Ivor Crewe and Clive Payne

Until the publication of the *Census 1966: General and Parliamentary Constituency Tables* in 1969, it was difficult to present factual information on the social composition of constituencies. Political analysts were forced to rely upon the impressions of M.P.s, journalists and academics, which were often misleading, for example, in their ready characterisation of seats as 'agricultural' or 'suburban'. However, with the publication of the sample census, we can obtain the relevant figures for constituencies in England, Scotland and Wales (but not Northern Ireland) and examine a number of phenomena in a more rigorous fashion. The figures are not in a form that is easy to digest and compare. We have selected, therefore, some of the key statistics and reduced them to percentage form. They are set out in pp. 358–78.

The figures on these pages in no way exhaust the interesting material available in the census tables. Restrictions of space forced us to leave out, for example, the rate of unemployment in each constituency, as well as the proportion of working women, married working women, retired working class, retired middle class, commuters of various kinds or foreign-born residents.[1]

[1] In addition, the census is rich in material on housing conditions, and provides figures on the number of rooms per house and the ratio both of rooms per household and persons per room. The proportion of households with over one person per room offers an obvious measure of overcrowding. The data on car ownership make it possible to use the percentage of households owning two or more cars as a rough indicator of relative prosperity, especially for comparison within the more middle-class areas. The occupational classifications make feasible further distinctions within the middle classes (between the professions, and managers and employers, for example) and within the working classes (between semi- and unskilled workers on the one hand, and skilled workers and foremen on the other).

With a little ingenuity and the occasional bold inference, composite indices can be derived from the variables. It would, for example, be possible to construct an index of class polarisation for each constituency (for example, by calculating the percentage constituted by professional workers and unskilled manual workers combined) and to distinguish between different patterns of working and middle-class composition. It would also be worthwhile to group constituencies according to whether they constituted areas of general immigration or contained predominantly only one category of immigrants; or by the various combinations of high immigration on the one hand, and different housing conditions, or social class composition, on the other.

Some fascinating and unexpected statistics emerge from the simple percentage form of the tables in Appendix I. It is not, perhaps, news that strictly speaking there are no farming seats — agriculture nowhere accounts for as much as a third of the labour force, and in only eight seats does it account for as much as a quarter. But is it commonly known how few middle-class seats there are? In fact, only forty-six constituencies — all but four of them in the Home Counties — contain more non-manual than manual workers, and this is to employ a generous definition of middle class. The established middle classes (the professions and semi-professions, managers and administrators, and most farmers and self-employed businessmen) exceed 25% in only forty-three constituencies, of which thirty-three are within commuting distance from London. The socially exclusive suburban constituency is largely a myth: next to the leafy avenues in the 'better' areas there is, as likely as not, a new council estate. Similarly, areas regarded as quintessentially 'Irish' or 'mining' turn out to be stereotypes based on conditions existing a generation ago. Of the 22 constituencies in which the Irish-born constitute over 5%, none is in Liverpool, and only one is in Glasgow (Gorbals). With less than 15% of their labour force down the pits Merthyr Tydfil and Ebbw Vale can no longer be considered mining seats. It is well known that housing conditions are particularly bad on Clydeside, but the extent would surprise most people. In terms of overcrowding the ten worst constituencies in Britain, are *all* in Glasgow; thirty-six of the worst fifty are on Clydeside and in the central Lowlands of Scotland. In terms of all these variables, the nearest to a microcosm of Britain turns out to be Gravesend,[1] closely followed by Nottingham South and Southampton Test.

The figures as they stand are clearly of intrinsic interest and many pages could be filled with tit-bits such as these. But much wider possibilities are opened up by the census data. The recent development of computer programmes, specifically designed for social and political research, makes it possible to extend analysis beyond the first simple stages of rankings and averages, and to explore

[1] The first publicised application of these Census figures, based on our calculations, appeared in a *Sunday Times* 'Insight' article (May 23, 1970) entitled 'Gravesend Man'. It explored the remarkable typicality of Gravesend by all kinds of criteria. Almost too neat a vindication of our calculation was provided on election night when a survey in Gravesend enabled the BBC to foreshadow a 4·4% swing before any results were declared. The Gravesend swing was actually 4·9%; the national swing was 4·8%.

with some sophistication the various complex relationships between the political behaviour and social composition of constituency electorates. In this appendix we describe briefly some of the newer techniques available, and indicate some of the political findings that can result from a rigorous analysis of the census data.[1] Readers who are interested less in the technical descriptions than in the results and political implications of the statistical procedures involved, should perhaps skip the next eight pages.

*Bivariate correlation.* If we wished to gauge the extent to which a social factor like housing conditions, class composition or concentration of immigrants was related to turnout, swing or partisanship, a natural initial step would be to calculate the correlation between the two appropriate variables. Correlations measure the degree of association and covariation between variables, and range from −1·0 (perfect inverse correlation) through 0·0 (perfect independence) to 1·0 (perfect positive correlation). For Census material involving 618 cases any 'product moment' correlation above +0·1 or below −0·1 may be considered of substantive interest. We calculated the product moment correlation (Pearson's *r*) between each of five dependent political variables (1970 % turnout, % turnout change 1966–70, % Conservative, % Labour and two-party swing) and (1) each of the appendix variables, and (2) sixteen other census variables not included in the appendix, for England, Wales and Scotland (see Table 1).

Bivariate correlations provide a rough outline of the social factors associated with voting patterns in the election. Yet there are serious limits to the possible interpretations. Various kinds of 'spurious correlation' are one pitfall. For example, there appears to be a strong inverse correlation between turnout and each of three variables, semi- and unskilled workers, car ownership and household density. It turns out, however, that it is the semi- and

[1] In the rapidly growing but rather uneven literature on aggregate data analysis the collection of original papers in M. Dogan and S. Rokkan, *Quantitative Ecological Analysis in the Social Sciences* (MIT Press, 1969), stand out as by far the most valuable single source on ideas, methods and recent empirical work. But see also the chapters by Erwin Scheuch and Erik Allardt in R. Merritt and S. Rokkan, *Comparing Nations* (Yale University Press, 1966), on methodological problems; and for the imaginative uses of aggregate data and techniques see in particular the pioneering study by André Siegfried, *Tableau Politique de la France de l'Ouest sous La Troisième Republique* (Librairie Armand Colin, 1964) as well as S. M. Lipset and S. Rokkan, *Party Systems and Voter Alignments* (Free Press, 1967), and Donald Mathews and James Prothro, *Negroes and the New Southern Politics*, pp. 101–172 (Harcourt, Brace, 1966).

## Table I

| | Con. % | | | Lab. % | | | Nat. % | | Turnout % | | | Two-party swing[4] | | |
|---|---|---|---|---|---|---|---|---|---|---|---|---|---|---|
| | Eng. | Wales | Scot. | Eng. | Wales | Scot. | Wales | Scot. | Eng. | Wales | Scot. | Eng. | Wales | Scot. |
| Non-manuals | 0·59 | 0·84 | 0·43 | −0·60 | −0·38 | −0·15 | −0·22 | 0·14 | 0·25 | −0·16 | 0·54 | 0·00 | −0·08 | −0·16 |
| Manuals | −0·31 | 0·14 | −0·27 | 0·38 | 0·33 | 0·41 | −0·12 | 0·42 | 0·11 | −0·55 | 0·28 | 0·18 | 0·07 | −0·01 |
| Prof. and managerial | 0·24 | 0·60 | 0·07 | −0·21 | −0·10 | 0·15 | −0·15 | 0·32 | 0·35 | −0·35 | 0·56 | 0·19 | −0·07 | −0·08 |
| Semi and unskilled | −0·08 | 0·34 | −0·09 | 0·14 | 0·27 | 0·33 | −0·24 | 0·39 | 0·05 | −0·60 | 0·42 | 0·05 | 0·13 | −0·07 |
| Owner-occupiers | 0·53 | 0·54 | 0·59 | −0·55 | −0·08 | −0·48 | −0·05 | −0·01 | 0·57 | −0·21 | 0·39 | 0·19 | −0·05 | −0·04 |
| Council-housing | −0·37 | 0·32 | −0·27 | 0·42 | 0·22 | 0·46 | −0·33 | 0·40 | −0·04 | −0·59 | 0·44 | 0·05 | 0·08 | −0·02 |
| With full plumbing | 0·39 | 0·75 | 0·17 | −0·39 | −0·18 | 0·06 | −0·29 | 0·38 | 0·45 | −0·30 | 0·66 | 0·11 | −0·06 | −0·10 |
| Household density[1] | −0·47 | 0·28 | −0·42 | 0·53 | 0·19 | 0·68 | −0·32 | −0·04 | −0·54 | −0·67 | −0·36 | −0·15 | 0·18 | −0·03 |
| Without cars | −0·38 | 0·26 | −0·19 | 0·46 | 0·35 | 0·60 | −0·18 | 0·09 | −0·31 | −0·72 | 0·08 | −0·07 | 0·07 | −0·04 |
| Born in New Commonwealth | −0·06 | 0·64 | 0·31 | 0·12 | −0·20 | −0·04 | −0·30 | −0·22 | −0·50 | −0·37 | −0·15 | −0·17 | −0·06 | −0·14 |
| Born in Ireland | −0·01 | 0·73 | −0·20 | 0·07 | −0·28 | 0·52 | −0·32 | −0·15 | −0·39 | −0·25 | −0·29 | −0·13 | −0·07 | −0·04 |
| All immigrants | 0·09 | 0·73 | 0·26 | −0·03 | 0·23 | 0·13 | −0·32 | −0·13 | −0·43 | −0·38 | −0·06 | −0·15 | −0·05 | −0·19 |
| Young voters | 0·03 | 0·53 | −0·01 | 0·02 | 0·07 | 0·25 | −0·28 | 0·29 | 0·20 | −0·54 | 0·45 | 0·05 | −0·01 | −0·11 |
| Aged over 64 | 0·42 | 0·72 | 0·37 | −0·49 | −0·33 | −0·20 | −0·06 | 0·26 | 0·31 | −0·17 | 0·54 | 0·08 | −0·10 | −0·11 |
| Retired | 0·27 | 0·37 | 0·20 | −0·34 | −0·13 | −0·19 | 0·14 | 0·45 | 0·39 | −0·24 | 0·59 | 0·10 | 0·01 | 0·03 |
| Employed in manufacturing | −0·17 | 0·36 | −0·22 | 0·29 | 0·33 | 0·51 | −0·39 | 0·21 | 0·00 | −0·65 | 0·28 | 0·15 | 0·06 | −0·02 |
| Employed in mining | −0·42 | −0·65 | −0·18 | 0·40 | 0·65 | 0·27 | 0·27 | 0·30 | 0·08 | −0·17 | 0·26 | 0·02 | 0·09 | 0·09 |
| Employed in services | 0·50 | 0·80 | 0·34 | −0·51 | −0·35 | −0·03 | 0·24 | 0·11 | 0·05 | −0·28 | 0·41 | −0·05 | −0·08 | −0·15 |
| Employed in agriculture | 0·40 | 0·15 | 0·35 | −0·44 | −0·66 | −0·74 | −0·22 | 0·25 | 0·42 | 0·60 | 0·25 | 0·14 | −0·10 | −0·16 |
| Females | 0·30 | 0·64 | 0·13 | −0·29 | −0·07 | 0·16 | −0·18 | 0·30 | 0·26 | −0·43 | 0·51 | 0·09 | −0·03 | −0·11 |
| Working women | 0·13 | 0·64 | 0·08 | −0·04 | −0·01 | 0·28 | −0·31 | 0·17 | −0·08 | −0·53 | 0·38 | 0·08 | −0·02 | −0·14 |
| In H.M. Forces | 0·32 | 0·37 | 0·14 | −0·33 | −0·26 | −0·34 | −0·02 | 0·35 | 0·14 | −0·17 | 0·25 | −0·05 | 0·01 | 0·15 |
| Commuters[2] | 0·12 | 0·12 | −0·07 | −0·08 | 0·22 | 0·17 | 0·04 | 0·49 | 0·04 | −0·09 | 0·52 | 0·07 | 0·06 | 0·03 |
| Migrants[3] | 0·44 | 0·67 | 0·23 | −0·46 | −0·18 | −0·20 | −0·17 | 0·42 | 0·16 | −0·17 | 0·55 | 0·05 | −0·11 | −0·02 |

*Note:* The small number of constituencies in Wales (36) tends to produce artificially high correlation coefficients.

[1] % of households with more than one person per room.
[2] % of employed working in another local authority area.
[3] % of persons having moved into local authority area within last five years.
[4] Swing to Conservatives is positive; to Labour is negative.

unskilled workers who are most likely to live in cramped conditions and least likely to own a car. All the three variables are highly inter-correlated, and therefore any one of them might not affect turnout in fact, only appearing to do so as a result of a strong association with the genuine independent variable. Even if turnout only varied with the proportion of semi- and unskilled workers in a constituency, it might seem to be determined by rates of household density and car ownership because the last two co-vary with the concentration of semi- and unskilled workers. Alternatively, all three social factors can correlate 'spuriously' because of a strong and common association with a fourth unconsidered variable. For instance, high household density, a heavy concentration of semi- and unskilled workers and a low degree of car ownership are all disproportionately characteristic of Scottish urban constituencies. Our original correlations may all have reflected the lower than average turnout in Scottish urban constituencies.

Various techniques are available for dealing with these forms of 'spurious correlation'. It is possible to calculate *partial correlations* which measure the degree of covariation between two variables but control for any other variables which one suspects, on the basis of bivariate correlations and other evidence, might have some independent effect. In the case mentioned above the correlation could be measured between turnout and each of the variables, car ownership, household density and semi- and unskilled workers, controlling for the other two in turn.

A further step would be to employ *path analysis* to test any hypothetical causal interpretation that might be deduced from the set of partial correlations.[1] Any rigorous attempt to trace the social factors that are linked to the percentage Labour and Conservative vote would inevitably involve working with a large group of inter-correlating variables. Let us say, for example, that positive and significant partial correlations occurred between the percentage Conservative vote and each of the variables, owner-occupancy, non-manual workers, ownership of two cars, professional and managerial workers, and employment in HM Forces, and that some of the partial intercorrelations between the five social variables were also significant and positive. We should therefore want

[1] No path analysis of aggregate data on British politics has been published so far. A good general review of the uses and procedures of path analysis is given in Otis Dudley Duncan, 'Path analysis: sociological examples', *American Journal of Sociology*, Vol. 72 (1), July 1966, pp. 1–16.

some indication of the structure of the causal network linking the social variables to each other and to the Conservative vote. We might hypothesize on the basis of our partial correlations that ownership of two cars had no direct effect on the Conservative vote, or that the proportion of professional and managerial workers rather than of non-manual workers generally was the stronger factor in the degree of owner occupancy, which in turn had a considerable independent impact on the Conservative vote. Path analysis cannot infer causal relations from correlations, but by providing us with a graphic and explicit representation of any proposed causal scheme, it can show which of our interpretations are invalid as a result of incompatible assumptions and empirical improbabilities. It shows that some causal hypotheses are wrong and so narrows the framework within which we interpret our set of correlation coefficients. It cannot show conclusively which particular hypotheses is right.

Path analysis is related to *structural modelling* — a form of data analysis in which the causal links between variables can be investigated by means of sets of simultaneous equations.[1] This approach would seem to offer great scope as it allows for the specification and examination of mathematical models of voting behaviour.

*Factor and cluster analysis.* Although the tendency for social variables to 'go together' places considerable obstacles in the way of any attempt at causal explanations, it nevertheless offers intriguing possibilities for other kinds of analysis. It suggests the possibility of reducing a large number of intercorrelating variables to a few underlying dimensions. It is normal to group British constituencies into seaside resorts, provincial suburbs, mining seats, urban twilight areas and so forth, on the assumption that each of these categories describes a distinctive pattern of social conditions and political behaviour. These conventional groupings, however, have rested more on personal impression than on rigorous empirical analysis. *Factor analysis* (and in particular, principal com-

[1] H. M. Blalock, *Causal Inferences in Non-Experimental Research* (Univ. of North Carolina Press, 1964), is the best introduction to the application of causal models in the social sciences. There is no example of their adoption for British data, but they have been increasingly used for American and cross-national aggregate data. See Warren E. Miller and Donald E. Stokes, 'Constituency Influence in Congress', *American Political Science Review*, Vol. 57 (1), March 1963, pp. 45–56; Arthur S. Goldberg, 'Discerning a causal pattern among Data on Voting Behaviour', *American Political Science Review*, Vol. 60 (4), December 1966, pp. 913–933; and Ted Gurr, 'A Causal Model of Civil Strife', *American Political Science Review*, Vol. 62 (4), December 1968, pp. 1104–24.

ponent analysis) provides that rigour.[1] It would be going too far to claim that in normal circumstances factor analysis can be used to test the validity of typical groupings. Nevertheless, as an exercise in data reduction, it may well suggest new ways in which to classify constituencies. It would be useful, moreover, to select as particularly 'representative' the variables with the highest 'loading', and the constituencies with the highest 'score', on any factor that turned out to be sociologically or politically interesting.

It would be necessary to factor analyse the total of 618 constituencies as well as smaller groups according to region, urban-rural differences and other appropriate classifications. Another sensible strategy would be to undertake separate factor analyses, one of Census variables only, the other combining both social and political variables.

A related but slightly different question concerns the constituencies which tend to 'hang together'. Are Eastbourne, Hove, Brighton Pavilion, Torquay, Poole and Folkestone and Hythe really distinctive and homogeneous in their social attributes (or in their social and political attributes combined) just because they all constitute 'seaside resorts'? *Cluster analysis* should prove fruitful for answering these questions.[2] It groups items (in our case, constituencies) according to their homogeneity on any group of variables or factors we wish to select. The statistical procedure involves grouping according to the degree of similarity that obtains on two or more variables for each possible pair of constituencies. There are various measures of similarity and numerous ways of clustering similarity scores; considerable experimentation with these procedures (and above all, with the variables incorporated in the analysis) would be necessary for the production of promising results.

An exploratory exercise on Scottish constituencies, using thirty-

[1] H. H. Harman, *Modern Factor Analysis* (University of Chicago Press, 1960) is the standard work. The chapters by Carl-Gunnar Janson and by Duncan Macrae Jnr. and James A. Meldrum in *Quantitative Ecological Analysis* discuss the problems of factor analysis that are peculiar to aggregate data. An early factor analysis of British urban boroughs, based on 1951 Census data, appears in C. Moser and W. Scott, *British Towns* (Oliver & Boyd, 1961), and there is a similar study of London suburbs by Kevin Cox (but with more political data) in *Quantitative Ecological Analysis*.

[2] Little cluster analysis has been undertaken on political data as yet. On its potential, see Geoffrey H. Ball, 'Data analysis in the social sciences: what about the details?', in *Proceedings of the Fall Joint Computer Conference* (Stanford Research Institute, 1965). The best standard work on classification techniques is R. R. Sokal and P. H. A. Sneath, *Principles of Numerical Taxonomy* (W. H. Freeman & Co., 1963).

four Census variables standardised to give each an equal weight, produced three major clusters. As might have been expected, one contained all the rural constituencies plus, surprisingly, Edinburgh South, but excluded semi-rural seats with substantial mining or heavy industry (e.g. South Ayrshire, Lanark, West Fife and Midlothian) — which, however, did not form a separate cluster. Most of the urban constituencies were divided into the other two clusters. The first consisted of exceptionally densely populated constituencies, with relatively little council housing, in the inner areas of Glasgow and Edinburgh: Glasgow Central, Gorbals, Kelvingrove, Woodside and, surprisingly, Hillhead, as well as Edinburgh Central, Leith and North. In the second were all the Lanarkshire boroughs including the remaining Glasgow seats, except Lanark; and the rest of the Central Lowlands except for Edinburgh and the semi-rural constituencies cited above. Edinburgh Pentlands and Edinburgh West, East Renfrewshire, the two Aberdeen seats and the two Dundee seats could not be assigned to major clusters, although the first four formed a loose group of relatively middle-class constituencies.

Given an appropriate choice of variables (based perhaps on principal component analysis) clustering should classify constituencies in a way that enables us to predict the political characteristics of most constituencies with some degree of reliability. For the classification to be meaningful and useful we should expect bivariate, partial and factor correlations to be stronger *within* most clusters than *between* most clusters or than across all 618 constituencies. We should also expect the clusters to hold good over two or more elections so that swing and turnout change would show a lower variation within than between clusters. On the basis of a cluster analysis the most typical constituencies might be selected from each cluster as an aid to sampling decisions and other problems of research design in future work on British voting. If, for example, seaside resorts or city centres were valid groups, it might be useful to pick out the archetypal seaside resort or city centre, so that students of British politics could point to a dozen or so constituencies as particularly reliable barometers of political trends in large blocks of seats.

*Regression analysis.* Does social class matter more than coloured immigration in determining differences of turnout in urban areas? If so, by how much? Is owner occupancy a more important factor in the suburban Conservative vote than the proportion of professional and managerial workers? If not, what is? How much of the variation in the Labour and Conservative vote is accountable to a single factor like social class? These questions can be answered with some accuracy by *multivariate regression analysis*[1] and in particular, a related technique, *analysis of variance*.[2] Whereas correlations indicate the degree of association between variables, regression coefficients measure the amount of change in the dependent variable per unit change in the independent variable. If each constituency's score on two variables were plotted on a graph, a correlation would reflect the extent to which the plotted points clustered around a line, whereas a bivariate (but not multivariate) regression would measure the line's steepness or curve. We use bivariate and multivariate regressions to predict the value of a dependent variable such as percentage party vote or swing, where the score of an independent variable like '% manual workers' or '% coloured immigrants' is known. As a result we can measure the relative importance of the many independent variables contributing to the total score and variation of any dependent variable. It is worth re-emphasising the need to control for region, social class, structure of party competition and the like for the purposes of regression analysis. This is best done by incorporating the appropriate variables, one by one, into the analysis. With data available on as many as 618 cases the use of controls is methodologically feasible as well as analytically necessary.

If numerous variables make an equally small contribution to the score of a dependent variable, multiple regression tends to produce results which, at first sight, appear to be politically uninteresting. We found that a multiple regression on the two-party swing was a case in point. Preliminary analysis suggested that no single independent social variable accounted for more than 8% of the total variation in the size of the two-party swing. This result is significant nevertheless in hinting at the possibility that national and uniform forces underly the swing. On stratified groups of constituencies, slightly more 'promising' results might emerge; the

[1] N. R. Draper and H. Smith, *Applied Regression Analysis* (John Wiley, 1966), is the best guide on applying regression techniques. For an impressive example of its value, see J. A. Laponce, 'Ethnicity, Religion and Politics in Canada: A Comparative Analysis of Survey and Census Data', in *Quantitative Ecological Analysis*.

[2] See H. Schaffé, *The Analysis of Variance* (Wiley, 1959).

most rewarding will only arise after a lengthy process of experimentation with the form of the regression equation and the groups of constituencies and variables selected for analysis.

An initial multiple regression analysis of the Labour percentage vote, however, showed that '% non-manual workers' was the single best predictor, and accounted for 28·7% of the variation. The best set of three variables — % employed in agriculture, % professional and managerial workers, and % manual workers — accounted for 74·0% of the variation. We can write the equation that most accurately predicts the Labour percentage vote on the basis of these three variables as:

42·3% + 0·03 × % manual workers − 0·04 × % employed in agriculture − 0·03 × % professional and managerial workers

As with other statistical techniques the value of multiple regression is also limited by the number and salience of the input variables, and the 1966 Census lacks data on crucial variables like religion and education. Nevertheless, comparisons of regression equations on the same set of variables between different elections, or between different regions in the same election, should prove interesting. An advanced research design could use cluster analysis as a guide to the groupings of constituencies, while relying on common sense for the selection of variables in the regression equations.

*Residuals analysis.* Correlations are never perfect and predictions based on regression analysis are always subject to random error. Out of 618 observations some must contribute more than others to the strength of a correlation and to the accuracy of a regression equation. We know that a constituency's proportion of manual workers is a major determinant of party fortunes across the country as a whole. But it is not the only determinant and it would be worth while, therefore, to discover the different extent to which each constituency 'deviated' from the overall association, and to explore the factors associated with these 'deviations'. Which constituencies 'deviated' from the normal class–party relationship, and by how much? Where did Labour receive substantially more or less votes than 'expected', given the countrywide relationship between % manual workers and the Labour vote? Did the constituencies in which Labour polled disproportionately well (or badly) possess something in common, or were class–party 'deviations' randomly distributed across all the constituencies?

These questions are the subject of *residuals analysis* which measures the discrepancy (or 'residual') between a constituency's *observed* and *expected* value on a dependent variable, given its value on an independent variable.[1] The expected value is based on the relation between the two variables that obtains for all the other constituencies in the analysis. In two-dimensional terms, where two variables are plotted against each other on a graph, one along the vertical and the other along the horizontal axis, residuals analysis measures and identifies the perpendicular from the intercept to the regression line. As this is a technique for delineating the irregularities rather than uniformities in a set of data, the exceptions rather than the rule, it is best restricted to those cases where the two variables strongly correlate and where one accounts for most of the variation in the other. In this limited context residuals analysis constitutes perhaps the most fruitful of all the statistical methods mentioned so far. Its potential is demonstrated by the initial residuals analysis we undertook on a regression of % manual workers on the % Labour vote. In order to control for the effects of substantial Liberal and nationalist strength, the Labour vote was expressed as a percentage of the two-party vote (i.e. Labour and Conservative vote combined). For each constituency we derived a 'residual score', which represented the difference between the actual and 'expected' % Labour vote.

In Table 2 we summarise the results of the analysis by listing the fifty British seats with the highest positive residual scores (i.e. the strongest 'deviation' *to* Labour) and the fifty with the highest negative residual scores (i.e. the strongest 'deviation' *from* Labour).[2] In Table 3 we do the same but for England only, because of the dominance of Wales and Scotland in Table 2. It is immediately apparent that Labour polled disproportionately well, or badly, in distinct types of constituency, and that it is possible to discern a rough hierarchy into which these groups can be ordered. In both tables we have therefore attempted to group the constituencies according to their social and regional attributes. What

[1] See N. R. Draper and H. Smith, op. cit., Chapter 3, and F. J. Anscombe and J. W. Tukey, 'The Examination and Analysis of Residuals', *Technometrics*, Vol. 5, 1963, pp. 141–60. For a very elementary form of residuals analysis on the Labour vote in English boroughs, see Anthony Piepe, Robin Prior and Arthur Box, 'The location of the Proletarian and Deferential Worker', *Sociology*, Vol. 3 (2), May 1969, pp. 239–44.

[2] The socially most typical of all constituencies, Gravesend, was also the closest of all to the norm, with a residual score of +0·003%.

follows is an outline of the pattern that emerges from Tables 2 and 3.

The Labour percentage vote was substantially *higher* than 'expected' in constituencies belonging to the following groups:

*Group A: Mining and heavy manufacturing areas of South Wales.* All 'deviated' significantly to Labour (except Newport), and all are concentrated in the top half of Table 2 (except Merthyr Tydfil).[1] It is possible to distinguish the less from the more predominantly mining seats. In Group A(1), mining accounts for at least 24% of the male labour force: all rank among the first thirteen seats and of all British seats Rhondda East deviates most to Labour with a score of 32·9%. In Group A(2), mining constitutes less than 20% of male employment, whereas manufacturing industry accounts for at least half. This group tends to occupy the next rung down our list of British constituencies.

*Group B: Mining and heavy manufacturing areas in the North-east.* In the tables we distinguish between predominantly mining seats (Group B(1)) and predominantly manufacturing seats (Group B(2)) on the same basis as in Group A, and the former clearly rank higher than the latter, as in South Wales. Five from Group B(2) (Chester-le-Street, Blyth, Easington, Durham and Houghton-le-Spring) rank between 26th and 39th among British constituencies (13·9% to 17·0%), and among the top ten of the English list (15·6% to 18·5%). Of the other three that clearly count as predominantly mining seats, Morpeth is 33rd in Table 3, but Consett and Durham North-west do not appear. Two from Group B(2), Blaydon and Gateshead East, rank 34th and 40th on the British list; another three, Sedgefield, Wallsend and Jarrow, appear among the fifty most 'deviant' English seats. It should be noted that as opposed to Tyneside, Teesside and Wearside (i.e. Stockton, Hartlepools, the two Middlesbrough and the two Sunderland seats), all dominated by heavy industry, show no marked tendency to 'deviate' to Labour.

*Group C: Other mining areas.* The West Riding (Group C(1)) is slightly less prone than the North-east but clearly more prone than the Derbyshire and Nottinghamshire coalfield (Group C(2)) to 'over-support' Labour. Dearne Valley, Barnsley, Pontefract, Hemsworth, Normanton and Rother Valley all rank between 2nd

[1] Where Labour came second to independent Labour, but as a percentage of the two-party vote still received 14% more than it 'ought' to have done.

and 28th among the most 'deviant' English constituencies (the first two are included on the British list) but only Bolsover from the East Midlands finds a place in Table 3 at 47th. Except for Sheffield, Yorkshire's most highly industrial seats (e.g. Rotherham, Dewsbury, Halifax, Brighouse and Spenborough) do not significantly 'deviate' to Labour. Two Scottish mining seats (Group C(3)) appear towards the bottom of the British list.

*Group D: London East End and Docks.* Most but by no means all of the seats in this category appear on the list of English 'deviants'. Bermondsey, Poplar, the two West Ham seats and Barking are also on the British list, but all in the bottom half. It is noticeable that nearly all the East End and docks seats not included in Table 3 contain substantial concentrations of coloured immigrants (e.g. Stoke Newington, Hackney Central and East Ham North) whereas the most high ranking seats from Group D (except for West Ham South) contain relatively small immigrant minorities.

Finally, a smaller number of constituencies were drawn from each of four additional groups:

*Group E: Exceptionally homogeneous working class constituencies in the provinces*, e.g. Hull East, Ince, Wigan, Swansea East, Sheffield Park and Brightside. Manual workers constituted at least 75% of the male workforce (and over 84% in the two Sheffield seats).

*Group F: Seats where a Liberal or Nationalist came second, or won*, e.g. Hamilton, West Lothian, Western Isles, Colne Valley, Carmarthen, Cardigan and Merioneth.

*Group G: 'Council estate' seats*, e.g. Huyton, Dagenham, East Dunbartonshire, Aberdeen North, Newcastle West. We define such a seat as one in which at least half the households are Council tenants (there are 58 in Britain altogether). It should be noted that the last three seats cited contain a proportion of non-manual workers somewhat above the national average.

*Group H: A mixed bag of relatively middle class, inner London suburbs in which the proportion of coloured, Irish or 'foreign' immigrants is usually well above average.* Greenwich, Woolwich West, Lewisham North, Lewisham South and Putney perhaps form one loose group, although the first two have only average levels of immigration, and might be thought to belong as much to Group D, the East End and Docks. Lewisham West, Brentford and Ealing North all narrowly miss inclusion on the English list and clearly belong to the same group. Hampstead features incongruously among the Welsh mining valleys as 11th most 'deviant' of British constituencies, and most 'deviant' of all among the English constituencies; its neighbour, Hendon South is 36th in Table 3. There remain a few seats which we could not group without stretching our categories e.g. Penistone, Feltham and Hull North.

One further point needs to be made about the two lists of seats 'deviating' to Labour. The majority consist of exceptionally high proportions of manual workers: in 49 of the 79 seats listed, manual workers account for over 75% of the male labour force (the national average is 67%; 157 seats exceed 75%). No analogous pattern occurs in the case of the constituencies that 'deviate' most strongly away from Labour. In only 6 of the 65 seats cited in the two tables (including the rather special cases of Orpington and Cheadle) do non-manual workers constitute over 40% (the national average is 33% and 130 constituencies in Britain exceed the 40% level). These figures suggest therefore that some further analysis and qualifications are required before we fully accept the recent argument that the working class Labour vote and the middle class Conservative vote increase, the greater the proportion of working class and middle class respectively in any area.[1]

The constituencies in which Labour support was markedly *lower* than 'expected' fall more readily into a few, slightly overlapping groups:

*Group A: Seats held or lost by Liberals in 1970.* Of the thirteen all but Colne Valley, Inverness and Ross and Cromarty appear in one of the tables. Cornwall North (−35·3%), Roxburgh (−33·2%) and Birmingham Ladywood (−27·1%) are the three most 'deviant' of all British seats, followed by Bodmin, Aberdeenshire West and North Devon at 8th, 11th and 16th places respectively. These results are hardly surprising: in all cases (except Ladywood) this massive slump in Labour strength is clearly due to Labour supporters voting Liberal as the stronger of the anti-Conservative parties in what would normally be safe Conservative territory.

*Group B: Scottish agricultural seats, excluding the crofting counties.* A 'major' agricultural seat is defined as one in which at least 15% of the total labour force (and thus about 20% of the *male* workforce) is employed on the land. A 'minor' agricultural seat is defined as

[1] See David Butler and Donald Stokes, *Political Change in Britain* (Macmillan, 1969), pp. 135–50.

one in which 10%–15% of the labour force (12·5%-20% of the *male* workforce) is employed on the land. All the 'major' agricultural seats in Scotland (B(1)), outside the crofting counties, are listed in Table 2 (except for Berwick and East Lothian), and most rank among the top twenty; three of the 'minor' seats (Group B(2)) stand lower down the same list.

*Group C: The West Midlands.* Nine seats are involved (excluding Ladywood), five in Birmingham, and all but two (Rowley Regis and Wednesbury) contain substantial proportions of coloured immigrants. Four Birmingham seats (All Saints, Aston, Handsworth and Sparkbrook) and Wolverhampton South-west are among the most 'deviant' English constituencies (and the 22 most 'deviant' in Britain), with the Labour percentage vote running between 17·8% and 22·3% below its 'expected' level for England as a whole.

*Group D: English 'major' agricultural seats.* Using the same definition as for Scotland, all the 'major' English agricultural seats with the exception of Eye, King's Lynn, North Norfolk, South West Norfolk and St. Ives count among the the fifty English seats in which Labour most markedly fails to mobilise its traditional social base. Within Group D there is clearly a hierarchy of 'deviation' according to region: the North and the South-west are most 'deviant', followed by the Welsh border, Lincolnshire and constituencies bordering East Anglia. Except for South Norfolk, East Anglia is distinctly less prone to 'deviate' from Labour than other agricultural regions in England.

*Group E: 'Minor' English agricultural seats.* Using the same definition as for Scotland, most of the remaining seats come under this category (E(1)) and are concentrated in the bottom half of the English list; seven more seats with a similar distribution of rankings and with an even smaller agricultural sector (employing between 7·5% and 10% of the total labour force) form a separate group (E(2)). It is generally the case that the smaller the agricultural sector in a listed constituency and the higher the rank of an agricultural seat, the more likely it is to include an exceptionally large proportion of (*a*) retired people (marked R) or (*b*) members of HM Forces (marked H). To be marked 'R' the proportion of retired people had to exceed 15% (there are 57 of such constituencies in Britain). To be marked 'H' the proportion employed by HM Forces had to exceed 7·5% of the total labour force (about 10% of the *male* labour force): this accounted for 40 constituencies in

Britain. These sub-groups overlap considerably as indicated by the number of double and treble group symbols entered against constituencies.

A final point is worth stressing. Hardly any seaside resorts or prosperous suburbs figure among the lists of constituencies that 'deviate' away from Labour.

Residuals analysis certainly has its fair share of methodological problems. How to deal with the nationalist and Liberal vote, or with the few 'quirky' results that occur in every election, are typical problems in the kind of exercise we have just described. Conducting separate analyses of two-party and multi-party contests, expressing the Labour or Conservative vote as a percentage of the two-party vote, combining the minor party poll with that of a major party, or taking the average party vote over the previous three elections are among the possible solutions. None are perfect but all are reasonably satisfactory.

It is worth seeking a way to circumvent these problems for the sake of the new ideas and fresh research directions on British voting that residuals analysis appears to provide. Consider the brief summary of results above. Why do some major cities like Birmingham and Leicester 'deviate' so strongly to the Conservatives? Why do the Welsh, Scottish, Yorkshire and North East mining areas differ in the additional boost they give to Labour? How would the results turn out if the same exercise were repeated separately for Scotland, Wales and England? Why does Labour fall substantially less below its 'expected' support in East Anglia than in other English rural areas? Why does Labour poll relatively better in Coventry than Birmingham, and comparatively worse in Bradford than Sheffield, given the similar occupational structures of the two pairs of towns? What is the explanation for the higher than expected Labour vote in some middle-class London suburbs like Hampstead, Hendon South and Putney, as against others like Southgate and Twickenham?

Residuals analysis can be applied to other pairs of variables and to smaller groups of constituencies. A pioneering attempt to investigate residuals from multivariate regressions, in which several appropriate variables are controlled before deviations from the predicted values are calculated, would be worth while. Restricting the same analysis of class and party to Scotland, or Wales, or

England, or to exceptionally middle-class or working-class constituencies, however, are the obvious next stages in residuals analysis. A residuals analysis of % immigrants and turnout would also be rewarding — or of % employed in agriculture and the nationalist vote in Wales and Scotland. The conditions for using residuals analysis mentioned before should, however, be borne in mind.

The value of residuals analysis lies partly in its capacity for interpreting party performance in different constituencies beyond the simple levels of swing and percentage majorities. It is common to talk in an impressionistic way of towns or areas being 'staunch' Labour or Conservative on the basis of swing or absolute majorities. But whether a constituency is staunch *enough* compared with other constituencies with a similar social composition is a question rarely asked. An instance is the popular belief that Liverpool in 1964, Birmingham in 1966 and Glasgow in 1970, manifested their exceptional strength as Labour areas. This impression is based on the especially high swings to Labour in the first two cases, and the particularly low swings to the Conservatives in the third. The traditional benefit accruing to the Conservatives from religious conflict in Liverpool, and from racial tension in the West Midlands had supposedly disappeared. In fact Labour has fared 'unexpectedly' badly in all three towns throughout the decade, considering their proportion of manual workers, and compared with the remainder of constituencies throughout Britain. Residuals analysis (indeed, multivariate analysis in general), may also encourage us to think afresh about the assumption of political homogeneity in Britain that derives from its reputation for a national uniform swing, by focusing on the long established heterogeneity of social forces that underly similar party performances, and on the variety of party performances that have long occurred in constituencies with ostensibly similar social structures.

Hitherto electoral research on Britain has tended to ignore aggregate analysis, for three reasons. One was the absence of suitable figures but, as Appendix I shows, this no longer holds. Another revolved around a major problem of analysis, usually called the *ecological fallacy*, which applies to all the statistical techniques that we have discussed.[1]

[1] The problem was initially raised by W. S. Robinson in his seminal article, 'Ecological Correlations and the Behaviour of Individuals', *American Sociological Review*, Vol. 15 (3), June 1950, pp. 351–7. For attempts to deal with the ecological fallacy, see Otis Dudley Duncan and Beverley Davis, 'An alternative to

The ecological fallacy is a type of spurious correlation peculiar to aggregate data. It refers to the illogical and dangerously misleading inferences commonly made from aggregate-level to individual-level relationships. We may know, for example, that at the constituency (i.e. aggregate) level there exists a substantial 'deviation' to the Conservatives in the coloured immigrant areas of the West Midlands. We cannot possibly infer, however, whether an unusually high working-class Conservative vote, or unusually low middle-class Labour vote, or working-class immigrant abstention, is primarily responsible. To discover the pattern of individual-level behaviour that produced this aggregate result we need a sample survey. The impossibility of calculating from a two-party swing figure alone what combination of straight conversions, abstentions and switches to third parties was responsible, is the same kind of problem.

It can be shown statistically that an aggregate-level correlation is nearly always stronger than that for the same variables at the individual-level, and is more misleading the fewer the aggregate units and the smaller the proportion of the unit constituted by the variable under scrutiny. So far no means has been found for circumventing the pitfalls of ecological inference without resort to unrealistic assumptions, but we can identify the cases in which aggregate-level relationships are likely to be better or worse indicators of individual behaviour. Thus we should feel less uneasy about interpreting an analysis of class and party on all 618 constituencies (a large number by aggregate-level standards) than we should on restricting ourselves to a single region, or when examining such variables as % coloured immigrants or % employed in agriculture. Generally it is wisest to limit interpretation of the Census data to statements about constituency or regional behaviour, to comparisons and description rather than explanation, to the raising rather than the answering of questions and to the posing rather than proving of hypotheses.

The third reason for the absence of aggregate analysis in Britain has been the belief that it is only a second best to sample surveys,

---

Ecological Correlation', *American Sociological Review*, Vol. 18 (6), December 1953, pp. 665–6; Hubert M. Blalock, op. cit., Chapter 4; Leo A. Goodman, 'Some Alternatives to Ecological Correlation', *American Journal of Sociology*, Vol. 64 (2), May 1959, pp. 610–15; Donald E. Stokes, 'Ecological Regression as a Game with Nature' (unpublished ms.), and W. Phillips Shrively, 'Ecological Inference: The Use of Aggregate Data to Study Individuals', *American Political Science Review*, Vol. 63 (4), December 1969, pp. 1183–96.

an unfortunate necessity for societies with high refusal rates in interviews, or other barriers to successful surveys, which are not problems in Britain. Census figures, however, do hold some advantages over exclusive reliance on sample surveys. They are geographically more comprehensive, but also more valuable for investigating residentially concentrated groups such as dockers and miners on which national sample surveys usually have too few cases. Moreover, the accumulation of census material over time, of 'aggregate panel data', allows for a historical depth in voting research that surveys can rarely provide. For the detection of regional variations, of the growth and decay of national uniformities in voting, of long term glacial changes in electoral cleavages and historical junctures in party fortunes, aggregate data is crucial. In addition, constituency-level data is ideally suited to the use of such communal characteristics as racial composition, occupational structure, social class polarisation and local social change, whereas sample surveys are rarely designed with such 'contextual' variables in mind. An amalgamation of the census figures with existing sample survey material (opinion polls, academic research, party sponsored surveys, etc.) would add to the value of both, and constitute a crucial development in the improvement of source material for students of British politics. It is to be hoped that the publication of Census data on a constituency basis marks a first step towards the integration of aggregate and survey data in future research on British voting.

## Table 2

*Britain: seats in which, given their proportion of manual workers, the Labour percentage of the two-party vote was most* above, *and* below, *the 'expected' level*

| | Residual score % | Group | | Residual score % | Group |
|---|---|---|---|---|---|
| 1. Rhondda, East | 32·9 | A(1) | 1. Cornwall, North | −35·3 | ADHR |
| 2. Hamilton | 30·0 | FG | 2. Roxburgh, Selkirk & Peebles | −33·2 | AB(1) |
| 3. Caerphilly | 29·9 | A(1) | 3. B'ham Ladywood | −27·1 | A |
| 4. Aberdare | 29·4 | A(1) | 4. Kinross & West Perthshire | −27·0 | B(1) |
| 5. Merioneth | 28·4 | F | 5. Angus North & Mearns | −26·5 | B(1) |
| 6. Rhondda, West | 28·3 | A(1) | 6. Leominster | −25·6 | DH |
| 7. Llanelly | 27·4 | A(2) | 7. B'ham All Saints | −25·6 | C |
| 8. Pontypridd | 26·4 | A(2) | 8. Bodmin | −24·8 | ADR |
| 9. Ebbw Vale | 25·8 | A(2) | 9. Galloway | −24·4 | B(1) |
| 10. Carmarthen | 25·3 | F | 10. B'ham Aston | −24·4 | C |
| 11. Hampstead | 22·0 | H | 11. Aberdeenshire, West | −24·4 | AB(1) |
| 12. Bedwellty | 21·0 | A(1) | 12. Aberdeenshire, East | −24·3 | B(1) |
| 13. Abertillery | 20·7 | A(1) | 13. Angus, South | −23·0 | B(1) |
| 14. Cardigan | 20·7 | F | 14. Torrington | −22·7 | DR |
| 15. Aberdeen, North | 20·6 | G | 15. Howden | −21·6 | D |
| 16. Ogmore | 20·5 | A(1) | 16. Devon, North | −21·3 | ADHR |
| 17. Neath | 20·0 | A(2) | 17. B'ham Handsworth | −20·7 | C |
| 18. Gower | 19·4 | A(2) | 18. B'ham Sparkbrook | −20·5 | C |
| 19. Swansea, East | 18·7 | A(2)E | 19. Banff | −20·2 | B(1) |
| 20. Glasgow Springburn | 18·3 | G | 20. Penrith & Border | −20·2 | D |
| 21. West Lothian | 18·3 | F | 21. Westmorland | −20·2 | D |
| 22. Dearne Valley | 17·9 | C(1) | 22. Wolverhampton, South-west | −20·1 | C |
| 23. Aberavon | 17·8 | A(2) | 23. Norfolk, South | −18·5 | D |
| 24. Caernarvon | 17·2 | F | 24. Chippenham | −17·4 | F(2)H |
| 25. Pontypool | 17·1 | A(2) | 25. Berwick | −17·0 | D |
| 26. Chester-le-Street | 17·0 | B(1) | 26. Dorset, North | −16·6 | B(1)R |
| 27. Western Isles | 16·6 | F | 27. Oswestry | −16·6 | DH |
| 28. Bermondsey | 15·7 | DG | 28. Isle of Ely | −16·5 | D |
| 29. Ince | 15·7 | E | 29. Orpington | −16·3 | A |
| 30. Barnsley | 15·2 | C(1) | 30. Horncastle | −16·1 | DR |
| 31. Blyth | 16·1 | B(1) | 31. Thirsk & Malton | −16·1 | DH |
| 32. Easington | 15·0 | B(1)G | 32. Wolverhampton, North-east | −16·1 | C |
| 33. Fife, West | 14·5 | C(2)G | 33. Fife, East | −16·0 | B(2) |
| 34. Dunbartonshire, East | 14·4 | G | 34. Montgomeryshire | −15·5 | A |
| 35. Gateshead, East | 14·3 | B(2)G | 35. Rowley Regis & Tipton | −15·5 | C |
| 36. Durham | 14·2 | B(1) | 36. Perth & E. Perth | −15·4 | B(2) |
| 37. Huyton | 14·1 | G | 37. Petersfield | −15·3 | E(2)H |
| 38. Merthyr Tydfil | 14·0 | A(2) | 38. Ludlow | −15·1 | D |
| 39. Houghton-le-Spring | 13·9 | B(1)G | 39. Orkney & Shetland | −15·1 | AB(1)RH |
| 40. West Ham, South | 13·6 | D | 40. Stratford | −15·1 | E(2) |
| 41. Dagenham | 13·4 | G | 41. Dumfriesshire | −14·8 | B(1) |
| 42. Poplar | 13·3 | DG | 42 Skipton | −14·8 | E(1) |
| 43. Colne Valley | 13·0 | F | 43. Worcestershire, South | −14·8 | E(1) |
| 44. Blaydon | 12·7 | B(2) | 44. Tavistock | −14·5 | E(1)H |
| 45. Anglesey | 12·6 | * | 45. Argyll | −14·4 | B(1) |
| 46. Wigan | 12·4 | E | 46. Scarborough & Whitby | −14·3 | E(2)R |
| 47. Midlothian | 12·4 | C(3)G | 47. Holland with Boston | −13·9 | D |
| 48. West Ham, North | 12·4 | D | 48. Tiverton | −13·5 | E(1)R |
| 49. Holborn & St. Pancras | 12·3 | H | 49. Derbyshire, West | −13·5 | E(1) |
| 50. Barking | 12·2 | DG | 50. Moray & Nairn | −13·1 | B(2)H |

* No clear grouping.

## TABLE 3

*England: seats in which, given their proportion of manual workers, the Labour percentage of the two-party vote was most* above, *and* below, *the 'expected' level*

| | Residual score % | Group | | Residual score % | Group |
|---|---|---|---|---|---|
| 1. Hampstead | 22·0 | H | 1. Cornwall, North | −34·5 | ADHR |
| 2. Dearne Valley | 19·9 | C(1) | 2. Leominster | −24·3 | DH |
| 3. Chester-le-Street | 18·5 | B(1) | 3. Bodmin | −23·8 | ADR |
| 4. Bermondsey | 17·5 | DG | 4. B'ham Ladywood | −23·5 | AC |
| 5. Barnsley | 17·0 | C(1) | 5. B'ham All Saints | −22·3 | C |
| 6. Easington | 17·0 | B(1)G | 6. Torrington | −21·7 | DR |
| 7. Ince | 17·0 | E | 7. B'ham Aston | −21·5 | C |
| 8. Blyth | 16·8 | B(1) | 8. Devon, North | −20·5 | ADHR |
| 9. Durham | 15·6 | B(1) | 9. Howden | −20·3 | D |
| 10. Houghton-le-Spring | 15·6 | B(1)G | 10. Westmorland | −19·1 | D |
| 11. West Ham, South | 15·6 | D | 11. Penrith & Border | −19·1 | D |
| 12. Gateshead, East | 15·5 | B(1)G | 12. Wolverhampton, South-west | −18·8 | C |
| 13. Poplar | 15·5 | DG | 13. B'ham Handsworth | −18·8 | C |
| 14. Huyton | 15·4 | G | 14. B'ham Sparkbrook | −17·8 | C |
| 15. Dagenham | 15·1 | G | 15. Norfolk, South | −16·6 | D |
| 16. Colne Valley | 14·3 | F | 16. Chippenham | −16·3 | E(2)H |
| 17. Sheffield Park | 14·2 | E(1)G | 17. Orpington | −16·2 | A |
| 18. Pontefract | 14·1 | C(1) | 18. Dorset, North | −15·9 | E(1)R |
| 19. West Ham, North | 14·1 | D | 19. Berwick-on-Tweed | −15·7 | D |
| 20. Blaydon | 14·0 | B(2) | 20. Oswestry | −15·3 | DH |
| 21. Wigan | 14·0 | E | 21. Horncastle | −15·0 | DR |
| 22. Barking | 13·8 | DG | 22. Isle of Ely | −14·9 | D |
| 23. Hemsworth | 13·8 | C(1) | 23. Thirsk & Malton | −14·9 | DH |
| 24. Normanton | 13·7 | C(1) | 24. Petersfield | −14·6 | E(2)H |
| 25. Bethnal Green | 13·1 | DG | 25. Stratford | −14·2 | E(2) |
| 26. Holborn & St. Pancras | 13·1 | H | 26. Ludlow | −13·9 | D |
| 27. Stepney | 13·1 | D | 27. Tavistock | −13·9 | E(1)H |
| 28. Rother Valley | 13·1 | C(1) | 28. Worcestershire, South | −13·9 | E(1) |
| 29. Woolwich, East | 12·8 | D | 29. Wolverhampton, North-west | −13·8 | C |
| 30. Woolwich, West | 12·7 | G | 30. Scarborough & Whitby | −13·6 | E(2)R |
| 31. Putney | 12·6 | G | 31. Skipton | −13·6 | E(1) |
| 32. Sedgefield | 12·6 | B(2) | 32. Rowley Regis & Tipton | −12·8 | C |
| 33. Morpeth | 12·4 | B(1) | 33. Tiverton | −12·6 | E(1)R |
| 34. Penistone | 12·4 | * | 34. Derbyshire, West | −12·2 | E(1) |
| 35. Newcastle, West | 12·3 | G | 35. Holland with Boston | −12·2 | D |
| 36. Hendon, South | 12·0 | H | 36. Melton | −11·7 | * |
| 37. Sheffield Brightside | 11·8 | E(1)G | 37. Cheadle | −11·6 | A |
| 38. Feltham | 11·7 | * | 38. Richmond (Yorkshire) | −11·3 | E(1)H |
| 39. Hull, North | 11·5 | * | 39 Honiton | −10·9 | E(1)HR |
| 40. St. Pancras, North | 11·4 | D? | 40. New Forest | −10·9 | R |
| 41. Hull, South | 11·2 | E | 41. Nottingham Central | −10·8 | * |
| 42. Greenwich | 11·1 | H | 42. Wednesbury | −10·8 | C |
| 43. Wakefield | 11·0 | C(1) | 43. Chichester | −10·7 | E(1)R |
| 44. Wallsend | 10·9 | E(2) | 44. North Fylde | −10·6 | E(1)R |
| 45. Don Valley | 10·8 | C(1) | 45. Eastbourne | −10·4 | R |
| 46. Battersea, North | 10·7 | D | 46. Rye | −10·4 | E(1)R |
| 47. Bolsover | 10·7 | C(2) | 47. Bury St. Edmunds | −10·2 | E(1)H |
| 48. Jarrow | 10·7 | B(2)G | 48. B'ham Selly Oak | −10·1 | C |
| 49. Lewisham, North | 10·7 | G | 49. Gainsborough | −10·1 | DH |
| 50. Lewisham, South | 10·7 | G | 50. Norfolk, South-west | −10·0 | DH |

* No clear grouping.

APPENDIX IV

# THE CONTENT OF ELECTION ADDRESSES AND LEADERS' SPEECHES

By David Robertson

## 1. *Election addresses*

Unlike the national manifestos of the parties, the election addresses issued by the individual candidates reach almost every household in the country (see pp. 310–11). Although they echo the themes put forward at the centre, they do so selectively, showing the themes that candidates consider most important or most attractive locally. An analysis of their content can therefore throw a special light on what an election seems to be about.

With the help of the parties it has been possible to obtain the addresses of 95% of Conservative candidates and of 87% of Labour candidates. The subjects mentioned in them have been tallied in Table 1, any mention, however brief, being included in the count.

Among the most interesting points to emerge from Table 1 are these:

Table 1

*Conservative and Labour election addresses in 1970*

| Subject | % of Conservative candidates mentioning subject | % of Labour candidates mentioning subject |
|---|---|---|
| A. Economic Issues | | |
| Abolish Selective Employment Tax | 63 | 0 |
| Introduce Value-added Tax | 3 | −21 |
| Shift tax burden towards indirect taxation | 58 | −15 |
| Cut taxation | 64 | −5 |
| Balance of payments strong | 0 | 77 |
| Economy strong | −12 | 82 |
| Unemployment | 76 | 12 |
| Nationalisation | −24 | 3 |
| Transport | 26 | 46 |
| Need to cut government expenditure | 50 | 0 |
| Remove economic controls/increase competition | 53 | 0 |
| Inflation | 92 | 25 |
| B. Social Services and Welfare | | |
| National superannuation scheme | −9 | 50 |
| Need to encourage occupational pension scheme | 19 | 0 |

Where figures are shown with a minus sign this indicates that the mentions are opposed to the policy mentioned. Some topics, such as 'Need to build more houses' cover both a perceived need for the future and a claim for a recent government achievement.

TABLE 1 (*cont.*)

| Subject | % of Conservative candidates mentioning subject | % of Labour candidates mentioning subject |
|---|---|---|
| B. Social Services and Welfare (*cont.*) | | |
| Gear pensions to cost of living | 28 | 8 |
| Make welfare benefits selective | 58 | 0 |
| Raise pensions | 10 | 67 |
| Increase council house building | −2 | 23 |
| Abolish council house subsidy | 16 | 0 |
| General housing need | 66 | 70 |
| Allow councils to sell council houses | 20 | 0 |
| Encourage owner-occupation | 57 | 36 |
| Fair rents | 14 | 43 |
| Health service | 22 | 73 |
| C. Education | | |
| Abolish 11+ | 0 | 63 |
| Retain grammar schools | 45 | 0 |
| Expand education generally | 28 | 84 |
| Concentrate on primary and nursery schools | 48 | 25 |
| D. Industrial Relations | | |
| Industrial democracy | 0 | 10 |
| Legal reform of unions | 72 | −10 |
| E. Social Issues | | |
| Expand police force | 44 | 17 |
| Compassionate or humane society | 13 | 45 |
| Anti-permissive society | 6 | 0 |
| Pro-civilised society | 2 | 13 |
| Law and order problem | 60 | 15 |
| F. Immigration | | |
| Advocate no further increase in immigration | 26 | 0 |
| Advocate voluntary repatriation | 12 | 0 |
| Mention ideal of multi-racial society | 6 | 2 |
| G. General | | |
| Need for devolution | 30 | 5 |
| Need to protect democracy through Bill of Rights/ Ombudsman, etc. | 0 | 11 |
| Mention agriculture other than in context of EEC | 33 | 34 |
| Mention Mr. Wilson | 33 | 21 |
| Mention Mr. Heath | 20 | 10 |
| H. Foreign Affairs and Defence | | |
| Europe | 38 | 23 |
| Support UN | 2 | 18 |
| Advocate foreign aid | 5 | 20 |
| Nuclear weapons policy | 1 | 4 |
| Presence East of Suez | 19 | −34 |
| Rhodesia | 7 | 4 |
| Arms to South Africa | 3 | 0 |

Where figures are shown with a minus sign this indicates that the mentions are opposed to the policy mentioned. Some topics, such as 'Need to build more houses' cover both a perceived need for the future and a claim for a recent government achievement.

There is at first sight a sharp difference between the parties in the salience of different issues. Table 2 shows the top ten on each side:

TABLE 2

| % of candidates mentioning issue | Conservative | % of candidates mentioning issue | Labour |
|---|---|---|---|
| 92 | Inflation | 84 | Expansion of education |
| 76 | Unemployment | 82 | Strength of the economy |
| 72 | Union reform | 77 | Balance of payments success |
| 66 | Housing | 73 | Health Service |
| 63 | Abolition of SET | 70 | Housing |
| 60 | Law and order | 67 | Pensions |
| 58 | Taxation cuts | 63 | Abolition of 11+ |
| 58 | Switch to indirect taxation | 50 | National superannuation scheme |
| 58 | Making welfare benefits selective | 46 | Transport improvement |
| 57 | Helping owner-occupiers | 45 | 'The Compassionate Society' |

Only housing appears in both lists. However, the overlap in subject area (though not in stress) is considerable. Five of the Conservative themes deal with the economy or taxation, three with housing and social services, two with union reform and law and order. Three of the Labour themes deal with the economy, six with social services and one with transport.

Since the economic theme was to be so prominent in the Conservatives' national campaign, it is interesting that, while 92% of Conservative candidates mentioned inflation, only 12% of them suggested directly that the economy was weak. On the other hand, 82% of Labour candidates boasted of its strength.[1]

It is perhaps with issues which cut across party lines — either at the elite or the mass level — that election addresses are most revealing. Two stand out in 1970 — immigration and Europe. Immigration provides a fascinating case. Despite the undoubted popularity of the official Conservative policy of checking still further the inflow from the Commonwealth, only 26% of Conser-

[1] Of course most election addresses must have been drafted in the last 10 days of May, before the warnings by Conservative leaders about impending economic difficulties.

vative candidates mentioned it at all and only 12% went on to suggest voluntary repatriation. A mere 2% of Labour candidates made any reference to immigration.

A surprising reticence was also evident in connection with the Common Market. Only 38% of Conservatives and 23% of Labour candidates referred to it, many of them in a way that did not make their own position clear.

TABLE 3

*Stands taken on joining Europe in election addresses*

| | Conservative | | Labour | | Liberal | |
|---|---|---|---|---|---|---|
| | % | % | % | % | % | % |
| Strongly pro-entry . . | 2 | (9) | 1 | (5) | 12 | (42) |
| Pro, with reservations . | 10 | (46) | 5 | (33) | 36 | (56) |
| Anti, with reservations . | 4 | (20) | 4 | (26) | 3 | (4) |
| Adamantly opposed . . | 7 | (25) | 5 | (35) | 2 | (3) |
| Total taking a stand . . | 23 | (100) | 15 | (100) | 53 | (100) |
| Ambiguous mention . . | 15 | | 8 | | 12 | |
| No mention . . . | 62 | | 77 | | 35 | |
| | 100 | | 100 | | 100 | |

All three parties were committed to joining Europe 'if the terms were right', and, although Mr. Wilson and Mr. Heath refused to promise a free vote on it, the issue was plainly one on which some M.P.s would feel obliged to take an individual stand. However, less than one major party candidate in sixteen committed himself to flat opposition to British entry, while two out of three made no mention of the subject at all.

One more point about 1970: Conservatives mentioned Mr. Wilson more often than they mentioned Mr. Heath (36% to 20%).

The priorities reflected in Table 1 stand in sharp contrast to those of previous years. Table 4 shows the themes that have predominated in these addresses at each election since 1950, as they have been recorded in the successive Nuffield studies. Unemployment, cited by 98% of Labour candidates in 1950, was mentioned by only 12% in 1970. References to nationalisation and the Empire declined almost as spectacularly. Housing, education and the health service have sustained or increased their prominence. But the most intriguing statistics are perhaps those dealing with the party leader. Conservative references to Mr. Heath were at only half the frequency of references to Sir Alec Douglas-Home in 1964 and a third of those to Mr. Macmillan in 1959. Mr. Wilson,

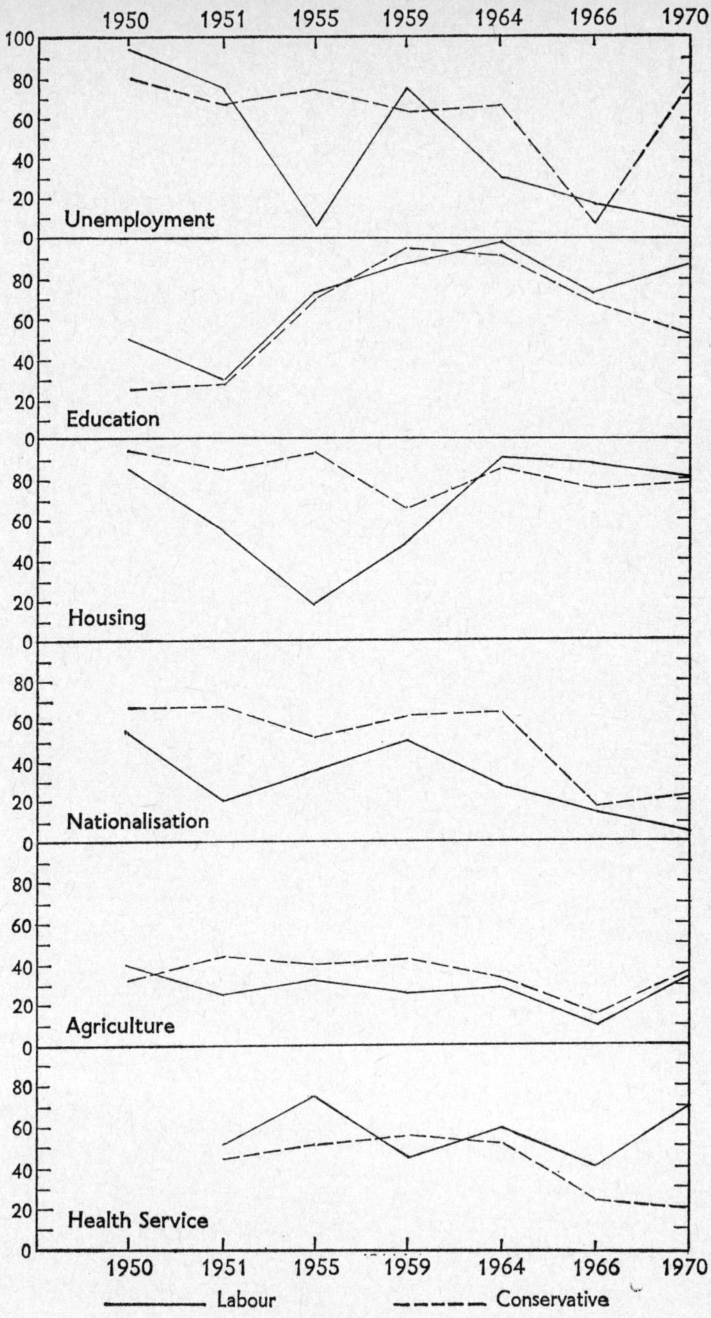


Variations in candidates' mentions of issues, 1950–70.

though far more prominent in Labour addresses than in 1964, was mentioned by barely one Labour candidate in five, compared to almost one in two in 1966. Certainly there was no evidence here of any trend towards a presidentialised election, with local party standard-bearers hanging on to their leaders coat-tails.

TABLE 4

*Historical comparison of some issues*

Figures denote percentage of candidates mentioning an issue

| | 1950 | | 1951 | | 1955 | | 1959 | | 1964 | | 1966 | | 1970 | |
|---|---|---|---|---|---|---|---|---|---|---|---|---|---|---|
| | C | L | C | L | C | L | C | L | C | L | C | L | C | L |
| 1. Unemployment | 80 | 98 | 69 | 74 | 75 | 18 | 62 | 73 | 63 | 30 | 8 | 16 | 76 | 12 |
| 2. Education | 25 | 49 | 30 | 29 | 71 | 73 | 97 | 87 | 89 | 93 | 66 | 71 | 52 | 86 |
| 3. Housing | 93 | 85 | 86 | 54 | 92 | 17 | 65 | 48 | 85 | 90 | 74 | 87 | 76 | 80 |
| 4. Nationalisation | 67 | 56 | 68 | 20 | 52 | 35 | 61 | 48 | 63 | 27 | 14 | 13 | 24 | 3 |
| 5. Empire/Commonwealth | 64 | 39 | 64 | 29 | 40 | 26 | — | — | 35 | 37 | 5 | 2 | — | — |
| 6. Nuclear weapons | — | — | — | — | 44 | 84 | 93 | 74 | 83 | 58 | 6 | 2 | 1 | 4 |
| 7. Comprehensive education | — | — | — | — | — | 65 | 40 | 60 | — | — | — | — | 45 | 63 |
| 8. Foreign aid | — | — | 26 | 25 | 0 | 38 | — | — | 50 | 27 | 2 | 10 | 5 | 20 |
| 9. Agriculture | 33 | 40 | 45 | 26 | 41 | 33 | 42 | 26 | 34 | 30 | 20 | 11 | 33 | 34 |
| 10. United Nations | 32 | 47 | 30 | 43 | 0 | 41 | — | — | 8 | 43 | 6 | 23 | 2 | 18 |
| 11. Health Service | — | — | 45 | 52 | 53 | 70 | 58 | 45 | 55 | 58 | 25 | 42 | 22 | 73 |
| 12. Industrial relations | — | — | 54 | — | — | — | 6 | 9 | 24 | 5 | 62 | 8 | 72 | 15 |
| 13. Mention of own party leader | — | — | 30 | — | — | — | 65 | 12 | 41 | 8 | 19 | 47 | 20 | 21 |

## 2. *Leaders' speeches*

In 1970 Transport House issued excerpts from 17 speeches and broadcasts by Mr. Wilson, amounting to 17,714 words. Conservative Central Office issued 15 handouts of Mr. Heath's remarks, amounting to 8,680 words. Although these formed only a small proportion of the leaders' total output, they include the passages that were considered most important at the party headquarters and which tended to be reported most fully in the press and on television. Tables 5 and 6 are based on a count of the number of words in these documents that were devoted to different categories of subjects.

Of the 25% of Mr. Wilson's words that were given to the case for his own side, four-fifths dealt with past achievements. Only by a generous interpretation of his remarks on social equality, the environment and one or two other themes could it be said that as much as one-fifth of his pro-Labour remarks (i.e. one-twentieth of his total output) was concerned with the discussion of plans for

## Table 5
*Mr. Wilson's speeches*

| | % | |
|---|---|---|
| Labour's economic achievement | 6 | |
| Labour's record on regional development | 2 | |
| Labour's welfare record | 5 | |
| Labour's housing record | 2 | |
| Labour's educational record | 1 | |
| Labour's record of law enforcement | 4 | |
| Labour's philosophy of social equality | 2 | |
| Labour's plan for the environment | 1 | |
| Labour party 'is responsible' | 2 | |
| | — | 25% |
| Conservatives are 'politically irresponsible' | 8 | |
| Conservative 'economic scare campaign' is irresponsible | 11 | |
| Conservative tax and spending policies 'do not add up' | 12 | |
| Conservative plans for VAT | 10 | |
| Conservative food policy | 4 | |
| Conservative rents policy | 5 | |
| Conservative prices policy | 3 | |
| Conservative policy for public sector wages | 3 | |
| Conservative law and order policy | 2 | |
| Conservative regional development policies and plans | 1 | |
| Conservatives' economic record | 2 | |
| Conservatives' housing record | 3 | |
| Reply to Conservative criticisms about inflation | 3 | |
| Charge that the Conservatives would reduce welfare spending | 2 | |
| General criticism of Conservative leadership | 3 | |
| Claim that Conservatives lack 'compassion' | 3 | |
| | — | 75% |
| | | 100% |

the future. 75% of the words in his handouts were devoted to castigating the Conservatives for their record, their attitude and their plans.

However, the handouts of Mr. Heath's offer a broadly similar picture. 70% of his words were criticisms of Labour. Of the remainder, 11% dealt with specific Conservative policies for the future — the rest being more general discussion of 'freedom' and 'a better life'.

Many of the attacking themes in both leaders' speeches were criticisms, not of what the other party had done or was committed to doing, but of things they *might* possibly do. For example, 10% of Mr. Wilson's output dwelt on the evils of the Value-added Tax,

## Table 6

*Mr. Heath's speeches*

| | % | |
|---|---|---|
| Labour's housing record | 2 | |
| Labour's record on inflation | 10 | |
| Labour's industrial relations record | 2 | |
| Labour's record on devaluation | 1 | |
| Labour's record on economic growth | 2 | |
| Labour's unemployment record | 1 | |
| Labour's welfare record | 1 | |
| Government spending too high | 4 | |
| Taxes too high | 5 | |
| Labour has reduced Britain's international prestige | 5 | |
| Claim that an economic crisis is impending | 16 | |
| Claim that Labour will impose another wage freeze if elected | 10 | |
| Claim that Labour has no policies for the election | 1 | |
| General criticism of the style of Labour government | 4 | |
| Claim that creeping socialism is crippling the economy | 4 | |
| Labour lacks integrity | 3 | |
| | | 70% |
| Conservative policy on Common Market | 3 | |
| Conservative tax policy | 1 | |
| Conservative industrial relations policy | 2 | |
| Conservative economic policy in general | 2 | |
| Conservative savings policy | 1 | |
| Conservative policy on prices | 1 | |
| Plan to pay for welfare out of increased prosperity | 2 | |
| Conservative plan to restore incentives by tax reduction | 1 | |
| Conservative policy for fair rents | 1 | |
| National desire for international prestige | 2 | |
| Promise that Conservatives will increase Britain's world-standing | 2 | |
| Conservative belief in freedom and opportunity | 4 | |
| Conservatives have integrity | 2 | |
| Claim that life will be better under Conservatives | 5 | |
| | | 30% |
| | | 100% |

although the Conservatives had avoided committing themselves to it, and 10% of Mr. Heath's output dealt with the freeze that would follow if Labour won the election, although Mr. Wilson denied that it was any part of his policy.

The picture that can be derived from Smith Square handouts of what the leading colleagues of Mr. Wilson and Mr. Heath were saying is potentially much more misleading: some of them had only a single speech or short passages from a few speeches distributed. But it is still instructive to look at their general thrust. The speeches of eleven leading Conservatives were circulated: 77% of their text were 'Labour-bashing' with the scores of individual spokesmen ranging from 95% down to 48%. Transport House handouts (less in number and in length) included nine Labour spokesmen: 47% of their texts were devoted to attacking the Conservatives, with the individual scores ranging from 81% down to 12%.

There was no very great correspondence between the subjects that, according to the polls, were of most concern to the public, and those that the politicians concentrated on. Mr. Wilson and his colleagues had little to say to those whose main anxieties were about taxation, strikes, housing or the cost of living. The Conservatives, as the opposition, could and did attack on all of these themes, but remarkably few of their speeches were devoted to the remedies which, for good or ill, they had offered in their manifesto. Certainly, it cannot be said that these handouts of campaign speeches offer the raw material for what the rational elector envisaged in democratic theory could regard as a well-reasoned argument over the real choices to be faced in the next five years. If one judged by the speech handouts, as distinct from the manifestos or the addresses, it was indeed a negative election.

APPENDIX V

# SCOTTISH NATIONALISM

By James G. Kellas[1]

Politics in Scotland since 1966 has been dominated by the flow and ebb of Scottish nationalism. Not since the late 1940s and early 1950s has the mood been so strongly nationalist, and even then the repercussions on the Scottish political system were much less. Yet by 1970 most people were convinced that the force was spent, and that normal politics would be resumed as soon as possible.

What, in Scotland, is 'normal' politics? Outside observers have usually supported the theory of 'British political homogeneity', which stresses that all parts of Great Britain (if not Northern Ireland) form one political community, in which party divisions are socio-economic rather than territorial.[2] Thus people in Scotland vote for the same parties as people elsewhere in Britain, and 'swing' from party to party at elections in the same direction as the rest of the country. There might be some difference in the intensity of support which the British parties receive in Scotland as compared to the average, and the swing in Scotland might sometimes actually go the other way (as it did in 1959), but these are minor variations.

Those who actually live in Scotland, however, are aware of considerable differences between Scotland and England, and when resident political analysts at last studied Scotland they discovered that it was at least 'a political region inside Britain', or even part of a 'multi-national United Kingdom'.[3]

After 1966, the homogeneity argument received a bad blow, from which perhaps not even the 1970 election can rescue it. The reason, of course, was the startling successes of the Scottish National Party (SNP), which drove the idea of a political region

[1] I should like to acknowledge the help and advice given to me by many people, particularly Iain McLean, Jim Craig, Roger Brooks, Jack Brand, Michael Dyer and Alan Betts.

[2] See especially J. Blondel, *Voters, Parties and Leaders* (Penguin Books, 1963), Chapter 2.

[3] I. Budge and D. W. Urwin, *Scottish Political Behaviour* (Longmans, 1966), p. 132; R. Rose, *The United Kingdom as a Multi-national State* (Survey Research Centre, University of Strathclyde, Occasional Paper no. 6, 1970).

much further forward, and indeed raised the spectre of a breakdown in the entire British political system. For if enough Scots were nationalists and believed with the SNP that Scotland should be a separate state, then the British political parties had failed to aggregate the interests of Scots with those of citizens in the rest of Britain.

Was there ever any evidence for this? In the 1966 general election, the SNP contested 23 of the 71 Scottish seats and achieved an overall average of 14·5% in the seats contested. Its vote was 5·0% of the Scottish total, and in only three seats did it even come second in the poll. These were in areas dominated by small towns, in the central lowland belt of Scotland. In the four major cities (Glasgow, Edinburgh, Dundee and Aberdeen) the SNP did not save a single deposit, and few rural and no Highland (crofting counties) seats were contested. At the same time, the Labour party recorded its greatest-ever victory in Scotland, with 46 M.P.s elected and 49·9% of the total votes cast. However, the SNP had doubled its vote since 1964, and it was possible to trace a steady rise in the SNP share of the vote since 1955, which had accelerated in 1964. Only the Conservatives were clearly in decline in Scotland, having fallen from 36 seats and 50·1% of the vote in 1955, to 20 seats and 37·7% of the vote in 1966. This was a greater dropping-off in Conservative support than in any other 'political region' of Britain.

The 1955 election was the high-point of British homogeneity, with the Scottish results mirroring those for the country as a whole, but by 1966 there were signs that political behaviour in Scotland was developing along more distinctive lines.

After the 1966 election, the SNP felt a new confidence, which showed itself in the large number of highly-visible young people who flocked to join its local branches, and who wore its newly-designed emblem ४, a simple combination of the St. Andrew's Cross and the thistle. The central organisation of the Party took on a new lease of life, and was able to build on the pioneering work of Ian Macdonald, an ex-farmer who became National Organiser in 1962. He had set out to establish the SNP as a grass-roots party with numerous local branches, some with as few as twenty members, and by rapidly increasing the number of such branches from 40 in 1963 to 486 in 1969, he made the SNP appear intensely active throughout Scotland at a time when the major parties were in their customary inter-election doldrums. In rural areas especially, the SNP organised concerts, dances and excursions, and this emphasis on social activities and togetherness attracted people whose interest in politics had previously been negligible. Of course, such tactics were less appropriate in the large towns, where the lack of community feeling was balanced by the availability of mass entertainments, but even in cities such as Glasgow their activities were far more noticeable than those of the other parties. Another achievement was the building-up of a sound financial base, through membership fees and functions, and the 'Alba Pools' (a lottery) which provided the main income.

To make any headway in the urban areas there had to be a political reaction against the major parties, which could somehow be channelled into the SNP. Already the Conservatives had reached their nadir in Scotland, and little could be gained from

TABLE

| Year | SNP vote at parliamentary elections, and % of total vote (Scottish total at general elections). | SNP vote at municipal elections, and % of total vote | Net emigration from Scotland (year to June) | % unemployment relative to GB (=100), March | Average weekly earnings of male manual workers in Scotland as % of UK (October) |
|---|---|---|---|---|---|
| 1966 | 128,474 (5·0) | 34,330 (4·1) | 47,000 | 210 | 96·4 |
| 1967 | Pollok (March) 10,884 (28·2) | 144,952 (15·6) (excluding landward areas of counties) | 45,000 | 170 | 97·2 |
| | Hamilton (November) 18,397 (46·0) | | | | |
| 1968 | | 343,491 (30·1) | 33,000 | 160 | 97·0 |
| 1969 | Glasgow, Gorbals (October) 3,671 (25·0) | 221,576 (22·0) | 25,000 | 155 | 97·0 |
| 1970 | South Ayrshire (March) 7,785 (20·3) | 131,337 (12·6) (excluding landward areas of counties) | 21,000 | 160 | n.a. |
| | 306,796 (11·4) | | | | |

Sources: Municipal elections. I am grateful to Iain McLean for providing me with these figures.
Net emigration. *Digest of Scottish Statistics*, HMSO (April 1970), p. 43, and Hansard, November 11, 1970.
Unemployment. *Digest of Scottish Statistics*, HMSO (April 1970), p. 37.
Earnings. Ibid., p. 41, *Abstract of Regional Statistics*, no. 5, HMSO (1969), pp. 70–71; *Employment and Productivity Gazette*, HMSO (July 1970), p. 635.

that side. Their severe decline was in large part a result of the feeling in Scotland of neglect under Conservative governments, aggravated by Mr. Macmillan's proclamations of prosperity. This sense of 'relative deprivation' accounted in part for the large migration from Scotland to England and overseas during this period, and heightened the discontent of those who remained behind. High unemployment, low wages, bad housing and a general lack of amenities were perhaps chronic features of Scottish life, but such regional imbalance now seemed to almost everyone (even in England where there were also regional problems) to be wrong. The Conservatives had belatedly begun a programme of regional economic development in the early 1960s, and by stressing that Scotland was indeed run down in comparison to the prosperous areas, they appeared to condemn their previous policy of inaction. At any rate, their Central Scotland Plan of 1963 (Cmnd. 2188) had no time to take effect before Labour came to power in the following year.

The Labour government believed strongly in regional development and established the Scottish Economic Planning Council and Board, and the Highlands and Islands Development Board. It also increased the size of the development area until it included all of Scotland except Edinburgh. In this area new, large grants were paid to incoming industries. Expenditure on services in Scotland was increased, and the presumed effect of these measures on emigration, unemployment and earnings is shown in the table on the opposite page.

However, these actions were quickly overtaken by events which strained the entire credibility of Labour policies. The optimism of the five-year plan for the Scottish economy, published in January 1966 (Cmnd. 2864), was dampened by the stringent 'squeeze' measures taken by the government in July 1966. Earlier that month the first Welsh Nationalist M.P. was returned to Parliament. In Scotland, a similar strengthening of nationalism could be predicted: both Wales and Scotland were Labour strongholds whose feelings (albeit temporary) against a Labour government could not easily be expressed in Conservatism. The Liberals failed to benefit because they did not appear to have a clear alternative economic policy, and could not build up an organisation in the towns. The Nationalists were both the strongest protest that could be found at the time, and the exponents of the most radical economic policy, for to cut adrift entirely from the ailing British state seemed eminently sensible when it appeared that the 'squeeze' was a result of Britain's unsatisfactory role as world banker and trader. Small nations, such as those in Scandinavia, did not have these problems, so would not Scotland (rather than Britain) be a more prosperous unit of government?

In this situation the SNP waited for a by-election. Eventually it came, at Pollok in Glasgow, on March 9, 1967. This seat had been highly marginal in 1964 and 1966, and no Labour or Conservative supporter could afford to 'waste' his vote on a protest candidate who might let the other side in. Yet the SNP got 28·2% of the vote, predominantly from Labour defectors, but also from a large number of Conservatives and previous abstainers, and the Conservatives gained the seat. At once, the SNP became a serious political force in the heartland of Scottish politics, where it had previously hardly counted. The SNP's Pollok campaign was something new in Scotland's dreary electioneering: it deliberately imported American-style motorcades, drum-majorettes, jazzy literature and an all-pervasive fly-posting. Crowds of helpers came from the surrounding districts, among whom were most of those who were to be candidates and officials of the party in Glasgow in the 1970 election. The SNP candidate himself, George Leslie, had returned from England specifically to help the SNP, and he later became the leader of the SNP group on Glasgow Corporation.

The Pollok result could be seen as another manifestation of the British-wide anti-Labour swing which was then current. The difference in Scotland was that the SNP benefited, rather than the Conservatives. Whether the Conservatives could have attracted these Labour defectors or previous abstainers in the absence of the SNP is an open question, but there is no doubt that the Conservatives suffered along with Labour by the SNP's intrusion.

Elated by their showing in Pollok, the SNP determined to make an onslaught on the local citadels of power. Up till then their local contests had been largely confined to small burghs, and in some of these (e.g. Stirling, Forfar and Bo'ness) they had been moderately successful. Now they wanted to attack the major parties where it hurt them most, and Labour was particularly vulnerable in Glasgow, since its majority on the council had been cut to ten. The decision to enter local politics on a large scale had disadvantages for the SNP, however, some of which were soon to become apparent. It exposed their candidates to enquiries as to their policies on council-house rents, rates and comprehensive schools — sensitive areas which divided rather than united the Scottish nation. The SNP's slogan of 'Put Scotland First' gave no answer to these issues. Moreover, as the SNP candidates were borne to the council chamber on the tide of nationalism, many of them were ill-prepared for the duties of councillor, and a few were even forced to resign because they could not afford to carry on.

In the long run, then, the SNP incursion into local politics proved to be a doubtful strategy, yet its advantage was that it kept the party before the public, and trained its parliamentary candidates. In 1967, 23 seats were gained at the burgh elections (compared to 4 in 1966), and the party won 15·6% of the votes cast (see Table). All the 37 Glasgow wards were contested, and the SNP came second in 15, gaining 9·5% of the total vote in Glasgow. This seemed to hit Labour more than the Progressives and Conservatives, who gained 3 seats, yet by comparison with the anti-Labour swing which was taking place in England at this time, the Scottish results again showed that the right-wing parties were suffering from the SNP intervention. Part of the anti-Labour vote was drained off to the SNP, while a number of Labour voters abstained. The turn-out was up, however, and in Glasgow was the highest since 1952. The Nationalists were attracting people to the polls who had abstained in previous elections.

A rather different situation arose when Hamilton (Lanarkshire) went to the polls at a parliamentary by-election on November 2, 1967. Unlike Pollok, this was the second safest Labour seat in Scotland. Thus, to the prevailing Labour discontent (devaluation was only days away) was here added the argument that a Conservative vote was a 'wasted' vote. The SNP virtually took over the constituency with their expanded Pollok electioneering team. The contrast between their flashy approach and Labour's time-worn machine came over in the personalities of the candidates: SNP's Mrs. Winifred Ewing was a bright and breezy, if emotional, Glasgow solicitor, who captured the attention and sympathies of a large section of the Scottish press and TV. Labour's Alex Wilson was a traditional trade unionist, who represented the 'old Hamilton' of bygone mining days. The Tory *Scottish Daily Express* headlined the result, 'WINNIE WINS FOR SCOTLAND'. Mrs. Ewing had gained the seat with a majority of 1,799 and a vote of 46% of the total poll.

The effect of this on Scottish politics was immediate, and shattering to the established order. Yet to most people in Scotland the *Express*'s sentiment rang true: this was a brave, defiant gesture in the supposed tradition of Scotland's past. Labour's promises had gone stale, the Conservatives had already been found wanting, the Liberals were too weak. SNP had made a big noise, and in politics a big noise is often heard. It was indeed heard throughout the world, and in Scotland itself it stunned most of the practical (and academic) politicians into silence. What they were witnessing was a curious inward-turning of the Scottish spirit: a collective assertion of Scottishness and Scotland's grievances, which was more spontaneous than led. If one looked to Scotland's social hierarchy for the inspiration of this nationalism one would be disappointed. Up to now, the establishment of Church of Scotland, Scots Law, Scottish education, Scottish industry, Scottish trade unionism and Scottish nobility had been silent. Only the Scottish press (especially the *Express* and *Scotsman*) fanned the flame. It was the amorphous, unled and unestablished Scotland that was stirring, and this startled the political parties, for they were not sure how (or whether) to adapt their 'image' to its demands.

It was a whole year before the Labour leadership felt confident enough to mount a scorching attack on the SNP, and even then it was Norman Buchan, an Under-Secretary of State at the Scottish Office, who spoke out and not Willie Ross, the Scottish Secretary. By this time the hatred felt by leading Labour men for the SNP was far greater than their hostility towards the Tories. Will Marshall, the Scottish secretary of the Labour party, had poured scorn on the 'Nats' (or 'Narks' as Mr. Ross liked to call them, using a Scots word for complainers) before the Pollok election, predicting that they would lose their deposit. This damaged his reputation as the 'hard-man' realist of the Labour party in Scotland. Nor were Labour's feelings in any way assuaged by the professed socialism of many of the SNP's leaders, including the Pollok candidate George Leslie and Mrs. Ewing herself. It was also seen that the Labour party's sympathies for devolution dating back to the days of Keir Hardie were now completely suppressed, although individuals in the Labour party in Scotland remained uncomfortably in its favour.[1]

[1] Most notably, John P. Mackintosh, M.P. for Berwick and East Lothian, and author of *The Devolution of Power* (Penguin, 1968). Other Labour devolutionists included Donald Dewar, M.P. for Aberdeen South; Andrew Hargrave, journalist and author of the Fabian Tract *Scotland: the third choice*, March 1969; and Norman Buchan himself.

As for the Tories, despite their long tradition as the 'Unionist' party in Scotland (it still called itself Conservative and Unionist party, and up to 1965 had been simply the Unionist party), they now adopted a policy of devolution. A working party had been studying the subject since June 1967, and in May 1968 Mr. Heath proposed to the Scottish Conservative conference that an elected Scottish Assembly, dealing with purely Scottish legislation but subject to the overriding power of Westminster, might become part of Conservative policy. While the Scottish Tories were somewhat taken aback by this proposal at first, the party leadership established a 'non-partisan' Constitutional Committee, under the chairmanmanship of Sir Alec Douglas-Home, to examine the subject thoroughly. In March 1970 it finally reported in favour of Mr. Heath's Assembly (now renamed the 'Scottish Convention').[1] This was endorsed by a large majority at the Scottish Conservative conference in May 1970, and Mr. Heath himself remained personally identified with the policy of Scottish devolution. It would be unfair to say that this was just a 'sop to nationalism'. Many leading Tories in Scotland were genuinely convinced that devolution was necessary, but they might not have considered the subject but for the challenge of the SNP.

The Scottish Liberal party (it claims independence from the 'Liberal party' as such) had for generations supported federal 'home-rule-all-round', and in 1967 its M.P.s formally promoted a Scottish Self-Government Bill. The Liberals were greatly agitated by the rise of the SNP, and at their conference in 1967 Ludovic Kennedy and Michael Starforth called for an electoral pact between the two parties. This was not made, however, and Kennedy and Starforth soon left the Liberals (but only Starforth joined the SNP). The Chairman of the Scottish Liberal party, George Mackie, M.P. for Caithness and Sutherland from 1964 to 1966, and Russell Johnston, M.P. for Inverness from 1964, strongly opposed a pact, but individual Liberals, including the other four Scottish M.P.s, Jo Grimond, David Steel, James Davidson and Alasdair Mackenzie, made unsuccessful approaches to the SNP. Only in Berwick and East Lothian did the Liberals support the SNP candidate, though this was declared unconstitutional by the party Executive. The distrust for the Liberals which

[1] *Scotland's Government: The Report of the Scottish Constitutional Committee*, Edinburgh, March 1970.

was felt by the SNP increased when the Liberal Assembly in Edinburgh in September 1968 revealed disagreement between the Scottish and English 'parties' over home rule (the English did not want a parliament for themselves while the Scots did). The SNP saw this as potential English domination of the Liberal party in Scotland, and the 'old guard' of the SNP, especially the Chairman Arthur Donaldson, and the President Dr. Robert McIntyre, opposed any dilution of the aim of sovereign independence for Scotland through an alliance with the Liberals. Both parties were therefore split, but the Liberals more badly so, and relations between the orthodox Scottish Executive and Jo Grimond and David Steel became distinctly cool.

The Hamilton by-election seemed, at the time, to the multitude of academics, journalists and politicians who tried to explain it, to be an event of great significance, revealing something about Scotland which to most had not been apparent. Scotland was a nation with its own laws, church, educational system and culture, and the natural result of all this was nationalism. It was for the moment forgotten that such strong credentials of nationality had not in the past in Scotland led to equally strong demands for political self-determination. They could, however, be pegs on which to hang a profound feeling of discontent with conventional politics, just as the Liberals had tapped such a feeling at Orpington in 1962. The discontent was basically with policy outcomes, rather than with the political structure as such, yet it was the structure which came under attack, for the SNP was avowedly 'anti-system'. On the other hand, the rise of the SNP could be seen as extending the party system in Scotland, rather than destroying it. It provided a new alternative, especially to Labour, and articulated many demands which the system could meet. But it undoubtedly tapped emotions which *might* destroy the system. The image of a nation oppressed and the belief that if liberated it could accomplish great things are notoriously powerful social forces, for good or ill. Scots have an alternative nationality, which they can wear in preference to their British statehood. Just how they would wear it, however, and for how long, no one could confidently predict in 1967.

This mood lasted for some considerable time (and in some places is still prevalent). The local elections of May 1968 were dominated by the successes of the SNP, most especially in the large cities, where their effect was painful to the established parties. In Glasgow the rout was complete, with SNP taking 35·9% of the vote, compared with 34·8% for Progressive/Conservative and only 25·5% for Labour. This gave SNP 13 seats on the Council, and the balance of power between the main groups. In all the municipal elections in Scotland, SNP took 30·1% of the votes, and pushed the turn-out up from 45·0% in 1967 to 48·9%. The extra voters were usually new SNP supporters who had not voted in the general election of 1966, but there were converts from the other parties, predominantly from Labour. At this time the SNP vote seemed to mirror socially the population as a whole, having a more even support in all classes than Labour or Conservative. But the average SNP voter was several years younger than the voter for the other parties, and in Glasgow there were few converts from the Roman Catholics. SNP candidates had nearly all joined the party during the previous two years, and had not been members of any other party before.[1] Their political inexperience was a handicap in the labyrinth of local government, and the SNP policy of allowing a free vote for its councillors confused the public as to where the party stood on many issues. Municipal press correspondents seemed hostile to the SNP, and it was difficult to learn what the party wanted to accomplish in the field of local government, far removed from the main battle-field of national self-determination. While the SNP brought a much needed jolt to the inefficient and at times corrupt local politicians in places like Glasgow, in general

[1] For accounts of surveys of SNP support, see J. P. Cornford and J. A. Brand, 'Scottish Voting Behaviour', in J. N. Wolfe (ed.), *Government and Nationalism in Scotland* (Edinburgh University Press, 1969), pp. 24–30. Iain McLean, 'Scottish Nationalism: Its growth and development, with particular reference to the period since 1961', unpublished B.Phil. thesis, Oxford, 1969, and 'The Rise and Fall of the Scottish National Party', *Political Studies*, September 1970, pp. 357–372. The following four surveys give a broad indication of SNP support during the period:

*Voting intention in the event of an immediate general election*
(adjusted to exclude 'Don't knows')

| | SNP % | Lab. % | Cons. % | Lib. % | Other % |
|---|---|---|---|---|---|
| NOP, November 1967 . . . . | 24·0 | 41·0 | 25·0 | 9·0 | 1·0 |
| Market Information Services, for BBC, May 1968 . . . . . . | 43·0 | 22·0 | 30·0 | 4·0 | 1·0 |
| NOP, January 1969 . . . . | 20·9 | 39·3 | 33·5 | 5·7 | 0·6 |
| Gallup, March 1970 . . . . | 12·5 | 37·5 | 43·0 | 6·5 | 0·5 |

its efforts to convince the electors that it was accomplishing something were not successful.

At the annual party conference shortly afterwards (June 1968), the Chairman, Arthur Donaldson, said, 'The argument until now has been for or against self-government. Now it will be about what kind of self-government. From now on then, the accent is to be on policies.'[1] This was in fact begging the question, for it was not at all clear that the majority of those who voted for the SNP did so because they wanted self-government. In fact, over the years, some surveys showed that only a minority of SNP supporters believed in the official policy of an independent Scotland. A large number were merely devolutionists of one kind or another, with the remainder (also quite large) uninterested in the self-government issue at all.[2] It was perhaps on these that the SNP now concentrated its appeal, and it was necessary to show the non-devolutionists that Scotland would be more prosperous as an independent country, and more awkwardly, that the SNP itself had attractive policies which went beyond the securing of that independence. The image of the SNP was carefully nurtured as a responsible, non-revolutionary, non-violent party (in contrast to well-publicised aspects of Irish and even Welsh nationalism). Cranks were expelled, including the semi-secret society which concentrated on romantic nationalism, the 1320 Club.

The question of Scotland's economic position in the event of independence was argued at length on TV and in print.[3] For a time, the SNP apparently convinced most Scots that independence would pay. But eventually Britain's economic position improved, and the Treasury issued a 'Scottish Budget' (October 1969), which was interpreted to mean that Scotland was being subsidised by England and would suffer if it became independent (though the 'Budget' itself did not specifically say that). This age-old argument was still rendered obscure by the absence of key financial statistics and the unknown effect of the policies of an independent Scottish government, but the doubters and apoliticals now shied back from

[1] *Scotsman*, June 3, 1968.

[2] See Cornford and Brand, op. cit., p. 27. McLean, *Political Studies*, September 1970, p. 369.

[3] Especially, 'Where do we go from here?', BBC-TV, April 4, 1968; 'In Camera', STV, November 1, 1969. G. McCrone, *Scotland's Future: The Economics of Nationalism* (Blackwell, 1969); D. Simpson, 'The Scales of Economic Independence', *Scotland*, November 1968.

a leap in the dark, leaving the SNP more dependent on the convinced devolutionists.

These devolutionists started to thrash out the details of their proposed Constitution for Scotland, as well as the other policies to be adopted. The party conference in June 1969 was the forum for these discussions, and it was somewhat dispirited from the beginning by the decline in SNP votes at the recent municipal elections (from 30·1% in 1968 to 22·0% in 1969). This was a severe check to the party, and badly damaged the 'credibility' of its claims to be the 'voice of Scotland'. Although it had been forecasting further sweeping gains, these amounted to only 20 seats, so that its position on the councils improved only marginally.

In this atmosphere, the conference debates on policies revealed deep divisions among party members. These could be described as between the left and right wings of the party, or between the new guard and the old guard (though these divisions did not always coincide). In general, the SNP had become something of a 'Social-Democratic' party, rather more collectivist than the Liberals, yet apparently opposed to centralisation and bureaucracy. Its policy tended to vary from place to place, partly because it did not believe in a strong party line, but also because it tended to promote issues which were locally popular. In defence matters, for example, if the local economy were threatened by the closure of a defence establishment (as at Alexandria), or if there were a popular campaign such as that to 'Save the Argylls', then SNP spokesmen might diverge from the predominant 'Little Scotland' policy of minimal defence. The same could be said about the attitude to land ownership, law and order, fee-paying schools and social services.

The main splits at the conference came over profit-sharing in industry, which the 'new guard' narrowly carried over the protests of the old; over social services, which was 'remitted back for further consideration'; and over the election of the Chairman of the party. Here the 'old guard' chairman, Arthur Donaldson, was defeated by William Wolfe by 544 to 238 votes.[1]

It is interesting to note that, as there was no further conference before the 1970 election, the party as a whole did not have the opportunity to endorse its election manifesto *The New Scotland*, despite the fundamental changes in emphasis in SNP policy be-

[1] *Scotsman*, May 31, 1969, June 2, 1969.

tween June 1969 and June 1970. For example, in December 1969 the National Council of the party renounced 'separatism and isolationism as outdated concepts' and said that the SNP aimed to establish 'an association of states of the British Isles' with co-operation in economic, social, cultural and scientific fields. William Wolfe added, 'We want a separate government: we want to be a separate country in political terms. Economic interdependence is obviously essential.'[1] Whatever this meant, it was difficult to reconcile with the other major change in policy adopted at the general election and greatly emphasised in the campaign — opposition to the Common Market.[2] Sensing that the dangers of entry into EEC were more appreciated by the Scottish electorate (especially in rural areas), the SNP saw this as a way of winning votes from outside the devolutionist sector. In this it may have been successful (at least in the Highlands and north-east Scotland), but the results did not clarify the degree of support for its purely Scottish constitutional aims.

Another electoral strategy which emerged at this time was that of refusing co-operation with the Liberals. Unlike the situation in 1966, when the SNP and Liberals fought each other in only two seats, the SNP was now determined to contest every seat in Scotland. Thus ended, at least until after the election, the tortuous history of attempted accommodation between the parties. Had there been a pact this would probably have benefited both parties: the SNP would have gained the support of well-known figures such as Jo Grimond, Ludovic Kennedy and David Steel, and the Liberals would have avoided the disastrous splitting of the 'third party vote' in such places as Ross and Cromarty, Banffshire and East Aberdeenshire. But both parties felt themselves strong enough to resist at a local level: the SNP because of its apparent strength in recent years, and the Liberals as the incumbents of five Scottish seats.

The general election was therefore fought by a record number of Scottish nationalist candidates (65 SNP and one independent Scottish nationalist). In Berwick and East Lothian the Liberals supported the SNP candidate, and in Greenock the SNP did not stand against the Liberal (neither did the Conservatives). Jo Grimond was not opposed in Orkney and Shetland, nor was the Liberal in Edinburgh North. Two Glasgow seats were left unfought. In one sense, it was a high-point in the history of the

[1] *Scotsman*, December 11, 1969. [2] *The New Scotland*, p. 6.

SNP. It was now an all-Scottish party in policy and candidatures, its membership had risen rapidly to over 100,000[1] (though not all of these were of voting age), and it had 515 local branches. The party had consistently 'made news' since 1967, and had strongly influenced opinion in a devolutionist direction throughout Scotland, and indeed England. The Crowther Commission on the Constitution had been set up by the government in December 1968 to review 'the relationships between the various parts of the United Kingdom', and the many organisations and individuals who gave evidence of favour of devolution (for example, the Church of Scotland and the Scottish Trades Union Congress) must have impressed the Commissioners that a real problem existed.

And yet the SNP entered the election as a party in decline. The Gorbals by-election (October 1969) and the South Ayrshire by-election (March 1970) had appeared failures, with 25% and 20% of the vote respectively, and the May 1970 local elections confirmed the downward trend of the previous year. Opinion polls showed the SNP as hovering between 13% and 21% in towns in the central lowlands, where in 1968 they had secured 35% of the vote.[2] Obviously, the 1968 vote had not been a 'threshold' from which the SNP would move rapidly forward (as some experts had predicted), but a temporary peak. Alternately, the 1970 figures might represent a 'plateau', from which a slow and steady advance could be expected, and the comparison should be with 1966 rather than with 1968.

If this were so, it made a sad anti-climax to the hopes of Hamilton. In the general election campaign of 1970, the SNP seemed to have lost its flair for capturing publicity, and in many constituencies there was little sign of its activities. More seriously, the press and TV found little that was newsworthy in the party's campaign — no large rallies, no great speeches, no visible leaders, but

[1] Membership claimed by the SNP:

| | |
|---|---|
| 1962 | 2,000 |
| 1963 | 4,000 |
| 1964 | 8,000 |
| 1965 | 16,000 (June) |
| | 20,000 (Nov.) |
| 1966 | 42,000 |
| 1967 | 80,000 |
| 1968 | 120,000 |

Since 1968, membership figures have not been supplied, but 'have remained fairly static'.

[2] See *Glasgow Herald* surveys, March 11, 13, 16 and 18, 1970.

just a vague tedium of 'narking'. There was no sense of urgency, and the SNP itself shifted its focus from 'national liberation' to opposition to the Common Market. The nation was bored, not oppressed.

Of the 65 SNP candidates who stood in the election, 43 lost their deposits. Hamilton returned to its normal Labour allegiance and the one seat which was gained (the Western Isles) could fairly be described as very untypical. Although the overall vote rose to 306,796 or 11·4% of the total Scottish poll, the average in the seats contested had dropped since 1966 from 14·5% to 12·2%. The SNP did best in the Highlands and north-east Scotland, but retained considerable strength in Hamilton, West Lothian and West Stirlingshire, where the party leaders stood. Its former strength in the cities vanished, though three Glasgow candidates saved their deposits.

There are many possible explanations for these results. One is that in the Lowlands the electors had already used their 'protest' nationalist vote and had seen the SNP councillors at work. They were dissatisfied, and returned to their traditional allegiances, based more on class interest than nationality. Further north and west, and especially in 'non-political' rural areas, voting SNP was still a novelty and SNP politics untried. There, too, opposition to centralisation and the Common Market was strong, and a feeling of neglect prevalent. The SNP fitted this mood, and its grass-roots activities with the emphasis on local branches and social functions could be maintained in rural communities much more successfully than in the towns. And the mass media, which stressed the British parties and the 'choice of government', had less influence in areas where local newspapers provided as much political information as the London press or TV.

The disadvantages faced by minor parties at a general election are well known, and it is difficult not to be sympathetic to the SNP regarding some of these. For example, the time given for party political broadcasting in 1970 (five minutes on both TV and radio) was exactly the same as in 1966, despite the greatly increased number of candidatures. Neither the BBC, the ITA, nor the Committee on Party Political Broadcasting moved one inch on this despite the SNP's protracted correspondence with each (see pp. 204–5). But other complaints by the party, that discussion programmes on TV and articles in the press were slanted against them, seem more open to question. A large number of features on Scottish nationalism were produced on TV and in the press between 1966 and 1970, and if the election campaign itself tended to neglect the constitutional issue, this was partly the fault of the SNP, which placed great emphasis on opposition to the Common Market and on socio-economic questions.

Perhaps the broadcasters and the newspapers should have initiated discussion on devolution (and some did, for example Grampian TV, the *Scotsman* and the *Scottish Daily Express*), but the public was clearly not very interested and the media men were by this time bored. They had to some extent created the wave of nationalism in 1967 and 1968, when nothing else in Scotland was political news. At that time, weekly columns by or about Mrs. Ewing appeared in the two best-selling Scottish newspapers (*Scottish Daily Express* and *Daily Record*, each read by over 40% of Scottish adults).[1] The Scottish press (with the exception of the *Glasgow Herald* and the Dundee *Courier and Advertiser*) was sympathetic towards the SNP, which was important, as only a small percentage of Scots read newspapers published in England.[2] Even the SNP's own weekly, the *Scots Independent*, rose to a circulation of 13,400 in 1968, falling by 1970 to 8,500. No other party in Scotland did so well in terms of publicity. But the mood had changed by June 1970, and the SNP probably got as much coverage as by ordinary news criteria it deserved.

Scotland remains an anomaly in the British political system, and the 1970 election did nothing to solve its constitutional and emotional problems. These relate essentially to the identity of Scotland within the British state, and the respect accorded to Scots and Scottishness in that state.[3] The first involves the tangled web of Scots Law, the Scottish Office and the Scottish Grand Committee of the House of Commons, which somehow co-exist

[1] *National Readership Survey*, January–December 1969, Vol. 3, Table 7. Joint Industry Committee for National Readership Surveys, London, 1970.

[2] The contrast is seen clearly in comparing readership figures for adults in Scotland with those in Great Britain as a whole (in brackets). *Daily Mirror* 3% (37%), *Daily Record* (Glasgow) 41% (4%), *Scottish Daily Express* (Glasgow) 47% (26%), *Daily Mail* 5% (13%), *Daily Telegraph* 2% (9%). On Sundays, the contrast is more striking: *Sunday Post* (Glasgow) 80% (11%), *Sunday Mail* (Glasgow) 51% (5%), *Scottish Sunday Express* (Glasgow) 26% (27%). The *Expresses*, though counterparts of the London editions, have approximately two-thirds of their contents Scottish. At an estimate, the *Glasgow Herald* is seen by 6% of Scottish readers and the *Scotsman* by 5%.

[3] On this, see J. P. Mackintosh, *The Devolution of Power* (Penguin, 1968), pp. 162–3; H. J. Paton, *The Claim of Scotland* (Allen and Unwin, 1968), Chapter 1.

with 'British Law' (if such a thing does really exist), the British government, and the British Parliament. How to improve this has been left to the Crowther Commission. But the Commissioners need to know what the Scots themselves want, which is not clear. That they want respect for their Scottishness goes without saying, yet London ignorance of, and indifference to, Scotland remains profound. More important is the rising expectation in Scotland that the standard of living should be equal to that of any part of England. The first desire leads Scots to say that Scotland should have more say in its own affairs, the second to putting pressure on London to give more to Scotland. Thus the intensity of the demand for participation in running Scotland is open to doubt.

The SNP has heightened Scottish national consciousness since 1966, and has committed many influential organisations and individuals to the support of devolution.[1] Some scheme will doubtless be adopted. But it has not explained the nature of Scottish nationalism, which remains enigmatic. Compared with nationalisms throughout the world, it is essentially of a non-violent nature, and its leaders are well-adjusted to living in their existing society.[2] Unlike Welsh nationalism, it has no linguistic basis, and Scottish culture seems to have had little influence on the SNP's policies, which have been mainly socio-economic in character. Scots, too, base their politics on such matters, and have relied on the British parties at general elections as vehicles for their realisation.

No one who lived in Scotland during the 1960s could fail to have been aware of an all-pervading Scottish national consciousness in every sector of public and private life. This was appealed to even by Labour, Conservative and Liberal politicians as a defence *against* the SNP. But they also tapped the other loyalty felt strongly in Scotland: to Britain. If England could develop this dual nationality, the narrower nationalisms would act in harmony with the larger throughout the United Kingdom.

[1] The most important of these organisations are the Conservative party, the Church of Scotland, the Scottish Trades Union Congress, the Scottish Chamber of Commerce, and the Scottish Council (Development and Industry). On the other hand, the Labour party and the Confederation of British Industry (Scottish Council) have not favoured devolution. Individuals include Professors of Politics, H. J. Hanham (author of *Scottish Nationalism*, Faber and Faber, 1969), J. P. Cornford and W. J. M. Mackenzie, and Law Professors Ian MacGibbon, David M. Walker and T. B. Smith. See also various contributors to N. MacCormick (ed.), *The Scottish Debate* (Oxford University Press, 1970).

[2] John E. Schwarz, 'The Scottish National Party: Non-violent Separatism and Theories of Violence', *World Politics*, July 1970, pp. 496–517.

APPENDIX VI

# SOURCES AND BIBLIOGRAPHY

BY DAVID R. STEEL

THIS bibliography was compiled in conjunction with the research for the main chapters of the book, especially the historical sections. Apart from a list of selected publications since 1966 on electoral studies and British government (Part II), it is confined to material bearing on the events from 1966 to 1970 that seem most relevant to the election. Part I is divided into two sections. The first deals with general sources; the second lists some useful articles and books relating to specific topics. In addition, a number of the most helpful writings not listed here are to be found in footnotes throughout the book.

## PART I

### (a) General Sources

The most concise summary of contemporary British history is to be found in *The Annual Register of World Events* (Longman). *The Times* remains the most convenient source of more detailed information as there is a full *Index*, published in two-monthly volumes, although these take several months to appear. *Keesing's Contemporary Archives* (Keesing's Publications Ltd.), a weekly summary of world events, has a cumulative subject index published fortnightly and a quarterly name index. It often includes the full texts of major speeches and agreements.

As general works of reference *Whitaker's Almanack* (J. Whitaker and Sons Ltd.) and the *Statesman's Year-Book* (Macmillan) are the most useful, the former paying special attention to the United Kingdom. The annual publication *Britain: An Official Handbook* (Central Office of Information: HMSO) contains a factual account of political and economic institutions. Specifically on politics and government, *British Political Facts, 1900–1968* (Macmillan) by D. E. Butler and J. Freeman is a comprehensive handbook. *The Political Year 1970* (Pitman) by R. Oakley and P. Rose, the first volume in a new series, is a detailed guide to the last session of the

1966 parliament. The quarterly *Political Companion* (Political Reference Publications) edited by F. W. S. Craig contains up-to-date information on by-elections and opinion polls. The *British Imperial Calendar and Civil Service List* (HMSO) provides details of all ministerial and civil service appointments. Of great interest is *1966 Census; General and Parliamentary Constituency Tables* (HMSO, November 1969). The privately circulated monthly reports issued by the Gallup Poll and National Opinion Poll contain details of their findings. *The Campaign Guide 1970* (Conservative Central Office, 1970) provides a major compendium of policy statements and quotations.

Economic and social statistics appear in the *Annual Abstract of Statistics* (HMSO), the annual Blue Book, *National Income and Expenditure* (HMSO) and the monthly *Economic Trends* (HMSO). The *National Institute Economic Review* (published quarterly by the National Institute of Economic and Social Research) and the less-publicised *Bank of England Quarterly Bulletin* (Bank of England Economic Intelligence Department) give accounts of current economic developments together with comments on likely trends.

The most useful guide to books published in the British Isles is the *British National Bibliography* which appears in weekly supplements classified by subject and with a monthly author, title and subject index. As comparatively few books have so far been published on British politics since 1966, articles are the main published source. The best list of articles in the major British journals and weeklies is the quarterly *British Humanities List* (The Library Association) which is classified by subject. More difficult, however, is the process of selecting those which are reliable and significant.

Official publications are catalogued in daily, monthly and annual lists. *Published by HMSO: A Brief Guide to Official Publications* (HMSO) and *An Introduction to British Government Publications* (Association of Assistant Librarians 1965) by J. G. Ollé are helpful guides to their use.

Those seeking information about the organisation and policies of the major political parties would be well advised to consult *Socialist Commentary* and *Tribune* (Labour), *Crossbow* (Conservative) and *New Outlook* and *Liberal News* (Liberal). Most of the national daily and weekly newspapers publish regular articles by their political columnists and the Sunday newspapers have established teams, such as 'Insight' and 'Spectrum' in the *Sunday Times* and 'Daylight' and 'Inquiry' in the *Observer*, which contribute occasional articles in depth on particular events. *The City Press* regularly contains articles of a high standard while *Private Eye* in a cryptic and often unreliable way has contained information too hot for established journals to use.

The academic journals, *Parliamentary Affairs*, *Political Quarterly* and *Public Administration* publish a number of articles on current developments. Defence policy is discussed in publications of the Royal United Service Institution.

It is clearly too soon for comprehensive general histories of the period to have been produced. Shortly before the election, however, Penguin published *The Labour Government 1964–70* by Brian Lapping, which one suspects will remain the best guide for some time. *The Pendulum Years: Britain and the Sixties* (Cape, 1970) by Bernard Levin contains a number of interesting comments on politics during the sixties.

*Election '70* (*Guardian*/Panther) by David McKie and Chris Cook provides a convenient analysis of Conservative and Labour records between 1959 and 1970 on the major issues and contains much statistical information that is not readily accessible elsewhere. On the election itself, *The Making of the Prime Minister 1970* (Macdonald Unit 75, 1970) by Andrew Alexander and Alan Watkins is the only general book yet available.

*Powell and the 1970 Election* (Elliott Right Way Books), edited by J. Wood, assesses the role of Enoch Powell during the campaign and includes some more general essays. Post mortems on the campaign appear in *Encounter* (Peter Jenkins: August 1970), *Political Quarterly* (October–December 1970) and *Socialist Commentary* (August 1970). *The Times Guide to the House of Commons 1970* provides a complete record of the results and short biographies of the candidates, but it contains some errors.

## (*b*) *Sources on specific topics*

*Economic Policy*

(i) General

The Task Ahead (Economic Assessment to 1972), DEA, 1969. (The second 'National Plan'.)

Brandon, H., *In the Red: the Struggle for Sterling, 1964–66* (Deutsch, 1966). (Factual account of the politics of economic policy, 1964–66.)

Brittan, S., *Steering the Economy: the Role of the Treasury* (Secker & Warburg, 1969). British economic policy from 1951 up to devaluation (contains valuable bibliography). (Also Penguin, 1971; updated to 1970).

Caves, R. E., *et al.*, *Britain's Economic Prospects* (Allen & Unwin, 1968). (Report of the Brookings Institution on Britain's economic performance.)

Davis, W., *Three Years Hard Labour: the Road to Devaluation* (Deutsch, 1968). (Straightforward account of government economic policy up to 1967.)

Brown, G., 'Why the DEA lost to the Treasury Knights', *Sunday Times*, March 31, 1968.

Jay, D., 'Government Control of the Economy: Defects in the Machinery', *Political Quarterly*, April/June 1968.

(ii) Incomes Policy

Prices and Incomes Standstill, Cmnd. 3073 1966.

Prices and Incomes Standstill: Period of Severe Restraint, Cmnd. 3150 1966.

Prices and Incomes Policy after June 30, 1967, Cmnd. 3235 1967.

Productivity, Prices and Incomes Policy in 1968 and 1969, Cmnd. 3590 1968.

Productivity, Prices and Incomes Policy after 1969, Cmnd. 4237 1969.

'Incomes Policy: What Next?', Special Supplement in *Socialist Commentary*, March 1967.

(iii) Regional and Industrial Policy

The Development Areas: Regional Employment Premium, Cmnd. 3310 1967.

Report of a Committee on the Intermediate Areas (Hunt), Cmnd. 3998 1969.

Shanks, M., *The Innovators: the Economics of Technology* (Penguin, 1967). (A study of government involvement in industrial performance.)

Broadway, F. E., *State Intervention in British Industry 1964–68* (Kaye and Ward, 1969).

Moonman, E., *Reluctant Partnership*: a critical study of the relationship between government and industry (Gollancz, 1970.)

*Industrial Relations*

Report of Royal Commission on Trade Unions and Employers' Associations 1965–68 (Donovan), Cmnd. 3623 1968.
*In Place of Strife: A Policy for Industrial Relations*, Cmnd. 3888 1969.
TUC General Council, *Industrial Relations: Programme for Action* (TUC, 1969).
Conservative Party, *Fair Deal at Work* (Conservative Political Centre, 1968).
Blackburn, R., and Cockburn, A. (eds.), *The Incompatibles: Trade Union Militancy and the Consensus* (Penguin, 1967). (Includes articles by Paul Foot on the Seamen's Strike 1966 and by Jack Jones and Clive Jenkins on the trade union movement.)
Castle, B., 'The Industrial Relations Bill', *Listener*, May 1, 1969. (Interview on *Panorama*, BBC-TV.)
Fay, S., *Measure for Measure: reforming the trade unions* (Chatto and Windus, 1970). (An analysis of the different proposals for reform.)
Jenkins, P., *The Battle of Downing Street* (Charles Knight, 1970). (An account of the events of the Industrial Relations Bill controversy, 1969.)
Turner, H. A., *Is Britain really Strike-Prone?* (CUP, 1969). (An attack on the assumptions underlying government policy on industrial relations.)
'Chronicle' of *British Journal of Industrial Relations* — Quarterly — (gives details of agreements, disputes, etc.).

*Race*

Rose, E. J. B., *Colour and Citizenship: a Report on British Race Relations* (OUP, 1969). (Contains full bibliography.)
Smithies, W., and Fiddick, P., *Enoch Powell on Immigration: An Analysis* (Sphere, 1969). (Powell's four speeches at Walsall, Birmingham, Eastbourne and on the Frost Programme, their background and a chapter on statistics.)
Steel, D. M. S., *No Entry: the Background and Implications of the Commonwealth Immigrants Act 1968* (Hurst, 1969). (An account

of events leading up to the introduction of the bill and of attempts to defeat it.)

*Ulster*

de Paor, L., *Divided Ulster* (Penguin, 1970). (A comprehensive account of the Ulster situation and its background.)

Devlin, B., *The Price of My Soul* (Deutsch/Pan, 1970). (The story of the Civil Rights movement.)

Hastings, M., *Ulster 1969: the fight for civil rights in Northern Ireland* (Gollancz, 1970). (Account of day-to-day events by *Evening Standard* reporter.)

O'Leary, C., 'Northern Ireland: the Politics of Illusion', *Political Quarterly*, July/September 1969. (Analysis of the Ulster situation up to O'Neill's resignation.)

O'Neill, T., *Ulster at the Crossroads* (Faber, 1969). (An edited collection of O'Neill's speeches.)

Riddell, P., *Fire over Ulster* (Hamish Hamilton, 1970). (O'Neillite account by a former civil servant and a columnist with a Belfast Sunday newspaper.)

*Foreign and Defence Policy*

(i) General

Report of the Review Committee on Overseas Representation 1968–1969 (Duncan), Cmnd. 4107 1969.

Brown, G., 'Why I shocked the Foreign Office Mandarins', *Sunday Times*, April 7, 1968.

Brown, N., *Arms without Empire: British defence role in the modern world* (Penguin, 1967).

Calleo, D. P., *Britain's Future* (Hodder and Stoughton, 1968). (An appraisal of the choices open to Britain in foreign affairs.)

Healey, D., 'Britain in a Changing World', *Socialist Commentary*, November 1969.

Heath, E., 'Realism in British Foreign Policy', *Foreign Affairs*, October 1969.

Heath, E., *Old World, New Horizons: Britain, the Common Market and the Atlantic Alliance* (OUP, 1970).

Vital, D., 'The Making of British Foreign Policy', *Political Quarterly*, July/September 1968. (The operation of the Foreign Office.)

Watt, D. C. 'Future Aims of British Foreign Policy', *Political Quarterly*, January/March 1970. (Discussion of British foreign policy in light of the strengths and weaknesses of the British position.)

(ii) East of Suez

Buchan, A., Zinkin, M., Tanham, G. K., Howard, M., 'Britain East of Suez', *Listener*, September 22, 29 and October 6, 13, 1966.

Mayhew, C. P., *Britain's Role Tomorrow* (Hutchinson, 1967). (Justification of his resignation from the government.)

Watt, D. C., 'The Decision to Withdraw from the Gulf', *Political Quarterly*, July/September 1968. (A critical review of the decision.)

Younger, K., 'Reflections on the Defence Review', *Political Quarterly*, July/September 1966; 'British Interests and British Foreign Policy', *Political Quarterly*, October/December 1967. (Advocates further reductions in Britain's role as a world policeman and concentration on European Atlantic security.)

(iii) Europe

Beloff, N., 'Getting Wilson to Market', *Observer*, October 23, 1966.

Jay, D., *After the Common Market: A Better Alternative for Britain* (Penguin, 1968). (The case against entry.)

Kitzinger, U. (ed.), *Britain and the Common Market* (BBC, 1967). (Articles by U. Kitzinger, W. Pickles and F. Mulley (at the time Minister responsible for Europe).)

Kitzinger, U., *The Second Try: Labour and the EEC* (Pergamon, 1968).

'Britain on her Way to Europe', *Times/Die Welt*, October 28, 1966.

'Britain and Europe: The Future', *Times/Die Welt*, October 28, 1967.

Uri, P. (ed.), *From Commonwealth to Common Market* (Penguin, 1968). (Includes chapter by Nora Beloff, 'What happened in Britain after the General said No?' (1963–67).)

Britain and the European Communities: An Economic Assessment, Cmnd. 4289 1970. (The cost of entry.)

(iv) Nigerian Civil War

Forsyth, F., *The Biafra Story* (Penguin, 1969). (Strongly in favour of Biafra.)

Mackintosh, J. P., 'Making sense of our Nigeria Policy', *The Times*, September 3, 1968. (General support of the policy of the government.)

*Government relations with the Press*

Benn, A. W., Speech attacking BBC for failure to bridge gap between politicians and people — and on editorial intervention in current affairs reporting. *The Times*, October 19, 1968.

Crossman, R. H. S., Granada Guidhall Lecture 1968. 'The Politics of TV', *New Statesman*, October 25, 1968. (Calls for radical change in coverage of current affairs to remove trivialisation, etc.)

Hedley, P., and Aynsley, C., *The 'D' Notice Affair* (Joseph, 1967).

Report of Committee of Privy Councillors Appointed to Inquire into 'D' Notice Matters (Radcliffe), Cmnd. 3309 1967.

The 'D' Notice System, Cmnd. 3312 1967. (The government's reply to the Radcliffe Report.)

Coady, M., 'The Premier and the Press', *New Statesman*, April 15, 1966.

Howard, A., 'Washington and Whitehall', *Listener*, July 21, 1966. (Political reporting in the two capitals compared.)

Jenkins, P., 'Bad P.M. or Bad Press?', *Guardian*, May 27, 1969. (Wilson's relationship with the press 1963–69.)

Wigg, G., 'Politicians and the Press', *Listener*, September 21, 1967. (Lecture to the Guild of British Newspaper Editors.)

'*The Machinery*'

(i) Electoral Reform

Report of the Committee on the Age of Majority (Latey), Cmnd. 3342 1967.

Conference on Electoral Law: Final Report, Cmnd. 3550 1968.

Conclusions on Review of the Law Relating to Parliamentary Elections, Cmnd. 3717 1968. (White Paper outlining government proposals.)

(ii) Civil Service Reform

Report of Committee on the Civil Service (Fulton) 1966–68, Cmnd. 3638 1968.

Armstrong, Sir W., 'The Fulton Report', *Listener*, January 30, 1969. (The Head of the Home Civil Service interviewed by Robert McKenzie.)

Brittan, S., 'Running the Civil Service without the Treasury', *Financial Times*, February 10, 1969.

Robson, W. A., 'The Fulton Report on the Civil Service', *Political Quarterly*, October/December 1968. (A critical review of the Fulton Report.)

Thomas, H. S. (ed.), *Crisis in the Civil Service* (Blond, 1968). (Includes essays by T. Balogh, R. Opie and D. Seers.)

(iii) Local Government Reform

Report of Royal Commission on Local Government in England 1966–1969 (Redcliffe-Maud), Cmnd. 4040 1969. (Short version, Cmnd. 4039.)

Report of Royal Commission on Local Government in Scotland 1966–1969 (Wheatley), Cmnd. 4150 1969.

Reform of Local Government in England, Cmnd. 4276 1970. (Government proposals for reform.)

Mackintosh, J. P., *The Devolution of Power* (Charles Knight, 1968).

Steed, M., Keith-Lucas, B., Hall, P., *The Maud Report* (New Society Publications, 1969). (Articles on the political complexion, the participatory and geographical aspects of the new authorities.)

(iv) Parliamentary Reform

House of Lords Reform, Cmnd. 3799 1968.

Report of Select Committee on Procedure 1968–69 H.C.410. (Scrutiny of public expenditure and administration.)

Public Expenditure: A New Presentation, Cmnd. 4017 1969.

Boulton, C. J., 'Recent Developments in House of Commons Procedure', *Parliamentary Affairs*, Winter 1969/70. (Includes reference list of changes in procedure, 1964–70.)

*'Biographical' works*

De'ath, W., *Barbara Castle: A Portrait from Life* (Clifton Books, 1970).

Donnelly, D., *Gadarene '68: The Crimes, Follies and Misfortunes of the Wilson Government* (Kimber, 1968).

Foot, P., *The Rise of Enoch Powell* (Penguin, 1969).

Foot, P., *The Politics of Harold Wilson* (Penguin, 1968).

George-Brown, Lord, *In My Way* (Gollancz, 1971).

Hutchinson, G., *Edward Heath: A Personal and Political Biography* (Longman, 1970).
Maude, A., *The Common Problem* (Constable, 1969). (An exposition of Conservative principles.)
Mayhew, C., *Party Games* (Hutchinson, 1969). (Semi-autobiographical; includes attack on party system.)
Nabarro, Sir G., *Nab 1: Portrait of a Politician* (Maxwell, 1969).
Roth, A., *Enoch Powell: Tory Tribune* (Macdonald, 1970).
Trevelyan, Sir H., *Revolution in the Middle East* (Macmillan, 1970). (Includes account of Aden withdrawal 1967.)
Utley, T. E., *Enoch Powell: the man and his thinking* (Kimber, 1968).
Young, K., *Sir Alec Douglas-Home* (Dent, 1970).
Jenkins, P., 'Jim, the Old Pro in Waiting', *Guardian*, January 21, 1969. (Profile of Jim Callaghan.)
Jenkins, P., 'Healey, white knight, dark horse?', *Guardian*, October 24, 1969.
Jenkins, P., 'The Radical Creed of a Civilised Man', *Guardian*, July 21, 1969. (Profile of Roy Jenkins.)
Wood, D., 'Callaghan, Man in the Middle of the Cabinet Crisis', *The Times*, March 31, 1969.
Wood, D., 'Intellectual in Politics', *The Times*, May 19, 1969. (Profile of Richard Crossman.)
Wood, D., 'A Safe Pair of Hands', *The Times*, March 24, 1969. (Profile of Michael Stewart.)

## PART II

### 1. *Electoral Studies*

Berrington, H. B., 'The General Election of 1964', *Journal of Royal Statistical Society*, Series A (General), Vol. 128, 1965, Part 1.
Berrington, H. B., 'The 1966 Election', *Swinton Journal*, Autumn 1966.
Berry, D., *The Sociology of Grass Roots Politics: a study of party membership* (Macmillan, 1970).
Budge, I., and Urwin, D. W., *Scottish Political Behaviour: a case study in British homogeneity* (Longman, 1966).
Butler, D. E., and Cornford, J., 'Britain', in Rokkan, S., and Meyriat, J. (eds.), *International Guide to Electoral Statistics* (Mouton, 1969).

Butler, D. E., and Freeman, J., *British Political Facts, 1900–68* (Macmillan, 1969).
Butler, D. E., and Stokes, D., *Political Change in Britain* (Macmillan, 1969).
Craig, F. W. S. (ed.), *British General Election Manifestos 1918–1966* (Political Reference Publications, 1970).
Craig, F. W. S. (ed.), *British Parliamentary Election Statistics 1918–68* (Political Reference Publications, 1968).
Craig, F. W. S. (ed.), *British Parliamentary Election Results*, Vol. 1, *1918–49* (Political Reference Publications, 1969).
Goldthorpe, J. H., Lockwood, D., Bechhofer, F., Platt, J., *The Affluent Worker: Political Attitudes and Behaviour* (CUP, 1968).
Goodhart, C. A. E., and Bhansali, R. J., 'Political Economy', *Political Studies*, March 1970.
Hodder-Williams, R., *Public Opinion Polls and British Politics* (RKP, 1970).
Holt, R. T., and Turner, J. E., *Political Parties in Action: the Battle of Barons Court* (Collier-Macmillan, 1968).
Janosik, E. G., *Constituency Labour Parties in Britain* (Pall Mall, 1968).
Kavanagh, D., *Constituency Electioneering in Britain* (Longman, 1970).
Kinnear, M., *The British Voter: an Atlas and Survey since 1885* (Batsford, 1968).
Leonard, R. L., *Elections in Britain* (Van Nostrand, 1968).
McKenzie, R. T., and Silver, A., *Angels in Marble* (Heinemann, 1968).
Moodie, G. C., and Studdert-Kennedy, G., *Opinions, Publics and Pressure Groups* (Allen & Unwin, 1970).
Nordlinger, E. A., *The Working-Class Tories* (MacGibbon & Kee, 1967).
Parkin, F., 'Working-class Conservatives: a theory of political deviance', *British Journal of Sociology*, September 1967.
Paterson, P., *The Selectorate* (MacGibbon & Kee, 1967).
Pulzer, P., *Political Representation and Elections in Britain* (Allen & Unwin, 1967).
Rose, R., *Influencing Voters: a study of campaign rationality* (Faber, 1967).
Rose, R. (ed.), *The Polls and the 1970 Election* (University of Strathclyde, Surrey Research Centre Occasional Paper No. 7, 1970).

Roth, A., *Business Background of M.P.s* (Parliamentary Profiles, 1967).

Rush, M., *The Selection of Parliamentary Candidates* (Nelson, 1969).

Sharpe, L. J. (ed.), *Voting in Cities: the 1964 Borough elections* (Macmillan, 1967).

2. *The Media*

Blumler, J. G., and McQuail, D., *Television in Politics* (Faber, 1968).

Seymour-Ure, C., *The Press, Politics and the Public* (Methuen, 1968).

*Sociology of Mass Media Communicators* (Sociological Review Monograph No. 13, 1969).

Tunstall, J., *The Westminster Lobby Correspondents: A Sociological Study of National Political Journalism* (RKP, 1970).

Whale, J., *The Half-Shut Eye: TV and Politics in Britain and America* (Macmillan, 1969).

Windlesham, Lord, *Communication and Political Power* (Cape, 1966).

3. *Government and Parliament*

Barker, A., and Rush, M., *The Member of Parliament and his Information* (Allen & Unwin, 1970).

Berkeley, H., *The Power of the Prime Minister* (Allen & Unwin, 1968).

Brown, R. G. S., *The Administrative Process in Britain* (Methuen, 1970).

Butt, R., *The Power of Parliament*, 2nd ed. (Constable, 1969).

Hanson, A. H., and Crick, B. (eds.), *The Commons in Transition* (Fontana, 1970).

Hanson, A. H., and Walles, M., *Governing Britain: A Guide-book to Political Institutions* (Fontana, 1970).

King, A., *The British Prime Minister: A Reader* (Macmillan, 1969).

Mackintosh, J. P., *The British Cabinet*, 2nd ed. (Stevens, 1968).

Mackintosh, J. P., *The Government and Politics of Britain* (Hutchinson University Library, 1970).

Punnett, R. M., *British Government and Politics* (Heinemann, 1968).

Rose, R. (ed.), *Policy-Making in Britain: A Reader in Government* (Macmillan, 1969).

Walker, P. Gordon, *The Cabinet* (Cape, 1970).

# INDEX